T0190393

# Communications in Computer and Information Science 1700

More information about this series at https://link.springer.com/bookseries/7899

Shuo Yang · Huimin Lu (Eds.)

# Artificial Intelligence and Robotics

7th International Symposium, ISAIR 2022
Shanghai, China, October 21–23, 2022
Proceedings, Part I

 Springer

*Editors*
Shuo Yang
Kyushu Institute of Technology
Kitakyushu, Japan

Huimin Lu
Kyushu Institute of Technology
Kitakyushu, Japan

ISSN 1865-0929 ISSN 1865-0937 (electronic)
Communications in Computer and Information Science
ISBN 978-981-19-7945-3 ISBN 978-981-19-7946-0 (eBook)
https://doi.org/10.1007/978-981-19-7946-0

This Springer imprint is published by the registered company Springer Nature Singapore Pte Ltd.
The registered company address is: 152 Beach Road, #21-01/04 Gateway East, Singapore 189721, Singapore

# Preface

In recent years, artificial intelligence (AI) has attracted attention as a key for growth in developed countries and developing countries. The attention has been focused mainly on developing new deep learning-based information communication technology (ICT) and Internet of Things (IoT) applications. Although recently developed deep learning technology certainly excels in extracting certain patterns, there are many limitations. Most of recent models are overly dependent on big data, lack a self-idea function, and are complicated. In order to overcome these limitations and to solve the real-world industrial problems, cognitive computing (CC) and computational neuroscience (CN) are driving some of the best tools for future brain-inspired robots.

Rather than merely focusing on the development of next-generation AI models, the 7th International Symposium on Artificial Intelligence and Robotics (ISAIR 2022) aimed to provide a platform to share up-to-date scientific and industrial achievements of general-purpose intelligence cognition methods. These methods provide efficient tools to solve the issues of recent AI models, and capture remarkable human learning abilities, combining the strengths of CC/CN and deep generative neural networks.

This proceedings collects the state-of-the-art contributions on the cognitive intelligence, computer vision, multimedia, the Internet of Things, robotics, and related applications presented at ISAIR 2022, held during October 21–23 in Shanghai, China.

We received 285 submissions from authors in over 10 countries around the world. After the careful single-blind review process, 67 papers were selected based on their originality, significance, technical soundness, and clarity of exposition. Each submission was reviewed by at least 2 members of the Program Committee and the accepted papers underwent further rigorous rounds of review.

It is our sincere hope that this volume provides stimulation and inspiration, and that it will be used as a foundation for works to come.

October 2022

Shuo Yang
Huimin Lu
Shenglin Mu
Rushi Lan

# Organization

## Steering Committee

| | |
|---|---|
| Manu Malek (Editor-in-Chief) | Computers and Electrical Engineering, USA |
| Seiichi Serikawa | Kyushu Institute of Technology, Japan |
| Huimin Lu | Kyushu Institute of Technology, Japan |

## General Chairs

| | |
|---|---|
| Tohru Kamiya | Kyushu Institute of Technology, Japan |
| Zongyuan Ge | Monash University, Australia |
| Jianru Li | Tongji University, China |

## Program Chairs

| | |
|---|---|
| Rushi Lan | Guilin University of Electronic Technology, China |
| Shenglin Mu | Ehime University, Japan |
| Shuo Yang | Kyushu Institute of Technology, Japan |

## Publicity Chairs

| | |
|---|---|
| Jože Guna | University of Ljubljana, Slovenia |
| Guangwei Gao | Nanjing University of Posts and Telecommunications, China |
| Shota Nakashima | Yamaguchi University, Japan |

## Award Chairs

| | |
|---|---|
| Quan Zhou | Nanjing University of Posts and Telecommunications, China |
| Jihua Zhu | Xi'an Jiaotong University, China |
| Zhibin Yu | Ocean University of China, China |
| Dong Wang | Dalian University of Technology, China |

## Area Chairs

| | |
|---|---|
| Csaba Beleznai | Austrian Institute of Technology, Austria |
| Hao Gao | Nanjing University of Posts and Telecommunications, China |

| | |
|---|---|
| Ainul Akmar Mokhtar | Universiti Teknologi Petronas, Malaysia |
| Ting Wang | Nanjing University of Technology, China |
| Weihua Ou | Guizhou Normal University, China |
| Wenpeng Lu | Qilu University of Technology, China |
| Xing Xu | University of Electronic Science and Technology of China, China |
| Xin Jin | Beijing Electronic Science and Technology Institute, China |
| Amit Kumar Singh | National Institute of Technology Patna, India |
| Zhe Chen | Hohai University, China |

## Program Committee

| | |
|---|---|
| Chiew-Foong Kwong | University of Nottingham, UK |
| Dario Lodi Rizzini | University of Parma, Italy |
| Danijel Skocaj | University of Ljubljana, Slovenia |
| Donald Dansereau | University of Sydney, Australia |
| Guangxu Li | Tianjin Polytechnic University, China |
| Giancarlo Fortino | Università della Calabria, Italy |
| Hossein Olya | University of Sheffield, UK |
| Iztok Humar | University of Ljubljana, Slovenia |
| Jianru Li | Tongji University, China |
| Jinjia Zhou | Hosei University, Japan |
| Keshav Seshadri | Carnegie Mellon University, USA |
| Levis Mei | Agilent, USA |
| Limei Peng | Kyungpook National University, South Korea |
| Liao Wu | University of New South Wales, Australia |
| Li He | Qualcomm Inc., USA |
| Mario G. C. A. Cimino | University of Pisa, Italy |
| M. Shamim Hossain | King Saud University, UAE |
| Matjaz Perc | University of Maribor, Slovenia |
| Oleg Sergiyenko | Baja California Autonomous University, Mexico |
| Sangeen Khan | COMSATS University, Pakistan |
| Shuai Chen | Chinese Academy of Sciences, China |
| Wendy Flores-Fuentes | Universidad Autonoma de Baja California, Mexico |
| Xin Li | Shanghai Jiao Tong University, China |
| Xinliang Liu | Beijing Technology and Business University, China |
| Yin Zhang | Zhongnan University of Economics and Law, China |
| Yichuan Wang | University of Sheffield, UK |

| | |
|---|---|
| Haitao Cheng | Nanjing University of Posts and Telecommunications, China |
| Fang Hu | Hubei University of Chinese Medicine, China |
| Xipeng Pan | Guilin University of Electronic Technology, China |
| Yun Liu | Southwest University, China |
| Huadeng Wang | Guilin University of Electronic Technology, China |
| Haigang Zhang | Shenzhen Polytechnic, China |
| Xianfeng Wu | Jianghan University, China |
| Zhihao Xu | Qingdao University, China |
| Junfei Wang | Jianghan University, China |
| Zhongyuan Lai | Jianghan University, China |
| Jianming Zhang | Changsha University of Science and Technology, China |
| Xiwang Xie | Dalian Maritime University, China |
| Heng Liu | Anhui University of Technology, China |
| Fenglian Li | Taiyuan University of Technology, China |

# Contents – Part I

# Contents – Part II

# Breast Ultrasound Tumor Detection Based on Active Learning and Deep Learning

Gen Liu[1], Jiyong Tan[1,2(✉)], Hongguang Yang[1], Yuanwei Li[1], Xi Sun[1], Jiayi Wu[3], and Baoming Luo[3]

[1] AISONO AIR Lab, Shenzhen, China
scutjy2015@163.com
[2] Harbin Institute of Technology, Harbin, China
[3] Department of Ultrasound, Sun Yat-Sen Memorial Hospital, Sun Yat-Sen University, Guangzhou, China

**Abstract.** Early breast cancer screening and diagnosis policy plays a significance role in reducing breast cancer mortality, which is the most common malignant tumor for women. Therefore, its accuracy and efficiency are very important. To cover these challenges in mass breast screening and diagnosis, including varied ultrasound image quality from different equipments, expensive professional annotation, we propose a novel method based on active learning and convolution neural networks for selecting more informative images and tumor detection, respectively. Firstly, we verify the effectiveness of active learning in the application of our breast ultrasound data. Secondly, we select the informative images from the origin training set using the Multiple Instance Active Learning (MIAL) with One-Shot Path Aggregation Feature Pyramid Network (OPA-FPN) structure. Through this way, we effectively balance the ratio of hard samples and simple samples in the origin training set. Finally, we train the model based on EfficientDet with specific and valid parameters for our breast ultrasound data. Through the corresponding ablation experiment, it is verified that the model trained on the selected dataset by combining MIAL with OPA-FPN exceeds the origin model in the metrics about sensitive, specificity and F1-score. Meanwhile, while keeping the corresponding metrics approximately the same, the confidence of inference images from the new model is higher and stable.

**Keywords:** Breast ultrasound · Tumor detection · AIBUS · Active learning · Breast Cancer screening and diagnosis

## 1 Introduction

Breast cancer is the most common malignant tumor for women [1]. Compare to the amount of world breast cancer cases and deaths each year, China accounts for 12.2% and 9.6%, respectively. As for the 5-year survival rate, China presents 82.0%, which 7.1% lower than the U.S. The literature [2] pointed out that the early diagnosis rate of breast cancer in China is less than 20%, and the proportion of breast cancer found through screening is less than 5%. Therefore, early screening and diagnosis of breast cancer based on ultrasound with its low cost and high efficiency play an important role in reducing the death rate of breast cancer [3]. However, ultrasound presents its unique challenges with low image quality, lack of experienced ultrasound operators and diagnosticians, the difference of ultrasound equipment and system [4]. To confront these challenges, more advanced automatic ultrasound image analysis methods have been proposed.

With the rapid development of deep learning, Convolutional Neural Networks (CNNs) have become popular and achieved desired results in breast tumor detection. In [5], several existing state-of-the-art object detection framework have been systematically evaluated on its breast ultrasound tumor datasets, including Faster R-CNN [6], SSD [7], YOLO [8]. It proved that the SSD with the input size as $300 \times 300$ achieved the best performance in terms of average precision, recall and F1-Score. In [9], a pre-trained FCN-AlexNet transfer learning method has been proposed, and its effectiveness in breast ultrasound tumor detection task has been verified. However, those data are all manually scanned by doctors, its image quality is relatively good. Therefore, it may lead to poor performance when simply applied the object detection network on other breast ultrasound data. In [10], an object detection framework is designed based on 3D convolution for the breast ultrasound data collected by the ABUS device. They got 100% and 86% sensitivity for tumor with different size on its defined statistics.

However, the above methods need a large amount of accurate annotation data which is very expensive in medical filed. Therefore, it is suitable for breast ultrasound that applying active learning to solve the problem. Active learning can select the important data from the original dataset for annotation and achieve better performance. In the deep learning eras, most of the active learning methods [11–13] remain falling into image-level classification tasks. Few methods are specified for active object detection, which faces complex instance distribution in the same images. The paper [14] simply sort the loss predictions of instance to evaluate the image uncertainly for the object detection. This paper [15] introduce spatial context to active detection and selected diverse samples according to the distances to the labeled set.

The existing breast ultrasound data and methods have certain deficiencies in breast cancer screening and diagnosis, including resource limitations in data acquisition and model performance caused by data. It cannot satisfy the strategy of early screening and diagnosis. Therefore, we collects standardized video data from 1603 cases based on AIBUS (AISONO) robots which adopt mechanical arm with US probe to realize full-automatic standardized fast scanning of breasts, and then generate at least 5 videos of each breast. Meanwhile, an algorithm framework based on the efficient EfficientDet with the reasonable dataset selected by the improved Multiple Instance Active Learning (MIAL) is proposed. Our contribution can be summarize as follows:

1.  An efficient mechanism for early screening and diagnosis of breast cancer based on AIBUS video, combing standard and efficient automatic robotic arm scanning.
2.  The improved MIAL active learning algorithm for obtaining diversified data from varied scenes and area of people.
3.  A robust tumor detection framework based on efficient EfficientDet. Specially, the model trained on smaller dataset selected through active learning has better performance on both accuracy and speed.

## 2   Materials and Method

In breast ultrasound, tumors have different complexity and difficulty. The more common tumor, the less complex it is, such as the simple cyst which belongs to Birads-2 [16]. On the contrary, more complex the tumor is, the more burdensome to obtain, such as the complicated tumor with unclear borders and varies shapes. Therefore, the dataset faces a serious imbalance in simple tumors and complex tumors. If the whole samples were used for training, it will cause the model to learn more on those simple breast tumors, and it also leads to a lack of robustness for more complicated tumors. Moreover, excessive redundant data consumes time and resources in model training.

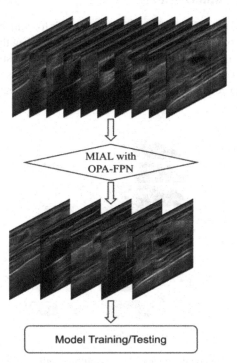

**Fig. 1.** Architecture diagram of the paper.

Consequently, this paper applies One-Shot Path Aggregation Feature Pyramid Network (OPA-FPN) [17] to improve the performance of MIAL [18] for better active learning in the instance level and more efficacious selection for samples with more information. Under the effect of the improved active learning, a smaller training dataset with more balanced simple and complicated tumors will be constructed. Then, a tumor detection model is trained based on EfficientDet [19]. The model can present more accurate information about tumors with different complexity in an effective and balanced manner way. The overall process is showed in Fig. 1. Each parts of our method will be described in details, including our dataset, the improved MIAL with OPA-FPN and the object detection framework named EfficientDet.

## 2.1 Dataset

The performance of our combined framework was mainly verified on our private dataset obtained by AIBUS robots which contains 5–8 videos with 20 FPS for a breast. The whole training datasets include 12666 breast ultrasound images from the videos of 1603 cases, which was acquired from varied areas. Meanwhile, each tumor region was labeled by two or three clinicians. For active learning, the selected data were all from the mentioned training dataset with 12666 breast ultrasound images. For detection task, the test dataset consists of 448 tumor images and 4207 normal images.

## 2.2 Improved MIAL with OPA-FPN

We apply the improved MIAL with OPA-FPN to select informative images for training RetinaNet detector. Compared to traditional method which using the mean of inference result directly, MIAL used the discrepancy learning and multi-instance learning (MIL) to learn and re-weight the uncertainty of instances. It also filters some negative sample instances in the inference process of RetinaNet, and select informative images from the unlabeled dataset.

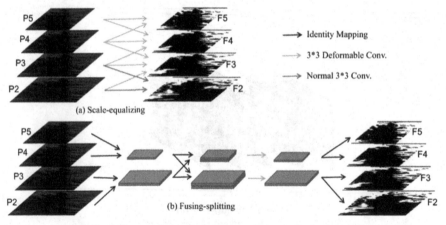

**Fig. 2.** Scale-equalizing and Fusing-splitting paths in OPA-FPN.

The improved MIAL selects informative images based on the sorted Top-K instances. The meaningful parameters K effects the Top-K instances uncertainty and the image uncertainty. According to the characteristics of each breast ultrasound image which contains less than 3 tumors per image, we set the parameters K as 5. Meanwhile, for the FPN structure in RetinaNet which plays an important role in feature fusion and expression at different scales, we replaced it with OPA-FPN, which is a novel search space of FPNs to fuse richer and reasonable features efficiently. The OPA-FPN contains 6 information paths as Top-down, Bottom-up, Scale-equalizing, None, Fusing-splitting, Skip-connect. The special Scale-equalizing and Fusing-splitting paths have been given in Fig. 2.

## 2.3  EfficientDet-Based Tumor Detection

We use EfficientDet as our tumor detector for its optional performance in terms of both speed and accuracy. For object detection, FPN structure and model depth have an important impact on model performance. Meanwhile, anchors effect the bounding box regression and selection of positive and negative samples during training. Therefore, we set the anchor ratio as [1, 1.5, 2] under the specific ultrasound dataset based on the aspect ratio distribution of the regression box. Then, compound scaling as the key contribution of EfficientDet, it proved that the scale of input resolution, model depth and width is effective. We only scale the model depth and width with the input resolution fixed because of the unique properties on ultrasound data. Specifically, we set the input resolution to 512 * 512 and the compound scaling coefficient to 2 taking into account of the model accuracy and inference speed, and other scaling configs for EfficientDet are shown in Table 1.

**Table 1.** Scaling configs for EfficientDet D0-D6.

| EfficientDet | Input size | Backbone network | BiFPN | | Box/class layers |
|---|---|---|---|---|---|
| | | | channel | layer | |
| D0 | 512 | B0 | 64 | 3 | 3 |
| D1 | 512 | B1 | 88 | 4 | 3 |
| D2 | 512 | B2 | 112 | 5 | 3 |
| D3 | 640 | B3 | 160 | 6 | 4 |
| D4 | 768 | B4 | 224 | 7 | 4 |
| D5 | 896 | B5 | 288 | 7 | 4 |
| D6 | 1024 | B6 | 384 | 8 | 5 |

# 3  Experiment

## 3.1  Implementation Details

The whole experiments were on the platform with two NVIDIA GeForce RTX 2080Ti GPU. In order to verify the validity of the improved MIAL, we also conducted experiments on PASCAL VOC Dataset. During the training for the improved MIAL on PASCAL VOC Dataset, we set the SGD optimizer with momentum as 0.9, learning rate as 1e–3 and the weight decay as 0.0001. Meanwhile, the initial training dataset ratio is 0.05, the selected quantity ratio is 0.025 for each cycle. For the experiments on our specific training dataset from AIBUS robots, we set the initial learning rate as 1e–4, the initial training dataset ratio is 0.1 and the selected quantity ratio is 0.05 for each cycle. The total cycle quantity is 8.

During the training for EfficientDet on the selected dataset from the improved MIAL, we set the SGD optimizer with momentum as 0.9, learning rate as 1e–4. The learning rate will be changed using dynamic learning rate reducing Strategy based on the valid dataset loss with patience as 3. Meanwhile, to implement the corresponding ablation experiment on the testing dataset based on tumor detection, we evaluate the model through the sensitive, specificity and F1-score.

## 3.2 The Improved MIAL Performance

To evaluate the effectiveness of our improved MIAL, we constructed the comparative experiment on the PASCAL VOC Dataset and our breast ultrasound dataset. Meanwhile, we compare our improved MIAL with random sampling, LAAL [20]. The mean average precision (mAP) is used as the metric. The result in Fig. 3 has shown the MIAL works well. It achieved the average detection accuracy of 72.3% when using the 20% samples. And it reached 93.5% of performance with whole samples in dataset.

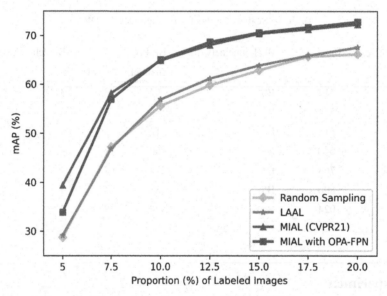

**Fig. 3.** Active Learning on PASCAL VOC.

Pleasantly, the improved MIAL with OPA-FPN outperformed MIAL by 0.5%. Finally, the detail results based on MIAL method on our dataset is shown in Fig. 4. It also proved the effectiveness.

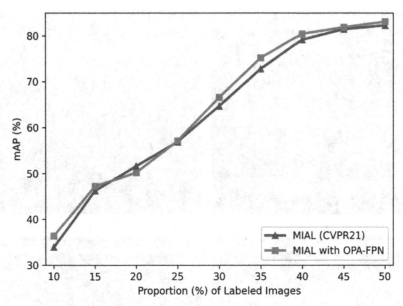

**Fig. 4.** Active learning on our dataset.

### 3.3 Tumor Detection Performance

For the tumor detection task, we use the CenterNet [21] on the whole dataset as the baseline on the metrics including the sensitive, specificity and F1-score. Meanwhile, we compared it with EfficientDet and the EfficientDet trained on the selected samples in Sect. 3.2 based on the improved MIAL. The experimental results have shown in Table 2. The number 12666 and 6333 in model name respectively represent the mounts of training set used in the corresponding model. Compared with the base model trained by CenterNet-12666, the EfficientDet performed well. In particular, the performance of sensitive and F1-score is respectively increased 0.028% and 0.009%, but the specificity is decreased 0.002%. In fact, the sensitive and F1-score is more important than the specificity in breast cancer screening tasks. Furthermore, the performance of sensitive, specificity and F1-score on EfficientDet-6333 is respectively increased 0.04%, 0.001% and 0.027% than the EfficientDet-12666. As for the model inference time on single image on our CPU, the time consumed by CenterNet and EfficientDet is 1.05s and 0.98s respectively. It is obvious that the model trained on the selected data from active learning performs well in accuracy and speed. The harder tumors that are only detected by EfficientDet have been shown in the Fig. 5.

However, there are some normal tissues which are similar with tumors on some single slices. As shown in Fig. 6, the region labeled by red box has some similarities on ith slice. However, it can be confirmed that it is fat tissue by observing the region labeled by green box on $(i + 1)$th slice. Therefore, the number of FP may be high if only reducing the threshold of inference for high TP or using the single-slice tumor detection. In the future work, it may be possible to combine continuous slices to reduce the False Positive (FP) without increasing the False Negative (FN).

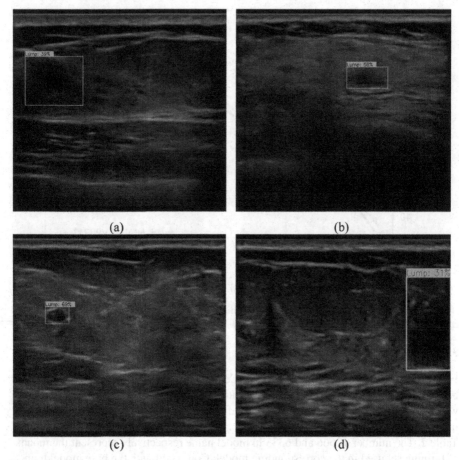

(a)                                      (b)

(c)                                      (d)

**Fig. 5.** Hard tumors detected by our model.The edges of tumor in (a) and (b) is blurred, and its borders is unclear. The tumor in (c) is tiny, but it has little calcification which is serious for patient. The shape of tumor in (d) is incomplete, and its edges and borders is unclear.

**Table 2.** Performance on different model with different training set.

| Model name | Sensitive | Specificity | F1-score |
|---|---|---|---|
| CenterNet-12666 | 0.729 | 0.963 | 0.706 |
| EfficientDet-12666 | 0.757 | 0.961 | 0.715 |
| EfficientDet-6333 | 0.797 | 0.962 | 0.742 |

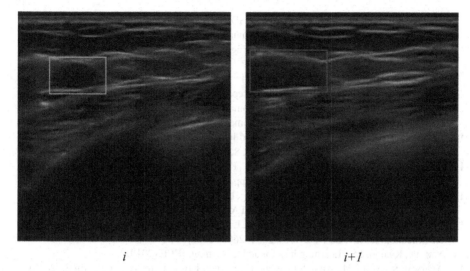

**Fig. 6.** Illustration of a normal fat tissue with similar features to tumor

## 4 Conclusion

We proposed the improved MIAL with OPA-FPN which automatically search the better FPN structure for object detection, to observe instance uncertainty. Based on the sorted uncertainty of all images in training dataset, we select the more difficult and reasonable images to create smaller training dataset. Using the selected small training dataset, we achieved more accurate performance. Meanwhile, the EfficientDet has shown it is more efficiency than CenterNet in MIAL with less model parameters. Specifically, we used the 50% of the whole training set and achieved result which exceeded the original model. Finally, the inference time of used model is 0.07s faster on our CPU.

**Acknowledgments.** This work was supported by Guangdong Basic and Applied Basic Research Foundation under Grant No. 2020B1515120098.

## References

1. Chen, W., et al.: CA Cancer J Clin **66**(2), 115–132 (2016)
2. Shen, H.-B., Tian, J.-W., Zhou, B.-S.: China guideline for the screening and early detection of female Breast Cancer. China Cancer **30**(3), 161–191 (2021)
3. Siegel, R.L., Miller, K.D., Fuchs, H.E., et al.: Cancer statistics. Cancer J. Clin. **71**(1) (2021)
4. Brem, R.F., Lenihan, M.J., Lieberman, J., Torrente, J.: Screening breast ultrasound: past, present, and future. Am. J. Roentgenol. **204**(2), 234–240 (2015)
5. Cao, Z., Duan, L., Yang, G., et al.: An experimental study on breast lesion detection and classification from ultrasound images using deep learning architectures. BMC Med. Imag. **19**(1) (2019)
6. Ren, S., He, K., Girshick, R., et al.: Faster R-CNN: towards real-time object detection with region proposal networks. IEEE Trans. Pattern Anal. Mach. Intell. **39**(6), 1137–1149 (2017)

7. Liu, W., Anguelov, D., Erhan, D., et al.: SSD: single shot multibox detector. In: Leibe, B., Matas, J., Sebe, N., Welling, M. (eds.) Computer Vision – ECCV 2016. ECCV 2016. Lecture Notes in Computer Science, vol. 9905. Springer, Cham (2016). https://doi.org/10.1007/978-3-319-46448-0_2

8. Redmon, J., Divvala, S., Girshick, R., et al.: You only look once: unified, real-time object detection. In: Computer Vision & Pattern Recognition. IEEE (2016)

9. Yap, M.H., Pons, G., Marti, J., et al.: Automated Breast ultrasound lesions detection using convolutional neural networks. IEEE J. Biomed. Health Inform. **22**(4), 1218–1226 (2017)

10. Deeply-supervised networks with threshold loss for Cancer detection in automated Breast Ultrasound. IEEE Trans. Med. Imag. **39**(4), 866–876 (2020)

11. Beluch, W.H., Genewein, T., Nürnberger, A., Köhler, J.M.: The power of ensembles for active learning in image classification. In CVPR, pp. 9368–9377 (2018)

12. Lin, L., Wang, K., Meng, D., Zuo, W., Zhang, L.: Active self-paced learning for cost-effective and progressive face identification. IEEE TPAMI **40**(1), 7–19 (2018)

13. Wang, K., Zhang, D., Li, Y., Zhang, R., Lin, L.: Cost-effective active learning for deep image classification. IEEE TCSVT **27**(12), 2591–2600 (2017)

14. Yoo, D., Kweon, I.S.: Learning loss for active learning. IEEE (2019)

15. Agarwal, S., Arora, H., Anand, S., et al.: Contextual Diversity for Active Learning (2020)

16. Balleyguier, C., Ayadi, S., Nguyen, K.V., et al.: BIRADS classification in mammography. Eur. J. Radiol. **61**(2), 192–194 (2007)

17. Liang, T., Wang, Y., Tang, Z., et al.: OPANAS: one-shot path aggregation network architecture search for object detection (2021)

18. Yuan, T., et al.: Multiple instance active learning for object detection. In: CVPR (2021)

19. Tan, M., Pang, R., Le, Q.V.: EfficientDet: scalable and efficient object detection. In: 2020 IEEE/CVF Conference on Computer Vision and Pattern Recognition (CVPR). IEEE (2020)

20. Jawahar, C.V., Li, H., Mori, G., Schindler, K. (eds.): ACCV 2018. LNCS, vol. 11365. Springer, Cham (2019). https://doi.org/10.1007/978-3-030-20873-8

21. Zhou, X., Wang, D., Krhenbühl, P.: Objects as points (2019)

22. Zhang, M., Xing, X.: Deep fuzzy hashing network for efficient image retrieval. IEEE Trans. Fuzzy Syst. (2020). https://doi.org/10.1109/TFUZZ.2020.2984991

23. Li, Y., Chen, M., et al.: Brain intelligence: go beyond artificial intelligence. Mob. Netw. Appl. **23**, 368–375 (2018)

24. Shenglin, M., et al.: Motor anomaly detection for unmanned aerial vehicles using reinforcement learning. IEEE Internet Things J. **5**(4), 2315–2322 (2018)

25. Qin, M., Zhang, F., et al.: RSCNN: a CNN-based method to enhance low-light remote-sensing images. Remote Sens. 62 (2020)

26. Zhang, Y., et al.: User-oriented virtual mobile network resource management for vehicle communications. IEEE Trans. Intell. Transp. Syst. **22**(6), 3521–3532 (2021)

# Adaptive Sliding Mode Control for a Hydraulic Position Servo System

Mingxing Yang[1,2]([⊠]), Yaxing Lu[1], Yulei Xia[1,2], and Kaiwei Ma[1,3]([⊠])

[1] Anhui Province Key Laboratory of Special Heavy Load Robot, Anhui University of
Technology, Maanshan 243032, China
mingxingyangvip@163.com, makaiwei@live.com
[2] College of Mechanical Engineering, Anhui University of Technology, Maanshan 243032,
China
[3] College of Automation and College of Artificial Intelligence, Nanjing University of Posts and
Telecommunications, Nanjing 210023, China

**Abstract.** The electro-hydraulic system is a typical complex system with nonlinear and high-order characteristics, which could seriously restrict the application of many advanced control algorithms. In this study, a sliding mode controller (SMC) based on adaptive neural network is proposed for a hydraulic position servo system with nonlinearity and parameter uncertainties. Structure design of a rotary hydraulic actuator is first introduced, and mathematical model of the hydraulic position servo system is constructed based on dynamic characteristics of the servo valve and the liquid flow continuity equation. Next, the adaptive neural network algorithm and sliding mode control technique are effectively combined to realize that the position signal of the hydraulic joint can be tracked along the desired command quickly and effectively. The SMC is adopted for its robustness against the uncertainty and nonlinearity of the target system, whereas the higher-order neural network observer is utilized to compensate parametric uncertainties to improve the accuracy. In addition, the closed-loop asymptotic stability of the designed control strategy is guaranteed by employing the Lyapunov theory. To investigate the tracking performance of the proposed controller, numerical simulation experiments have carried out and the results demonstrated the effectiveness of proposed control scheme.

**Keywords:** Electro-hydraulic system · Parameter uncertainties · Sliding mode controller · High-order neural network

## 1 Introduction

The electro-hydraulic servo system (EHSS) is considered the most promising choice for many engineering fields since it combines many merits of small size-to-power ratios, fast response speed and large torque output [1–3]. However, the EHSS is a typical nonlinear system with parametric uncertainties caused by the presence of servo valve dynamics, flow-pressure characteristics, internal leakage and dead zone, which seriously affects accuracy of position tracking and dramatically affects the performance of electro-hydraulic servo mechanisms [4]. Therefore, developing high performance controllers to realize accurate position control for hydraulic servo systems is of great importance.

In previous works, various advanced control strategies have been studied, such as adaptive control [5, 6], backstepping control [7], sliding mode control [8, 9], fuzzy methods [10], and neural network algorithms [11]. To a certain extent, these approaches can improve the control ability of the servo system, but still have their own limitations and shortcomings. The control of some indefinite parameters can be realized by adaptive control. Still, when the system is complex and the working conditions change, the adaptive algorithm is difficult to meet the high stability requirements [12]. It is well known that backstepping technology is a suitable means to deal with uncertainties. However, when some adaptive laws are used to deal with uncertainties to enhance the compensation ability of the controller, the backstepping with adaptive laws is no longer relevant [13]. Though the neural network and fuzzy control can approximate any nonlinear function to the desired accuracy, they require substantial computational power due to the complexity of the process [14]. Compared with other control schemes, the sliding mode control is the ideal method to control uncertain nonlinear systems with high dynamic uncertainties due to the advantages of insensitivity to model errors and high robustness. However, it should be noted that the inherent chattering phenomenon of sliding mode control will take place with the change of external disturbance and system structure parameters [15]. Therefore, the EHSS studied in this paper has nonlinear dynamics with many uncertainties, and single-use of the conventional control approach cannot realize satisfactory control performance.

In this paper, an innovation of adaptive sliding-mode controller based on a higher-order neural network is proposed for a hydraulic position servo control system. The novelty of this paper comes from (1) the adaptive part is constructed to handle the generalized uncertain parameters of the system, which improves the mismatch between the control model as well as the practical system and effectively reduces chattering. (2) The sliding mode control strategy is designed as the vital part to deal with the errors coming from state estimation, load disturbance and other un-modeled dynamics. The paper is organized as follows. Section 2 presents an electro-hydraulic manipulator dynamic, and consisting a manipulator dynamic and an electro-hydraulic dynamic. The control design and the proof of stability and robustness are depicted in Sect. 3. Numerical simulation results and some discussions are shown in Sect. 4. Concluding remarks are drawn in Sect. 5.

## 2  Introduction Mathematical Model of the Electro-hydraulic Position System

The rotary electro-hydraulic actuator studied in this paper is depicted in Fig. 1(a), which is utilized for power driving of the hip exoskeleton to assist human walking. It is mainly consists of an arc-shaped bent piston rod, a center-mounted supporting shaft, an angular sensor, two rigid links attached to the shaft, etc. To ensure the machining accuracy and convenience of installation, the cylinder is composed of left and right cylinder blocks

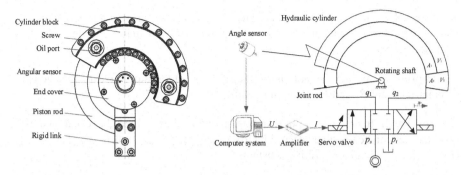

**Fig. 1.** The rotary electrohydraulic actuator and its corresponding schematic diagram of position servo system.

tightly fastened by bolts and elastic washers [16]. In addition, some essential sealing components are taken into account to prevent oil's internal and external leakages.

The schematic diagram of the valve-controlled hydraulic position servo system is shown in Fig. 1(b), where $P_s$ is the pump supply pressure, and $P_r$ is the tank pressure, and $x_v$ is the spool displacement of the slide valve. Meanwhile, $Q_1, A_1$, and $V_1$ represent the flow, effective area, and initial volume of the cylinder chamber with the hydraulic rod, respectively. $V_{10}$ and $V_{20}$ denote flow volumes from the servo valve to the rod and rodless cavities in the hydraulic cylinder respectively. Correspondingly, $Q_2, A_2$, and $V_2$ are the flow, effective area, an initial volume of the cylinder chamber without the hydraulic rod, respectively.

In addition, the other symbols of the EHSS are defined as follows: $w$ represents the area gradient of the throttle window, $\varepsilon$ is the piston-area ratio, $\beta_e$ and $B_t$ represent the effective bulk modulus and the viscous damping coefficient, respectively. $C_d, k_q$ and $k_c$ represent the flow coefficient, flow gain and flow pressure-coefficients of the servo valve, respectively. Moreover, $k_v$ denotes the gain of the servo amplifier, $R$ is the curvature radius of the piston rod, $T_L$ implies the external disturbance torque, and $J_L$ denotes the inertia moment of the piston rod and payload.

According to previous studies in reference [16], the system state variable is selected as $[x_1, x_2, x_3]^T = [\theta_p, \dot{\theta}_p, \ddot{\theta}_p]^T$. Then, in terms of the load-torque balance equation, load pressure dynamics and load flow equation, the state-space form of the valve-controlled hydraulic system will be described as follows:

$$\begin{cases} \dot{x}_1 = x_2 \\ \dot{x}_2 = x_3 \\ \dot{x}_3 = -\varphi_1\varphi_2 x_2 - (\varphi_3 + \varphi_1\varphi_4)x_2 - (\varphi_1\varphi_5 + \varphi_6) + \varphi_1\varphi_7 u \end{cases} \tag{1}$$

where $u$ is the input command voltage, and the unknown parameter set $\varphi = [\varphi_1, \varphi_2, \varphi_3, \varphi_4, \varphi_5, \varphi_6, \varphi_7]$ will be expressed as $\varphi_1 = \beta_e(\varepsilon^2 V_{10} + V_{20})/V_{10}V_{20}J_L$, $\varphi_2 = (A_1^2 + k_c B_t) R^2$, $\varphi_3 = B_t R^2/J_L$, $\varphi_4 = k_c J_L$, $\varphi_5 = k_c T_L$, $\varphi_6 = T_L/J_L$, and $\varphi_7 = k_q k_v A_1 R$.

Because it is difficult to accurately identify and changes with oil temperature and pressure, the internal parameters $C_i, C_e, C_d$ and $\beta_e$ are uncertain. In addition, the variation of working conditions and the difference in load torque always lead to the inability to accurately obtain external interference. Therefore, the following assumptions should be considered in the subsequent controller design to make the actuator track the trajectory as closely as possible.

**Assumption 1.** Assuming that four throttle windows of the slide valve are matched and symmetrical, and $P_1$ and $P_2$ are both bounded by $0 < Pr < P_1, P_2 < Ps$.

**Assumption 2.** In practical applications, the parameter set defined above and modeling uncertainties can be restricted according to $\varphi_{i\,min} \leq \varphi_i \leq \varphi_{i\,max}$, where $\varphi_{i\,min}$ and $\varphi_{i\,max}$ ($i = 1, 2, ...,7$) are given positive constants.

## 3   Problem Formylation and Preliminary

The controlled hydraulic system (1) can be simplified into the following third-order system

$$\begin{cases} \dot{x}_1 = x_2 \\ \dot{x}_2 = x_3 \\ \dot{x}_3 = f(x) + g(x)u \end{cases} \tag{2}$$

where $x_i \in \Re(i = 1, 2, 3)$ are known as the system states, $f(x) = -\varphi_1\varphi_2x_2 - (\varphi_3 + \varphi_1\varphi_4)x_3 - (\varphi_1\varphi_5 + \varphi_6)$ and $g(x) = \varphi_1\varphi_7$ represent unknown general continuous nonlinear functions, and $u \in \Re$ is the control signal. Considering that the general parameter $g(x)$ is positive in hydraulic systems, it's reasonable to assume that $g(x) > 0$ without losing generality.

Let $y = c_1x_1 + c_2x_2 + x_3$, a nonlinear system with variable control gain will be considered as

$$\dot{y} = c_1x_2 + c_2x_3 + f(x) + g(x)u \tag{3}$$

where $c_1, c_2$ are strictly positive constants to be specified according to the desired dynamics of the closed-loop system.

Since the $g(x) > 0$ is a given fact, the nonlinear system (3) can be restated as

$$u = g^{-1}(x)\dot{y} - g^{-1}(x)[c_1x_2 + c_2x_3 + f(x)] = \phi_1(x)\dot{y} - \phi_2(x) \tag{4}$$

where $\phi_1(x) = g^{-1}(x)$ and $\phi_2(x) = g^{-1}(x)[c_1x_2 + c_2x_3 + f(x)]$.

To identify the unknown control signal (4), a higher-order neural network (HONN) is employed to approximate the unknown function $\phi_1(x)$ and $\phi_2(x)$ as

$$\begin{cases} \phi_1(x) = W_1^*H_1(x) + \sigma_1 \\ \phi_2(x) = W_2^*H_2(x) + \sigma_2 \end{cases} \tag{5}$$

where $H_1(x) = [h_{11}(x), h_{12}(x), ..., h_{1n}(x)]^T \in \Re^n$ and $H_2(x) = [h_{21}(x), h_{22}(x), ..., h_{2n}(x)]^T \in \Re^n$ are the basis vectors of the nonlinear functions. $W_1^* = [w_{11}^*, w_{12}^*, ..., w_{1n}^*]$

$\in \mathfrak{R}^n$ and $W_2^* = [w_{21}^*, w_{22}^*, \ldots, w_{2n}^*] \in \mathfrak{R}^n$ denote the weight vectors of an ideal neural network. In addition, normal numbers $\sigma_1$ and $\sigma_2$ represent the approximation errors of the two neural networks, which satisfy $|\sigma_1| \leq \sigma_{1N}, |\sigma_2| \leq \sigma_{2N}$.

Therefore, the Eq. (4) will be re-expressed as

$$u = W_1^* H_1 \dot{y} - W_2^* H_2 + \sigma_{12} \tag{6}$$

where $\sigma_{12} = \sigma_1 \dot{y} - \sigma_2$ is a bounded estimation error, satisfying $|\sigma_{12}| \leq \sigma_{12N}$.

According to paper [17], filter variables $H_{1f}, H_{2f}$, and $H_{12f}$ can be defined as

$$\begin{cases} \lambda \dot{H}_{1f} + H_{1f} = H_1, & H_{1f}(0) = 0 \\ \lambda \dot{H}_{2f} + H_{2f} = H_2, & H_{2f}(0) = 0 \\ \lambda \dot{\sigma}_{12f} + \sigma_{12f} = \sigma_{12}, & \sigma_{12f}(0) = 0 \end{cases} \tag{7}$$

where $\lambda > 0$ is a filter parameter.

Furthermore, the following equation is considered

$$(H_1 \dot{y})_f = H_{1f} \dot{y}_f + \varsigma_1 \tag{8}$$

where $\varsigma_1$ is a high-order approximation error after filtering.

By using the filter on both sides of Eq. (6), we can get that

$$u_f = W_1^* H_{1f} \dot{y}_f - W_2^* H_{2f} + \bar{\delta}_f = W_{12} H_{12f} + \bar{\delta}_f \tag{9}$$

where $\bar{\delta}_f = W_1^* \varsigma_1 + \sigma_{12f}$ is the bounded integration error that satisfying $|\bar{\delta}_f| < \bar{\delta}_{fN}$, $W_{12} = [W_1^*, W_2^*]$ is the augmented weight vector, and $H_{12f} = [H_{1f} \dot{y}_f - H_{2f}]^T$ is the augmented regression vector.

The HONN output will be expressed as follows:

$$\begin{cases} \hat{\phi}_1(x) = \hat{W}_1 H_1 \\ \hat{\phi}_2(x) = \hat{W}_2 H_2 \end{cases} \tag{10}$$

where $\hat{W}_1$ and $\hat{W}_2$ are the estimated values of $W_1^*$ and $W_2^*$, respectively.

Therefore, the neural network estimation of Eq. (9) can be re-expressed as

$$\hat{u} = \hat{W}_1 H_{1f} \dot{y}_f - \hat{W}_2 H_{2f} = \hat{W}_{12} H_{12f} \tag{11}$$

where $\hat{W}_{12} = [\hat{W}_1, \hat{W}_2]$.

By introducing the estimation error as $\delta_u = u_f - \hat{u}$ and subtracting Eq. (11) from Eq. (9), we can get that

$$\delta_u = \tilde{W}_{12} H_{12f} + \bar{\delta}_f \tag{12}$$

where $\tilde{W}_{12} = W_{12} - \hat{W}_{12}$, $\tilde{W}_1 = W_1^* - \hat{W}_1$ as well as $\tilde{W}_2 = W_2^* - \hat{W}_2$ represent estimation errors of $W_1^*$ and $W_2^*$, respectively.

In addition, the learning law for the augmented weight vector is proposed as

$$\dot{\hat{W}}_{12} = \left( \frac{H_{12}^T \delta_u}{\kappa + H_{12}^T H_{12}} - \sigma \hat{W}_{12} \right) \Lambda \tag{13}$$

where $\kappa > 0$ is a small constant, $\Lambda = \text{diag}(\Gamma_1 E_n, \Gamma_2 E_n)$ is a positive definite matrix satisfying $\Gamma_1, \Gamma_2 \in \mathfrak{R}^+$, and $\sigma \in \mathfrak{R}^+$ is a small constant used to enhance the robustness of HONN identification algorithm.

## 4   Controller Design and Stability Analysis

### 4.1   Design of the Sliding Mode Controller

After system identification, it is necessary to design an adaptive sliding mode controller for nonlinear system (3) with variable control gains. Considering that the design objective is to make $x_1 \to x_d$, the reference signal of the controlled system will be defined as

$$y_d = c_1 x_d + c_2 \dot{x}_d + \ddot{x}_d \tag{14}$$

The tracking error vector of system (3) is $e = [e_1, e_2, e_3]^T = [x_d - x_1, \dot{x}_d - x_2, \ddot{x}_d - x_3]^T$, and choosing the sliding surface function as $s = c_1 e_1 + c_1 e_2 + e_3$, we can get that

$$s = c_1 x_d + c_2 \dot{x}_d + \ddot{x}_d - c_1 x_1 - c_2 x_2 - x_3 \tag{15}$$

Accordingly, the derivative of Eq. (15) can be obtained as

$$\dot{s} = c_1 \dot{x}_d + c_2 \ddot{x}_d + \dddot{x}_d - c_1 x_2 - c_2 x_3 - f(x) - g(x)u \tag{16}$$

By introducing $g^{-1}(x)$ to both sides of Eq. (16), we can get that

$$\begin{aligned}
g^{-1}(x)\dot{s} &= g^{-1}(x)(c_1 \dot{x}_d + c_2 \ddot{x}_d + \dddot{x}_d) - g^{-1}(x)[c_1 x_2 + c_2 x_3 + f(x)] - u \\
&= \phi_1(x)\dot{y}_d - \phi_2(x) - u
\end{aligned} \tag{17}$$

Based on the above analysis, the controller is designed as follows:

$$u = \hat{W}_1 H_1 \dot{y}_d - \hat{W}_2 H_2 + \eta \mathrm{sgn}(s) + ks \tag{18}$$

where $\dot{s} = -\eta sgn(x) - ks$, $k > 0$ and $\eta > 0$.

Finally, taking Eq. (5–16) and Eq. (5–22) into (5–21) that

$$\begin{aligned}
\phi_1(x)\dot{s} &= W_1^* H_1 \dot{y}_d - W_2^* H_2 - \sigma_2 + \sigma_1 \dot{y}_d - \hat{W}_1 H_1 \dot{y}_d + \hat{W}_2 H_2 - \eta \mathrm{sgn}(s) - ks \\
&= (W_1^* - \hat{W}_1) H_1 \dot{y}_d - (W_2^* - \hat{W}_2) H_2 - \eta \mathrm{sgn}(s) - ks - \sigma_2 + \sigma_1 \dot{y}_d \\
&= \tilde{W}_1 H_1 \dot{y}_d - \tilde{W}_2 H_2 - \sigma_2 + \sigma_1 \dot{y}_d - \eta \mathrm{sgn}(s) - ks \\
&= \zeta - \eta \mathrm{sgn}(s) - ks
\end{aligned} \tag{19}$$

where $\zeta = \tilde{W}_1 H_1 \dot{y}_d - \tilde{W}_2 H_2 - \sigma_2 + \sigma_1 \dot{y}_d$.

**Remark 1.** It should be noted that $\sigma_1, \sigma_2, \tilde{W}_1$ and $\tilde{W}_2$ are bounded, and $\dot{y}_d$ is a bounded signal simultaneously, so $\zeta$ will also be bounded.

## 4.2  Stability Analysis

Consider the following Lyapunov function:

$$V = \frac{1}{2}\phi_1 s^2 \qquad (20)$$

According to Eq. (19), the derivative of $V$ can be expressed as

$$
\begin{aligned}
\dot{V} = \phi_1 s\dot{s} &= s\zeta - s[ks + \eta\mathrm{sgn}(s)] \\
&= s\zeta - (ks^2 + \eta|s|) \le -ks^2 - \eta|s| + |\zeta||s| \\
&= -ks^2 - (\eta - |\zeta|)|s|
\end{aligned} \qquad (21)
$$

which means that $\dot{V}$ is negative when $k > 0$ and $\eta \ge |\zeta|$, and it can be concluded that the closed-loop system is asymptotically stable at this time. As a result, the state $x_1$ of the system will track $x_d$.

## 5  Simulation Verification of the Proposed Controller

In order to investigate the effectiveness of the designed control method, the proposed sliding mode controller based on adaptive neural network is simulated and analyzed based on Matlab/Simulink. Ignoring the influence of fluid leakage and the elastic damping in the cylinder, initial parameters of EHSS are chosen based on the preliminary work [16]. Thus, the initial dynamic model that based on the system state equation will be expressed as

$$
\begin{cases}
\dot{x}_1 = x_2 \\
\dot{x}_2 = x_3 \\
\dot{x}_3 = -3.18 \times 10^5 x_2 - 60.912 x_3 + 8.8 \times 10^5 u
\end{cases} \qquad (22)
$$

**Table 1.** Control parameters of the proposed controller.

| HONN | | SMC | |
|---|---|---|---|
| Parameters | Value | Parameters | Value |
| $\chi$ | 0.02 | $c_1$ | $3.8 \times 10^4$ |
| $\Gamma_1$ | 0.01 | $c_2$ | 600 |
| $\Gamma_2$ | 1.0 | $k$ | $1.5 \times 10^{-3}$ |
| $K$ | 0.01 | $\eta$ | 0.01 |
| $\sigma$ | 0.05 | | |

Taking a sinusoidal signal as the desired trajectory, where the amplitude is $20°$ and the frequency is $0.25$ Hz that $x_d = 20\sin(\pi t/2)$. For the proposed controller, the activation functions of basis vectors $H_1(x)$ and $H_2(x)$ are selected as $h_{11} = h_{21} = 1/(1 + e^{-0.005x1})$, $h_{12} = h_{22} = 1/(1 + e^{-0.01x1})$, $h_{13} = h_{23} = 1/(1 + e^{-0.015x1})$, $h_{14} = h_{24} = 1/(1 + e^{-0.025x1})$, $h_{15} = h_{11}^2$, $h_{16} = h_{12}^2$, $h_{17} = h_{13}^2$, $h_{18} = h_{11}h_{12}h_{13}$, $h_{25} = h_{21}^2$, $h_{26} = h_{22}^2$, $h_{27} = h_{23}^2$, and $h_{28} = h_{21}h_{22}h_{23}$. Besides, parameters of the proposed controller are summarized in Table 1. The initial value of the neural network weight and system state are set zero at the beginning, while the simulation time is 160 s. The simulation results are shown in Fig. 2 and Fig. 3, which illustrate the effectiveness of the designed controller.

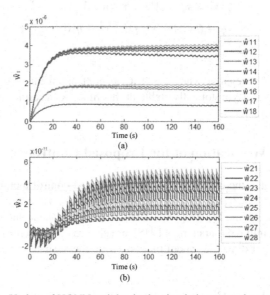

**Fig. 2.** Update of HONN weights in the simulation control experiment

In Fig. 2, it is demonstrated that weights $\hat{W}_1$ and $\hat{W}_2$ can converge to their stable state in a short period of time. Meanwhile, in Fig. 3, it is evident that the system state $x_1$ is close to the reference signal $x_d$, while a more significant gap between the system state and the reference signal can be observed at the beginning of the time. In particular, the system structure estimated by HONN is quite different from the actual value at the beginning of the simulation, which causes the weights of the neural network to show a wide range of adjustments. Then, the HONN estimation gradually approaches the structure of the system, and its weight estimation shows a minor adjustment. Therefore, fast response and a very accurate tracking procedure for the hydraulic position servo system are realized through the proposed controller.

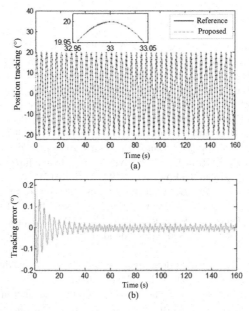

**Fig. 3.** Tracking performance of the joint in the simulation experiment

## 6 Conclusion

A novel method for the design of an adaptive sliding-mode controller for a nonlinear hydraulic position servo system with unknown dynamics and parameter uncertainties. The main idea of this method is to introduce a high-order neural network to adjust the sliding mode parameters of the system, and the SMC ensures the robustness and rapidity of the entire system. The target joint of the valve-controlled system and its corresponding mathematical model are first introduced, and the unknown parameters of matching and mismatching are considered. Second, the proposed adaptive sliding-mode controller is presented, and the stability and convergence of the entire closed-loop system by adjusting the weight of the adaptive neural network, and the stability of the closed loop system is analyzed. In addition, the reliability and effectiveness of the proposed control strategy are verified by simulation experiments, and the results reveal that the presented method exhibits good tracking performance in reducing the position tracking error and well dynamic regulation. Future work will be focused on the generalization of this idea to hydraulic control systems with engineering practice.

**Acknowledgement.** This work was partially supported by the National Natural Science Foundation of China under grant 52005006, partially supported by the Open fund of Anhui Province Key Laboratory of Special Heavy Load Robot under grant TZJQR001-2022, and partially supported by the Postdoctoral Research Fund of Anhui Province under grant 2021B504.

# References

1. Han, H., Liu, Y., Ma, L., Liu, Z., Quan, L.: Analyze the characteristics of electro-hydraulic servo system's position-pressure master-slave control. Adv. Mech. Eng. **10**(6), 1–9 (2018)
2. Yao, J., Jiao, Z., Ma, D., Yan, L.: High-accuracy tracking control of hydraulic rotary actuators with modeling uncertainties. IEEE/ASME Trans. Mechatron. **19**(2), 633–641 (2014)
3. Na, J., Li, Y., Huang, Y., Gao, G., Chen, Q.: Output feedback control of uncertain hydraulic servo systems. IEEE Trans. Industr. Electron. **67**(1), 490–500 (2019)
4. Yang, G., Yao, J.: High-precision motion servo control of double-rod electro-hydraulic actuators with exact tracking performance. ISA Trans. **103**, 266–279 (2020)
5. Yao, J., Deng, W., Jiao, Z.: RISE-based adaptive control of hydraulic systems with asymptotic tracking. IEEE Trans Autom Sci Eng **14**(3), 1524–1531 (2017)
6. Mohanty, A., Gayaka, S., Yao, B.: An adaptive robust observer for velocity estimation in an electro-hydraulic system. Int. J. Adapt. Control Sig. Process. **26**(12), 1076–1089 (2012)
7. Guo, K., Wei, J.H., Fang, J.H., Feng, R.L., Wang, X.C.: Position tracking control of electro-hydraulic single-rod actuator based on an extended disturbance observer. Mechatronics **27**, 47–56 (2015)
8. Palli, G., Strano, S., Terzo, M.: Sliding-mode observers for state and disturbance estimation in electro-hydraulic systems. Control. Eng. Pract. **74**, 58–70 (2018)
9. Shu, W., Burton, R., Habibi, S.: Sliding mode controller and filter applied to an electro-hydraulic actuator system. In: ASME International Mechanical Engineering Congress and Exposition (2011)
10. Lu, H., Zhang, M., Xu, X., Li, Y., Shen, H.: Deep fuzzy hashing network for efficient image retrieval. IEEE Trans. Fuzzy Syst. **29**(1), 166–176 (2020)
11. Li, Y., Wang, Q.: Adaptive neural finite-time trajectory tracking control of hydraulic excavators. Proc. Inst. Mech. Eng. Part I J. Syst. Control Eng. **232**(7), 909–925 (2018)
12. Yang, M., Zhang, Q., Lu, X., Xi, R., Wang, X.: Adaptive sliding mode control of a nonlinear electro-hydraulic servo system for position tracking. Mechanika **25**(4), 283–290 (2019)
13. Tran, D., Truong, H., Ahn, K.K.: Adaptive backstepping sliding mode control based RBFNN for a hydraulic manipulator including actuator dynamics. Appl. Sci. **9**(6), 1265 (2019)
14. Lu, H., Li, Y., Chen, M., Kim, H., Serikawa, S.: Brain intelligence: go beyond artificial intelligence. Mob. Netw. Appl. **7553**, 1 (2017)
15. Yuan, X., Chen, Z., Yuan, Y., Huang, Y., Li, X., Li, W.: Sliding mode controller of hydraulic generator regulating system based on the input/output feedback linearization method. Math. Comput. Simul. **119**, 18–34 (2016)
16. Yang, M., Ma, K., Shi, Y., Wang, X.: Modeling and position tracking control of a novel circular hydraulic actuator with uncertain parameters. IEEE Access **7**, 181022–181031 (2020)
17. Na, J., Ren, X., Zheng, D.: Adaptive control for nonlinear pure-feedback systems with high-order sliding mode observer. IEEE Trans. Neural Netw. Learn. Syst. **24**(3), 370–382 (2013)
18. Zhang, M., Xing, X.: Deep fuzzy hashing network for efficient image retrieval. IEEE Trans. Fuzzy Syst. (2020). https://doi.org/10.1109/TFUZZ.2020.2984991
19. Huimin, L., Li, Y., Chen, M., et al.: Brain Intelligence: go beyond artificial intelligence. Mob. Netw. Appl. **23**, 368–375 (2018)
20. Shenglin, M., et al.: Motor anomaly detection for unmanned aerial vehicles using reinforcement learning. IEEE Internet Things J. **5**(4), 2315–2322 (2018)
21. Zhang, F., et al.: RSCNN: a CNN-based method to enhance low-light remote-sensing images. Remote Sens. 62 (2020)
22. Li, Y., et al.: User-oriented virtual mobile network resource management for vehicle communications. IEEE Trans. Intell. Transp. Syst. **22**(6), 3521–3532 (2021)

# Multimodal Interaction Fusion Network Based on Transformer for Video Captioning

Hui Xu, Pengpeng Zeng[✉], and Abdullah Aman Khan

Sichuan Artificial Intelligence Research Institute, Yibin 644000, China
pengpengzeng@gmail.com

**Abstract.** Learning to generate the description for a video is essentially a challenging task as it involves an understanding of vision and language. Existing methods are mainly based on Recurrent Neural Networks (RNN). Nevertheless, there are some limitations, such as feeble representation power and sequential nature. The transformer-based architecture was proposed to address such issues, and it is widely used in the domain of image captioning. Although it has achieved success in existing methods, the applicability to video captioning is still largely under-explored. To fully explore its significance in video captioning, this paper proposes a novel network by utilizing the transformer for video captioning named Multimodal Interaction Fusion Network (MIFN). To effectively learn the relationship between multiple features, a cross-attention module is introduced within the encoder, which provides a better representation. Moreover, in the decoder, we use a gated mechanism for filtering the essential information to produce the next word. Moreover, we evaluate the proposed approach by using the benchmark MSR-VTT and MSVD video captioning datasets to illustrate its quantitative and qualitative effectiveness and employ extensive ablation experiments to fully understand the significance of each component of MIFN. The extensive experimental results demonstrate that MIFN obtains performance comparable to the state-of-the-art methods.

**Keywords:** Multimodal · Transformer · Video captioning · Attention

## 1 Introduction

Recently, the task of vision and language has attracted widespread attention due to one of the key initiatives to achieve artificial intelligence (AI). Meanwhile, the development of deep learning has promoted many multimodal learning tasks such as image-text matching [1], visual question answering (VQA) [2–4] and captioning [5–9]. Captioning task is defined as generating the natural language descriptions of an image or a video. Captioning requires a deep understanding of visual concepts, linguistic semantics, and the alignment of the two. The model needs to recognize the visual information provided to generate accurate and descriptive sentences. However, compared with image captioning, video captioning presents many challenges. First, reasoning over the sequence of images rather than the static image can be more difficult. To describe the video, the model

S. Yang and H. Lu (Eds.): ISAIR 2022, CCIS 1700, pp. 21–36, 2022.
https://doi.org/10.1007/978-981-19-7946-0_3

needs to identify the content of each frame in the video. Secondly, the model needs to consider long-range temporal structures without missing the relationship between the frames in the video. Thirdly, it is a common problem for both image captioning and video captioning to build the relationships between the visual and language to generate descriptions consistent with visual semantics. Thus, video captioning models require reasoning ability on spatial and long-range temporal structures of both video and text to generate an accurate sentence.

The well-known encoder-decoder framework with a Recurrent Neural Network (RNN) is usually used as the basic structure for video captioning tasks. First, a convolutional neural network (CNN) has been adept in our framework to extract frame-based features from an input video. And then, the encoder captures the temporal information to obtain video-based features. Finally, the decoder generates the caption words about the video by taking the output of the encoder. The encoder-decoder framework was optimized end-to-end through a word-level cross-entropy loss. Based on this framework, some researchers have proposed plenty of improved algorithms to upgrade the model for video captioning tasks. For instance, to build the relationship between the caption words and their related frames in the video, an attention mechanism has also been adopted for video captioning, including spatial and temporal attention. To provide a better visual representation of the video, multiple features (appearance and motion) can be extracted from different networks to represent the diverse information.

Although it has succeeded in existing methods, the applicability to video captioning is still largely under-explored. Although it has succeeded in existing methods in video captioning, we observed the following limitations: First, when encoding the multiple features, the encoder neglects intra-modal interactions (e.g., appearance to appearance or motion to motion) and inter-modal interactions (e.g., appearance to motion or motion to appearance). Secondly, the decoder also ignores the self-attention between the output caption words (*i.e.,* word-to-word). Third, the fusion strategy in the decoder is to simply fuse different features, such as concatenation and element-wise adding.

To deal with the above-mentioned issues, we design a novel Multimodal Interaction Fusion network with a transformer (MIFN) to upgrade the effectiveness of the video captioning task. Especially, the property of transformer [10] can capture some intra-modal interactions (e.g., appearance-to-appearance, motion-to-motion, and word-to-word) and inter-modal interactions (e.g., word-to-motion and word-to-appearance) which can address partial limitation and the second limitations. To resolve the first limitation, we inject the cross-attention module to learn the relationship between the input visual features (*i.e.,* appearance-to-motion and motion-to-appearance). Furthermore, we apply a gated mechanism to select the key information from the multiple features.

Our MIFN model achieves comparable performance with the competing methods over MSR-VTT and MSVD datasets, two large-scale video captioning benchmarks. In summary, the major contributions of the proposed method include:

- This paper proposes a novel approach, Multimodal Interaction Fusion Network (MIFN), based on a transformer for video captioning by jointly modeling the interactions with self-attention and co-attention. The MIFN model uses a modular attention block to model a better representation by extracting five types of relationships, e.g., word-to-word, appearance-to-motion, motion-to-appearance, word-to-appearance, and word-to-motion.

- We introduce a Gated mechanism in the decoder part of the MIFN model to obtain key information across different modalities.
- The extensive ablation experiments illustrate that MIFN obtains performance improvement over two publicly available MSR-VTT and MSVD datasets for video captioning tasks. In addition, our experimental results obtained comparable results to the state-of-the-art methods.

## 2 Related Work

Here, we review the last few years studies about video captioning and transformer.

### 2.1 Video Captioning

Learning to generate video descriptions is a very challenging task that involves understanding both vision and language. Early approaches [11–14] on video captioning is often based on template methods, which apply the word and language rules to design a sentence template. According to the predefined template, the model can align with video content and languages. For example, the work in [13] adopted a Conditional Random Field (CRF) to generate the semantic features for description by modeling the relationships of each two different components from visual inputs. In [14], they proposed a unified framework with two joint models to model two types of features, compositional semantics language and video, in video-text space. However, fixed templates also limit the capabilities of the model for language generation.

The well-known encoder-decoder framework is broadly used in neural machine translation and captioning, which is more flexible than the aforementioned method. The encoder-decoder framework includes encoder and decoder components. In captioning tasks, the former is used to encode video information, and the latter is used to produce human-specific sentences. The work in [7] first averaged each frame feature and then used an LSTM to decode it into captions. The temporal information of video is not adequately used. The attention mechanism is introduced into video captioning to focus on a specific frame in the video relevant to the generated word [15]. The work in [16] proposes a general video caption method (S2VT) without an explicit attention model which learns the temporal structure of the video (optical flow) and applies an LSTM in both encoder and decoder. In [6], they adapt a parallel two-stream 3D-CNN to gain better visual features from the video. Since then, numerous works have adopted multimodal visual features to upgrade the effectiveness of video captioning. The work in [17] proposes an adaptive attention (hLSTMat) hierarchical LSTM framework to select the key information between the visual content and the language context content and adapt the multi-modal features too.

However, the works mentioned above directly input the various visual outputs from the encoder into the decoder while ignoring the relationship between those features. To learn such a relationship, MIFN injects a cross-attention into the encoder to learn the relationship between the multiple features and a gated mechanism into the decoder to generate the video's description by selecting the key information.

## 2.2 Video Captioning

The first work on the transformer network [10] introduced a new encoder-decoder architecture. This architecture was applied to machine translation and it achieved better results than the previous works [18–20]. The transformer includes self-attention and cross-attention. The former can characterize the intra-modal interaction within each modality (e.g., appearance-to-appearance), and the latter can characterize inter-modal interaction across different modalities (*i.e.,* Chinese to English). Some work also attempted to use the transformer to solve the captioning task since the captioning involves multimodal interactions. The work in [21] proposed the Object Relation transformer (ORT), explicitly modeling the spatial relationships. The work in [9] introduced EnTangled Attention (ETA) for image captioning that enables the transformer to bridge the relationship between semantic and visual information simultaneously. The work in [8] proposed $\hat{M2}$, a meshed transformer with memory that model the prior knowledge between the low and high two-level information.

Nevertheless, there are only a few studies that use transformers to deal with video captioning tasks. In our work, we adopt the transformer architecture that introduces the different encoder and decoder designs to deal with video captioning tasks. The encoder learns a better representation from different multimodal features. The decoder can select more important information with the gate mechanism.

# 3  Preliminaries

Next, this section introduces the primary formulation of the transformer, which is the core structure for our model. The transformer has two basic blocks: the multi-head attention module and the feed-forward network (FFN).

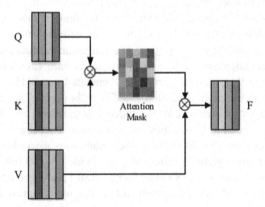

**Fig. 1.** The Scaled Dot-Product Attention network.

**Multi-Head Attention module layer (MHA):** The core component of the multi-head attention module is h paralleled scaled independent dot-product attention layers, namely

'Head', as shown in Fig. 1. Specifically, the input of 'Head' contains $q \in R^d$, $k^t \in R^d$, and $v^t \in R^d$, where $q$ is the query, $k$ is the key and belongs to set $K$, $v$ is the value and belongs to set $V$, $t \in \{1, 2, ..., n\}$ is the number of key-value pairs, and $d$ is the dimension number. Then, we can achieve the attention weights for the values by calculating the dot products of the query with all keys through a softmax function. Eventually, through this dot-product attention mechanism, we obtain queries-based aware attended feature defined as $F$. For matrices $Q = [q_1, ..., q_m] \in R^{m \times d}$, $K = [k_1, ..., k_n] \in R^{n \times d}$ and $V = [v_1, ..., v_n] \in R^{n \times d}$, we formulate the above process as:

$$F = \text{Attention}(Q, K, V) = \sigma \left( \frac{QK^T}{\sqrt{d}} \right) V, \tag{1}$$

where the dimension of $F$ is $m \times d$, $\delta$ is the softmax function.

MHA allows the model not only conduct with a single attention layer but also to explore subspaces. Thus, the final attended feature $F$ will be obtained as follows:

$$M - \text{head}(Q, K, V) = \text{Concat}(H_1, \ldots, H_h) W^O,$$
$$H_i = \text{Attention}\left( QW_i^Q, KW_i^K, VW_i^V \right), \tag{2}$$

where M-head is the short form of multihead, $W_i^K$, $W_i^V \in R^{d \times d_h}$ are linear function parameters of the $i - th$ 'Head' which respectively project $Q$, $K$ and $V$ into the latent space. $W_i^V \in R^{d \times d_h}$ is the output projection matrix. We denote the sequence number of the 'Head' as $h$ and set $d_h = d/h$.

**Feed-Forward Network layer (FFN):** Another basic block of the transformer is FFN. FFN takes the output from the MHA as input and it is implemented by two linear projections to obtain the high-level representation. This process is formulated as:

$$FFN(x) = FC(\text{ReLU}(FC(x))), \tag{3}$$

where both input and output dimensions are $d$, ReLU is the ReLU activation function. And the dimensionality of inner-layer is usually $d_{ff} = 2048$.

Both encoder and decoder of transformer consist of multiple above building blocks where each building block is composed of the MHA and FFN modules. According to whether the input features are the same, the MHA module can be divided into self-attention and cross-attention two types. The original encoder of the transformer only has self-attention, which can characterize the intra-modal interaction within each modality. The difference in the decoder is that it has these two attention mechanisms, and cross-attention can characterize Inter-modal interaction across different modalities. Besides, each layer follows layer normalization (LayerNorm), and the residual connection is used for all building blocks.

## 4  Methodology

For a video sequence $V = [v_1, ..., v_m]$, the goal of video captioning is to produce a natural sentence $S = [s_1, ..., s_n]$ that expresses the semantic meaning of the video, where $m$ is the length of frames, $n$ is the length of a sentence.

26    H. Xu et al.

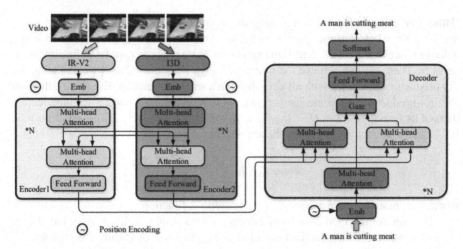

**Fig. 2.** The framework of the proposed MIFN. We first inject the cross-attention module into the encoder of the transformer to fully exploit the differential but related semantic information. Then, we select the key information to generate textual captions by representing various features through the encoder.

Next, we detail the proposed framework, *i.e.*, Multimodal Interaction Fusion Network (MIFN) based on the transformer for video captioning, which can upgrade the quality of the produced sentence descriptions. In our method, we first adopt the basic structure of the transformer and then modify its internal structure to meet our specific needs. Specifically, a cross-attention module is injected into the encoder of the transformer to fully utilize the different but relevant semantic information. Furthermore, since we get representations of various features through the encoder, we need to produce textual captions by choosing the key information. Thus, we propose a gated mechanism to deal with such issue. The overall framework of the MFIN is illustrated in Fig. 2. The following sections provide details about each component.

## 4.1 Encoder with Multimodal Features

The process of the encoder includes two stages. The first stage aims to extract the different visual representations, namely appearance and motion features, defined as a multimodal feature extraction module. Moreover, the second stage aims to learn the relationship between the multimodal visual representation to obtain the final video features.

## 4.2 Multimodal Feature Extraction Module

For appearance representation, we utilize Inception-Resnet-v2 (IR-v2) network [22] pre-trained on ILSVRC-2012-CLS dataset [23] to extract it. The input of each frame $v_i$ in the video to the IR-v2 network is resized to $299 \times 299$. The output feature of the last pooling layer is used to encode the frame-based visual feature $a_i \in R^{1536}$, where 1536 is the dimension. Therefore, the total appearance features $A$ of video $V$ is defined as follows:

$$A = [a_1, \ldots, a_m], a_i \in R^{1536}$$
$$a_i = IR - v2(v_i),$$

(4)

where $v_i$ represents the RGB image of the frame in the video.

For motion representation, we adopt the Inflated 3D ConvNet (I3D) [24] pre-trained on the Kinetics dataset [12] to obtain clip-based visual features. First, we use both horizontal and vertical directions between each frame and adjacent frames, using TVL1-flow networks [25], to calculate the optical flow information. Then, each continuous 64 optical flow flips are input to the I3D network to obtain 2048-dimensional motion features $m_i \in R^{2048}$. We formulate this process as below:

$$M = [m_1, \ldots, m_m], a_i \in R^{1536}$$
$$m_i = I3D(c_i)$$

(5)

where $c_i$ represents a clip, the clip duration is 64 frames.

In order to represent sequence order for the transformer model, the model uses position encoding (PE) to encode the position information of the frames.

We formulate the process of PE as:

$$PE_{(\text{position},2i)} = \sin\left(\frac{p}{10000^{\frac{2i}{d}}}\right)$$
$$PE_{(\text{position},2i+1)} = \cos\left(\frac{p}{10000^{\frac{2i}{d}}}\right)$$

(6)

where $i$ is the dimension. The $PE$ chose the sinusoidal version.

### 4.3 Cross-Attention Module with Multi-modal Features

The cross-attention module is composed of two identical encoders, and each encoder encodes a different video feature. Each encoder encodes its features without interaction, and there is no relationship between the learned features. To deal with this issue, this paper introduces a cross-attention strategy to the encoder that modifies the transformer's original encoder. Each encoder stack $L$ cross-attention block, and each cross-attention block has three sub-networks, a self-attention network, a cross-attention network, and a FFN. Take the outputs of the $l - th(0 \leq l < N)$ block of two encoders $V_A^i \in R^{m \times d}$ and $V_M^i \in R^{m \times d}$ as an example. Specifically, the input from the $(i + 1) - th$ self-attention network is the output for the $i - th$ block, which learns Intra-modal interaction within each modality.

$$D_{.,t}^{l+1} = MHA_{\text{self}}\left(H_{.,t}^l, H_{\leq t}^l, H_{\leq t}^l\right),$$

(7)

And then the $V_A^i$ and $V_M^i$ are input to the $(i + 1) - th$ cross-attention network to learn inter-modal interaction across different modalities. This process is formulated as follows:

$$g^a = MHA_{\text{cross}}\left(d_t, V_A^L, V_A^L\right)$$
$$g^m = MHA_{\text{cross}}\left(d_t, V_M^L, V_M^L\right),$$

(8)

Before feeding into this module, the appearance feature $A$ and the motion feature $M$ are mapped into $V_A^0 \in R^{m \times d}$ and $V_M^0 \in R^{m \times d}$, and the residual connection and layer normalization are used.

### 4.4 Decoder with Gated Mechanism

Given previously generated words and video features, the decoder generates the next tokens of the output caption. Note that the video features extracted from multiple encoders focus on aspects of the video that have different importance to the generated words, making it challenging to select key information from different features. To address such an issue, our decoder block inserts a gated mechanism module between the MHA sub-layer and FFN sub-layer, which can empower the ability of the decoder block to perform attention over the difference encoder outputs simultaneously.

Given the previously generated words$S_{<t} = [s_0, ..., s_{t-1}]$, the decoder is to generate the next $t - th$ word. Each word $w_t \in R^d$ is represented by a vector for the word at position t in the sentence. Moreover, $w_t$ is obtained by word embedding and positional encoding. Notably, $w_0$ represents the start of a sentence.

Similar to the encoder, the decoder has $N$ identical blocks, and each block consists of five sub-layers, namely one$MHA_{self}$, two$MHA_{cross}$, one a gated mechanism and one FFN. For the $(l + 1) - th$ block, the output of the $l - th$ block $H^l \in R^{t \times d} = [h_1^l, ..., h_t^l]$, are fed into a $(l + 1) - th$ $MHA_{self}$ sub-layer in the $(l + 1) - th$ block, notice that $h_0^l$ corresponds to $w_{t-1}$ :

$$
\begin{aligned}
c\_a_t &= sigmoid(W_a[d_t, g^a] + b_a \\
c\_m_t &= sigmoid(W_m[d_t, g^m] + b_t \\
c_t &= Relu([(c\_a_t \odot f(g^a)) \oplus (c\_m_t \odot f(g^m))])
\end{aligned}
\tag{9}
$$

where $H_{.,t}^l \in R^{1 \times d}$, $E_{.,t}^{l=1} \in R^{1 \times d}$, and $h_0^l = s_{t-1}$. Subsequently, the $MHA_{self}$ output $D_{.,t}^{l+1}$ is passed into the two $MHA_{cross}$ to provide the proper guidance for the attention in different target modalities. The process can be formulated as follows:

$$
L_\theta = -\sum_{t=1}^{N} \log P(w_t|w_{<t}, V, \theta),
\tag{10}
$$

where $V_A^L$ and $V_M^L$ are the output of the two encoders.

The gating mechanism is to select key information between the different modalities and flow to the subsequent layers. Such a gate is good at dealing with gradient explosion and vanishing, enabling information to spread unimpeded through a long time step or a deeper layer. The context gates $c_{a_t}$ and $c_{m_t}$ are determined by the current self-attention output $d_t$, the appearance guidance $g^a$ and the motion guidance $g^m$.

$$
F = Attention(Q, K, V) = \text{MultiH}(QUOTE \ ta_l h_{V_l^{enc}}^u, W_{k_1}^{TA_l} h_{TA_l}^u, W_{v_1}^{TA_l} h_{TA_l}^u
$$

where $W_a$ and $W_m$ are parameters that needed to be learned, and $b_a$ and $b_t$ are bias terms. Note that $[,]$, $\odot$, and $\oplus$ is the concatenation, element-wise multiplication and element-wise addition operation separately. $f(.)$ can be an activation function. We feed the $c_t$ into the FFN sub-layer to obtain the final feature $H_{\leq t}^{t+1} \in R^{t \times d}$.

$$F = Attention(Q, K, V) = \text{MultiH(QUOTE ta}_1 h_{V_l^{enc}}^u, W_{k_1}^{TA_l} h_{TA_l}^u, W_{v_1}^{TA_l} h_{TA_l}^u$$

Suppose the decoder is generating the $n - th$ word of the target sentence. Similar to the encoder, the decoder also consists of $N$ uniform multi-head layers. Each layer consists of three MHA modules, more preciously, two FFN modules and one gated mechanism module. Moreover, the first two MHA modules learn motion-guided attention from the caption words separately (appearance to word and motion to word) and the appearance-guided attention from the caption words. The last MHA module models the self-attentions on the caption words (word to word).

### 4.5 Training Processing

In the training process, we follow the standard protocol of video captioning to implement the training process. Specifically, we pre-train the model by using a word-level cross-entropy objective:

$$F = Attention(Q, K, V) = \text{MultiH(QUOTE ta}_1 h_{V_l^{enc}}^u, W_{k_1}^{TA_l} h_{TA_l}^u, W_{v_1}^{TA_l} h_{TA_l}^u$$

where $N$ denotes the length number of the sentence, and $\theta$ denotes the model parameter.

## 5 Experiments

In this section, we demonstrate the effectiveness through extensive experiments. we first introduce two public datasets used for the video captioning task. Then, we compare MIFN with other competing baselines. Finally, qualitative results of ablation experiments are conducted to verify the effectiveness of each component.

### 5.1 Datasets

To evaluate the effectiveness of the proposed video captioning models, this part reports the results over MSR-VTT and MSVD, two large-scale video captioning datasets.

**MSR-Video to Text (MSR-VTT) dataset:** MSR-VTT dataset collected by [5] is one of the largest video captioning datasets for generating the description of the video, which contains 10,000 video clips. The duration of each clip is between 10 and 30 s, and each video clip is annotated with approximately 20 different captions by Amazon Mechanical Turk (AMT) workers. The total of video-sentence pairs is 200K. Following the existing work, we use the splits provided by [5], *i.e.,* 6,513 for training, 497 for validation, and 2,990 for testing respectively.

**Microsoft Video Description (MSVD) dataset:** MSVD dataset consists of 1,970 video clips, each of them also annotated by AMT workers. Each video clip has roughly 40 descriptions and the dataset has approximately 80,000 video-sentence pairs. Similar to the existing works [16, 26], there are 1,200 training video clips, 100 validation video clips, and 670 test video clips.

**Table 1.** The experiment results over MSR-VTT dataset.

| Model | B@1 B@2 B@3 B@4 M R C |
|---|---|
| MP-LSTM [7] | - - - 30.4 23.7 52.0 35.0 |
| Soft-Attention [15] | - - -28.5 25.0 53.3 37.1 |
| Res-Attention [31] | 77.1 62.1 48.7 37.0 26.9 – 40.7 |
| S2VT [16] | - - - 28.5 25.0 52.0 37.1 |
| v2t_navigater [32] | - - - 40.8 28.2 60.9 44.8 |
| Aalto [33] | - - - 39.8 26.9 59.8 45.7 |
| VideoLAB [34] | - - - 39.1 27.7 60.6 44.1 |
| hLSTMat [17] | 76.2 62.9 50.6 39.7 27.0 – 42.1 |
| RecNet [35] | - - - 39.1 26.6 59.3 42.7 |
| PickNet [36] | - - - 41.3 27.7 59.8 44.1 |
| LSGN + LNA [37] | - - - 39.5 27.4 60.9 46.5 |
| baseline (our) | - - - 38.5 26.8 58.9 44.8 |
| MIFN (our) | 78.6 65.1 51.9 41.0 27.6 60.1 46.6 |

## 5.2 Implementation Details

**Preprocessing.** To preprocess the text information, we first convert all words to lower-case letters, remove the punctuation and add three additional tokens, namely unknown $< UNK >$, the begin-of-sentence $< BOS >$, and the end-of-sentence $< EOS >$. Thus, it yields a vocabulary of 23,665 and 15,906 in size for the MSR-VTT and MSVD datasets, respectively.

**Evaluation Settings:** Following the previous works, we employ the same captioning metrics: BLEU [27], METEOR [28], ROUGE [29], and CIDEr [30].

**Model Settings & Training:** All MHA layers and FFN layers have 512-dimensional, and the input feature's dimension of the co-encoder is mapped into 512 with a linear projection. We represent words with word embeddings, whose size is also set as 512. During training, the model is optimized using Adams' optimizer. The batch size is set as 50, and a beam size is equal to 5. Besides, we introduce gradient clipping and dropout technology during training.

## 5.3 Comparison with Competing Baselines

Here, we present the results of our evaluation followed by a comparison of the proposed method with several competing baselines over MSR-VTT and MSVD datasets.

### 5.3.1 The Experiment Results Over MSR-VTT Dataset

**Comparing Methods.** We first consider the MSR-VTT dataset and compare the performance of the proposed approach to other competing methods. Specifically, we compare MIFN with Mean-Pooling [7], Soft-Attention [15], Res-Attention [31] S2VT [16], v2t_navigater [32], Aalto [33], VideoLAB [34], hLSTMat [17], RecNet [35], PickNet [36], and LSGN + LNA [37].

**Results:** The experimental results are demonstrated in Table 1. In this experiment, the proposed method (MIFN) achieves better performance than other baseline models. The results show that the Cider of our MIFN can achieve 47.6, which exceeds the highest performance reported over MSR-VTT dataset. For the rest of the evaluation metrics, our model obtains comparable scores with 41.0 B@4 (vs. 41.3 B@4), 27.6 Meteor (vs. 28.2 Meteor), and 60.1 Rough (vs. 60.0 Rough). It proves the effectiveness of our approach.

### 5.3.2 The Experiment Results over MSVD Dataset

**Comparing Methods:** Next, we assess our model over MSVD dataset. For the experiments, we compare the proposed MIFN with previous works, *i.e.,* S2VT [16], Res-Attention [31], hLSTMat [17], HRNE [38], MA [39], SCN [40], SCN [40], TSA [41], RecNet [35], PickNet [36], and ASGN + LNA [37].

**Results:** We demonstrate the experimental results in Table 2. We can see that the proposed MIFN model outperforms other competing baselines. The proposed method achieves improvements of 1.3 B@4, 0.6 Meteor, 1.1 Rough, and 2.3 Cider respectively, compared to the LSGN + LNA model [37].

**Table 2.** The Experiment Results over MSVD Dataset.

| Model | B@4 M R C |
|---|---|
| S2VT [16] | - 29.2 - |
| Res-Attention [31] | 53.4 34.3 72.9 |
| hLSTMat [17] | 33.5 – 72.8 |
| HRNE [38] | 43.8 33.1 - - |
| MA [39] | 50.4 31.8 – 69.9 |
| SCN [40] | 51.1 33.5 – 77.7 |
| TSA [41] | 51.7 34.0 – 74.9 |
| RecNet [35] | 52.3 34.1 69.8 80.3 |
| PickNet [36] | 52.3 33.3 69.6 76.5 |
| ASGN + LNA [37] | 52.1 33.3 70.3 80.3 |
| MIFN (Our) | 53.4 33.9 71.4 82.6 |

### 5.4 Ablation Study

We employ extensive ablation studies to illustrate the effectiveness of each component over the MSR-VTT dataset.

### 5.4.1 The Effect of Transformer

Here, we demonstrate the effectiveness of the transformer. The results are shown in Table 3 which has three blocks, and each block takes a different feature as an input. Especially, $A$ and $M$ denote appearance features and motion features, respectively.

Moreover, $A + M$ denotes the fusing of the appearance feature and motion feature by simple concatenating. Furthermore, each block is divided into three categories: 1) LSTM-ATT model, which uses a two-layer LSTM with attention mechanism, 2) transformer with three layers, and 3) transformer with six layers.

As shown in Table 4, we first see that the performance of $A + M$ is better than $A$ and $M$. This result shows the beneficial effects of multiple features. Then, the result illustrates that the original transformer for video captioning in effectiveness. The original configuration of the transformer is six layers and self/cross attention. Comparing LSTM (Row 1) with transformer (Row 3) in the first block of Table 4, it has obtained the improvement by the original transformer, by 0.4 in B@4, 0.3 in Meteor, 0.3 in Rough, and 1.5 in Cider, respectively. Furthermore, by changing the number of layers of the transformer (three layers vs. six layers), we notice that the performance has also slightly increased. This validates the impact of the number of transformer layers. The possible reason is that training data quantity is reduced, and the complexity of the sentence is lower for video description compared with machine translation. In the following experiments, we utilize multiple features ($A + M$) to train our model and adopt the transformer with three layers.

### 5.4.2 Effects of Proposed Individual Components

Here, an ablation study is designed to verify the effect of our MIFN individual component in MIFN. The results are shown in Table 3. The baseline model is the basic-transformer encoder with three layers, which takes input by simply concatenating multiple features into one visual feature. Comparing Row 0 and Row 1, we observe the efficiency of the total model MIFN. The improvement over the baseline is significant, by 2.5 in B@4, 0.8 in Meteor, 1.2 in Rough, and 2.0 in Cider, respectively. Then we start with the MIFN model and successively remove Cross-attention from the encoder and the Gated mechanism from the decoder to demonstrate their importance.

**Effects of the encoder with cross-attention:** By removing the Cross-attention in the encoder (Row 2), we notice that the model has fallen on the MSR-VTT dataset and have fallen by 0.2, 0.7, 0.7, and 0.4 on B@4, Meteor, Rough, and Cider, respectively, almost fallen on all evaluation metrics. These results show the effectiveness of such cross-attention from the encoder to generate a better visual feature from the video.

**Effects of decoding with gated mechanism:** Further, we verify the strength of decoding with a gated mechanism by comparing it (Row 1) with the other model (Row 5) that replaces the gated mechanism with the concatenation operation in the decoder. The result of Row 4 (the RCM model with only supervised learning) validates the superiority of the gated mechanism in the decoder. The gated mechanism in the decoder improves the performance of video caption, particularly for B@4 by 0.6, Meteor by 0.5, Rough by 0.4, and cider by 0.9, respectively.

**Table 3.** The effectiveness of the transformer in the MSR-VTT dataset. The table has three blocks, and each block uses a different feature to train the model. A and M denotes the appearance feature and motion feature, respectively. A + M denotes the fusing between the appearance feature and motion feature by simple concatenation. L represents the number of the transformer's layers.

| Model | | B@4 M R C |
|---|---|---|
| A | LSTM | 37.8 26.0 58.3 41.4 |
| | transformer (L = 3) | 38.0 26.5 58.7 43.5 |
| | transformer (L = 6) | 38.2 26.3 58.6 42.9 |
| M | LSTM | 37.2 25.3 57.9 39.9 |
| | transformer (L = 3) | 37.8 26.2 58.3 42.5 |
| | transformer (L = 6) | 37.5 25.8 58.2 41.8 |
| A + M | LSTM | 38.0 26.2 58.5 42.3 |
| | transformer (L = 3) | 38.5 26.8 58.9 44.8 |
| | transformer (L = 6) | 38.3 26.4 58.7 44.3 |

**Table 4.** Ablation study on MSR-VTT. The result demonstrates the performance of the basic transformer as the baseline, which takes features by simply concatenating multiple features as input. Row 1–3 shows the influence of individual components by removing them from the final model (Row 1).

| # | Model | B@4 | M | R | C |
|---|---|---|---|---|---|
| 0 | Baseline (transformer with three layers) | 38.5 | 26.8 | 58.9 | 44.8 |
| 1 | MIFN | 41.0 | 27.6 | 60.1 | 46.6 |
| 2 | —Cross-attention in the encoder | 39.8 | 26.9 | 59.4 | 45.5 |
| 3 | —Gated mechanism in the decoder | 39.4 | 27.1 | 59.7 | 45.9 |

## 6 Conclusion

In this paper, we propose a novel framework, named Multimodal Interaction Fusion Network (MIFN) which is based on the transformer, for the video captioning task. Firstly, we inject the cross-attention module into the original transformers' encoder to learn the relationship between the input visual feature which provides a better visual representation of video. Besides, we apply a gated mechanism to replace the simple fusion strategy, which can select the key information from the multiple features in the decoder. Experimental results on MSR-VTT and MSVD datasets illustrate that MIFN achieves performance comparable with the competing methods. Moreover, extensive ablation studies also indicate the effectiveness of the proposed model for video captioning.

**Acknowledgment.** This work is supported by the Sichuan Science and Technology Program (No. 2022119).

# References

1. Li, K., Zhang, Y., Li, K., Li, Y., Fu, Y.: Visual semantic reasoning for image-text matching. In: Proceedings of the IEEE International Conference on Computer Vision, pp. 4654–4662 (2019)
2. Antol, S., et al.: VQA: visual question answering. In: 2015 IEEE International Conference on Computer Vision, ICCV 2015, Santiago, Chile, December 7–13, 2015, pp. 2425–2433 (2015)
3. Teney, D., Anderson, P., He, X., Van Den Hengel A.: Tips and tricks for visual question answering: Learnings from the 2017 challenge. In: Proceedings of the IEEE Conference on Computer Vision and Pattern Recognition, pp. 4223–4232 (2018)
4. Gao, L., Zeng, P., Song, J., Liu, X., Shen, H.T.: Examine before you answer: multi-task learning with adaptive-attentions for multiple-choice vqa. In: Proceedings of the 26th ACM international conference on Multimedia, pp. 1742–1750 (2018)
5. Xu, J., Mei, T., Yao, T., Rui, Y.: MSR-VTT: a large video description dataset for bridging video and language. In: Proceedings of the IEEE conference on computer vision and pattern recognition (CVPR), pp. 5288–5296 (2016)
6. Zhang, C., Tian, Y.: Automatic video description generation via lstm with joint two-stream encoding. In: 2016 23rd International Conference on Pattern Recognition (ICPR), pp. 2924–2929, IEEE (2016)
7. Venugopalan, S., Xu, H., Donahue, J., Rohrbach, M., Mooney, R., Saenko, K.: Translating videos to natural language using deep recurrent neural networks. In: Proceedings of the 2015 Conference of the North American Chapter of the Association for Computational Linguistics: Human Language Technologies, pp. 1494–1504 (2015)
8. Cornia, M., Stefanini, M., Baraldi, L., Cucchiara, R.: M ^2: Meshed-memory transformer for image captioning. arXiv preprint arXiv:1912.08226 (2019)
9. Li, G., Zhu, L., Liu, P., Yang, Y.: Entangled transformer for image captioning. In: Proceedings of the IEEE International Conference on Computer Vision, pp. 8928–8937 (2019)
10. Vaswani, A.: Attention is all you need. In: Advances in Neural Information Processing Systems, pp. 5998–6008 (2017)
11. Guadarrama, S.: Youtube2text: Recognizing and describing arbitrary activities using semantic hierarchies and zero-shot recognition. In: Proceedings of the IEEE International Conference on Computer Vision, pp. 2712–2719, (2013)
12. Kay, W., et al., The kinetics human action video dataset. arXiv preprint arXiv:1705.06950 (2017)
13. Rohrbach, M., Qiu, W., Titov, I., Thater, S., Pinkal, M., Schiele, B.: Translating video content to natural language descriptions. In: Proceedings of the IEEE International Conference on Computer Vision, pp. 433–440 (2013)
14. Xu, R., Xiong, C., Chen, W., Corso, J.J.: Jointly modeling deep video and compositional text to bridge vision and language in a unified framework. In: Twenty-Ninth AAAI Conference on Artificial Intelligence (2015)
15. Yao, L., Torabi, A., Cho, K., Ballas, N., Pal, C., Larochelle, H., Courville, A.: Describing videos by exploiting temporal structure. In: Proceedings of the IEEE International Conference on Computer Vision, pp. 4507–4515 (2015)
16. Venugopalan, S., Rohrbach, M., Donahue, J., Mooney, R., Darrell, T., Saenko, K.: Sequence to sequence-video to text. In: Proceedings of the IEEE International Conference on Computer Vision, pp. 4534–4542 (2015)
17. Gao, L., Li, X., Song, J., Shen, H.T.: Hierarchical LSTMs with adaptive attention for visual captioning. IEEE Trans. Pattern Anal. Mach. Intell. p. 1 (2019)

18. Gehring, J., Auli, M., Grangier, D., Yarats, D., Dauphin, Y.N.: Convolutional sequence to sequence learning. In: Proceedings of the 34th International Conference on Machine Learning-Volume 70, pp. 1243–1252 (2017)
19. Shazeer, N., et al.: Outrageously large neural networks: The sparsely-gated mixture-of-experts layer. arXiv preprint arXiv:1701.06538 (2017)
20. Wu, Y., et al.: Google's neural machine translation system: bridging the gap between human and machine translation. arXiv preprint arXiv:1609.08144 (2016)
21. Herdade, S., Kappeler, A., Boakye, K., Soares, J.: Image captioning: transforming objects into words. In: Advances in Neural Information Processing Systems, pp. 11135–11145 (2019)
22. Szegedy, C., Ioffe, S., Vanhoucke, V., Alemi, A.A.: Inception-v4, inception-resnet and the impact of residual connections on learning. In: Thirty-first AAAI Conference on Artificial Intelligence (2017)
23. Russakovsky, O., et al.: Imagenet large scale visual recognition challenge. Int. J. Comput. Vis. **115**(3), 211–252 (2015)
24. Carreira, J., Zisserman, A.: Quo vadis, action recognition? a new model and the kinetics dataset. In: Proceedings of the IEEE Conference on Computer Vision and Pattern Recognition, pp. 6299–6308 (2017)
25. Pérez, J.S., Meinhardt-Llopis, E., Facciolo, G.: TV-L1 optical flow estimation. Image Processing On Line 2013, pp. 137–150 (2013)
26. Pan, Y., Mei, T., Yao, T., Li, H., Rui, Y.: Jointly modeling embedding and translation to bridge video and language. In: Proceedings of the IEEE conference on computer vision and pattern recognition, pp. 4594–4602 (2016)
27. Papineni, K., Roukos, S., Ward, T., Zhu, W.: BLEU: a method for automatic evaluation of machine translation. In: Proceedings of the 40th Annual Meeting of the Association for Computational Linguistics (ACL), pp. 311–318 (2002)
28. Banerjee, S., Lavie, A.: METEOR: an automatic metric for MT evaluation with improved correlation with human judgments. In: Proceedings of the Workshop on Intrinsic and Extrinsic Evaluation Measures for Machine Translation and/or Summarization, pp. 65–72 (2005)
29. Lin, C.-Y.: ROUGE: a package for automatic evaluation of summaries. In: Text Summarization Branches Out, pp. 74–81. Association for Computational Linguistics, (Barcelona, Spain) (2004)
30. Vedantam, R., Zitnick, C. L., Parikh, D.: CIDER: consensus-based image description evaluation. In: Proceedings of the IEEE Conference on Computer Vision and Pattern Recognition (CVPR), pp. 4566–4575 (2015)
31. Li, X., Zhou, Z., Chen, L., Gao, L.: Residual attention-based LSTM for video captioning. World Wide Web **22**(2), 621–636 (2019)
32. Jin, Q., Chen, J., Chen, S., Xiong, Y., Hauptmann, A.: Describing videos using multi-modal fusion. In: Proceedings of the 24th ACM International Conference on Multimedia, pp. 1087–1091 (2016)
33. Shetty, R., Laaksonen, J.: Frame-and segment-level features and candidate pool evaluation for video caption generation. In: Proceedings of the 24th ACM International Conference on Multimedia, pp. 1073–1076 (2016)
34. Ramanishka, V., et al.: Multimodal video description. In: Proceedings of the 24th ACM International Conference on Multimedia, pp. 1092–1096 (2016)
35. Wang, B., Ma, L., Zhang, W., Liu, W.: Reconstruction network for video captioning. In: Proceedings of the IEEE Conference on Computer Vision and Pattern Recognition, pp. 7622–7631 (2018)
36. Chen, Y., Wang, S., Zhang, W., Huang, Q.: Less Is More: Picking Informative Frames for Video Captioning. In: Ferrari, V., Hebert, M., Sminchisescu, C., Weiss, Y. (eds.) ECCV 2018. LNCS, vol. 11217, pp. 367–384. Springer, Cham (2018). https://doi.org/10.1007/978-3-030-01261-8_22

37. Xiao, X., Wang, L., Fan, B., Xiang, S., Pan, C.: Guiding the flowing of semantics: Interpretable video captioning via POS tag. In: Proceedings of the 2019 Conference on Empirical Methods in Natural Language Processing and the 9th International Joint Conference on Natural Language Processing (EMNLP-IJCNLP), pp. 2068–2077 (2019)
38. Pan, P., Xu, Z., Yang, Y., Wu, F., Zhuang, Y.: Hierarchical recurrent neural encoder for video representation with application to captioning. In: Proceedings of the IEEE Conference on Computer Vision and Pattern Recognition, pp. 1029–1038 (2016)
39. Hori, C., et al.: Attention-based multimodal fusion for video description," in Proceedings of the IEEE International Conference on Computer Vision, pp. 4193–4202 (2017)
40. Gan, Z., et al.: Semantic compositional networks for visual captioning. In: Proceedings of the IEEE Conference on Computer Vision and Pattern Recognition, pp. 5630–5639 (2017)
41. Wu, X., Li, G., Cao, Q., Ji, Q., Lin, L.: Interpretable video captioning via trajectory structured localization. In: Proceedings of the IEEE Conference on Computer Vision and Pattern Recognition, pp. 6829–6837 (2018)
42. Lu, H., Li, Y., Chen, M., et al.: Brain Intelligence: go beyond artificial intelli-gence. Mobile Netw. Appl. **23**, 368–375 (2018)
43. Lu, H., Zhang, Y., Li, Y., et al.: User-oriented virtual mobile network resource management for vehicle communications. IEEE Trans. Intell. Transp. Syst. **22**(6), 3521–3532 (2021)

# An Image Enhancement Method Based on Multi-scale Fusion

Haoming Wang[✉]

College of Electrical and Control Engineering, Xi'an University of Science and Technology,
Xi'an 710054, China
1850042634@qq.com

**Abstract.** To solve the problem of low contrast and poor visual effect of video capture image in coal mine underground, a method based on multi-scale fusion is adopted to enhance coal mine underground image. Firstly, the improved homomorphic filtering and the contrast-limited adaptive histogram equalization are used respectively for the to obtain an underground image with uniform brightness and a contrast enhanced. Then, the enhanced image is obtained by multi-scale fusion of the two images with above processing. Experimental results show that the algorithm can solve the problem of distortion, and effectively improve the contrast and brightness in the image.

**Keywords:** Multi-scale fusion · Image enhancement · Coal mine underground

## 1 Introduction

Coal resource is one of the widest used energy in China, it is widely applied to the production and living of people. Now, coal resources account for 70% of China's energy consumption, and will still be the major energy in China for a long time in the future [1].

However, the poor environment of coal mines underground has brought about great pressure to controlling safety and frequently caused coal mine accidents [2, 3]. With the progress of science and technology, underground video monitoring has been widely used in coal mine production, which can reduce accidents rates. Influenced by large dust, uneven light distribution and low contrast in underground coal mine [4–7], the image quality of video capture is relatively poor, which makes it difficult to monitor the safety in production of mine staff. Therefore, it is of great significance to enhance images in coal mine [8, 9].

At present, the commonly used image enhancement methods mainly include gray transformation method, Retinex algorithm [10] and histogram equalization (HE) [11, 12]. Gray scale transformation enhancement methods can mainly be divided into linear gray scale enhancement, piecewise linear gray scale enhancement and nonlinear gray scale enhancement. When processing coal mine underground images, parameters cannot be adjusted adaptively and image enhancement cannot be carried out accurately. Due to the dark and uneven brightness distribution of coal mine underground images, HE

S. Yang and H. Lu (Eds.): ISAIR 2022, CCIS 1700, pp. 37–42, 2022.
https://doi.org/10.1007/978-981-19-7946-0_4

may bring about color deviation and cause the loss of image details when processing underground coal mine images. The essence of traditional Retinex is to obtain reflected image by subtracting brightness image from original image, so as to enhance the image. Retinex has a better effect on images with uniform overall brightness, but it is easy to over-enhance images with uneven brightness.

An image enhancement algorithm based on multi-scale fusion is proposed in this paper. The improved homomorphic filtering and CLAHE are used to process the low illumination images respectively, and then the two images are processed by multi-scale fusion to obtain the enhanced image.

## 2   Proposed Method

### 2.1   The Improved Homomorphic Filtering

In order to equalize the brightness of the image, an improved homomorphic filtering algorithm is used to enhance the image. The traditional homomorphic filter is used to obtain the unbalance of the overall brightness of the image, and the processing effect of dark region is not well. The low frequency part is mainly used to represent the key content of the image, and the high frequency part is mainly used to represent the details and edge information of the image. Therefore, this paper improves the homomorphic filter, processes the high and low frequency of the image separately, so as to reduce the loss of image details, and finally integrates the results obtained. The improved homomorphic filter function expression is:

$$H_h(u, v) = (r_H - r_L) \cdot [-e^{-c[\frac{D^2(u,v)}{d_0^2}]}] + r_L \tag{1}$$

$$H_l(u, v) = 1 - \{(r_H - r_L) \cdot [-e^{-c\left[\frac{D^2(u,v)}{d_0^2}\right]}] + r_L\} \tag{2}$$

In the above two formulas, $H_h(u, v)$ represents the high frequency filter and $H_l(u, v)$ represents the low frequency filter. $r_H$ is the increase multiple of high frequency, $r_L$ is the attenuation multiple of low frequency, $C$ is the sharpening coefficient, $r_L < c < r_H$, $d_0$ is the cut off frequency, and $D(u, v)$ represents the distance from $(u, v)$ to the filtering center.

### 2.2   CLAHE Algorithm

ContrasT-Limiting adaptive histogram equalization (CLAHE) algorithm [13] reduces noise by limiting the height of part of the histogram so as to reduce the excessive enhancement of local contrast. Compared with the HE algorithm, the CLAHE optimizes the image detail information, some areas in the image also have excessive enhancement, but this problem can be improved by fusing with other input images.

## 2.3 Multi-scale Fusion

Due to the single scale image distortion and halo phenomenon, this paper uses the multi-scale fusion algorithm. In order to obtain images with significant advantages, this paper uses three weights to determine the proportion of input images in the fusion process, including brightness weight, local contrast weight and saturation [14].

The algorithm in this paper is aimed at enhancing low-light images in coal mines. On the one hand, it is based on homomorphic filtering to reduce noise so as to obtain a uniformly illuminated image. On the other hand, it uses CLAHE to improve the contrast. Finally, the fusion algorithm is used for these two images with significant advantages to obtain enhanced image. The flow of the fusion algorithm in this paper is shown in the Fig. 1.

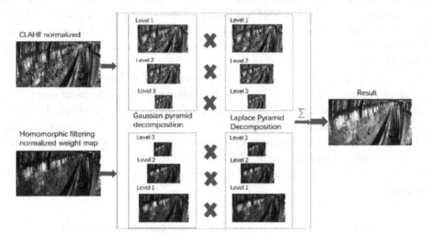

**Fig. 1.** Visualization of multi-scale fusion map

## 3   Analysis of Simulation Results

In order to verify the effectiveness of the algorithm, the low-illuminated images of coal mines are selected for enhancing process, and they are verified by both subjective evaluation and objective quality evaluation. This paper chooses HE, single-scale Retinex algorithm [10] (SSR) and adaptive histogram equalization algorithm (AHE) as comparisons. The experimental results are shown in the Fig. 2.

(a)            (b)            (c)            (d)            (e)

**Fig. 2.** Different algorithm comparison; (a) Original image (b) HE algorithm (c) SSR algorithm (d) AHE algorithm (e) Ours algorithm

From the different scenes in the above figure, it can be seen that the original image has obtained uneven light and low illuminance, which is not conducive to subsequent target tracking and recognition. HE algorithm improves the brightness of the image, but the exposure caused is unexpected in that excessive enhancement occurs. The brightness of the image processed by the SSR has increased, but the enhanced image is slightly blurred. Moreover, the image has also been over-enhanced by the AHE. The algorithm in this paper improves the contrast and sharpness, and the edge information of the image is reflected, The image visual effect is better.

In this paper, three performance indicators are used to evaluate images objectively. Peak signal-to-noise ratio (PSNR), structural similarity (SSIM), and mean square error (MSE) are used as the evaluation indicators of the enhancement algorithm. The PSNR evaluates the level of image noise. The larger the value may bring the smaller the image distortion. SSIM is used as a measure of the similarity of two images. The larger value may lead to smaller image distortion. The MSE demonstrates the amount of noise introduced into the image in which the smaller mean square error may lead to smaller noise introduced.

**Table 1.** Evaluation indicators of different enhancement algorithms

| Algorithm | PSNR | SSIM | MSE |
|---|---|---|---|
| Original image | – | – | 4049.08 |
| He | 13.46 | 0.4334 | 2925.61 |
| SSR | 12.60 | 0.3318 | 3565.35 |
| AHE | 14.03 | 0.4891 | 2568.84 |
| Ours | 16.09 | 0.6796 | 1011.68 |

As shown in Table 1, the MSE of the image processed by the HE algorithm is greatly reduced; the MSE of the image processed by the SSR does not change much, and the peak value is relatively small, HE PSNR and SSIM are relatively small, which indicates that the improvement of the image after SSR processing not as excepted, the MSE of the image processed by the AHE is greatly reduced; the algorithm in this paper is due to the other three algorithms in all evaluation indicators, the MSE of the image processed by the proposed in this paper has been greatly reduced, and the noise of the image is significantly reduced compared with other algorithms, the PSNR and SSIM of the image are larger, indicating that the image distortion after the algorithm processed in this paper is small. Various indicators show that the image processed by the proposed in this paper is better than the image processed by the algorithm mentioned. It can be seen that the algorithm in this paper has achieved a good enhancement in processing low-light images in coal mines. Compared with others, our PSNR has improved by 2.63, 3.49, 2.06 respectively, our SSIM has improved by 0.2462, 0.3478, 0.1905 respectively, our MSE has reduced by 1913.93, 2553.67, 1557.16 respectively.

## 4  Conclusion

Due to the harsh underground environment of coal mines, the acquired images have the characteristics of low illumination and low contrast, which have a great impact on the subsequent work. Therefore, this paper proposes a coal mine image enhancement algorithm based on multi-scale fusion. Firstly, the improved homomorphic filtering algorithm and the contrast-limited adaptive histogram equalization algorithm are used respectively for the coal mine underground image to obtain an image with uniform brightness and a contrast-enhanced image. Then, the enhanced image with excellent subjective and objective performance is obtained by multi-scale fusion of the two images after above processing.

## References

1. Sun, J.P.: Review and prospect of coal mine automation and information technology. Ind. Mine Autom. **36**(06), 26–30 (2010)
2. Jin, Y.F., Jin, Y.Z.: Several problems and countermeasures in coal mine safety production in my country. Coal Mine Safety **46**(04), 234–236+240 (2015)
3. Li, Y.: Research on classification algorithm of coal mine underground video scene based on AlexNet and LSTM. Xi'an University of Science and Technology (2019)
4. Wang, X., Bai, S.W., P, L. H., Chen, L.C.: A mine image enhancement algorithm. Ind. Mine Autom. **43**(03), 48–52 (2017)
5. Yang, Y., Yue, J.H., Li, Y.L., Wang, Q.F.: A method of mine dynamic image enhancement. Ind. Mine Autom. **41**(11), 48–52 (2015)
6. Zhao, Q., Wang, Y.T., Zeng, Z.H., Hou, Y.B., Zhao, S.: An algorithm for edge detection of mine tunnel images. Ind. Mine Autom. **39**(02), 71–75 (2013)
7. Wang, Y., Guan, N.N., Liu, H.T.: Improved multi-scale Retinex downhole image enhancement algorithm. J. Liaoning Tech. Univ. (Nat. Sci. Edn.) **35**(04), 440–443 (2016)
8. Zhang, X.H., Zhang, S., Fang, S., Cao, Y.: Research on the clarification of fog and dust images in intelligent video surveillance of coal mines. J. China Coal Soc. **39**(01), 198–204 (2014)
9. Zhao, Q.: Research on image processing of dynamic target video monitoring in coal mine. Xi'an University of Science and Technology (2014)
10. Rahman, Z.U., Jobson, D.J., Woodell, G.A.: Retinex processing for automatic image enhancement. IS&T/SPIE Electron. Imaging (2002)
11. Wang, X., Bai, S.W., Pan, L.H., Chen, L.C.: A mine image enhancement algorithm. Ind. Mine Autom. **43**(03), 48–52 (2017)
12. Wu, C.M.: Research on the mathematical model of histogram equalization. Acta Electron. Sin. **41**(03), 598–602 (2013)

13. Karel, Z.: Contrast limited adaptive histogram equalization. Graphics Gems IV. San Diego: Academic Press Professional. 474–485 (1994)
14. Dhivya, R., Prakash, R., Mohanraj, M.R.: Color balance and fusion for underwater image enhancement. Digital Image Process. 11(2) (2019)
15. Huimin, L., Li, Y., Chen, M., et al.: Brain intelligence: go beyond artificial intelligence. Mob. Netw. Appl. 23, 368–375 (2018)
16. Huimin, L., Li, Y., Shenglin, M., et al.: Motor anomaly detection for unmanned aerial vehicles using reinforcement learning. IEEE Internet Things J. 5(4), 2315–2322 (2018)
17. Huimin, L., Zhang, Y., Li, Y., et al.: User-oriented virtual mobile network resource management for vehicle communications. IEEE Trans. Intell. Transp. Syst. 22(6), 3521–3532 (2021)

# Research on Construction Technology of Graph Data Model

Wei Rao[1(✉)], Fan Yang[1], Zeyang Tang[1], and Junjie Wang[2]

[1] State Grid Hubei Electric Power Co. Ltd, Electric Power Research Institute,
Wuhan 430077, China
310714175@qq.com
[2] College of Automation, Nanjing University
of Posts Telecommunications, Nanjing 210003, China

**Abstract.** As the scale of the power grid continues to expand, the traditional distribution network management model cannot meet the requirements of power grid development under the new situation. The current distribution network operation inspection still lacks in data collection, and it is impossible to establish an informative and intelligent operation inspection management system. The upper-level production management system is also unable to integrate due to the lack of operation inspection marketing data. Aiming at the performance problem of the visualization of topology data in the distribution network operation and inspection, this paper uses the graph data model to build knowledge, designs graphic elements for data migration, and forms a topology map for the intelligent operation and inspection of the distribution network. The research clearly and intuitively displays the specific information of the power system equipment and the physical relationship between the equipment, thus forming a data model of the grid diagram.

**Keywords:** Graph database · Topological graph · Graph data model for power grid · Distribution network inspection

## 1 Introduction

The distribution network is at the end of the power system and has the characteristics of wide area, large scale, many types, and multiple connections. With the urbanization construction and the growth of electricity demand, the scale of the distribution network is constantly expanding while constantly transforming and expanding. With the expansion of the power grid and the increase in the amount of topology management data, the attribute dimension of the data will also increase. The traditional distribution network management model can no longer meet the requirements of power reform and smart grid development under the new situation. The current distribution network operation inspection still lacks in data collection, and it is impossible to establish an informative and intelligent operation inspection management system. The upper production management system is also unable to integrate due to the lack of operation inspection marketing data,

© The Author(s), under exclusive license to Springer Nature Singapore Pte Ltd. 2022
S. Yang and H. Lu (Eds.): ISAIR 2022, CCIS 1700, pp. 43–54, 2022.
https://doi.org/10.1007/978-981-19-7946-0_5

which makes it impossible to achieve fault research and judgment and fault location based on multiple data. We should use the application layer to strengthen the application of big data, from the traditional "passive repair" to "active operation and maintenance".

At the same time, data analysis and processing technologies are developing rapidly, and non-relational databases (NoSQL, Not Only SQL) are leading the database technology revolution. This paper analyzes and studies the knowledge of graph data model construction, designs graph elements for data migration, forms topological graphs for intelligent operation and inspection of distribution networks, and constructs grid graph database models. A storage method which uses a graph database is proposed to combine the grid big data with the grid's own network topology characteristics, so as to effectively use graph theory and topology theory to analyze and optimize the power grid under the power of big data. Because different data models in the graph database deal with different problems, the efficiency difference is obvious. Therefore, it is necessary to study different modeling methods and their applicable conditions.

The rest of this paper is organized as follows: The first part describes the current research status of graph data model construction at home and abroad. The second part analyzes the methods and advantages of Neo4j graph data model and GraphX graph database model construction. The third part analyzes the design of graph data model for intelligent operation and inspection of distribution network. The fourth part introduces the CIM model, the data model with electrical nodes as domain entities, the data model of materialized attributes, the application scenarios of the materialized time data model and their respective performance. The fifth part proposes the future prospects and challenges of graph data model construction.

## 2  Related Work

Pan et al. [1] proposed the principle of grid data modeling based on domain modeling theory and following the CIM model. According to these principles, some power grid data models and their applicable occasions are proposed, as well as methods to convert these models to each other. Finally, three graphical database models are established using the modeling method proposed in this paper. The graphic database model proposed in this paper can greatly improve the retrieval efficiency, which proves the effectiveness of the modeling method and the effectiveness of the graphic database in specific retrieval. Pavkovic et al. [2] introduced the use of Neo4j graph database to model and manage power system data. Hu et al. [3] regards the data model as an entity in the knowledge graph, and combines semantic analysis technology and entity similarity calculation technology for the data model in the power grid field, and proposes a model diagnosis method based on the knowledge graph. Consistency of sex and diagnosis. Research shows that this method can more fully utilize the relevant information of the data model and expand the thinking of traditional diagnostic methods. Gonzalez et al. [4] shows that the motion graph model can be better organized around gateway nodes, which act as a bridge to connect different areas of the motion graph. The graph-based object moving cube can be constructed by merging and collapsing nodes and edges according to the application-oriented topology. Risi et al. [5] proposed a method using visual language coding based on logic paradigm. CoDe allows visualization to be organized through the CoDe model, which graphically represents the relationship between information items and can be regarded as a conceptual diagram of the view. Xue et al. [6] relies on the commercial bank system architecture, reuses the external business data query service of the commercial bank system, integrates the data processing capabilities of the data warehouse, provides related data for the map display tool, and builds the corporate relationship map data model, which helps to improve the bank¡¯s acquisition of new The ability of customers, as well as fully understand existing customers, establish customer profiles, and help banks prevent group risks from group customers. Wu et al. [7] proposes a fast graph construction method based on the existing SG-CIM model data of the State Grid Interconnection Department. It can fully support the company's various analysis and recommendation applications based on the unified knowledge graph. Scarselli et al. [8] proposed a new neural network model, called the graph neural network (GNN) model, which extends the existing neural network method to process the data represented in the graph domain. In order to deal with the graph uncertainty in the spatial and topological relationships between objects in the graph, Majumdar et al. [9] proposed an object-oriented graph theoretical model for representing graphs, which allows the use of the concept of (fuzzy) graph matching to assess the similarity between the graphs. Compared with traditional relational databases, graph databases can naturally fit the characteristics of grid data due to the similarity of basic structures, showing their potential advantages in processing power system data and performing real-time data analysis and calculation. Lee et al. [10] uses a path ranking algorithm to extract relational paths from the knowledge graph and uses it to construct training data. In order to learn the characteristics of the relationship, the extracted relationship path is used to create a circuitous path between nodes as training data. Combi et al. [11] proposed the Multimedia Time Graphical Model (MTGM), which represented a clinical database of cardiac patients undergoing cardio angiography, and then described it in a formal way. Designed and implemented a prototype based on XML native database system. Zhang et al. [12] proposed a method of expressing high-order features of graph-based dependent analytical models depending on language models and beam search, which solved the problem of enriching high-order features without increasing decoding complexity. Huimin Lu et al. [13] propose a fuzzy attentionbased DenseNet-BiLSTM Chinese image captioning method to solve some Chinese image description generation tasks. Huimin Lu et al. [14] propose a novel hashing method termed deep fuzzy hashing network (DFHN) to overcome the shortcomings of existing deep hashing approaches for efficient image retrieval.Qi Ge et al. [15] propose a graph regularized Bayesian tensor factorization based on KDSDL model to solve the problem that existing matrix factorization methods cannot deal with the non-i.i.d outliers and the non-uniform incoherence well.

## 3    Graph Database

NoSQL databases not only allow storing relational data models, but also allow to store other models, the most prominent of which is the graph database. The graph database model is based on graph theory, and provides data storage by introducing the concepts of nodes and relationships, where the relationship is the most important element in the graph data model. Each node directly contains a relationship list, which stores the relationship records between the node and other nodes. The relationship records in the graph organize all nodes by type and direction, and attributes can be added into nodes and relationships. The graph database implements all the operations of the database on this structure. When the graph database performs a connection operation which is similar to a relational database, it uses the relation list to directly access the connected node, without searching for records and calculating matching operations.

### 3.1 Neo4j Graph Database

Neo4j is an open source NoSQL graph database implemented in Java. The architecture of Neo4j graph database is designed to optimize the rapid management, storage and traversal of nodes and relationships. Neo4j has strong scalability, enabling it to be able to process large-scale and complex relational graph data on one machine, and it can also support parallel processing on multiple machines. Compared with other relational databases, Neo4j has better performance to deal with a large amount of complex, related and structured sparse data. The graph database model is shown in Fig. 1.

### 3.2 GraphX Database

GraphX is a graph computing framework built on Spark. GraphX describes a directed graph with vertex attributes and edge attributes. GraphX provides three views: Vertex, Edge, and EdgeTriplet. Various graph operations of GraphX are also completed on three views. It uses Resilient Distributed Data Set (RDD) to store graph data and provides practical graph manipulation methods. RDD is a partitioned data structure, which is processed by calculation primitives provided by Spark Core. Each Spark application can be deployed in a cluster. According to the characteristics of elastic distributed data sets, GraphX can efficiently realize distributed storage and proceeding of graphs, and can be applied into large-scale graph computing scenarios such as social networks. GraphX has optimized the storage of graph vertex information and edge information, so that the performance of the graph computing framework can be greatly improved compared to the native RDD implementation, which is close to the performance of professional graph computing platforms such as GraphLab. GraphX graph database architecture is shown in Fig. 2.

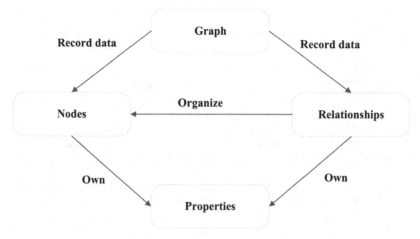

**Fig. 1.** Neo4j graph database model.

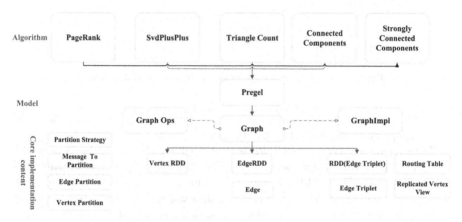

**Fig. 2.** GraphX graph database architecture.

## 4  Model Design

### 4.1  Data Analysis Framework of Power Grid Topology

In order to transform the abstract grid topology data into an intuitive graph database that is helpful to analyze and understand, this paper designs a grid topology graph data analysis framework based on the characteristics of the graph data of the power system, which mainly includes data collection and processing, data storage, There are several levels of data analysis, as shown in Fig. 3.

(1) The collection and processing layer mainly collects various topological data of the power system, physical equipment, connection lines, equipment operation data, historical data, etc. At the same time, the collected data is classified and screened, the missing data is counted or reported, and graph data modeling is performed based

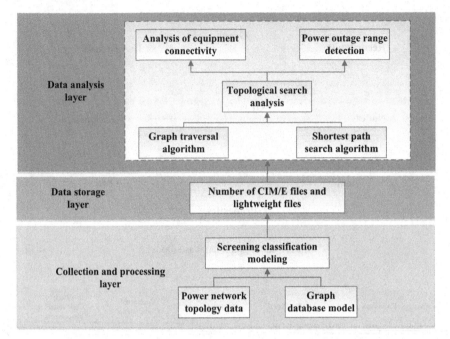

**Fig. 3.** Data model analysis framework of power grid diagram.

on the collected data. The collection and processing layer plays a vital role in the stable operation and maintenance of the power system.

(2) The data storage layer uses CIM/E files and lightweight file databases as model data solidification storage media, and different data information is stored in different systems. The CIM/E file mainly stores the cross-section model extracted by the operating system. The lightweight file database mainly uses two-dimensional tables for structured storage of historical and future version of the grid model data, providing support for the recall and viewing of historical data.

(3) The purpose of the data analysis layer to build the grid graph database model is to use some algorithm framework to analyze the graph database, find out the correlation, potential problems and operating conditions between the grid equipment, and ensure the stable operation of the power system.

## 4.2 Power Grid Data Model Construction

The construction of the data model of the grid diagram includes four steps: data acquisition, data processing, data import, and data management, as shown in Fig. 4.

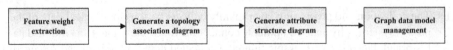

**Fig. 4.** Modeling flowchart.

According to the correlation of the big data collected by the power system, the feature weights of the nodes are extracted, and the priority is divided according to the feature weights to form a topological structure diagram. Then we use the Pearson product-moment correlation coefficient method to judge the correlation between equipment and equipment, and form a topological correlation diagram. The establishment of a power grid model must be complete and consistent. The model must be able to fully describe the characteristics of the power system objects, and be consistent with existing definitions as much as possible; in addition, the power grid model must also efficiently adapt to the characteristics of the graph database to improve the efficiency of data access. The basic principle of establishing a power grid model based on a graph database must follow the CIM/E standard. In the graph database, power system equipment such as generators, loads, and lines are defined as vertices. Due to the large number of switches and equipments, the switches and the connecting line between each device is defined as an edge, and an attribute structure diagram is generated.

The number of vertices and edges in the grid database is greatly reduced, which improves the query access efficiency of the graph database.

## 5  Graph Data Model

### 5.1  CIM Model

In order to make the distribution network data model unique, applicable and shareable among various applications and companies, a standard method for describing these data must be provided. The most commonly used and generally accepted standard for the data model of power system data is the CIM standard. CIM was introduced by the IEC (International Electrotechnical Commission) and is defined as part of the IEC 61970-301 standard [16].

The CIM model is an abstract object model that represents all the main entities and their relationships in the power system, transmission and distribution networks. All objects from the distribution network (such as current transformers, generators, etc.) are displayed in the form of corresponding types in the CIM model. All entities of the distribution network use identification objects, equipment, equipment containers, conductive equipment, power system resources, PSRType, and terminal types for data modeling in CIM. At the top of the type hierarchy, there are defined object classes, and other types in CIM are derived from the defined object types. The equipment type describes all distribution network equipment, which are grouped in containers represented by the equipment container class. The conductive equipment category represents all conductive equipment. The parts of the equipment that can be operated as follows: such as switches, busbars and other related conductive equipment. There is a special category in the model, namely the PSRType class. The main function of the PSRType class is to classify instances of the same class, that allows a small amount of non-standard modifications to the CIM model without changing the model. In the modeling of the distribution network, in addition to basic entities, it is also necessary to provide a mechanism for connecting conductive equipment. This is done through the terminal and CIM connection node class. These classes do not perform data modeling on the resources of the distribution network, but provide information about the physical connections of the equipment. The connection node class connects two or more parts of the conductive device through the terminal class (describes the access point that connects two or more connection nodes) [17]. Since all devices are modeled as objects of the class, and the relationship between them is related, as shown in the figure, by representing objects as nodes, representing relationships as relationships, and representing all object data as attributes, it can be easy to map it to the surface. Using CIM to represent power system data has the advantage of using the General Data Access (GDA) standard defined in IEC 61970-403 for data exchange. Some methods of general data access standards are executed on this graph model as query operations. The CIM topology model is shown in Fig. 5.

## 5.2  Data Model with Electrical Nodes as Domain Entities

The network structure of the power grid is the basis of the analysis of the power grid topology. In order to reflect the structure of the power grid, this paper proposes a data model with electrical nodes as domain entities. The electrical node is the connection point of physical equipment, which combines the topology and physical characteristics of the electrical connection point and the physical bus [18]. The electrical node is used as the node of the graph database, the straight line is used as the relationship, and the physical properties of the two are used as the respective property. In addition, other types of data in topology analysis are also stored in the graph database, but in this article, by defining different "node labels", these irrelevant data can be stored in the database in an "other dimension" manner.

This model can fully restore the topological structure of the power grid, it facilitates the rapid topology analysis of the power grid and it is convenient to introduce graph theory related algorithms, such as the shortest path algorithm, the maximum flow algorithm, and so on. By combining equation solving theory with graph theory, calculations related to the network structure can be quickly performed, such as power flow calculations. Therefore, the model provides strong support when using grid topology for grid analysis. By using this model, the power industry-related algorithms based on graph theory can also be effectively calculated and verified [19]. The advantage of this model is that it can use the topology structure to store data, which facilitates grid topology analysis. However, in the storage process, irrelevant data is placed in another dimension or be ignored, which is equivalent to hiding switches, circuit breakers, generators, etc., so this model is not suitable with analyzing problems related to the abovementioned equipment.

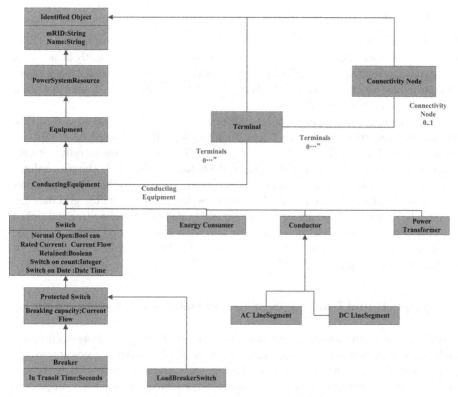

**Fig. 5.** CIM topology model.

## 5.3 Data Model of Materialized Attributes

This paper proposes a data model with materialized attributes, when the grid attributes occupy the main part of the analysis, the main attributes can be materialized as domain entities, and some attributes can be stored as database nodes. The model is based on a data model with electrical nodes as domain entities, and mathematical modeling is performed. For example, when calculating the power flow of the power grid, you can use the sparsity of the Jacobian matrix and use the graph theory solving algorithm of the sparse matrix to solve the problem.

The data model of materialized attributes refers to storing the attributes as nodes, and then calculating and analyzing the graphs based on the attributes. Therefore, when analyzing problems such as power flow calculation and reactive power optimization based on Newton's method or pre-return method, the model can make full use of the performance of the graph database. This model is a mathematical model and has almost no physical meaning. This model emphasizes the attributes in the grid, so it can be used in scenarios where specific problems are analyzed or grid calculations are performed. However, this model also changes the topology of the mesh itself, so it is not suitable for topology analysis.

## 5.4   Materialized Time Data Model

In traditional modeling methods, time is usually used as the attribute of the event. Time is a special attribute, because some physical quantities change dynamically at any time, while some are relatively fixed. This paper proposes a power data model that materializes time attributes, which uses time as the database node, and connects the events that occur at this time through relationship.

The materialized time data model is suitable for storing "events" because event data has unstructured characteristics that are difficult to describe with fixed fields. Time is an important characteristic when an event occurs. Therefore, when recording events that occur on a node, a data model of materialized time can be used. The materialized time model separates time from events, but is also related to each other. Different times are also related to each other, so the key events of the time nodes in the grid data can be quickly retrieved. There are two main modeling methods: timeline tree and linked list. The timeline tree model is suitable for retrieving a time period within a specific range, such as within a month or a year, and so on. The linked list model is suitable for continuous time retrieval.

# 6   Prospects and Challenges of Graph Data Model Construction

Based on the domain modeling theory and the CIM model, this paper proposes the principle of grid data modeling and the principle of using Neo4j to model the power grid data graph database. According to this principle, four basic graph database models are proposed. With the rapid development of society, as the amount of topological management data increases, the attribute dimension of the data will also increase. A single data model no longer has the ability to handle complex data. This is bound to change the model primitives. Changes of the model primitives can easily cause the instability of the graph model. In the future, when analyzing data processing problems in different scenarios for the distribution network, the four basic models can be combined or expanded to form a new optimal model. The model construction of graph data also faces the following challenges.

1) The challenge of data quality. High-quality data is the key to good application of grid graph data and it ensures the high quality of graph data. The accuracy, completeness, and real-time of the data have a great influence on the results of decision analysis, and even give wrong suggestions.

2) The challenge of multi-data fusion. Data fusion is the key to the application of electric power big data. Information data fusion is the multi-level processing of multi-source data, each level represents a different degree of abstraction of the original data, which includes data detection, correlation, estimation, and combination processing. According to the degree of abstraction in the data processing level, data fusion can be divided into three levels: data-level fusion (before feature extraction), feature-level fusion (before attribute description), and decision-level fusion (after independent attribute description of each sensor data).

3) The challenge of data visualization and information transmission. Electric power data visualization can effectively convey the value of data. Electric power data contains the laws and characteristics of power production and economic and social development, which are generally abstract and difficult to discover. Visual analysis of big data will make it easy to mine and analyze the laws contained in big data, which is conducive to transferring data value and sharing knowledge.
4) Challenges of big data storage and processing. Electric power big data requires huge data storage and computing capabilities. Power big data analyzes and processes structured and unstructured data from multiple data sources, and needs to store massive amounts of data and provide fast computing capabilities. Distributed data storage and calculation is an effective way to solve power big data storage and calculation.

## 7 Conclusion

This paper summarizes the domestic and foreign research status of graph data model construction technology, introduces graph databases commonly used in graph data model construction, expounds the relevant steps of using graph databases for data modeling, and summarizes four commonly used data models and their respective characteristics. In the future, the scalability of Neo4j database can be used to combine and apply commonly used data models to solve complex problems in different scenarios. Finally, the challenges of graph data model in data quality, multi-data fusion, data visualization information, storage and processing are explained.

**Acknowledgements.** We would like to thank the anonymous reviewers for their comments and constructive suggestions that have improved the paper. The subject is sponsored by the Science and Technology Project of State Grid Corporation of China (No. 5700-202058480A-0-0-00).

## References

1. Pan, Z., Jing, Z.: Modeling methods of big data for power grid based on graph database, pp. 4340–4348 (2018)
2. Pavković, V., Čapko, D., Vukmirović, S., Erdeljan, A.: Modeling power system data using nosql database. In: 2017 25th Telecommunication Forum (TELFOR), pp. 1–4. IEEE (2017)
3. Hu, J., Zhao, S., Nie, Q.: Research on modeling of power grid information system based on knowledge graph. In: 2021 IEEE International Conference on Power Electronics, Computer Applications (ICPECA), pp. 648–651. IEEE (2021)
4. Gonzalez, H., Han, J., Cheng, H., Li, X., Klabjan, D., Wu, T.: Modeling massive rfid data sets: a gateway-based movement graph approach. IEEE Trans. Knowl. Data Eng. **22**(1), 90–104 (2009)
5. Risi, M., Sessa, M.I., Tucci, M., Tortora, G.: Code modeling of graph composition for data warehouse report visualization. IEEE Trans. Knowl. Data Eng. **26**(3), 563–576 (2013)
6. Xue, C.: Method for constructing data model of enterprise relationship graph based on industrial and commercial data. In: 2019 4th International Conference on Mechanical, Control and Computer Engineering (ICMCCE), pp. 876–8763. IEEE (2019)

7. Wu, G., et al.: An automatic and rapid knowledge graph construction method of sg-cim model. In: 2020 IEEE International Conference on Smart Cloud (SmartCloud), pp. 193–198. IEEE (2020)

8. Scarselli, F., Gori, M., Tsoi, A.C., Hagenbuchner, M., Monfardini, G.: The graph neural network model. IEEE Trans. Neural Networks **20**(1), 61–80 (2008)

9. Majumdar, A.K., Bhattacharya, I., Saha, A.K.: An object-oriented fuzzy data model for similarity detection in image databases. IEEE Trans. Knowl. Data Eng. **14**(5), 1186–1189 (2002)

10. Lee, W.K., et al.: A path-based relation networks model for knowledge graph completion. Expert Syst. Appl. **182**, 115273 (2021)

11. Combi, C., Oliboni, B., Rossato, R.: Merging multimedia presentations and semistructured temporal data: a graph-based model and its application to clinical information. Artif. Intell. Med. **34**(2), 89–112 (2005)

12. Zhang, M., Chen, W., Duan, X., Zhang, R.: Improving graph-based dependency parsing models with dependency language models. IEEE Trans. Audio Speech Lang. Process. **21**(11), 2313–2323 (2013)

13. Lu, H., Yang, R., Deng, Z., Zhang, Y., Gao, G., Lan, R.: Chinese image captioning via fuzzy attention-based densenet-bilstm. ACM Trans. Multimedia Comput. Commun. Appl. (TOMM) **17**(1), 1–18 (2021)

14. Lu, H., Zhang, M., Xu, X., Li, Y., Shen, H.T.: Deep fuzzy hashing network for efficient image retrieval. IEEE Trans. Fuzzy Syst. **29**(1), 166–176 (2020)

15. Ge, Q., Gao, G., Shao, W., Wang, L., Wu, F.: Graph regularized bayesian tensor factorization based on kronecker-decomposable dictionary. Comput. Electr. Eng. **90**, 106968 (2021)

16. IEC61970, D.: Energy management system application program interface (emsapi) part 301: Common information model (cim) base. Geneva, Switzerland: IEC (2003)

17. McMorran, A.W.: An introduction to iec 61970–301 & 61968–11: the common information model. University Strathclyde **93**, 124 (2007)

18. Wenchuan, W., Boming, Z.: A graphic database based network topology and its application. Power Syst. Technol.-Beijing- **26**(2), 14–18 (2002)

19. Liu, K., Liu, G., Xie, K., Wang, Z.: A faster non-linear iteration solver using graph computing and its application in power flow calculation. Energy Procedia **142**, 2534–2540 (2017)

20. Lu, H., Li, Y., Chen, M., Kim, H., Serikawa, S.: Brain Intelligence: Go beyond Artificial Intelligence. Mob. Networks Appl. **23**(2), 368–375 (2017). https://doi.org/10.1007/s11036-017-0932-8

21. Huimin, L., Zhang, Y., Li, Y., et al.: User-Oriented virtual mobile network resource management for vehicle communications. IEEE Trans. Intell. Transp. Syst. **22**(6), 3521–3532 (2021)

# Optimal SVM Using an Improved FOA of Evolutionary Computing

Xing Chen, Mei Wang$^{(\boxtimes)}$, Shuai Wu, Chaofei Yu, and Yuancheng Li

Xi'an University of Science and Technology, Xi'an 710054, China
20206227094@stu.xust.edu.cn

**Abstract.** To solve the problem that the traditional model has the problem of low recognition accuracy, this paper proposes a dynamic step size factor to realize the dynamic change of step size, which makes the fruit fly optimization algorithm (FOA) have strong local optimization ability and improve the convergence accuracy. The smell concentration determination formula is improved to realize the search of the algorithm in the negative value range. This paper constructs an improved FOA-SVM model and uses the heart dataset to evaluate the classification performance of the improved FOA-SVM algorithm. Finally, the gray texture joint feature parameters of coal and gangue are extracted as the input vector of the improved FOA-SVM and gangue are carried out. The experimental results show that the classification results of the improved FOA-SVM model proposed in this paper are good, and the average accuracy are 96.30%, which improves the classification performance by 2.1% compared with the original algorithm.

**Keywords:** First keyword · SVM · Fly optimization algorithm · Recognition · Model

## 1 Introduction

High speed and accurate identification of coal gangue is the key to realize the intelligence of coal industry [1], and it is very important to improve the production efficiency of coal mining and coal preparation. Therefore, the research on coal gangue identification has always been the focus and hotspot in the field of coal intelligent technology. It is related to the further improvement of coal mining technology and the development of safe and green mining. In recent years, ray transmission coal preparation method has developed rapidly, including γ Ray detection technology [2], X-ray detection [3], laser detection [4] and so on. Ray detection techniques are easy to achieve integration, but X-ray transmission coal preparation method has some defects, such as high cost, difficult maintenance and great harm to human body. At the same time, the technology of image processing and pattern recognition has been developing continuously, and the use of image recognition technology [5] has promoted the development of coal gangue recognition. Eshaq et al. [6] used the infrared camera to obtain the image of coal and gangue, and used the gray level co-occurrence matrix to extract the gray level features of the image. Finally, SVM was combined with the gray level features to classify coal

S. Yang and H. Lu (Eds.): ISAIR 2022, CCIS 1700, pp. 55–68, 2022.
https://doi.org/10.1007/978-981-19-7946-0_6

and gangue, and achieved good classification results. Singh V et al. [7] compared and summarized the gray histogram of coal gangue through image processing technology, and set the recognition threshold to distinguish coal and gangue. Hu et al. [8] Proposed a method to identify coal and gangue by using spectral imaging technology, which overcomes the influence of light, dust and other environmental factors on the detection of ordinary images. Su et al. [9] proposed an automatic recognition method of coal gangue image based on convolutional neural network, and the recognition rate of coal gangue reached 95.88%.

The fruit fly optimization algorithm (FOA) is an intelligent optimization algorithm proposed by Pan [10] according to the foraging behavior of Drosophila. Compared with genetic algorithm (GA) [11, 12], particle swarm optimization (PSO) [13, 14], ant colony optimization (ACO) [15, 16], FOA has the advantages of easy understanding and simple calculation process. It has been widely used in various fields, but in practical application, the algorithm is easy to fall into local optimization and other problems. Huang. H et al. [17] Proposed the twin swarm Drosophila optimization algorithm (LFOA) with Levy flight characteristics, which effectively solved the problem of FOA falling into local optimization and improved the performance of the algorithm. In order to overcome the shortcomings of the original FOA algorithm, Wu [18] and others proposed an improved fruit fly optimization algorithm (IAFOA). Compared with the original FOA, IAFOA also includes four additional mechanisms. Pan et al. [19] proposed an improved fruit fly optimization algorithm (IFFO), which introduces a new control parameter to adaptively adjust the search range around the population position. Specifically, after setting the maximum and minimum radius of the search range, the iteration step value decreases with the increase of the number of iterations. Hu et al. [20] proposed the fruit fly optimization algorithm (SFOA) with decreasing step size. In SFOA, the current step value RI can be calculated according to the formula, where R is the initial step value, M is the maximum number of iterations, and M is the current number of iterations.

In view of the fruit fly algorithm adopts a fixed search radius in the fruit fly foraging stage, the convergence speed and accuracy of the algorithm are poor. In this paper, the dynamic step factor and the improved fruit fly smell concentration judgment formula are proposed to improve the algorithm, then an improved fruit fly optimization algorithm is proposed, and several commonly used test functions are selected to optimize and verify the improved FOA. The experimental results show that the improved FOA has better optimization performance and higher stability. On the basis of improving FOA, this paper proposes to optimize the SVM algorithm with the improved FOA. Then, the gray texture joint feature parameters of coal and gangue are extracted as the input vector of the improved FOA-SVM classification model, and the classification experiments of coal and gangue are carried out. The improved FOA-SVM, FOA-SVM, PSO-SVM (based on the particle swarm optimization algorithm) and SVM were compared in detail. Experimental results show that the proposed improved FOA-SVM method is superior to other methods in average accuracy, average accuracy, average recall and average F1 score.

## 2   SVM Classifier

SVM (Support Vector Machine) is to find a hyperplane with the largest distance from the edge. That is to solve the following problems:

$$
\begin{cases}
\min \frac{1}{2}\|\omega\|^2 + C\sum_{i=1}^{n}\varepsilon_i \\
s.t. \ y_i[(\omega \times x_i) + b] \geq 1 - \varepsilon_i, \varepsilon_i \geq 0, i = 1, \cdots, n
\end{cases}
\tag{1}
$$

where $\omega$ is weight vector, $C$ is penalty parameter, $\varepsilon_i$ is relaxation variable, and $b$ is the classification threshold. By introducing Lagrange function and solving the dual problem, and a new objective function is obtained.

$$
\begin{cases}
\max \frac{1}{2}\alpha_i - \frac{1}{2}\sum_{i,j=1}^{n} y_i y_j \alpha_i \alpha_j \\
s.t. \ \sum_{i=1}^{n}\alpha_i y_i = 0, 0 \leq \alpha_i \leq c, i = 1, \cdots, n
\end{cases}
\tag{2}
$$

where $\alpha$ is the Lagrange multiplier and $K$ is the kernel function. We consider radial basis function (RBF) as the kernel function, and $k(x_i, x) = \exp(-g \cdot \|x_i - x\|^2)$, $g$ is the parameter of the kernel function. SVM decision function can be represented as.

$$
f(x) = \text{sgn}(\sum_{i=1}^{n}\alpha_i y_i K(x_i, x) + b)
\tag{3}
$$

According to the above derivation, the classification of support vector machine needs to determine the parameters $C$ and $g$. when we use SVM and radial basis kernel function to deal with a classification problem, it is of great significance to select the best parameter $C$ and penalty parameter $g$, which directly determines the performance of the classifier and the effect of processing the problem. Therefore, this paper optimizes the parameters $C$ and $g$ with the improved FOA, and then obtains the optimal support vector classification model, so as to improve the classification performance of SVM model.

## 3   Fruit Fly Optimization Algorithm

### 3.1   The Basic Fruit Fly Optimization Algorithm

According to the foraging principle of fruit fly population, we can summarize the fruit fly optimization algorithm into the following steps:

Step 1: The initial population size of fruit fly is $G$, the maximum number of iterations is $M$, the initial position of the population is randomly set as $X_{axis}, Y_{axis}$, and the direction and distance of searching food are randomly set for fruit fly individuals, where $R$ is the search distance.

$$
\begin{cases}
X_i = X_{axis} + R \\
Y_i = Y_{axis} + R
\end{cases}
\tag{4}
$$

Step 2: Calculate the distance $D_i$ from fruit fly individual to the origin, and then calculate the judgment value $S_i$ of smell concentration.

$$\begin{cases} D_i = \sqrt{X_i^2 + Y_i^2} \\ S_i = 1/D_i \end{cases} \qquad (5)$$

Step 3: Substituting $S_i$ into the fitness function to calculate the food smell concentration of each fruit fly individual.

$$Smell_i = f(S_i) \qquad (6)$$

Step 4: Save the information of fruit fly individuals with the largest fitness value $Smell_i$ in the fruit fly population.

$$[bestSmell, bestindex] = \max(smell_i) \qquad (7)$$

Step 5: Record and retain *bestsmell* and its corresponding coordinate $X, Y$, and its remaining fruit flies are updated from the previous position to the position of this coordinate.

$$\begin{cases} Smellbest = bestSmell \\ X_{axis} = X(bestIndex) \\ Y_{axis} = Y(bestIndex) \end{cases} \qquad (8)$$

Step 6: Judge whether the algorithm reaches the maximum number of cycles or target accuracy. If not, the algorithm executes step 2–step 5. If it reaches, the optimal fruit fly individual is returned and the algorithm ends.

## 3.2  A Improved FOA

Because FOA uses a fixed search radius in the fruit fly foraging stage, it has a great impact on the speed and accuracy of the algorithm. Therefore, in order to improve the optimization accuracy of FOA, improve the calculation efficiency, enhance the global search ability and search range of the algorithm, this paper will make the following improvements to the algorithm:

The dynamic step size factor is proposed to realize the dynamic change of the step size, and then realize the dynamic decrease of the search radius. Under the condition of ensuring a certain global search ability, the convergence speed and solution accuracy of the algorithm are improved at the same time.

The determination formula of fruit fly smell concentration in the algorithm is improved to realize the search of the algorithm in the negative value area, expand the search range and improve the ability to solve complex problems.

### 3.2.1  Decreasing Radius Strategy

Using fixed radius to search, the algorithm can not be improved from two aspects of convergence speed and accuracy. When the search radius remains large, the algorithm has strong global search ability, which can accelerate the convergence speed of the algorithm, but at the same time, the accuracy will decline, and it is difficult to find an accurate global optimal solution. When the search radius remains small, the global optimization ability will decline, which will slow down the convergence speed of the algorithm, but improve the optimization accuracy. In this paper, an improved method of dynamic step size is proposed to solve the shortcomings of fixed radius. While ensuring the global search ability of the algorithm, the accuracy can be significantly improved. The dynamic step factor proposed in this paper is as follows:

$$\begin{cases} w = w_0 \times e^{-(\alpha d)/\max gen} \\ X_i = X_{axis} + wR \\ Y_i = Y_{axis} + wR \end{cases} \tag{9}$$

where $w$ represents the weight, $w_0$ represents the initial weight, $\alpha$ represents the weight coefficient, $d$ represents the current number of iterations, and *maxgen* represents the maximum number of iterations.

### 3.2.2 Improved Taste Concentration Formula

The judgment value of smell concentration of FOA algorithm is the reciprocal of the distance between the individual fruit fly and the coordinate origin, and its value range is always positive, which can not realize the search of negative spatial solutions, and lacks the ability to solve high latitude and complex problems. Therefore, the smell concentration determination formula is optimized, as shown in formula (10):

$$S_i = \exp^{-L_i} \times sgn(X_i \times Y_i) \tag{10}$$

In Eq. (10), the exponential function ensures the negative correlation between the candidate solution and the position of fruit fly. At the same time, the function is used. When the individual fruit fly is within the two and four image limits of two-dimensional coordinates, it is negative. Equation (10) can realize the comprehensive search of negative value space, increase the application scenario of the algorithm, and improve the ability of the algorithm to solve high latitude and complex problems.

## 4 Implementation of Improved FOA-SVM Algorithm

### 4.1 Improved FOA-SVM Classification Algorithm Flow

The improved FOA-SVM algorithm flow is as follows:

Step 1: Initialize the population size $G$, the maximum evolution times $M$, and set the initial positions as $X_{-axis}$ and $Y_{-axis}$. Since there are two optimization parameters, when the initial position of fruit fly, $X_{-axis}$ and $Y_{-axis}$ should take two random numbers respectively, then the initial coordinates $(X_1^c, Y_1^c)$ and $(X_1^g, Y_1^g)$.
Step 2: The distance d from fruit fly to the origin was calculated, and the judgment values $S_1^C$ and $S_1^g$ of smell concentration were obtained by using the improved judgment formula.

Step 3: Through the 5-fold cross validation method, the accuracy is the fitness value of fruit fly, and the information of the best fitness individual is saved.

Step 4: The information of fruit fly individuals with the highest accuracy is saved, and the other individuals gather to the optimal individual location.

Step 5: Judge whether the set maximum evolution times is reached. If not, return to step 2. Otherwise, the optimal parameter of the output model, that is, $C = S_1^C, g = S_1^g$.

Step 6: The SVM recognition model is established by using the optimal parameters $C$ and $g$, and the test samples are classified to obtain the test results.

## 4.2 Classifier Performance Evaluation Index

At present, various classifier evaluation indexes have been used in different classification models and achieved good results. Among the evaluation indicators, accuracy, accuracy, recall and F1 score are the most commonly used.

Accuracy: measure the proportion of all samples classified accurately. The calculation formula is:

$$Accuracy = \frac{TP + TN}{TP + FP + TN + FN} \tag{11}$$

Precision: also known as precision, it measures the classification accuracy of positive samples. The calculation formula is:

$$\Pr ecision = \frac{TP}{TP + FP} \tag{12}$$

Recall: the proportion of positive samples with correct classification in the total positive samples. The calculation formula is:

$$Recall = \frac{TP}{TP + FN} \tag{13}$$

F1 score: harmonic average of accuracy rate and recall rate, and its calculation formula is:

$$\frac{2}{F_1} = \frac{1}{P} + \frac{1}{R} \Rightarrow F_1 = \frac{2PR}{P + R} = \frac{2TP}{2TP + FP + TN} \tag{14}$$

TP: it was originally a positive sample, but it was also judged as a positive sample by the model, that is, the category judged by the classification result is consistent with the category to which the sample belongs.

TF: It is originally a negative sample, but it is also judged as a negative sample by the model, that is, the category judged by the classification result is consistent with the category to which the sample belongs.

FP: originally a negative sample, but it is also judged as a positive sample by the model, that is, the category judged by the classification result is inconsistent with the category to which the sample belongs.

FN: originally a positive sample, but it is also judged as a negative sample by the model, that is, the category judged by the classification result is inconsistent with the category to which the sample belongs.

Accuracy rate is used to measure the proportion of real positive samples in the total number of predicted positive samples, which describes the accuracy of classifying positive samples. Recall rate is used to measure the proportion of positive samples with correct classification in the total samples. The recall rate reflects the recall rate of the classifier. F1 score is the harmonic average of accuracy and recall. The larger the value of F1 score, the better the overall performance of the classifier. The above indicators have the characteristics of independence, small amount of calculation and easy to understand. It can evaluate the classification results well, so it is widely used in the research of classification problems.

### 4.3   Performance Evaluation Results of Classifier Based on UCI Data Set

UCI data set, as a standard test data set, is often used to train machine learning models. The data set contains 559 sub data sets. In this experiment, the heart dataset in UCI dataset is selected to verify the performance of the classifier. The heart sub dataset contains 303 samples, 2 categories and the feature dimension is 13. In the experiment, the number of training samples was 153 and the number of test samples was 150.

When evaluating the classifier performance, this paper uses the heart dataset in UCI dataset to verify the improved FOA optimized SVM algorithm, and calculates the selected indicators to evaluate the classifier performance. Run the program 10 times in MATLAB 2018, keep the parameters consistent before and after each run, and count the mean value of each index of the classification results 10 times to evaluate the performance of the model.

**Table 1.** Evaluation indexes of improved FOA-SVM model

| Serial number | Accuracy | Precision | Recall | F1-score |
|---|---|---|---|---|
| 1 | 0.9571 | 0.9477 | 0.9667 | 0.9571 |
| 2 | 0.9604 | 0.9542 | 0.9669 | 0.9605 |
| 3 | 0.9538 | 0.9412 | 0.9664 | 0.9537 |
| 4 | 0.9472 | 0.9412 | 0.9536 | 0.9473 |
| 5 | **0.9406** | 0.9346 | **0.9470** | **0.9407** |
| 6 | 0.9571 | 0.9477 | 0.9667 | 0.9571 |
| 7 | 0.9505 | 0.9412 | 0.9489 | 0.9450 |
| 8 | 0.9439 | **0.9346** | 0.9600 | 0.9471 |
| 9 | **0.9670** | **0.9608** | 0.9533 | **0.9606** |
| 10 | 0.9604 | 0.9477 | **0.9732** | 0.9602 |
| Average value | 0.9538 | 0.9451 | 0.9603 | 0.9530 |

Table 1 shows the final evaluation results of the classifier using UCI dataset. As can be seen from Table 2, the average accuracy of the results of these 10 experiments is about 95.38%, the average accuracy is about 94.51%, the average recall is about 96.03%, and the average F1 score is about 95.30%. According to the above indicators, the improved FOA optimized SVM algorithm proposed in this paper has good classification effect. Except that the accuracy rate is 0.9451, the values of other indicators are more than 0.95, which has high classification performance.

**Table 2.** Comparison of classification performance of several models

| Classification model | Accuracy | Precision | Recall | F1-score |
|---|---|---|---|---|
| FOA-SVM | 92.08 | 90.85 | 93.29 | 92.06 |
| LFOA-SVM | 93.40 | 92.16 | 94.63 | 93.38 |
| Improved FOA-SVM | 95.38 | 94.51 | 96.03 | 95.30 |

In order to verify the reliability of the algorithm proposed in this paper, the heart data set in UCI is selected and classified by FOA optimized support vector machine and LFOA optimized support vector machine. The classification effect is evaluated by the above four indicators: average accuracy, average accuracy, average recall and F1 score. Compared with each index of improved FOA optimized support vector machine classification results in this paper, Table 2 shows the final results.

It is obvious from Table 2 that the improved FOA-SVM algorithm in this paper has better classification effect than the other two algorithms. The accuracy, accuracy, recall and F1 score of the classification results are higher than the corresponding index values of the other two algorithms in Table 1, and a good classification effect is obtained.

## 5   Experiment and Analysis

### 5.1   Image Preprocessing

The coal gangue images used in this paper are from a coal preparation plant in Han Cheng. A total of 1500 coal gangue images are taken, including 750 coal and 750 gangue. In order to easily distinguish and facilitate the experiment, the coal and gangue images are numbered respectively in the shooting, and finally the coal gangue image sample data set is established. In this paper, CCD industrial camera is used to capture the image of coal gangue. Its model is $MV - VS030FM - L$, the shooting resolution is $640 \times 480$, and the pixel size is 5.6 μm. It is developed on the basis of MOS integrated circuit, which can realize the automatic scanning of coal gangue.

In the process of image preprocessing, [21] image enhancement is an important step. Due to various factors and problems such as unclear picture and quality degradation in the process of image transmission, it will affect the later feature extraction and final recognition effect. Therefore, it is very necessary to enhance the picture. Image enhancement can highlight the target area in the image and weaken the useless or unimportant information, so as to increase the readability of the image. The reinforcement diagram of coal and gangue is shown in Fig. 1.

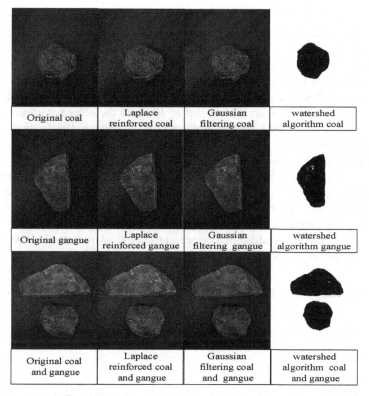

**Fig. 1.** Reinforcement diagram of coal and gangue

## 5.2 Coal Gangue Classification Based on Improved FOA-SVM

The gray mean, gray variance and skewness in the limestone features of coal gangue have low correlation [22], and the contrast and entropy in the texture features have low correlation. By comparing the classification results based on gray features, texture features and gray texture joint features, it is concluded that compared with gray features or texture features, the combination of gray and texture features has a high recognition rate for coal gangue recognition. In this paper, the gray texture joint feature parameters of coal and gangue will be extracted as the input vector of the improved SVM classification model.

**Table 3.** Range of gray texture joint feature parameters

| Sample | Gray mean | Gray variance | Skewness | Contrast ratio | Entropy |
|---|---|---|---|---|---|
| Coal | 26.3–70.9 | 15.8–64.4 | 19.1–66.3 | 3.2–6.5 | 2.5–40.1 |
| Waste | 57.1–114.7 | 5.2–27.8 | 4.7–37.6 | 1.9–4.6 | 0.6–9.2 |

In this experiment, 750 photos of coal and gangue are selected, a total of 1500 photos are selected, and their gray texture joint feature parameters are analyzed. The distribution range is shown in Table 3. The above parameters are used as the input vector of the support vector machine model, the recognition model is established, and the improved FOA algorithm is used to optimize the parameters of the recognition model, so as to obtain the optimal accuracy. The population number of the improved FOA algorithm is set to 30, the number of iterations is set to 100, and the other parameters remain unchanged. Figures 2, 3 and 4 are the results of coal and gangue classification.

As can be seen from Fig. 2 above, the accuracy of traditional FOA optimized support vector machine for coal gangue classification is 95.3%, and the corresponding optimal parameter C is 6.1610 and G is 0.9827; In the identification error results, the total number of test samples is 300, and the number of error identification is 14. It can be seen from Fig. 3 that the classification accuracy of the improved FOA optimized support vector machine for coal gangue is 96.3%, the corresponding optimal parameter C is 22.4804, and G is 13.8065; In the identification error results, the total number of test samples is 300, and the number of error identification is 11.

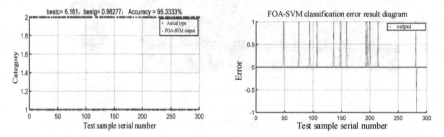

**Fig. 2.** Accuracy and error of coal gangue classification by FOA-SVM

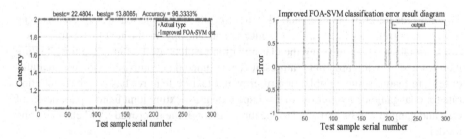

**Fig. 3.** Accuracy and error of coal gangue classification by improve FOA-SVM

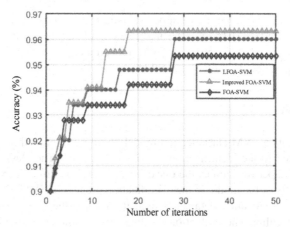

**Fig. 4.** Comparison of iterative evolution curves of three algorithms for coal gangue classification

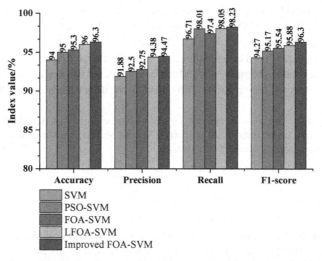

**Fig. 5.** Comparison of evaluation indexes of coal gangue classification results of several models

It can be seen from Fig. 4 that the improved FOA algorithm optimized support vector machine has fewer iterations and higher accuracy in coal gangue recognition than the other two algorithms. From the above comparison, it can be seen that the improved FOA optimized support vector machine has good results in coal gangue recognition.

In order to verify the reliability and effectiveness of the algorithm proposed in this paper, support vector machine, PSO optimized support vector machine [23], FOA optimized support vector machine and other algorithms are used to classify coal and gangue, and the corresponding evaluation index values are calculated, which are compared with the evaluation index values of the classification algorithm proposed in this topic to verify the feasibility of this algorithm for coal gangue classification. It can be seen intuitively from Fig. 5 that the optimized support vector machine is used to classify coal gangue, and each evaluation index is higher than that before optimization. Among the indexes of the improved FOA optimized support vector machine classification algorithm in this paper. Therefore, the improved FOA optimized SVM has better classification performance and good classification effect than other algorithms.

## 6 Conclusion

This paper presents a SVM classification model based on improved the fruit fly algorithm. It is applied to the identification of coal and gangue. The classification model proposed in this paper overcomes the disadvantage that it is difficult to determine the optimal parameters of the model in the classification process of SVM algorithm. In this paper, the heart classification data set is used to evaluate the classification results of the improved algorithm. The evaluation results show that the algorithm has good classification performance. Finally, taking the coal gangue image as the research object, PSO-SVM algorithm, FOA-SVM algorithm, LFOA-SVM algorithm and the improved FOA-SVM are used to classify the coal gangue image. Compared with the classification results, the improved FOA-SVM algorithm in this paper has the best classification effect on the coal gangue image, and its accuracy reaches 96.3%, Therefore, the algorithm proposed in this paper has a certain application value in coal gangue recognition. In the future research, the deep learning method can be considered to recognize the coal gangue image, and the specific recognition results need to be further analyzed and proved.

**Acknowledgement.** This work is supported by The Chinese Society of Academic Degrees and Graduate Education under grant B-2017Y0002-170, and Shaanxi Province Key Research and Development Projects under grants 2016GY-040.

## References

1. Zou, L., Yu, X., Li, M., et al.: Nondestructive identification of coal and gangue via near-infrared spectroscopy based on improved broad learning. IEEE Trans. Instrum. Meas. **69**(10), 8043–8052 (2020)
2. Yazdi, M., Esmaeilnia, S.A.: Dual-energy gamma-ray technique for quantitative measurement of coal ash in the Shahroud mine Iran. Int. J. Coal Geol. **55**(2), 151–156 (2003)
3. Dong, Z., Xia, J., Duan, X., Cao, J.: Based on curing age of calcined coal gangue fine aggregate mortar of X-ray diffraction and scanning electron microscopy analysis. Spectrosc. Spectral Anal. **36**(3), 842–847 (2016)
4. Wang, W., Zhang, C.: Separating coal and gangue using three-dimensional laser scanning. Int. J. Miner. Process. **169**, 79–84 (2017)
5. Fu, K.-S.: Pattern recognition and image processing. IEEE Trans. Comput. **C–100**(12), 1336–1346 (1976)
6. Eshaq, R.M.A., Hu, E., Li, M., et al.: Separation between coal and gangue based on infrared radiation and visual extraction of the YCbCr color space. IEEE Access **08**, 55204–55220 (2020)
7. Singh, V., Singh, T.N., Singh, V.: Image processing applications for customized mining and ore classification. Arab. J. Geosci. **4**(7), 1163–1171, 28–36 (2011)

8. Hu, F., Zhou, M., Yan, P., Bian, K., Dai, R.: Multispectral imaging: a new solution for identification of coal and gangue. IEEE Access **7**, 169697–169704 (2019). https://doi.org/10.1109/ACCESS.2019.2955725
9. Su, L., Cao, X., Ma, H., Li, Y.: Research on coal gangue identification by using convolutional neural network. In: Proceedings of the 2018 2nd IEEE Advanced Information Management, Communicates, Electronic and Automation Control Conference (IMCEC), pp. 810–814 (2018). https://doi.org/10.1109/IMCEC.2018.8469674
10. Pan, W.T.: A new fruit fly optimization algorithm: taking the financial distress model as an example. Knowl.-Based Syst. **26**, 69–74 (2012)
11. Mirjalili, S.: Genetic algorithm. In: Evolutionary Algorithms and Neural Networks, vol. 780, pp. 43–55. Springer, Cham (2019). https://doi.org/10.1007/978-3-319-93025-1_4
12. Deng, W., Zhao, H., Zou, L., et al.: A novel collaborative optimization algorithm in solving complex optimization problems. Soft. Comput. **21**(15), 4387–4398 (2017)
13. Nebro, A.J., Durillo, J.J., Garcia-Nieto, J., et al.: SMPSO: a new PSO-based metaheuristic for multi-objective optimization. In: Proceedings of the 2009 IEEE Symposium on Computational Intelligence in Multi-criteria Decision-Making (MCDM), pp. 66–73. IEEE (2009)
14. Ishaque, K., Salam, Z., Amjad, M., et al.: An improved particle swarm optimization (PSO)–based MPPT for PV with reduced steady-state oscillation. IEEE Trans. Power Electron. **27**(8), 3627–3638 (2012)
15. Liu, Y., Cao, B.: A novel ant colony optimization algorithm with Levy flight. IEEE Access **8**, 67205–67213 (2020)
16. Deng, W., Xu, J., Zhao, H.: An improved ant colony optimization algorithm based on hybrid strategies for scheduling problem. IEEE Access **7**, 20281–20292 (2019)
17. Huang, H., Zhou, S., Jiang, J., et al.: A new fruit fly optimization algorithm enhanced support vector machine for diagnosis of breast cancer based on high-level features. BMC Bioinformatics **20**(8), 1–14 (2019)
18. Wu, L., Liu, Q., Tian, X., et al.: A new improved fruit fly optimization algorithm IAFOA and its application to solve engineering optimization problems. Knowl.-Based Syst. **144**, 153–173 (2018)
19. Pan, Q.K., Sang, H.Y., Duan, J.H., et al.: An improved fruit fly optimization algorithm for continuous function optimization problems. Knowl.-Based Syst. **62**, 69–83 (2014)
20. Hu, R., Wen, S., Zeng, Z., et al.: A short-term power load forecasting model based on the generalized regression neural network with decreasing step fruit fly optimization algorithm. Neurocomputing **221**, 24–31 (2017)
21. Jeong, H.J., Park, K.S., Ha, Y.G.: Image preprocessing for efficient training of YOLO deep learning networks. In: Proceedings of the 2018 IEEE International Conference on Big Data and Smart Computing (BigComp), pp. 635–637. IEEE (2018)
22. Wang, M., Ma, C., Li, Z.L., et al.: Alertness estimation using connection parameters of the brain network. IEEE Trans. Intell. Transp. Syst. (2021). https://doi.org/10.1109/TITS.2021.3124372
23. Wang, M., Huang, Z.Y., Li, Y.C., et al.: Maximum weight multi-modal information fusion algorithm of electroencephalographs and face images for emotion recognition. Comput. Electr. Eng. **94**(2021), 107415:1-107415:13 (2021)
24. Lu, H., Zhang, M., Xu, X.: Deep fuzzy hashing network for efficient image retrieval. IEEE Trans. Fuzzy Syst. (2020). https://doi.org/10.1109/TFUZZ.2020.2984991
25. Lu, H., Li, Y., Chen, M., et al.: Brain intelligence: go beyond artificial intelligence. Mobile Netw. Appl. **23**, 368–375 (2018)
26. Lu, H., Li, Y., Mu, S., et al.: Motor anomaly detection for unmanned aerial vehicles using reinforcement learning. IEEE Internet Things J. **5**(4), 2315–2322 (2018)
27. Lu, H., Qin, M., Zhang, F., et al.: RSCNN: A CNN-based method to enhance low-light remote-sensing images. Remote Sens. **13**, 62 (2020)

28. Lu, H., Zhang, Y., Li, Y., et al.: User-oriented virtual mobile network resource management for vehicle communications. IEEE Trans. Intell. Transp. Syst. **22**(6), 3521–3532 (2021)

# Analysis and Control for Bilateral Teleoperation Systems with Part Active Power

Dekun Zheng[1], Yanfeng Pu[2(✉)], and Jing Bai[3,4]

[1] College of Electrical Engineering and Control Science, Nanjing Tech University,
Nanjing 21816, China
[2] Nanjing Customs District P.R. China, 360, Longpanzhong Road, Qinhuai District, Nanjing,
China
64016663@qq.com
[3] Industrial Technology Research Institute of Intelligent Equipment,
Nanjing Institute of Technology, Nanjing 211167, China
[4] Jiangsu Provincial Engineering Laboratory of Intelligent Manufacturing Equipment,
Nanjing 211167, China

**Abstract.** Bilateral operation systems have been widely used in daily life and many filed. Generally, both master manipulators and slave manipulators are assumed to be passive devices. However, master manipulators may always bring part active power in the integral network due to the active haptic device. In this paper, we study the bilateral system with part active power, analyze the stability condition is analyzed and a PD bilateral controller is proposed on the basis of four channel two-wave network. Numerical simulations are performed and results prove that the proposed method is better than the conventional method.

**Keywords:** Teleoperation system · Four-channel control · Double wave-variable method · Bilateral teleoperation

## 1 Introduction

Tele-operation systems are widely applied to many hard-to-reach environments, such as aerospace [1], medical surgery [2], deep-sea exploration [3] and so on. Especially, in the medical surgery tele-operation system, at the console, the surgeon commands the master surgical manipulator to perform surgery on the patient. In teleoperation systems, the human operates the master manipulator, and the slave manipulator may follow the trajectory of the master side. Normally, there is a communication channel between the master side and the slave side since they are located in different sites.

In the bilateral teleoperation system, the time delay may be occurred owing to the communication channel between the master and the remote slave side. Many researchers devote themselves to various control methods in order to realize trajectory tracking as well as to enhance the accurate force feedback of the slave side. Some researchers studied the stability of the force feedback bilateral teleoperation system are analyzed from the direction of Lyapunov-Krasovskii theory and hybrid system theory [4–7]. Others use

© The Author(s), under exclusive license to Springer Nature Singapore Pte Ltd. 2022
S. Yang and H. Lu (Eds.): ISAIR 2022, CCIS 1700, pp. 69–76, 2022.
https://doi.org/10.1007/978-981-19-7946-0_7

the four-channel structure to carry out bilateral coordinated control of the teleoperation system [8, 9]. However, in most exist work, the integral network of teleoperation systems are assumed to be passive. The part active power may be produced due to the development and the introduce of more soft master manipulators and devices.

Ensuring the stability of bilateral teleoperation systems with part active power, we design a control structure based on the four-channel wave variables under the condition under constant time delay. The advantage of the four-channel is the clear structure and the parameters are relatively transparent. At the same time, the wave variable algorithm may ensure the stability of the system under different time delays. In the view of the network energy, the stability condition is discussed and a PD bilateral controller is applied, so as to achieve high tracking performances. The rest of paper is organized as follows. The bilateral teleoperation system with part active power is introduced in Sect. 2. The stability is detailed analyzed and the stability condition is discussed in Sect. 3. The PD bilateral controller and numerical simulations are explained in Sect. 4. Conclusions are drawn in the conclusion part.

## 2   Bilateral Teleoperation System with Part Active Power

The passive theory is similar to Lyapunov theory, both of which analyzes the stability of the system from the perspective of the energy. Many physical systems in reality, such as electromechanical systems, have the nature of passive theory. The basic idea of the passive theory is that if a physical system consumes energy, then this system is passive. Thus, it can be obtained that the system is stable.

For a certain physical system, as shown in Fig. 1, the input vector and output vector are defined as x and y respectively, then the input power Pin of the system is:

$$P_{in} = x^T y \tag{1}$$

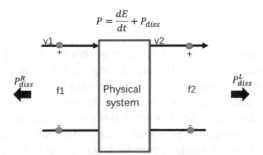

**Fig. 1.** Single port physical system.

For the physical system shown in Fig. 1, the input power is equal to the sum of the system power consumption $P_{diss}$ and the change of the system energy storage $E_{store}$,

$$P_{in} = \frac{dE_{store}}{dt} + P_{diss} \tag{2}$$

(2) indicates that the power input to the system may be consumed or stored by the system. Integrating (2) from any initial time t0 to a certain time t, the energy change relationship can be obtained as follows:

$$\int_{t0}^{t} P_{in} d\tau = \int_{t0}^{t} x^T y d\tau = E_{store}(t_0) - E_{store}(t_0) + \int_{t0}^{t} P_{diss} d\tau \qquad (3)$$

If (3) always satisfies following relation,

$$\int_{t0}^{t} P_{in} d\tau \geq -E_{store}(t_0) \qquad (4)$$

Then the system can be determined to be passive, which can further conclude that the system is stable.

Figure 1 displays a single-port network, while our current teleoperation system is generally simplified into a two-port network analysis as shown in Fig. 2.

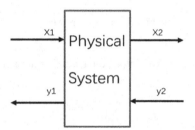

**Fig. 2.** Two-port physical system

The input power $P_{in}$ of the two-port physical system shown in Fig. 2 can be expressed as follows,

$$P_{in} = x_1^T y_1 - x_2^T y_2 \qquad (5)$$

Assuming that the initial energy storage of the two-port network is 0, from any time t0 to the current time t, if (6) is satisfied, the two-port network is considered passive.

$$\int_{t0}^{t} (x_1^T y_1 - x_2^T y_2) \, d\tau \geq 0 \qquad (6)$$

Currently, the majority of bilateral teleoperation systems addressed in existed litteratures are recommended for the passive input of master terminal. However, we discover through theoretical derivation that adds certain part active components to the input of main terminal which may still achieve system stability control and position tracking. The integral network may be regarded as the combination of an active part and passive part. Our work is focused on arrange the limitation of the active part so that the overall system can be still stable and energy dissipative. In this case, the stability of the integral system, and the relationship between input and output power may be examined from an energy standpoint to determine and discussed.

## 3   Stability Analysis of Part Active Four Channel Network

### 3.1   Network Power

The entire working network can be simplified into a two-port network, as illustrated in Fig. 3.

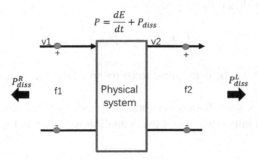

**Fig. 3.** Network power

Figure 3 shows the power flow into the part active network and the power flow is given as follow,

$$P = f_1 V_1 - f_2 V_2 = \frac{dE}{dt} + P_{diss} \qquad (7)$$

In formula (7), $f_1$, $V_1$ represents the force input and speed input information of the left port, and $f_2$, $V_2$ represents the force input and speed input information of the right port. $P_{diss}^L$ and $P_{diss}^R$ represents the power dissipation of the left and right ports. From Eq. (7), we can extend it appropriately, because the framework of the entire system is based on the four-channel structure and wave variable algorithm, so b represents the wave impedance, and the following equation can also be obtained:

$$P_1 = \frac{1}{2b} f_1^2 + \frac{b}{2} V_1^2 - \frac{1}{2b} (f_1 - bV_1)^2 = f_1 V_1 \qquad (8)$$

$$P_2 = \frac{1}{2b} f_2^2 + \frac{b}{2} V_2^2 - \frac{1}{2b} (f_2 + bV_2)^2 = f_2 V_2 \qquad (9)$$

Making the difference between (8) and (9) to get the power consumed by the entire network $\Delta P$, we may get

$$\Delta P = f_1 V_1 - f_2 V_2 = \frac{1}{2b} f_1^2 + \frac{b}{2} V_1^2 - \frac{1}{2b} (f_1 - bV_1)^2 - [\frac{1}{2b} f_2^2 + b/2 V_2^2 - \frac{1}{2b} (f_2 + bV_2)^2] \qquad (10)$$

## 3.2 The Asymmetric Delay of Vm, Fs

Since the entire communication channel has time delay, considering following asymmetric delay characteristics of $V_m$ and $F_s$, we can get:

$$P = \tfrac{1}{b}f_1^2 - \tfrac{b}{2}T_f^2 V_2^2 - \tfrac{1}{2b}(f_1 - bV_1)^2$$
$$+ bV_2^2 - \tfrac{1}{2b}T_b f_1^2 - \tfrac{1}{2b}(f_2 + bV_2)^2 \tag{11}$$
$$+ \tfrac{d}{dt}(\int_{t-Tb}^t \tfrac{1}{2b}f_2^2(\tau)d\tau) + \tfrac{d}{dt}(\int_{t-Tf}^t \tfrac{b}{2}V_1^2(\tau)d\tau) + D.$$

$T_b$ and $T_f$ in (11) are respectively the time delays of the communication channel, $\tau$ is input torque, and D is a function about time t. From (11), it can be seen that the system energy E(t) and the dissipation power $P_{diss}$ have following relations,

$$E(t) = \int_{t-Tb}^t \frac{1}{2b}f_2^2(\tau)d\tau + \int_{t-Tf}^t \frac{b}{2}V_1^2(\tau)d\tau \tag{12}$$

$$P_{diss} = \frac{1}{b}f_1^2 - \frac{1}{2b}(f_1 - bV_1)^2 + bV_2^2 - \frac{1}{2b}(f_2 + bV_2)^2 - \frac{b}{2}T_f V_2^2 - \frac{1}{2b}T_b f_1^2 \tag{13}$$

## 3.3 Analysis of the Stability Condition of Part Active Network

The energy of the entire system can be derived from the following (14):

$$E_{flow}(t) = \int_0^t P(\tau)d\tau$$
$$= \int_0^t (\tfrac{dE}{dt} + P_{diss} + D)(\tau)d\tau \tag{14}$$
$$= E(t) - E(0) + \int_0^t P_{diss}(\tau)d\tau + \int_0^t D(\tau)d\tau$$

It can be easily seen that if E(t) in (12) contains a square term, then $E(t) \geq 0$. To make the entire system satisfy the passive condition, the following relation must be established $E_{flow}(t) \geq 0$. Therefore, we deduced following conditions that $D(\tau)$ and $\int_0^t D(\tau)d\tau$ must be satisfied,

(1)  D(t) = f(t).
(2)  D(t) can be differential, and $\exists \frac{dD(t)}{dt}$, $\left| \frac{dD(t)}{dt} \right| \leq D$, $\frac{d^2D(t)}{dt^2} \geq 0$.
(3)  $\int_0^t D(\tau)d\tau = \frac{D}{2}t^2 \geq 0$.

According to above three conditions (1) (2) (3), we can use the way of squeeze for the $\int_0^t D(\tau)d\tau$:

$$E_{flow}(t) \geq -E(0) + \int_0^t P_{diss}(\tau) \tag{15}$$

Assuming that E(0) = D, the quantitative relationship between the initial energy and the extreme value identity at the adjacent active energy can be derived. Therefore, we can obviously get the inequality of $E_{flow}(t) \geq \int_0^t P_{diss}(\tau)d\tau$. In this way, the passivity of the entire system can be proven.

## 4 Numerical Simulations and Results

In the numerical simulation, both master and slave manipulators are used same two-degree-of-freedom manipulators as shown in Fig. 4. The dynamics model, inertia, Coriolis and Centrifugal, Jacobian matrices in the dynamic function are written as follows. Both of the master and the slave side take PID motion controls.

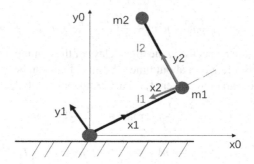

**Fig. 4.** Model of two-degree-of-freedom manipulators of both master and slave side.

The parameters are applied the same as in [3]. The two links lengths of the manipulators are l1 and l2, and the masses of manipulators are m1 and m2 respectively. Let the rotation angle of the connecting joint at a certain time be $\theta_1, \theta_2$. The angular velocity of its rotations are the differential of the rotation angle, which is $\dot{\theta}_1, \dot{\theta}_2$. q is the joint angle, which can be represented by a matrix containing the angle parameter of $\theta_1, \theta_2$, which is expressed as $q = (\theta_1\ \theta_2)^T$. $\tau$ is the torque on each joint, and it can express as $\tau = (\tau_1\ \tau_2)^T$. $F_h$ is the force exerted by the operator on the main manipulator, while $F_e$ is the force of the salve manipulator and the operating environment.

The four channel network diagram of the entire system is showed in Fig. 5. First, we input a step wave and pulse wave in the x and y directions of the master and the slave sides. The position tracking is displayed in Fig. 6. The first joint's torque of the master side is represented by a yellow solid line, and the second joint torque is represented by a purple solid line. From the results, it can be seen that the control effect of the entire system has high efficiency. Meanwhile, the tracking performance is relatively excellent. The force signal tracking is illustrated in Fig. 7. The force of the master terminal is represented by blue and red curves, and the force of the slave terminal is marked with yellow and purple curves. From the results, it can be seen that the transparency and feedback of the force control effect in the entire system are all pretty superior.

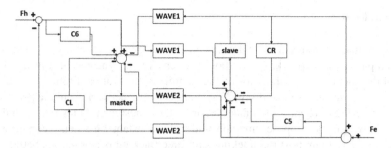

**Fig. 5.** The diagram of part active teleoperation system.

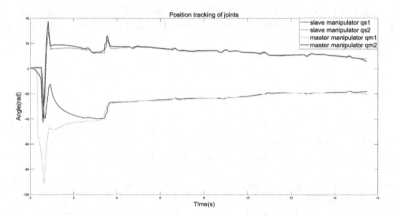

**Fig. 6.** Position tracking of joints of master and slave manipulators.

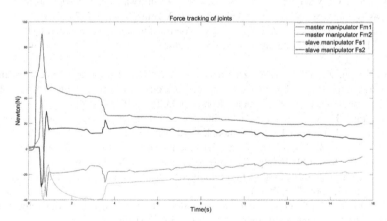

**Fig. 7.** Force tracking of joints of master and slave manipulators.

# 5 Conclusion

This paper firstly introduces a new four-channel double-wave variable control structure based on part active network. The purpose is to ensure the synchronous tracking of the force of the manipulator without losing the stability of the motion. From the theoretical point of view, we analyze and discuss the stability of the network from the perspective of network energy. Then, a PD bilateral controller is designed. Numerical simulation results show that the proposed method under the constant time delay condition has comparatively brilliant position tracking and force tracking performances between the master and slave manipulators.

**Acknowledgements.** This work was supported by the National Natural Science Foundation of China [grant numbers No. 61906086], Natural Science Foundation of Jiangsu Province of China [No. BK20210930].

# References

1. Cheng, R., Liu, Z., Ma, Z., Huang, P.: Approach and maneuver for failed spacecraft detumbling via space teleoperation robot system. Acta Astronaut. **181**, 384–395 (2021)
2. Liu, C., Guo, J., Poignet, P.: Nonlinear model-mediated teleoperation for surgical applications under time variant communication delay. In: SyRoCo (2018)
3. Wang, T., Li, Y., Zhang, J., Zhang, Y.: A novel bilateral impedance controls for underwater tele-operation systems. Appl. Soft Comput. **91**, 106194 (2020)
4. Estrada, E., Yu, W., Li, X.: Stable bilateral teleoperation with phase transition and haptic feedback. J. Franklin Inst. **358**, 1940–1956 (2021)
5. Kostyukova, O., Vista, F.P., Chong, K.: Design of feedforward and feedback position control for passive bilateral teleoperation with delays. ISA Trans. **85**, 200–213 (2019)
6. Higashino, A., Yamashita, Y., Kobayashi, K.: Control of bilateral teleoperation system consisting of heterogeneous manipulators with communication delay. IFAC-PapersOnLine **52**(16), 747–752 (2019)
7. Mohammadi, K., Talebi, H.A., Zareinejad, M.: A novel position and force coordination approach in four channel nonlinear teleoperation. Comput. Electr. Eng. **56**, 688–699 (2016)
8. Hashemzadeh, F., Tavakoli, M., et al.: Robotica **33**, 1003–1016 (2014)
9. Li, L., Yang, H., Liu, J.: Bilateral coordination control of flexible maste' slave manipulators using a partial differential equation model. J. Vib. Control **27**, 1561–1572 (2020)
10. Lu, H., Zhang, M., Xu, X.: Deep fuzzy hashing network for efficient image retrieval. IEEE Trans. Fuzzy Syst. (2020). https://doi.org/10.1109/TFUZZ.2020.2984991
11. Lu, H., Li, Y., Chen, M., et al.: Brain Intelligence: go beyond artificial intelligence. Mobile Netw. Appl. **23**, 368–375 (2018)
12. Lu, H., Li, Y., Mu, S., et al.: Motor anomaly detection for unmanned aerial vehicles using reinforcement learning. IEEE Internet Things J. **5**(4), 2315–2322 (2018)
13. Lu, H., Qin, M., Zhang, F., et al.: RSCNN A CNN-based method to enhance low-light remote-sensing images. Remote Sens. **13**, 62 (2020)
14. Lu, H., Zhang, Y., Li, Y., et al.: User-oriented virtual mobile network resource management for vehicle communications. IEEE Trans. Intell. Transp. Syst. **22**(6), 3521–3532 (2021)

# Content Extraction of Chinese Archive Images via Synthetic and Real Data

Xin Jin[1], Xinning Li[1], Xiaoyu Chen[2], Yijian Liu[1], and Chaoen Xiao[1(✉)]

[1] Beijing Electronic Science and Technology Institute, No. 7, Fufeng Street, Fengtai District, Beijing 100070, China
xcecd@qq.com

[2] China North Industries Group Corporation Limited, Beijing 100089, China

**Abstract.** With the development of the information age, the awareness of archives informatization of governments, organizations and groups at all levels is constantly increasing. The key content extraction of scanned archive images has been widely concerned by researchers. Based on the deep learning method, we extract text and key elements (ID photo, seal, date of birth) by analyzing the archive images. Based on the real archive images data set and synthetic archive images data set, we use the PP-OCR [1] model to finish the text structured extraction and YOLOv5 [2] to train a target detection model of ID photos, seals, and dates of birth to achieve the extraction of key elements. Since the real data set cannot be made public, we use ordinary archive data for explanation.

**Keywords:** Archive images · Synthetic archive images · PP-OCR · YOLOv5 · Text structured extraction · Key elements extraction

## 1 Introduction

In recent years, the demand for digitization of archive images and the extraction of key elements during archive review have been increasing. The method of automatically extracting the text and key content of archive images is crucial for related fields. The specific table structure of the archive image also provides some references and methods for the structured extraction of its text content and the extraction of key elements. With the development of deep learning technology, academia and industry have also proposed many methods for text extraction and object detection. We use these methods to extract the key content of the archive image based on the specific table structure in the archive image.

The key content extraction of archive images is mainly divided into two parts. One part is the structured extraction of text, and the other part is the extraction of key elements. The key elements extracted in this paper are ID photo, seal and date of birth. The key to the extraction of text content is to structure the output of the extracted text, which is convenient for management and operation. At present, there are many OCR models with good text extraction effects, but the text extracted by the OCR model cannot be output in a structured manner. At the same time, none of the mainstream target detection

© The Author(s), under exclusive license to Springer Nature Singapore Pte Ltd. 2022
S. Yang and H. Lu (Eds.): ISAIR 2022, CCIS 1700, pp. 77–91, 2022.
https://doi.org/10.1007/978-981-19-7946-0_8

algorithms can simultaneously extract key elements such as ID photos, seals, and dates of birth. In order to solve the problems mentioned above, our key contributions are:

(1) Utilize the specific table structure of the archive image, and use the PP-OCR model to realize the text structure extraction of the archive image.
(2) For the three key elements of ID photo, seal, and date of birth, the target detection module is constructed separately, and YOLOv5 is used to train the target detection module of ID photo, seal, and date of birth.
(3) For different key element detection modules, construct different data sets for training.

## 2 Structured Extraction of Archive Image Text

### 2.1 Text Extraction

We use PP-OCR to extract text from archive images. The PP-OCR model mainly includes three parts: text detection, text boxes rectify and text recognition. The overall process is as follows (Fig. 1):

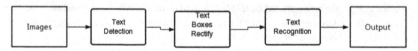

**Fig. 1.** PP-OCR model architecture, which mainly includes three parts: text detection, text boxes rectify and text recognition.

PP-OCR uses a differentiable binary text detection method. PP-OCR uses a differentiable binary text detection method. Use six technologies: Light Backbone, Light Head, Remove SE, Cosine Learning Rate Decay, Learning Rate Warm-up, FPGM Pruner to enhance the model's representation ability and reduce the size of the model. In a large amount of text detection, the detected text needs to be rotated. Use the direct classification method for judgment, and also use MobieNetv3 for feature extraction. Finally, use CRNN for text recognition.

### 2.2 Structured Extraction of Text

Archive images have unique structural characteristics. Based on the unique table structure, we preprocess the archive images. Use OpenCV to identify the table structure of the archive image, process the image to grayscale, and then perform the binarization process. Finally, after corrosion and expansion operations, the grid point coordinates of the table are identified.

Based on the identified grid points, the file picture is cut into grids according to the grid point coordinates. The cut archive image is as follows (Fig. 2):

Input the sub-images into the trained PP-OCR model, and the prediction results of each file are written into a text file, and then converted, and finally saved as a CSV file that is easy for statistical analysis.

**Fig. 2.** The archive image is cut into sub-pictures.

## 3    Data Set Construction

The key element extraction part includes three modules: ID photo extraction module, seal extraction module, and date of birth extraction module. Using the YOLOv5 target detection model, the data set training model was constructed separately, and three modules were obtained to detect the ID photo, seal and date of birth. Due to the limited number of real archive images, in order to achieve an ideal detection effect, we generate some archive images based on the real archive images data set. The generated images and the real images together constitute the training set.

Analyze the real archive images data set, and get Table 1.

**Table 1.** Analysis of real archive image data set.

| Category | Number of images |
| --- | --- |
| Archive images with ID Photo | 120 |
| Archive images with Seal | 80 |
| Archive images with the date of birth | 46 |
| Real archive images | 500 |

### 3.1    ID Photo Extraction Data Set Construction

There are only 120 archive images with ID photos in the real archive images data set, which cannot satisfy YOLOv5 target detection model training. So based on the real archive image data set, we used OpenCV face recognition to filter out 120 real archive images with ID photos and 300 real archive images without ID photos. Among the 120 real file images with ID photos, the images were cut according to the size and location of the ID photos, and finally 100 ID photos with appropriate size and clarity were obtained. We also obtained 100 ID photos through Internet searches. At the same time, 300 real archive images without ID photos are used as the background of the synthetic archive images. The materials of the synthetic ID photo archive images are shown in the Fig. 3.

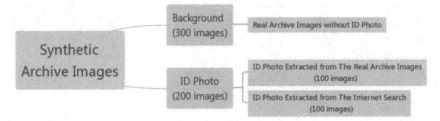

**Fig. 3.** The materials of the synthetic ID photo archive images.

Based on the above materials, the archive images are synthesized through different combinations. The synthetic archive images and the real archive images together constitute the training set for the ID photo extraction. The composition of the ID photo extraction training set is shown in the Table 2.

**Table 2.** The composition of the ID photo extraction training set.

| ID photo extraction training set | Number of images |
|---|---|
| Total archive images | 1120 |
| Real archive images | 120 |
| Synthetic archive images | 1000 |

In some old archives, the ID photos are gray or even black and white. In modern archives, they are generally in color. In order to restore the real effect as much as possible, the synthetic file images also consider the color of the ID photo, and the distribution of the generated data is shown in the Fig. 4.

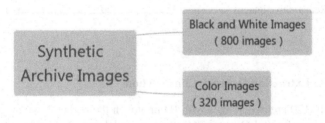

**Fig. 4.** The distribution of the generated data.

After the ID photo extraction training set is constructed, use the LabelImg annotation tool to label the ID photos to generate YOLOv5 format annotation files for subsequent training of the YOLOv5 ID photo detection model. The overall process of ID photo extraction training set generation is shown in the Fig. 5.

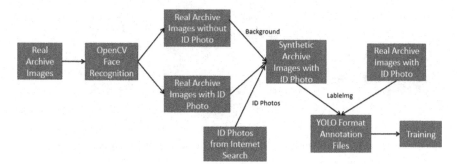

**Fig. 5.** The overall process of ID photo extraction training set generation.

The synthetic picture is shown in Fig. 6.

个人信息简表

| 姓 名 | 王冰宦 | | 性别 | 男 | 民族 | 汉族 | |
|---|---|---|---|---|---|---|---|
| 身份证号 | 311111199988881111 | | 准考证号 | | 100100100100100 | | |
| 本科就读院校名称 | 湖北农业大学 | | 籍贯 | 山东省 | 身高(cm) | 179 | |
| 已通过的英语等级 | 六级 | 政治面貌 | 入团时间: 2000 年 12 月 地点: xx 市 xx 中学 入党时间: 2009 年 12 月 地点: 湖北农业大学 | | 本科毕业设计题目 | 基于 xx 技术的 xx 的设计与实现 | |
| 考研总分 | 400 | 政治 | 100 | 英语 | 100 | 数学 100 | 专业课 100 |
| 个人情况 | 学习情况: 认真学习, 多次获得奖学金 科研情况: 多次承担学校科研课题 个人性格: 做事勤恳认真, 待人真诚 | | | | | | |

**Fig. 6.** Synthetic archive images with ID photo.

### 3.2 Seal Extraction Data Set Construction

Because the color of the seal in the real archive images is either blue or red, we use OpenCV color recognition to filter out the red or blue part of the real archive images. Then, the seal is extracted through contour extraction, shape filtering, and color restoration. We selected 100 seals of suitable size and shape from the real archive images as synthetic materials. We also used the seal generator to generate 30 seals after adding noise and blurring. At the same time, real archive images without a seal served as the synthetic background. The materials of the synthetic Seal archive images are shown in the Fig. 7.

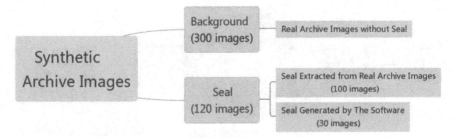

**Fig. 7.** The materials of the synthetic Seal archive images.

Based on the above materials, we synthesized the archive images with the seal, and then used the LabelImg labeling tool to label seals, and obtained some label files in the YOLO format to implement the training of the seal extraction module. The overall process of seal extraction training set generation is shown in the Fig. 8.

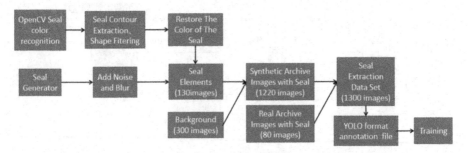

**Fig. 8.** The overall process of seal extraction training set generation.

The synthetic picture is shown in Fig. 9.

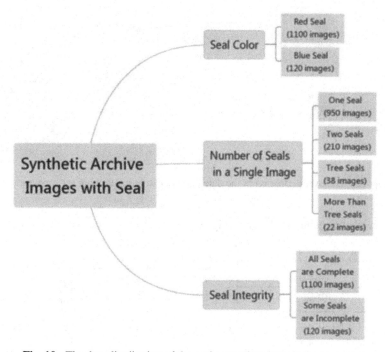

**Fig. 9.** Archive images in the synthetic seal data set.

At the same time, considering the color, quantity and completeness of the seal in the real archive images, the data distribution of the seal extraction data set we generated is shown in the Fig. 10.

**Fig. 10.** The data distribution of the seal extraction data set we generated.

### 3.3   Seal Extraction Data Set Construction

There are two ways to generate the date of birth: handwriting and extraction. Handwriting generation is to write "date of birth" on white paper, use Opencv for color extraction and outline extraction after taking a picture, and finally add a table border to imitate the actual situation. The extraction and generation is to deploy the Easyocr model to process all the real archive images, find the archives containing the words "date of birth", and determine the location of the text. This recognition is not accurate, but it is sufficient for preliminary filter. Cut out the borders of the surrounding table according to the text position to get an image of the date of birth. With 300 real files of undocumented photos as the background, 70 birth dates were combined in a certain arrangement and combined into 754 images with different sizes and positions. The overall process of the date of birth extraction training set generation is shown in the Fig. 11.

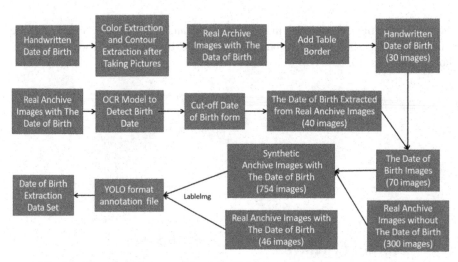

**Fig. 11.**  The overall process of the date of birth extraction training set generation.

The synthetic picture is shown in Fig. 12.

**Fig. 12.**  On the left is the date of birth generated by handwriting, and on the right is the date of birth generated by extraction.

# 4  Key Elements Extraction

The YOLOv5 target detection algorithm network is mainly composed of two main components: Backbone and Head. The Backbone convolutional neural network part is used to aggregate and form image features at different image granularities. It is the core step of deep learning. The Head part is used to predict image features, generate corresponding bounding boxes and predict object categories. The network structure of the YOLOv5 target detection algorithm is shown in the Fig. 13.

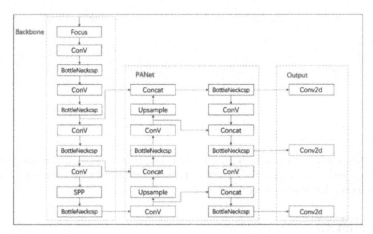

**Fig. 13.** The network structure of the YOLOv5 target detection algorithm.

We use the constructed ID photo extraction data set, seal extraction data set, and date of birth extraction data set to train the YOLOv5 target detection models, and finally obtain the ID photo extraction module, seal extraction module and date of birth extraction model to achieve the extraction of key elements. The extraction effect is shown in Fig. 14.

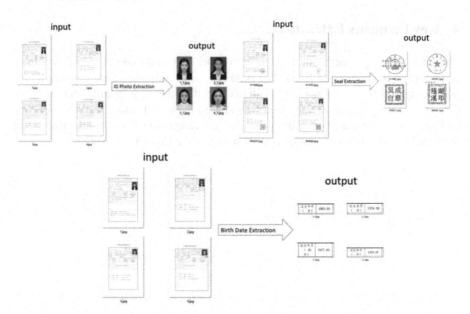

**Fig. 14.** The upper left corner is the extraction effect of the ID photo extraction module, the upper right corner is the extraction effect of the seal extraction module, and the bottom is the extraction effect of the birth date extraction module.

## 5  Experiment

We use real archive images and synthetic archive images to form a total data set. Based on the constructed total data set training model, we conduct relevant experimental analysis.

### 5.1  Text Structured Extraction Experiment

There are two open source OCR models, one is the ultra-lightweight Chinese OCR model, and the other is the general Chinese OCR model. Based on the two trained models, the text recognition effect is tested. The experiment found that the main difference between the two models is the number of detection frames. The number of detection frames for the two models is counted as shown in Table 3.

**Table 3.** Comparison of the number of detection boxes.

| ID | 1 | 2 | 3 | 4 | 5 | 6 | 7 | 8 | 9 |
|---|---|---|---|---|---|---|---|---|---|
| Lightweight boxes | 98 | 90 | 79 | 84 | 86 | 88 | 92 | 86 | 90 |
| Universal boxes | 105 | 105 | 96 | 96 | 95 | 104 | 113 | 105 | 103 |
| ID | 10 | 11 | 12 | 13 | 14 | 15 | 16 | 17 | 18 |
| Lightweight boxes | 96 | 84 | 78 | 84 | 91 | 93 | 96 | 92 | 97 |
| Universal boxes | 110 | 98 | 95 | 100 | 110 | 107 | 108 | 107 | 110 |

Use the prediction confidence of all check boxes in the appointment and dismissal approval form of all cadre files in the sample set to find the average accuracy rate. The average accuracy rate of Chinese ultra-lightweight OCR is above 98.5%, and the average accuracy rate of Chinese universal OCR is above 98%. Combined with the data in the table, it is concluded that the number of detection frames in the Chinese universal OCR model is more than that of the Chinese ultra-lightweight. OCR model, but the model's accuracy of predicting the results of the cadre appointment and dismissal approval form is lower than the Chinese ultra-lightweight OCR model, so the Chinese ultra-lightweight OCR model is selected for file identification.

Using the lightweight Chinese OCR model, the CSV file of the archive image text extraction processed by the cutting algorithm is shown in Fig. 15.

| Name | Bei Wang |
|---|---|
| Gender | Male |
| Birth | 2015.02 |
| Nationality | Han |
| Place of birth | Hebei |
| Hometown | Shijiazhuang |
| Admission time | 2020.10 |
| Health Status | Healthy |
| Specialty | Top-level Architecture Design |
| Full-time Education | Postgraduate Master of Engineering |
| Graduated Colleges and Majors | Peking University Software Engineering |
| On-the-job Education | Part-time Postgraduate |
| Graduated Colleges and Majors | Peking University Software Engineering |

**Fig. 15.** CSV file of archive image text extraction.

## 5.2 ID Photo Extraction Experiment

Configure the training parameters for neural network training, choose YOLOv5s as the pre-training model, which can effectively improve the training efficiency, and select the configuration file of the corresponding model architecture. The number of training in each batch is set to 16, and a total of 300 epochs are trained. The test results of the ID photo model is shown in Fig. 16.

GIoU (mean value of loss function, the smaller the box, the more accurate), Objectness (the average value of target detection loss, the smaller the target detection, the more accurate) all reached a lower level. Precision (accuracy rate) and Recall (recall rate) have reached a high level. The average accuracy of all classes (mAP, also known as the average accuracy of all classes, the number behind @ indicates the threshold for judging iou as a positive or negative sample, @0.5:0.95 indicates that the threshold is 0.5:0.05:0.95 and then the average is taken) mAP@0.5 reaches 0.99, MAP@0.5:0.95 reaches 0.88. In summary, the comprehensive recognition accuracy of the ID photo model is relatively high, and it is suitable for the ID photo extraction module.

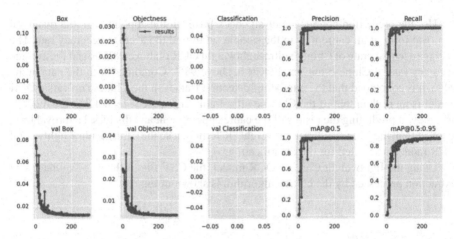

**Fig. 16.** The test results of the ID photo model.

## 5.3 Seal Extraction Experiment

Configure training parameters for neural network training, choose YOLOv5s as the pre-training model, which can effectively improve training efficiency, and select the configuration file of the corresponding model architecture. The number of training in each batch is set to 16, and a total of 300 epochs are trained. The test effect of the seal model is shown in Fig. 17.

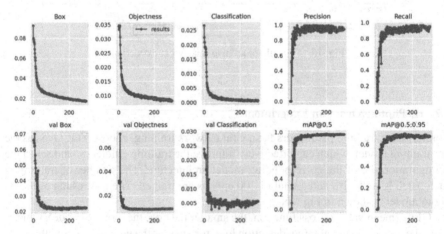

**Fig. 17.** The test effect of the seal model.

GIoU (mean value of loss function, the smaller the box, the more accurate), Objectness (the average value of target detection loss, the smaller the target detection is more accurate), and the Classification (the average value of classification loss, the smaller the more accurate the classification), all reached a low level. Precision (accuracy rate) and Recall (recall rate) have reached a high level. The average accuracy of all classes (mAP, also known as the average accuracy of all classes, the number behind @ indicates the threshold for judging iou as a positive or negative sample, @0.5:0.95 indicates that the threshold is 0.5:0.05:0.95 and then the average is taken) mAP@0.5 reaches 0.97. In summary, the comprehensive recognition accuracy of the seal model is relatively high, and it is suitable for use in the seal extraction module.

## 5.4  Date of Birth Extraction Experiment

Configure training parameters for neural network training, choose YOLOv5s as the pre-training model, which can effectively improve training efficiency, and select the configuration file of the corresponding model architecture. The number of training in each batch is set to 16, and a total of 300 epochs are trained. The date of birth model test effect is shown in Fig. 18.

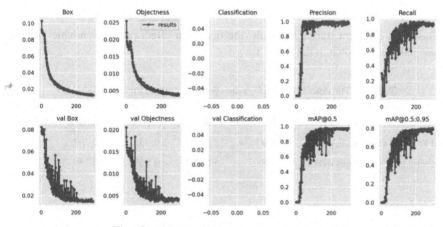

**Fig. 18.** The test effect of the date of birth model.

GIoU (mean value of loss function, the smaller the box, the more accurate), Objectness (the average value of target detection loss, the smaller the target detection, the more accurate) all reached a lower level. Precision (accuracy rate) and Recall (recall rate) have reached a high level. The average accuracy of all classes (mAP, also known as the average accuracy of all classes, the number behind @ indicates the threshold for judging iou as a positive or negative sample, @0.5:0.95 indicates that the threshold is 0.5:0.05:0.95 and then the average is taken) mAP@0.5 reaches 0.97, MAP@0.5:0.95 reaches 0.79. In summary, the comprehensive recognition accuracy rate of the birth date model is relatively high, and it is suitable for application to the birth date extraction module.

## 5.5  Crossover Experiment

In order to prove the effectiveness of the synthetic data set, we train separately on the real data set and the synthetic data set with roughly the same number of labels. Among them, there are 400 real data sets with 830 tags; 756 synthetic data sets with 815 tags. In order to make the transformed data more suitable for the shape of the extracted part, we limit the size of the candidate frame, and set the value of the parameter ar_thr to 10 and the value of area_thr to 0.4. Except for the different data sets during the training process, all training parameters remain the same. The obtained model is tested for performance on the same test set. Based on different training models, the detection effect on the real archive images data set is shown in the Table 4.

**Table 4.** The detection effect on the real archive images data set.

|  | Precision | Recall | mAP0.5 | mAP@0.5:0.95 |
|---|---|---|---|---|
| Real archive images data set | 0.923 | 0.824 | 0.896 | 0.695 |
| Synthetic archive images data set | 0.892 | 0.862 | 0.898 | 0.667 |

Based on different training models, the detection effect on the synthetic archive images data set is shown in the Table 5.

**Table 5.** The detection effect on the synthetic archive images data set.

|  | Precision | Recall | mAP0.5 | mAP@0.5:0.95 |
|---|---|---|---|---|
| Real archive images data set | 0.970 | 0.907 | 0.930 | 0.702 |
| Synthetic archive images data set | 0.986 | 0.960 | 0.969 | 0.759 |

## 6　Conclusion

We propose a method and system for extracting key content of archive images based on deep learning, which extracts key content such as text, ID photo, seal, date of birth and so on by analyzing the archive image. The method and system consist of two parts: the text extraction part and the key element extraction part. Text extraction is mainly used in personnel file content extraction, which can extract and save text in images in editable csv format; key element extraction can identify and extract and save ID photos, seals, and dates of birth in archive images in batches. This method is based on a large amount of data collection and sorting, augmenting the data through various image processing algorithms, using neural network for training, and the obtained model has good test performance and practical value. Our method provides a way to realize the digitization of archive images. It can not only extract text content, but also extract key content in file review such as ID photos, seals, and dates of birth in batches, reducing the workload of review.

**Acknowledgements.** We thank all the ACs and reviewers. This work is partially supported by the National Natural Science Foundation of China (62072014 & 62106118), the Beijing Natural

Science Foundation (L192040), the Open Fund Project of the State Key Laboratory of Complex System Management and Control (2022111), the Project of Philosophy and Social Science Research, Ministry of Education of China (20YJC760115).

# References

1. Du, Y., et al.: PP-OCR: a practical ultra lightweight OCR system. arXiv preprint arXiv:2009.09941
2. Dabai Jiang, N.: In-depth explanation of the core basic knowledge of YOLOv5 of the Yolo series. Zhihu, 17 November 2021. https://zhuanlan.zhihu.com/p/172121380

# An Active Robotic Detumbling Method Based on Deep Reinforcement Learning for Non-cooperative Spacecraft

Hao Liu[1]([✉]), Haidong Hu[1], Yingzi He[2], and Hao Gao[2]

[1] Beijing Institute of Control Engineering, Beijing, China
liuhao_stsicl@outlook.com
[2] Nanjing University of Posts and Communications, Nanjing, China

**Abstract.** Active contact detumbling method using a brush-type contactor is an effective way for damping the angular momentum of rotating target in order to make it easy to capture. In this paper, we propose a new brush-type detumbling method base on deep deterministic policy gradient (DDPG) for achieving the autonomous detumbling trajectory planning and control strategy of robot arm for the first time. We propose a recommended racemization point as a state space input based on the relative position to avoid the curse of dimensionality. The rewards are designed to associate with the recommended point and continuous damped collisions. Then the agent is trained to learn to find the racemization point and generate smooth trajectory action. The robot arm can track the motion of target panel and automatically select the optimal detumbling point. The proposed method can provide a new control strategy for active contact detumbling application.

**Keywords:** Space non-cooperative spacecraft · Reinforcement learning · Deep deterministic policy gradient · Active robotic detumbling method · Flexible decelerating brush

## 1 Introduction

### 1.1 A Subsection Sample

With the increasingly serious problem of space debris, more and more attention has been paid to the space on orbit active capture technology. Under the influence of complex space environment, failed spacecraft without control will eventually exhibit free rolling motion. The Active capture for the rotating target requires very high pose synchronization, resulting in the reliability and safety issues. Therefore, a detumbling phase before the capture of high-speed spinning spacecraft out of control may be necessary.

A variety of active detumbling method have been proposed, which can be divided into contactless and contact detumbling method. Active contactless detumbling method usually applies torque to reduce the spinning rate of the debris by using electricity [1], magnetism [2] or gas [3]. Since this method does not directly require physical contact the target, low requirements for accuracy and control are permitted. However, it shows applicability limitations with the complex structure and long braking time. On the other hand, active contact detumbling method has the advantages of simple structure, short braking time and easy engineering application. Contact method uses a damper tool mounted on the end of the robot arm to apply force to the target, mainly including brush type contactor [4], cushion-type damper [5], etc. Therefore, this paper adopts the method of brush type contactor to carry out the active contact detumbling research.

The concept of brush type contactor [6] was first proposed by Japan aerospace exploration agency (JAXA). The decelerating brush is driven by a robot arm to contact with the accessories of the failed satellite, such as the sails and antennas, so as to exert a torque to reduce the rotational rate of the target. However, trajectory planning of the robot arm needs to be executed accurately to achieve reasonable collision of the target. At the same time, due to the large feedback force acting on the robot arm during the collision, the controller should be designed to ensure the safety of the robot arm.

At present, many arm controller have been applied in the brush-type detumbling method., such as PD control [4] and sliding mode control [7]. Unfortunately, the above method has poor adaptability and efficiency in the braking task. The robot arm operation based on machine learning can realize compliant and human-like natural operation, so as to safely achieve braking task for rotating target which are not affected by communication delay between the spacecraft and the ground. Therefore, it is necessary to study the control method of flexible brush contact detumbling method based on machine learning.

Deep reinforcement learning (DRL) is an important research hotspot in machine learning, which combines the perception of deep learning with the decision-making ability of reinforcement learning. DRL has greatly improved the autonomy and flexibility of robot control, and has provided a broad prospect for the automation of space manipulator operation tasks. Since the first DRL called deep Q-Network (DQN) [8] was proposed in 2013 by Deepmind, many improved algorithms have emerged for overcoming the problem of convergence, including Double DQN [9], Deep Deterministic Policy Gradient (DDPG) [10], Trust Region Policy Optimization (TRPO) [11], Asynchronous Advantage Actor-Critic (A3C) [12], Distributed Proximal Policy Optimization (DPPO) [13] etc. A number of approaches have sought to apply DRL methods for solving tasks on robot arm. Lampe [14] explore deep reinforcement learning algorithms for vision-based robotic grasping. Tadanobu [15] used reinforcement learning to train a recursive neural network to complete pin insertion task, which was used for high-precision assembly of mechanical parts. Rajeswaran [16] improved the training efficiency and completed the grasping action of the manipulator by combining manual teaching with self-learning based on the DRL. Wen [17] planned the trajectory of the robot arm to avoid obstacles based on the DDPG algorithm, and verified the correctness of the algorithm through the simulation model of the Nao robot arm.

In this paper, we explore deep reinforcement learning algorithms for robotic detumbling of non-cooperative spacecraft by using flexible brush for the first time. The state and reward appropriate to brush racemization is designed in our experiment based on deep deterministic policy gradient (DDPG), so as to achieve autonomous and smooth detumbling of non-cooperative spacecraft and ensure the safety of capture. The major contributions of this paper are shown as:

1. We formulate the decelerating brush application in spatial contact detumbling task as a reinforcement learning problem to achieve the autonomous trajectory planning and control strategy. DDPG based on the actor-critic algorithm is firstly used to solve the problem, which could generate an optimal policy with continuous states and actions.
2. Considering the characteristics of brush racemization, we rewrite the problem into a state, action, and reward. To avoid the curse of dimensionality, we propose a recommended racemization point as a state space input based on the relative position between the robot arm base and the outer corner point of the solar panel of non-cooperative target. Moreover, in order to obtain better optimization results, the reward is designed to provide feedback on whether the recommended pose has been reached and whether a reasonable collision has occurred, and is more related to the state space. Also, the training and validation processes of the proposed algorithm are discussed in detail.
3. Based on the Mujoco physics engine, the single-axis de-tumbling simulation scenario is built, including the target, air bearing table and the capture spacecraft. Simulations are conducted to evaluate the performance of the proposed detumbling policy. The robot arm realizes the compliant application of damping through learning.

The rest of the paper is organized as follows. Section 2 explains the problem. Details of our proposed method is described in Sect. 3. Simulation analysis of the method on a single-axis racemization platform is presented in Sect. 4. Finally, Sect. 5 concludes this paper.

## 2 Problem Formulation

### 2.1 System Description

The single-axis detumbling system is constructed, including the capture spacecraft, target, both of which are mounted on an air bearing table (see Fig. 1). The capture spacecraft is equipped with two robot arms and a binocular camera. The camera is used to identify and estimate the pose and rotational speed of the racemized target, and to provide input for racemization and capture. The robot arm uses a UR10 robot arm, which has six degrees of freedom, a payload of 10 kg, a joint range of $[-360°, +360°]$, and a working radius of 1300 mm. A flexible deceleration brush is installed at the end of a robot arm, which is composed of a 30 mm long brush rod and 8 stainless steel wires with a length of 30 mm. The other robot arm is used for cooperative capture, which will not be studied in this article. The detumbling target is a central rigid body (size of 1 m * 1 m * 1 m) with two solar panel (size of 1 m * 1.3 m * 0.03 m). The quality of the target is 100 kg. A system reference coordinate system is established. Among them, $\Sigma_o$, $\Sigma_b$, $\Sigma_c$, and $\Sigma_t$ represents the inertial coordinate system, coordinate system of the race arm base, the camera coordinate system and coordinate system of the target respectively.

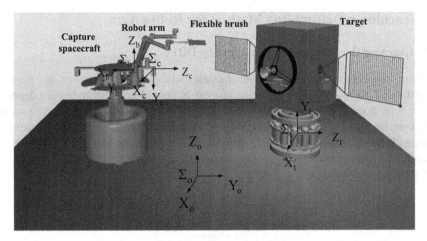

**Fig. 1.** Reference frames

## 2.2 Task Flow

In this paper, the target solar panel is selected as the part where the brush touches. By touching the outer edge of the solar panel with the brush, the momentum exchange between the captured spacecraft and the target is performed to achieve the detumbling of the rolling target.

First, the camera vision based on the full convolutional neural network [18] and the PnP algorithm [19] is used to detect and measure the pose of the four apex feature points on the outside of the two solar panels. Then, the recommended racemization position is given based on the relative position between the base of the robotic arm and the four outer corner points. After continuous training and learning, the agent finds a racemization position that makes the reward bigger. DDPG generates a continuous and smooth joint sequence of robot arm, driving the robotic arm so that the end brush can flexibly collide with the target panel continuously. At the same time, the robot arm should avoid touching the target body or the capture spacecraft. When the target's rotation angular velocity is less than 0.01 rad/s, the braking task is considered to have been accomplished successfully (see Fig. 2).

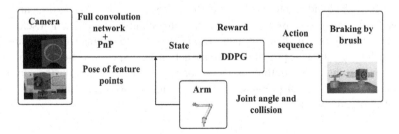

**Fig. 2.** Task flow

# 3  Learning a Detumbling Method for Robot Arm

## 3.1  Learning the Detumbling Behaviors by DDPG

There is a mapping relationship between the state and the action of the robot, and the next state that the robot arm can reach in the process of detumbling operation only depends on the current state and the selected action. Therefore, the flexible brush braking model based on the robot arm is a typical Markov Decision Process (MDP) reinforcement learning Process. In this paper, a deep deterministic strategy gradient algorithm (DDPG) is used, and active contact detumbling method based on the robot arm is trained in a Gym/Mujuco environment (see Fig. 3).

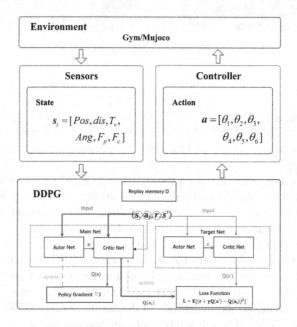

**Fig. 3.** Reinforcement learning with DDPG

DDPG can be divided into Actor and Critic. Actor network is used to train and select actions. Critic network is used to evaluate the value obtained by the action selected by Actor network. Actor usually uses function approximation to estimate the value function. Actors no longer output the probability of each action, but a specific action, which is more helpful for learning in the continuous action space. The DDPG can solve the continuous state and continuous motion problems in the environment and is very suitable for training the control of a robot arm.

The neural networks of DDPG are trained from the set $(s_t, a_t, r_t, s_{t+1})$. Therefore, we must define appropriate state and action sets of racemization task for DDPG. Next, the design of the state set, action set and reward is described in detail, respectively.

**State Space Construction**

The state space is formed by processing the environmental information that can be obtained by the sensor. In the collision process of rolling target and decelerating brush, because the collision force acting on the target is not on its center of mass, it will not only cause the target's angular velocity to decrease, but also cause its position to change. Therefore, it is necessary to control the capture spacecraft to ensure its position relative to the target. In order to simplify the analysis, the relative displacement between the capture spacecraft and the target is temporarily not considered. In this paper, it is assumed that the relative position of the capturing spacecraft and the target remains unchanged. The target has an initial angular velocity around the z-axis in the inertial frame. The environmental states that can be obtained by the system through sensors include: the pose of the end of the arm, the position of the feature points of the panels, the speed of the target, the joint angle of the robot arm, whether the brush touches the outer vertical edge of the target panel, and whether there is a reasonable collision, etc. However, the dimension of the state vector should not be too large, otherwise it will cause the curse of dimensionality problem, thus reducing the convergence and learning rate. According to the characteristics of brush detumbling task, we have further processed the environmental information to improve the success rate of training while ensuring that the state information is sufficient. The definition of state space is as follows:

$$s_t = [Pos, dis, T_v, Ang, F_p, F_c]  \qquad (1)$$

where, $Pos$ is Recommended point, $dis$ is distance between the end of the arm and the recommended point, $T_v$ is target angular velocity, $Ang$ is robot arm joint angle, $F_p$ means whether the robot arm reaches the desired attitude, $F_c$ means whether a racemic collision occurs.

For the brush detumbling task, it is difficult to describe the relationship between the robot arm, the target (or rather the target sail), and braking task in simple mathematical terms. We can measure the pose of the feature points on the target by visual, such as the edge point of the solar panels and body. However, for the purpose of this paper, the useful points are the four points on the outer edge of the solar panel, including {lower left $P_1$, upper left $P_2$, upper right $P_3$, lower right $P_4$} (see Fig. 4). The inner point is not used for policy generation because the brush does not extend into the inner side of the solar panel to avoid unreasonable collisions. Considering that the corner point information of the solar panel is not good for the DDPG to find the learning law, we propose a recommended racemization point as a state space input based on the relative position between the robot arm base $P_b$ and the outer corner point of the solar panel of target. Then the agent is trained to learn to find the racemization point that makes the reward bigger.

The pose of the recommended points are selected according to the following principles:

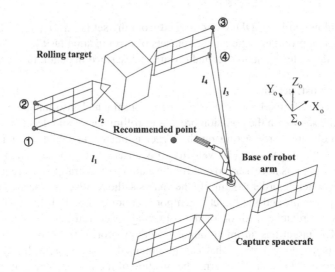

**Fig. 4.** Diagram of brush pose selection

1. The collision surface between the brush and the solar panel should be as large as possible to obtain the maximum damper effect. Therefore, considering the installation attitude of the brush at the end of the robot arm, the fixed recommended point attitude was adopted, [1.567, 0, −3.141] rad.
2. In order to ensure the maximum probability of collision, the z-axis of the recommended point should be the middle position between the end of the robot arm and the near side of the solar panel. The x and y axis positions of the recommended points are defined by the deviation between the center of the panel and the base of the arm. The detailed procedure of the recommended point assign is listed in Table 1.

$l_1$ $l_2$ $l_3$ $l_4$ are the vector of the base $P_b$ of the robot arm pointing to the corner points $P_1$ $P_2$ $P_3$ $P_4$ of the solar panel, shown in Fig. 4. Pos is a one-step recommended point that being assigned. A_P is the end position of the robot arm. x_L is a constant value selected by preliminary experiments that specified the minimum position error threshold that was suitable for detumbling. x_U is a constant value that specified the maximum position error threshold. $\lambda_x$ is the adjustment coefficient, which is related to the relative position of the capture spacecraft and target. y_L, y_U, $\lambda_y$ are constant value that similar to the definition above, but suitable for the Y-axis.

There are two types of collision, one is the collision between the brush and the solar panel that we need, and the other is the unreasonable collision between the robot arm and itself or the target body that is dangerous. The detailed procedure of the collision detection thread is listed in Table 2.

$C_d$ is a constant value selected by preliminary experiments that specified the minimum position threshold for the end of robot arm that won't touch itself. $F_{tcp}$ and $T_{tcp}$ are the communication data with UR10 that representing the forces and torques applied to the joints of the robot arm. $F_{td}$ and $T_{td}$ are the constant value selected by preliminary experiments that specified the maximum force threshold during reaching episode. c_Ur is

Table 1. Algorithm of assign recommended point.

| **Algorithm1** Assign recommended point |
|---|
| At final timestep of each movement: |
| **if** $norm(l_1) < norm(l_4)$ **then** |
| $\quad$ Pos(z)=0.5* $(l_1(x) + l_2(x))$ |
| $\quad$ Error=0.5*$(P_1 + P_3) - P_b$ |
| **else** |
| $\quad$ Pos(z)=0.5* $(l_3(x) + l_4(x))$ |
| $\quad$ Error=0.5*$(P_2 + P_4) - P_b$ |
| **end if** |
| **if** Error(x)>x_L **and** Error(x)<x_U **then** |
| $\quad$ Pos(x) =A_P(x)-$\lambda_x$ |
| **else if** Error(x)<x_L |
| $\quad$ Pos(x) =A_P(x)-$\lambda_x$+ Error(x)- x_L |
| **else** Pos(x) =A_P(x)-$\lambda_x$+ Error(x)+ x_U |
| **end if** |
| **if** Error(y)>y_L **and** Error(y)<y_U **then** |
| $\quad$ Pos(y) =A_P(y)+$\lambda_y$ |
| **else if** Error(y)<y_L |
| $\quad$ Pos(y) =A_P(y)-$\lambda_y$+ Error(y)- y_L |
| **else** Pos(y) =A_P(y)-$\lambda_y$+ Error(y)- y_U |
| **end if** |

a binary value indicating whether there was an unreasonable collision of the robotic arm, determined from c_Fd and c_Ff. $S_{im}$ is a binary-valued state indicating whether there is a collision between the brush and the target, determined from force sensor mounted on brush. GetImpact is a binary-valued state indicating the damping effect of the robot arm with the brush controlled by agent on the target.

Combining Algorithm 1 and Algorithm 2, we give the state thread, shown in Table 3. It needs to pay attention that the arm joints *Ang* should be normalized for a much easier and faster training. GetAttitude is a binary-valued state indicating whether the end attitude of robot arm was within an experimentally-selected value of 0.3 rad from that of recommended point.

**Action Space.** After perceiving the status information, DDPG would select an action by estimating the appropriate policy. Since the attitude control of the capture spacecraft is not considered, the controllable mechanism of the system is the robot arm. Therefore, the sequence of joint angles of the robot arm is taken as the action set.

$$a_t = [\theta_1, \theta_2, \theta_3, \theta_4, \theta_5, \theta_6] \tag{2}$$

**Table 2.** Algorithm of collision detection thread.

| Algorithm2 Collision detection thread |
|---|
| At final timestep of each movement: |
| **if** A_P(y)< $C_d$ **then** |
|     c_Fd=true |
| **else** c_Fd =false |
| **end if** |
| **if** $F_{tcp}$> $F_{td}$ **or** $T_{tcp}$ > $T_{td}$ **then** |
|     c_Ff=true |
| **else** c_Ff=false |
| **end if** |
| **if** c_Fd **or** c_Ff **then** |
|     c_Ur =true |
| **else** c_Ur =false |
| **end if** |
| **if !** c_Ur **and** $S_{im}$>0 **then** |
|     GetImpact =true |
| **else** GetImpact =false |
| **end if** |

**Table 3.** Algorithm of state thread.

| Algorithm3 State thread |
|---|
| **Input:** |
|     Joint angle of arm *Ang*, $P_1$, $P_2$, $P_3$, $P_4$, A_P, $P_b$, $F_{tcp}$, $T_{tcp}$, $S_{im}$ |
| **Output** |
|     Assign recommended point Pos |
|     Dis=norm (A_P- Pos) |
|     Normalized Joint *Ang=Ang*/PI |
|     Collision detection |
| **Return S**= (Pos, dis, $T_v$, *Ang* , GetAttitude , GetImpact) |

where, $\theta_i \in [-1, 1]$, $i = 1, 2, 3, 4, 5, 6$ is the normalized value of the joint angle of the robot arm, so the expected joint angle of the arm is $a_t$*PI (see Fig. 5).

**Reward Function.** The environment could return a reward to the agent from the reward function after getting a decision action. A suitable reward function should be designed to provide a learning guideline for the agent in order to obtain better optimization results. Inspired by the design of the state space, we give a positive reward for the action reaching

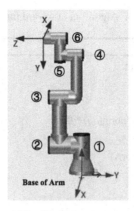

**Fig. 5.** Action space

the recommended pose. The behavior of the brush colliding with the solar panel of target will get a greater positive reward, and unreasonable collision behavior should be punished. The goal of braking task is to get the target to reduce the angular velocity as quickly as possible, so it is a good scheme to increase the damping effect in a single collision period. Therefore, we give a greater positive reward for damped collisions at least 5 timesteps consecutively. The detailed procedure of the reward assign is listed in Table 4.

ErrorD is the 2-norm of the position error between the end of the robot arm(A_P) and the recommended point(R_P). ErrorA is the error vector between the end attitude of the robot arm(A_Rpy) and the recommended attitude(R_Rpy), which is described by RPY angle rotating around the fixed axis X-Y-Z. TimestepR is a one-step reward that being assigned, which has an initial value inversely proportional to the ErrorD and the action $a_t$. For each reaching movement, GetPosition is a binary value defined based on whether the end of robot arm was within a distance of 0.01m from the recommended point, determined experimentally. InPos is a binary value indicating whether the end of robot arm had been located within the recommended point zone for at least 5 timesteps consecutively. InAttitude is a binary value indicating whether the end attitude of robot arm had been located within the recommended point zone for at least 5 timesteps consecutively. $T_v(t-1)$ and $T_v(t)$ are the angular velocity of the target at time $t$-1 and time $t$, respectively. InImpact is a binary value indicating whether there was a collision between brush and target panel for at least 5 timesteps consecutively.

## 3.2  Network Training Methods

The network training process is divided into four stages in order to improve training efficiency and ensure safety (see Fig. 6). Firstly, pose network training is conducted to reduce the difficulty of detumbling network training. Then the detumbling network is trained on the basis of the trained pose network.

**Table 4.** Algorithm of reward function.

| Algorithm4 Assign Rewards |
| --- |
| At final timestep of each movement: |
| ErrorD=norm (A_P – R_P) |
| ErrorA= A_Rpy – R_Rpy |
| TimestepR = (-0.1* ErrorD - 0.01*norm($a_t$)) * 0.25 |
| **if** $G_p$ **and** InPos **then** |
|     TimestepR += 10- norm (ErrorA) |
| **end if** |
| **if** $G_p$ **and** $G_a$ **and** InAttitude **then** |
|     TimestepR += 10 |
| **else if** GetPosition **and** GetAttitude **and** ! InAttitude **then** |
|     TimestepR += 50 |
| **end if** |
| **if** NotPos **and** c_Ur **then** |
|     TimestepR-=50 |
| **end if** |
| **if** GetImpact **then** |
|     TimestepR = 50+(1e2*($T_v(t$-1)- $T_v(t)$)-norm($a_t$)) |
| **end if** |
| **if** InImpact **then** |
|     TimestepR += 200 |
| **end if** |

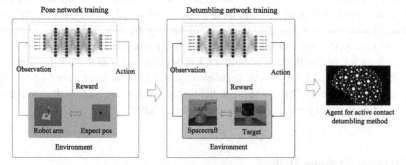

**Fig. 6.** Network training process

**Pose Network Training.** The training of detumbling network without prior strategy is too difficult for DDPG. Therefore, in order to reduce the difficulty of training, robot arm is first trained to learn to reach the expected pose. Since no collisions occur during this process, state and reward are redefined:

$$s_t = [Pos2, dis2, T_v, Ang2, F_p] \tag{3}$$

where, $Pos2$ is the position error between the end of the robot arm and the desired point, $dis2$ is distance between the end of the arm and the desired point. $Ang2$ is robot arm joint angle, $F_p$ means whether the robot arm reaches the desired attitude.

The reward function is the same as algorithm 4, except for the reward portion of the collision. $a_t \in [-1, 1]$ is the action for agent. The number of learning episode is 200 times. The robot arm in each simulation trains 300 times per round. In the learning process, when robot arm achieve target 5 timesteps consecutively, an episode is terminated.

**Detumbling Network Training.** The detumbling neural networks of DDPG are trained on the basis of the trained pose network. The design of the set $(s_t, a_t, r_t, s_{t+1})$ are based on Sect. 3.1. DDPG algorithm of parameter settings are as follows, Action network learning rate is set to 0.0001, the critic network learning rate is set to 0.001, the discount rate of rewards is set to 0.99, updated mode parameter based on Soft update mode is set to 0.001, the smallest BATCH_SIZE is set to 64. CUDA is used to accelerate network training. The Adam optimizer is selected to iteratively optimize the network parameters, and the noise in the action network adopts OU random noise.

In order to further reduce the difficulty of learning and improve the success rate of training, joint range of robot arm can be constrained. Considering that the target is in front of the arm, the rotation range of the arm joint can be limited so that the arm does not move backwards.

The number of learning episode is 300 times. The robot arm in each simulation trains 600 times per round. In the learning process, when the flexible brush applied a damping to the target panel at least 5 timesteps consecutively or an unreasonable collision occurred, an episode is terminated.

# 4 Experiments and Results

## 4.1 Simulation Settings

The algorithm in this paper is trained in the framework of PyTorch. The simulation environment was built using the 1.50 version of Mujoco. SolidWorks was used to build and generate STL models of the spacecraft and UR10 robot arm. The model is equipped with an XML file so that it can be simulated in Mujoco. Mujoco is responsible for collision dynamics calculations and robotic arm kinematics planning (see Fig. 7).

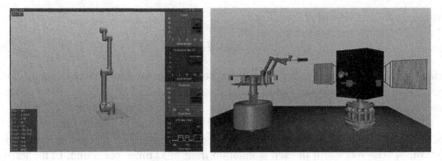

**Fig. 7.** Simulation environment

The settings of joint range are listed in Table 5. Next, based on the DDPG algorithm, experiments in Mujoco simulation environment will be introduced respectively.

**Table 5.** .

| Number of joint | Range | Action bound | Initial value |
|---|---|---|---|
| 1 | [0.323, 1.716] | [−1, 1] | 1.57 |
| 2 | [−1.2, 0.2] | [−1, 1] | −1.40 |
| 3 | [−0.3, 1.571] | [−1, 1] | 1.04 |
| 4 | [−4.713, −3.3] | [−1, 1] | −3.14 |
| 5 | [−3.14, −0.9] | [−1, 1] | −1.75 |
| 6 | [−0.523, 0.523] | [−1, 1] | 0 |

## 4.2  Pose Training Experiment

The simulation result of pose network training is shown in Fig. 8. The base of UR10 arm is fixed to a rigid plane. The red ball in the picture is the expected point in 3D space, which was randomly generated. It is observed that the UR10 arm will reach the desired target point successfully after training.

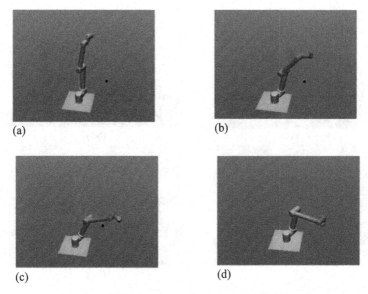

**Fig. 8.** Result of pose training

Figure 9(a) shows the number of learning steps required for the robot arm to get to the expected pose for each episode. With the increase of the training epoch, the number of steps needed to reach the desired pose of the robot arm becomes less. Figure 9(b) shows the reward for the agent each episode. The stable positive reward indicates that the robot arm can get to the desired pose stably and quickly in the 200 episode.

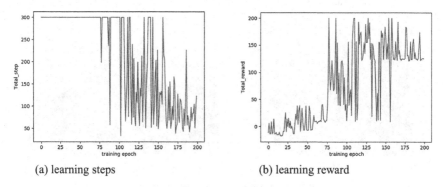

(a) learning steps                              (b) learning reward

**Fig. 9.** Learning curve for the robot arm

### 4.3   Detumbling Training Experiment

On the basis of the trained pose network, the detumbling training for the rolling target is carried out. The braking task for the rolling target which initial angular velocity is 0.3rad/s

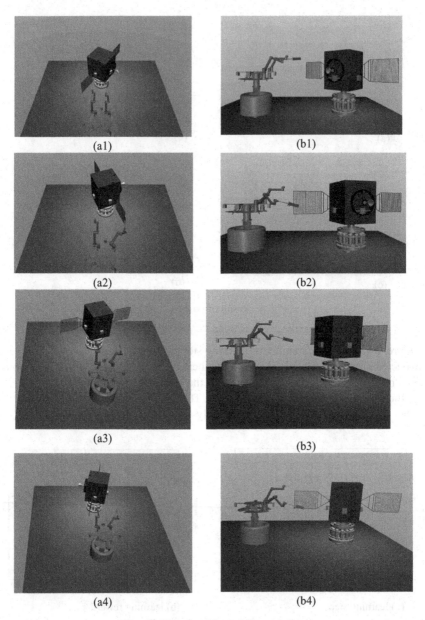

(a1)    (b1)

(a2)    (b2)

(a3)    (b3)

(a4)    (b4)

**Fig. 10.** Result of detumbling training

has been implemented by using the trained detumbling network. The simulation result is shown in Fig. 10. Figure 10(a) is the top view and Fig. 10(b) is the front view during the movement of the robot arm. The robot arm based on trained DDPG can autonomously plan the trajectory and reach to the next optimal detumbling position after touching the target through reasonable control strategies. Thus, the rolling target can be damped continuously and the angular velocity of the target can decrease eventually. The reward for training of each episode is shown in Fig. 11. Because of the trained pose network, some positive rewards can be obtained during the first half of detumbling training. In the latter stage, the robot arm learned to apply damping to the target in order to get a higher reward. The simulation process will be analyzed in detail.

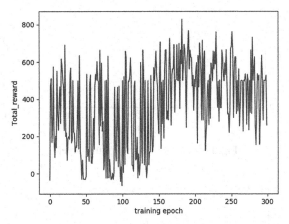

**Fig. 11.** Learning curve of detumbling training

The angular velocity curve of the target is shown in Fig. 12. It can be seen that the target's angular velocity is reduced from 0.3 rad/s to 0.01 rad/s after a 40 s braking operation. The angular velocity curve falls in the form of a step because the damping applied to the target by the brush is the step response. Figure 13 shows the collision force curve between brush and target. The change frequency of the collision force is consistent with that of the angular velocity. Since the angular velocity of the target is larger at the beginning, its collision force is larger. As the angular velocity of the target decreases, its collision force also decreases. Distance curve between the end of the arm and the recommended point is shown in Fig. 14. After each collision, the robot arm is able to quickly reach the next detumbling point. At the same time, we noticed that the distance was larger than before 20 s. This is because the robot arm realizes the compliant application of damping through learning. The robot arm will track the panel movement within the limit of its maximum travel distance, thereby continuously applying damping to it to obtain a single maximum damping effect. We zoom and observe the collision curve at 30s, shown in Fig. 13. From 30.1 s to 30.15 s, the collision continued to occur, which is consistent with the conclusion of Fig. 14. Joint angle curve of robot arm is shown in Fig. 15. It can be seen that the robot arm performs detumbling motion until the angular velocity of the target is reduced to the index requirement. In one collision period, the joint angles change smoothly to achieve continuous damping to target. The detumbling efficiency is higher than that of the traditional control.

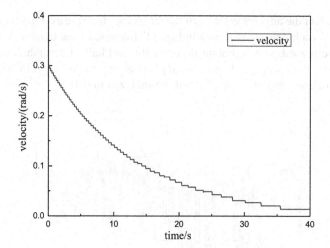

**Fig. 12.**  Angular velocity of the target

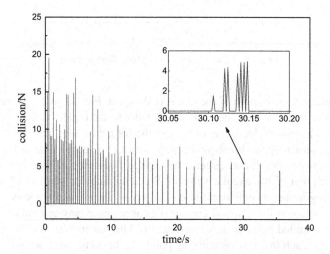

**Fig. 13.**  Collision force between brush and target

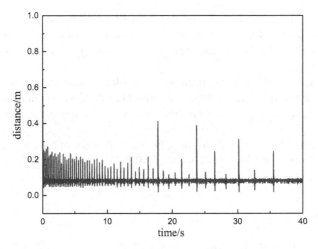

**Fig. 14.** Distance between the end of the arm and the recommended point

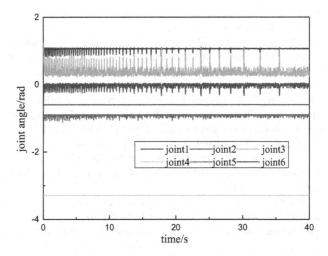

**Fig. 15.** Joint angle of robot arm

## 5 Conclusion

Classical detumbling strategy of robot arm is poor in autonomy and efficiency for rotating targets. In this paper, we propose a new brush-type detumbling method base on deep deterministic policy gradient (DDPG) for achieving the autonomous detumbling trajectory planning and control strategy of robot arm for the first time. Considering the characteristics of brush racemization, we rewrite the problem into a state, action, and reward. Thus, the curse of dimensionality problem is avoided and the convergence efficiency and learning rate are improved. The simulation scenario is built based on the Mujoco physics engine. The results show the excellent performance of path planning and smooth detumbling control of robot based on DDPG. The target's angular velocity is successfully reduced from 0.3 rad/s to 0.01 rad/s after a 40 s braking operation. The method proposed in this paper can provide a new control strategy for active contact detumbling application.

In future work, a physical platform will be built, including the target, air bearing table and the capture spacecraft with the UR arm. Then the network trained in the virtual environment could to be transferred the physical experiment so as to get better robustness.

**Acknowledgments.** This work was supported by Nature Program of National Natural Science Foundation of China (Grant No. 61690210 and 61690215).

# References

1. Bennett, T., Schaub, H.: Touchless electrostatic three-dimensional detumbling of large axisymmetric debris. J. Astronaut. Sci. **62**(3), 233–253 (2015). https://doi.org/10.1007/s40295-015-0075-8
2. Gómez, N.O., Walker, S.J.I.: Guidance, navigation, and control for the Eddy Brake method. J. Guidance Control Dyn. **40**, 52–68 (2017)
3. Nakajima, Y., Mitani, S., Tani, H., Murakami, N., Yamamoto, T., Yamanaka, K.: Detumbling space debris via thruster plume impingement. In: AIAAAAS Astrodynamics Specialist Conference, Long Beach, California. American Institute of Aeronautics and Astronautics (2016)
4. Cheng, W., Li, Z., He, Y.: Strategy and control for robotic detumbling of space debris by using flexible brush. In: Proceedings of the 3rd International Conference on Robotics and Automation Sciences ICRAS, Wuhan, China, pp. 41–47. IEEE (2019)
5. Matunaga, S., Kanzawa, T., Ohkami, Y.: Rotational motion-damper for the capture of an uncontrolled rotating satellite. Control Eng. Pract. **9**, 199–205 (2001)
6. Nishida, S.-I., Kawamoto, S.: Strategy for capturing of a tumbling space debris. Acta Astronaut. **68**, 113–120 (2011)
7. Sun, S., Wu, H., Wei, C., Zhao, Y.: Dynamic analysis of rotating satellite de-spun using flexible brush. Sci. Sin. Phys. Mech. Astron. **49**, 024515 (2019)
8. Mnih, V., et al.: Human-level control through deep reinforcement learning. Nature **518**, 529–533 (2015)
9. Zhang, Q., Lin, M., Yang, L.T., Chen, Z., Khan, S.U., Li, P.: A double deep q-learning model for energy-efficient edge scheduling. IEEE Trans. Serv. Comput. **12**, 739–749 (2019)
10. Casas, N.: deep deterministic policy gradient for urban traffic light control (2017)
11. Schulman, J., Levine, S., Moritz, P., Jordan, M.I., Abbeel, P.: Trust region policy optimization. In: Computer Science, pp. 1889–1897 (2015)
12. Alghanem, B., Keerthana, P.G.: Asynchronous advantage actor-critic agent for starcraft II (2018)
13. Zhang, Z., Luo, X., Xie, S., Wang, J., Wang, W., Li, Y.: Proximal policy optimization with mixed distributed training (2019)
14. Jagodnik, K.M., Thomas, P.S., van den Bogert, A.J., Branicky, M.S., Kirsch, R.F.: Training an actor-critic reinforcement learning controller for arm movement using human-generated rewards. IEEE Trans. Neural Syst. Rehabil. Eng. **25**, 1892–1905 (2017)
15. Inoue, T., De Magistris, G., Munawar, A., Yokoya, T., Tachibana, R.: Deep reinforcement learning for high precision assembly tasks. arXiv170804033 Cs (2017)

16. Rajeswaran, A., Kumar, V., Gupta, A., Vezzani, G., Schulman, J., Todorov, E., et al.: Learning complex dexterous manipulation with deep reinforcement learning and demonstrations. In: Robotics Science and Systems XIV. Robotics: Science and Systems Foundation (2018)

17. Wen, S., Chen, J., Wang, S., Zhang, H., Hu, X.: Path planning of humanoid arm based on deep deterministic policy gradient. In: Proceedings of the 2018 IEEE International Conference on Robotics and Biomimetics ROBIO, Kuala Lumpur, Malaysia, pp. 1755–1760. IEEE (2018)

18. Sharma, S., Beierle, C., D'Amico, S.: Pose estimation for non-cooperative spacecraft rendezvous using convolutional neural networks (2018)

19. Sharma, S., D'Amico, S.: Comparative assessment of techniques for initial pose estimation using monocular vision. Acta Astronaut. **123**, 435–445 (2016)

20. Huimin, L., Zhang, M., Xing, X.: Deep fuzzy hashing network for efficient image retrieval. IEEE Trans. Fuzzy Syst. (2020). https://doi.org/10.1109/TFUZZ.2020.2984991

21. Huimin, L., Li, Y., Chen, M., et al.: Brain Intelligence: go beyond artificial intelligence. Mob. Netw. Appl. **23**, 368–375 (2018)

22. Huimin, L., Li, Y., Shenglin, M., et al.: Motor anomaly detection for unmanned aerial vehicles using reinforcement learning. IEEE Internet Things J. **5**(4), 2315–2322 (2018)

23. Lu, H., Qin, M., Zhang, F., et al.: RSCNN: A CNN-based method to enhance low-light remote-sensing images. Remote Sens. **13**, 62 (2020)

24. Huimin, L., Zhang, Y., Li, Y., et al.: User-oriented virtual mobile network resource management for vehicle communications. IEEE Trans. Intell. Transp. Syst. **22**(6), 3521–3532 (2021)

# A Bilateral Controller for Pharyngeal Swab Test Teleoperation System

Yanfeng Pu[1][✉], Liang Li[2], Ting Wang[2], and Zhenxing Sun[2]

[1] Nanjing Customs District P. R. China, 360, Longpanzhong Road, Qinhuai District, Nanjing, China
64016663@qq.com
[2] College of Electrical Engineering and Control Science, Nanjing Tech University, Nanjing 21816, China

**Abstract.** Due to the novel pneumonia virus outbreak and gradual normalization, throat swab detection has become an important means for customs entry and exit personnel. However, the current detection methods make the medical staff exposed to the dangerous environment for a long time, which is very easy to cause the infection of medical staff. In view of the relative shortage of medical staff, this paper proposes to use the teleoperation system for pharyngeal swab detection, and puts forward the corresponding bilateral teleoperation controller. Finally, its feasibility is verified by numerical simulations.

**Keywords:** Teleoperation system · Bilateral teleoperation controller · Numerical simulation

## 1 Introduction

Nearly 300, 000 people worldwide died from complications caused by COVID-19 virus, and more than 4.3 million cases were infected. According to data from the Asian Development Bank (ADB), the global economic losses caused by the COVID-19 epidemic this year may be more than doubled over the period of 5 trillion and 800 billion minus 8.8 trillion dollars. Reuters reported that the ADB's estimate is equivalent to 6.4%9.7% of global GDP, worse than its April forecast. The ADB estimated in April that the global economic loss may be between $2.0 trillion and $4.1 trillion, depending on the duration time of the anti epidemic blockade measures are implemented. This new analysis shows novel coronavirus pneumonia (COVID-19) that may cause a very significant economic impact. At the same time, it also highlights that policy intervention can play an important role in helping reduce economic losses. After the health crisis caused China's economy to actually stagnate in the first quarter, the number of reported infection cases and deaths in several countries and regions increased, leading to extensive travel restrictions and home orders. The Asian Development Bank (ADB) said that the measures taken to control the spread of the epidemic may cause economic losses of US $1.7 trillion to US $2.5 trillion in Asia and US $1.1 trillion to US $1.6 trillion in China. Travel restrictions

S. Yang and H. Lu (Eds.): ISAIR 2022, CCIS 1700, pp. 112–117, 2022.
https://doi.org/10.1007/978-981-19-7946-0_10

and blockades could reduce global trade by $1.7 trillion to $2.6 trillion, resulting in the unemployment of 158 million to 242 million people [1, 2].

Novel coronavirus pneumonia test reagent, currently approved by the China CDC researcher Feng Luzhao, mainly includes two categories, one is nucleic acid detection reagent, the other is antibody detection reagent. So far, the State Food and drug administration has approved 12 nucleic acid detection reagents and 8 antibody detection reagents, including 5 kinds of colloidal gold method and 3 kinds of magnetic particle chemiluminescence method. The nucleic acid detection process includes sample processing, nucleic acid extraction, PCR detection and other steps. The average detection time takes 23 h. Since it directly detects the viral nucleic acid in the collected samples, it has strong specificity and relatively high sensitivity. It is the main detection method at present. Antibody detection includes colloidal gold method and magnetic particle chemiluminescence method. The average detection time of colloidal gold method is about 15 min. However, if the serum is used instead of whole blood, this serum treatment still needs some time. If whole blood is used, it is about 15 min. Magnetic particle chemiluminescence generally takes 3060 min. Antibody detection is to detect the antibody level in human blood. In the early stage of disease infection, there may be no antibody in human body, so it has a detection window. Therefore, antibody detection can be used for auxiliary diagnosis of cases with negative nucleic acid detection and screening of cases, but it can not replace nucleic acid detection method. With the normalization and scattered development of the epidemic situation, pharyngeal swab detection is still the most frequently used method in countries all over the world [3, 4].

In China and many other countries in the world, pharyngeal swab detections are heavily relying on medical staff which causes the shortage of medical staffs owing to the close contact. In addition, it also aggravates the infection risk of medical staff although medical staffs wear protective clothing. Therefore, in this paper, we introduce of using teleoperation system to achieve accurate and fast pharyngeal swab test. In the pharyngeal swab test teleoperation system, the medical staff operates the master haptic manipulator to make the slave manipulator to lamp the cotton swab and to realize pharyngeal swab sampling. In this case, medical staffs may located at the place far from the person to be sampled.

The rest of the paper is organized into the following 4 sections. Section 2 analyzes the dynamic equation of pharyngeal swab test teleoperation system. Section 3 describes the bilateral sliding mode control method. Section 4 performs the numerical simulation and discusses results. Conclusions are discussed in the Conclusions section.

## 2 Dynamic Equation of Pharyngeal Swab Test Teleoperation System

Assuming both the master and the slave manipulators apply the same two degree of freedom (2-DOF) manipulator with two links and three joints, the dynamic equation of the pharyngeal swab test teleoperation system can be expressed as follows:

$$M_i(q_i)\ddot{q}_i + C_i(q_i, \dot{q}_i)\dot{q}_i + G_i(q_i) = \tau_i + d_i, \ i = m, s \qquad (1)$$

where, Subscribes m and s are respectively represented the master side and the slave side. $q_i \in R^n$ is the rotation angle vector of three joints of both the master and the slave manipulators. $\dot{q}_i \in R^n$ and $\ddot{q}_i \in R^n$ are angular velocity and angular accelerations of the master and the slave manipulators in the joint space. $d_i \in R^n$ is the lump disturbances involving the model uncertainties and external disturbances and has the upper boundedness. $M_i(q_i) \in R^{n \times n}$ are the inertia matrix of the master and the slave sides. $C_i(q_i, \dot{q}_i) \in R^{n \times n}$ are the combination of centrifugal force and Coriolis force matrix of the master and the slave sides. $G_i(q_i) \in R^{n \times n}$ are the gravitational matrix of the master and the slave sides. $\tau_i \in R^n$ are respectively torque vectors of the master and the slave manipulators. The teleoperation dynamic equation satisfied following properties.

1. The inertia matrix $M_i(q_i)$ are symmetric and positive definite. Its norm is bounded:

$$M_i(q_i) = M_i(q_i)^T > 0 \tag{2}$$

$$M_i(q_i)_{\min} \leq \|M_i(q_i)\| \leq M_i(q_i)_{\max} \tag{3}$$

2. $\dot{M}_i(q_i) - 2C_i(q_i, \dot{q}_i)$ are skew-symmetric matrix and it satisfies:

$$\left[\dot{M}_i(q_i) - 2C_i(q_i, \dot{q}_i)\right]^T = -\left[\dot{M}_i(q_i) - 2C_i(q_i, \dot{q}_i)\right] \tag{4}$$

3. The 2-norm of $M_i(q_i)$ is bounded with an upper limit $\zeta$ and it satisfies:

$$\forall q_i \in D_i q_i, \left\|\dot{M}_i(q_i)\right\| \leq \zeta_i \tag{5}$$

## 3   Bilateral Teleoperation Control of Pharyngeal Swab Test Teleoperation System

In order to get high accuracy of the pharyngeal swab test, the disturbance observer is designed as follows.

$$\begin{cases} \dot{z}_i = L_i(q_i)\big(C_i(q_i, \dot{q}_i)\dot{q}_i + G_i(q_i) - \tau_i - \hat{\tau}_{di}\big) \\ \hat{\tau}_{di} = z_i + p_i(\dot{q}_i) \end{cases} i = m, s \tag{6}$$

$$L_i(q_i) = X_i^{-1} M_i^{-1}(q_i) \, i = m, s \tag{7}$$

$$p_i(q_i) = X_i^{-1} \dot{q}_i \, i = m, s \tag{8}$$

where $X_i$ are an invertible matrix, $M_i(q_i) = M_i(q_i)^T > 0$, $i = m, s$.

The lumped disturbance and uncertainties is estimated by $\hat{\tau}_{di}$. Then, based on the disturbance observer, the bilateral controller is designed as follows.

Define the error as follows:

$$\tilde{q}_i(t) = q_i(t) - q_{di}(t) \tag{9}$$

where $\tilde{q}_i$ is tracking error and $q_{di}$ are the desired trajectories of manipulators. Then define the auxiliary variable $q_{ri}$ as:

$$\dot{q}_{ri} = \dot{q}_{di} - \Lambda_i \tilde{q}_i$$
$$\ddot{q}_{ri} = \ddot{q}_{di} - \Lambda_i \dot{\tilde{q}}_i \tag{10}$$

where $\dot{q}_{di}$ and $\ddot{q}_{di}$ are the velocity and acceleration of the desired trajectories respectively and $\Lambda_i = diag(\lambda_{1i} \cdots \lambda_{ni})$, $\lambda_i > 0$. The control law are designed as

$$s_i = \dot{\tilde{q}}_i + \Lambda_i \tilde{q}_i \tag{11}$$

$$\tau_i = M_i(q_i)\ddot{q}_{ri} + C_i(q_i, \dot{q}_i)\dot{q}_{ri} + G_i(q_i) - K_{di}s_i - \eta_i \mathrm{sgn}s_i - \hat{\tau}_{di} \tag{12}$$

where $K_{di} = diag(K_{d1} \cdots K_{dn})$, $K_{di} > 0$, $\eta_i \geq \max(|d_{1i}|, |d_{2i}|)$, and $\mathrm{sgn}s_i$ is a symbolic function.

**Proof**: Lyapunov function $V_i$ is considered as follows

$$V_i = \frac{1}{2}s_i^T M_i(q_i)s_i + V_{1i} \tag{13}$$

$$\dot{V}_i = s_i^T M_i(q_i)\dot{s}_i + \frac{1}{2}s_i^T \dot{M}_i(q_i)s_i + \dot{V}_{1i}$$

$$= s_i^T(u_i - C_i(q_i, \dot{q}_i)\dot{q}_i - G_i(q_i) - M_i(q_i)\ddot{q}_{ri}) + \frac{1}{2}s_i^T \dot{M}_i(q_i)s_i + \dot{V}_{1i}$$

$$= -s_i^T K_{di}s_i - \eta_i\|s_i\| + \frac{1}{2}s_i^T(\dot{M}_i(q_i) - 2C_i(q_i, \dot{q}_i))s_i + \dot{V}_{1i} \text{ From above, when } \dot{V} \equiv 0, \text{ It}$$

$$= -s_i^T K_{di}s_i - \eta_i\|s_i\| + \dot{V}_{1i} \leq 0$$

It is easily seen that $s_i \equiv 0$, $\tilde{q}_i \equiv 0$. Depending on the theory of LaSalle, the teleoperation system is asymptotically stable using the above controller. As $t \to \infty$, $s_i$ and $\tilde{q}_i$ converge exponentially to zero. That is, the teleoperation system may accomplish accurate trajectory tracking.

## 4  Numerical Simulations

In numerical simulations, parameters are set as the same as [5]. The observed initial value of the disturbance td is taken as $[0, 0]$. Other parameters are set as follows, $\Upsilon_m = \Upsilon_s = \begin{bmatrix} 0.5 & 0 \\ 0 & 0.6 \end{bmatrix}$, $X_m = X_s = \begin{bmatrix} 0.3 & 0 \\ 0 & 0.4 \end{bmatrix}$, $K_{dm} = K_{ds} = \begin{bmatrix} 100 & 0 \\ 0 & 100 \end{bmatrix}$, $\Lambda_m = \Lambda_s = \begin{bmatrix} 150 & 0 \\ 0 & 150 \end{bmatrix}$. After numerical simulations, results are illustrated as follows. Trajectory tracking of the master and the salve side are displayed respectively in Fig. 1 and Fig. 2. From results of numerical simulations, the teleoperation system may accomplish precise trajectory tracking due to the bilateral teleoperation controller.

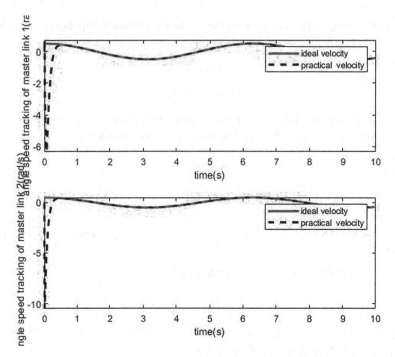

**Fig. 1.** Trajectory tracking of the master manipulator.

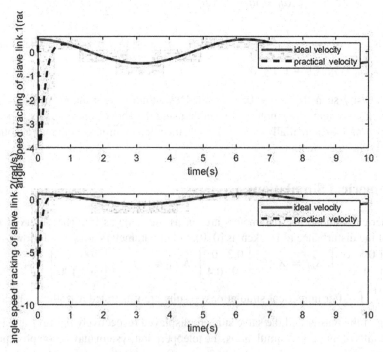

**Fig. 2.** Trajectory tracking of the slave manipulator.

# 5 Conclusion

In the paper, a teleoperation system is used to achieve accurate and fast pharyngeal swab test avoiding the infection risk of medical staff. Both of the master and the slave side take 2 DOF manipulators. A bilateral teleoperation controller is proposed for accurate trajectory tracking. The stability is analyzed and numerical simulations are performed to verify the proposed method. Results show the efficiency of the tracking performances.

**Acknowledgements.** This work was supported by the National Natural Science Foundation of China [grant numbers No. 61906086].

# References

1. Hase, R., Kurita, T., Muranaka, E., et al.: A case of imported COVID-19 diagnosed byPCR-positive lower respiratory specimen but with PCR-negative throat swabs.Taylor& Francis, pp. 1–4 (2020). https://doi.org/10.1080/23744235.2020.1744711
2. Huang, K., Sun, Y., Chen, B., et al.: New COVID-19 saliva-based test: how good is it compared with the current nasopharyngealor throat swab test? J. Chin. Med. Assoc. **83**(10), 891 (2020). https://doi.org/10.1097/JCMA.0000000000000396
3. Vlek, A.L.M., Wesselius, T.S., Achterberg, R., Thijsen, S.F.T.: Combined throat/nasal swab sampling for SARS-CoV-2 is equivalent to nasopharyngeal sampling. Eur. J. Clin. Microbiol. Infect. Dis. **40**(1), 193–195 (2020). https://doi.org/10.1007/s10096-020-03972-y
4. Bertalan, G., Klein, C., Schreyer, S., et al.: Biomechanical properties of the hypoxic and dying brain quantified by magnetic resonance elastography. Acta Biomater. **101**, 395–402 (2020)
5. Wang, T., Li, Y., Zhang, J., Zhang, Y.: A novel bilateral impedance controls for underwater tele-operation systems **91**, 106194 (2020)
6. Huimin, L., Zhang, M., Xu, X.:Deep fuzzy hashing network for efficient image retrieval. IEEE Trans. Fuzzy Syst. **29**(1), 166176 (2020). https://doi.org/10.1109/TFUZZ.2020.2984991
7. Huimin, L., Li, Y., Chen, M., et al.: Brain intelligence: go beyond artificial intelligence. Mobile Networks Appl. **23**, 368–375 (2018)
8. Huimin, L., Li, Y., Shenglin, M., et al.: Motor anomaly detection for unmanned aerial vehicles using reinforcement learning. IEEE Internet Things J. **5**(4), 2315–2322 (2018)
9. Huimin, L., Qin, M., Zhang, F., et al.: RSCNN: A CNN-based method to enhance low-light remote-sensing images. Remote Sensing **13**(1), 62 (2020)

# Enhanced Feature Fusion and Multiple Receptive Fields Object Detection

Hailong Liu, Jinrong Cui$^{(\boxtimes)}$, Haowei Zhong, and Cheng Huang

College of Mathematics and Informatics, South China Agricultural University,
Guangzhou 510642, China
tweety1028@163.com

**Abstract.** CenterNet is a widely used single-stage anchor-free object detector. It only uses single feature map to detect all size objects, and does not effectively use different levels of feature maps. We present an enhanced feature fusion and multi receptive field object detector, named EM-CenterNet. Our detector first fuses different levels of feature maps, and then enhances feature fusion through semantic information transfer path. Besides, we design another key component, which is composed of continuous several dilated convolutions and shortcut connections, so that our detector can cover all object's scales. We compare the EM-CenterNet method with the baseline on the Pascal VOC and COCO datasets. Experiments show that our method increases the AP by 12.2% on the Pascal VOC dataset, and increases the AP by 5.9% on the COCO dataset.

**Keywords:** Deep learning · Object detection · Receptive field · Feature fusion

## 1 Introduction

Computer vision technology has played a powerful role in many fields [1, 2]. At present, object detection technology is widely used. The accuracy of object detector has a great influence on the accuracy of subsequent tasks based on object detection. In recent years, more and more excellent detectors have been proposed. According to different detection processes, the types of object detectors generally include one-stage detectors [3, 4] and two-stage detectors [5, 6]. Two-stage detectors predict boxes proposals and one-stage detectors slide several specific bounding boxes over the image and classify them directly. Whether one-stage detector or two-stage detector, most of them are anchor-based detectors. Specifically, they need to place many carefully set anchors on the image in advance. And it is very complex and needs to adjust the hyper-parameters of the anchors according to different datasets.

Recently, anchor-free detector, as an emerging framework for object detection with a simple strategy and excellent performance, has received increasing attention. FCOS [7] is a widely used anchor-free object detector. It treats all samples in the ground truth as positive samples, and then obtains the distance from the center point to the four sides directly through regression. At the same time, FCOS adds a center-ness branch to

© The Author(s), under exclusive license to Springer Nature Singapore Pte Ltd. 2022
S. Yang and H. Lu (Eds.): ISAIR 2022, CCIS 1700, pp. 118–129, 2022.
https://doi.org/10.1007/978-981-19-7946-0_11

obtain higher quality detection boxes. Another anchor-free object detector, CornerNet [8], detects two bounding box corners as keypoints.

Different from the above two anchor-free detector, CenterNet [9] only regards the center point of the object as the positive sample, and other points are regarded as positive samples, and then regresses at the center point to obtain the size of the object. CenterNet is simpler and faster because it only needs to detect all the objects of different sizes on a single high resolution feature map. However, CenterNet only obtain the feature map by upsampling the smallest high-level feature map for detection, but does not effectively use the low-level feature maps. The research of Li et al. shows that objects with different scales have different needs for the best receptive field of the network [10]. In addition, our investigation found that the receptive field of CenterNet is not enough to cover all objects' scales.

In this paper, two key components, Enhanced feature fusion and Residual dilated convolution are proposed, which bring considerable improvements. First, we propose a semantic information transmission path to enhance feature fusion. Specifically, we fuse feature maps at different levels, and we use semantic information transfer path to transfer the semantic information, so as to significantly enhance feature fusion. Then we design a continuous dilated convolution module with shortcut connections. Experiments on two datasets which are challenging, Pascal VOC and COCO datasets, demonstrate the effectiveness of our method. The main contributions of our work are as follows:

1) We fusing the low-level feature maps of the backbone to improve the performance of CenterNet. And we propose a semantic information transfer path to enhance feature fusion.
2) We verify the influence of the receptive field of CenterNet on the detection performance of objects with different scales, and the current receptive field of CenterNet is not enough to cover targets with all scales. And we propose a continuous dilated convolutions module with shortcut connections, which can generate a feature with multiple receptive fields.
3) Sufficient experiments show the advantages of our proposed detector.

## 2 Related Work

### 2.1 Anchor-Based Detector

**Two-Stage Method.** R-CNN [11] innovatively uses convolutional neural network to detect objects. The detection steps of R-CNN are complex. Firstly, it obtains redundant candidate boxes through selective search, and then classifies the candidate boxes and obtains the size of the objects through regression in the second stage. R-CNN has good detection performance, but its slow inference speed limits its application. Faster R-CNN [5] uses the Regional Proposal Network (RPN) to speed up the generation of candidate boxes. At present, the two-stage detectors have the most advanced accuracy.

**One-Stage Method.** Different from the above object detectors, the earliest one-stage object detector YOLOv1 [12] based on deep learning does not need to form excessive candidate boxes, but directly divides the image into many regions, classifies each region and predicts the size of the objects. This method significantly shortens the inference speed, but it is less accurate than two-stage detectors. SSD [13] uses multi-scale feature maps to predict the location and category of objects, so it has better detection performance for small objects. Thereafter, many object detectors have followed this approach [14, 15]. YOLOv3 [3] draws on the multi-scale feature maps of SSD and introduces feature pyramid network (FPN) [16] to improve the detection accuracy of small objects. RetinaNet [4] is a relatively new detector, which uses focal loss to alleviate the problem of category imbalance in the process of network training.

### 2.2 Anchor-Free Detector

The first successful universal anchor-free detector is YOLOv1 [12]. The inference speed of YOLOv1 is surprising, but it is not as accurate as the anchor-based object detectors. Therefore, its successor, YOLOv2, abandons the anchor-free design. Recently, the proposal of CornerNet [8] has turned the attention of the academic to the anchor-free object detectors. CornerNet does not need to regress the size of the objects, but only needs to predict two key points of the objects, and determine the category and location through the key points. Another successful anchor-free detector, FCOS [7], introduces FPN to detect objects with different scales and has achieved competitive performance. CenterNet [9] determines the location and category by predicting the center point of the objects, and then predicts the size of the objects at the center point. CenterNet detects objects at all scales only through a high-resolution feature map, thus its reasoning speed is very fast.

### 2.3 Feature Fusion

Different levels of feature maps contain different semantic information or spatial information. Feature pyramid network (FPN) [16] fuses different level feature maps, and significantly improves the detection effect of small objects. Zhang et al. added semantic information to the low-level feature maps to enhance the fusion effect, which slightly improved the performance of the instance segmentation method [17]. We use a similar way to improve the object detector. The experimental results show that the low-level feature map containing more semantic information can be better fused with the high-level feature map.

### 2.4 Dilated Convolutions

Dilated convolution is a common component in many semantic segmentation methods [18, 19]. It increases the receptive field without losing information. Now, many object detectors [20, 21] also use dilated convolution to improved accuracy. In this paper, we stack convolution layers with different dilated rates to obtain feature map that can cover objects of different scales.

## 3 Receptive Field of CenterNet

In this section, we will introduce CenterNet at length, and then we design a scientific experiment to investigate the influence of receptive field on CenterNet object detector.

### 3.1  CenterNet

Different from other target detectors, CenterNet's approach is similar to key point detection. [22, 23], which represents objects by a single center point. In the reasoning stage, we only need to input the image into the network to get the heatmap representing the location and category of the objects, and the size of the objects.

The construction of CenterNet is very sample, the backbone network generates a low-resolution feature map, and then obtains a high-resolution feature map after three consecutive up sampling. After the image is input into the network, four feature maps with width and height gradually reduced by half are obtained from the bottom-up pathway, that is, the backbone network. Then the smallest high-level feature map is upsampled for three consecutive times to obtain a high-resolution feature map for subsequent detection.

Specifically, for ResNets [24] we choose the last four output feature maps as the selection and mark them as C2, C3, C4, and C5. The top-down pathway generates feature maps with higher resolution by upsampling the high-level feature maps, and we mark them as P2, P3, P4, and P5. It should be noted that P5 is produced applying one $1 \times 1$ convolutional layer on C5. CenterNet determines the location and category by detecting the center point of the objects, and directly predicts the width and height of the objects. At the same time, to compensate for the center point offset caused by downsampling, CenterNet predicts the center point offsets.

**Table 1.** Results with different receptive fields using CenterNet [9] evaluated on the Pascal VOC dataset [26].

| Dilation rate | AP | $AP_S$ | $AP_M$ | $AP_L$ |
|---|---|---|---|---|
| 1 | 38.6 | **6.2** | 25.0 | 48.5 |
| 2 | 40.3 | 5.2 | **25.1** | 51.3 |
| 4 | **41.2** | 5.7 | 25.0 | **52.6** |

### 3.2  Investigation of Receptive Field

The receptive field of the network is one of the key factors affecting the performance of object detectors [25]. To investigate the relationship between receptive field and CenterNet detection effect, we add a dilated convolution layer between the backbone network and the upsampling structure. We use three different dilation rates to generate networks with three different receptive fields.

We conduct our experiment using the CenterNet with the ResNet18 backbone on the VOC dataset. The dilation rates used in the experiment are 1, 2 and 4. And we report Average Precision (AP) on object of small ($AP_S$), medium ($AP_S$) and large sizes ($AP_L$).

We can find that the detection performance of objects with different scales is positively correlated with the dilation rate from Table 1. In other words, larger receptive fields are better for detecting large objects. This phenomenon strongly shows that the receptive field of CenterNet is not enough to cover all objects' scales. These findings inspire the following improvements to the CenterNet object Detector.

## 4   EM-CenterNet

This section will describe the main components of our proposed EM-CenterNet detector in detail. The proposed EM-CenterNet consists of Enhanced feature fusion and Residual dilated convolution. The brief structure of EM-CenterNet as shown in Fig. 1. First, we describe the proposed components of EM-CenterNet. Then, we also introduce several loss functions for training in detail.

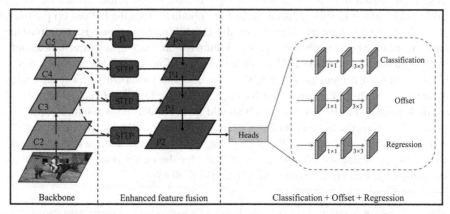

**Fig. 1.** The brief structure of EM-CenterNet detector, in which C2, C3, C4 and C5 are the feature maps of different scales in the backbone network respectively, D is residual dilated convolution, the bule dotted line is the path of semantic information transmission, SITP means semantic information transmission path, and P2 to P5 are the feature levels.

### 4.1   Enhanced Feature Fusion

To effectively use the low-level feature map rich in spatial information, we improve the structure of CenterNet. After sampling on the feature maps, we fuse them with the feature maps in the backbone, and finally get a feature map containing rich information. And to enhance the effect of feature fusion, we introduce semantic information transmission path. We will describe it in detail later.

**Feature Fusion.**  The construction of our feature fusion as like FPN [16]. We upsample the high-level feature maps and add them pixel by pixel with the feature maps in the backbone to get the final high-resolution feature map for detection. The detailed design of feature fusion is illustrated in Fig. 2.

**Semantic Information Transmission Path.**  In object detection, semantic information is conducive to the classification of objects, and spatial information is more conducive to the positioning of objects. Previous studies [17] believe that due to the large difference of semantic information between them, it is not the best way to directly fuse them.

To enhance the effect of feature fusion, we introduce three semantic information transmission paths. Specifically, we first sample the three high-level feature maps in

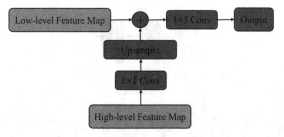

**Fig. 2.** The network architecture of feature fusion. The " +" sign means element-wise addition.

the backbone, then multiply them pixel by pixel with the feature maps in the previous stages in the backbone, and finally add the obtained feature maps pixel by pixel with the feature maps in the top-down path. The detailed design of the semantic information transmission path is illustrated in Fig. 3.

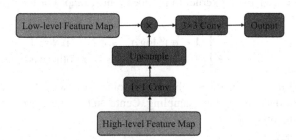

**Fig. 3.** The network architecture of Semantic information transmission path. The " ×" sign means element-wise multiplication.

### 4.2 Residual Dilated Convolution

From Sect. 3, we can see that the detection effect of CenterNet object detector on objects of different sizes is closely related to its receptive field. And the receptive field of CenterNet is not enough to cover all objects' scales.

To increase the receptive field of the CenterNet, we first designed a continuous dilated convolution structure. We add four continuous convolution layers with different dilation rates between the backbone network and the upsampling structure. At the same time, we reduce the channel dimension of the feature map by applying one $1 \times 1$ convolution layer and then add a $3 \times 3$ convolution layer. The dilation rates are 2, 4, 6, and 8, respectively.

The above structure is very simple, but continuous dilated convolution will lead to a large receptive field, which is not friendly for small objects. To solve this problem, we add a shortcut connection after each dilated convolution layer. The residual dilated convolution structure is shown in Fig. 4.

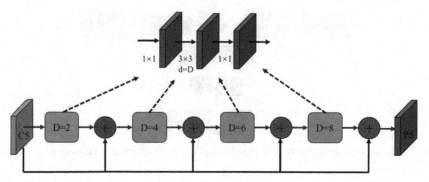

**Fig. 4.** The network architecture of Residual Dilated Convolution. The D means dilation rate.

### 4.3 Loss Function

The training process of our EM-CenterNet is consistent with CenterNet. For center localization, we use Gaussian kernel to produce a heat-map. For the prediction $\sigma$ and the target y, we have:

$$L_K = \frac{-1}{N} \sum_{xyc} \begin{cases} (1-\sigma)^\alpha \log\sigma & \text{if } y = 1 \\ (1-y)^\beta (\sigma)^\alpha \log(1-\sigma) & \text{otherwise} \end{cases} \tag{1}$$

where $\alpha = 2$ and $\beta = 4$, $N$ is the number of keypoints, following CenterNet [9].

Center point offset due to downsampling, CenterNet predict the offset of the center of the objects. The offset loss:

$$L_{off} = \frac{-1}{N} \sum |p - q| \tag{2}$$

where $p$ is the true offset and $q$ is the offset of the network output.

For size regression, we use an L1 loss:

$$L_{size} = \frac{-1}{N} \sum |S - \hat{S}| \tag{3}$$

where $S$ is the true width and height, and $\hat{S}$ is the predicted width and height.

The total loss L includes localization loss $L_K$, offset loss $L_{off}$ and size loss $L_{size}$, weight by two scalars. The total loss is:

$$L = L_K + w_1 L_{off} + w_2 L_{size} \tag{4}$$

where $w_1 = 1$ and $w_2 = 0.1$ in our setting as in CenterNet.

## 5 Experiments

We evaluate our EM-CenterNet on the Pascal VOC [26] and MS COCO datasets [27]. We first introduce our experimental setting, including datasets and training details. Then we compare the results of EM-CenterNet on the test-dev set of MS COCO dataset with CenterNet and other methods. Finally, we provide detailed ablation experiments of each component of our proposed EM-CenterNet object detector and provide quantitative results and analysis.

## 5.1 Experimental Setting

**Datasets.** In this section, we first describe the datasets and experimental settings we used, then we show the main results, and finally we show the ablation results. We experimented on Pascal VOC and COCO datasets. Pascal VOC datasets include VOC 2007 and VOC 2012 datasets. VOC 2007 includes 5011 training images and 4952 test images. VOC 2012 has 11540 training images, and the annotation of the test images is not disclosed. We test the performance of the detector on the test images of the VOC 2007 dataset.

**Training Details.** ResNet-18 is the backbone in our method for experiments and we resize the images to $512 \times 512$. The initial learning rate is 0.001, and the mini-batch size is 16. We reduced the learning rate by a factor of 10 at epoch 90 and 120 for 140 total epochs. Our optimizer is SGD, and weight decay is 0.0005. Warm-up is applied for the first epoch.

## 5.2 Main Results

We evaluate our EM-CenterNet on the COCO dataset and VOC dataset, and we adopt ResNet-18 as the backbone. As shown in Table 2, the AP of our detector is improved by 5.9% compared with baseline on the VOC dataset. As shown in Table 3, the AP of our detector is improved by 5.9% compared with baseline on the COCO dataset. And compared with other popular detectors, our method also has strong competitiveness with the same backbone.

**Table 2.** The experimental results on VOC dataset are compared with several newer detectors.

| Method | Backbone | AP | $AP_{50}$ | $AP_{75}$ | $AP_S$ | $AP_M$ | $AP_L$ |
|---|---|---|---|---|---|---|---|
| FCOS [7] | R50 | 44.1 | 73.5 | 46.2 | 14.9 | 32.2 | 51.9 |
| RetinaNet [4] | R50 | 44.8 | 73.1 | 46.9 | 13.3 | 32.2 | 52.6 |
| YOLOF [28] | R50 | 49.6 | **76.6** | 54.1 | 11.2 | 35.4 | 59.6 |
| EM-CenterNet | R50 | **51.4** | 74.6 | **56.3** | **17.1** | **36.7** | **61.2** |

## 5.3 Visualization Results

Figure 5 visualizes the detection results of CenterNet and EM-CenterNet. We can see that the detection result of our proposed method is better than the baseline. Specifically, the detection boxes of our method are more accurate and have higher classification confidence.

**Table 3.** Comparison with CenterNet and other popular object detectors on COCO test-dev. Using the same backbone resnet-18, EM-CenterNet outperforms the baseline counterpart CenterNet by 5.9% in AP. EM-CenterNet also outperforms the CenterNet with ResNet-18-DCN as its backbone.

| Method | Backbone | AP | $AP_{50}$ | $AP_{75}$ | $AP_S$ | $AP_M$ | $AP_L$ |
|---|---|---|---|---|---|---|---|
| SSD [13] | VGG16 | 25.7 | 43.9 | 26.2 | 6.9 | 27.7 | **42.6** |
| YOLOv3 [3] | D53 | 28.2 | - | - | - | - | - |
| FCOS [7] | R18 | 26.9 | 43.2 | 27.9 | **13.9** | 28.9 | 36.0 |
| CenterNet [9] | R18-DCN | 28.1 | 44.9 | 29.6 | - | - | - |
| CenterNet | R18 | 23.9 | 41.6 | 25.0 | 9.1 | 26.1 | 33.4 |
| EM-CenterNet | R18 | **29.8** | **47.3** | **31.6** | 11.3 | **30.7** | **42.6** |

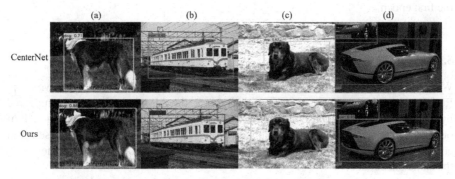

**Fig. 5.** Visualization of CenterNet and EM-CenterNet detection results.

## 5.4 Ablation Experiments

**Enhanced Feature Fusion.** As shown in Table 4, we first add feature pyramid network to CenterNet, and the result of ablation experiment result show that feature fusion can significantly improve the performance of CenterNet (36.8 vs. 41.3). Then we add the semantic information transfer path to feature pyramid network. The result of ablation experiment show that the semantic information transfer path significantly enhances feature fusion (41.3 vs. 42.4). After adding semantic information transfer path, the performance of large objects is significantly improved, and the performance of medium objects and small objects is slightly increased.

**Residual Dilated Convolution.** Based on the enhanced feature fusion component, we further add the residual dilated convolution component. As shown in Table 4, residual dilated convolution also significantly improves the performance of baseline (41.3 vs. 48.3). Finally, EM-CenterNet achieve significant improvements (12.2 AP increase) on the baseline.

**Table 4.** Results on the Pascal VOC dataset with ResNet-18. Starting from our baseline, we gradually add Enhanced feature fusion, Residual dilated convolution in our EM-CenterNet for ablation studies. FPN means feature pyramid network.

| FPN | Enhanced feature fusion | Residual dilated convolution | AP | $AP_{50}$ | $AP_{75}$ | $AP_S$ | $AP_M$ | $AP_L$ |
|-----|-----|-----|-----|-----|-----|-----|-----|-----|
| - | - | - | 36.8 | 60.0 | 39.9 | 9.1 | 27.8 | 44.6 |
| √ | - | - | 41.3 | 65.8 | 44.7 | 13.1 | 30.5 | 49.4 |
| √ | √ | - | 42.4 | 66.7 | 46.0 | 13.3 | 31.0 | 50.7 |
| √ | - | √ | 48.3 | 73.2 | 52.8 | **14.2** | 32.2 | 58.3 |
| √ | √ | √ | **49.0** | **73.4** | **53.5** | 13.7 | **32.8** | **59.1** |

## 6 Conclusion

In this work, we find that fusing the low-level features of the backbone can significantly improve the performance of CenterNet. And we propose a semantic information transfer path to enhance feature fusion. In addition, to make the receptive field of our detector can cover all objects of different sizes, we propose residual dilated convolution. We conducted experiments on two challenging data sets. The performance of our proposed detector, EM-CenterNet, is significantly improved compared with the baseline. We hope that our EM-CenterNet object detector can provide insights for designing anchor-free detectors.

## References

1. Gao, G., Yang, J., Jing, X.Y., et al.: Learning robust and discriminative low-rank representations for face recognition with occlusion. Pattern Recogn. **66**, 129–143 (2017)
2. Gao, G., Yu, Y., Yang, M., et al.: Cross-resolution face recognition with pose variations via multilayer locality-constrained structural orthogonal procrustes regression. Inf. Sci. **506**, 19–36 (2020)
3. Redmon, J., Farhadi, A.: Yolov3: an incremental improvement. arXiv preprint arXiv:1804. 02767 (2018)
4. Lin, T.Y., Goyal, P., Girshick, R., et al.: Focal loss for dense object detection. In: Proceedings of the IEEE International Conference on Computer Vision, pp. 2980–2988 (2017)
5. Ren, S., He, K., Girshick, R., et al.: Faster r-cnn: Towards real-time object detection with region proposal networks. Adv. Neural Inf. Processing Syst. **28** (2015)
6. He, K., Gkioxari, G., Dollár, P., et al.: Mask r-cnn. In: Proceedings of the IEEE International Conference on Computer Vision, pp. 2961–2969 (2017)
7. Tian, Z., Shen, C., Chen, H., et al.: Fcos: fully convolutional one-stage object detection. In: Proceedings of the IEEE/CVF International Conference on Computer Vision, pp. 9627–9636 (2019)
8. Law, H., Deng, J.: Cornernet: detecting objects as paired keypoints. In: Proceedings of the European Conference on Computer Vision (ECCV), pp. 734–750 (2018)
9. Zhou, X., Wang, D., Krähenbühl, P.: Objects as points. arXiv preprint arXiv:1904.07850 (2019)

10. Li, Y., Chen, Y., Wang, N., et al.: Scale-aware trident networks for object detection. In: Proceedings of the IEEE/CVF International Conference on Computer Vision, pp. 6054–6063 (2019)

11. Girshick, R., Donahue, J., Darrell, T., et al.: Rich feature hierarchies for accurate object detection and semantic segmentation. In: Proceedings of the IEEE Conference on Computer Vision and Pattern Recognition, pp. 580–587 (2014)

12. Redmon, J., Divvala, S., Girshick, R., et al.: You only look once: unified, real-time object detection. In: Proceedings of the IEEE Conference on Computer Vision and Pattern Recognition, pp. 779–788 (2016)

13. Liu, W., Anguelov, D., Erhan, D., et al.: Ssd: Single shot multibox detector. In: European Conference on Computer Vision. Springer, Cham, pp. 21–37 (2016). https://doi.org/10.1007/978-3-319-46448-0_2

14. Fu, C.Y., Liu, W., Ranga, A., et al.: Dssd: deconvolutional single shot detector. arXiv preprint arXiv:1701.06659 (2017)

15. Yi, J., Wu, P., Metaxas, D.N.: ASSD: Attentive single shot multibox detector. Comput. Vis. Image Underst. **189**, 102827 (2019)

16. Lin, T.Y., Dollár, P., Girshick, R., et al.: Feature pyramid networks for object detection. In: Proceedings of the IEEE Conference on Computer Vision and Pattern Recognition, pp. 2117–2125 (2017)

17. Zhang, Z., Zhang, X., Peng, C., Xue, X., Sun, J.: ExFuse: enhancing feature fusion for semantic segmentation. In: Ferrari, V., Hebert, M., Sminchisescu, C., Weiss, Y. (eds.) ECCV 2018. LNCS, vol. 11214, pp. 273–288. Springer, Cham (2018). https://doi.org/10.1007/978-3-030-01249-6_17

18. Yu, F., Koltun, V., Funkhouser, T.: Dilated residual networks. In: Proceedings of the IEEE Conference on Computer Vision and Pattern Recognition, pp. 472–480 (2017)

19. Yu, F., Koltun, V.: Multi-scale context aggregation by dilated convolutions. arXiv preprint arXiv:1511.07122 (2015)

20. Li, Z., Peng, C., Yu, G., et al.: Detnet: A backbone network for object detection. arXiv preprint arXiv:1804.06215 (2018)

21. Liu, S., Huang, D., Wang, Y.: Receptive field block net for accurate and fast object detection. In: Ferrari, V., Hebert, M., Sminchisescu, C., Weiss, Y. (eds.) ECCV 2018. LNCS, vol. 11215, pp. 404–419. Springer, Cham (2018). https://doi.org/10.1007/978-3-030-01252-6_24

22. Cao, Z., Simon, T., Wei, S.E., et al.: Realtime multi-person 2d pose estimation using part affinity fields. In: Proceedings of the IEEE Conference on Computer Vision and Pattern Recognition, pp. 7291–7299 (2017)

23. Zhou, X., Karpur, A., Luo, L., Huang, Q.: StarMap for category-agnostic keypoint and viewpoint estimation. In: Ferrari, V., Hebert, M., Sminchisescu, C., Weiss, Y. (eds.) ECCV 2018. LNCS, vol. 11205, pp. 328–345. Springer, Cham (2018). https://doi.org/10.1007/978-3-030-01246-5_20

24. He, K., Zhang, X., Ren, S., et al.: Deep residual learning for image recognition. In: Proceedings of the IEEE Conference on Computer Vision and Pattern Recognition, pp. 770–778 (2016)

25. Cai, Z., Fan, Q., Feris, R.S., et al.: A unified multi-scale deep convolutional neural network for fast object detection. In: European Conference on Computer Vision. Springer, Cham, pp. 354–370 (2016). https://doi.org/10.1007/978-3-319-46493-0_22

26. Everingham, M., Van Gool, L., Williams, C.K.I., et al.: The pascal visual object classes (voc) challenge. Int. J. Comput. Vision **88**(2), 303–338 (2010)

27. Lin, T.Y., Maire, M., Belongie, S., et al.: Microsoft coco: Common objects in context. In: European Conference on Computer Vision. Springer, Cham, pp. 740–755 (2014). https://doi.org/10.1007/978-3-319-10602-1_48

28. Chen, Q., Wang, Y., Yang, T., et al.: You only look one-level feature. In: Proceedings of the IEEE/CVF Conference on Computer Vision and Pattern Recognition, pp. 13039–13048 (2021)
29. Huimin, L., Zhang, M., Xing, X.: Deep fuzzy hashing network for efficient image retrieval. IEEE Trans. Fuzzy Syst. (2020). https://doi.org/10.1109/TFUZZ.2020.2984991
30. Huimin, L., Li, Y., Chen, M., et al.: Brain Intelligence: go beyond artificial intelligence. Mobile Networks Appl. **23**, 368–375 (2018)
31. Huimin, L., Li, Y., Shenglin, M., et al.: Motor anomaly detection for unmanned aerial vehicles using reinforcement learning. IEEE Internet Things J. **5**(4), 2315–2322 (2018)
32. Huimin, L., Qin, M., Zhang, F., et al.: RSCNN: A CNN-based method to enhance low-light remote-sensing images. Remote Sensing **13**(1), 62 (2020)
33. Huimin, L., Zhang, Y., Li, Y., et al.: User-oriented virtual mobile network resource management for vehicle communications. IEEE Trans. Intell. Transp. Syst. **22**(6), 3521–3532 (2021)

# An Object Detection and Pose Estimation Method for AR Application

Tengteng Ji[1], Fengquan Zhang[2(✉)], and Huibai Wang[1]

[1] School of Information Science and Technology, North China University of Technology, Beijing, China
[2] School of Digital Media and Design Arts, Beijing University of Posts and Telecommunications, Beijing, China
zhangfq@bupt.eiidu.cn

**Abstract.** With the continuous development of computer technology and deep learning, object detection technology has received great attention in recent years. Especially on the problem of 3D object detection in AR field, a variety of novel algorithms are in bloom. However, these algorithms are either low precision or slow speed. Therefore, we propose an object detection and pose estimation method for AR Application, which is a model for 6D pose estimation of 3D object based on 2D object detection. In our model, we firstly input the 2D projection image of the 3D model into the improved RetinaNet model, and detect the coordinates of the vertex and center point of the object on the image. Then the coordinates on the image and the coordinates on the CAD are matched by point matching. Then, the EPnP improved by Perspective-n-Point (PnP) algorithm is used to complete the pose estimation of 3D object. Finally, we test the performance of our algorithm. The results show that our accuracy has reached the average level of the mainstream algorithms.

**Keywords:** Pose estimation · Object detection · Deep learning · Convolutional neural network

## 1 Introduction

In the AR field, 3D object detection is one of an important research area. It refers to detecting the position and category of objects in three-dimensional space [1]. There are some ways to try to solve this problem. The method based on feature matching has high accuracy, but it is heavily dependent on the detected environment. The deep learning method based on RGBD camera needs to consider the calculation of z-axis, so the camera cannot be moved in order to prevent the z-axis from changing [2]. The 3D object detection method based on point cloud has high accuracy, but it is difficult to meet the real-time requirements due to its huge amount of calculation and time-consuming [3].

Considering on the above problems, 2D object detection has become our preferred solution [4]. We designed an end-to-end model based on 2D projection to solve the problem of 3D object detection in AR application. In order to enable it to complete the training of 6D pose estimation of the object, we have adjusted the output dimension of the detection model, which can map point coordinates corresponding to the 3D bounding box of the object. In addition, we also use new confidence and loss functions to adjust the output results. Finally, we use efficient perspective-n-point (EPnP) algorithm to solve the 3D object pose information.

In this paper, we first introduce the current mainstream 2D object detection algorithms. Then the 6D pose estimation, EPnP algorithm and our model in 3D object detection system are introduced. Finally, we use 2D re-projection error and ADD error to evaluate and analyze the model, and compare it with other mainstream algorithms. Finally, we achieve faster speed while the accuracy reaches the average level of mainstream algorithms.

## 2  Object Detection Algorithms

Object detection algorithm for 2D image is one of the most popular and most effective fields. In recent years, researchers proposed many novel and intelligent algorithms, which are mostly developed based on deep learning. These methods greatly improve the speed and accuracy of object detection. In this part, we will introduce these mainstream algorithms.

S. Ren et al. [5] proposed faster R-CNN in 2016. Compared with SPPNet [6] and fast R-CNN [7], it uses a Region Proposal Network (RPN) instead of the time-consuming selective search to extract region proposals. The calculation process of faster R-CNN is as follows: First, CNN is used to extract features and obtain feature maps. Then RPN layer is used to obtain region proposals. Finally, softmax classifier and linear regression are used to calculate the category and location of object respectively. It uses the feature map obtained by convolution network and "anchor" boxes to obtain region proposals without other calculations, which is the most prominent contribution of faster R-CNN. Finally, the method achieves a mAP of 69.9% on pascal VOC 2007 [8].

In 2017, K. He et al. [9] Proposed mask R-CNN. It is the extending work of faster R-CNN. They used a ResNet [10] -FPN [11] as the backbone network. In ROI, they proposed ROI align instead of ROI pooling to solve the problem of asymmetry between the feature map and the original image. To classification and regression branches, they also added mask branches for instance segmentation. Mask R-CNN achieves higher performance than the previous algorithms.

In 2018, T. Y. Lin et al. [12] proposed RetinaNet, which mainly solves the problem of class imbalance in network training. This method proposes a new loss function, focal loss, which can make the model pay more attention to difficult samples in the training process. In addition, the backbone network uses ResNet-FPN. After that, it uses two sub networks in each pyramid layer to obtain the category and location of objects. Finally, RetinaNet obtained an AP of 39.1% and an AP50 of 59.1%.

In 2020, M. Tan et al. [13] Proposed EfficientDet, which was a lightweight, multi-scale and high-accuracy object detection network. In this method, EfficientNet [14] is used as the backbone network, and BiFPN layer is used to realize the upper and lower feature fusion to obtain the feature map. Finally, it uses class prediction net and box prediction net to get the category and location of the object. EfficientDet-D7 achieved an AP of 51.0% on the MS COCO [15] dataset, which has 77M parameters and 410B FLOPs.

## 3 Methods

### 3.1 6D Pose Information

The 6D pose information is one of the most important information reflecting the current position of the object [16]. 6D refers to six pieces of information, which are the position and the rotation on x-axis, y-axis and z-axis.

The 6D pose of the camera can be calculated through the transformation matrix of the world coordinate system. The calculation formula is as formula (1).

$$T_c = R_{cw} \times T_w \times t_{cw} \tag{1}$$

where, $T_c$ represents the 3D point under the camera system, $R_{cw}$ represents the rotation matrix from the world system to the camera system, $T_w$ represents the 3D point under the world system, and $t_{cw}$ represents the translation component from the world system to the camera system.

The 6D pose of an object refers to the translation and rotation of the camera coordinate system relative to the world system. The 6D pose of an object can be calculated through the transformation matrix that converts coordinates from the world coordinate system to the camera coordinate system [17]. The calculation formula is as formula (2).

$$T_c = R_{cm} \times T_m \times t_{cm} \tag{2}$$

where, $T_c$ represents the 3D point of the object under the camera coordinate system, $R_{cm}$ represents the rotation matrix from the world coordinate system to the camera coordinate system. $T_m$ represents the 3D point of the object under the world coordinate system, $t_{cm}$ represents the translation component from the world coordinate system to the camera coordinate system. Therefore, when the world system is aligned with the object itself, the 6D pose of the camera is equivalent to the 6D pose of the object.

### 3.2 EPnP Algorithm

As shown in Eq. (3). It is the calculation formula of EPnP algorithm [18]. We just provide more than 4 sets of corresponding point data, and EPnP can calculate $R$, $t$ and $\lambda$.

$$\lambda \begin{bmatrix} u \\ v \\ 1 \end{bmatrix} = K[R|t] \begin{bmatrix} x \\ y \\ z \\ 1 \end{bmatrix} \tag{3}$$

where, $\lambda$ represents the depth information of the object, $[u, v, 1]$ represents the pixel point on the image, $K$ represents the camera internal parameter. $[R|t]$ is the translation matrix and rotation matrix of the required solution, $[x, y, z, 1]$ is the coordinate point of 3D space. As shown in Eq. 4 and Eq. 5, $R$ is a 3x3 matrix and $t$ is a 1x3 matrix.

$$R = \begin{bmatrix} r_{11} & r_{12} & r_{13} \\ r_{21} & r_{22} & r_{23} \\ r_{31} & r_{32} & r_{33} \end{bmatrix} \tag{4}$$

$$t = \begin{bmatrix} t_1 \\ t_2 \\ t_3 \end{bmatrix} \tag{5}$$

### 3.3  3D Object Detection Model

Our model calculation process is shown in Fig. 1. First, input an RGB image into the improved RetinaNet, and predict the center and 8 corner point coordinates that is the projection of 3D object bounding box included on 2D image. Then, match the 2D point coordinates and corresponding 3D point coordinates. The required camera internal parameters are obtained by camera calibration. Finally, the EPnP algorithm is used to establish the mapping relationship from 2D to 3D, and the object pose is output.

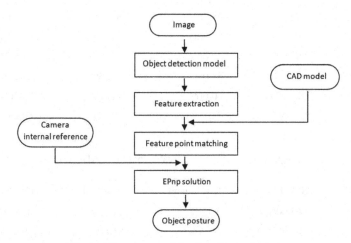

**Fig. 1.** The process of the algorithm calculation

In the object detection model, we changed the output dimension to $S \times S \times (2 \times 9 + 1 + C)$. S represents dividing the original image into $S \times S$ cells, 9 represents the point coordinates of 8 corner points and 1 center point on the 2D image, 1 represents a confidence, and $C$ represents the prediction probability of each category.

## 4  Results

### 4.1  Normal Evaluation

We evaluated the algorithm using 2D re-projection error and ADD error, and compared it with other mainstream algorithms. As shown in Table 1 and Table 2. We show the accuracy on each category of objects. From the 2D re-projection error evaluation, it can be seen that SSD-6D [16], Brachmann [19] and YOLO6D [20] methods have high detection accuracy. This is due to posture refinement. We did not use these additional optimizations or others but still got high accuracy. From the ADD error evaluation, it can be seen that we still obtained a relatively high accuracy without the additional knowledge such as complete 3D model and posture refinement.

**Table 1.** Comparison of test results based on 2D re-projection error

| Model | SSD-6D | Brachmann | YOLO6D | OURS |
|---|---|---|---|---|
| Ape | 76.30% | 85.20% | 92.10% | 93.24% |
| Benchvise | 97.10% | 67.90% | 95.06% | 91.18% |
| Cam | 92.20% | 58.70% | 93.24% | 86.96% |
| Can | 93.10% | 70.80% | 97.44% | 93.80% |
| Cat | 89.30% | 84.20% | 97.41% | 94.31% |
| Driller | 97.80% | 73.90% | 79.41% | 73.44% |
| Duck | 80.00% | 73.10% | 94.65% | 93.80% |
| Eggbox | 93.60% | 83.10% | 90.33% | 83.94% |
| Glue | 76.30% | 74.20% | 96.53% | 94.98% |
| Irco | 98.20% | 83.60% | 82.94% | 83.53% |
| Lamp | 93.00% | 64.00% | 76.86% | 87.10% |
| Phone | 92.40% | 60.60% | 86.07% | 94.20% |
| Average | 88.55% | 73.70% | 90.37% | 89.29% |

**Table 2.** Comparison of test results based on ADD error

| Model | SSD-6D | Brachmann | YOLO6D | OURS |
|---|---|---|---|---|
| Ape | 65.00% | 33.20% | 21.62% | 21.90% |
| Benchvise | 80.00% | 64.90% | 81.80% | 69.48% |
| Cam | 78.00% | 38.40% | 36.57% | 30.49% |
| Can | 86.00% | 62.90% | 68.80% | 65.85% |
| Cat | 70.00% | 42.70% | 63.51% | 37.23% |
| Driller | 73.00% | 61.90% | 41.82% | 62.64% |
| Duck | 66.00% | 30.20% | 27.23% | 23.19% |
| Eggbox | 100.00% | 49.90% | 69.58% | 19.44% |
| Glue | 100.00% | 31.20% | 80.02% | 38.80% |
| Irco | 98.20% | 80.00% | 74.97% | 59.86% |

(*continued*)

**Table 2.** (*continued*)

| Model | SSD-6D | Brachmann | YOLO6D | OURS |
|---|---|---|---|---|
| Lamp | 93.00% | 64.00% | 71.11% | 55.76% |
| Phone | 92.40% | 38.10% | 47.74% | 56.20% |
| Average | 88.55% | 50.20% | 55.95% | 44.61% |

In order to achieve the augmented reality effect. In this work, we put the virtual object into the corresponding position by using the posture information of the object. The augmented reality effect is shown in Fig. 2.

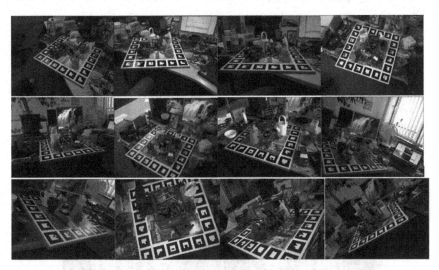

**Fig. 2.** 3D object detection and virtual object rendering renderings

The system renders the virtual model to the real environment by using the posture information output from the object detection model. From the figure, we can see that the virtual model can accurately align with the detection model, which further verifies the accuracy of the system.

### 4.2 Video Stream Based Evaluation

In order to test the object tracking [21] effect of the system on the object, we conducted an experiment under different conditions. Three groups with different conditions were set in the experiment: (1) video stream tracking under normal conditions. (2) video stream tracking under occlusion conditions. (3) video stream tracking under complex background. In this paper, the current object tracking results are recorded randomly in the detection process, and we take the average value as the final result. The experimental results are shown in Table 3.

**Table 3.** Object tracking accuracy results under different conditions

| Group number | Conditions | Accuracy |
|---|---|---|
| (1) | Normal | 90% |
| (2) | Occlusion | 82% |
| (3) | Complex | 86% |

from the above table we can see that the system can maintain high accuracy for the object tracking under three conditions, which proves the robustness and superiority of our system. However, due to the need to complete the rendering of 3D objects in real time, the running speed of the system will decrease with the complexity of the rendering model.

**Fig. 3.** A rendering of real-time object tracking and superimposing virtual object

Figure 3 shows the final effect. We can see that the system can effectively detect and track the objects. The experimental results show that the real-time detection rate of our system can reach about 25FPS, which basically meets the needs of real-time detection.

## 5    Conclusions

In this paper, an AR-oriented object detection and position estimation system is implemented, and we also test it in the tasks of two-dimensional object detection and three-dimensional object detection respectively. The experimental results show that the system has great accuracy and robustness for both detection tasks, and the detection speed basically meets the real-time requirements. However, because there are few 3D models in the LineMod dataset, the generalization of model may be low. In the future, we need to build a large number of 3D model datasets that includes more scenarios to improve the generalization of 3D detection models.

**Acknowledgements.** This research was supported by the Humanities and Social Sciences Fund of the Ministry of Education (No. 19YJC760150).

# References

1. Qian, R., Lai, X., Li, X.: 3D Object Detection for Autonomous Driving: A Survey (2021)
2. Zhou, T., Fan, D.P., Cheng, M.M., et al.: RGB-D salient object detection: A survey (2021)
3. Guo, Y., Wang, H., Hu, Q., et al.: Deep learning for 3D point clouds: a survey. IEEE Trans. Pattern Analysis Machine Intelligence **43**(12), 4338-4364 (2020)
4. Zou, Z., Shi, Z., Guo, Y., Ye, J.: Object Detection in 20 Years: A Survey. IEEE TPAMI (2019)
5. Ren, S., He, K., Girshick, R., Sun, J.: Faster R-CNN: towards real-time object detection with region proposal networks. IEEE Trans. Pattern Anal. Mach. Intell. **39**(6), 1137–1149 (2017)
6. He, K., Zhang, X., Ren, S., Sun, J.: Spatial pyramid pooling in deep convolutional networks for visual recognition. IEEE Trans. Pattern Anal. Mach. Intell. **37**(9), 1904–1916 (2015)
7. Girshick, R.: Fast R-CNN. In: 2015 IEEE International Conference on Computer Vision (ICCV), pp. 1440–1448 (2015)
8. Everingham, M., Gool, L., Williams, C.K., Winn, J., Zisserman, A.: The PASCAL Visual Object Classes Challenge, VOC 2007 Results (2007)
9. He, K., Gkioxari, G., Dollár, P., Girshick, R.: Mask R-CNN. In: 2017 IEEE International Conference on Computer Vision (ICCV), pp. 2980–2988 (2017)
10. He, K., Zhang, X., Ren, S., Sun, J.: Deep residual learning for image recognition. In: 2016 IEEE Conference on Computer Vision and Pattern Recognition (CVPR), pp. 770–778 (2016)
11. Lin, T.Y., Dollár, P., Girshick, R., He, K., Hariharan, B., Belongie, S.: Feature pyramid networks for object detection. In: 2017 IEEE Conference on Computer Vision and Pattern Recognition (CVPR), pp. 936–944 (2017)
12. Lin, T.Y., Goyal, P., Girshick, R., He, K., Dollár, P.: Focal loss for dense object detection. In: 2017 IEEE International Conference on Computer Vision (ICCV), pp. 2999–3007 (2017)
13. Tan, M., Pang, R., Le, Q.V.: EfficientDet: scalable and efficient object detection. In: 2020 IEEE/CVF Conference on Computer Vision and Pattern Recognition (CVPR), pp. 10778–10787 (2020)
14. Tan, M., Le, Q.V.: EfficientNet: Rethinking Model Scaling for Convolutional Neural Networks. arXiv preprint, arXiv:1905.11946v5 (2020)
15. Lin, T.-Y., et al.: Microsoft COCO: common objects in context. In: Fleet, D., Pajdla, T., Schiele, B., Tuytelaars, T. (eds.) ECCV 2014. LNCS, vol. 8693, pp. 740–755. Springer, Cham (2014). https://doi.org/10.1007/978-3-319-10602-1_48
16. Kehl, W., Manhardt, F., Tombari, F., Ilic, S., Navab, N.: SSD-6D: Making RGB-based 3D detection and 6D pose estimation great again. In: 2017 IEEE International Conference on Computer Vision (ICCV), pp. 1530–1538 (2017)
17. Chen, J., Zhang, L., Liu, Y., et al.: Survey on 6D pose estimation of rigid object. In: 39th Chinese Control Conference (2020)
18. Lepetit, V., Moreno-Noguer, F., Fua, P.: EPnP: an accurate O(n) solution to the PnP problem. Int. J. Comput. Vision **81**(2), 155–166 (2009)

19. Brachmann, E., Krull, A., Michel, F., Gumhold, S., Shotton, J., Rother, C.: Learning 6D object pose estimation using 3D object coordinates. In: Fleet, D., Pajdla, T., Schiele, B., Tuytelaars, T. (eds.) ECCV 2014. LNCS, vol. 8690, pp. 536–551. Springer, Cham (2014). https://doi.org/10.1007/978-3-319-10605-2_35

20. Tekin, B., Sinha, S.N., Fua, P.: Real-time seamless single shot 6D object pose prediction. In: 2018 IEEE/CVF Conference on Computer Vision and Pattern Recognition, pp. 292–301 (2018)

21. Yilmaz, A., Javed, O., Shah, M.: Object tracking: a survey. ACM Comput. Surv. 38(4), 13 (2006)

22. Lu, H., Zhang, M., Xu, X.: Deep fuzzy hashing network for efficient image retrieval. IEEE Trans. Fuzzy Systems 29(1), 166176 (2020). https://doi.org/10.1109/TFUZZ.2020.2984991

23. Huimin, L., Li, Y., Chen, M., et al.: Brain intelligence: go beyond artificial intelligence. Mobile Networks Appl. 23, 368–375 (2018)

24. Huimin, L., Li, Y., Shenglin, M., et al.: Motor anomaly detection for unmanned aerial vehicles using reinforcement learning. IEEE Internet Things J. 5(4), 2315–2322 (2018)

25. Huimin, L., Qin, M., Zhang, F., et al.: RSCNN: A CNN-based method to enhance low-light remote-sensing images. Remote Sensing 13(1), 62 (2020)

26. Huimin, L., Zhang, Y., Li, Y., et al.: User-oriented virtual mobile network resource management for vehicle communications. IEEE Trans. Intell. Transp. Syst. 22(6), 3521–3532 (2021)

# Learning Visual Tempo for Action Recognition

Mu Nie[1], Sen Yang[2], and Wankou Yang[2(✉)]

[1] School of Cyber Science and Engineering, Southeast University, Nanjing 210096, China
[2] School of Automation, Southeast University, Nanjing 210096, China
wkyang@seu.edu.cn

**Abstract.** The variation of visual tempo, which is an essential feature in action recognition, characterizes the spatiotemporal scale of the action and the dynamics. Existing models usually use spatiotemporal convolution to understand spatiotemporal scenarios. However, they cannot cope with the difference in the visual tempo changes, due to the limited view of temporal and spatial dimensions. To address these issues, we propose a multi-receptive field spatiotemporal (MRF-ST) network in this paper, to effectively model the spatial and temporal information. We utilize dilated convolutions to obtain different receptive fields and design dynamic weighting with different dilation rates based on the attention mechanism. In the proposed network, the MRF-ST network can directly obtain various tempos in the same network layer without any additional learning cost. Moreover, the network can improve the accuracy of action recognition by learning more visual tempo of different actions. Extensive evaluations show that MRF-ST reaches the state-of-the-art on the UCF-101 and HMDB-51 datasets. Further analysis also indicates that MRF-ST can significantly improve the performance at the scenes with large variances in visual tempo.

**Keywords:** Action recognition · Spatiotemporal · Multi-receptive field · Visual tempo

## 1 Introduction

Video is the lifeblood of the internet, which means analyzing and understanding video content is critical for the most modern artificial intelligence agents [1, 2]. Deep neural networks play an important role in many aspects [3, 4]. Although the accuracy of video action recognition has been greatly improved [5, 6], in the design of these recognition networks, an important aspect that characterizes different actions - the visual tempo of action instances is often overlooked. Unfortunately, existing models [7, 8] mainly focus on using spatiotemporal factorization to reduce computational cost and model parameters.

Visual tempo actually describes the speed at which an action is performed, which often determines the effective temporal of recognition. Therefore, we need to consider the differences in the temporal and spatial feature of action instances, when designing an action recognition network. For example, walking action is slower than running class in temporal and spatial change frequency. Action tempo not only exists inter-class actions, but also has significant differences in the intra-class. In Fig. 1, we show examples of the video clips and coefficients of variations from the HMDB-51 dataset.

© The Author(s), under exclusive license to Springer Nature Singapore Pte Ltd. 2022
S. Yang and H. Lu (Eds.): ISAIR 2022, CCIS 1700, pp. 139–155, 2022.
https://doi.org/10.1007/978-981-19-7946-0_13

(a) Riding bike on a fast-variation

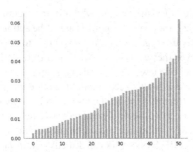

(b) Riding bike on a slow-variation

(c) Coefficient of variation of action classes in the hmdl51

**Fig. 1.** Examples from the HMDB-51 dataset. The subfigures (a) and (b) show that videos tend to vary at different spatiotemporal rates for the same action (ride bike). The subfigure (c) shows the coefficients of variation of each class in the HMDB-51 dataset.

As shown in Fig. 1, the speed of riding bike in Fig. 1 (a) is faster than that in Fig. 1 (b). The action of riding a bicycle is very subtle in Fig. 1 (b), and the change on the temporal scale is very small. Note that conspicuous differences can be seen in the changes in the temporal feature. Simultaneously, the visual appearance changes in Fig. 1 (a) are also at a different rate from those in Fig. 1 (b) because of the different positions of the cameras. There are also a great number of different visual tempos variations in reality or the action recognition datasets. Figure 1 (c) show that the coefficient of variation is significant different for inter-class. For example, the fall floor has the giant view variance in the spatial-temporal frequency of the instances, while the sit-up has the smallest. We introduce the details of the coefficient of variation in Sect. 4.5 of the paper. We show that it can be exploited to improve accuracy significantly for action recognition.

Current representative models, such as R(2 + 1)D [9] and GST [10], usually decompose 3D convolutions into temporal and spatial convolutions and stack them. Although, as the number of layers increases, so does their receptive field. However, adapting to different rhythms in a single model is challenging. These models struggle to cope with the identification challenges posed by various frequency variations inter-classes and intra-classes. On the other hand, redundant model parameters inevitably lead to difficulties in model training and computational burden. To extract the multi-scales feature of action instances, previous works [11–13] mainly rely on constructing a frame pyramid for the visual tempo. These methods obtain different spatial scales through splicing the feature of different layers of the backbone network. Other methods [14, 15] obtain different temporal scales by sampling the input frames from different stride. However, they due to need to use additional models to experience variation at different visual tempos. As can be seen, the development of action recognition remains an ongoing challenge due to strict requirements for learning dynamic features of visual tempos that need a model with good perform and low cost.

In this paper, we introduce a novel and concise Multi-Receptive Field SpatioTemporal (MRF-ST) network to tackle the problem above. Similar to the decomposition convolution, we first divide the 3D convolution into temporal convolution and spatial convolution, and then implement them by two dilated convolutions [16] with different dilation rates. We realize a two-path unit Multi-Receptive Field Temporal (MRF-T) and Multi-Receptive Field Spatial (MRF-S), both of which achieve various visual tempos at the same unit. Our MRF-ST network can fuse different receptive fields for the spatiotemporal feature on the same layer without extra parts. Our major contributions can be summarized as follows:

- Firstly, we propose a new 3D convolution decomposition method, Based on our exploration of visual tempo, that can effectively model the spatial and temporal information of different receptive fields.
- Next, we can capture different visual rhythm features and model their relationships from the proposed MRF-ST network using multiple receptive fields. To the best of our knowledge, this is the first action recognition unit that simultaneously fusions different visual tempo features in the same layer of the network. In this way, dynamic characteristics can be captured more robustly.
- Then, the method utilizes an attention mechanism to assign different weights according to different contributions of different receptive fields. This allows for a more efficient adaptation to different visual tempos.
- Lastly, we evaluate MRF-ST on two action benchmarks (HMDB-51 [17] and UCF-101 [18]). Experimental results show that MRF-ST significantly improves performance. We further analyze the contribution of MRF-ST to learning visual tempos and it achieves stellar performance on several datasets with much less parameters.

The rest of this paper is organized as follows. We introduce related work progress and our advantages in Sect. 2. In Sect. 3, we detail the MRF-ST network. We perform experiments and analysis of our model in Sect. 4. The summary and outlook of this paper are in Sect. 5.

## 2 Related Work

In this section, we introduce the related work of action recognition in the era of deep learning networks. In particular, we discuss the work related to visual tempo in the final.

### 2.1 Deep Learning in Action Recognition

The related work can be divided into two categories for video action recognition. Methods in the first category often adopt a 2D + 1D paradigm, where 2D CNNs are applied over per-frame inputs, followed by a 1D module that aggregates per-frame features. Temporal relational networks [19, 20] explored the temporal relation between learning and reasoning video frames. In particular, moving features along the temporal dimension, the method [21] only maintains the complexity of 2D CNN while achieving the performance of 3D CNN without optical flow. [22, 23] explored different fusion models for action recognition. [24, 25] studied the sequential models based on RNN and LSTM for video. For 2D CNNs deployed in these methods, the semantics of input frames cannot interact with each other early on, which limits their ability to capture visual rhythmic dynamics.

Methods [10] in the second category alternatively apply 3D CNNs that stack 3D convolutions to jointly model temporal and spatial semantics. To capture the spatiotemporal information from multiple adjacent frames, a 3D convolutional kernel [26, 27] is mainly utilized in several deep neural networks instead of a two-dimensional (2D) convolutional one. However, 3D convolution brings more parameters than 2D, making it difficult to train and requiring more hardware resources. The heavy calculation requirement and the great number of parameters are still two burdens for 3D CNN development. CoST [28] learns spatial appearance and temporal motion information using 2D convolution with weight sharing to capture three orthogonal views from video data. [29] captures spatiotemporal information from both snippet-level and long-term context by using the dilated dense blocks. [30] can obtain semantic relevance in spatial and channel dimensions through two types of attention modules. In the channel module, the attention mechanism emphasizes interdependent channel characteristics by integrating the correlation characteristics among all channel maps. And the spatial module does weighted fusion at all positions, selectively aggregating the features of each position. GST [10] employs two groups to pay attention to static and dynamic feature prompts by decomposing 3D convolution into spatial and temporal convolution in parallel.

Nevertheless, it may be not able to understand the temporal and spatial dynamics of the video. Our proposed model is also inspired by the above ideas, which can effectively utilize the most active context from a broader 3D perspective. Our model can collaboratively learn the key spatiotemporal representations of different visual rhythms by fusing two different reception fields in this paper.

## 2.2 Visual Tempo in Action Recognition

Understanding action semantics and temporal information is a difficult task in action recognition, especially in the variety of visual rhythms. Recently, many researchers concentrate on solving this problem [14, 31]. [11] handles multi-rate videos by randomizing the sampling rate during training. DTPN [12] also samples frames with different frames per second to construct a natural pyramidal representation for arbitrary-length input videos. In SlowFast [14], an input-level frame pyramid structure is established to encode changes in visual rhythm, which is fast and slow networks by inputting video frames sampled at different rates. The slow network tends to capture the slow rhythm while the fast network tends to capture the fast rhythm. The different rhythm features of the two networks are fusion through lateral connections. With the frame pyramid and information fusion, SlowFast can robustly capture changes in visual rhythm. S-TPNet [15] and TPN [32] take full advantage of the temporal pyramid module. They reuse the video features and exploit various spatial scale and temporal scale pooling approaches to efficiently obtain different spatial-grained and temporal-grained features. CIDC [33] can encode the temporal sequence information of actions into the feature maps to learn the temporal association among local features in a temporal direction fashion by introducing a directional convolution unit independent of the channel.

However, this coding scheme often extracts multiple frames or multiple middle layer features, especially when we need a large pyramid scale. Note that we could deal with the concerns about visual speed in a single network. Thus, we only need to sample frames at a single rate at the input level and deal with changes in the visual tempo at the feature level using multiple receptive fields to capture different rhythms.

## 3  Proposed Model

In this section, we implement a baseline by the conventional 3D convolution architectures. Then we introduce the proposed MRF-ST and discuss the differences between different networks. The MRF-ST networks can be described as a spatiotemporal architecture that operates at two various receptive fields to capture visual tempos changes. Our generic architecture has MRF-T and MRF-S units (Sec. 3.2). We use the attention mechanism to capture the contributions of different receptive field modules (Sec. 3.3). Finally, complete network architecture and some discussions are given (Sec. 3.4).

### 3.1  3D ConvNets in Action Recognition

To verify our ideas, we implement 3D ResNet50 network as a baseline model. The video clip sampled from a 64-frame with a temporal stride of 4 as input. For a general 3D convolutional kernel with $C_i$ input channels and $C_o$ output channels, T, H, W are the kernel sizes along the temporal and spatial dimensions. As shown in Table 1, we decompose the 3D convolution kernel into the temporal and spatial kernel with the sizes of $w_t \in \mathbb{R}^{C_0 \times C_i \times T \times 1 \times 1}$ and $w_s \in \mathbb{R}^{C_0 \times C_i \times 1 \times H \times W}$. It is worth noting that the instead model learns temporal and spatial features, rather than jointly.

### 3.2  Multi-receptive Field Unit

There are very helpful that learning the spatiotemporal features of different visual tempos and performing good fusion for video recognition. A good strategy should preserve the spatial and temporal information to the greatest extent and capture the interaction between features of different visual tempos. Unlike the idea of constructing two input frames with two sampling rates in the SlowFast model, we use another method to use the group convolution to integrate the temporal or spatial convolution into two parts, and then use different dilation rates to achieve the effect of learning different visual tempos information.

As shown in Fig. 2, for the temporal convolution of $w_t \in \mathbb{R}^{C_{0n} \times C_{in} \times T \times 1 \times 1}$, we split it into two dilated convolutions with different dilation rates, and similar operations are also applied to the spatial convolution. We can get MRF-T and MRF-S units, with the convolution sizes of $w_t \in \mathbb{R}^{C_{0m} \times C_{im} \times T \times 1 \times 1}$ and $w_s \in \mathbb{R}^{C_{0m} \times C_{im} \times 1 \times H \times W}$. Among them,

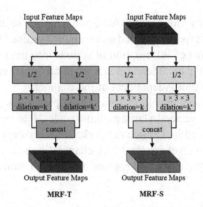

**Fig. 2.** Our proposed method for MFT and MFS.

**Table 1.** The 3D ResNet50 configuration.

| Stage | Layer | Output size |
|---|---|---|
| conv1 | $1 \times 7 \times 7$, 64, stride $1 \times 2 \times 2$ | $16 \times 112 \times 112$ |
| pool1 | $1 \times 3 \times 3$ max, stride $1 \times 2 \times 2$ | $16 \times 112 \times 112$ |
| res2 | $\begin{bmatrix} 3 \times 1^2, 64 \\ 1 \times 3^2, 64 \\ 1 \times 1^2, 256 \end{bmatrix} \times 3$ | $16 \times 56 \times 56$ |
| res3 | $\begin{bmatrix} 3 \times 1^2, 128 \\ 1 \times 3^2, 128 \\ 1 \times 1^2, 512 \end{bmatrix} \times 4$ | $16 \times 28 \times 28$ |
| res4 | $\begin{bmatrix} 3 \times 1^2, 256 \\ 1 \times 3^2, 256 \\ 1 \times 1^2, 1024 \end{bmatrix} \times 6$ | $16 \times 14 \times 14$ |
| res5 | $\begin{bmatrix} 3 \times 1^2, 512 \\ 1 \times 3^2, 512 \\ 1 \times 1^2, 2048 \end{bmatrix} \times 3$ | $16 \times 7 \times 7$ |
| global average pool, FC | | $1 \times 1 \times 1$ |

$C_{0m} = C_{0n}/2$ and $C_{im} = C_{in}/2$, in other words, $m$ is half of $n$. Take MRF-T as an example. Formally, we can formulate MRF-T as:

$$X^t = \left( x_1^t, x_2^t, \ldots x_m^t, x_{m+1}^t, \ldots x_n^t \right) \tag{1}$$

$$w_t = (w_1^t, w_2^t, \ldots, w_m^t) \tag{2}$$

We denote the feature maps as $X^t$ in the input temporal convolution, where $n = T \times H \times W$. We divide $X^t$ along the channel into $X_1^t$ and $X_2^t$.

Formally, we can formulate MRF-T as:

$$\theta_1^t(X_1^t) = X_1^t \otimes \cdot w_t \tag{3}$$

$$\theta_2^t(X_2^t) = X_2^t \otimes \cdot w_t \tag{4}$$

$$y^t = \theta_1^t(X_1^t) \oplus \theta_2^t(X_2^t) \tag{5}$$

where $\otimes$ denotes 3D convolution, $w_t$ is temporal convolution filters shared among the two dilation rates. The $\theta_1^t(X_1^t)$ and $\theta_2^t(X_2^t)$ are the result of convolution, and then concatenate them to get $y^t$.

Similarly, the above formula is the operation in the temporal convolution of MRF-T, and the spatial convolution in MRF-S is also the same.

$$y^s = \theta_1^s(X_1^s) \oplus \theta_2^s(X_2^s) \tag{6}$$

MRF-T and MRF-S can encourage each group's channels to focus on the dynamic features of different rates convenient for training. MRF-TS can thus combine various tempos features naturally. Then, the $w_m$ is the number of parameters for multi-receptive field spatiotemporal unit, we reduce the number of parameters by reducing the input channels $C_{im}$ and output channels $C_{om}$.

$$w_m = (H \cdot W + T) \cdot C_{im} \cdot C_{om} \tag{7}$$

### 3.3 Attention for the Multi-receptive Field Unit

To make the model more suitable for learning spatiotemporal features of visual tempo changes, we design dynamic weighting for different dilation rates, which a parameter $\alpha$. Since the convolution of different receptive fields contributes differently to learning, we predict $\alpha$ according to the network's feature map. The attention method [45] inspired us to make the attention unit. For MRF-T, we can use the formula:

$$y_a^t = \alpha_1 \theta_1^t(X_1^t) \oplus \alpha_2 \theta_2^t(X_2^t) \tag{8}$$

$\theta_1^t(X_1^t)$ and $\theta_2^t(X_2^t)$ are the result of temporal convolution with different dilation rates. $\alpha_1$ and $\alpha_2$ are the weights calculated by the attention module, which is shown in Fig. 3.

Specifically, we divide the input feature map into $X_1^t$ and $X_2^t$ along the channel, and then send them into two temporal convolutions with different dilation rates to get $\theta_1^t(X_1^t)$ and $\theta_2^t(X_2^t)$, which are concatenated to get $y^t$. The above process is consistent with the MRF-T described in Sect. 3.2. The difference is that we evaluated the contribution of $X_1^t$ and $X_2^t$ through attention operations. As shown in Fig. 3, we first use the adaptive

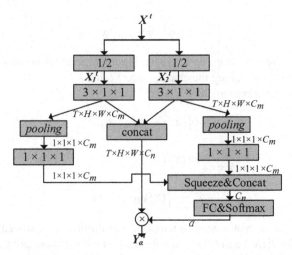

**Fig. 3.** Attention for the multi-receptive field unit

max pooling to reduce the feature map to $1 \times 1 \times 1 \times C_m$, along the dimensions $T$, $H$, and $W$. The pooled features are input into the $1 \times 1 \times 1$ convolution to capture the channels' context information. Then, the features of two sets obtained in the previous step are concatenated and fed into a fully connected layer. This FC layer can capture the contextual information among different visual tempos. Then, we use the Softmax function to normalize the output to get $\alpha$. Finally, $\alpha$ multiply the corresponding $y^t$ introduced above, and the final process is formally expressed as Eq. (8). In the model, the weight coefficient of each feature depends on itself.

### 3.4 Network Architecture

Here we introduce the network architecture of MRF-ST for action recognition. To better study the different receptive field of visual tempo, we have proposed the following structure.

The proposed MRF-ST unit is flexible and can easily replace the convolution modules in most current networks. As shown in Fig. 4, we put the proposed units on the backbone network composed of 3D ResNet50. In our architecture, we enter 16 video clips into the network to obtain the final classification result.

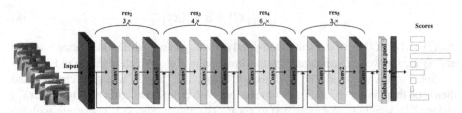

**Fig. 4.** The architecture of a multi-receptive field spatiotemporal network. We build it based on 3D ResNet50.

To verify the temporal and spatial effect, we design different models, as shown in Fig. 4. Compared with 3D ResNet50, we replace the temporal convolution and spatial convolution with MRF-T and MRF-S, respectively. First, we apply a separate spatial-temporal unit for baseline, which consists of three layers i.e., a 3 temporal convolution layer, a $3 \times 1 \times 1$ temporal convolution, a $1 \times 3 \times 3$ spatial convolution, and a $1 \times 1 \times 1$ convolution layer, namely Conv1, Conv2 and Conv3. Then, we just replace Conv1 with MRF-T, in order to demonstrate the effect of fusion of multiple receptive fields in the temporal dimension. Similarly, we replace Conv2 with MRF-S, to fuse multiple receptive fields in spatial dimension. Finally, we consider the combined impact of two factors and replace both Conv1 and Conv2. These are four units with comparison, and we conduct ablation study on them in Sect. 4.3.

# 4 Experiment

To evaluate the performance of the proposed MRF-ST network on visual tempo feature learning and action recognition tasks, we conduct experiments and ablation studies on two wild datasets, UCF-101[17] and HMDB-51[18]. In this section, we introduce the implementation details of the experiments involved in this paper. We discuss the effectiveness of each component and the correctness of the visual tempo learning concept.

## 4.1 Datasets

UCF-101 and HMDB-51 have been very popular in research, which are challenging benchmarks for action recognition. Table 2 lists the general information of the datasets we used.

**Table 2.** Details of the datasets used for evaluation. The Clips show the total number of short video clips extracted from the Videos available in the dataset..

| dataset | # Clips | # Videos | # Classes |
|---------|---------|----------|-----------|
| UCF-101 | 13320 | 2500 | 101 |
| HMDB-51 | 6766 | 3312 | 51 |
| Kinetics400 | 306,245 | 306,245 | 400 |

There are 2500 videos and 13320 clips with 101 classes from YouTube in the UCF-101. The short clips are extracted from the videos available. In this dataset, 25 people are performing each behavior, and each of them performs multiple operations. The UCF-101 datset offers the greatest diversity in action, with large variations in camera motion, object appearance and pose, object scale, viewpoint, cluttered backgrounds, lighting conditions, and more.

The HMDB-51 with 51 different categories is mainly collected from movies. There are 3312 videos and 6766 clips, which contain a lot of facial actions and object interaction. We can divide HMDB-51 into five action categories: Common facial actions, Complex facial movements, Common body movements, Complex body movements, and Multi-person interactive body movements.

They all have three training and testing splits for action recognition. Unless otherwise stated, our final result is the average of these splits. Our models are pre-trained on a large dataset kinetics400 [34], which contains 236763 training videos and 19095 validation videos.

### 4.2  Implementation Detail

In our model, we sample 64 consecutive frames from the clip and then take one every three frames to get 16 frames as input. During the inference time, we do the random crop for each frame. We use PyTorch to implement our networks, which train on the TITAN Xp GPU machine. We train the models using the CrossEntropyLoss function and the SGD optimizer. Meanwhile, we set the momentum to 0.9, the weight decay to 0.0001, and the minimum batch size to 16. We train 80 epochs to optimize all models. The learning rate is initialized to 0.01 and reduced by a factor of 10 every 30 epochs. The total training epochs are about 80.

### 4.3  Comparisons with the State-Of-The-Arts

**Table 3.** Top-1 accuracy performance on UCF-101 and HMDB-51 compared with state-of-the-art methods. All accuracies are averaged over three splits.

| Method | UCF-101 | HMDB-51 |
|---|---|---|
| C3D [27] | 82.3 | 51.6 |
| C3D + IDT[27] | 90.4 | - |
| P3D [35] | 88.6 | - |
| STC-ResNet 101[36] | 93.7 | 66.8 |
| 3D ResNeXt-101[37] | 94.5 | 70.2 |
| I3D RGB [38] | 95.1 | 74.3 |
| MiCT-Net [39] | 88.9 | 63.8 |
| MiCT-Net two-stream[39] | 94.7 | 70.5 |
| Two-stream ConvNet[40] | 88.0 | 59.4 |
| Two-Stream Fusion [41] | 92.5 | 65.4 |
| TSN [42] | 94.9 | 71.0 |
| TSM[43] | 94.5 | 70.7 |
| STM[44] | 96.2 | 72.2 |
| Our MRF-ST | 96.3 | 73.1 |

We evaluate the Top-1 accuracy of our MRF-ST module embedded in the 3D ResNet-50 network against state-of-the-art methods. As Table 3 shows, our method approaches the best performance compared with the state-of-the-art methods using only RGB, such as 3D methods [27, 38] and temporal shift methods [43, 44]. And it is also close to the results of using optical flow, such as Two-stream based methods [40, 41].

We can infer from the table that the use of optical flow information can effectively improve the competitiveness of the model. However, optical flow needs to be pre-calculated and stored on the hard disk, which requires a lot of costs. There is also not conducive to the application and migration of the model. Our model is easy to replace by the 3d convolution model to achieve a competitive effect without additional cost. Table 4 lists the Top-1 and TOP-5 accuracies. MRF-ST can achieve fine performance results in different split situations, which shows that our model has not lost its robustness due to the addition of the multi-receptive field module.

**Table 4.** Top-1 and TOP-5 accuracy on different splits of UCF-101 and HMDB-51

| split | UCF-101 | | HMDB-51 | |
|---|---|---|---|---|
| | Top-1 acc | Top-5 acc | Top-1 acc | Top-5 acc |
| 1 | 96.51 | 99.86 | 73.73 | 93.46 |
| 2 | 96.63 | 99.57 | 73.59 | 93.86 |
| 3 | 96.02 | 99.59 | 72.09 | 91.31 |

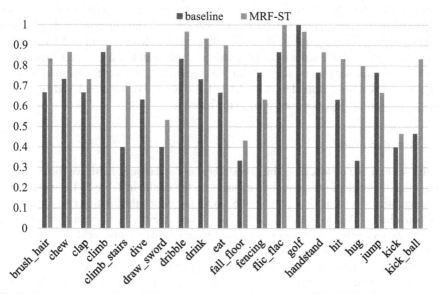

**Fig. 5.** Accuracy comparisons for the top-20 classes on the split1 of HMDB-51 dataset between MRF-ST (Ours) and the baseline (3D ResNet-50) model

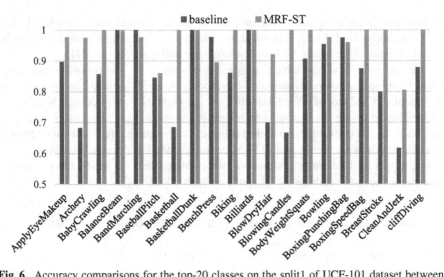

**Fig. 6.** Accuracy comparisons for the top-20 classes on the split1 of UCF-101 dataset between MRF-ST (Ours) and the baseline (3D ResNet-50) model

To further investigate the performance over different actions, Fig. 5 and 6 show the comparison between our model (MRF-ST) and the baseline (ResNet-50) for different categories of HMDB-51 and UCF-101 datasets. Figure 5 shows the top 20 classes' accuracy from HMDB-51, where our model outperforms the original model. For some classes with fast visual tempo variations such as *Kick_ball* and *Dive*, our model obtains a significant performance gain (36.7% and 23.3%) over the ResNet-50 model. Our method faithfully captures the visual tempo information in both spatial and temporal dimensions. A similar conclusion can be found from Fig. 6, which demonstrates the performance improvements using our model on the UCF-101 dataset. We have achieved significant progress in most categories compared to the baseline.

### 4.4 Ablation Study

In this section, we conduct the ablation studies on the datasets. First, we further investigate the influence of receptive field changes on the model in Table 5. T represents the dilation rate for the temporal convolution, and S represents the dilation rate for the spatial convolution. We study that add different dilation rates to the original convolution to change the receptive field. However, we find that a single receptive field change, which, only replace with dilation convolution, cannot improve the effect or be negative. In the deep network, convolutional of different depths implicitly learn different receptive field information. At the same time, we need to perform the padding operation, when using the dilated convolution. But if the dilation rate is set too large, a lot of information will be lost. And then, we study the different units proposed in Sect. 3.2 for our action recognition model. As shown in Table 5, we improve the effect compared to the baseline by MRF-T or MRF-S units, but the effect did not increase as the dilation rate increased. Not listed in the table, when we use more dilated convolutions (more than two) to get worse experimental results in spatial or temporal convolution. This consequence shows that the network has different receptive field fusions that can better fit the feature of visual tempos changes. However, the model will lose some feature information because the dilation rate is too large. In summary, we set the dilation rate to 1 and 2 in the MRF-T and MRF-S units.

**Table 5.** Top-1 accuracy performance on UCF-101 and HMDB-51 split1 compared with different dila-tion rates.

| Model | Dilation rate | UCF-101 | HMDB-51 |
|-------|---------------|---------|---------|
|       |               | Top-1 acc | Top-1 acc |
| baseline | $T = 1, S = 1$ | 88.9 | 66.5 |
| baseline | $T = 2, S = 1$ | 88.3 | 65.9 |
| baseline | $T = 3, S = 1$ | 87.5 | 63.9 |
| baseline | $T = 1, S = 2$ | 88.8 | 64.5 |
| baseline | $T = 1, S = 3$ | 88.6 | 64.3 |
| MRF-T | $T = (1,2), S = 1$ | 92.5 | 70.5 |
| MRF-T | $T = (2,3), S = 1$ | 91.6 | 68.9 |
| MRF-S | $T = 1, S = (1,2)$ | 91.8 | 68.6 |
| MRF-S | $T = 1, S = (2,3)$ | 90.3 | 67.4 |

We show the parameters and accuracy of different models in Table 6. Their structure is shown in Fig. 4 above, but the attention module is implied. Our model has improved compared with baseline, and the parameters have been significantly reduced. For example, comparing MRF-ST with baseline, we reduce the number of parameters by 12.2 $\times 10^6$. Meanwhile, we improve the accuracy of top-1 and top-5 by 7.6% and 2.86% in UCF-101. And with more attractive results in HMDB-51, we improve by 7.19% and 5.36%. This result fully shows that our model has better results with fewer parameters.

**Table 6.** The parameters and accuracy of different models are compared on split1 of UCF-101 and HMDB-51.

| Model | Param $\times 10^6$ | UCF-101 | | HMDB-51 | |
|-------|---------------------|---------|---------|---------|---------|
|       |                     | Top-1 acc | Top-5 acc | Top-1 acc | Top-5 acc |
| baseline | 32.4 | 88.91 | 97.00 | 66.54 | 88.10 |
| MRF-S | 26.7 | 93.16 | 99.18 | 70.26 | 91.57 |
| MRF-T | 23.7 | 94.13 | 99.49 | 71.37 | 92.16 |
| MRF-ST | 20.2 | 96.51 | 99.86 | 73.73 | 93.46 |

### 4.5 Empirical Analysis

To verify whether MRF-ST has captured the variance of visual tempos, we used the parameter α to conduct some experimental analysis. We measure the coefficient of variation of the action instance to distinguish the visual tempos of the action instance accurately. Specifically, we calculate the cosine acquaintance of adjacent frames of the video to characterize the difference in video motion pixel level. Then we use the coefficient of variation to measure the difference in cosine similarity changes inter-classes and intra-classes. The coefficient of variation can well reflect the visual tempo. However, the model-based method, which measures the probability change of action category to express the visual tempo, will be greatly affected by its measure model of bias. Accuracy comparisons for the top-20 classes of variation coefficients, as shown in Fig. 7. Comparing with the results shown in Fig. 5, the MRF-ST model can achieve better results in categories with fast changes, which shows that our model can effectively model visual tempo.

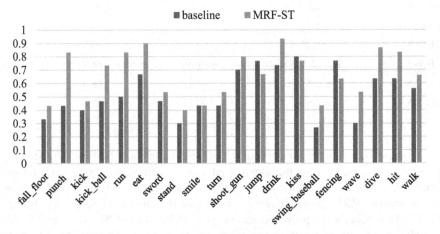

**Fig. 7.** Accuracy comparisons for the top-20 classes of variation coefficients on the split1 of HMDB-51 dataset between MRF-ST (Ours) and the baseline (3D ResNet50) model.

## 5   Conclusion

Feature learning from visual tempo variation is the unneglectable challenge in video action recognition. We propose a novel spatiotemporal feature learning operation, which learns visual tempos fusion from multiple receptive fields. Although we do not have a deeper model to achieve the best results, we verified learning visual tempos is essential. Experiments on the datasets illustrate the availability of the proposed architecture and the easiness of learning visual tempo variation features for action recognition. We hope that these explorations will inspire more video recognition to design models.

# References

1. Kang, S., Wu, H., Yang, X., et al.: Discrete-time predictive sliding mode control for a constrained parallel micropositioning piezostage. IEEE Trans. Systems, Man, Cybernetics: Systems **52**(5), 3025–3036 (2021)
2. Zheng, Q., Zhu, J., Tang, H., et al.: Generalized label enhancement with sample correlations. IEEE Trans. Knowledge Data Eng. (2021)
3. Lu, H., Zhang, Y., Li, Y., et al.: User-oriented virtual mobile network resource management for vehicle communications. IEEE Trans. Intell. Transp. Syst. **22**(6), 3521–3532 (2020)
4. Lu, H., Zhang, M., Xu, X., et al.: Deep fuzzy hashing network for efficient image retrieval. IEEE Trans. Fuzzy Syst. **29**(1), 166–176 (2020)
5. Jin, X., Sun, W., Jin, Z.: A discriminative deep association learning for facial expression recognition. Int. J. Mach. Learn. Cybern. **11**(4), 779–793 (2020)
6. Zhuang, D., Jiang, M., Kong, J., et al.: Spatiotemporal attention enhanced features fusion network for action recognition. Int. J. Mach. Learn. Cybern. **12**(3), 823–841 (2021)
7. Ziaeefard, M., Bergevin, R.: Semantic human activity recognition: a literature review. Pattern Recogn. **48**(8), 2329–2345 (2015)
8. Chen, L., Song, Z., Lu, J., et al.: Learning principal orientations and residual descriptor for action recognition. Pattern Recogn. **86**, 14–26 (2019)
9. Tran, D., Wang, H., Torresani, L., et al.: A closer look at spatiotemporal convolutions for action recognition. In: Proceedings of the IEEE Conference on Computer Vision and Pattern Recognition, pp. 6450–6459 (2018)
10. Luo, C., Yuille, A.L.: Grouped spatial-temporal aggregation for efficient action recognition. In: Proceedings of the IEEE/CVF International Conference on Computer Vision, pp. 5512–5521 (2019)
11. Zhu, Y., Newsam, S.: Random temporal skipping for multirate video analysis. In: Asian Conference on Computer Vision. Springer, Cham, pp. 542–557 (2018). https://doi.org/10.1007/978-3-030-20893-6_34
12. Zhang, D., Dai, X., Wang, Y.F.: Dynamic temporal pyramid network: A closer look at multi-scale modeling for activity detection. In: Asian Conference on Computer Vision. Springer, Cham, pp. 712–728 (2018). https://doi.org/10.1007/978-3-030-20870-7_44
13. Du, Y., Yuan, C., Li, B., Zhao, L., Li, Y., Hu, W.: Interaction-aware spatio-temporal pyramid attention networks for action classification. In: Ferrari, V., Hebert, M., Sminchisescu, C., Weiss, Y. (eds.) ECCV 2018. LNCS, vol. 11220, pp. 388–404. Springer, Cham (2018). https://doi.org/10.1007/978-3-030-01270-0_23
14. Feichtenhofer, C., Fan, H., Malik, J., et al.: Slowfast networks for video recognition. In: Proceedings of the IEEE/CVF International Conference on Computer Vision, pp. 6202–6211 (2019)
15. Zheng, Z., An, G., Wu, D., et al.: Spatial-temporal pyramid based convolutional neural network for action recognition. Neurocomputing **358**, 446–455 (2019)
16. Yu, F., Koltun, V.: Multi-scale context aggregation by dilated convolutions. arXiv preprint arXiv:1511.07122 (2015)
17. Kuehne, H., Jhuang, H., Garrote, E., et al.: HMDB: a large video database for human motion recognition. In: 2011 International Conference on Computer Vision. IEEE, pp. 2556–2563 (2011)
18. Soomro, K., Zamir, A.R., Shah, M.: UCF101: A dataset of 101 human actions classes from videos in the wild. arXiv preprint arXiv:1212.0402 (2012)
19. Zhou, B., Andonian, A., Oliva, A., Torralba, A.: Temporal relational reasoning in videos. In: Ferrari, V., Hebert, M., Sminchisescu, C., Weiss, Y. (eds.) ECCV 2018. LNCS, vol. 11205, pp. 831–846. Springer, Cham (2018). https://doi.org/10.1007/978-3-030-01246-5_49

20. Shi, Y., Tian, Y., Huang, T., et al.: Temporal attentive network for action recognition. In: 2018 IEEE International Conference on Multimedia and Expo (ICME). IEEE, pp. 1–6 (2018)

21. Lin, J., Gan, C., Han, S.: Tsm: Temporal shift module for efficient video understanding. In: Proceedings of the IEEE/CVF International Conference on Computer Vision, pp. 7083–7093 (2019)

22. Feichtenhofer, C., Pinz, A., Zisserman, A.: Convolutional two-stream network fusion for video action recognition. In: Proceedings of the IEEE Conference on Computer Vision and Pattern Recognition, pp. 1933–1941 (2016)

23. Zolfaghari, M., Singh, K., Brox, T.: ECO: efficient convolutional network for online video understanding. In: Ferrari, V., Hebert, M., Sminchisescu, C., Weiss, Y. (eds.) ECCV 2018. LNCS, vol. 11206, pp. 713–730. Springer, Cham (2018). https://doi.org/10.1007/978-3-030-01216-8_43

24. Du, W., Wang, Y., Qiao, Y.: Recurrent spatial-temporal attention network for action recognition in videos. IEEE Trans. Image Process. **27**(3), 1347–1360 (2017)

25. Li, C., Zhang, B., Chen, C., et al.: Deep manifold structure transfer for action recognition. IEEE Trans. Image Process. **28**(9), 4646–4658 (2019)

26. Li, J., Liu, X., Zhang, M., et al.: Spatio-temporal deformable 3d convnets with attention for action recognition. Pattern Recogn. **98**, 107037 (2020)

27. Tran, D., Bourdev, L., Fergus, R., et al.: Learning spatiotemporal features with 3d convolutional networks. In: Proceedings of the IEEE International Conference on Computer Vision, pp. 4489–4497 (2015)

28. Li, C., Zhong, Q., Xie, D., et al. Collaborative spatiotemporal feature learning for video action recognition. In: Proceedings of the IEEE/CVF Conference on Computer Vision and Pattern Recognition, pp. 7872–7881 (2019)

29. Xu, B., Ye, H., Zheng, Y., et al.: Dense dilated network for video action recognition. IEEE Trans. Image Process. **28**(10), 4941–4953 (2019)

30. Fu, J., Liu, J., Jiang, J., et al.: Scene segmentation with dual relation-aware attention network. IEEE Trans. Neural Networks Learning Syst. **32**(6), 2547–2560 (2020)

31. Wang, Z., Chen, K., Zhang, M., et al.: Multi-scale aggregation network for temporal action proposals. Pattern Recogn. Lett. **122**, 60–65 (2019)

32. Yang, C., Xu, Y., Shi, J., et al.: Temporal pyramid network for action recognition. In: Proceedings of the IEEE/CVF Conference on Computer Vision and Pattern Recognition, pp. 591–600 (2020)

33. Li, X., Shuai, B., Tighe, J.: Directional temporal modeling for action recognition. In: European Conference on Computer Vision. Springer, Cham, pp. 275–291 (2020). https://doi.org/10.1007/978-3-030-58539-6_17

34. Kay, W., Carreira, J., Simonyan, K., et al.: The kinetics human action video dataset. arXiv preprint arXiv:1705.06950 (2017)

35. Qiu, Z., Yao, T., Mei, T.: Learning spatio-temporal representation with pseudo-3d residual networks. In: proceedings of the IEEE International Conference on Computer Vision, pp. 5533–5541 (2017)

36. Diba, A., et al.: Spatio-temporal channel correlation networks for action classification. In: Ferrari, V., Hebert, M., Sminchisescu, C., Weiss, Y. (eds.) ECCV 2018. LNCS, vol. 11208, pp. 299–315. Springer, Cham (2018). https://doi.org/10.1007/978-3-030-01225-0_18

37. Feichtenhofer, C., Pinz, A., Wildes, R.P.: Spatiotemporal multiplier networks for video action recognition. In: Proceedings of the IEEE Conference on Computer Vision and Pattern Recognition, pp. 4768–4777 (2017)

38. Carreira, J., Zisserman, A.: Quo vadis, action recognition? a new model and the kinetics dataset. In: Proceedings of the IEEE Conference on Computer Vision and Pattern Recognition, pp. 6299–6308 (2017)

39. Zhou, Y., Sun, X., Zha, Z.J., et al.: Mict: Mixed 3d/2d convolutional tube for human action recognition. In: Proceedings of the IEEE Conference on Computer Vision and Pattern Recognition, pp. 449–458 (2018)

40. Simonyan, K., Zisserman, A.: Two-stream convolutional networks for action recognition in videos. Adv. Neural Inf. Processing Syst. **27** (2014)

41. Christoph, R., Pinz, F.A.: Spatiotemporal residual networks for video action recognition. Adv. Neural Inf. Processing Syst. 3468–3476 (2016)

42. Wang, L., Xiong, Y., Wang, Z., et al.: Temporal segment networks for action recognition in videos. IEEE Trans. Pattern Anal. Mach. Intell. **41**(11), 2740–2755 (2018)

43. Lin, J., Gan, C., Han, S.: Temporal shift module for efficient video understanding. CoRR abs/1811.08383 (2018)

44. Jiang, B., Wang, M.M., Gan, W., et al.: Stm: Spatiotemporal and motion encoding for action recognition. In: Proceedings of the IEEE/CVF International Conference on Computer Vision, pp. 2000–2009 (2019)

45. Yin, M., Yao, Z., Cao, Y., et al.: Disentangled non-local neural networks. In: European Conference on Computer Vision. Springer, Cham, pp. 191–207 (2020). https://doi.org/10.1007/978-3-030-58555-6_12

46. Huimin, L., Zhang, M., Xu, X.: Deep fuzzy hashing network for efficient image retrieval. IEEE Trans. Fuzzy Syst. **29**(1), 166176 (2020). https://doi.org/10.1109/TFUZZ.2020.2984991

47. Huimin, L., Li, Y., Chen, M., et al.: Brain intelligence: go beyond artificial intelligence. Mobile Networks Appl. **23**, 368–375 (2018)

48. Huimin, L., Li, Y., Shenglin, M., et al.: Motor anomaly detection for unmanned aerial vehicles using reinforcement learning. IEEE Internet Things J. **5**(4), 2315–2322 (2018)

49. Huimin, L., Qin, M., Zhang, F., et al.: RSCNN: A CNN-based method to enhance low-light remote-sensing images. Remote Sensing **13**(1), 62 (2020)

50. Huimin, L., Zhang, Y., Li, Y., et al.: User-oriented virtual mobile network resource management for vehicle communications. IEEE Trans. Intell. Transp. Syst. **22**(6), 3521–3532 (2021)

# Research on the Identification Method of Audiovisual Model of EEG Stimulation Source

Zhaoxiang Lu[1]($\boxtimes$), Mei Wang[1], and Wenbin Chai[2]

[1] Xi'an University of Science and Technology, Xi'an 710054, China
20206043038@stu.xust.edu.cn
[2] Xi'an Nuclear Instrument Co., Ltd., Xi'an 710000, China

**Abstract.** For the cloud center of the mining industry, one of the most important tasks is to obtain the special environment safety state information because the hidden dangers of the water and fire, as well as the gas, always threaten human life and the production.In addition, audiovisual model of EEG stimulation source is integrated by using the convolutional neural network model with the inception network. It fuses the EEG information with the additional environment sensor information to increase the environment safety classification accuracy.Through brain network visualization and brain connection, we can get the density and weight change of global network connection in different audio-visual stimulation stages, which makes the analysis of EEG signals more intuitive. The experimental results indicate that the environment safety recognition accuracy of the audiovisual model can respectively reach 87.98%, 88.4%, and 90.12% for the single visual, the single auditory, and the audiovisual stimulus. The audio-visual modality has the best performance for the audiovisual evocation than the single visual or auditory stimuli.

**Keywords:** Safety state information · Audiovisual model · EEG · Brain network · Improved CNN

## 1 Introduction

Neuromorphic computing science has the potential to lead the next generation of computing science because of its high computing efficiency [1]. The neuromorphic computing model draws from the human brain computation mechanism, which performs the critical functions of perception and cognition [2, 3]. Due to the 80% of external environment information is obtained through the visual neural mechanism, and the 90% of external environment information is obtained through the audiovisual neural mechanisms, then the neuromorphic computing model of audiovisual evocations is absolutely important for human perception and cognition mechanism. Meanwhile, the audiovisual neuromorphic computing model is equally significant for the patrol robot using the human perception and cognition model [4–6].

For the perception and cognition mechanism modeling by using human electroencephalograph (EEG) signals of audiovisual evocations, a specific filtering algorithm is

S. Yang and H. Lu (Eds.): ISAIR 2022, CCIS 1700, pp. 156–166, 2022.
https://doi.org/10.1007/978-981-19-7946-0_14

firstly needed to eliminate the noises from the raw EEG signals [7–9]. Researchers have used different filtering methods to remove the noises, such as the filter bank method to decompose the EEG signals into sub-band and have overlapped frequency cutoffs, and the coincidence filtering method to remove the different types of noises [10, 11]. Besides, scientists propose a denoising method of an empirical mode decomposition (EMD) fused with the principal component analysis for the seizure EEG processing [12]. However, the different descriptions of EEG signals of the different evocation patterns have particular characteristics, and different filtering methods are required [13–15].

The paper is proposed an improved convolutional neural network (CNN) parallel computation strategy for the convolutional layer and Brain source estimation. Results and comparisons are provided in conclusions.

## 2 Related Works

In this section,we introduce the existing studies related to our approach and desvribe the differences.

For neural computing, the researchers performed a simple fusion of EEG and neuro-computing [16–18]. Besides, the neuromorphic feature extraction is secondly required. There is usually the one-dimensional time-frequency feature of a single tunnel EEG feature [19], the two-dimensional EEG energy feature of the multiple tunnels [20–22], and the three-dimensional EEG connection feature of the brain network [23]. Furthermore, researchers propose the EEG feature of the composite multivariate multiscale fuzzy entropy to describe the motor imagery [24–26]. Besides, the EEG and the electrooculogram (EOG) are fused to represent the brain-muscle feature [27]. However, the evocation of EEG signals is a time process, the dynamic characteristic should be considered [28].

Moreover, the neuromorphic computation model is also an important part of modeling human perception and cognition mechanisms [29]. The hidden Markov models and recurrent neural networks are used for event detection. In addition, the multi-modal neural network is constructed for person verification using signatures and EEGs [30]. In addition, scientists give the brain informatics-guided systematic fusion method and propose a predictive model to build a bridge between brain computing and the application services. The self-regulated neuro-fuzzy framework and the hierarchical brain networks via volumetric sparse deep belief network are developed to conduct neuromorphic computation.

## 3 Estimation of Brain Network Source Model

Brain networks are novel methods to study the interactions between important brain regions, combined with brain inverse activity is possible to extract nonlinear information about the source of local electrical activity using nonlinear potential information generated directly from the activity of local organismal neural circuits in the cerebral cortex. The source model is calculated from the segmentation of Magnetic Resonance Image (MRI). Usually, the white matter-gray matter interface is chosen as the main source space generating region. The MRI anatomy and channel locations are used with the same anatomical landmarks (left and right ear anterior points and nasal tip).

According to dipole theory, the EEG signal $X(t)$ recorded from the $M$ channel can be considered as a linear combination of $P$ time-varying current dipole sources $S(t)$.

$$X(t) = \begin{pmatrix} x_1(t) \\ \cdots \\ x_M(t) \end{pmatrix} = G \cdot \begin{pmatrix} s_1(t) \\ \cdots \\ s_p(t) \end{pmatrix} + N(t) = G \cdot S(t) + N(t) \tag{1}$$

where $G$ is the guide field matrix describing the deterministic quasi-instantaneous projection of the source onto the scalp electrodes. $N(t)$ is the measurement noise inherent in any acquisition process, and $G$ is calculated from the head model and the position of the electrodes. If the source distribution is constrained to a current dipole field uniformly distributed across the cortex and normal to the cortical surface, the position of the source is defined and direction.

Using a validated mind model as well as an internally generated source model, each two elements within the network are connected to function as a whole network, and the effect of this network on EEG signals under audiovisual modal stimulation is then analyzed by the following experiments.

## 4   Experiments and Results

### 4.1   Experimental Environment

The EEG signals were collected by the 40 leads electrode cap of Neuroscan. The international 10–20 system electrode placement method is adopted to standardize the position of each lead electrode. And that distance between potential is moderate. According to the analysis of the visual and auditory experimental areas in previous studies, the electrode can accurately and effectively collect the original data of EEG signals, which can meet the requirement of this study. Moreover, the symmetry between potentials can guarantee the accuracy of the following brain source inverse estimation results. The placement of standard 10–20 system electrodes is shown in Fig. 1.

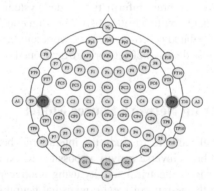

**Fig. 1.** Electrode distribution diagram of standard 10–20 system

The reference electrode is between Fz and Cz, and the ground electrode is between Fz and Pz. EEG signals are synchronously collected at a sampling frequency of 1 kHz, and the impedance between scalp and electrode is less than 5 kΩ. Electrodes are placed on each lobe of the brain, and electrode labels identify their location. The odd number is left, the even number is right, and the middle electrode is "z". For example, the F3 electrode comes from the left frontal lobe, and Cz is placed at the vertex on the top of the head.

In this experiment, five subjects were selected, the age distribution was about 25 years old, both sexes were male, without any history of brain diseases, and all of them had normal hearing and normal or corrected vision. Before the experiment, make sure that the subjects have enough rest time, and keep their hair clean within one hour before the experiment, to ensure less interference in the collection process. The experiment was conducted in a shielded room, Including three kinds of stimuli: visual, auditory, and audio-visual stimuli.

### 4.2 Experiment and Analysis of Brain Source Estimation Under Audiovisual Stimulation

In this experiment, the 30s scalp EEG sequence of the subjects in the EEG acquisition experiment under audio-visual mixed stimulation was selected, and then the collected EEG signals were denoised by the CEEMDAN-FastICA algorithm, and then the source was estimated in different periods. Finally, the brain network connection model under audio-visual stimulation was constructed by the collected EEG signals.

As shown in Fig. 2, Fig. 3 and Fig. 4 from top to bottom, the audio-visual mixed modal stimuli collected in three different periods are used for brain source estimation. Figure 5. is a diagram of brain network connection under audio-visual mixed-mode simulation.

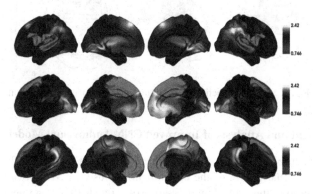

**Fig. 2.** Estimated images of brain sources under audio-visual stimulation in different periods(R0)

Through brain network visualization and brain connection, we can get the density and weight change of global network connection in different audio-visual stimulation stages, which makes the analysis of EEG signals more intuitive.

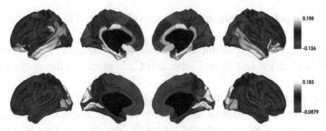

**Fig. 3.** Estimated images of brain sources under audio-visual stimulation in different periods(R1)

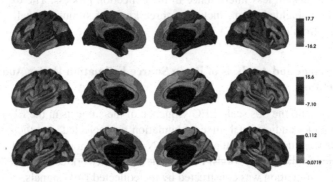

**Fig. 4.** Estimated images of brain sources under audio-visual stimulation in different periods(R2)

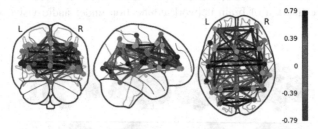

**Fig. 5.** Brain connection diagram under audio-visual stimulation

### 4.3 Experiment and Analysis of Improved CNN Audiovisual Model

In the experiment, binary cross-entropy is used as the cost function, L2 regularization is used, and the penalty term of the cost function is used to avoid overfitting. Visual stimulation is used as the evoked modality of EEG signals to obtain relevant EEG data. Taking the MSE value of the data as the input of the improved CNN, the curves of training accuracy and loss function are shown in Fig. 7.

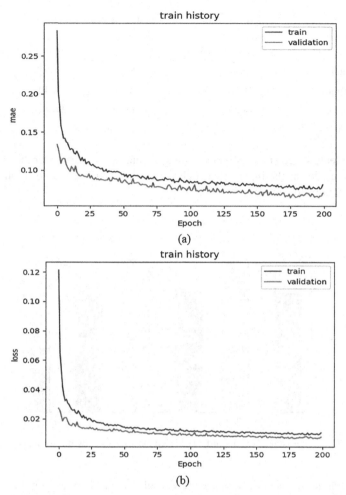

**Fig. 6.** Model performance under auditory stimuli: (a) Model accuracy under auditory stimuli; (b) Model loss value under the auditory stimulus

For visual stimulation, the best training effect is achieved at about the 200th time, when the training accuracy of the model is 82.34% and the loss value is 0.0117. For auditory stimulation, the best training effect is achieved at about the 870th time, and the training accuracy rate is 84.78%. The loss value is 0.0072. When the visual and auditory stimuli are mixed, the best training effect is achieved around the 200th time, when the training accuracy is 90.12% and the loss value is 0.0041 (Fig. 6).

By discussing the modes of visual stimulation, auditory stimulation, and audio-visual mixed stimulation, the following is the classification accuracy of the recognition model. The EEG signals denoised by the CEEMDAN-FastICA algorithm are finally used as the input of linear classifier, Support Vector Machine (SVM), and improved CNN. The classification accuracy is as shown in Table 1.

**Table 1.** Accuracy of EEG classification (%)

| Stimulation mode | Linear classifier | SVM | Improved CNN |
|---|---|---|---|
| Visual stimulus | 69.31 | 82.09 | 87.98 |
| Acoustic stimuli | 71.78 | 84.17 | 88.40 |
| Audio-visual stimuli | **74.25** | **85.60** | **90.12** |

For the feature vectors constructed with scale entropy values under the above three stimulation modes as the input of each classifier, the accuracy visualization results of the classifier are shown in Fig. 8.

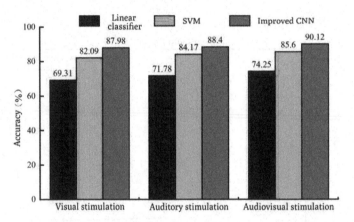

**Fig. 7.** Comparison of results of EEG Signal classification by different classifiers

According to the classification accuracy results in the chart, among the linear classifier, the SVM, and the improved CNN, the classification results of the improved CNN are better than those of the other two. Meanwhile, for visual stimuli, auditory stimuli, and mixed audio-visual stimuli, the classification results of mixed audio-visual stimuli are better.

In this experiment we assess the significance of correlations between the first canonical gradient and data from other modalities (curvature, cortical thickness and T1w/T2w image intensity). A normal test of the significance of the correlation cannot be used, because the spatial auto-correlation in EEG data may bias the test statistic. In Fig. 9. we will show three approaches for null hypothesis testing: spin permutations, Moran spectral randomization, and autocorrelation-preserving surrogates based on variogram matching.

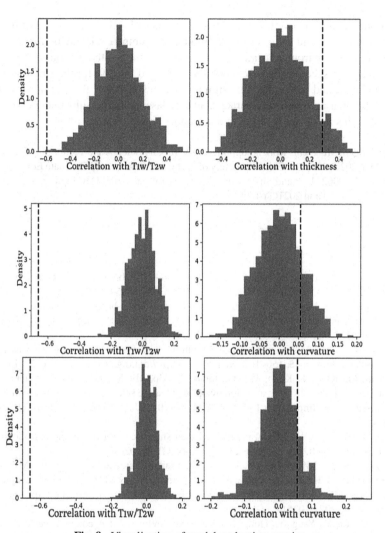

**Fig. 8.** Visualization of model evaluation metrics

## 5    Conclusions

EEG signals in different periods under audio-visual stimulation are analyzed by constructing a brain connection network and brain source map visualization, Thereby providing a powerful guarantee for the processing of EEG signals of audio-visual stimuli.

Brain source estimation and model of audiovisual evocations, that is, the parallel computing strategy of the convolutional layer is proposed. The convolutional kernel in the convolutional layer is set as a vector to extract only spatial features, and the regularization operation is added to the network structure to prevent over-fitting. The audio-visual model is integrated by using the improved CNN model with the inception network.

Through experiments, the classification effects of EEG signals by traditional classification methods and improved CNN model are compared. The experimental results indicate that the environment safety recognition accuracy of the neuromorphic computing model can respectively reach 87.98%, 88.4%, and 90.12% for the single visual, the single auditory, and the audiovisual stimulus. The results show that the improved CNN model has better recognition accuracy, and the classification results under audio-visual mixed stimulus mode are better than those under single stimulus mode.

**Acknowledgements.** This work is supported by Yulin City Science and Technology Project under grants CXY-2020–026, The Chinese Society of Academic Degrees and Graduate Education under grant B-2017Y0002–170, and Shaanxi Province Key Research and Development Projects under grants 2016GY-040 and 2021GY-029.

# References

1. Zhang, Y., Qu, P., Ji, Y., et al.: A system hierarchy for brain-inspired computing. Nature **586**(7829), 378–384 (2020). https://doi.org/10.1038/s41586-020-2782-y
2. Kaushik, R., Akhilesh, J., Priyadarshini, P.: Towards spike-based machine intelligence with neuromorphic computing. Nature **575**(7784), 607–617 (2019). https://doi.org/10.1038/s41 586-019-1677-2
3. Kuai, H., et al.: Multi-source brain computing with systematic fusion for smart health. Information Fusion **75**, 150–167 (Mar.2021). https://doi.org/10.1016/j.inffus.2021.03.009
4. Bhatti, M., Khan, J., Khan, M.U.G., Iqbal, R., Aloqaily, M., Jararweh, Y., Gupta, B.: Soft computing-based EEG classification by optimal feature selection and neural networks. IEEE Trans. Industrial Informatics **15**(10), 5747-5754 (2019). https://doi.org/10.1109/TII.2019.292 5624
5. Lu, Y., Bi, L., Li, H.: Model predictive-based shared control for brain-controlled driving. IEEE Trans. Intell. Transp. Syst. **21**(2), 630–640 (Feb.2020)
6. Chakraborty, M., Mitra, D.: A novel automated seizure detection system from EMD-MSPCA denoised EEG: Refined composite multiscale sample, fuzzy and permutation entropies based scheme. Biomedical Signal Processing and Control **67**, 102514 (2021). https://doi.org/10.1016/j.bspc.2021.102514
7. Gao, Z., Li, Y., Yang, Y., Dong, N., Yang, X., Grebogi, C.: A coincidence filtering-based approach for CNNs in EEG-based recognition. IEEE Trans. Industr. Inf. **16**(11), 7159–7167 (Nov.2020). https://doi.org/10.1109/TII.2019.2955447
8. Saini, M., Satija, U., Upadhayay, M.D.: Wavelet-based waveform distortion measures for assessment of denoised EEG quality concerning noise-free EEG signal. IEEE Signal Process. Lett. **27**, 1260–1264 (Jul.2020)
9. Bhattacharyya, A., Ranta, R., Cam, S.L., et al.: A multi-channel approach for cortical stimulation artifact suppression in-depth EEG signals using time-frequency and spatial filtering. IEEE Trans. Biomed. Eng. **66**(7), 1915–1926 (Jul.2019)
10. Teng, T., Bi, L., Liu, Y.: EEG-Based detection of driver emergency braking intention for brain-controlled vehicles. IEEE Trans. Intelligent Transportation Syst. **19**(6), 1766–1773 (2018)
11. Tryon, J., Trejos, A.L.: Classification of task weight during dynamic motion using EEG–EMG fusion. IEEE Sens. J. **21**(4), 5012–5021 (Feb.2021)
12. Wu, W., Wu, Q.M.J., Sun, W., et al.: A regression method with subnetwork neurons for vigilance estimation using EOG and EEG. IEEE Trans. Cognitive Developmental Syst. **13**(1), 209–222 (Mar.2021)

13. Around, A., Mirkovic, B., De Vos, M., Doclo, S.: Impact of different acoustic components on EEG-based auditory attention decoding in noisy and reverberant conditions. IEEE Trans. Neural Syst. Rehabil. Eng. **27**(4), 652–663 (Apr.2019)

14. Wang, M., Huang, Z., Li, Y., Dong, L., Pan, H.: Maximum weight multi-modal information fusion algorithm of electroencephalographs and face images for emotion recognition. Computers and Electrical Eng. **94**, 107319 (2021). https://doi.org/10.1016/j.compeleceng.2021.107319

15. Li, P., Liu, H., Si, Y., Li, C., et al.: EEG based emotion recognition by combining functional connectivity network and local activations. IEEE Trans. Biomed. Eng. **66**(10), 2869–2881 (Oct.2019)

16. Cai, J., Wang, Y., Liu, A., McKeown, M.J., Wang, Z.J.: Novel regional activity representation with constrained canonical correlation analysis for brain connectivity network estimation. IEEE Trans. Med. Imaging **39**(7), 2363–2373 (Jul.2020)

17. Wang, M., Ma, C., Li, Z., Zhang, S., Li, Y.: Alertness estimation using connection parameters of the brain network. IEEE Trans. Intelligent Transportation Syst. (2021) https://doi.org/10.1109/TITS.2021.3124372

18. Ting, C.M., Sandin, S.B., Tang, M., Ombao, H.: Detecting dynamic community structure in functional brain networks across individuals: a multilayer approach. IEEE Trans. Med. Imaging **40**(2), 468–480 (Feb.2021)

19. Mammone, N., et al.: Brain network analysis of compressively sensed high-density EEG signals in AD and MCI subjects. IEEE Trans. Industr. Inf. **15**(1), 527–536 (Feb.2019)

20. Masulli, P., Masulli, F., Rovetta, S., Lintas, A., Villa, A.E.P.: Fuzzy clustering for exploratory analysis of EEG event-related potentials. IEEE Trans. Fuzzy Syst. **28**(1), 28–38 (Feb.2020)

21. Li, M., Wang, R., Yang, J., Duan, L.: An improved refined composite multivariate multiscale fuzzy entropy method for MI-EEG feature extraction. Computational Intelligence and Neuroscience (2019). https://doi.org/10.1155/2019/7529572

22. Bhattacharyya, A., Tripathy, R.K., Garg, L., Pachori, R.B.: A novel multivariate-multiscale approach for computing EEG spectral and temporal complexity for human emotion recognition. IEEE Sens. J. **21**(3), 3579–3591 (Jun.2021)

23. Zhang, G., Etemad, A.: Capsule attention for multimodal EEG-EOG representation learning with application to driver vigilance estimation. IEEE Trans. Neural Syst. Rehabil. Eng. **29**, 1138–1149 (Jun.2021)

24. Zhang, G., Cai, B., Zhang, A.Y., Stephen, J., et al.: Estimating dynamic functional brain connectivity with a sparse hidden Markov model. IEEE Transactions on Medical Imaging **39**(2), 488–498 (2020)

25. Khalifa, Y., Mandic, D., Sejdić, E.: A review of hidden Markov models and recurrent neural networks for event detection and localization in biomedical signals. Information Fusion **69**, 52–72 (May2021)

26. Chakladar, D.D., Kumar, P., Roy, P.P., Dogra, D.P., Scheme, E., Chang, V.: A multimodal-siamese neural network (MSN) for person verification using signatures and EEG. Information Fusion **71**, 17–27 (Jul.2021). https://doi.org/10.1016/j.inffus.2021.01.004

27. Jafarifarmand, A., Badamchizadeh, M.A., Khanmohammadi, S., Nazari, M.A., Tazehkand, B.M.: A new self-regulated neuro-fuzzy framework for classification of EEG signals in motor imagery BCI. IEEE Trans. Fuzzy Syst. **26**(3), 1485–1497 (Jun.2018)

28. Dong, Q., Ge, F., Ning, Q., Zhao, Y., et al.: Modeling hierarchical brain networks via volumetric sparse deep belief network. IEEE Trans. Biomed. Eng. **67**(6), 1739–1748 (Jun.2020)

29. Wang, Y., Song, W., Tao, W., et al.: A systematic review on affective computing: Emotion models, databases, and recent advances. Information Fusion (2022)

30. Kumar, S., Yadava, M., Roy, P.P.: Fusion of EEG response and sentiment analysis of products review to predict customer satisfaction. Information Fusion **52**, 41–52 (2019)

31. Lu, H., Zhang, M., Xu, X.: Deep fuzzy hashing network for efficient image retrieval. IEEE Trans. Fuzzy Systems **29**(1), 166176 (2020). https://doi.org/10.1109/TFUZZ.2020.2984991
32. Huimin, L., Li, Y., Chen, M., et al.: Brain Intelligence: go beyond artificial intelligence. Mobile Networks Appl. **23**, 368–375 (2018)
33. Huimin, L., Li, Y., Shenglin, M., et al.: Motor anomaly detection for unmanned aerial vehicles using reinforcement learning. IEEE Internet Things J. **5**(4), 2315–2322 (2018)
34. Huimin, L., Qin, M., Zhang, F., et al.: RSCNN: A CNN-based method to enhance low-light remote-sensing images. Remote Sensing **13**(1), 62, 2020
35. Huimin, L., Zhang, Y., Li, Y., et al.: User-oriented virtual mobile network resource management for vehicle communications. IEEE Trans. Intell. Transp. Syst. **22**(6), 3521–3532 (2021)

# Deep Learning-Based Virtual Trajectory Generation Scheme

Jiaji Pan[1], Jingkang Yang[1], Hongbin Fan[1,2(✉)], and Yining Liu[1]

[1] Guangxi Key Laboratory of Trusted Software, Guilin University of Electronic Technology, Guilin 541004, China
[2] College of Computer and Artificial Intelligence, Xiangnan University, Chenzhou 423000, China
hongbinfan@xnu.edu.cn

**Abstract.** At present, location based service (LBS) has developed rapidly, it is extensive use in the applications of various intelligent mobile terminals. The trajectory privacy of users is protected by virtual trajectory generation algorithm constructed by statistical method. Since the user's motion model is a complex equation, it is difficult to model it mathematically, because the user's trajectory model does not consider its motion model, limiting the formation of the trajectory. As a result, previous virtual trajectory generation algorithms were not resistant to deep learning-based data mining attacks. In this paper, real and virtual trajectory discriminators are designed using LSTM (Long Short-Term Memory) technology, and a deep learning-based virtual trajectory generation scheme is proposed. Experiments show that the false trajectory can be identified with a success rate of at least 96%, while for the real trajectory, the false positive rate is only 6.5%. The virtual trajectory generated by the proposed scheme has human motion patterns similar to the real trajectory, and protects against colluding, inference, and channel attacks. The generated virtual trajectory points will not be distributed in the map inaccessible areas. On the premise that the users obtain the service quality, the user trajectory privacy is effectively protected to reduce the loss as much as possible.

**Keywords:** Virtual trajectory · Motion model · LSTM

## 1 Introduction

At present, LBS [1, 2] is widely used in intelligent mobile terminals to carry out information interaction with the Internet as the carrier. In the process of interaction, many track data will be generated. Users' personal privacy data can be obtained through data mining. Major accidents often occur due to location privacy leakage [3]. For example, Area 51 Air Force Base in Nevada used a mobile APP called Strava to reveal its location; Shanghai Consumer Rights Protection Commission evaluated the personal information permissions involved in map mobile apps in 2018, and the results showed that Tencent Map applied for seven sensitive permissions and Baidu Map applied for 14 sensitive permissions in Android system. In recent years, researchers have proposed a series of LBS

© The Author(s), under exclusive license to Springer Nature Singapore Pte Ltd. 2022
S. Yang and H. Lu (Eds.): ISAIR 2022, CCIS 1700, pp. 167–182, 2022.
https://doi.org/10.1007/978-981-19-7946-0_15

trajectory privacy protection algorithms, but these algorithms can only resist traditional data mining attacks, but cannot resist deep learning-based data mining attacks.

The user's trajectory data contains rich spatio-temporal information. For example, a school often appears in a person's trajectory, and the time of occurrence is regular. The attacker can infer that the user has a high probability of being a teacher. If the attacker's trajectory of a user shows that he or she often appears in a high-end venue, the attacker can infer that the user is a political dignitary, track it, kidnap, and extort a lot more than a random user. Much more. Such cases occur in society, and the reason is that their trajectory is leaked, and the attacker analyzes his general identity through data mining attacks to make corresponding criminal actions. The arrival of big data Era, it is especially important that our track privacy is protected to the maximum extent.

The solution to the trajectory privacy protection of smart mobile terminals can be divided into a trusted authority-based approach and a distributed approach based on mobile terminals. The virtual trajectory method without trusted third party is the most practical.

Our contributions are summarized as follows:

1) It is proposed to use a four-dimensional vector to define the trajectory points and the spatiotemporal distribution of the trajectory section composed of n points is described by an n × 4 matrix.
2) An LSTM-based trajectory detector is designed, which can detect most trajectories with very low error rate.
3) A real-time continuous trajectory privacy-preserving solution against map background recognition and deep learning-based discriminator recognition is proposed.

## 2 Related Work

Hara et al. [4] designed a virtual trajectory generation algorithm based on the trajectory characteristics of vehicle motion. Shokri et al. [5] proposed a pseudo-trajectory generation solution that generates each pseudo-position independently of a uniform probability distribution, making it have the same distribution. Lei et al. [6] designed a false trajectory privacy-preserving solution based on spatio-temporal correlation that fully considered the trajectory direction trend. The research results proved that the temporal reachability of adjacent positions on the trajectory, the distance moved by the user and the adjacent positions of the trajectory had spatio-temporal correlation. Dong et al. [7] proposed a false trajectory generation scheme with five parameters considering the privacy requirements of users' personalized trajectories. These schemes use probability to fabricate many false trajectory data to mask the real trajectory, which can easily be inferred to be invalid, resulting in data being completely useless statistically.

Pingley et al. [8] designed a scheme based on query disturbance to protect query privacy in continuous LBS. Wang et al. [9] introduced location awareness to protect privacy and find the smallest hidden region. But these schemes are too simple and easy to be cracked by attackers, exposing user private information.

Komishani et al. [10] proposed a combination of sensitive data generalization and sensitive trajectory suppression scheme, which generalizes a part of the sensitive data in the user trajectory that is easy to leak the user's privacy, meanwhile, the trajectory inhibition operation of some trajectories that are easy to expose the sensitive location of the user is carried out, and the combination of these two technologies protects the user's trajectory privacy to the greatest extent.

As the accumulation of pseudo-trajectories and position distributions is added to the trajectory data, the difference between the trajectory data and its raw data increases. Therefore, it is difficult to obtain practical application.

Algorithms MN [11]: MN means moving in a neighborhood, and the next position of the dummy is determined in the neighborhood of the dummy's current position. In this algorithm, the user's communication device memorizes the previous position of each dummy.

Algorithms MLN [11]: MLN means moving in a limited neighborhood, and the next location of the dummy is determined in the neighborhood of the dummy's current location. However, the next location is limited by regional density. This algorithm is suitable for the situation that user communication equipment acquires location data of other users. Firstly, the user equipment obtains the location data of other users.

Algorithms ADTGA [12]: ADTGA generates virtual trajectories based on user privacy model. The privacy model proposed by the algorithm includes three privacy indicators. Users can set these metrics as privacy-preserving requirements. Use these stricter privacy-preserving requirements can reduce the probability of actual location and trajectory leakage.

## 3 Preliminary Tools

### 3.1 Introduction of Deep Learning

Deep learning (DL) is a machine learning technique that implements artificial intelligence in computer systems by establishing hierarchical artificial neural networks (ANNs).

The hierarchical ANN used in deep learning has many forms, and its complexity is commonly referred to as "depth" [13]. Depending on the type of architecture, the form of deep learning includes depth confidence network and other hybrid structures [14]. DL uses data to update the parameters in its construction to achieve training objectives. This process is commonly referred to as "learning". The common method of learning is gradient descent algorithm and its variant [15]. Some statistical learning theories are used to optimize the learning process.

In application, DL is used to learn high-dimensional data of complex structures and large samples. According to the research fields, it includes automatic control, computer vision, etc. DL has been successfully applied to the practical problems of image translation, automatic driving and so on.

### 3.2 Introduction of LSTM Model

LSTM is a special RNN that can learn long dependencies. The identification of trajectory needs to synthesize the information of each historical trajectory point. Therefore, it is necessary to analyze and establish the identification model from the perspective of time series. LSTM is suitable for this task.

LSTM adds a cell state c to the hidden layer of RNN to realize long-term learning. Cell State c consists of three special gates. The gate structure is a selective structure. It takes any value in [0,1] through a sigmoid or tanh network layer. Its function is to determine whether the previous state information can be used for the next sample. When the output value is 1, all the information of the current sample can be used for the next sample. When the output value is 0, the next sample has nothing to do with the current sample.

For a single LSTM memory module, the forward propagation process is shown in Fig. 1. $h_t$ and $x_t$ are the hidden output at t time and the input vector at t time, respectively. $f_t$ is the output of the forgotten gate, $o_t$ is the output of the output gate, and the output of input gate includes $i_t$ and $a_t$. $W_f$, $U_f$, $W_a$, $U_a$, $W_i$, $U_i$, $W_o$ and $U_o$ are respectively the weight matrix corresponding to the gate structure; $b_f$, $b_a$, $b_i$ and $b_0$ are bias. LSTM backpropagation calculates the error terms of backpropagation direction from two levels of network and time in order to reduce the error of backpropagation. Secondly, according to the error terms, the gradient of each weight is calculated. Then, the steepest descent method is adopted to iteratively update the weight parameters of ownership until the error satisfies the demand.

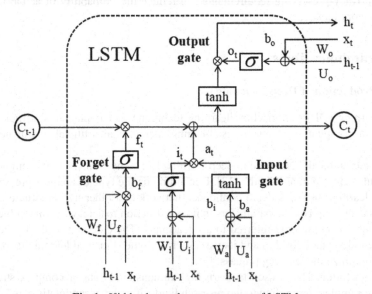

**Fig. 1.** Hidden layer element structure of LSTM.

## 4   Virtual Trajectory Recognition Scheme Based on LSTM

Traditional mathematical modeling means that mathematicians build models based on expert experience and understanding of the real world. Deep learning modeling is another completely different way of modeling. Machine learning algorithm describes some objective facts in a more covert way. Although human beings cannot fully understand the description process of the model, in most cases, deep learning model is more accurate than the mathematical model built by human experts.

### 4.1  Virtual Trajectory Identification Scheme

The trajectory is divided into n trajectory segments. The model framework of virtual trajectory recognition is shown in Fig. 2.

Since a complete trajectory is often very long, and the lengths of each trajectory in the trajectory dataset are uneven, it is difficult to design an effective virtual trajectory discriminator to discriminate trajectories of all lengths. Therefore, using the segmentation method, a complete trajectory is divided into trajectory segments with equal time intervals, and then each trajectory segment is put into the false trajectory discriminator. If the number of false trajectory segments obtained is greater than the set threshold, this track is determined to be a false track. The higher the threshold is set, the lower the detection rate of false trajectories and the lower the false positive rate of true trajectories.

When processing trajectory data in this paper, a trajectory point is taken every 5 s to form a trajectory. When this complete trajectory is divided into several trajectory segments, each trajectory segment has $n$ points, and the last trajectory segment is truncated.

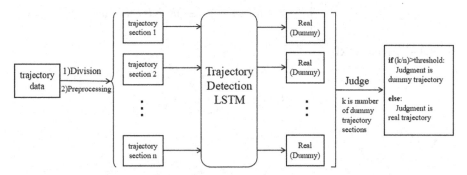

**Fig. 2.** The model framework of virtual trajectory identification

### 4.2  Preprocessing of Trajectory Data Set

We take n points as a trajectory section, $\text{tra}_j = \{loc_1, loc_2, \ldots, loc_n\}$.

We use a four-dimensional vector $(Roa_{ti}, Rl_{ti}, X_{ti}, Y_{ti})$ to describe the location state $LS_i$ of $loc_{ti}$.

As shown in Fig. 3, $\vec{a}$ denotes the vectors from $loc_{i-2}$ to $loc_{i-1}$, so do $\vec{b}$ and $\vec{c}$. $\vec{d}$ is the extension line of $\vec{a}$.

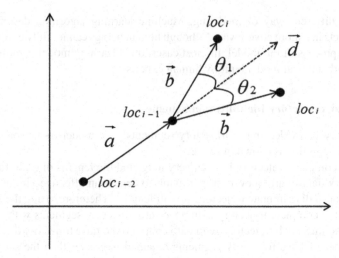

**Fig. 3.** Trajectory point definition

**1)  Relative offset angle (Roa)**

$$\text{Roa}_i = \begin{cases} \theta_1 = arccos(\dfrac{\vec{d} \times \vec{b}}{|\vec{d}| \times |\vec{b}|}) if \ \vec{b} \ is \ above \ \vec{d} \\[4mm] \theta_2 = -arccos(\dfrac{\vec{d} \times \vec{b}}{|\vec{d}| \times |\vec{b}|}) if \ \vec{b} \ is \ below \ \vec{d} \end{cases}$$

**2)  Relative length (Rl)**

$$\text{Rl}_i = \frac{\left| \overrightarrow{loc_{i-1}loc_i} \right|}{\sum_{j=1}^{n} \left| \overrightarrow{loc_{j-1}loc_j} \right|}$$

**3)  X, Y**

$$X_i = loc_x^i - loc_x^0$$

$$Y_i = loc_y^i - loc_y^0$$

We represent the position state of trajectory in time series as a matrix as shown in Table 1.

For the sake of improve the accuracy of training results, the three dimensions of the trajectory point are normalized according to the order of magnitude of the four dimensions describing the trajectory point.

$$Roa_i := \frac{Roa_i}{\pi}$$

**Table 1.** Sequential characteristic matrix of trajectory.

| $Roa_1$ | $Rl_1$ | $X_1$ | $Y_1$ |
|---------|--------|-------|-------|
| $Roa_2$ | $Rl_2$ | $X_2$ | $Y_2$ |
| ... | ... | ... | ... |
| $Roa_n$ | $Rl_n$ | $X_n$ | $Y_n$ |

$$X_i := \frac{X_i - X_{min}}{X_{max} - X_{min}}$$
$$Y_i := \frac{Y_i - Y_{min}}{Y_{max} - Y_{min}}$$

Among them, $X_{max}$ is the maximum values of X in training samples, $X_{min}$ is the minimum values of X in training samples, $Y_{max}$ is the maximum values of Y in training samples, $Y_{min}$ is the minimum values of Y in training samples.

### 4.3 LSTM Trajectory Discriminator Framework

The track discriminator framework based on LSTM is shown in Fig. 4.

**Input Layer:** Firstly, the trajectory is converted from latitude and longitude to plane cartesian coordinate system. Secondly, the trajectory is divided into equal trajectory segments. The last, the trajectory points are preprocessed into time series matrix.

**Network Layer:** The first position state of the track segment is entered into the LSTM network in chronological order, and then the results are transmitted to the output layer via the fully connected layer.

**Output Layer:** By performing the Softmax operation on the output of the fully connected layer, the classification result is finally obtained.

**Network Training Layer:** The output of the output layer is combined with the label (true or false) of the track segment to calculate the loss value during the training phase of the network. Gradient descent method is used to update the weight matrix and deviation of network layer to make the predicted value closer to the real value.

### 4.4 Experiments and Analysis of Result

We randomly select 20,000 track segments from the track data set as the real track set, the random virtual trajectory generation algorithm is used to generate 20000 virtual trajectory segments from the real trajectory as the virtual trajectory set. 40,000 trajectory sections are trained according to the flow of Fig. 1. After the training, we use dummy trajectory test set, real trajectory test set, ATGA-based generation trajectory, MLN-based generation trajectory, and MN-based generation trajectory to evaluate the detection performance of LSTM, as shown in Fig. 5.

Experiments show that the false trajectory can be identified with a success rate of at least 96%, while the false positive rate of real trajectories is only 6.5%.

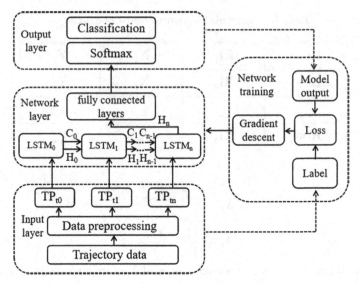

**Fig. 4.**  The framework of trajectory discriminator based on LSTM

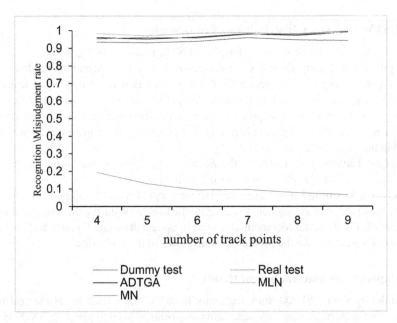

**Fig. 5.**  LSTM detection performance of virtual trajectory detector

# 5 Virtual Trajectory Generation Scheme Based on Deep Learning

## 5.1 Constraints for Virtual Trajectory Generation

1) External map background restrictions, such as water, green space and other inaccessible areas. Enemy is easy to grasp the user background map, if the generated virtual track points on the inaccessible areas on the map, such as lakes, rivers, etc., or frequent falls in the most inaccessible areas, an attacker can know that the big probability path for the generated virtual path, so do not conform to the background information of the trajectory is easy to be ruled out. Since the background map information of the user is the easiest to obtain, and the method of screening virtual trajectories through the background map is the easiest, we set the priority of considering the restrictions of the map background as high.

2) The characteristic limitation of the trajectory itself (human movement pattern): the trajectory is not a combination of a series of randomly distributed points, but a broken line segment restricted in a certain spatial and temporal distribution space (deep neural network can learn the complex difference between the trajectory generated by the real trajectory and the algorithm. These differences, it is difficult to use equation can only use neural network black box, two classification methods are used to distinguish the real trajectory from the generated virtual trajectory). Since attackers have similar attacks, this paper proposes a method based on deep learning, the existing algorithm to generate virtual trajectory can big probability are identified, thus unable to effectively protect user privacy. Since the neural network discriminator has a high recognition rate for the virtual trajectory generated by the existing virtual trajectory generation scheme, and a low misjudgment rate for the real trajectory, we set the priority of considering the feature limitation of the trajectory as medium.

3) Inter-trajectory restrictions, spatial restrictions of trajectory point distribution, etc., namely, some restrictions of virtual trajectories modeled by mathematical methods such as statistics and probability in existing virtual trajectory generation schemes. Such virtual trajectories have simple characteristics and are easy to be expressed by equations. Since the researchers constructed the trajectory features empirically when constructing virtual trajectories, feature descriptions may not be accurate or related to trajectories. Since deep learning has a stronger ability to obtain deep information than in mathematical modeling, neural network-based data mining attacks are given priority when generating virtual trajectory points. The virtual trajectory generation scheme combines the advantages of the existing virtual trajectory generation algorithm to construct the virtual trajectory based on considering the background information and the inherent properties of the trajectory itself, so that the generated virtual trajectory can be identified by the attacker with a little success rate after being mixed with the user's real trajectory.

## 5.2 The Premise of Constructing Reasonable Virtual Trajectory

1) **Information held by the adversary**

When facing an opponent, we assume that the opponent has all the information, namely:

(1) When the user requests the LBS service from the provider, the adversary has the map background of the user.
(2) The adversary has mastered the false trajectory identification method based on neural network.
(3) The adversary can also distinguish false trajectories by other methods, which are listed in relevant literature.

Therefore, the virtual trajectory generation needs to know all the information of the adversary and these three constraints.

2) Map background information

Using simplified background map information, the background map is divided into three levels, as shown in Fig. 6.

(1) Hotspots areas:

Hotspot areas are represented by green grids, representing densely populated areas. When the trajectory is generated, first select the trajectory point in the hot spot area.

(2) Normal area:

The common area is represented by a yellow grid, and the yellow grid represents an area with relatively sparse human flow, which is a secondary consideration area for trajectory points when the trajectory is generated.

(3) Prohibited areas:

Prohibited areas are represented by a red grid, representing inaccessible areas. Track points should avoid these areas when generating tracks.

The collection and modeling of background information is relatively simple and effective, and can be divided by combining empirical methods and pedestrian flow data.

Empirical method: For non-scenic lakes and mountainous areas, they are generally set as restricted areas, and streets and residential areas are generally set as hot spots.

Pedestrian flow: According to the pedestrian flow data, set a reasonable pedestrian flow threshold, and then divide it into three areas.

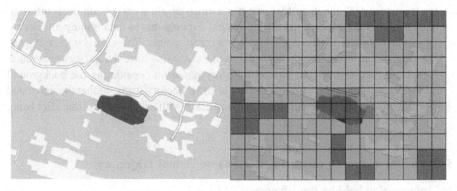

**Fig. 6.** Level division of map information

### 5.3  Virtual Trajectory Generation Scheme

Suppose Alice goes to a tourist scenic spot, starting from point A of the scenic spot, she wants to know hotels, attractions, places to stay, etc. She opened an APP to ask about scenic spots of interest, but she didn't want to reveal the privacy of her trajectory. She faces the risk of trajectory privacy leakage. After preprocessing the LBS request on the mobile phone, she sends the real trajectory points and the $k$-1 trajectory points generated by the virtual trajectory method to the LBS supplier.

The process of virtual trajectory generating trajectory points is shown in Fig. 7.

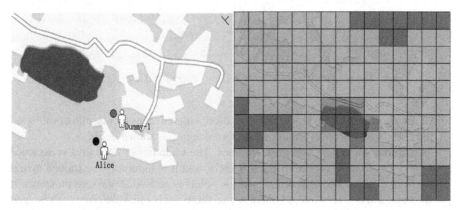

**Fig. 7.** The first step of virtual trajectory generation

**The first step:** Initialize the starting point of $k - 1$ virtual trajectory so that it is located in the green area less than or equal to a certain distance near Alice.

**The first operation:** Alice sends a service request for k locations to the LBS provider. The service request returned by the LBS provider is filtered out by Alice's mobile terminal k − 1 pseudo-request, and then the returned result is given to Alice.

**The second step:** Since the designed neural network discriminator needs more than three positions to judge whether the trajectory conforms to the spatiotemporal distribution of the actual trajectory, the traditional false trajectory generation algorithm is used to generate false trajectory points (the classical false trajectory generation algorithm MLN is used). The restriction is that the generated virtual trajectory points must located in the yellow or green area, as shown in Fig. 8.

If the virtual track point area generated by algorithm MLN does not intersect the background graph area, the virtual trajectory points that conform to the constraints of the background graph are first selected to be as close to the region of the virtual trajectory points generated by algorithm MLN as possible. Then perform the first operation.

**The third step:** From the beginning to the end of the service request, Alice's mobile terminal will perform the following operations:

1)  First, according to the point at the previous moment, the range of the virtual point at the current moment is determined. Then, the grids are divided, and the priority

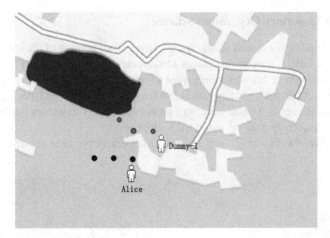

**Fig. 8.** The second step of virtual trajectory generation (Color figure online)

of each grid is identified by a different color, with red areas representing prohibited areas and green areas representing preferred areas, as shown in Fig. 9.

2) Iterate over all yellow and green meshes. The midpoint of each grid is assumed to be a feasible point of a virtual trajectory, and it is input into the trained neural network together with the virtual position points generated at previous moments. If the trained neural network judgment is true, this point is a feasible point (represented by a hollow pentagon); otherwise, it is an infeasible point, as shown in Fig. 10.

3) The feasible area of the virtual trajectory point is determined according to the MLN algorithm, that is, the virtual frame region, as shown in Fig. 11.

4) After determining the feasible areas of a virtual track point, the selection of virtual track points follows the priority of three constraints, namely:

   After the feasible area of the virtual trajectory points is determined, the selection of the virtual trajectory point follows the priority of three constraints, namely:

(1) If there are hollow five-pointed stars in the intersection of the dotted box and the green grid, select these points as the point set of candidate trajectory points, and select a point in the point set as the false trajectory point. Selectable points are shown by solid five-pointed stars.

(2) If there is no five-pointed star in the dashed-line box, look for the five-pointed star outside the dashed-line box as a false track point.

(3) If there is no five-pointed star in the feasible domain of the map background, select the point in the dotted box, such as the dotted box and the ground.

### 5.4   Experience and Analysis

In this paper, MN, MLN and ADTGA are selected among the classical virtual trajectory generation algorithms to generate virtual trajectories, and the virtual trajectory discriminator based on deep learning is used to identify the generated virtual trajectories.

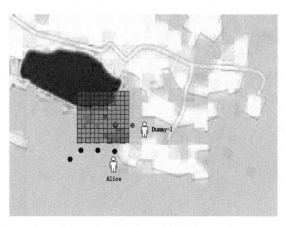

**Fig. 9.** Case 1 of the third step of the virtual trajectory generation (Color figure online)

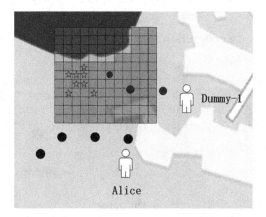

**Fig. 10.** Case 2 of the third step of the virtual trajectory generation (Color figure online)

Figure 12 shows that the proposed solution has a very low probability of being recognized.

Divide a complete trajectory into several trajectory segments with 4 to 9 points per trajectory segment, and then train the corresponding neural network with these different trajectory segment sets. Figure 13 shows the recognition effect of the neural network on false trajectories after training. On the whole, as the number of trajectories in each trajectory segment increases, the recognition rate of false trajectories shows an upward trend until the number of trajectories peaked and stabilized at 7, while the misjudgment rate of true trajectories shows a downward trend until the number of trajectories in each trajectory segment reaches the lowest and tends to be stable at 7. Therefore, when the discriminator based on neural network identifies false trajectories, every 7 points of the trajectory should be regarded as a trajectory segment.

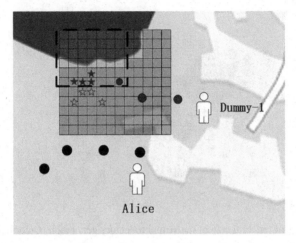

**Fig. 11.** Case 3 of the third step of the virtual trajectory generation

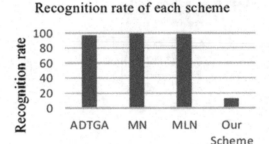

**Fig. 12.** Performance of LSTM based schemes against discriminators

### 5.5 Security Analysis

**Theorem 1** Resists collusion attacks

Since the proposed scheme does not require cooperate with other entities, the scheme is resistant to collusion attacks.

**Theorem 2** Resists inference attacks

The proposed scheme takes full account of map background. Each selected trajectory point conforms to the space-time distribution of the actual trajectory. The opponent does not know the prior knowledge of the map information and query probability, so it can resist the inference attack.

**Theorem 3** Resist channel attack

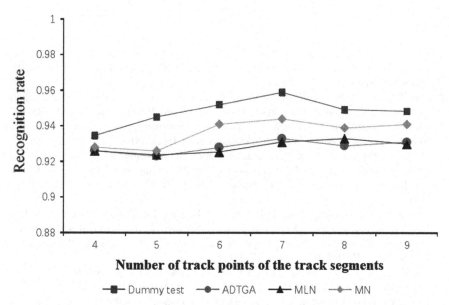

**Fig. 13.** False track recognition rate of false track discriminator based on LSTM

Since the virtual trajectory points are generated and published in the mobile intelligent terminal, and the communication channel is not passed before the fusion of $k$ trajectory points, the attacker cannot obtain the real track points from the channel, so it can resist inference attacks.

## 6 Conclusion

In this paper, a deep learning-based virtual trajectory generation scheme and a virtual trajectory detection scheme based on LSTM are designed. According to the shortcomings of existing algorithms, a whole set of virtual trajectory generation solutions are designed. In the process of false trajectory generation, the generation of trajectory points is placed under three constraints, which not only considers the constraints of the background map, but also considers the constraints between trajectories proposed in existing papers, and the spatial constraints on the distribution of trajectory points. The trajectory itself hides some constraints of human movement patterns, that is, the generated false trajectory can resist the recognition of the neural network-based false trajectory identification scheme. The virtual trajectories generated by this scheme have similar human movement patterns to the real trajectories, which can resist collusion attacks, reasoning attacks and channel attacks, and the generated virtual trajectory points will not be distributed in the unreachable area of the map, so as to minimize losses as much as possible on the premise that users obtain service quality, the user's trajectory privacy is effectively protected.

# References

1. Li, M., Gao, S., Lu, F., Tong, H., Zhang, H.: Dynamic estimation of individual exposure levels to air pollution using trajectories reconstructed from mobile phone data. Int. J. Environ. Res. Public Health **16**(22), 4522 (2019)
2. Park, Y.M., Kwan, M.P.: Individual exposure estimates may be erroneous when spatiotemporal variability of air pollution and human mobility are ignored. Health & Place **43**, 85–94 (2017)
3. Chow, C.Y., Mokbel, M.F., Liu, X.: Spatial cloaking for anonymous location-based services in mobile peer-to-peer environments. GeoInformatica **15**(2), 351–380 (2011)
4. Hara, T., Arase, Y., Yamamoto, A., et al.: Location anonymization using real car trace data for location based services. In: Proceedings of the 8th International Conference on Ubiquitous Information Management and Communication (ICUIMC '14), pp.1–8. ACM, New York (2014)
5. Shokri, R., Theodorakopoulos, G., Danezis, G., Hubaux, J.P., Boudec, J.Y.L.: Quantifying location privacy: the case of sporadic location exposure. In: International Symposium on Privacy Enhancing Technologies Symposium, pp. 57–76. Springer, Berlin, Heidelberg (2011). https://doi.org/10.1007/978-3-642-22263-4_4
6. Lei, K., Li, X., Liu, H.: Privacy protection scheme of fake trajectory based on spatiotemporal correlation in trajectory publishing. J. Communications **37**(12), 156–164 (2016)
7. Dong, Y., Pi, D.: A novel trajectory privacy protection model based on fake data. Computer Science **044**(008), 124–128 (2017)
8. Pingley, A., Zhang, N., Fu, X., Choi, H.A., Subramaniam, S., Zhao, W.: Protection of query privacy for continuous location based services. In: 2011 Proceedings IEEE INFOCOM, pp. 1710–1718. IEEE (2011)
9. Wang, Y., Xu, D., He, X., Zhang, C., Li, F., Xu, B.: L2P2: Location-aware location privacy protection for location-based services. In: 2012 Proceedings IEEE INFOCOM, pp. 1996–2004.IEEE (2012)
10. Komishani, E.G., Abadi, M., Deldar, F.: PPTD: Preserving personalized privacy in trajectory data publishing by sensitive attribute generalization and trajectory local suppression. Knowl.-Based Syst. **94**, 43–59 (2016)
11. Kido, H., Yanagisawa, Y., Satoh, T.: An anonymous communication technique using dummies for location-based services. In :ICPS'05. Proceedings. International Conference on Pervasive Services, 2005, pp. 88–97. IEEE (2005)
12. Wu, X., Sun, G.: A novel dummy-based mechanism to protect privacy on trajectories. In: 2014 IEEE International Conference on Data Mining Workshop, pp.1120–1125. IEEE (2014)
13. Bengio, Y.: Learning deep architectures for AI. Foundations and trends® in Machine Learning **2**(1), 1–127 (2009)
14. Gibson, A., Patterson, J.: Deep Learning: O'Reilly Media, Inc. (2017)
15. Zhang, J.: Gradient Descent based Optimization Algorithms for Deep Learning Models Training. arXiv preprint arXiv:1903.03614 (2019)

# Intrusion Tolerance Quantitative Calculation for Energy Internet Data

Zhanwang Zhu[1] and Song Deng[2(✉)]

[1] College of Automation, Nanjing University of Posts Telecommunications, Nanjing 210003, China
[2] Institute of Advanced Technology, Nanjing University of Posts Telecommunications, Nanjing 210003, China
dengsong@njupt.edu.cn

**Abstract.** In the energy Internet, the deep integration of various en- ergy networks and information communication systems, as well as the operation characteristics of openness, interconnection and sharing, lead to more complex network security risks. Data security is another huge challenge facing the energy Internet. In this paper, a quantitative model of energy Internet data intrusion tolerance is constructed by studying the data autonomy and the quantitative principle of data survival based on set theory. Based on the quantitative model of data intrusion tol- erance, an adaptive intrusion response model based on game theory is proposed. By analyzing the gains and losses of both sides of the game, the profit model of both sides is derived, The optimal Nash equilibrium of both sides is obtained based on game theory. The analysis shows that the proposed data intrusion tolerance quantification and adaptive intru- sion response model can provide theoretical basis and support for active defense of energy Internet data security under network attacks.

**Keywords:** Energy Internet · Intrusion tolerance · Information security · Data security · Quantitative calculation of intrusion tolerance

## 1 Introduction

The large-scale development and utilization of renewable energy will become the development trend of global energy field. The emergence of energy Internet promotes the coupling of power, solar energy, natural gas and other energy net- work systems, and changes the traditional energy utilization mode [1, 2]. As an important part of renewable energy development and energy conservation and emission reduction of the whole society, energy Internet has the characteristics of complex structure, wide data sources, huge data scale and open data sharing, which brings great challenges to the security protection of energy Internet data. In the energy Internet, the security protection of data basically

Supported by the National Natural Science Foundation of China (No.51977113), BAGUI Scholar Program of Guangxi Zhuang Autonomous Region of China (201979) and NUPTSF (No.NY219095).

stays in the aspects of data encryption, access control, authorization and log audit. It is difficult to resist the increasingly complex network intrusion attacks only relying on these security means. At the same time, these security technologies are de- signed to maximize the avoidance of network attacks, and do not consider how to comprehensively assess the threat of data security risks to information systems and physical systems in the case of network intrusion. The existing quantitative calculation methods for data security in the energy Internet generally calculate the security risk value or its state value according to the confidentiality, integrity and availability of the data in the information and physical system, without considering the response of data under the incentive of intrusion attacks and the response mechanism of data after intrusion. Therefore, this paper analyzes and constructs the energy Internet data intrusion tolerance quantitative model from the per- spective of data survival quantification principle, describes the data autonomous domain, the basic data security component chain corresponding to the attack scenario, and the evolution of data attack resistance, identifiability and data recoverability, so as to enrich the data security protection means of energy Internet [3, 4].

The traditional means of data security protection are to avoid the occurrence of intrusion attacks, but these technical means are difficult to truly avoid the occurrence of intrusion attacks and provide timely response after the occurrence of intrusion, and ultimately cannot provide normal business system data services in the energy Internet. Therefore, under the premise of considering attacks, this paper constructs an adaptive intrusion response game model for energy Internet data services from the perspective of data service effectiveness and response cost, so as to enhance the robustness of energy Internet data services.

The remaining of this paper is organized as follows. Section 2 analyzes related work. The energy Internet architecture and data security risk analysis under business scenarios is presented in Sect. 3. Section 4 introduces the quantitative calculation method of energy Internet data intrusion tolerance. And we conclude the whole paper in Sect. 5.

## 2 Related Work

The research on intrusion tolerance technology by foreign scholars was about 20 years earlier than that in China. The concept of intrusion tolerance was first proposed by Fraga and Powel [5]. Huimin LU et al. [6] propose the decentralized blockchain-based route registration framework-decentralized route registration system based on blockchain (DRRS-BC).Foreign scholars have achieved rich results in the research of this hot topic. Wang et al. [7] conducted intrusion detection on the system from various levels, and established a supervision system with functions such as policy reconfiguration and service monitoring. Liu et al. [8] proposed an intrusion tolerance technology based on incomplete information dynamic game, which combines game theory with intrusion tolerance technology, and determines the optimal strategy of both sides of the game by solving the Nash equilibrium. Mostefaoui et al. [9] proposed a digital signature protocol that is conditionally tolerant of intrusions against network attacks based on cryptographic systems to ensure that the system can still provide minimal authentication services when the system is under attack.

In recent years, domestic scholars have also done corresponding research on intrusion tolerance technology. Li et al. [10] combined threshold cryptography with intrusion tolerance technology, and proposed a threshold ECC-based intrusion-tolerant CA private key protection scheme, which ensured that even if the system is attacked. Wang et al. [11] proposed a network distance election calculation model that supports intrusion tolerance, which had a stronger predictive ability than traditional benchmark algorithms. Yu et al. [12] proposed an intrusion tolerant public key encryption scheme to reduce the harm of key leak- age to the encryption system. Zhao et al. [13] proposed a virtual machine-based intrusion tolerance system quantitative performance evaluation method, which improves the security of the computer compared with traditional methods. Wei et al. [14] used an improved semi-Markov process model to describe the process of normal and penetration attacks against the intrusion tolerance system in the data acquisition and monitoring (SCADA) system.

Energy Internet, as a research field that has only emerged in recent years, has been highly valued at home and abroad. Due to the open intercommunication of the Energy Internet, the interaction between various energy data is extremely vulnerable to intruders. As a newly developed field, quantitative calculation and adaptive intrusion response for energy Internet data intrusion tolerance technology are rarely involved.

## 3  Data Security Risk Analysis for Energy Internet

### 3.1  Energy Internet Architecture

The development of the Energy Internet not only breaks the shackles that the use and transmission of traditional energy can only rely on electric energy, so that various types of energy can be dispatched and transformed into each other in a unified manner, and the power system network is closely connected with the natural gas network and other types of energy networks. Combine to form an energy sharing network with multiple energy interoperability. Energy flow of Energy Internet is shown in Fig. 1.

The function of the energy center is mainly to realize the conversion between various types of energy, or to store the energy inside the energy center and use it for load consumption [15, 16]. It can be seen from Fig. 1 that the energy Internet is mainly composed of four parts: the primary energy side, the energy center, the power generation unit, and the load side. The primary energy side is mainly composed of the power grid, the natural gas grid, the cooling grid, and the heating grid. The power generation unit mainly includes wind power, solar power, thermal power, etc. The energy center is responsible for the conversion between various types of energy, as well as the input and output of energy, including energy storage equipment, refrigerators, fuel cells, boilers, etc. The load end corresponds to primary energy side input fully meets the diverse needs of users.

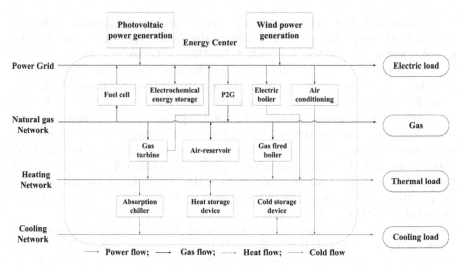

**Fig. 1.** Energy flow of energy internet.

The complete life cycle of the Energy Internet can be described as the energy flow process from the generation of energy to the transmission and conversion of energy, as well as energy storage and energy use. Figure 2 summarizes the entire life cycle of energy input, conversion, transmission and output of the Energy Internet, including the energy supply layer, energy production control layer, energy consumption layer and energy storage layer. The energy supply layer is the energy source of the entire energy Internet, which mainly includes primary energy such as solar energy and petroleum. The energy production control layer is mainly responsible for receiving the collected primary energy, taking the primary energy as input, and converting the primary energy into electrical energy through the energy router and as the input of the next level. The energy consumption layer is the most frequent link of data interaction in the entire energy Internet, which mainly includes users' inquiries on electric and thermal energy and transmission rights transactions. The energy storage layer is the "warehouse" of the entire energy Internet. When the physical system fails, it can ensure the normal operation of the business and improve the stability of the grid.

## 3.2 Data Security Risk Analysis

The information network of the Energy Internet has the characteristics of open- ness and sharing, and more levels of data sources, generally showing the characteristics of wide sources, large scale and complex types. Information in the Energy Internet accompanies the flow of energy, forming a wide-area distributed data application environment in all fields. However, the openness, interconnection and sharing mechanism of the Energy Internet will cause malicious network attacks to occur continuously. This section will analyze the various links of data flow in the Energy Internet, expounding possible data security risks from three aspects.

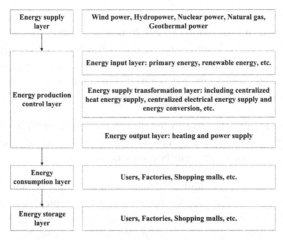

**Fig. 2.** The architecture of energy internet.

The security of energy Internet-related business scenarios mainly includes infrastructure security, system and interaction security, and smart terminal se curity. The specific analysis is as follows:

(1) The stable operation of infrastructure is inseparable from data transmission. The information transmission of the energy Internet usually uses traditional transmission methods such as optical fiber, local area network, and wire. Common data risks mainly include fiber-optic eavesdropping, tampering with status data and misoperation by operators.

(2) With the development of the Energy Internet, business exchanges between users and systems are increasing. The gradual improvement of information ser vices enhances user experience and increases system data security risks. Typical data attacks include DOS attacks and fake data attacks.

(3) The security threats of smart terminals mainly come from traditional devices such as mobile handheld terminals, energy Internet data collection terminals, and smart energy efficiency terminals. The information communication between the system and the terminal makes the security of the system inevitably threatened. The main threats are data loss, tampering, and Dos and DDos attacks initiated by intruders.

## 4  Quantitative Calculation Method of Data Intrusion Tolerance for Energy Internet

In order to carry out the quantitative analysis and calculation of the cyber- physical system data of each link of the Energy Internet after being attacked, what must be solved is to analyze the survival situation of the cyber-physical system of each link of the Energy Internet (that is, whether these systems can still provide external information. Service), this article draws on the traditional theory and methods of system intrusion tolerance to analyze the quantitative calculation method of data intrusion tolerance from the perspective of data sur vivability.

**Definition 1.** Let $A_i$ denote the source of energy Internet data collection, $T_i$ denote the type and mode of transmission, $S_i$ and $P_i$ denote the data storage and processing platforms, respectively, $E_i$ denote the data interaction between energy Internet links, and $D_i$ denote the means of data destruction. Then we call $AS_i = \{A_i, T_i, P_i, S_i, E_i, D_i\}$ as the autonomous domain of energy Internet data securety {ASi = Ai, Ti, Pi, Si, Ei, Di}.N autonomous domains $AS_i$ form the autonomous domain set $\{AS_i, i = 1, 2, \ldots\}$.

**Definition 2.** Let $AS_i$ denote the i-th autonomous domain and $CS_i$ denote the basic security logic components contained in the i-th autonomous domain, then we call{ $CS_i$,i = 1, 2}, denotes the set of basic security components.

Based on the data location and environment in the energy Internet and the overall posture of the data security autonomous domains, N typical data attack scenarios against $AS_i$ are constructed to form a data attack scenario set Fi (e.g., virus and malware attacks, DoS, eavesdropping, tampering, etc.). The data attack flow formed by the whole data attack scenario $Fi$ is mapped to the data logical components to form another security component set $SC_i$, which finally forms the basic security component chain corresponding to the autonomous domain and attack scenarios as shown in Fig. 3.

### 4.1 Resistability Quantification Calculation

Resistance refers to the ability of the Energy Internet as a whole to provide data services normally when the system is under attack. The emphasis is on the overall system rather than the performance of individual components. This article constructs the criticality value of the event set {$E_{qn}$}of the data-attack damage level $q$ from indicators such as

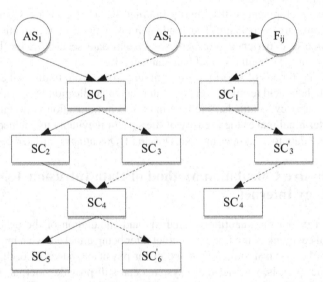

**Fig. 3.** Basic security component chain corresponding to autonomous domain and attack scenario.

autonomous domain and criticality weight, as shown in the following formula:

$$\omega_q = \frac{\sum_{n=1}^{N} \omega_{qn}}{N} \tag{1}$$

where $N$ is the number of data attack events and $w_{qn}$ is the harm value of the $n$-th data attack event.

On this basis, $AS_i$ constructs the data security domain to the data attack scenario set and the data security autonomy domain resistibility quantification formula respectively, as shown in formula (2) and (3):

On this basis, the resistibility quantification formulas of data security au- tonomous domain $AS_i$ to data attack scenario set $F_{ij}$, and data security au- tonomous domain $AS_i$ are constructed respectively.

$$Resis\_F_{ij} = \Sigma_k(\Sigma_k(W_q \times p\_res_q \times d_q) \times m_{ijk}). \tag{2}$$

$$Resis\_AS_i = \Sigma_j(Resis\_F_{ij} \times f_{ij}). \tag{3}$$

where $p\_res_q$ is the resistance rate of data to attack events at this level, $d_q$ is the distribution rate of data attack events at all levels, $m_{ijk}$ is the weighted value of logical relationship and attack scenario relationship among data sets in data security autonomous domain, and $f_{ij}$ is the jeopardy weight value of $F_{ij}$ in data attack scenario.

If the importance of each data security domain $AS_i$ is represented by a weight $s_i$, then the resistibility of energy Internet is shown as follows:

$$Resis = \Sigma_i(Resis\_AS_i \times s_i). \tag{4}$$

### 4.2 Recognizability Quantification Calculation

Recognizability emphasizes the monitoring and identification of the data security status in the cyber-physical system of the entire energy Internet, not just for a certain event. This paper intends to construct the overall recognition time of the event set {Eqn} of the attack hazard level q by the data as shown as follows:

$$T_q = \frac{\sum_{n=1}^{N} t_{qn}}{N} \times n. \tag{5}$$

where N is the number of data attack events, and tqn is the regularized value of the recognition time of the nth data attack event.

On this basis, the data attack scenario Fij and the data security autonomous domain $AS_i$ identifiable quantitative model are constructed respectively, as shown in Eqs. (6) and (7).

$$Recog\_F_{ij} = \Sigma_k(\Sigma_q(W_q \times p\_recog_q \times d_q \times T_q) \times m_{ijk}). \tag{6}$$

$$Recog\_AS_i = \Sigma_j(Recog\_F_{ij} \times f_{ij}). \tag{7}$$

where $p\_recog_q$ is the recognition rate of $q$ level attack events in the attack scenario event set by data, $d_q$ is the distribution rate of data attack events at this level, and $m_{ijk}$ is the weighted value of the logical relationship between each data set in the data security autonomous domain and the data attack scenario relationship, $f_{ij}$ is the hazard weight of $F_{ij}$ in the data attack scenario.

The recognizability of the Energy Internet can be summarized as the weighting of the recognizability values of all data security autonomous domains, as shown in Eq. (8)

$$Recog = \Sigma_i(Recog\_AS_i \times s_i). \tag{8}$$

### 4.3  Recoverability Quantitative Calculation

The recoverability of data is defined as whether the impact on the data caused by a network attack is recoverable, and the extent to which the data autonomous domain can be recovered within a certain period of time.

This paper intends to construct the recoverability function model of each link $N_{ik}$ in the data security autonomous domain $AS_i$, as shown in Eqs. (9) and (10), respectively.

$$Recov\_N_{ik} = \Sigma_j[f_{ij} \times p\_recov_{kj} \times p\_recov_{kj}. \times recovT_{ik}/TureT_{kj}]. \tag{9}$$

$$Recov\_AS_i = \Sigma_k(Recov\_N_{ik} \times a_{ik}). \tag{10}$$

where $recovT_{ik}$ is the recovery time requirement of each link of the $N_{ik}$ in the data security autonomous domain $AS_i$, $TureT_{kj}$ is the time interval from the start of the data attack scenario set $F_{ij}$ to the complete recovery of each link in the data security autonomous domain $AS_i$, and $p\_recov_{kj}$ is the data within the $TureT_{kj}$ time interval The degree of recovery of the $N_{ik}$ of each link in the security autonomous domain $AS_i$, $a_{ik}$ is the recoverability weight of each link of the $N_{ik}$ in the data security autonomous domain $AS_i$.

On this basis, the formula for summarizing the recoverability of Energy Internet data is shown as follows:

$$Recov = \Sigma_i(Recov\_AS_i \times s_i). \tag{11}$$

## 5  Conclusions

This article gives a detailed introduction to the concept of data intrusion tolerance and its quantitative calculations in the context of the Energy Internet. On the basis of constructing the basic security component chain of the cyber- physical system data for each link of the Energy Internet, from the aspects of resistance, identifiability and The data intrusion tolerance is quantitatively calculated at three levels of recoverability, and the adaptive intrusion response based on game theory is theoretically deduced. Compared with other existing models, the adaptive intrusion response model based on game theory analyzes the cost of intrusion tolerance and the benefits obtained, and the decision made fully considers the gains and losses of both parties in the game and is reasonable.

**Acknowledgements.** We would like to thank the anonymous reviewers for their comments and constructive suggestions that have improved the paper. The subject is sponsored by the National Natural Science Foundation of P. R. China (No. 51977113) and BAGUI Scholar Program of Guangxi Zhuang Autonomous Region of China (201979).

# References

1. Wang, K., et al.: A survey on energy internet: architecture, approach, and emerging technologies. IEEE Syst. J. **12**(3), 2403–2416 (2017)
2. Zhou, K., Yang, S., Shao, Z.: Energy internet: the business perspective. Appl. Energy **178**, 212–222 (2016)
3. Sani, A.S., Yuan, D., Jin, J., Gao, L., Yu, S., Dong, Z.Y.: Cyber security framework for internet of things-based energy internet. Futur. Gener. Comput. Syst. **93**, 849–859 (2019)
4. Wang, H., Ruan, J., Ma, Z., Zhou, B., Fu, X., Cao, G.: Deep learning aided interval state prediction for improving cyber security in energy internet. Energy **174**, 1292–1304 (2019)
5. Veríssimo, P.E., et al.: Intrusion-tolerant middleware: the road to automatic security. IEEE Secur. Priv. **4**(4), 54–62 (2006)
6. Lu, H., Tang, Y., Sun, Y.: Drrs-bc: Decentralized routing registration system based on blockchain. IEEE/CAA J. Automatica Sinica **8**(12), 1868–1876 (2021)
7. Wang, F., Gong, F., Sargor, C., Goseva-Popstojanova, K., Trivedi, K., Jou, F.: Sitar: A scalable intrusion-tolerant architecture for distributed services. In: Workshop on Information Assurance and Security. vol. 1, p. 1100 (2003)
8. Liu, P.: Engineering a distributed intrusion tolerant database system using cots components. In: Proceedings DARPA Information Survivability Conference and Exposition. vol. 2, pp. 284–289. IEEE (2003)
9. Mostéfaoui, A., Raynal, M.: Intrusion-tolerant broadcast and agreement abstractions in the presence of byzantine processes. IEEE Trans. Parallel Distrib. Syst. **27**(4), 1085–1098 (2015)
10. Li, X.: An intrusion tolerant protection scheme of ca private key based on threshold ecc. Computer Simulation **26**(12), 115–117 (2009)
11. Wang, C., Zhang, F.L., Yang, X.X., Li, M., Wang, R.J.: A voter model supporting intrusion-tolerance for network distance estimation. J. Electron. Inf. Technol. **35**(11), 2637–2643 (2013)
12. Yu, J., Cheng, X.G., Li, F.G., Pan, Z.K., Kong, F.Y., Hao, R.: Provably secure intrusion-resilient public-key encryption scheme in the standard model. Ruanjian Xuebao/Journal of Software **24**(2), 266–278 (2013)
13. Zhao, F., Jin, H., Jin, L., Yuan, P.: Vfrs: a novel approach for intrusion tolerance in virtual computing environment. J. Computer Res. Development **47**(3), 493 (2010)
14. Wei, K., Zhang, F.: Based on markov network tolerate invasion ability evaluation model. Computer Simulation **33**(7), 289–292 (2016)
15. Deswarte, Y., Powell, D.: Internet security: an intrusion-tolerance approach. Proc. IEEE **94**(2), 432–441 (2006)
16. Moniz, H., Neves, N.F., Correia, M., Verissimo, P.: Ritas: Services for randomized intrusion tolerance. IEEE Trans. Dependable Secure Comput. **8**(1), 122–136 (2008)
17. Huimin, L., Zhang, M., Xu, X.: Deep fuzzy hashing network for efficient image retrieval. IEEE Trans. Fuzzy Syst. **29**(1), 166176 (2020). https://doi.org/10.1109/TFUZZ.2020.2984991

18. Huimin, L., Li, Y., Chen, M., et al.: Brain Intelligence: go beyond artificial intelligence. Mobile Networks Appl. **23**, 368–375 (2018)
19. Huimin, L., Li, Y., Shenglin, M., et al.: Motor anomaly detection for unmanned aerial vehicles using reinforcement learning. IEEE Internet Things J. **5**(4), 2315–2322 (2018)
20. Huimin, L., Qin, M., Zhang, F., et al.: RSCNN: A CNN-based method to en-hance low-light remote-sensing images. Remote Sensing 13(1), 62 (2020)
21. Huimin, L., Zhang, Y., Li, Y., et al.: User-oriented virtual mobile network resource management for vehicle communications. IEEE Trans. Intelligent Transportation Syst. **22**(6), 3521–3532 (2021)

# Data Security Knowledge Graph for Active Distribution Network

Qianliang Li[1], Renjie Dai[2], Siming Wei[2], Jie Zhang[1], and Song Deng[3(✉)]

[1] College of Automation, Nanjing University of Posts Telecommunications, Nanjing 210003, China
[2] State Grid Shanghai Municipal Electric Power Company, Shanghai 200122, China
[3] Institute of Advanced Technology, Nanjing University of Posts Telecommunications, Nanjing 210003, China
dengsong@njupt.edu.cn

**Abstract.** The openness, interconnection and sharing mechanism of the active distribution network bring great security risks to business system data. The existing data security protection strategies for the active distribution network are basically based on encryption, access control, and blockchain technology, which cannot enable the active distribution network operation and maintenance and management personnel to intuitively understand the data security situation affecting the active distribution network from a global perspective. Therefore, this paper combines the concept of knowledge graph to explore the key technologies of data security knowledge graphs for the active distribution network. First, the key technologies for constructing knowledge graph are explained in detail from named entity recognition, entity relation extraction and entity alignment. And then, with the active distribution network data as the object, the process of constructing data security knowledge graph for active distribution network is explained. Finally, the challenge of constructing a data security knowledge map for active distribution network is given.

**Keywords:** Active distribution network · Data security · Knowledge graph named entity recognition · Entity relation extraction

## 1 Introduction

The energy interaction, communication and information interaction among various energy sources in the active distribution network are mostly realized by industrial control systems. Information in the active distribution network accompanies the flow of energy to form a wide-area distributed data application environment [1]. However, the openness, interconnection and sharing mechanism of the active distribution network will lead to continuous malicious network attacks. These malicious cyber-attacks use the coupling between hyperphysical systems in the active distribution network to generate cross-space (from information space to physical space, feedback from physical space to information space), cross-system (from energy management system to intelligent control system and transaction prediction system between various energy forms, etc.), and cross-platform

© The Author(s), under exclusive license to Springer Nature Singapore Pte Ltd. 2022
S. Yang and H. Lu (Eds.): ISAIR 2022, CCIS 1700, pp. 193–204, 2022.
https://doi.org/10.1007/978-981-19-7946-0_17

(from embedded devices to smart PDAs, from Windows systems to Linux systems, etc.) chain reactions of interactive propagation. This inevitably poses a great threat to the security of the entire life cycle process of data collection, transmission, storage, processing, exchange and destruction in the active distribution network [2].

The existing technologies to ensure data security of the active distribution network mainly include encryption and blockchain. However, these technologies cannot enable users to grasp the entire active distribution network data security situation from a global perspective. Knowledge graph is a kind of semantic network that uses visualization technology to describe knowledge resources and their carriers, mines, analyzes, constructs, draws and displays knowledge and their interrelationships [3]. This paper constructs a data security knowledge map for the energy Internet, which is to describe the relationship between entities and entities that affect the data security of the Energy Internet through the knowledge map, forming an energy Internet data security network with clear entities and association relationships. Eventually, the knowledge in the field of data security for the active distribution network will be materialized, relational, and visualized. By constructing an active distribution network-oriented data security knowledge graph, management and operation personnel can intuitively understand security intelligence and security situations, and sort out the relationships between entities that affect active distribution network data security.

The remainder of this paper is organized as follows. The related work is first introduced in Sect. 1. And then the key technology of constructing knowledge graph is described in Sect. 2. The detailed process of constructing the data security knowledge graph of the active distribution network is presented in Sect. 3. The key technical difficulties of the data security knowledge map for the active distribution network are shown in Sect. 4. And we conclude the whole paper in Sect. 5.

## 2   Related Work

In recent years, domestic and foreign researches have been conducted on the hot issue of active distribution network information security, especially data security protection. Shahzad et al. [4] analyzed the system framework of the energy Internet, and discussed the challenges and solutions of data integrity protection on the open and interconnected architecture of the Energy Internet. Zhang et al. [5] described the information security threats faced by the energy Internet, discussed the data security protection of distributed energy stations in the energy Internet, and built a corresponding data security protection framework. It can be seen that data security occupies an important position in energy Internet information security protection.

To deal with the security protection problems of energy big data in the storage and processing process, Chin et al. [6] comprehensively analyzed and investigated the security threats faced by energy big data under the existing communication protocols. And it is pointed out that attackers can use replay attacks to launch concealed attacks on energy big data, which is not easy to be detected and identified. To address the security problem of energy Internet data storage under network attacks, Deng et al. [7] proposed a data lossless recovery algorithm based on network coding and rough sets for the energy Internet, which solved the recovery problem of multi-modal data in the energy

Internet scenario after being damaged by some attacks. In turn, the continuous and stable operation of the energy Internet business system is guaranteed. Thomas et al. [8] proposed a hybrid intrusion detection system oriented to the active distribution network, which can reduce the attack detection time and improve the accuracy of anomaly detection. Wang et al. [9] proposed a defense mechanism based on the interval state predictor to effectively detect malicious attacks on data in the active distribution network. In this mechanism, any state beyond the estimated range can be identified as an anomaly, indicating that the data has been maliciously attacked. Hou et al. [10] proposed a multi-objective optimization algorithm based on RBF neural network and dynamic adjustment of weights to optimize and evaluate the network security defense strategies of different components of the active distribution network data, network and system. And a system-level comprehensive optimization is achieved to ensure the optimal overall security of the active distribution network. Abubakar et al. [11] proposed a network security framework based on identity authentication to provide security and privacy protection for energy Internet data, and proved the security and reliability of the proposed scheme through the Nash equilibrium theory. Ref. [12-14] used lightweight two way terminal authentication, access control and encryption to ensure the security of data transmission in the energy Internet. Guan et al. [15] proposed a blockchain-based energy Internet transaction strategy, which not only guarantees the privacy in the data transaction process, but also meets the protection needs of data security. To reduce the impact of false data injection attacks on the accuracy of multiple energy state estimation, Tu et al. [16] deeply studied the mechanism and countermeasures of stealth false data injection attacks in the energy Internet. The experimental results verified that the proposed false data injection attack protection strategy greatly improves the accuracy of energy Internet state estimation. Ref. [17, 18] analyzed the impact of false data injection attacks on power system state estimation, and used spatiotemporal correlation and Kalman filtering methods to detect false data. These methods could provide ideas for false data detection in complex scenarios of the Energy Internet.

It can be seen from the above documents that most of the existing active distribution network data security defense systems use single methods such as intrusion detection, authentication and encryption, and blockchain to build a defense system to block or isolate external intrusions, so as to ensure the security of data transmission, data storage and application of active distribution network. Because the active distribution network is a cyber-physical system that integrates humans, machines and physics. Risks affecting data security will propagate between information systems, which in turn will affect the safe and stable operation of physical systems. However, the existing single or combined active distribution network security defense system cannot master the entire data security situation as a whole, nor can it find the correlation between data security risks from the details. Therefore, building a data security knowledge graph for active distribution network is very important for in depth discovery of the relationship between humans, machines and physics in the active distribution network.

# 3    Key Technology of Knowledge Graph

## 3.1    Named Entity Recognition

Named entity recognition [19] is an important task in information extraction and information retrieval. Its purpose is to identify the components of the text that represent named entities and classify them, so it is sometimes called named entity recognition and classification (NERC). The methods of named entity recognition mainly include rule-based [20], and deep learning-based methods [21, 22].

In recent years, due to the continuous development of deep learning technology, especially the continuous progress of text vectorization methods, deep learning methods have become the mainstream method for solving named entity recognition. Ji et al. [Power entity recognition based on bidirectional long short-term memory and conditional random fields] used the BILSTM-CRF model to extract power grid text features, and completed the labeling of the sequence and achieved good training results. The BILSTM-CRF model is divided into three layers: input layer, hidden layer, and annotation layer. The model is shown in Fig. 1.

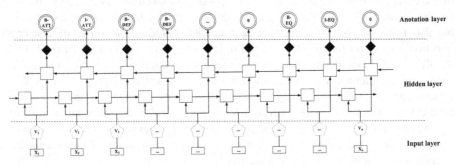

**Fig. 1.** BILSTM-CRF model.

The input layer is based on the WORD2VEC model to realize the vectorization of text data, so that the text data completes the mapping of high-dimensional vectors. The hidden layer is based on the BILSTM model to obtain the characteristics of the text. The input vector sequence $(x1, x2, ..., xn)$ is used as the input of the two-way LSTM network. In BILSTM, the input vector sequence is used as the input of the forward LSTM, and the reverse sequence is used as the input of the backward LSTM [23]. Then, the model spliced the hidden state sequence $\overrightarrow{h_1}, \overrightarrow{h_2}, ..., \overrightarrow{h_n}$ output by the forward LSTM and the hidden sequence $\overleftarrow{h_1}, \overleftarrow{h_2}, ..., \overleftarrow{h_n}$ utput by the reverse LSTM into $h_t = [\overrightarrow{h_t}, \overleftarrow{h_t}] \in R^m$ get the complete hidden state sequence $(h_1, h_2, ..., h_t) \in R^{n \times m}$ where m is the dimension of the hidden state vector. In order to automatically extract sentence features, a linear transformation layer is connected to the hidden layer, and the previously obtained hidden state sequence is mapped from m-dimension to k-dimension, where $k$ represents the number of labels in the annotation set, and the result is recorded as matrix $P = (p_1, p_2, ..., p_n) \in R^{n \times k}$. And each $P_{ij}$ of $P_i \in R^k$ is regarded as a scoring value for classifying to the $j$-th label.

The annotation layer is based on the CRF model to complete the annotation task. CRF introduces a state transition matrix $M$, each element $M_{ij}$ of the matrix $M$ represents the conditional probability of changing from $i$ to $j$, and uses the labeled information to label a new position. If a label sequence is denoted as $y = (y_1, y_2, \ldots, y_n)$, for sentence $x$, the model predicts the score of labels $y$ as $score(x, y) = \sum_{i=1}^{n}(M_{y_iy_{i+1}} + P_{i,y_i})$. We can see that the scoring result consists of two parts. One is determined by the output pi of the LSTM, and the other is determined by the change matrix $M$ of the CRF. Finally, the Softmax function is used for normalization and the result is obtained:

$$P(y|x) = \frac{exp(score(x, y))}{\sum_{u'} exp(score(x, y'))} \tag{1}$$

## 3.2 Entity Relation Extraction

Entity relation extraction [24] is the core task of text mining and information extraction. It mainly uses text information modeling to automatically extract the semantic relation between entity pairs and effective semantic knowledge. The main methods of relation extraction can be divided into supervised [25, 26], unsupervised [27], and semi-supervised [28].

Traditional relation extraction based on supervised learning requires a large amount of artificially labeled data to complete the training of the model, and complete the classification task of specific relations through the trained model. Relation extraction based on unsupervised learning does not require a training method of manually labeling data. Generally, clustering algorithms are used to classify context entities with high similarity into the same category, and the phrase representing the relationship with the highest occurrence frequency in the same category is selected as the relationship type [29].

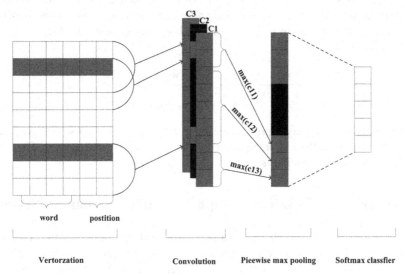

**Fig. 2.** PCNN Model.

Relation extraction based on semi-supervised learning first needs to construct a relation set. The training sample contains a small amount of labeled data and a large amount of unlabeled data, and then through the learning and matching of the samples, the final relationship model is generated. Semi supervised learning gets rid of the dependence of supervised learning on the need for a large amount of labeled data.

The PCNN model is a classic model of supervised relation extraction in the current knowledge graph, as shown in Fig. 2. The first layer of the PCNN model is the vector coding layer, which contains vector coding and position coding, to realize the vectorized representation of text and position. The second layer of the model is a convolutional layer containing three convolutions, which divides the sentence into three parts. A part is from the beginning of the sentence to the first entity. The second part is from the first entity to the second entity, and the third part is from the second entity to the end of the sentence. Each part is subjected to convolution operation separately, and the maximum pooling output vector of each part is calculated. The third layer of the model is the SoftMax layer, which implements the classification and prediction of relation attributes to complete the task of relation extraction.

### 3.3 Entity Alignment

Entity alignment [30] refers to finding out the same entity in the real world for each entity in the knowledge base of heterogeneous data sources. Traditional entity alignment methods can be divided into Trans E model and text similarity matching. In the Trans E model, the triple information is embedded in the lowdimensional space, and the entity alignment is completed through the operation of the vector. Zhu et al. [31] improved the traditional Trans E model through iteration and parameter sharing, thereby enhancing the performance of entity alignment. In this work, we propose an entity alignment method based on Word2Vec and text similarity. The word vector model is trained through Word2Vec, and the similarity is determined by calculating the cosine similarity of different feature words to complete the entity alignment task. The cosine similarity calculation formula is shown in formula Eq. 1.The greater the cosinvalue, the greater the similarity.

$$\frac{w \cdot s}{|w| \times |s|} = \frac{\sum_{i=1}^{n}(w_i \times s_i)}{\sqrt{\sum_{i=1}^{n} w_i^2} \times \sqrt{\sum_{i=1}^{n} s_i^2}} \tag{2}$$

where w and s respectively represent the word vectors of the two words, $w_i$ and $S_i$ respectively represent the $i$-th value in the two n-dimensional word vectors. The entire Word2Vec model is shown in Fig. 3.

## 4    Data Security Knowledge Graph for Active Distribution Network

As a domain knowledge graph, the data security knowledge graph for the active distribution network follows the process and framework of general knowledge graph construction and adopts a top-down construction model. Based on the existing data security protection knowledge system for the active distribution network, the entities and the relationships between entities that affect the data security of the active distribution network are obtained from the data through information extraction and other technologies. And the fragmented active distribution network data security knowledge is linked together through the framework of graph database. Finally, it will be displayed in the form of diagrams.

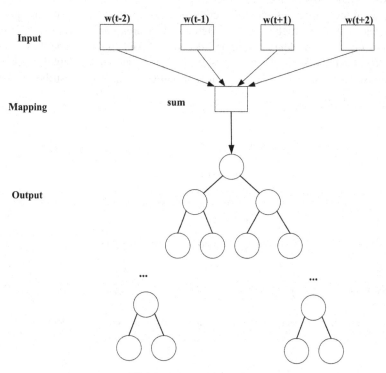

**Fig. 3.** Word2Vec model.

## 4.1 Data Security Entity Construction for Active Distribution Network

The definition of the type of knowledge entity refers to the data security protection rules in the existing active distribution network data security protection and power information security protection plan. Then, we extract multiple entity types, including attack targets, attack methods, attack sections, attack types, attack effects, common detection methods, communication methods, attack equipment, defense measures, tools, etc. The data security knowledge graph for the active distribution network must standardize the dictionary, and carry out a unified and standardized description of the attributes of different entities in order to facilitate the construction of the knowledge graph.

Attack targets include specification descriptions such as availability, integrity, and confidentiality. Attack methods include DDOS attacks, black hole attacks, man-in-the-middle attacks, false data injection attacks, etc. The attack section includes specification descriptions such as the transmission side, the power generation measurement, the distribution side, and the power consumption side. Attack types include obstruction of traffic, delay of communication, illegal data tampering, injecting wrong data, and cracking of passwords. Attack effects include fault cascading, voltage instability, load loss, system disassembly, and data leakage. Detection methods include machine learning, neural networks, statistical knowledge, residual detection, and risk assessment. Communication methods include optical fiber, Ethernet, Zigbee, and power communication network. Attack equipment includes data collection devices, switchgear, terminal equipment, switchgear, and smart meter devices. Defense measures include detection, isolation, rejection, interruption, degradation, and deception. And tools include Trojan horses, agents, and backdoors. All these entities closely focus on data security through attacks and defenses. The entire data security entity structure for the active distribution network is shown in Fig. 4.

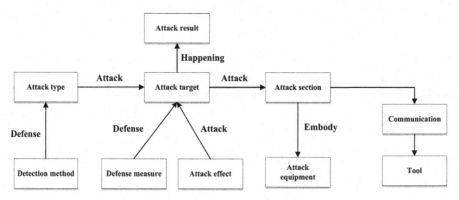

**Fig. 4.** Data security entity construction for active distribution network.

## 4.2 Construction of Data Security Entity Relation for Active Distribution Network

The definition of data security for the active distribution network can only form isolated information nodes in the knowledge graph. There is no relation between nodes and nodes, and in-depth mining and analysis cannot be completed. Through the data security report and logical analysis of active distribution network, the entity relation of the data security knowledge graph for active distribution network is constructed. Then it sums up a set of entity relations that include attack relations, defense relations, containment relations, and occurrence relations that are applicable to active distribution network-oriented data security relations. Finally, a data security knowledge map for the active distribution network is shown in Fig. 5.

# 5   Key Technical Difficulties

## 5.1   Key Technical Difficulties of General Knowledge Graph

First of all, entity naming recognition is the basic task of constructing a knowledge graph. However, the construction of general knowledge graphs usually depends on knowledge crowdsourcing, which is huge in terms of human resource consumption. Secondly, in relation extraction, the mainstream method is based on the relation of supervised learning, and the relation model is gradually constructed through continuous learning of samples. However, the introduction of relation samples will create inevitable data noise and reduce the efficiency of entity relation recognition. Entity alignment usually relies on prior knowledge to align samples, but it is inefficient for massive entity alignment.

**Fig. 5.** Data security knowledge graph for active distribution network.

## 5.2   Key Technical Difficulties of Data Security Knowledge Graph for Active Distribution Network

According to the key technical difficulties of the general knowledge graph, the complexity of named entity recognition and the accuracy of samples in the entity relation models will be the challenges that must be faced when constructing a data security knowledge graph for active distribution network.

(1) To build a data security knowledge map for the active distribution network, entity relation extraction not only requires large-scale and high-quality entity annotations, but also requires the participation of experts in the energy field. This will undoubtedly increase the difficulty of constructing a knowledge graph.

(2) In the data security knowledge map for the active distribution network, knowledge about data security needs to be summarized in advance, and data noise will also increase the difficulty of constructing relational models

## 6  Conclusions

To better grasp the data security situation of the active distribution network from the overall perspective, this paper explores the key technologies of the data security knowledge map for the active distribution network. Firstly, the key technologies of general knowledge graph are analyzed from named entity recognition, entity relation extraction and entity alignment. Then, by identifying the entities that affect the data security of the active distribution network, and extracting the relations between these entities, a knowledge graph of data security for the active distribution network is explored. Finally, the key technical difficulties of constructing a data security knowledge map for the active distribution network.

**Acknowledgment.** This work was supported by the State Grid Shanghai Municipal Electric Power Company Technology Projects (B30935210005).

## References

1. Wang, J., et al.: Review on information and communication key technologies of energy internet. Smart grid **3**(6), 473–485 (2015)
2. Lu, H., Zhang, M., Xu, X., Li, Y., Shen, H.T.: Deep fuzzy hashing network for efficient image retrieval. IEEE Trans. Fuzzy Syst. **29**(1), 166–176 (2020)
3. Mendsaikhan, O., Hasegawa, H., Yamaguchi, Y., Shimada, H.: Quantifying the significance and relevance of cyber-security text through textual similarity and cyber-security knowledge graph. IEEE Access **8**, 177041–177052 (2020)
4. Shahzad, Y., Javed, H., Farman, H., Ahmad, J., Jan, B., Zubair, M.: Internet of energy: opportunities, applications, architectures and challenges in smart industries. Comput. Electr. Eng. **86**, 106739 (2020)
5. Zhang, J.: Distributed network security framework of energy internet based on internet of things. Sustainable Energy Technol. Assess. **44**, 101051 (2021)
6. Chin, W.L., Li, W., Chen, H.H.: Energy big data security threats in iot-based smart grid communications. IEEE Commun. Mag. **55**(10), 70–75 (2017)
7. Deng, S., Yuan, C., Yang, L., Qin, X., Zhou, A.: Data recovery algorithm under intrusion attack for energy internet. Futur. Gener. Comput. Syst. **100**, 109–121 (2019)

8. Rose, T., Kifayat, K., Abbas, S., Asim, M.: A hybrid anomaly-based intrusion detection system to improve time complexity in the internet of energy environment. J. Parallel Distributed Comput. **145**, 124–139 (2020)
9. Wang, H., Ruan, J., Ma, Z., Zhou, B., Fu, X., Cao, G.: Deep learning aided interval state prediction for improving cyber security in energy internet. Energy **174**, 1292–1304 (2019)
10. Hou, R., Ren, G., Gao, W., Liu, L.: Research on cyberspace multi-objective security algorithm and decision mechanism of energy internet. Futur. Gener. Comput. Syst. **120**, 119–124 (2021)
11. Sani, A.S., Yuan, D., Jin, J., Gao, L., Yu, S., Dong, Z.Y.: Cyber security framework for internet of things-based energy internet. Futur. Gener. Comput. Syst. **93**, 849–859 (2019)
12. Hou, R., Ren, G., Zhou, C., Yue, H., Liu, H., Liu, J.: Analysis and research on network security and privacy security in ubiquitous electricity internet of things. Comput. Commun. **158**, 64–72 (2020)
13. Wang, P., Xiang, T., Li, X., Xiang, H.: Access control encryption without sanitizers for internet of energy. Inf. Sci. **546**, 924–942 (2021)
14. Sani, A.S., Yuan, D., Bao, W., Dong, Z.Y.: A universally composable key exchange protocol for advanced metering infrastructure in the energy internet. IEEE Trans- actions on Industrial Informatics **17**(1), 534–546 (2020)
15. Guan, Z., Lu, X., Wang, N., Wu, J., Du, X., Guizani, M.: Towards secure and efficient energy trading in iiot-enabled energy internet: a blockchain approach. Futur. Gener. Comput. Syst. **110**, 686–695 (2020)
16. Tu, C., He, X., Liu, X., Shuai, Z., Yu, L.: Resilient and fast state estimation for en- ergy internet: a data-based approach. IEEE Trans. Industr. Inf. **15**(5), 2969–2979 (2019)
17. Liu, X., Wu, Z.: Online defense research of spatial-hidden malicious data injection attacks in smart grid. In: Proc. Chin. Soc. Electr. Eng. vol. 13, pp. 1520–1534 (2020)
18. Rawat, D.B., Bajracharya, C.: Detection of false data injection attacks in smart grid communication systems. IEEE Signal Process. Lett. **22**(10), 1652–1656 (2015)
19. Huang, X., Tang, J., Tan, Z., Zeng, W., Wang, J., Zhao, X.: Knowledge graph embedding by relational and entity rotation. Knowl.-Based Syst. **229**, 107310 (2021)
20. Liao, X., Yuan, K., Wang, X., Li, Z., Xing, L., Beyah, R.: Acing the ioc game: Toward automatic discovery and analysis of open-source cyber threat intelligence. In: Proceedings of the 2016 ACM SIGSAC Conference on Computer and Communications Security, pp. 755–766 (2016)
21. Hung, J.C., Chang, J.W.: Multi-level transfer learning for improving the performance of deep neural networks: theory and practice from the tasks of facial emotion recognition and named entity recognition. Appl. Soft Comput. **109**, 107491 (2021)
22. Santoso, J., Setiawan, E.I., Purwanto, C.N., Yuniarno, E.M., Hariadi, M., Purnomo, M.H.: Named entity recognition for extracting concept in ontology building on indonesian language using end-to-end bidirectional long short term memory. Expert Syst. Appl. **176**, 114856 (2021)
23. Lu, H., Yang, R., Deng, Z., Zhang, Y., Gao, G., Lan, R.: Chinese image caption- ing via fuzzy attention-based densenet-bilstm. ACM Trans. Multimedia Computing, Communications, and Applications (TOMM) **17**(1s), 1–18 (2021)
24. Wan, Q., Wei, L., Chen, X., Liu, J.: A region-based hypergraph network for joint entity-relation extraction. Knowl.-Based Syst. **228**, 107298 (2021)
25. Shi, Y., Xiao, Y., Quan, P., Lei, M., Niu, L.: Distant supervision relation extraction via adaptive dependency-path and additional knowledge graph supervision. Neural Netw. **134**, 42–53 (2021)
26. Wen, H., Zhu, X., Zhang, L., Li, F.: A gated piecewise cnn with entity-aware enhancement for distantly supervised relation extraction. Inf. Process. Manage. **57**(6), 102373 (2020)
27. Hou, S., Lu, R.: Knowledge-guided unsupervised rhetorical parsing for text summarization. Inf. Syst. **94**, 101615 (2020)

28. Zeng, D., Liu, K., Chen, Y., Zhao, J.: Distant supervision for relation extraction via piecewise convolutional neural networks. In: Proceedings of the 2015 Conference on Empirical Methods in Natural Language Processing, pp. 1753–1762 (2015)
29. Zheng, Q., Zhu, J., Tang, H., Liu, X., Li, Z., Lu, H.: Generalized label enhancement with sample correlations. IEEE Transactions on Knowledge and Data Engineering (2021)
30. Zeng, K., Li, C., Hou, L., Li, J., Feng, L.: A comprehensive survey of entity alignment for knowledge graphs. AI Open 2, 1–13 (2021)
31. Zhu, H., Xie, R., Liu, Z., Sun, M.: Iterative entity alignment via knowledge embeddings. In: Proceedings of the International Joint Conference on Artificial Intelligence (IJCAI) (2017)
32. Huimin, L., Zhang, M., Xu, X.LDeep fuzzy hashing network for efficient image retrieval. IEEE Transactions on Fuzzy Systems (2020). https://doi.org/10.1109/TFUZZ.2020.2984991
33. Huimin, L., Li, Y., Chen, M., et al.: Brain Intelligence: go beyond artificial intelligence. Mobile Networks Appl. 23, 368–375 (2018)
34. Huimin, L., Li, Y., Shenglin, M., et al.: Motor anomaly detection for unmanned aerial vehicles using reinforcement learning. IEEE Internet Things J. 5(4), 2315–2322 (2018)
35. Huimin, L., Qin, M., Zhang, F., et al.: RSCNN: A CNN-based method to en-hance low-light remote-sensing images. Remote Sensing 13(1), 62 (2020)
36. Huimin, L., Zhang, Y., Li, Y., et al.: User-oriented virtual mobile network resource management for vehicle communications. IEEE Trans. Intelligent Transportation Syst. 22(6), 3521–3532 (2021)

# Design of MobileNetV1 SSD Target Detection Accelerator Based on FPGA

Luojia Shi, Chunyu Long, Jitong Xin, Jianhong Yang, Peng Wang$^{(\boxtimes)}$,
and Fangcong Wang

Institute of Microelectronics, School of Physical Science and Technology, Lanzhou University,
Lanzhou, China
{wangpeng,wangfc}@lzu.edu.cn

**Abstract.** Object detection based on convolutional neural network has become one of the important algorithms in the field of computer target detection. However, due to the speed and power limitation brought by convolution computation, the algorithm of the convolutional network used for target recognition generally needs to be accelerated by the convolution accelerator before it can be effectively deployed to edge computing devices. In this paper, a new architecture of the convolution accelerator is proposed. On this basis, the convolution accelerator is used to build and complete the convolutional acceleration system, and the MobileNetV1 SSD detection algorithm network is realized. The convolution accelerator has a special operation channel, which can normalize convolution kernels of different sizes. Besides, it innovatively optimizes the addition operation mode in the convolution kernels, realizes pipeline convolution calculation, shortens the image recognition time and increases the versatility of the convolution accelerator.

**Keywords:** Convolution accelerator · Architecture improvement · Target detection · MobileNetV1 SSD · FPGA

## 1 Introduction

In recent years, target detection technology has become an important research tool in the field of computer vision. As an important content of computer vision research, target detection is applied to judge the category of the target in the static image and generate multiple detection information such as the location of the target by using a certain target detection technology or calling some database for comparative analysis.

The algorithm for target detection is based on the convolutional neural network system, which has high image category detection accuracy, it supports high-precision positioning, and is more powerful than traditional target detection algorithms. Therefore, this algorithm has become the primary choice for the research and development of target detection schemes.

The MobileNet model is a lightweight deep neural network proposed by Google for mobile phones and other embedded devices using deeply separable convolution [1]. Compared with the traditional convolutional neural network, it has the advantage of

S. Yang and H. Lu (Eds.): ISAIR 2022, CCIS 1700, pp. 205–217, 2022.
https://doi.org/10.1007/978-981-19-7946-0_18

effectively reducing the amount of computation, saving a large number of parameters, speeding up the operation speed, and alleviating the training problems caused by excessive fitting [2]. MobileNet SSD [3] (Single Shot MultiBox Detector) algorithm is a target detection model based on MobileNet model, The MobileNetV1 SSD algorithm is very commonly used and has potential, so this paper chooses it as a research tool for the test of the target detection accelerator.

However, the convolutional neural network algorithm used in the target detection is not fast enough in CPU, but its power consumption is greatly limited. Therefore, the task of convolution calculation is generally assigned to a special convolution accelerator for calculation, and such a convolution accelerator generally takes logical resources of FPGA (Field Programmable Gate Array) [4] or ASIC (Application Specific Integrated Circuit) [5] as the carrier.

Although many architectures have been designed using FPGA, single-core convolution accelerators with traditional architectures have fixed operators, slow speed and poor compatibility on the one hand. On the other hand, few breakthroughs have been made in the architecture improvement of the accelerators recently, which requires research and improvement on the architecture of the accelerators.

Although at present there have been many FPGA convolution accelerator, but on the other hand due to the present most accelerators are doing translation software engineers and scholars of the algorithm based on convolution algorithm, using C language, the use of conversion tool for circuit transformation and generate the convolution accelerator [6], the convolution accelerator for algorithm architecture direct translation, Most of these convolution accelerators are single-core convolution accelerators [7]. The convolution accelerator with traditional architecture has fixed operator, slow speed and poor compatibility, so it is necessary to optimize the convolution accelerator from the perspective of hardware. On the other hand, there are few breakthroughs in the architecture innovation of the accelerator recently, which requires research and innovation on the architecture of the accelerator.

In this paper, a special pipeline convolution accelerator is designed, which has high flexibility and calculation speed. The MobileNetV1 SSD detection algorithm network can be implemented by this accelerator and complete the target detection function.

The rest of this paper is organized as follow. We first introduce the MobileNet SSD algorithm introduction in Sect. 2, we then describe the system configuration in Sect. 3. We give the accelerator design in Sect. 4, and experimental results and analysis are provided in Sect. 5. Finally, we conclude this paper in Sect. 6.

## 2 Algorithm Introduction

The architecture of the MobileNet SSD detection algorithm network is based on the VGG16-SSD algorithm structure [8]. It uses regression-based mode to directly return the category and location of the object in the network, and the concept of region-based makes it possible to use many candidates in the detection process which uses the anchor point method [9], and the idea of multi-scale detection is introduced. Feature maps of different sizes are used. The larger feature maps are used to detect relatively small targets, while the small ones are responsible for detecting large targets and predicting the next target, and generating target detection results by regression of the location [10].

Figure 1 shows the structure of the MobileNet SSD algorithm framework:

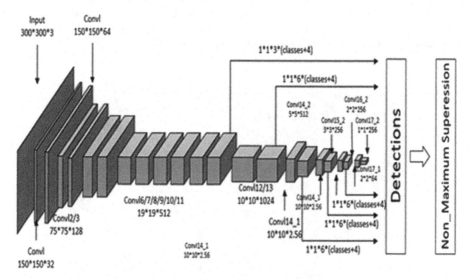

**Fig. 1.** The diagram of MobileNet-SSD algorithm framework structure

The MobileNet SSD network structure is similar to the VGG-SSD network structure, except that the number of convolutional layers is increased on the basis of the conv13 layer, and 6 layers are extracted from the 8 convolutional layers for target inspection, thereby improving the performance of target detection. The clever decomposition of convolutional kernel accelerates computation and effectively reduces network parameters. The backbone network of the MobileNet SSD algorithm studied in this work is the MobileNet network structure. Its core is the use of depthwise separable convolution [11], which is a typical mobile operating network structure. In the case that the detection accuracy is not affected, but the redundancy of convolution kernel of target detection is greatly reduced, which reduces the computation amount of the algorithm and the size of the model, thus helping to improve the efficiency of target detection.

## 3   System Configuration

The system as a whole is divided into two parts, namely PL part and PS part [12]. PL is the logic part, which is the FPGA, and the PS part is the ARM. Among them, the PL side mainly includes the accelerator, and the PS side mainly includes the fpgadrv driver, the ssd_detection user program, the Paddlelite framework [13], the mobilenet_v1 SSD model, the lib library, and the opencv library [14]. The PL side mainly realizes the acceleration of the convolution; the PS side mainly transmits the image data and the convolution kernel operator for the PL, and further processing of the result of the convolution operation is also required. The overall block diagram of the system is shown in Fig. 2, and the specific functions of each unit are shown below. The accelerator unit mainly accelerates the convolution part. The data enters the convolution kernel through the Avalon bus [15], and the weight data and the image data are convolved through the convolution kernel [16]. Fpgadrv: Fpgadrv is the driver of FPGA accelerator on Linux side. Mobilenet_v1 SSD: Mobilenet_v1 SSD stores the SSD model and parameters. Lib [17] contains the library files needed to run the demo. Ssd_detection_src: Contains the demo source code. Opencv: The compiled opencv library.

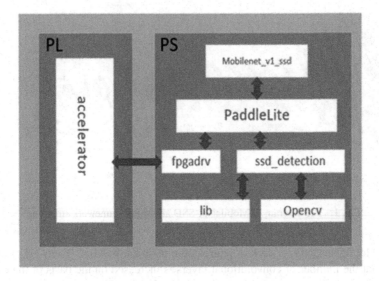

**Fig. 2.** System overall block diagram

# 4   Accelerator Design

## 4.1   Structure of Accelerator

As shown in Fig. 3, The accelerator consists of AvalonBusUpSizer ABUS module, AvalonBusMatrix MTX module, ConvCore module and sysCtrl module.

Among them, the Sysctrl module completes the configuration of the convolution kernel register through the configuration mode register. The AvalonBusUpsizer ABUS module mainly adapts the bus bandwidth. The data bit width of the Avalon bus on the ARM side is 128-bit, and the data bit width of the internal Avalon bus of the convolution acceleration kernel is 512-bit, so bus adaptation is required. The AvalonBusMatrix MTX module judges the data that enters the module, judges whether it is image data or convolution kernel data, transmits different types of data to the corresponding storage module, and provides the ARM side with a read map of the convolution result data.

As shown in Fig. 4, the ConvCore module is composed of din_fifo unit, ConvCompute unit, and dout_fifo unit:

Among them, din_fifo mainly completes the buffering of the input weight data and image data and splicing them into the convolution calculation module. As shown in

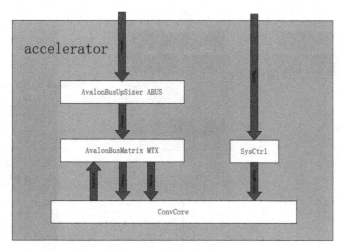

**Fig. 3.** Structure diagram of accelerator

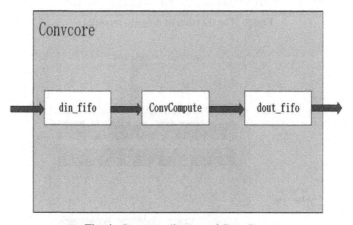

**Fig. 4.** Structure diagram of ConvCore

Fig. 5, the figure is a structural diagram of din_fifo. Input fifo completes the buffering of the input image data, and Kernal fifo completes the buffering of the weight data. When the data enters, the two fifo units perform pipeline operation at the same time. Convheight counts the number of kernel rows in each batch of kernel, and each 32-bit in the convolution kernel operator is regarded as a minimum arithmetic unit, and then it is expanded to 512-bit by repeating the 32-bit unit. Finally, the weight data and the image data are spliced, and the spliced result is input to the convolution calculation unit.

The structure of dout_fifo is shown in Fig. 6. This module is configured with a buffer with depth of 4096 and width of 512-bit. Each row contains 64-byte and 16 result points.

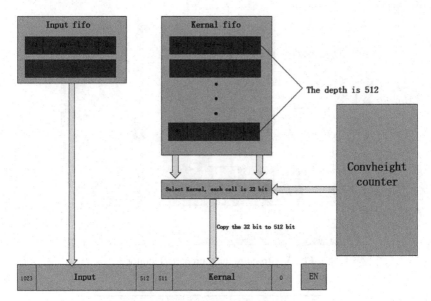

**Fig. 5.** The diagram of din_fifo module

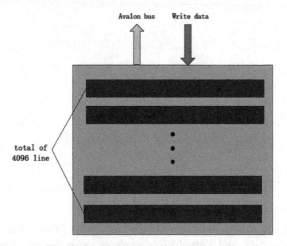

**Fig. 6.** The diagram of dout_fifo module

The overall architecture of ConvCompute is shown in Fig. 7. The function of the convolution calculation module is to perform multiplication and addition operations by the input image data and weight data, where the weight data and image data are multiplied by the 8 × 8 multiplier unit, and the result enters the adder array unit for addition calculation, where the ConvHeight counts the number of kernel rows in each batch, and the control output is effectively enabled.

For the multiplication calculation unit, as shown in Fig. 8. We use 64 multipliers to perform 8-bit fixed-point multiplication calculations on the input image data and weight

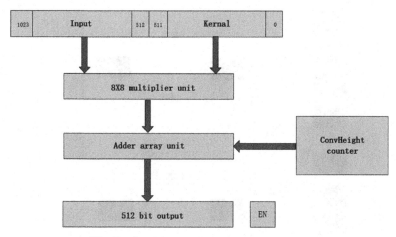

**Fig. 7.** The diagram of ConvCompute module

data, and insert registers for pipeline operation. Then the result into the addition module for addition operation. The multiplication calculation consumes 32 DSPs (Digital Signal Processor) [18].

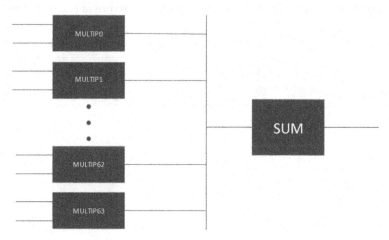

**Fig. 8.** The diagram of multiplier unit structure

For the addition calculation unit, as shown in Fig. 9, the adder array unit is composed of three-layer adders. The data first passes through 32 adders to complete an addition operation, then the calculation result is added again, next the data is registered. Then through a layer of adder to complete the self-adding operation. For the adder, we chose the Koggle-Stone tree adder parallel algorithm [19], which greatly improves the speed of the addition operation.

The Koggle-Stone adder is a tree adder generated by a parallel algorithm proposed by Peter M. Koggle and Harold S. Stone in 1972. In the tree adder, this kind of adder

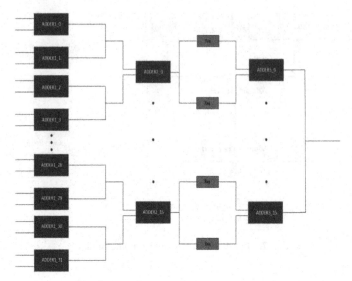

**Fig. 9.** The diagram of the adder array unit

has the characteristics of low logic layers and low fan-in and fan-out. This type of adder trades area for speed. The simulation of this algorithm is shown in Fig. 10 below.

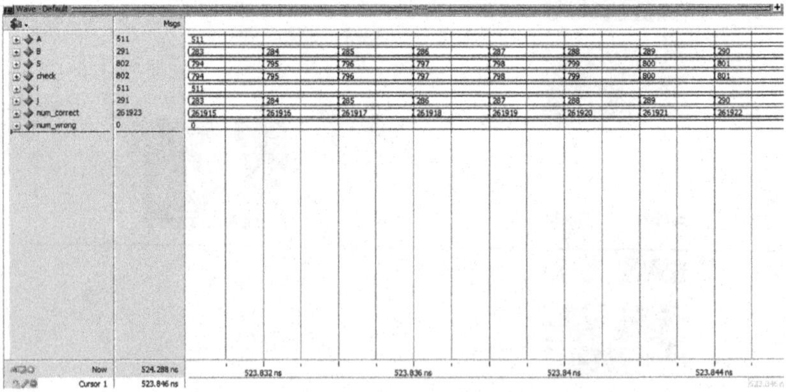

**Fig. 10.** Simulation result of Koggle-Stone adder

As shown in Fig. 11, the figure is a simulation diagram of the ConvCore module, in which LUT consumes 4226, DSP consumes 64, and bram consumes 2359296. The maximum operating clock frequency of the accelerator is 144.18 MHz.

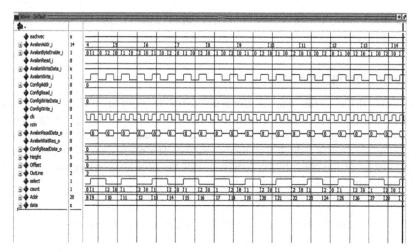

**Fig. 11.** Simulation of the ConvCore module

## 4.2  The Overall Use and Function of Accelerator

The driver on the ARM side integrates and assembles the image data according to the same batch of data of different channels. Each row of data is 64-bit, and the row of data contains 16 points of data. Each point data needed for segmentation and assembly, according to each of the 4-byte. The ConvHeight is the amount of data needed to calculate the result of a row divided by 4-byte and insufficient rounded up. And then output to the output memory with 16 points per row, and only the calculation depth (ConvHeight) and the result Depth (ConvOutMax) need to be configured in the configuration parameters, the ARM side needs to configure the kernel of each batch first, and then the data is fragmented and transmitted to the FPAG side (transmitted to the convolution kernel information through the AXI bus [20] to the Avalon bus [15]), and the accelerator performs convolution calculations as it receives data. After the transmission is completed, the data processing is obtained by reading the status register, and then the driver on the ARM side reads the results and reorganizes the data. Theoretically, the processing time is almost equal to the ARM data preprocessing time plus transmission time and then plus read back time, because of the accelerator architecture belongs to stream processing as transmission goes along. It only needs to store part of the input. In this design, the input memory is a 2-line memory structure (128-byte in total), while the Kernel memory is 512 row memory (following the original design), the output memory is 4096 row of memory (which can store 65536 result points). The input memory uses similar the structure of the ping-pong operation [21] ensures the accuracy of the input data (one row of memory is used to store the input data, and the other row is used to output the convolution calculation), and realizes a streaming architecture that transmits and processes at the same time, saving transmission time and storage space, use the limited embedded storage block as much as possible to store output data and kernel information. In addition, the convolution accelerator supports channel fusion and convolution kernel normalization [22] of convolution data, because any convolution calculation is regarded as a $1 \times 1 \times$ multi-channel convolution calculation, which improves the versatility of the convolution accelerator.

### 4.3 Control Group Experiment

In the case of the same hardware platform and software configuration, only the accelerator was replaced. And the accelerator generated by a company using C language was used as the control group. The accelerator was a traditional fixed-point and single-core convolution accelerator, which was representative. The results are compared with the running results of the convolution accelerator of the new architecture adopted in this paper, as shown in Table 1:

**Table 1.** Performance comparison of convolution accelerators

| Convolution accelerator | Accelerator frequency | Accelerator power consumption | Total system running time |
|---|---|---|---|
| The traditional architecture accelerator generated by C language | 142.13 MHz | 424.88 mW | 3.42 s |
| The convolution accelerator of the paper used | 144.18 MHz | 430.55 mW | 2.28 s |

## 5  Experimental Results and Analysis

This system driver runs on the Linux-C5 SOC platform [23], the operating system is CentOS7. After the development board is powered on, configure the rbf file generated by quartus to the FPGA, then start the Linux kernel, and the Linux kernel loads the device tree file. The hardware development platform used in this experiment is Quartus 18.1 Standard. The simulation software is modelsimModelSim SE-64 10.5 [24], and the PL accelerator part is written in Verilog language. When recognizing a picture with three targets to be recognized, the recognition results are shown in Fig. 12 below. The total operation time of the system using the accelerator is 2.28 s. The recognition accuracy is more than 90%, and the target detection function can be realized. The working frequency of the accelerator is 144.18 MHz. The power consumption of the accelerator is 430.55 mW. Compared with the traditional convolution accelerator, the overall running time of the system is shortened from 3.42 s to 2.28 s under the premise that the accelerator's frequency and power consumption are not much different. These results show that the performance of convolution accelerator with the new architecture is improved, and its architecture innovation method has positive value.

**Fig. 12.** Recognition effect using the MobileNet SSD network structure

## 6 Conclusion

The architecture of accelerator commonly used in target recognition network is innovated and the configurable storage computing system is redesigned. At the same time, we also use a high speed Koggle-Stone adder to optimize the addition operation, which has never been used in previous accelerators before. At the algorithm level, this accelerator adopts the method of channel fusion, which processes all the data of a batch of convolution operation at a time, normalizes the accelerator, and converts the acceleration kernel into a multi-channel $1 \times 1$ volume, which improves the calculation speed. In addition, because of the normalization process, the accelerator's universality is greatly enhanced. The working frequency of the accelerator is 144.18 MHz, and the power consumption is 430.55 mW. It takes about 2.28 s for the system to recognize images with three targets using the accelerator, and the target detection algorithm is successfully realized. The new architecture and method are of reference value to the future architecture innovation of the accelerator used for target recognition.

## References

1. Li, D., et al.: Fast detection and location of longan fruits using UAV images. Comput. Electron. Agric. **190**, 106465 (2021)

2. Bilbao, I., Bilbao, J., Feniser, C.: Adopting some good practices to avoid overfitting in the use of machine learning. WSEAS Trans. Math **17**, 274–279 (2018)
3. Liu, W., et al.: Ssd: Single shot multibox detector. In: Proceedings European Conference on Computer Vision. Springer, Cham, pp. 21-37 (2016). https://doi.org/10.1007/978-3-319-464 48-0_2
4. Zhang, C., Li, P., Sun, G., Guan, Y., Cong, J.: Optimizing FPGA-based accelerator design for deep convolutional neural networks. In: Proceedings The 2015 ACM/SIGDA International Symposium. ACM (2015)
5. Pan, H., Wang, M., Li, J.: Design of the key Structure of Convolutional Neural Network Reconfigurable Accelerator Based on ASIC. Proc.2018 International Conference on Network, Communication, Computer Engineering (NCCE 2018). Atlantis Press, pp. 301–304 (2018)
6. Cornu, A., Derrien, S., Lavenier, D.: HLS tools for FPGA: Faster development with better performance. In: Proceedings International Symposium on Applied Reconfigurable Computing. Springer, Berlin, Heidelberg, pp. 67-78 (2011). https://doi.org/10.1007/978-3-642-194 75-7_8
7. Johnson, D., Johnson, M., Kelm, J., Tuohy, W., Lumetta, S., Patel, S.: Rigel: A 1,024-core single-chip accelerator architecture. IEEE Micro, Papers **31**(4), 30–41 (2011)
8. Kang, H.J.: Real-time object detection on 640x480 image with vgg16+ ssd. In: 2019 International Conference on Field-Programmable Technology (ICFPT). IEEE, pp. 419–422 (2019)
9. Yamada, Y., Ishida, M., Tsuzuki, S., Tazaki, S.: Simplified anchor point method for fast nearest neighbor search algorithm. Technical Research Report of Electronic Information Commun. Society **96**(78–88), 71–76 (1997)
10. Bao, D., Hao, L.: Survey of target detectionbased on neural network. J. Phys: Conf. Ser. **1952**(2), 022055 (2021)
11. Chollet, F.: Xception: Deep Learning with Depthwise Separable Convolutions. IEEE, pp. 1251–1258 (2017)
12. Zhang, Y., Liu, P., Wang, X.: Design of high speed 1553B bus test system based on ARM and FPGA. J. Changchun University of Science and Technology (Natural Science Edition) (2016)
13. Paddlepaddle: Paddle Lite (2021). https://www.paddlepaddle.org.cn/paddle/paddlelite
14. Culjak, I., Abram, D., Pribanic, T., Dzapo, H., Cifrek, M.: A brief introduction to OpenCV. In: 2012 Proceedings of the 35th International Convention MIPRO. IEEE, pp. 1725–1730 (2012)
15. Xu, N.Y., Zhou, Z.C.: Avalon bus and an example of SOPC system. Semiconductor Technology **28**(2), 17–20 (2003)
16. Gu, J., Wang, Z., Kuen, J., Ma, L., Shahroudy, A., Shuai, B., Chen, T.: Recent advances in convolutional neural networks. Pattern Recognition **77**, 354–377 (2018)
17. Zheng, J.Y., Wang, L.: Static link library in implementing radar simulation system component. Communications Technology (2011)
18. Pailoor, R., Pradhan, D.: Digital signal processor (DSP) for portable ultrasound. Texas Instruments, Application Report SPRAB18A (2008)
19. Kogge, P.M., Stone, H.S.: A parallel algorithm for the efficient solution of a general class of recurrence equations. IEEE Trans. Comput. **100**(8), 786–793 (1973)
20. Math, S.S., Manjula, R.B., Manvi, S.S., Kaunds, P.: Data transactions on system-on-chip bus using AXI4 protocol. In: Proceedings IEEE, pp. 423–427 (2011)
21. Rui, L.I., Xiao, L.I., Wang, Z., Wang, G.: Design of data acquisition system based on SRAM ping-pong operation. J. University of Jinan (Science and Technology) (2015)
22. Sledevic, T.: Adaptation of convolution and batch normalization layer for CNN implementation on FPGA. In: 2019 Open Conference of Electrical, Electronic and Information Sciences (eStream) IEEE (2019)

23. El-Moursy, M.A., Sheirah, A., Safar, M., Salem, A.: Efficient embedded SoC hard-ware/software codesign using virtual platform. In: Proceedings 2014 9th International Design and Test Symposium (IDT). IEEE, pp. 36–38 (2014)

24. Alsharef, A.A., Ali, M., Sanusi, H.: Direct digital frequency synthesizer simulation and design by means of quartus-modelSim. J. Applied Sciences **12**(20), 2172–2177 (2012)

25. Huimin, L., Zhang, M., Xu, X.:Deep fuzzy hashing network for efficient image retrieval. IEEE Trans. Fuzzy Systems **29**(1), 166176 (2020). https://doi.org/10.1109/TFUZZ.2020.298 4991

26. Huimin, L., Li, Y., Chen, M., et al.: Brain Intelligence: go beyond artificial intelligence. Mobile Networks Appl. **23**, 368–375 (2018)

27. Huimin, L., Li, Y., Shenglin, M., et al.: Motor anomaly detection for unmanned aerial vehicles using reinforcement learning. IEEE Internet Things J. **5**(4), 2315–2322 (2018)

28. Huimin, L., Qin, M., Zhang, F., et al.: RSCNN: A CNN-based method to en-hance low-light remote-sensing images. Remote Sensing **13**(1), 62, 2020

29. Huimin, L., Zhang, Y., Li, Y., et al.: User-oriented virtual mobile network resource man-agement for vehicle communications. IEEE Trans. Intelligent Transportation Syst. **22**(6), 3521–3532 (2021)

# Transformer-Based Point Cloud Classification

Xianfeng Wu[1,2,3,4], Xinyi Liu[2], Junfei Wang[1,2,4], Xianzu Wu[6,7],
Zhongyuan Lai[1,2,3,4(✉)], Jing Zhou[2(✉)], and Xia Liu[5(✉)]

[1] State Key Laboratory of Precision Blasting, Jianghan University, Wuhan 430056,
People's Republic of China
laizhy@jhun.edu.cn
[2] School of Artificial Intelligence, Jianghan University, Wuhan 430056,
People's Republic of China
zhj131@jhun.edu.cn
[3] Bingling Honorary School, Jianghan University, Wuhan 430056, People's Republic of China
[4] Institute for Interdisciplinary Research, Jianghan University, Wuhan 430056,
People's Republic of China
[5] School of Intelligent Manufacturing, Jianghan University, Wuhan 430056,
People's Republic of China
23761854@qq.com
[6] College of Geophysics and Petroleum Resources, Yangtze University, Wuhan 430100,
People's Republic of China
[7] Key Laboratory of Oil and Gas Resources and Exploration Technology of Ministry
of Education, Yangtze University, Wuhan 430100, People's Republic of China

**Abstract.** In this paper, we propose a transformer-based point cloud classification method. We introduce different transformer modules into the three key networks of PointNet, to improve the discriminability and the stability of features extracted at different stages. Experimental results show that compared with the PointNet, our method has not only a higher classification accuracy but also a higher stability, especially when the points in the point cloud are extremely few.

**Keywords:** Point cloud classification · PointNet · Transformer · Classification accuracy · Stability

## 1 Introduction

The sampled points on the surface of an object for a set of points called a point cloud. Compared with images, point clouds have richer spatial information and are less affected by illumination changes, so point cloud-based object classification is paid more and more attention to in the application server autonomous driving, robotics, and augmented reality. However, its intrinsic properties of disorder, irregularity and nonuniform distribution makes it challenging to design a deep neural network for classification that directly uses point clouds as inputs.

PointNet is one of the pioneers of deep neural networks that directly use point clouds as inputs [1]. This method consists of spatial alignment network, a feature extraction

S. Yang and H. Lu (Eds.): ISAIR 2022, CCIS 1700, pp. 218–225, 2022.
https://doi.org/10.1007/978-981-19-7946-0_19

network, and a classification network. The key network among them is the feature extraction network, which can be divided three sub-networks: the low-level feature extraction network, the low-level feature alignment network, and the high-level feature extraction network. Since the process of feature extraction does not involve the local partition and the neighborhood calculation of point clouds, it cannot effectively utilize the local information of point clouds, and thus the classification accuracy is not high. To effectively improve the classification accuracy, many local feature-based methods and neighborhood feature-based methods have been developed. Although these methods effectively improve the classification accuracy, they involve the local partition and the neighborhood calculation, and thus their classification accuracies are inevitably affected by the local absence and density variation of point clouds.

In practical applications, the captured point cloud of an object is often affected by the view angle, the distance from the camera, and the occlusion by the other object, which may result in local absent and density variation. Therefore, whether a point cloud classification method is good or bad does not only depends on the classification accuracy under idea situation but also depends on whether it is stable against point variations in the real world.

Then the question arises, can we find a method that can achieve a high classification accuracy while at the same time performing stable against point variations? To answer the above question, on the one hand, we choose PointNet method as our backbone to guarantee the stability; on the other hand, it is shown that transformer can make full use of the correlation of all the point features [2], enhancing both the discriminability and stability of the extracted features. Therefore, we introduce transformer into the feature extraction network of PointNet. We also find that the offset-attention (OA) mechanism works best among the existing transformer mechanisms, so we choose the OA mechanism for our implementation. Specifically, we introduce the OA mechanism into the low-level feature extraction network and introduce the cascaded-attention (CA) mechanism into the low-level feature transformation network and the high-level feature extraction network, to enhance the discriminability and stability of the features at different feature extraction stages. Experimental results show that compared with PointNet, our method can improve not only classification accuracy but also stability.

## 2  Our Method

In this section, we first revisit the PointNet method [1], then briefly introduce the OA mechanism, and finally show how to embed the OA mechanism into the PointNet method.

### 2.1  Revisiting PointNet

The PointNet network consists of a spatial alignment network, a feature extraction network, and a classification network, as shown in Fig. 1(a). The workflow of this network is as follows. First, the coordinate matrix of size $N \times 3$ is put into the spatial alignment network to obtain an aligned coordinate matrix of size $N \times 3$, where $N$ denotes the number of points in the input point cloud. And then the aligned coordinate matrix is put

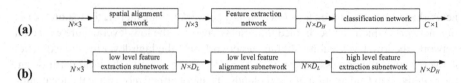

**Fig. 1. (a)** Block diagram of PointNet **(b)** Feature extraction network

into the feature extraction network to obtain a high-level feature matrix of size $N \times D_H$. This matrix is put into the classification network to obtain a $C$-dimensional class vector.

The feature extraction network is the core network of PointNet, which consists of three sub-networks, the low-level feature extraction subnetwork, the low-level feature alignment subnetwork, and the high-level feature extraction subnetwork, respectively, as shown in Fig. 1(b). The workflow of this network is as follows. Firstly, the aligned coordinate matrix of size $N \times 3$ is put into low-level feature extraction subnetwork to obtain a low-level feature extraction matrix of size $N \times D_L$. And then this low-level feature matrix is put into the low-level feature aligned subnetwork to obtain an aligned low-level feature matrix of size $N \times D_L$. Finally, the aligned low-level feature matrix is put into the high-level feature extraction subnetwork to obtain a high-level feature matrix of size $N \times D_H$.

The above workflow does not involve the local partition or the neighborhood calculation, which brings both positive and negative effects. On the positive side, at each stage of feature extraction, the feature of each point is either directly generated from itself, or generated by the features of all points, so the obtained features are global in nature and not easily affected by the part absence and density variations. On the negative side, the local characteristics of the object are not fully utilized, resulting in low classification accuracy.

## 2.2   Offset-Attention Mechanism

As mentioned previously, to improve the classification accuracy while at the same time preserving the stability of PointNet, we introduce the transformer mechanism. The common transformer mechanisms include self-attention (SA) and offset-attention (OA). As pointed out by [3], compared to SA, OA has better performance, so we choose OA for our implement. Next, we give a brief introduction to OA.

Let $\mathbf{F}_{in}$ denote the input feature matrix of size $N \times D$, where $D$ denotes the dimension of the input feature of each point in the point cloud. Let $\mathbf{Q}, \mathbf{K}, \mathbf{V}$ denote the query matrix of size $N \times D_A$, key matrix of size $N \times D_A$ and value matrix of size $N \times D$, respectively, then we have.

$$(\mathbf{Q}, \mathbf{K}, \mathbf{V}) = F_{in} \cdot (\mathbf{W}_q, \mathbf{W}_k, \mathbf{W}_v), \tag{1}$$

where $\mathbf{W}_q, \mathbf{W}_k, \mathbf{W}_v$ is the shared learnable linear transformation matrices of size $D_A \times D, D_A \times D, D \times D$.

Next, we performed dot-product between the query matrix and the key matrix to obtain the attention weights matrix $\widetilde{\mathbf{A}}$ as follows:

$$\widetilde{\mathbf{A}} = (\widetilde{a})_{ij} = \mathbf{Q} \cdot \mathbf{K}^T. \tag{2}$$

Then we perform softmax normalization for each column of matrix $\tilde{\mathbf{A}}$ as follows:

$$\bar{a}_{ij} = soft \max(\tilde{a}_{ij}) = \frac{\exp(\tilde{a}_{ij})}{\sum_k \exp(\tilde{a}_{kj})}. \tag{3}$$

After that, we perform linear normalization row of matrix $\overline{\mathbf{A}} = (\bar{a})_{ij}$ as follows:

$$a_{ij} = \frac{\bar{a}_{ij}}{\sum_k \bar{a}_{ik}}. \tag{4}$$

Now we obtain the normalized attention matrix $\mathbf{A} = (a)_{ij}$. We performed the dot-product between the normalized attention matrix and the value matrix, and we obtain the self-attention feature matrix $\mathbf{F}_{sa}$ as follows:

$$\mathbf{F}_{sa} = \mathbf{A} \cdot \mathbf{V}. \tag{5}$$

Finally, we calculate the offset-attention feature matrix of size $N \times D$ as follows:

$$\mathbf{F}_{out} = MLP(\mathbf{F}_{in} - \mathbf{F}_{sa}) + \mathbf{F}_{in}, \tag{6}$$

where MLP denotes multi-layer perceptron.

## 2.3 Point Cloud Classification Based on Transformer

To improve the classification accuracy while at the same time maintaining the stability advantage of PointNet, we introduce the above OA mechanism into each of the three sub-networks of the feature extraction network of PointNet, as described below.

Firstly, we introduce the OA mechanism into the low-level feature extraction sub-network. As shown in Fig. 2, the OA-based low-level feature sub-network consists of a MLP and OA module. It works as follows. Firstly, the aligned coordinate matrix of size $N \times 3$ is put into MLP to obtain the feature matrix of size $N \times D_L$, where $D_L$ is the dimension of the low-level feature. And then this feature matrix is put into the OA module to obtain the performance enhanced feature matrix of size $N \times D_L$. Finally, these two feature matrices of size $N \times D_L$ are summarized to obtain the low-level feature matrix of size $N \times D_L$.

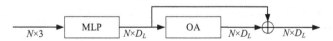

**Fig. 2.** OA-based low-level feature extraction subnetwork

Then we concatenate four OA modules to form cascaded attention (CA) mechanism, as show in Fig. 3, which can enhance performance of feature at different scales. Then we introduce the CA mechanism into the low-level feature alignment subnetwork. As shown in Fig. 4, the CA-based low-level feature alignment subnetwork consists of four MLP, a CA module, a max-pooling layer and a fully connected (FC) network. It works

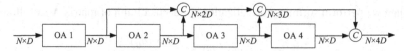

**Fig. 3.** Cascaded-attention mechanism

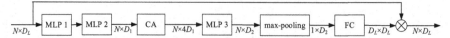

**Fig. 4.** CA-based low-level feature alignment subnetwork

**Fig. 5.** CA-based high-level feature extraction subnetwork

as follows. Firstly, the low-level feature matrix of size $N \times D_L$ is put into two MLPs to obtain the feature matrix of size $N \times D_1$, followed by a CA module to obtain the feature matrix of size $N \times 4D_1$. And then this feature matrix is put into MLP 3 to obtain the feature matrix of size $N \times D_2$. After that, the above feature matrix is put into the max-pooling layer to obtain a $D_2$-dimensional feature vector. Finally, this vector is put into the FC network to obtain the feature transformation matrix of size $D_L \times D_L$. The dot product between the aligned low-level feature matrix of size $N \times D_L$ and the feature transformation matrix of size $D_L \times D_L$ is performed to obtain an aligned low-level feature matrix of size $N \times D_L$.

Finally, we introduce the CA mechanism into the high-level feature extraction subnetwork. As shown in Fig. 5, the CA-based high-level feature extraction subnetwork consists of two MLP and a CA module. It works as follows. Firstly, the aligned low-level feature matrix of size $N \times D_L$ is put into MLP 1 to obtain the feature matrix of size $N \times D_3$, followed by the CA module to obtain the feature matrix of size $N \times 4D_3$. Finally, this feature matrix is put into MLP 2 to obtain the high-level feature matrix of size $N \times D_H$.

From the above, we introduce the transformer mechanism at each key stage of feature extraction to improve the discriminability and the stability of the features, which in turn leads to the improvement of the overall classification accuracy and stability.

## 3   Experiments

To verify that our method can improve the classification accuracy while at the same time maintaining the stability of PointNet [1], we conduct a series of experiments. In Sect. 3.1 we compare the classification accuracies of various methods, and in Sect. 3.2 we compare the stability of different methods under the variation of the number of points in the point cloud. In Sect. 3.3, we give the results of the ablation study.

## 3.1  Comparison of Classification Accuracy

To verify that our method can effectively improve the accuracy of PointNet, we select ModelNet40 as our dataset [4]. This dataset contains 12311 point cloud samples, of which 9843 samples are used for training, and 2468 for testing. For each sample, we perform the farthest point downsampling method to obtain 1024 points as input. Table 1 shows the overall accuracy and average accuracy of the existing method and our method. When the number of input points is 1024, the overall accuracy of our method is 92.9%, which achieves a 3.7% gain over the 89.2% overall accuracy of PointNet. Compared with other methods, our method is second only to Paconv [12] in terms of classification accuracy, which further reveals the advantage of our method in terms of classification accuracy.

## 3.2  Stability Comparison

In order to verify that our method can maintain the stability even under the change of the number of points, we select PointNet [1], PointNet + + [6] and DGCNN [13] as the counterpart of our method. Here the testing samples are randomly downsampled to 1024, 768, 512, 256, 128, 64 and 32 points and then put to the above trained model for testing. As shown in Fig. 6, we can see that the classification accuracy of DGCNN starts to drop rapidly when the sampling points drop to 512, and the classification accuracy of PointNet + + starts to drop rapidly when the sampling points drop to 128, while both PointNet and our method can maintain the stability of the classification accuracy. Furthermore, as the number of points in the point cloud decreases, our classification accuracy decreases more slowly compared to PointNet, which fully demonstrates the greater stability of our method in the face of drastic changes in the number of points.

**Table 1.** Overall and mean accuracies of various point cloud classification methods

| Year | Methods | Overall accuracy (%) | Mean accuracy (%) | Frame |
|------|---------|----------------------|-------------------|-------|
| 2017 | PointNet [1] | 89.2 | 86.2 | PyTorch |
| 2017 | Deep Sets [5] | 87.1 | - | PyTorch |
| 2017 | PointNet + + [6] | 90.7 | - | PyTorch |
| 2018 | Mo-Net [7] | 89.3 | 86.1 | PyTorch |
| 2019 | PATs [8] | 91.7 | - | PyTorch |
| 2018 | SRN [9] | 91.5 | - | PyTorch |
| 2019 | PointWeb [10] | 92.3 | 89.4 | PyTorch |
| 2021 | PCT [3] | 93.2 | - | Jittor |
| 2020 | Point ASNL [11] | 92.9 | - | TensorFlow |
| 2021 | Paconv [12] | 93.6 | - | PyTorch |
| 2022 | Our method (1k) | 92.9 | 90.0 | Pytorch |
| 2022 | Our method (2k) | 93.6 | 91.2 | Pytorch |

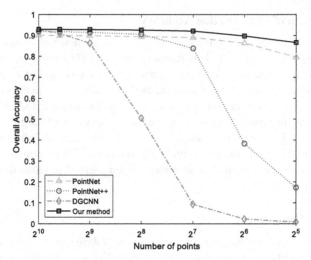

**Fig. 6.** Stability comparison of four different methods

### 3.3 Ablation Study

Table 2 gives the contributions of different modules in our method to the overall classification accuracy. We can see that, compared with PointNet, the OA-based low-level feature extraction subnetwork, the CA-based low-level feature alignment subnetwork, and the CA-based high-level feature extraction subnetwork can bring 1.5%, 0.8%, and 1.4% gain in classification accuracy, respectively, while these three subnetworks together can bring 3.7% gain, which verifies the effectiveness of our method in the way of transformer introduction.

**Table 2.** Ablation study: contribution of each transformer module to the overall classification accuracy for different number of points.

|  | Accuracy |
|---|---|
| **PointNet** | 89.2 |
| **PointNet with OA-based low-level feature extraction** | 90.7 |
| **PointNet with CA-based low-level feature alignment** | 90.0 |
| **PointNet with CA-based high-level feature extraction** | 90.6 |
| **Our method** | 92.9 |

## 4    Conclusion

In this paper, we propose a transformer-based point cloud classification method. Our main idea is to introduce the transformer mechanism into the feature extraction network of PointNet. Experimental results show that compared with PointNet, our method not only improves the classification accuracy significantly, but also improves the stability.

**Acknowledgment.** This work is supported by Key Research and Development program projects of Hubei Province (No. 2020BCB054).

# References

1. Qi, C.R., Su, H., Mo, K., Guibas, L.J.: Pointnet: Deep learning on point sets for 3d classification and segmentation. In: Proceedings of the IEEE Conference on Computer Vision and Pattern Recognition, pp. 652–660 (2017)
2. Vaswani, A., et al.: Attention is all you need. Adv. Neural Inf. Processing Syst. **30** (2017)
3. Guo, M., Cai, J., Liu, Z., Mu, T., Martin, R.R., Hu, S.: PCT: point cloud transformer. Computational Visual Media **7**(2), 187199 (2021)
4. Wu, Z., et al.: 3D shapenets: a deep representation for volumetric shapes. In IEEE Conference on Computer Vision and Pattern Recognition, CVPR 2015, Boston, MA, USA, June 7–12, 2015, pp. 1912–1920. IEEE Computer Society (2015)
5. Zaheer, M., Kottur, S., Ravanbakhsh, S., Poczos, B., Salakhutdinov, R.R., Smola, A.J.: Deep sets. Adv. Neural Inf. Process. Syst. **30** (2017)
6. Qi, C.R., Yi, L., Su, H., Guibas, L.J.: Pointnet++: deep hierarchical feature learning on point sets in a metric space. Adv. Neural Inf. Processing Syst. **30** (2017)
7. Joseph-Rivlin, M., Zvirin, A., Kimmel, R.: Momen(e)t: Flavor the moments in learning to classify shapes. In: Proceedings of the IEEE/CVF International Conference on Computer Vision Workshops (2019)
8. Duan, Y., Zheng, Y., Lu, J., Zhou, J., Tian, Q.: Structural relational reasoning of point clouds. In: Proceedings of the IEEE/CVF Conference on Computer Vision and Pattern Recognition, pp. 949–958 (2019)
9. Yang, J., et al.: Modeling point clouds with self-attention and gumbel subset sampling. In: Proceedings of the IEEE/CVF Conference on Computer Vision and Pattern Recognition, pp. 3323–3332 (2019)
10. Zhao, H., Jiang, L., Fu, C., Jia, J.: Pointweb: Enhancing local neighborhood features for point cloud processing. In: Proceedings of the IEEE/CVF Conference on Computer Vision and Pattern Recognition, pp. 5565–5573 (2019)
11. Yan, X., Zheng, C., Li, Z., Wang, S., Cui, S.: Pointasnl: Robust point clouds processing using nonlocal neural networks with adaptive sampling. In: Proceedings of the IEEE/CVF Conference on Computer Vision and Pattern Recognition, pp. 5589–5598 (2020)
12. Xu, M., Ding, R., Zhao, H., Qi, X.: Paconv: Position adaptive convolution with dynamic kernel assembling on point clouds. In: Proceedings of the IEEE/CVF Conference on Computer Vision and Pattern Recognition, pp. 3173–3182 (2021)
13. Wang, Y., Sun, Y., Liu, Z., Sarma, S.E., Bronstein, M.M., Solomon, J.M.: Dynamic graph CNN for learning on point clouds. Acm Transactions On Graphics (tog) **38**(5), 1–12 (2019)

# Underwater Object Tracking Based on Error Self-correction

Huibin Wang[✉], Qinxu Jia, Zhe Chen, and Lili Zhang

Hohai University, No. 8 Focheng West Road, Nanjing, Jiangsu, China
hbwang@hhu.edu.cn

**Abstract.** Underwater object tracking is more challenging than tracking on land due to the image distortion. Underwater illumination changes, motion blur and other problems will greatly degrade the performance of various tracking methods, especially when using underwater cameras. To overcome these limitations, we proposed an underwater tracking method based on error self-correction. We combine the SiamFC tracker and correlation filter trackers into one framework. In this framework, the correlation filter tracker is used to guide the update of SiamFC tracker. In addition, this framework contains a multi-peak suppression module, which comprehensively improves the tracking accuracy of our tracker in underwater scenarios. Experimental results on the underwater dataset we established demonstrate that the success rate of the AUC criterion is 68.2%, which has a 11.4% improvement over the baseline tracker. Also, our proposed algorithm achieves a 12.6% improvement over the conventional correlation filter tracker BACF, especially in challenging scenarios.

**Keywords:** Underwater object tracking · Error self-correction · SiamFC · Correlation filter

## 1 Introduction

Visual object tracking is one of the research hotspots in the field of computer vision. It has important research significance in the fields of video surveillance, unmanned driving, and intelligent transportation [1]. Underwater object tracking plays an important role in marine resource measurement, marine engineering and marine biology [2]. However, Most recent deep-sea mining machines have little intelligence in visual monitoring systems [3] and complex underwater imaging environments like light changes [4], surface wave motion [5] and motion blur caused by rapid bring huge challenges to underwater target tracking.

Compared with the underwater scenarios, the object tracking research on land is more mature. The existing target tracking approaches can be divided into two main categories: discriminative methods and generative methods. Due to the development of correlation filter and deep learning in recent years, generative methods have gradually become the mainstream. The core idea of the correlation filter-based tracker is to find an optimal filter template, and use the template to calculate the target location by correlation with

© The Author(s), under exclusive license to Springer Nature Singapore Pte Ltd. 2022
S. Yang and H. Lu (Eds.): ISAIR 2022, CCIS 1700, pp. 226–241, 2022.
https://doi.org/10.1007/978-981-19-7946-0_20

the target area. MOSSE [6] achieved an astonishing 669 frames per second using gray-scale features [7], but it does not guarantee accurate tracking when the appearance of an object changes. Henriques et al. designed a CSK tracker [8] using ridge regression and kernel tricks. KCF [9] extends multi-channel features and efficiently incorporate them in Fourier domain. Bertinetto incorporate color statistical in STAPLE [10], this tracker combines two image patch representation that are sensitive to complementary factor to learn a model that is inherently robust to both color changes and deformation. Yang et al. incorporated the scale factor into SAMF [11] to improve the scale adaptability of the correlation filter.

With the development of computer technology, Convolutional Neural Networks [12] have gradually become dominant in the field of object tracking by virtue of their powerful feature extraction capabilities and generalization capabilities. CNNs are used frequently in vision tasks because of their excellent extraction ability. Before Siamese network, researchers incorporate depth features into the correlation filter tracker, Give full play to the ability of depth features and the speed of correlation filter tracker, Such as Ma et al. proposed HCFT [13], Danelljan et al. proposed ECO [14]. However, while the accuracy is improved, the speed of the correlation filter tracker is greatly affected. Recently, Tao proposed SINT [15] which applied Siamese network to object tracking. In the same year, Bertinetto proposed SiamFC [16], using the Siamese network to achieve end-to-end tracking. The features extracted by the Siamese network from the template given to the first frame are used to match the current frame, and the high-confidence part is used as the target appearance position. SiamFC achieves the most advanced performance while maintaining a very great tracking speed. Later, in order to solve the problem that the SiamFC tracking frame is not flexible enough, some reachers proposed SiamRPN [17] which introduces a region proposal network (RPN) [18] to improve the tracker's ability at target-scale estimation. Zhang et al. proposed SiamDW [18] and fully analyzed the important reasons affecting the tracking results. SiamFC++ [19] proposed by Wang introduce both classification and target state estimation branch to further improve the tracking success rate.

Object tracking based on Siamese network makes full use of the feature extraction advantages of neural network in simple frames. Depth features have great robustness to appearance changes. SiamFC only uses the extracted features for template matching, so the requirements for features are very high, and the features must be sufficiently strong and robust enough to achieve better tracking results.

However, due to problems such as illumination changes and motion blur under water, only using depth features may lack positioning information, resulting in tracking failure. As shown in Fig. 1, Fig. 2.

During our researches, the correlation filter tracker based on some traditional hand-crafted features perform well in difficult scenes like illumination change and motion blur. The HOG feature can obtain local shape information of underwater objects, and have good invariance to geometric and illumination changes; The CN feature is a great tool to describe the color information of underwater objects, and is robust to blurring caused by fast movement. Although handcrafted features lack generalization ability compared with depth features, handcrafted features have good positioning ability, can better extract foreground information and keep up with the target in some difficult scenes (Fig. 3).

**Fig. 1.** Tracking drift when encountering illumination changes.

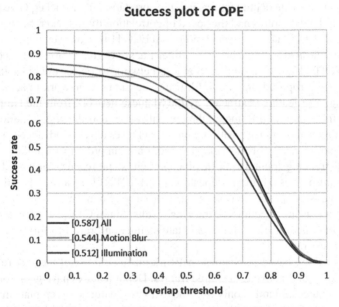

**Fig. 2.** Success rate in illumination and motion blur scenes.

Therefore, we propose an underwater object tracking method based on error self-correction to solve problems exposed by SiamFC during underwater object tracking. Main tasks as follows:

1) Error self-correction. The correlation filter tracker is used to guide SiamFC to update at low-confidence to realize self-correction.
2) Reliability evaluation. We propose a tracking reliability evaluation standard combining APCE and PSR.
3) Introduce timing information. Taking into account the continuity of object tracking, the movement displacement of the object between two adjacent frames will not be too large, which is used as the multi-peak suppression standard under low-confidence

Input image                                    Histogram of Oriented Gradients

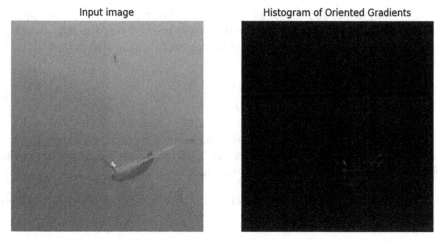

**Fig. 3.** HOG feature under illumination changes scenes.

conditions to reduce the tracking drift in the case of underwater background noises and illumination changes

4) Dataset establishment. A novel underwater target tracking dataset is established with multiple interesting targets. It provides a benchmark to fairly evaluate underwater target tracking models.

## 2 Related Works

### 2.1 SiamFC Tracker

SiamFC consists of two branches that use the same network structure: one branch is used to process the groundtruth in the first frame of the object to be tracked, denoted as $z$. While the other branch is used to process the search region cropped from the frame to be searched, denoted as $x$. The input image sizes of the two branches are 127 * 127 pixels and 255 * 255 pixels, respectively. Input the two pictures into the upper and lower branches respectively to generate 6 * 6 * 128 and 22 * 22 * 128 feature maps. In the cross-correlation layer, the feature map from the example branch is used as a sliding window to calculate similarity scores with all sub-regions of the feature map from the example branch and generate a response map. Cross-correlation operations are as follows:

$$f(z, x) = \varphi(z) * \varphi(x) + b_1 \tag{1}$$

where $\varphi(z)$ can be regarded as a convolution kernel, do cross-correlation operation with $\varphi(x)$. $b_1$ represent the value of each position in the score map.

A hanning window is introduced to punish the large drift. Then, the maximal value of the whole response map is considered as the target. Throughout the training process, the positive and negative samples are trained using the discriminant method. The loss function is defined as:

$$l(y, v) = \log(1 + \exp(-yv)) \tag{2}$$

where $y$ is the groundtruth, labeled as $-1$ or $+1$. $v$ is the real-valued response map.

Since the search image is larger than the sample image, a response map $D$ will be generated during training. The final loss of the score map is defined as the mean of each pixel's loss:

$$L(y, v) = \frac{1}{|D|} \sum_{u \in D} l(y[u], v[u]) \tag{3}$$

$D$ is the whole area of the response map and $u$ represents each position on it.

Finally, use Stochastic Gradient Descent (SGD) to update the parameters of the following formula to obtain the optimal tracking model.

$$\arg \min L(y, f(z, x; \theta)) \tag{4}$$

## 2.2 Correlation Filter Tracker

In the correlation filter model, the training samples are obtained by cyclic shifting the image blocks containing the target and surrounding information. The correlation filter can be obtained by minimizing the following loss function:

$$\varepsilon(f) = \left\| \sum_{l=1}^{d} h^l * f^l - g \right\|^2 + \lambda \sum_{l=1}^{d} \left\| h^l \right\|^2 \tag{5}$$

where $f^l$ represents the HOG feature, $h^l$ represents the filter in different dimension, $*$ denotes the circular convolution, $\lambda$ is the regularization parameter.

The calculation can be accelerated by FFT in the Fourier domain.

As the tracking process continues, filters are updated iteratively in each frame by the linear interpolation method, as shown in the following formula:

$$A_t^l = (1 - \eta)A_{t-1}^l + \eta \overline{G_t} F_t^l \tag{6}$$

$$B_t^l = (1 - \eta)B_{t-1}^l + \eta \sum_{k=1}^{d} \overline{F_t^k} F_t^k \tag{7}$$

where $\eta$ represents the learning rate.

The calculation method of the response map $y_{CF}$ of the new frame is:

$$y_{CF} = F^{-1} \left\{ \frac{\sum_{l=1}^{d} \overline{A^l} z}{B + \lambda} \right\} \tag{8}$$

The target location is determined by the location of the maximum score.

## 3  Proposed Algorithm

Although SiamFC tracker has achieved great results in accuracy and speed in object tracking, it still exposes the following problems when applied to underwater:

1) Single feature type. Using only deep features results in the lack of effective positioning information, and will lead to tracking failures when encountering complex scenes.
2) Lack of correction mechanism. Each frame update of SiamFC is adjusted based on the tracking result of the previous frame. When an error occurs in one of the frames, subsequent frame errors will gradually accumulate. The entire tracking process will not perform error correction and repositioning of the tracked object.
3) For the response map obtained after template matching, only the highest score position is taken as the tracking result, and the reliability is poor.
4) Only using the appearance information of the template itself and ignoring the continuity of object tracking in time, resulting in tracking drift in search area.

In response to the above problems, the algorithm in this paper proposes an underwater object tracking based on error self-correction. The tracking frame is shown in Fig. 4:

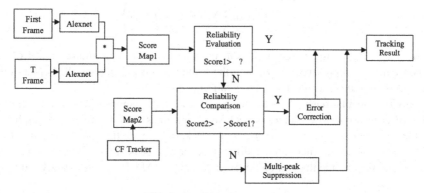

**Fig. 4.** Tracking framework.

### 3.1  Tracking Framework Combining SiamFC and Correlation Filter

In this paper, the tracking method we proposed is to design SiamFC and the related filter tracker in one framework. When the confidence of SiamFC tracker is low, the correlation filter is used to complete the error correction and guide SiamFC updates. As shown in Fig. 1, when SiamFC encounters complex scenarios, the tracking results may incorrect due to missing location information. Through experimental analysis, the handcrafted features used in correlation filtering have certain advantages in such complex scenes. The HOG feature is more stable when encountering underwater illumination changes and background noises; The CN feature performs better in the face of motion blur.

Since the update of SiamFC is based on the result of the previous frame, when the confidence of SiamFC is low, we use the result of the correlation filter tracker as the basis for correction. The update of SiamFC by the correlation filter tracker in time will make the overall performance of the tracker better. During the whole tracking process, when SiamFC tracker's confidence is lower than the threshold and the correlation filter tracker's score is higher, the system determines that the result of the correlation filter is more reliable, and uses it to modify the tracking result of SiamFC, so that SiamFC is guided and updated. The search area in next frame will also be adjusted accordingly.

## 3.2 Reliability Evaluation Standard

In the SiamFC tracking process, the response map obtained through correlation calculation is an important basis for judging the tracking result. Traditional tracking algorithms use the maximum value of the response graph $F_{max}$ as the object position. However, we found that when the tracking drifts caused by illumination change, background noises and other issues, the response value is still very high, but it follows the wrong target. In response to this phenomenon, we introduce APCE and Peak Sidelobe Ratio(PSR) for reliability evaluation.

$$F_{APCE} = \frac{|F_{max} - F_{min}|}{mean\left(\sum_{w,h} (F_{w,h} - F_{min})\right)} \tag{9}$$

where $F_{max}$, $F_{min}$ respectively represent the maximum and minimum values of the response map, $w$ represents the width of the response graph, $h$ denotes the height of the response graph, $mean$ is the average operation.

APCE is the relationship between the peak value of the response map and the response value of each point. When there is occlusion, blur, loss, etc., the response graph will fluctuate. The more prominent the response peak, the greater the corresponding APCE value. When the target encounters a difficult scene, the peak value of the response map becomes lower and the fluctuation becomes larger, the APCE value is greatly reduced.

$$F_{PSR} = \frac{y_{t,max} - \mu_t}{\sigma_t} \tag{10}$$

where $y_{t,max}$ is the peak value of the t-th frame response map, $\mu_t$ and $\sigma_t$ are the mean and standard deviation of the are around the maximum response position.

The higher the $F_{PSR}$ score, the higher the peak intensity in the response distribution.

Therefor we combine PSR and APCE as the reliability evaluation of the current response graph.

$$Score = a_1 F_{PSR} + a_2 F_{APCE} \tag{11}$$

When the score of SiamFC tracker is low, the correlation filter is used to guide the tracking. When the scores of both are lower than the threshold $\varphi$, the system judges that the current tracking result is unreliable and activates the multi-peak suppression module to find the optimal tracking result.

### 3.3 Multi-peak Suppression Module Based on Time Information

Object tracking is performed in simple scenes in most cases. The peak point of the response map is the location of the target. However, in complex scenes, the response map will have multiple peaks. Although SiamFC uses the Hanning window strategy to suppress the larger displacement response, through the analysis of the tracking failure frame, we found that there are still multiple peaks in the response map after only the Hanning window suppression, resulting in tracking failure (Fig. 5).

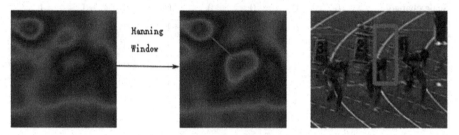

**Fig. 5.** Tracking failed after using Hanning window.

Therefore, we introduced another drift point removal strategy, using timing information to detect and calculate the distance from the center of the previous frame to the response graph with multiple peaks. The obtained result is compared with the average of the displacement of the previous three frames, the obvious drift points are removed, and the best point is finally selected as the tracking result of the current frame. The movement distance between two adjacent frames is:

$$D_t = \sqrt{(x_t - x_{t-1})^2 + (y_t - y_{t-1})^2} \tag{12}$$

$D_t$ is the movement distance of the target from frame $t-1$ to frame $t$.
The formula for multimodal suppression is:

$$D_t < \beta \times Mean(D_{t-3} + D_{t-2} + D_{t-1}) \tag{13}$$

Considering that the object will accelerate instantaneously when it is in motion, while the growth rate of the target between adjacent frames will not be too large, so $\beta$ takes a smaller value. When the above conditions are met, it is judged that the coordinates of the current tracking point are the optimal tracking result.

## 4 Data

In order to evaluate the performance of different tracking models, we established a new underwater data benchmark. There are 16 underwater videos collected in our dataset with 3556 frames in total. LabelImg tool is used to mark the ground-truth of interest targets (including underwater creatures, divers, underwater submarines, etc.). In our dataset, there are various attributes that affect tracking performance, such as illumination changes, rotation, scale changes, occlusion, deformation, motion blur, high-speed motion, out of view, background noise, and low resolution, as shown in Table 1 and Table 2.

**Table 1.** Underwater dataset.

| Sequence | Fish1 | Fish2 | Fish3 | Fish4 | Fish5 | Fish6 | Fish7 | Fish8 |
|---|---|---|---|---|---|---|---|---|
| Frames | **200** | **149** | **150** | **350** | **196** | **434** | **93** | **217** |
| Illumination change | 0 | 0 | 0 | 0 | 0 | 0 | 0 | 0 |
| Out-plane rotation | 0 | 1 | 1 | 1 | 0 | 1 | 0 | 1 |
| In-plane rotation | 1 | 1 | 0 | 1 | 0 | 0 | 0 | 0 |
| Scale change | 0 | 0 | 0 | 0 | 0 | 0 | 1 | 1 |
| Occlusion | 1 | 0 | 1 | 1 | 1 | 0 | 0 | 1 |
| Deformation | 0 | 1 | 1 | 1 | 1 | 0 | 0 | 0 |
| Motion blur | 1 | 1 | 1 | 1 | 1 | 0 | 0 | 0 |
| High-speed motion | 1 | 1 | 1 | 1 | 1 | 1 | 0 | 1 |
| Out of view | 1 | 1 | 0 | 0 | 0 | 1 | 1 | 1 |
| Background noise | 1 | 0 | 1 | 1 | 1 | 0 | 1 | 0 |
| Low resolution | 1 | 0 | 1 | 1 | 1 | 0 | 0 | 0 |

**Table 2.** Underwater dataset.

| Sequence | Fish9 | Person1 | Person2 | Person3 | Jellyfish | Seahorse | Shark | AUV |
|---|---|---|---|---|---|---|---|---|
| Frames | **177** | **200** | **168** | **175** | **377** | **191** | **100** | **379** |
| Illumination change | 1 | 1 | 0 | 1 | 1 | 0 | 1 | 1 |
| Out-plane rotation | 1 | 0 | 0 | 0 | 1 | 0 | 0 | 0 |
| In-plane rotation | 0 | 1 | 0 | 1 | 1 | 0 | 1 | 1 |
| Scale change | 0 | 0 | 1 | 0 | 0 | 1 | 0 | 0 |
| Occlusion | 0 | 0 | 0 | 1 | 1 | 1 | 1 | 0 |
| Deformation | 1 | 0 | 1 | 1 | 0 | 0 | 1 | 1 |
| Motion blur | 0 | 1 | 0 | 0 | 1 | 0 | 1 | 0 |
| High-speed motion | 0 | 0 | 0 | 0 | 1 | 0 | 0 | 0 |
| Out of view | 1 | 1 | 0 | 1 | 0 | 1 | 0 | 0 |
| Background noise | 0 | 0 | 1 | 0 | 1 | 1 | 1 | 0 |
| Low resolution | 1 | 0 | 1 | 0 | 0 | 0 | 0 | 1 |

# 5 Experiments

We conducted a comprehensive experiment on the underwater dataset proposed in Sect. 4 to evaluate the effectiveness of our proposed tracking method. All experiments are performed on personal computers. We used Intel Core i7-8700K CPU and NVIDIA RTX 2070 GPU. The operating system is 64-bit Windows 10 Professional. We continued the training method of SiamFC itself. Initial parameters are set as $a_1 = 0.85$, $a_2 = 0.15$, $\beta = 1.2$. Our tracker enable real-time tracking with a speed of 29 FPS.

## 5.1 Benchmark and Evaluation Metric

OTB2013 [20] and OTB2015 [21] are classic benchmarks designed especially to evaluate the tracker's performance in visual object tracking. We followed the metric introduced in OTB to evaluate the trackers' performance. This indicator uses one-pass evaluation (OPE) to evaluate tracker performance, which means that the tracker processes each image sequence only once from start to finish, and then evaluates the tracking performance based on the tracking results. The metric contains a success plot and a precision plot, which are based on the Center Location Error (CLE) and Intersection Over Union (IOU). CLE compares the Euclidean distance between the center locations of the tracking result provided by the tracker and the corresponding groundtruth of each frame with a given threshold to determine whether the tracking is successful. A smaller Euclidean distance in CLE denotes better tracking. IOU is defined as:

$$IOU = \frac{area(R_T \cap R_G)}{area(R_T \cup R_G)} \tag{14}$$

where $R_T$ is the tracked result, $R_G$ is the groundtruth. $\cup$ and $\cap$ are the intersection area and union area between $R_T$ and $R_G$. Area under curve (AUC) value is used to represent the tracker's performance in IOU. A bigger AUC value denotes better tracking.

## 5.2 Overall Performance

We first tested our tracker on the OTB100 dataset. Our tracking framework has 8.3% improvement in success rate than the baseline tracker SiamFC. Success rate and precision score are recorded in Table 3.

Table 3. Experimental comparison on the OTB100 dataset.

|              | SiamFC | Ours  |
|--------------|--------|-------|
| Success rate | 0.528  | 0.611 |
| Precision    | 0.712  | 0.816 |

Figure 6 shows the overall performance of five trackers on the underwater dataset in terms of precision based on CLE and success based on IOU.

As we can see, in dataset we established, performance of our tracker is significantly better than the baseline tracker (SiamFC tracker), which proves the correctness and effectiveness of the framework we built.

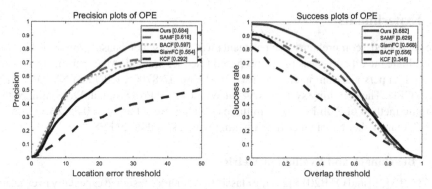

**Fig. 6.** Performance comparison between our proposed tracker and other trackers.

## 5.3  Scenario-Based Performance

The performance of the tracker will be affected by many factors, such as deformation, scale changes, and lighting. In order to better evaluate the tracker, we further evaluated the performance of the tracker under different tracking attributes and compared it with common trackers. It can be seen from the conclusion that our method has better performance for most scenes, and the scores on all attributes are better than the baseline tracker. We can see in Fig. 7, in the face of illumination changes, our tracker ranked first with a 70.1% success rate. Under the interference of background noise, our tracker ranked first with a 73.9% success rate due to the introduction of error correction mechanism timing information, which is 14.4% higher than SiamFC. In general, our model has better performance in underwater target tracking, especially suitable for use in challenging scenes such as motion blur, background noise, and illumination changes.

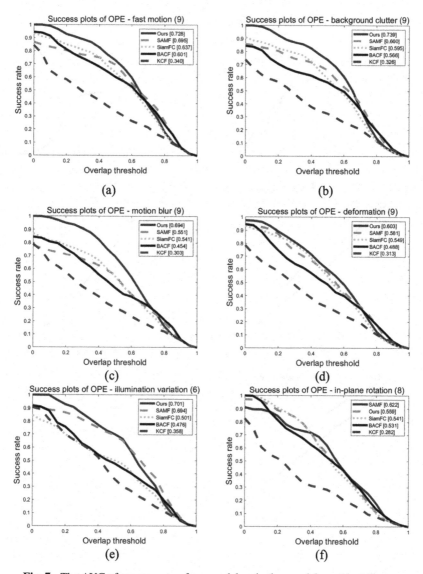

**Fig. 7.** The AUC of success rate of our model and other models on 11 attributes.

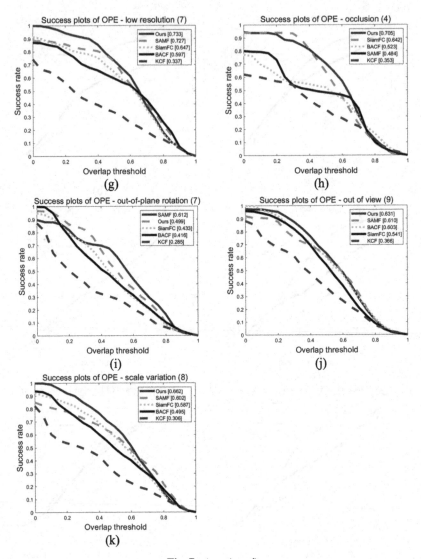

**Fig. 7.** (*continued*)

## 5.4 Qualitative Experiment

In this section, we visualize the tracking results of the proposed tracker and other advanced trackers on our underwater dataset. Details are shown in Fig. 8. The five rows of image sequences are (a–f) Person3, Fish9, Shark, Fish6, AUV. The color of each tracker's bounding box is listed at the bottom of Fig. 8.

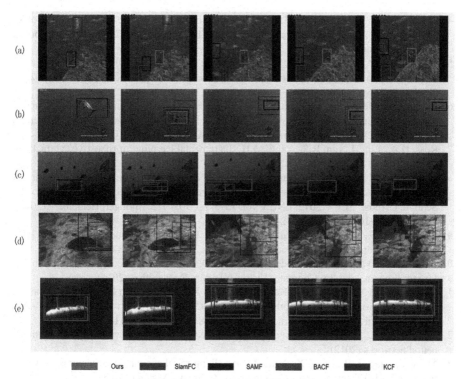

**Fig. 8.** Visualization and comparison of tracking results.

## 6  Conclusion

In this paper, we propose a new tracking framework to solve the problems exposed when SiamFC tracker is applied to underwater object tracking. In order to solve the problem of weak expressiveness of depth features in complex underwater environment, a correlation filter tracker is used to guide SiamFC tracker updating. A new reliability evaluation standard and a multi-peak suppression module are also set within the framework. Through comparing the proposed tracker with other advanced trackers in underwater dataset, the effectiveness of the proposed tracker is verified. Experimental results show our proposed model has good adaptability to the challenging underwater environment and can be efficiently applied in complex underwater scenes.

## References

1. Li, P., Wang, D., Wang, L., Lu, H.: Deep visual tracking: review and experimental comparison. Pattern Recogn. **76**, S0031320317304612 (2017)
2. Zhang, S.Y., Xin-Yi, H.E., Zhang, C., Zhu, L., Chen, S., Academy, N.: Present situation and prospect of underwater multi-target tracking technologies. J. Unmanned Undersea Syst. (2018)
3. Ma, C., Li, X., Li, Y., et al.: Visual information processing for deep-sea visual monitoring system. Cogn. Robot. **1**, 3–11 (2021)

4. Lin, C., Fan, Z., Yu, S., Xiang, T., Chen, Y.: Illumination insensitive efficient second-order minimization for planar object tracking. In: 2017 IEEE International Conference on Robotics and Automation (ICRA) (2017)
5. Wang, P., Wang, D., Zhang, X., et al.: Numerical and experimental study on the maneuverability of an active propeller control based wave glider. Appl. Ocean Res. **104**, 102369 (2020)
6. Bolme, D.S., Beveridge, J.R., Draper, B.A., Lui, Y.M.: Visual object tracking using adaptive correlation filters. In: The Twenty-Third IEEE Conference on Computer Vision and Pattern Recognition, CVPR 2010, San Francisco, CA, USA, 13–18 June 2010 (2010)
7. Ross, D.A., Lim, J., Lin, R.S., Yang, M.H.: Incremental learning for robust visual tracking. Int. J. Comput. Vision **77**(1–3), 125–141 (2008)
8. Henriques, J.F., Caseiro, R., Martins, P., Batista, J.: Exploiting the circulant structure of tracking-by-detection with Kernels. In: Fitzgibbon, A., Lazebnik, S., Perona, P., Sato, Y., Schmid, C. (eds.) ECCV 2012. LNCS, vol. 7575, pp. 702–715. Springer, Heidelberg (2012). https://doi.org/10.1007/978-3-642-33765-9_50
9. Henriques, J.F., Caseiro, R., Martins, P., Batista, J.: High-speed tracking with kernelized correlation filters. IEEE Trans. Pattern Anal. Mach. Intell. **37**(3), 583–596 (2015)
10. Bertinetto, L., Valmadre, J., Golodetz, S., Miksik, O., Torr, P.: Staple: complementary learners for real-time tracking. In: Computer Vision & Pattern Recognition (2016)
11. Li, Y., Zhu, J.: A scale adaptive Kernel correlation filter tracker with feature integration. In: Agapito, L., Bronstein, M.M., Rother, C. (eds.) ECCV 2014. LNCS, vol. 8926, pp. 254–265. Springer, Cham (2015). https://doi.org/10.1007/978-3-319-16181-5_18
12. Krizhevsky, A., Sutskever, I., Hinton, G.E.: ImageNet classification with deep convolutional neural networks (2012)
13. Ma, C., Huang, J.-B., Yang, X., Yang, M.-H.: Hierarchical convolutional features for visual tracking. In: IEEE International Conference on Computer Vision (2016)
14. Danelljan, M., Bhat, G., Khan, F.S., Felsberg, M.: ECO: efficient convolution operators for tracking. In: IEEE Computer Society (2016)
15. Tao, R., Gavves, E., Smeulders, A.W.M.: Siamese instance search for tracking. In: 2016 IEEE Conference on Computer Vision and Pattern Recognition (CVPR), 2016, pp. 1420–1429 (2016)
16. Bertinetto, L., Valmadre, J., Henriques, J.F., Vedaldi, A., Torr, P.H.S.: Fully-convolutional siamese networks for object tracking. In: Hua, G., Jégou, H. (eds) Computer Vision – ECCV 2016 Workshops. ECCV 2016, vol. 9914. Springer, Cham (2016).https://doi.org/10.1007/978-3-319-48881-3_56
17. Bo, L., Yan, J., Wei, W., Zheng, Z., Hu, X.: High performance visual tracking with siamese region proposal network. In: 2018 IEEE/CVF Conference on Computer Vision and Pattern Recognition (CVPR) (2018)
18. Zhang, Z., Peng, H.: Deeper and wider siamese networks for real-time visual tracking (2019)
19. Xu, Y., Wang, Z., Li, Z., et al.: SiamFC++: towards robust and accurate visual tracking with target estimation guidelines (2019)
20. Wu, Y., Lim, J., Yang, M.-H.: Online object tracking: a benchmark. In: Computer Vision & Pattern Recognition (2013)
21. Wu, Y., Lim, J., Yang, M.H.: Object tracking benchmark. IEEE Trans. Pattern Anal. Mach. Intell. **37**(9), 1834–1848 (2015)
22. Lu, H., Zhang, M., Xu, X.: Deep fuzzy hashing network for efficient image retrieval. IEEE Trans. Fuzzy Syst.https://doi.org/10.1109/TFUZZ.2020.2984991
23. Huimin, L., Li, Y., Chen, M., et al.: Brain Intelligence: go beyond artificial intelligence. Mob. Netw. Appl. **23**, 368–375 (2018)
24. Huimin, L., Li, Y., Shenglin, M., et al.: Motor anomaly detection for unmanned aerial vehicles using reinforcement learning. IEEE Internet Things J. **5**(4), 2315–2322 (2018)

25. Linshu, H., Qin, M., Zhang, F., Zhenhong, D., Liu, R.: RSCNN: a CNN-based method to enhance low-light remote-sensing images. Remote Sensing **13**, 62 (2020)
26. Huimin, L., Zhang, Y., Li, Y., et al.: User-oriented virtual mobile network resource management for vehicle communications. IEEE Trans. Intell. Transp. Syst. **22**(6), 3521–3532 (2021)

# Novel Elimination Method of Baseline Drift Basedon Improved Least Square Method

Ruhao Zhang, Xin Xu$^{(\boxtimes)}$, Yin Zhan, and Tingting Xu

School of Communication and Information Engineering, Nanjing University of Posts and Telecommucations, Nanjing, China
xuxin@njupt.edu.cn

**Abstract.** With the development of brain computer interface (BCI), the application of bioelectrical signals in the field of intelligent medical devices has been flourishing. Currently, how to remove the interference in the electrical signal and improve the recognition accuracy has attracted great attention. In the process of electromyographic (EMG) signal acquisition, baseline drift is a serious issue, which can affect the signal recognition accuracy, the traditional least square method (LSM) cannot remove the filtered baseline drift component within the window. To address this issue efficiently, a modified least method is designed in this paper, which employs a polynomial fit to remove the baseline drift component within the window by the curvature of the polynomial. The designed method can not only retain the advantages of the LSM in terms of small operation size, but also improve the baseline drift removal capability, providing a solution for a high-precision embedded bioelectric signal acquisition device. Experimental results show that the improved least square method (ILSM) improves the baseline drift removal capability by about 5% over the LSM. In addition; In addition, compared to LSM, the ILSM can reduced the number of window openings.

**Keywords:** Baseline drift · Electromyography · Improved least square method · Wavelet decomposition

## 1 Introduction

It is Known that there exist many wheelchair users. However, most of the existing wheelchairs on the market use joystick control, which is big challenge, for patients with disabilities in their hands. To address this problem, some scholars have tried to use voice and blowing as the control means of wheelchairs. However, in practical usage, it has been found that these means are affected by the environment, e.g., the surrounding noise. Thus, more efficient methods need to be proposed urgently. Recently, the bioelectrical signal based on control methods have received a lot attention [1]. The friction and pressure between the skin and the myoelectric acquisition sensor, which results in the fluctuations of the output signal from the sensor. This fluctuation can cause the output signal to jitter and drift up and down around the baseline. It was found by experiments that the baseline drift varies with the degree of friction between the skin, and the electromyographic

(EMG) sensor is also affected by breathing, sweating, etc. [4]. Since baseline drift causes up and down jitter in the electrical signal with random variations in amplitude and frequency, the usage of conventional high-pass filters is inefficient in addressing the baseline drift problem. In addition,the existence of baseline drift can also affect the various time and frequency domain indicators of EMG signal. Therefore, solving the baseline drift problem is one of the keys to improve the recognition accuracy of the system [5]. Currently, some schemes have been proposed the baseline drift problem in EMG signals. For example: 1) Adaptive trap filter scheme [4]. 2) Butterworth filter [6, 7]. 3) Ensemble empirical modal method [8, 9]. 4) Wavelet transform [10]. 5) Wavelet decomposition. 6) least square method (LMS) [11].

In the above scheme, LSM is very suitable for embedded medical devices because of its small computation and good effect. However, the traditional LSM cannot remove the baseline drift component within the window. To deal with this problem, this paper designs the improved least square method (ILSM), which polynomial and removes the baseline drift component. From the EMG signal by the curvature of the polynomial. The experimental results show that ILSM can effectively remove the baseline drift component within the window. In addition, the computational complexity of the designed method is still low, which can guarantee that the designed method is suitable for the real-time applications.

We first introduce the relevant principles of the algorithm in Sect. 2 and demonstrate that ILSM has the advantage of small operation size by time complexity analysis. Experimental results are demonstrated in Sect. 3. A comparative analysis of the performance metrics of the algorithms is presented in Sect. 4. Finally, the conclusion and future work are given in Sect. 5.

## 2 Principle and Proof of Algorithm

### 2.1 Principle of LSM

The traditional LSM is a computational tool widely used in error estimation, data prediction. It can be used to find trends in data and is often used for curve fitting.

EMG signal is a one-dimensional time series signal during the activity of the neuromuscular system. Through the electrical signal acquisition sensor, a set of electrical signals is recorded, which is denoted by $\{x_i\}$, where $i = 0, 1, \ldots, m-1$, is the sampling order.

To find a function that can match the trend of recorded data well, it is necessary compute the summation of distances from the function to each data point. It is noted that the best function is typically used, which can formulated as $P(x) = a + bx$. The mean square error function can be obtained as:

$$Q(a, b) = \sum_{i=0}^{m-1} (p(x_i) - i)^2 = \sum_{i=0}^{m-1} (a + bx_i - i)^2 \tag{1}$$

If there is a point $(a, b)$ that minimizes $Q(a, b)$, the function $P(x) = a + bx$ at the point (a, b) is the best-fit function of the EMG signal. Let $a, b$ be the minimum point of $Q(a, b)$, then the partial derivative of $Q(a, b)$ with respect to point $(a, b)$ is 0. After calculation, the fitting function can be obtained as shown in (2):

$$P(x) = \frac{\sum_{i=0}^{m-1} i \sum_{i=0}^{m-1} x_i^2 - \sum_{i=0}^{m-1} x_i \sum_{i=0}^{m-1} x_i i}{m \sum_{i=0}^{m-1} x_i^2 - (\sum_{i=0}^{m-1} x_i)^2} + \frac{m \sum_{i=0}^{m-1} x_i i - \sum_{i=0}^{m-1} x_i \sum_{i=0}^{m-1} i}{m \sum_{i=0}^{m-1} x_i^2 - (\sum_{i=0}^{m-1} x_i)^2} x \tag{2}$$

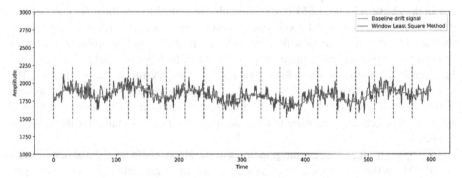

**Fig. 1.** The fitting function based on least square method.

Figure 1 depicts the fitting function based on LSM, where the red dashed line is the splitting line between the windows, the orange is the fitting function, and the blue is the original EMG signal. As can be seen from Fig. 1, the orange line can show the trend of the EMG signal within the window, However, it cannot show the baseline drift trend of the EMG signal within the window. To address this problem, we can reduce the size of window to enhance the removal performance of baseline drift. However, this operation cannot totally remove the baseline drift component. According to [11] the window size is positively correlated with the performance of baseline drift removal. Decreasing the size of window is a way of removing the baseline drift component. However, as the window size increases, the computational complexity will increase exponentially.

## 2.2 Principle of ILSM

In order to solve the problems of traditional LSM, we design the ILSM in this subsection. For the ILSM, a quadratic polynomial fitting is used to replace the linear segment fitting. Thus, the baseline drift component with the considered window can be removed by curvature of the quadratic function. By replacing the linear segment fitting used in the LSM with the polynomial $K_i(x) = a_i x^2 + b_i x + c_i$, and setting each segment to consist of n (n < m) data, the ILSM equation can be obtained as follows:

$$P(x) = \begin{cases} a_1 x^2 + b_1 x + c_1, x \in (1, N) \\ a_2 x^2 + b_2 x + c_2, x \in (N, 2N) \\ \vdots \\ a_N x^2 + b_N x + c_N, x \in (m - N, m) \end{cases} \tag{3}$$

In (3), m is the total number of collected points of the electromyographic data, and n is the number of sampling points in each segment. The sum of the square of the distances between each point on $P(x)$ to each sampling point is called the cost function denoted as $Q(a, b, c)$, which is expressed as:

$$Q(a, b, c) = \sum_{i=0}^{m-1} (p(x_i) - i)^2 = \sum_{i=0}^{m-1} (ax_i^2 + bx_i + c - i)^2 \tag{4}$$

The best-fit curve is obtained when $Q(a, b, c)$ is minimum, each partial derivative is 0. Thus, setting the partial derivative of (4) with respect to $a$, $b$, $c$, to be zero, we have:

$$\begin{pmatrix} 2(\sum_{i=0}^{m-1} x_i^2)^2 & 2\sum_{i=0}^{m-1} x^2 \sum_{i=0}^{m-1} x & 2\sum_{i=0}^{m-1} x_i^2 \\ 2\sum_{i=0}^{m-1} x^2 \sum_{i=0}^{m-1} x & 2(\sum_{i=0}^{m-1} x)^2 & 2\sum_{i=0}^{m-1} x \\ 2\sum_{i=0}^{m-1} x^2 & 2\sum_{i=0}^{m-1} x & 2m \end{pmatrix} \begin{pmatrix} a \\ b \\ c \end{pmatrix} = \begin{pmatrix} 2\sum_{i=0}^{m-1} x^2 \sum_{i=0}^{m-1} i \\ 2\sum_{i=0}^{m-1} x^2 \sum_{i=0}^{m-1} i \\ 2\sum_{i=0}^{m-1} i \end{pmatrix} \tag{5}$$

As the determinant equation is not full-rank, more than one solution can be found for it. Thus, so the gradient descent algorithm can be used to find the optimal solution.

$$\begin{cases} a' = a - W \times d_a \\ b' = b - W \times d_b \\ c' = C - W \times d_c \end{cases} \tag{6}$$

In (6), $a', b', c'$ are the updated polynomial coefficients after calculation, and $a$, $b$, and $c$ are the previous polynomial coefficients. $W$ is the learning rate. $d_a, d_b, d_c$ are the partial derivatives of $a$, $b$, and $c$. Using (6) to obtain updated polynomial coefficients $a', b', c'$, we can then update the cost function, which is given by coefficients. Let the difference between the cost function calculated from the new polynomial coefficients and the previous cost function be the gradient, denoted as $Q(a, b, c, a', b', c')$, which is giving by:

$$Y(a, b, c, a', b', c')$$
$$= \sum_{i=0}^{m-1} (i - ax_i^2 - bx_i - c) - \sum_{i=0}^{m-1} (i - a'x_i^2 - b'x_i - c') \tag{7}$$

By computing (7), we can obtain the updated gradients of $a$, $b$, $c$. If the gradient is less than 0.01, the updated parameters $a$, $b$, $c$ are considered to be the coefficients of the best-fit curve. Otherwise, the parameters $a$, $b$, $c$ are not considered to be the optimal solutions at this time, and the above process is repeated until the optimal solution is found.

## 2.3 Comparative Analysis of the Time Complexity

Since wavelet decomposition and LSM are close to each other in terms of computation and denoising effect, and the time complexity of the ILSM is slightly increased, the time complexity of the two algorithms is compared to demonstrate the superiority of the ILSM. In order to explore the time consumed by the two algorithms in the same environment, this paper models the time complexity of the two algorithms in order to explore the time efficiency of the two algorithms. With $N$, $I$, $A$ denoting the scale of the algorithm, the input of the algorithm, and the overall of the algorithm, respectively, and with $T$ denoting the time complexity of the algorithm, there should be $T = (N, I, A)$. Since wavelet decomposition requires decomposing the signal into $I$ layers, removing the low frequency part and then wavelet reconstruction to get the processed signal. According to the principle of wavelet decomposition algorithm, the time complexity model of wavelet decomposition algorithm can be constructed as:

$$T = 2n[1 - (\frac{1}{2})^{I}]$$

(8)

In (8), $n$ is the number of sampling points, and $I$ is the number of wavelet decomposition layers. Where $2 \leq I \leq \log_2 n$.

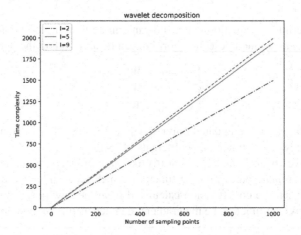

**Fig. 2.** Time complexity of wavelet decomposition algorithm under different I condition.

Figure 2 expresses the variation curve of time complexity with respect to the number of layers of wavelet decomposition $I$. Where, the time complexity of wavelet decomposition is a positive function with respect to $I$.

In the ILSM, the gradient descent algorithm is used to solve for the three coefficients of the second order polynomial. To solve the partial derivatives with respect to the coefficients it is also necessary to calculate the cumulative sum of each sampling point, which is used to solve the partial derivatives of each coefficient during each iteration.

In ILSM, in the process of solving the second-order polynomial coefficients with the help of gradient descent algorithm, it is necessary to iterate $\frac{n}{A}$ windows cyclically $I$ times, and the time complexity of this step is denoted as $I * \frac{n}{A}$. It is also necessary to calculate the cumulative sum of each sampling point for use in the partial derivative calculation, and the time complexity of this step is $n$. Therefore, the time complexity model of ILSM can be obtained as:

$$T = n + I * \frac{n}{A} \tag{9}$$

where $n$ is the number of sampling points, $A$ is the window size, and $I$ ($10 \leq I \leq 30$) is the number of iterations.

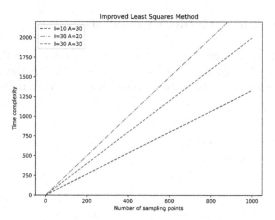

**Fig. 3.** Time complexity of improved least square method in different I cases.

Figure 3 expresses the variation curve of time complexity with respect to the number of wavelet decomposition layers $I$ and the window size $A$. Where, as can be seen from Fig. 3, the time complexity of ILSM is proportional to $I$ and inversely proportional to $A$.

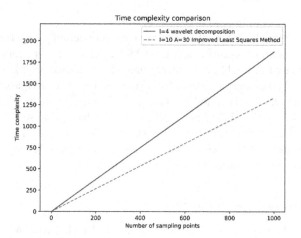

**Fig. 4.** Comparison of improved least square and wavelet decomposition algorithms.

Figure 4 depicts the comparative relationship between the time complexity of the ILSM and the wavelet decomposition method. As can be seen in Fig. 4, the time complexity of the ILSM is smaller than that of the wavelet decomposition algorithm when the window size is 30 and the number of iterations is 10.

In summary, when the window size is larger than a certain value, the time complexity of the ILSM is much smaller than that of the wavelet decomposition method [12, 13].

## 3    Experiment and Performance Analysis

In this chapter, the experimental data set used in the experiments is the humeral radial EMG signal acquired through the EMG single-lead muscle electrical sensor developed by Brain Lab. The hardware and software environment is shown in the following table (Table 1).

**Table 1.** Experimental environment.

| CPU | I7-9th |
|---|---|
| Operating Memory | 32G |
| System | Win10 |
| Simulation Software | VS code |
| Simulation Environment | Python3.0 |
| High-pass filtering order | 5 |
| Low-pass filtering order | 5 |
| Wavelet decomposition | Db1 |

To investigate the algorithm effectiveness, and reproducibility, experimental analysis is done in this section using own acquired sEMG signals of the brachioradialis muscle and sEMG signals from publicly available datasets, respectively [14, 15]. Since own acquisition of sEMG ensures a low baseline drift component, a baseline drift component can be added to investigate the ability of the algorithm to remove baseline drift and the effect on the useful signal. In the public dataset, since the signal itself already contains a more obvious baseline drift problem, it is not possible to add quantitative addition of baseline drift components to explore the metrics of the algorithm, only to demonstrate the effectiveness and generalizability of the algorithm.

### 3.1    ILSM to Remove Baseline Drift

Figure 5 shows the fitted data trend function of ILSM with a window size of 30. The blue line is the original EMG acquisition signal, the orange line is the fitted function for each segment of the EMG acquisition signal, and the red vertical segmentation line is the segmentation line for each segment. As can be seen from Fig. 5, the fitted function can accurately fit the trend function of the original EMG signal.

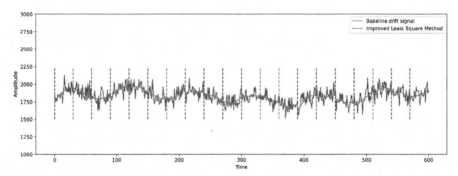

**Fig. 5.** Improved least square method fitting curve with a window size of 30 sampling points.

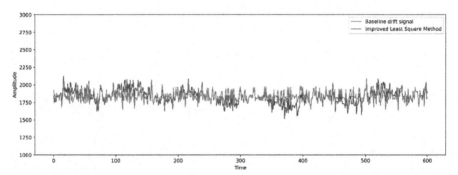

**Fig. 6.** Comparison pre and post improved least square method processing with a window size of 30 sampling points.

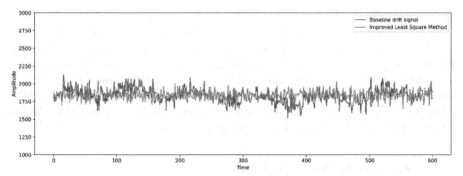

**Fig. 7.** Comparison pre and post improved least square method processing with a window size of 10 sampling points.

As shown in Fig. 6 and Fig. 7, Plots of amplitude versus time after ILSM processing are shown for window sizes of 10 and 30 sampling points, respectively. From the figures, it can be seen that the processing effect with a window size of 10 sampling points fits the baseline better than the one with a window size of 30 sampling points.

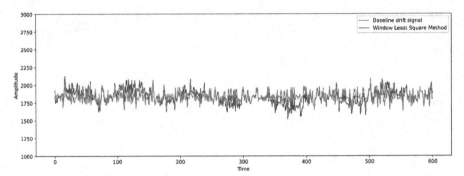

**Fig. 8.** Comparison of pre and post least square method processing with a window size of 30 sampling points.

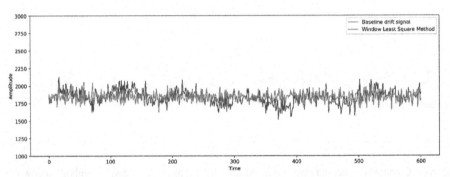

**Fig. 9.** Comparison of pre and post least square method processing with a window size of 10 sampling points.

Figure 8 and Fig. 9, respectively, show the relationship between magnitude and time after LSM processing under the window size of 10 and 30 sampling points. Comparing Fig. 6 and Fig. 7 with Fig. 8 and Fig. 9, we can see that the baseline drift still exists in the window of the function after using LSM processing, and changing the window size can optimize the problem, but it cannot remove the baseline drift from the root. After using ILSM, the baseline drift in the window is effectively filtered out, so the filtering effect of ILSM is better than LSM with the same window size.

### 3.2 Comparative Analysis of the Time Complexity

In the previous subsection, the 2nd order polynomial ILSM is compared with the linear fit LSM, and the pictures in the time and frequency domains show that the 2nd order polynomial based LSM is better than the ILSM in terms of effectiveness. In this section, we investigate whether the LSM based on 3rd order polynomials outperforms the LSM based on 2nd order polynomials in terms of filtering effect and performance.

Figure 11 shows the effect of the 3rd order ILSM after processing. The orange line in the figure is the processed EMG signal waveform, and it can be seen that the baseline drift problem has been effectively improved.

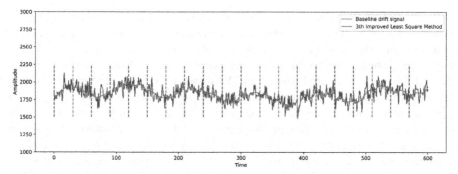

**Fig. 10.** 3rd order improved least square method curve fitting graph.

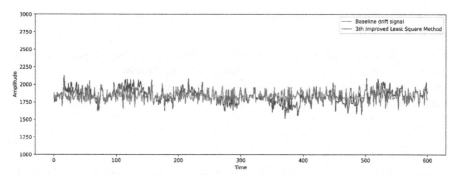

**Fig. 11.** Comparison of the 3rd order improved least square method with the original data.

**Table 2.** Comparison of the timeliness of the two algorithms.

| Order | Time ms |
|-------|---------|
| 2rd order | 4.05 |
| 3rd order | 11.97 |

In order to investigate the timeliness of the 2nd and 3rd order ILSM [16, 17], the time consumed by the two algorithms for processing data with the same window size is tested with a window size of 30 and 600 sampling points, as shown in Table 2. As shown in Table 2, the time required for the 3rdorder LSM is 2.95 times longer than that required for the 2ndorder LSM, which is not acceptable in embedded wearable devices because it consumes too much arithmetic power, so the performance of higher-order ILSM is not analyzed and discussed in this paper.

## 4   Performance Analysis

To measure the effectiveness of an algorithm, quantitative analysis of the signal is usually done in the time and frequency domains. In the time domain, a quantitative analysis of the algorithm's baseline drift removal metrics is done to observe the time domain metrics before and after the algorithm improvement. In the frequency domain, a spectral analysis of the EMG signal before and after the algorithm processing is done to observe two metrics whether the baseline drift component is effectively removed and whether the useful signal is attenuated. Since the EMG signals provided in the Ninapro database are unprocessed raw EMG signals, there is no guarantee that the EMG signals in the Ninapro database do not contain baseline drift components, so they are not suitable for quantitative analysis. Therefore, in this paper, an EMG single-conductor EMG sensor containing a hardware filter was used to acquire the signals and further filtered by a band-pass filter to ensure the purity of the raw signals. A sine wave superimposed at 2 Hz and 5 Hz with 1 signal-to-noise ratio is added to the original signal as the baseline drift content for quantitative analysis.

### 4.1 Time Domain Analysis

In the time domain, the degree of signal deviation from the baseline is mainly analysed. Therefore, Sample Mean Square Error (sMSE) can be used to observe the overall degree of variation of the signal and thus the ability of the algorithm to remove the baseline drift problem.

$$sMSE = \frac{\sum_{i=0}^{m} (x_i - \bar{x})^2}{m - 1} \tag{10}$$

where $m$ is the number of sampling points, $x_i$ is the $I$ sampled EMG signal value, and $\bar{x}$ is the average of EMG signal sampling points.

**Table 3.** Sample variance values before and after algorithm improvement.

| Signal | sMSE |
| --- | --- |
| Original signal | 5819 |
| Baseline drift signal | 10375 |
| LSM with a window size of 10 | 4381 |
| ILSM with a window size of 10 | 4150 |
| LSM with a window size of 30 | 5533 |
| ILSM with a window size of 10 | 5331 |

As shown in Table 3, the sMSE value of the EMG signalwith the baseline drift added was 10375 and the sMSE of the original EMG signal was 5819, which shows that the EMG signal was significantly deviated after the baseline drift was added. With a window size of 10, the sMSE value of the LSM is 231 higher than that of the ILSM, and it can be seen that the ILSM is more effective in removing the baseline drift compared to before the improvement.

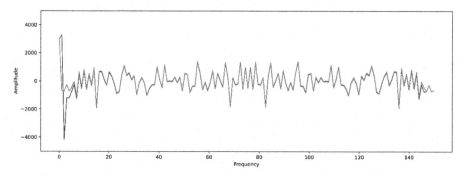

**Fig. 12.** Comparison of the spectrum of the original signal and the baseline drift signal.

## 4.2 Frequency Domain Analysis

Figure 12 shows a comparison of the spectrum of the original signal and the signal with baseline drift, where the orange color is the spectrum of the original signal and the blue color is the spectrum of the signal with baseline drift. It can be observed that both the original signal and the signal with baseline drift have a high frequency density at 0 Hz, i.e., a high DC component is present. The signal with baseline drift has a high energy density at 1–5 Hz, which corresponds to the frequency range where the baseline drift frequency is located.

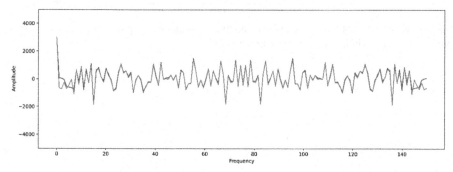

**Fig. 13.** Comparison of the original signal and the spectrum after least square method processing with a window size of 30 sampling points.

Figure 13 and Fig. 14 show the comparison of the original signal and the spectrum after processing by LSM for a window size of 30 and 10 sampling points, respectively. In the frequency domain of 10 Hz–150 Hz, comparing Fig. 10 and Fig. 15, it can be found that the original signal and the processed signal completely overlap in the frequency domain when the window size is 30 sampling points. In contrast, when the window size is 10 sampling points, there is a slight deviation in the frequency domain waveform after the LSM processing. This phenomenon indicates that LSM has a slight effect on the useful signal portion at smaller windows. In the 0 Hz–5 Hz frequency domain band, comparing Fig. 13 and Fig. 14, it can be found that when the window size is 10 sampling

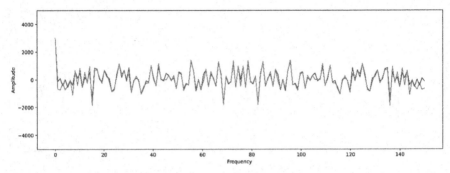

**Fig. 14.** Comparison of the original signal and the least square method processed spectrum with a window size of 10 sampling points.

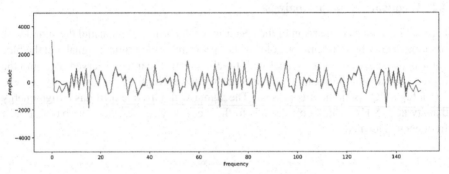

**Fig. 15.** Comparison of the original signal and the spectrum after improved least square method processing with a window size of 30 sampling points.

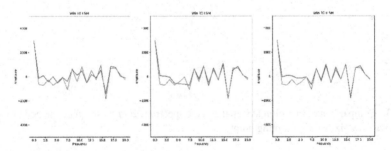

**Fig. 16.** Comparison of 0–20 Hz waveforms in Figs. 14, 15 and 16.

points, the frequency domain content after LSM processing is smaller than the content after LSM processing with a window size of 30 sampling points. In summary, it can be concluded that by reducing the window size, the ability of the LSM algorithm to remove the baseline drift content can be improved. However, when the window is smaller than a certain value, it will have some effect on the useful signal segment.

Figure 15 depicts the comparison of the spectra of the original signal and the signal containing baseline drift after ILSM processing at a window size of 30 sampling points. In the 10 Hz–150 Hz frequency domain, comparing Fig. 13 and Fig. 15, it can be found that neither LSM nor ILSM has any effect on the useful signal components for the same window size. In the 0 Hz–5 Hz frequency domain, it can be found from Fig. 16 that the baseline drift component in the ILSM-processed waveform is smaller than that in the LSM-processed waveform. In summary, ILSM has no significant effect on the useful signal compared to LSM with the appropriate window size, but ILSM has stronger attenuation effect on the baseline drift component in 0 Hz–5 Hz. Through Fig. 12, Fig. 13, Fig. 14, and Fig. 15, the advantages of ILSM over the LSM algorithm are perceptually observed from the spectrum, and the superiority of ILSM over LSM will be quantitatively analyzed by mathematical equations in the following. In order to measure the ability of the two algorithms to remove baseline drift, a Signal Removal Rate (sRR) metric is used in this paper to measure the ability of the algorithm to remove baseline drift before and after the improvement of the algorithm, and its expression is:

$$sRR = 1 - \frac{\sum_{i=1}^{5}(|\widehat{p_i}| - |p_i|)}{\sum_{i=1}^{5}(|\ddot{p_i}| - |p_i|)} \tag{11}$$

where, $p_i$ is the $i$ frequency power density of the original signal, $\sum_{i=1}^{2}|\widehat{p_i}|$ is the power density of 1–5 Hz at which the baseline drift content is processed by the algorithm, $p_i$ is the $i$ frequency power density of the original signal, $\sum_{i=1}^{2}\ddot{p_i}$ is the power density of 1–5 Hz at which the baseline drift of the signal with the baseline drift is added.

**Table 4.** Signal removal rate before and after algorithm improvement.

| Signal | sRR% |
| --- | --- |
| With baseline drift signal | 0 |
| Original signal | 100 |
| Window size of 10 LSM | 85.9 |
| Window size of 10 ILSM | 88.9 |
| Window size of 30 LSM | 79.0 |
| Window size of 30 ILSM | 81.9 |

Table 4 shows the signal removal rate of each algorithm under different window sizes. As can be seen from Table 4, under the same window, the improved algorithms are all improved by about 3% compared with the previous ones. In addition, it can be observed that the removal of baseline drift is better than before improvement under any window size. In order to measure whether the useful signal components are attenuated after the algorithm processing, this paper defines a Single Attenuation Rate (sAR) indicator to measure the attenuation of the useful signal, which is defined as:

$$sAR = 1 - \frac{\sum_{i=20}^{n}|\widehat{p_i}|}{\sum_{i=20}^{n}|p_i|} \tag{12}$$

where $n$ denotes the number of frequency analyses, $p_i$ is the $i$ frequency power density of the original signal, and $\widehat{p_i}$ is the $i$ frequency power density after the algorithm removes the baseline drift problem.

**Table 5.** Signal attenuation rate pre and post-algorithm improvement.

| Signal | sAR% |
|---|---|
| Window size of 10 LSM | 10.0 |
| Window size of 10 ILSM | 10.2 |
| Window size of 30 LSM | 1.8 |
| Window size of 30 ILSM | 2.1 |

Table 5 shows the signal attenuation rates of each algorithm for different window sizes. From Table 5, it can be seen that the effects on the useful signals are similar pre and post algorithm improvement with the same window size, and there is no big difference. However, it can be seen from Table 5 that although the smaller the window is, the better the baseline drift removal effect is, but it will cause some distortion of the signal and affect the useful signal content. In summary, from both the time domain and frequency domain, several indicators are summarized, based on the ILSM for the removal of baseline drift is about 3% more effective than the LSM, and the attenuation rate of the signal is similar to that before the improvement, so it can be seen that the algorithm is better than before the improvement in all aspects of the comprehensive indicators, with good baseline drift removal effect.

### 4.3 Comparative Analysis of Wavelet Decomposition Performance

In the previous subsection, it is verified that the performance index of ILSM is better than that of LSM in all aspects. Since the wavelet decomposition algorithm is similar to LSM in terms of denoising effect, and the time complexity is close to that of LSM, this section will explore the performance comparison between ILSM and traditional wavelet decomposition algorithm. In this section, db1 wavelet is used to decompose the EMG signal, and after obtaining the wavelet coefficients of each layer, the low frequency content is removed and then the wavelet reconstruction is performed to analyze the parameters of the reconstructed EMG signal. According to the wavelet decomposition principle, the EMG sampling signal can be decomposed into 9 layers of wavelet coefficients, and the wavelet coefficients are removed in order from the first to the highest in the frequency domain, and the baseline drift problem is effectively filtered out when wavelet coefficients from 1 to 4 layers are retained.

As can be seen from Fig. 17, the signal content at this time between 1 and 3 Hz is very close to the original signal.

As shown in Table 6, the performance indexes of wavelet coefficients of each layer are shown. From the data in the table, it can be found that the 3-layer wavelet coefficients have the best effect on the removal of baseline drift. Increasing or decreasing the number of

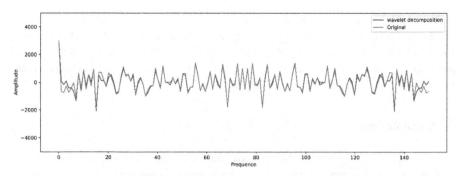

**Fig. 17.** Spectrum after reconstruction of 4-layer wavelet coefficients.

**Table 6.** Performance indexes of wavelet coefficients of each layer.

| layers | sMSE | sAR % | Time ms | sRR % |
|--------|------|-------|---------|-------|
| 4 | 5403 | 4.2 | 6.18 | 80.4% |
| 3 | 4919 | 8.0 | 4.98 | 83.0% |
| 2 | 4094 | 10.6 | 2.95 | 79.3% |

wavelet layers will reduce the baseline drift removal effect. Therefore, it can be concluded that the number of wavelet layers has a non-linear relationship with the removal effect of the baseline drift problem. In terms of processing time and loss rate, the higher the number of wavelet layers, the more time the algorithm takes, and conversely the lower the attenuation rate of the useful signal. In terms of mean square deviation, the lower the number of layers, the smaller the mean square deviation, indicating that the lower the number of layers the closer the signal is to the baseline and the less jitter, at the cost of reducing the useful signal content. Because of the large signal decay rate of the two-layer coefficients, the 3 and 4-layer wavelet coefficients are selected for performance comparison with LSM with different window sizes. As shown in Table 6.

**Table 7.** Performance indexes of wavelet coefficients of each layer.

| Signal | sMSE | sAR % | Time ms | sRR % |
|--------|------|-------|---------|-------|
| Window size of 30 ILSM | 5331 | 2.1 | 4.05 | 81.9 |
| 4 layers of small waves | 5403 | 4.2 | 6.18 | 80.4 |
| 3 layers of small waves | 4919 | 8.0 | 4.98 | 83.0 |
| Window size of 20 ILSM | 4816 | 7.7 | 7.97 | 83.9 |

As shown in Table 7, the 3-layer wavelet coefficients and the ILSM with a window size of 20 are close to each other in removing the baseline drift problem, but the wavelet decomposition algorithm takes less time. The sAR of both the 3-layer wavelet coefficients and the ILSM with a window size of 20 are large. sAR of both the 4-layer wavelet coefficients and the ILSM with a window size of 30 are smaller, and the sAR metric of the ILSM with a window size of 30 is half of that of the 4-layer wavelet coefficients. In terms of time, the ILSM is 2.13 ms faster than the four-layer wavelet coefficients, and the sRR metric is 1.5% higher.

## 5  Conclusion

In this article, we proposed ILSM to remove baseline drift, and some achievements are as follows: (1) This method improves the baseline drift removal rate. (2) The method can reduce the number of windows. (3)The ILSM used in this paper is close to the filtering effect of traditional wavelet transform and empirical modal methods in terms of performance, but the computation is much lower than traditional methods and the attenuation of useful signals is smaller. (4)And the method contributes to the less impact on the signal-to-noise ratio of the output signal.

## References

1. Abayasiri, R.A.M., Jayasekara, A.G.B.P., Gopura, R.A.R.C., et al.: EMG Based Controller for a Wheelchair with Robotic Manipulator (2021)
2. Atrisandi, A.D., Adiprawita, W., Mengko, T.L.R., et al.: Noise and artifact reduction based on EEMD algorithm for ECG with muscle noises, electrode motions, and baseline drifts (2015)
3. Atzori, M., Muller, H.: The Ninapro database: A resource for sEMG naturally controlled robotic hand prosthetics. Annual International Conference of the IEEE Engineering in Medicine and Biology Society, IEEE Engineering in Medicine and Biology Society, Annual International Conference, pp.7151–7154 (2015)
4. Boualem, A., Meryem, J., Ravier, P., et al.: Legendre polynomial modeling of time-varying delay applied to surface EMG signals—derivation of the appropriate time-dependent CRBs. Signal Process. p. 114 (2015)
5. De Luca, C.J., Gilmore, L.D., Kuznetsov, M., et al.: Filtering the surface EMG signal: movement artifact and baseline noise contamination. J. Biomech. **43**, 1573–1579 (2010)
6. Hossain, M.-B., Bashar, S.K., Lazaro, J., et al.: A robust ECG denoising technique using variable frequency complex demodulation. Comput. Methods Programs Biomed. **200**, 105856 (2021)
7. Huang, C., Li, W., Han, S., et al.: A novel image dehazing algorithm based on dual-tree complex wavelet transform. KSII Trans. Internet Inf. Syst. **12**, 5039–5055 (2018)
8. Luo, Y., Hargraves, R.H., Belle, A., et al.: A hierarchical method for removal of baseline drift from biomedical signals: application in ECG analysis. Sci. World J. **2013**, e896056 (2013)
9. Nudra Bajantika Pradivta, I.W., Arifin, A., Arrofiqi, F., et al.: Design of Myoelectric Control Command of Electric Wheelchair as Personal Mobility for Disabled Person (2019)
10. Paul, D., Mukherjee, M.: Automation of wheelchair using brain computer interface (BCI) technique. AIP Conf. Proc. **2072**, 020004 (2019)
11. Sbriccoli, P., Bazzucchi, I., Rosponi, A., et al.: Amplitude and spectral characteristics of biceps Brachii sEMG depend upon speed of isometric force generation. J. Electromyogr. Kinesiol. Off. J. Int. Soc. Electrophysiol. Kinesiol. **13**, 139–147 (2003)
12. Ma, C., et al.: Visual information processing for deep-sea visual monitoring system. Cogn. Robot. **1**, 3–11 (2021). https://doi.org/10.1016/j.cogr.2020.12.002

13. Lu, H., Zhang, Y., Li, Y., Jiang, C., Abbas, H.: User-oriented virtual mobile network resource management for vehicle communications. IEEE Trans. Intell. Transp. Syst. **22**(6), 3521–3532 (2021). https://doi.org/10.1109/TITS.2020.2991766
14. Chinese image captioning via fuzzy attention-based DenseNet-BiLSTM, ACM Transactions on Multimedia Computing Communications and Applications (2021)
15. Sun, J., Li, Y.: Multi-feature fusion network for road scene semantic segmentation. Comput. Electr. Eng. **92**, 107155 (2021). https://doi.org/10.1016/j.compeleceng.2021.107155
16. Tyastuti, F.H., Aniroh, Y., Muslimin, D., et al.: Classification of EMG signal on arm muscle motion using special fourier transformation to control electric wheelchair (2017)
17. Zhang, F., Tang, X., Tong, A., et al.: An automatic baseline correction method based on the penalized LSM. Sensors **20**, E2015 (2020)
18. Lu, H., Zhang, M., Xu, X.: Deep fuzzy hashing network for efficient image retrieval. IEEE Trans. Fuzzy Syst. (2020). https://doi.org/10.1109/TFUZZ.2020.2984991
19. Lu, H., Yujie, L., Min, C., et al.: Brain Intelligence: go beyond artificial intelligence. Mobile Networks Appl. **23**, 368–375 (2018)
20. Lu, H., Yujie, L., Mu, S., et al.: Motor anomaly detection for unmanned aerial vehicles using reinforcement learning. IEEE Internet Things J. **5**(4), 2315–2322 (2018)
21. Lu, H., Qin, M., Zhang, F., et al.: RSCNN: a CNN-based method to en-hance low-light remote-sensing images. Remote Sens. **13**, 62 (2020)
22. Lu, H., Yin, Z., Yujie, L., et al.: User-Oriented Virtual Mobile Network Resource Management for Vehicle Communications. IEEE Transactions on Intelligent Transpor-tation Systems **22**(6), 3521–3532 (2021)

# Point Cloud Driven Object Classification: A Review

Junfei Wang[1,2,4], Luxin Hu[1,2,4], Xianfeng Wu[1,2,3,4], Zhongyuan Lai[1,2,3,4($\boxtimes$)], and Qian Jia[1]

[1] State Key Laboratory of Precision Blasting, Jianghan University, Wuhan 430056, People's Republic of China
laizhy@jhun.edu.cn
[2] School of Artificial Intelligence, Jianghan University, Wuhan 430056, People's Republic of China
[3] Bingling Honorary School, Jianghan University, Wuhan 430056, People's Republic of China
[4] Institute for Interdisciplinary Research, Jianghan University, Wuhan 430056, People's Republic of China

**Abstract.** The rapid development of 3D sensors makes it very easy to obtain large amounts of point cloud data. Point cloud data can reflect the rich real world in real time and is widely used in face recognition, intelligent transportation and other fields. As the basis of computer vision, point cloud classification technology has received extensive attention. The application of deep learning further improves the accuracy and robustness of point cloud classification. This paper first introduces the ModelNet40 data set and evaluation indicators in detail. Then, two methods for directly processing point cloud data are introduced, namely point-based method and graph-based method. After that, the basic ideas and improvement points of representative methods in each category are introduced, and the error sources of these methods are analyzed. Then the experimental results are analyzed. Finally, the future of point cloud classification is prospected.

**Keywords:** Point cloud · Deep learning · Classification · Error sources

## 1 Introduction

In recent years, with the rapid development of three-dimensional sensors, more and more three-dimensional data have been obtained. These data are closely related to people's lives, so how to deal with these data has become a hot research direction. For different types of data, such as voxel, grid, processing methods are not the same. However, these methods applied to point cloud data processing have some limitations. For example, the voxelization method will incur additional memory overhead and slow down the running speed; converting 3D to 2D will lose some spatial information. The traditional methods of processing point cloud data include point feature histogram, shape context, surface feature description, etc. Although these methods can identify point clouds, they are all hand-designed features for specific problems. Such methods have poor adaptability and low recognition in new scenarios. The introduction of deep learning perfectly solves this problem, and its powerful learning and analysis capabilities have been recognized by researchers.

Previous review papers on point cloud classification [1–3] mainly focus on adapting point cloud data to existing network models. That is to say, what data the existing network is good at, and then we convert the point cloud into this type of data. This paper analyzes and compares point cloud classification from the perspective of information loss for the first time.

Our main contributions are as follows.

1. Detailed description of the ModelNet40 dataset;
2. We take the lead in analyzing and comparing point cloud classification from the perspective of information loss, and predict its classification performance according to the degree of information loss.
3. We conducted a comprehensive comparison of existing point cloud classification methods on the ModelNet40 dataset, and the results are consistent with our predictions;
4. We provide some suggestions to improve the performance of point cloud classification from the perspective of information loss.

## 2  Data

### 2.1  Dataset

The dataset used for point cloud classification experiments is ModelNet40 [6]. Model-Net40 is a list of the most common object categories in the world compiled by Princeton University using statistics obtained from the SUN database. 3D CAD models belonging to each object category were then collected using an online search engine by querying each object category term. Then manually determine whether each CAD model belongs to the specified category, and then delete the ones that are not, and get 40 categories of CAD models. The number of samples, points, and faces of each category are shown in Table 1, and then each model is uniformly sampled to obtain 10,000 points, and their point cloud models are obtained. Figure 1 shows the conversion from a CAD model to a point cloud model. Figure 2 shows the 40 categories of images in this dataset. Figures 3 and 4 show some images of people and chairs in this dataset, respectively. There are 9843 training samples and 2468 test samples in this dataset, and all grids are selected from 1024 points in the experiment.

The ModelNet40 dataset has the following characteristics:

1. The number of samples is large, and the shapes are different.
2. The intra-class difference is large, but the inter-class difference is small.
3. The distribution is not uniform and the number of sample points in each type is very different.
4. It comes from the real world and can fully reflect the real world.

**Fig. 1.** CAD drawing converted to point cloud.

**Table 1.** ModelNet40 dataset. Numbers means number of samples. Points means CAD drawing point range. Surfaces means range of surfaces in CAD drawings

| Model | Numbers | Points | Surfaces |
|---|---|---|---|
| Airplane | 726 | 1107–2286376 | 1253–2583632 |
| Bathtub | 156 | 202–261711 | 206–88205 |
| Bed | 615 | 100–246191 | 84–208716 |
| Bench | 193 | 28–60733 | 48–36088 |
| Bookshelf | 672 | 104–566973 | 64–361179 |
| Bottle | 435 | 96–678733 | 152–555549 |
| Bowl | 84 | 48–29549 | 118–19098 |
| Car | 297 | 1920–1039614 | 1218–838922 |
| Chair | 989 | 114–250056 | 74–165408 |
| Cone | 187 | 19–83397 | 7–72481 |
| Cup | 99 | 72–30982 | 116–27040 |
| Curtain | 158 | 96–2501688 | 48–4548836 |
| Desk | 286 | 152–83896 | 76–76918 |
| Door | 129 | 16–80412 | 10–80882 |
| Dresser | 286 | 112–176097 | 72–283606 |
| Flower_pot | 169 | 56–313753 | 36–489823 |
| Glass_box | 271 | 44–65444 | 22–121320 |
| Guitar | 255 | 501–152374 | 430–166819 |
| Keyboard | 165 | 36–337240 | 18–455368 |
| Lamp | 144 | 52–35119 | 60–36826 |
| Laptop | 169 | 24–210138 | 28–118568 |
| Mantel | 384 | 142–113534 | 84–99974 |
| Monitor | 565 | 106–137115 | 60–127656 |
| Night_stand | 286 | 130–189046 | 84–286433 |
| Person | 108 | 299–127838 | 292–119850 |

(*continued*)

**Table 1.** (*continued*)

| Model | Numbers | Points | Surfaces |
|---|---|---|---|
| Piano | 331 | 195–786234 | 147–666600 |
| Plant | 340 | 104–1587572 | 60–1193536 |
| Radio | 124 | 145–167899 | 122–162353 |
| Range_hood | 215 | 76–86206 | 42–57668 |
| Sink | 148 | 104–83615 | 84–82762 |
| Sofa | 780 | 110–502603 | 62–403575 |
| Stairs | 144 | 82–1246107 | 118–616816 |
| Stool | 110 | 40–151644 | 72–59750 |
| Table | 492 | 104–370056 | 68–221734 |
| Tent | 183 | 14–408876 | 4–479542 |
| Toilet | 444 | 212–131605 | 192–164155 |
| Tv_stand | 367 | 74–85559 | 36–101429 |
| Vase | 575 | 102–161820 | 56–119800 |
| Wardrobe | 107 | 34–36094 | 42–21928 |
| Xbox | 123 | 24–101507 | 12–77847 |

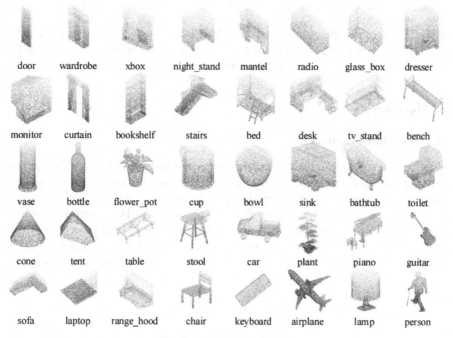

**Fig. 2.** ModelNet40 dataset.

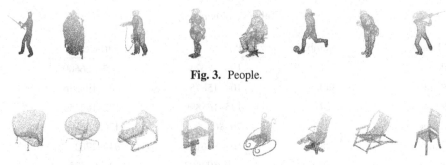

**Fig. 3.** People.

**Fig. 4.** Chair.

## 2.2 Evaluation Indicators

The evaluation indicators selected for object recognition are generally overall accuracy and mean class accuracy. The overall accuracy calculation formula for the class $i$ is:

$$Acc_i = \frac{TP_i + TN_i}{TP_i + FP_i + FN_i + TN_i} \tag{1}$$

The formula for calculating the mean class accuracy among $N$ types of objects is:

$$mAcc = \frac{1}{N} \sum_{i=1}^{N} Acc_i \tag{2}$$

where $TP$ means that the positive class is judged as a positive class, $FP$ means that the negative class is judged as a positive class, $FN$ means that a positive class is judged as a negative class, and $TN$ means that a negative class is judged as a negative class.

## 3  Methods

### 3.1  Point-Based Approach

Point-based approach has been a research hotspot in recent years. Since this method directly processes point cloud data and does not require other transformations, it will not lose some information like other approaches. Therefore, we can infer that this method performs better in object recognition from 3D point clouds. The unified idea of such approaches is to obtain local features of points through a multi-layer perceptron (MLP) [4], and then use pooling [5] to aggregate local features to form global features. Finally, this global feature is input into the classifier to obtain the classification result (Fig. 5).

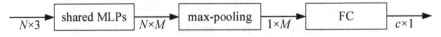

**Fig. 5.** Basic structure of the point-based approach.

**Point-Based Networks:**

*PointNet*: This network is the pioneering work of directly processing point cloud data. [6] proposed a new network model for processing point cloud data, by stacking shared weights of MLP to obtain global features for recognition. It achieves good results on point cloud classification, but does not consider the local structural relationships of points.

*PointNet++:* [7] designed this layered network to improve the accuracy of point cloud classification. The local structural features of points are obtained through the set abstraction layer (the set abstraction layer consists of the sampling layer, the grouping layer and the PointNet layer), and the global features are finally obtained by stacking the set abstraction layer.

*Moment Networks (Mo-Net):* [8] increased the input of the network on the basis of PointNet++, changed the input from $(x, y, z)$ to $(x, y, z, x^2, y^2, z^2, xy, yz, zx)$.

*Structural Relational Reasoning (SRN):* [9] introduced a self-attention mechanism, which allows it to select points with high attention scores when sampling. And change the sampling method to Gumbel Subset Sampling to make it adaptable to input with varying sizes.

*PointWeb:* [10] used the Adaptive Feature Adjustment module to form regional local features, which considered the relationship between all points in the local region, and used this local region feature to represent the local feature of this point.

*Point Clouds Adaptive Sampling Nonlocal Neural Networks (PointASNL):* [11] designed an adaptive sampling module, which designed an attention mechanism with adaptive offset for feature learning. Its principle is to first re-weight the points near the selected sampling points, and then let it adaptively adjust the overall outer edge sampling points of the point cloud. This method has a good effect on dealing with noise points.

*Point Cloud Transformer (PCT):* [12] improved the self-attention mechanism by supporting farthest point sampling and nearest neighbor search to enhance the features of input points.

*Position Adaptive Convolution (PAConv):* [13] used a way of dynamically assembling weight matrices to construct the kernel. A weight matrix is designed, and the coefficients of the weight matrix are generated by the relative positions of the points obtained by self-learning, so that it has greater flexibility and can better deal with irregular and disordered point cloud data.

**Error Sources of Point-Based Approach:**

There are three main sources of error in point-based approach. First, Independent processing of points leads to lack of local topological relationships between points. Second, when sampling, a random method is generally used for sampling, which will lead to the loss of some key points, resulting in errors. Third, when using the K-nearest neighbor method or the spherical radius method to select the neighborhood, its robustness cannot be guaranteed.

The point-based method directly uses the point cloud data as input, which can ensure the robustness of the input and the source of error is relatively small. Therefore, we speculate that this method performs well in point cloud classification.

**Graph-Based Approach:**
This method still processes the point cloud data directly, and the difference from the point-based method is that instead of processing each point independently, the points are connected into a graph and then processed. The unified idea of this type of method is to first connect the points into a graph, then obtain the local features of the graph through a multi-layer perceptron (MLP), and then use pooling to aggregate the local features to form global features. Finally, this global feature is input into the classifier to obtain the recognition result (Fig. 6).

**Fig. 6.** Basic structure of the graph-based approach.

**Graph-Based Networks:**
*Edge-Conditioned Convolutional (ECC):* [14] pioneered this approach. First, the points are connected into a graph, and the eigenvalues of all adjacent points of the vertex are weighted and summed as the eigenvalues of the point, and then the voxelization method is used to sample the point cloud data.

*Kernel Correlation Network (KCNet):* [15] performed kernel association by exploiting the local geometric structure of the graph. The local network was used to enhance the robustness of the network.

*Adaptive Graph Convolutional Neural Networks (AGCN):* [16] Considering that real graphs differ in size and structure, and previous networks require fixed-size graphs as input. Therefore, a Spectral Graph Convolution layer with graph Laplacian Learning layer is designed to learn the adaptive graph topology, which effectively solves the problem of different local topologies of training samples.

*Dynamic Graph CNN (DGCNN):* [17] designed edge convolution to obtain local structural features of points and reconstruct the graph after each feature is obtained. Edge convolution is portable and can be easily integrated into existing network architectures. This effectively solves the shortcomings that the previous methods do not consider the local structural features of the point cloud and the graph-based methods generally do not update the graph after the graph is constructed.

*Linked Dynamic Graph CNN (LDGCNN):* [18] Considering that MLP can guarantee transformation invariance to a certain extent, the transpose network of DGCNN is removed. The acquired features of different dimensions are connected by jump links, thus avoiding the problem of gradient disappearance.

*Grid-GCN:* [19] achieved efficient data structure and computation through Coverage-Aware Grid Query. The space coverage is improved, the time complexity is reduced, and the running speed is improved.

*Geometry disentangled network (GDANet):* [20] give higher weights to the contour parts of the point cloud and lower weights to the plane parts, so that the network pays more attention to the contour parts.

**Error Sources of Graph-Based Approach:**
There are two main sources of error in graph-based approach. First, when sampling, a random method is generally used for sampling, which will lead to the loss of some key points, resulting in errors. The other is that when using the K-nearest neighbor method or the spherical radius method to select the neighborhood, its robustness cannot be guaranteed.

The graph-based methods have a good performance in detail processing. Since the point cloud data is directly used as input, the robustness of the input can be guaranteed, and the source of error is relatively small. Therefore, we speculate that such methods should perform best in point cloud classification.

The graph-based method makes up for the shortcoming of the point-based method to obtain the local topological relationship of points, and does better in obtaining details. So, we speculate that this method performs better in point cloud classification.

## 4    Results Analysis

Table 2 shows the point cloud classification accuracy and code framework of some classic models on ModelNet40. It can be seen from Table 2 that the point-based method is one of the mainstream methods for object recognition at present, with extensive research and many network models. Using point cloud data directly can use more point information and cause fewer errors, so it has good performance in point cloud classification accuracy. The graph-based method effectively considers the local topological relationship between points and has a deeper consideration of local information, so the accuracy of point cloud classification is higher.

The experimental results are in good agreement with our predicted results, proving that our analysis is correct, and the following research hotspots should still focus on methods that directly use point cloud data. And it can be seen from the table that most of the frameworks are PyTorch and TensorFlow, so it proves that these two frameworks are relatively complete and can meet our needs.

**Table 2.** Comparison of Point Cloud Classification Accuracy. OA means overall accuracy. MA means mean class accuracy.

| Type | Year | Models | OA | MA | Frame |
|------|------|--------|----|----|-------|
| Point-based | 2017 | Pointnet [6] | 89.2 | 86.2 | PyTorch |
|  | 2017 | PointNet++ [7] | 90.7 | – | PyTorch |
|  | 2018 | Mo-Net [8] | 89.3 | 86.1 | PyTorch |
|  | 2018 | SRN [9] | 91.5 | – | PyTorch |
|  | 2019 | PointWeb [10] | 92.3 | 89.4 | PyTorch |
|  | 2020 | Point ASNL [11] | 92.9 | – | TensorFlow |
|  | 2021 | PCT [12] | 93.2 | – | Jittor |
|  | 2021 | PAConv [13] | 93.6 | – | PyTorch |
| Graph-based | 2017 | ECC [14] | 87.4 | 83.2 | Torch |
|  | 2018 | KCNet [15] | 91 | – | PyTorch |
|  | 2019 | DGCNN [17] | 92.2 | 90.2 | PyTorch |
|  | 2019 | LDGCNN [18] | 92.9 | 90.3 | TensorFlow |
|  | 2020 | Grid-GCN [19] | 93.1 | 91.3 | PyTorch |
|  | 2021 | GDANet [20] | 93.8 | – | PyTorch |

## 5 Outlook

Although existing methods model point cloud classification from different perspectives and improve the recognition accuracy, these networks still have some limitations. Based on these limitations, this section provides an outlook on point cloud classification techniques.

**Datasets.** Massive datasets are the basis for deep learning-based point cloud classification. At present, the dataset used by most networks is still ModelNet40, which can no longer meet the current needs of point cloud classification. The construction of richer and broader datasets is currently the top priority.

**Real-Time.** After years of research, although the accuracy of the current point cloud classification model has been greatly improved, the complexity of the entire model has increased and the running speed has decreased. Now, autonomous driving and unmanned delivery vehicles have entered people's lives, which has higher requirements for the real-time performance of point cloud classification. Therefore, while improving the accuracy of point cloud classification, the network model should be designed as light as possible to make it run faster and more accurately, so as to meet the real-time requirements, which will become a research direction of point cloud classification.

**Acknowledgment.** This work was supported by the Scientific Research Program of Jianghan University (No. 2021yb052).

# References

1. Placitelli, A.P., Gallo, L.: Low-cost augmented reality systems via 3D point cloud sensors. In: Proceedings of the Seventh International Conference on Signal Image Technology & Internet-Based Systems (SITIS), pp. 188–192. Dijon, France (2011)
2. Rukhovich, D., Vorontsova, A., Konushin, A.: Imvoxelnet: Image to voxels projection for monocular and multi-view general-purpose 3D object detection. In: Proceedings of the IEEE/CVF Winter Conference on Applications of Computer Vision (WACV), pp. 2397–2406. Waikoloa, USA (2022)
3. He, P., Emami, P., Ranka, S., et al.: Learning scene dynamics from point cloud sequences. Int. J. Comput. Vis. **130**, 1–27 (2022)
4. Pinkus, A.: Approximation theory of the MLP model in neural networks. Acta Numer **8**, 143–195 (1999)
5. Liu, N., Jian, S., Li, D., et al.: Hierarchical adaptive pooling by capturing high-order dependency for graph representation learning. IEEE Transactions on Knowledge and Data Engineering (TKDE) (2021)
6. Qi, C.R., Su, H., Mo, K., et al.: PointNet: deep learning on point sets for 3D classification and segmentation. In: Proceedings of the IEEE/CVF Conference on Computer Vision and Pattern Recognition (CVPR), pp. 652–660. Honolulu, USA (2017)
7. Qi, C.R., Yi, L., Su, H., et al.: Pointnet++: deep hierarchical feature learning on point sets in a metric space. In: Advances in Neural Information Processing Systems (NIPS). Long Beach, USA (2017)
8. Joseph-Rivlin, M., Zvirin, A., Kimmel, R.: Moment: flavor the moments in learning to classify shapes. In: Proceedings of the IEEE/CVF International Conference on Computer Vision Workshops (ICCVW), pp. 4085–4094. Seoul, Korea (2019)
9. Duan, Y., Zheng, Y., Lu, J., et al.: Structural Relational Reasoning (SRN) of point clouds. In: Proceedings of the IEEE/CVF Conference on Computer Vision and Pattern Recognition (CVPR), pp. 949–958. Long Beach, USA (2019)
10. Zhao, H., Jiang, L., Fu, C. W., et al.: PointWeb: enhancing local neighborhood features for point cloud processing. In: Proceedings of the IEEE/CVF Conference on Computer Vision and Pattern Recognition (CVPR), pp. 5565–5573. Long Beach, USA (2019)
11. Yan, X., Zheng, C., Li, Z., et al.: PointASNL: robust point clouds processing using nonlocal neural networks with adaptive sampling. In: Proceedings of the IEEE/CVF Conference on Computer Vision and Pattern Recognition (CVPR), pp. 5589–5598 (2020)
12. Guo, M.H., Cai, J.X., Liu, Z.N., et al.: PCT: point cloud transformer. Comput. Visual Media **7**(2), 187–199 (2021)
13. Xu, M., Ding, R., Zhao, H., et al: PAConv: position Adaptive Convolution with dynamic kernel assembling on point clouds. In: Proceedings of the IEEE/CVF Conference on Computer Vision and Pattern Recognition (CVPR), pp. 3173–3182 (2021)
14. Simonovsky, M., Komodakis, N.: Dynamic edge-conditioned filters in convolutional neural networks on graphs. In: Proceedings of the IEEE Conference on Computer Vision and Pattern Recognition (CVPR), pp. 3693–3702. Honolulu, USA (2017)
15. Shen, Y., Feng, C., Yang, Y., et al.: Mining point cloud local structures by kernel correlation and graph pooling. In: Proceedings of the IEEE Conference on Computer Vision and Pattern Recognition (CVPR), pp. 4548–4557. Salt Lake City, USA (2018)
16. Li, R., Wang, S., Zhu, F., et al.: Adaptive Graph Convolutional Neural Networks (AGCNN). In: Proceedings of the AAAI Conference on Artificial Intelligence (AAAI), pp. 3546–3553. New Orleans, USA (2018)
17. Wang, Y., Sun, Y., Liu, Z., et al.: Dynamic Graph CNN (DGCNN) for learning on point clouds. ACM Trans. Graph. **38**(5), 1–12 (2019)

18. Zhang, K., Hao, M., Wang, J., et al.: Linked Dynamic Graph CNN (LDGCNN): learning on point cloud via linking hierarchical features, arXiv preprint arXiv:1904.10014 (2019)
19. Xu, Q., Sun, X., Wu, C. Y., et al.: Grid-GCN for fast and scalable point cloud learning, In: Proceedings of the IEEE/CVF Conference on Computer Vision and Pattern Recognition (CVPR), pp. 5661–5670 (2020)
20. Xu, M., Zhang, J., Zhou, Z., et al.: Learning geometry-disentangled representation for complementary understanding of 3d object point cloud, Proceedings of the AAAI Conference on Artificial Intelligence, vol. 35(4), pp. 3056–3064 (2021)

# Intelligent Identification of Similar Customers for Electricity Demand Estimation Based on Metadata of Household Background

Jing Jiang[1,2]($\boxtimes$), Menghan Xu[2], Sen Pan[1,2], and Lipeng Zhu[1,2]

[1] State Grid Smart Grid Research Institute Co., LTD., Beijing 102200, China
395937369@qq.com

[2] Information and Telecommunication Branch, State Grid Jiangsu Electric Power Co., LTD., Nanjing 210024, China

**Abstract.** Electricity consumption plays an extremely crucial role in influencing the economic development of the world. To guarantee the residential electricity demand, it is necessary to analyze the electricity consumption behaviors of customers. Due to a large number of customers in real life, it is required to group similar customers for a better understanding of their behaviors. Household income is a vital and appropriate indicator to discover similar customers in a group. However, sometimes it is difficult to collect the income information of customers because of the privacy protection and deliberate hiding of information. To address this issue, this paper proposes a method to intelligently identify similar customers by exploiting their metadata of public household background information associated the household income. To evaluate the proposed method, we adopt the real datasets collected by Pullinger et al. [1] to conduct the experiments. This dataset comprises gas, electricity, and contextual data from 255 UK homes over a 23-month period ending in June 2018, in which a mean participation duration is 286 days. The results demonstrate that the proposed method is effective in grouping the customers with similar household income based on their metadata of public household background information only.

**Keywords:** Electricity demand · Electricity consumption · Metadata · Intelligent identification · Household income · Classification · Ensemble learning

## 1 Introduction

Electricity power, as the main clean energy, has received more and more attention from all over the world [2, 3]. Since it is the key to reducing carbon emission, the shift towards electricity consumption is becoming a trend in the future energy systems of the world [4]. For example, Fig. 1 shows the situation of the world's electricity generation from 1985 to 2020 [5]. From it, we see that electricity generation keeps increasing in the main seven economies. Hence, electricity consumption plays an extremely crucial role in influencing the economic development of the world [6].

© The Author(s), under exclusive license to Springer Nature Singapore Pte Ltd. 2022
S. Yang and H. Lu (Eds.): ISAIR 2022, CCIS 1700, pp. 271–280, 2022.
https://doi.org/10.1007/978-981-19-7946-0_23

Since household electricity demand increases every year with the increase of economic growth, community income, and population, electricity generation is vital in performing daily activities [7]. It is the duty of the government to provide sufficient electrical energy for industrial, commercial as well as household demands [2, 3]. Especially with the process of urbanization is accelerating, electricity becoming the most important energy source in household life. In households, electrical energy is required mainly by the use of home electronic appliances [8]. To guarantee the residential electricity demand, it is necessary to analyze the electricity consumption behaviors [2, 9].

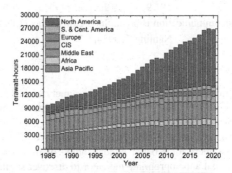

**Fig. 1.** The situation of electricity generation of the world from 1985 to 2020.

In fact, there is diversity and variation in electricity consumption among different households, which makes it difficult to understand the electricity consumption behaviors of residents in detail [10]. Notably, due to a large number of customers, it is impossible to design policies tailored to individual customers. Hence, it is necessary to segment or group the customers into distinguished groups by considering their unique characteristics [11, 12]. To this end, many researchers pay attention to how electricity prices influence the residential behaviors of electricity consumption [13]. Some studies have found that electricity prices have a minor influence on residential electricity consumption behaviors [14, 15].

Except for electricity prices, household income is also a crucial factor to influence household electricity consumption [8]. Many studies have researched the relationship between residential electricity consumption and per capita income. Recent examples of such studies mainly assume a linear relationship between residential electricity consumption and per capita income [16]. However, some evidence shows that the linear assumption may have biases associated with estimation [17]. Hence, household income is a vital and appropriate indicator to discover similar customers in a group, helping analyze the residential electricity consumption demand.

However, due to the privacy protection and deliberate hiding of information, sometimes it is difficult to collect the income information of customers. Hence, it is necessary to find an alternative and easier way to group the similar customers associated with household income. To this end, we propose a method to intelligently identify similar customers by exploiting their metadata of public household background information associated the household income, where an Ensemble Household Income Classification

(EHIC) model is also developed based on four kinds of machine learning classifier. We use the real datasets collected by Pullinger et al. [1] to conduct the experiments. The results demonstrate that the proposed method is effective in grouping the customers with similar household income based on their metadata of public household background information only. The main contributions of this paper are concluded as follows.

1. We propose an approach to intelligently identify similar customers by exploiting their metadata of public household background information associated with the household income.
2. We propose a concrete method to preprocess the dataset in terms of the metadata of public household background information associated the household income with making it be suitable for machine learning algorithms.
3. We conduct extensive experiments to validate the proposed method.

## 2 Related Work

### 2.1 Machine Learning-Based Analysis of Household Electricity Demand

Many prior studies focus on the relationship between household income and the ownership of specific electrical appliances. They find that household income is a key predictor of appliance ownership, which can help to estimate the growth of household electricity demand [2, 6]. With the household level data, most prior studies rely on traditional statistical methods to analyze the aforementioned relationship. However, such a relationship is complex and nonlinear, traditional statistical methods are difficult to handle. To address this issue, many researchers pay attention to machine learning [14]. In general, there are two kinds of methods, i.e., supervised and unsupervised [9]. The unsupervised method aims at finding the underlying groups or patterns based on a set of features associated with household electricity demand. In terms of the supervised method, also known as classification [18], the groups are classified based on a labelled set of features associated with household electricity demand. In this paper, we focus on grouping customers with similar household income by exploiting their metadata of public household background information, which has never been studied as far as we know.

### 2.2 Classification Methods

The classification problem is the basis of supervised machine learning [19–21]. Up to now, many well-known classification algorithms are proposed, deep neural networks (DNN), support vector machines (SVM), k-nearest neighbor (KNN), random forest (RF), eXtreme gradient boosting (XGBoost), etc. In this paper, we group similar customers by exploiting their metadata of public household background information associated the household income, which is also modeled as a classification problem. Hereby, we select the SVM, KNN, RF, and XGBoost as the classification algorithms [22–24].

### 2.3  Dataset Description

We conduct the experiments by using the IDEAL household energy dataset collected by Pullinger et al. [1]. This dataset comprises gas, electricity, and contextual data from 255 UK homes over a 23-month period ending in June 2018, in which a mean participation duration is 286 days. Please refer to https://datashare.ed.ac.uk/handle/10283/3647 to see more details. To group similar customers by exploiting their metadata of public household background information associated the household income, we select the metadata of home and room of IDEAL dataset. They are recorded in 'home.csv' and 'room.csv', respectively.

## 3  The Proposed Method

### 3.1  The Structure of the Proposed Method

The proposed method has several parts as shown in Fig. 2. It works as follows.

1. Input: inputting the metadata of home and room;
2. Conducting the feature engineering to preprocess the metadata of home and room;
3. Conducting the feature selection to delete the irrelevant and redundant features;
4. Training four classifiers of SVM, KNN, RF, and XGBoost based on the selected features, respectively;
5. Ensembling the four classifiers to obtain a final estimation;

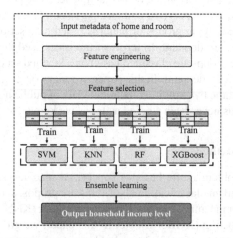

**Fig. 2.** The flowchart of the proposed method.

## 3.2    Feature Engineering

Since the two datasets of 'home.csv' and 'room.csv' have the same attribute of home id, we can fuse the 'room.csv' into the 'home.csv'. Concretely, we encode the categorical data in the home dataset, and the format description of the encoding is shown in Table 1. By trying different classification methods, we classify the income band into three categories, as shown in Table 1, making the income band have the maximum correlation with other attributes describing housing quality.

**Table 1.**  Encoding format description

| Coding | 0 | 1 | 2 |
|---|---|---|---|
| install_type | standard | enhanced | x |
| hometype | flat | house_or_bungalow | x |
| occupancy | multiple | single | other |
| urban_rural_class | 3+ | 2 | 1 |
| entry_floor | Attic | Basement (level -1) | other |
| outdoor_space | No | Yes- shared with neighbors | Yes - private |
| outdoor_drying | other | No | Yes |
| income_band | £10,800 to £26,999 or less | £27,000 to £37,799 | £37,800 to £90,000 or more |

## 3.3    Feature Selection

To conduct the feature selection, we first analyze the correlation between the fused data attributes. The heat map of the data after alignment fusion and encoding is shown in Fig. 3(a). The top 16 attributes with the strongest correlation with the income band and their corresponding correlations value are shown in Fig. 3(b). After correlation analysis, we use the feature selection algorithm to select the most relevant features. The variance selection method is used to filter out features with a variance lower than 1.

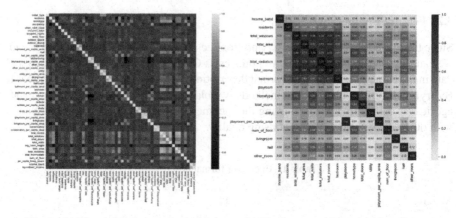

**Fig. 3.** (a) The global data attributes heatmap; (b) The heatmap of the top 16 attributes.

### 3.4 Ensemble Learning

In this part, we explain how to conduct ensemble learning based on the selected features. We employ SVM, KNN, RF, and XGBoost as the base classifiers. Supposing we classify an instance $x$ which belongs to the testing dataset with a $t$ classes problem, i.c., the label $\omega = (\omega_1, \omega_2, ..., \omega_t)$. Let a $t$-dimensional vector $c_i(x) = (c_i^1(x), c_i^2(x), ..., c_i^t(x))$ represent the prediction label vector for the instance $x$ by classifier $C_i$, $i = 1, 2, 3$, and 4 corresponding to SVM, KNN, RF, and XGBoost, respectively. According to the plurality voting, the label of instance $x$ can be obtained by:

$$\omega(x) = \arg\max_j \sum_{i=1}^{4} c_i^j(x) \tag{1}$$

## 4  Experiments and Results

### 4.1  General Settings

We normalize the data of the total area, per capita area, and floor height in the results obtained by the previous fusion to reduce the computational cost and make the feature distribution of the data more uniform. Table 2. Summarizes all the parameters of the four base classifiers of SVM, KNN, RF, and XGBoost. In addition, five-fold cross-validation is used to obtain the objective average results. Additionally, we use ensemble learning to soft-vote the results of the four base classifiers according to formula (1).

**Table 2.** Parameter settings of the four base classifiers and ensemble learning

| Classifier | Parameters |
|---|---|
| SVM | LIBSVM: all the parameters are set as default values |
| KNN | Number of neighbors = 3 |
| RF | Tree = 6 |
| XGBoost | learning_rate = 0.3, n_estimators = 100, max_depth = 7, min_child_weight = 2, subsample = 0.8 colsample_bytree = 0.6, objective = 'multi:softprob' |
| EHIC | Ensemble household income classification model proposed in this paper |

### 4.2 Experimental Designs

We conduct three sets of experiments where each set contains different feature combinations. Firstly, there is no performed feature filtering on the preprocessed data, and full features are used for classification training. Secondly, according to the heatmap in Fig. 5, 16 features that are most closely related to the income band are selected as the second feature combination. Finally, the variance selection method is used to filter out features with variance lower than 1, and the last remaining ten features are used as the third feature combination.

### 4.3 Experimental Results

The final classification results of three sets of experiments are recorded in Tables 3, 4 and 5, respectively. From these tables, we have the following findings.

- The classification results on full features, 16 manually selected features datasets, and the ten features selected by variance selection are progressively more accurate.
- The ensemble classifier of EHIC steadily performs better than the four base classifiers can on the three sets of experiments.

From the two findings, it can be found that classification performance on the full features is not ideal as there are some irrelevant and redundant features. After simply selecting the features manually by correlation, the classification accuracy can be slightly improved. Finally, by selecting features with variance selection method, the classification accuracy can be further improved, which verifies that appropriate feature selection can boost the accuracy of classifiers. Besides, we also see that ensemble learning is a useful method to further improve the classification results.

In summary, the experimental results demonstrate that the proposed method can intelligently identify similar customers by exploiting their metadata of public household background information associated the household income.

**Table 3.** Classification results on full features.

| Five-fold | SVM | KNN | RF | XGBboost | EHIC |
|---|---|---|---|---|---|
| #1 | 48.98% | 61.22% | 61.22% | 61.22% | 63.27% |
| #2 | 45.83% | 58.33% | 54.17% | 62.50% | 58.33% |
| #3 | 60.42% | 56.25% | 50.00% | 60.42% | 62.50% |
| #4 | 60.42% | 64.58% | 64.58% | 60.42% | 64.58% |
| #5 | 56.25% | 60.42% | 62.50% | 60.42% | 62.50% |
| **Mean** | **54.38%** | **60.16%** | **58.49%** | **60.99%** | **62.24%** |

**Table 4.** Classification results on 16 closely related features.

| Five-fold | SVM | KNN | RF | XGBboost | EHIC |
|---|---|---|---|---|---|
| #1 | 61.22% | 65.31% | 57.14% | 65.31% | 63.27% |
| #2 | 60.42% | 58.33% | 50.00% | 64.58% | 62.50% |
| #3 | 60.42% | 62.50% | 58.33% | 64.58% | 64.58% |
| #4 | 60.42% | 60.42% | 66.67% | 64.58% | 64.58% |
| #5 | 60.42% | 60.42% | 60.42% | 58.33% | 60.42% |
| **Mean** | **60.58%** | **61.39%** | **58.51%** | **63.48%** | **63.07%** |

**Table 5.** Classification results on 10 features selected by variance selection method.

| Five-fold | SVM | KNN | RF | XGBboost | EHIC |
|---|---|---|---|---|---|
| #1 | 61.22% | 61.22% | 65.31% | 69.39% | 63.27% |
| #2 | 60.42% | 60.42% | 58.33% | 64.58% | 64.58% |
| #3 | 60.42% | 60.42% | 52.08% | 62.50% | 62.50% |
| #4 | 60.42% | 60.42% | 66.67% | 64.58% | 68.75% |
| #5 | 60.42% | 60.42% | 62.50% | 60.42% | 64.58% |
| **Mean** | **60.58%** | **60.58%** | **60.98%** | **64.29%** | **64.74%** |

## 5  Conclusion

This paper proposes a method to intelligently identify similar customers by exploiting their metadata of public household background information associated the household income, where an Ensemble Household Income Classification (EHIC) model is also proposed based on four kinds of machine learning classifier. To evaluate the proposed method, we use the real datasets collected by Pullinger et al. [1] to conduct the experiments. The experimental results demonstrate that the proposed method is effective in grouping the customers with similar household income based on their metadata of public household background information only. In the future, we plan to use the proposed method to help estimate the household electricity demand.

**Acknowledgement.** This work is supported by the Science and Technology Project of State Grid Corporation of China (Research on Intelligent Data Management and Feature Engineering Technology for Middle Platform, No. 5700-202058480A-0- 0-00).

# References

1. Pullinger, M., et al.: The ideal household energy dataset, electricity, gas, contextual sensor data and survey data for 255 uk homes. Sci. Data **8**(1), 1–18 (2021)
2. Liddle, B., Huntington, H.: How prices, income, and weather shape household electricity demand in high-income and middle-income countries. Energy Econ. **95**(2021), 104995 (2021)
3. Athukorala, W., Wilson, C., Managi, S., Karunarathna, M.: Household demand for electricity: the role of market distortions and prices in competition policy. Energy Policy **134**(2019), 110932 (2019)
4. Atalla, T., Bigerna, S., Bollino, C.A.: Energy demand elasticities and weather worldwide. Economia Politica **35**(1), 207–237 (2018)
5. Spencer Dale: Bp statistical review of world energy (2021). https://www.bp.com/en/global/corporate/energy-economics/statistical-review-of-world-energy.html
6. Poblete-Cazenave, M., Pachauri, S.: A model of energy poverty and access: estimating household electricity demand and appliance ownership. Energy Econ. **98**(2021), 105266 (2021)
7. Li, M., Allinson, D., He, M.: Seasonal variation in household electricity demand: a comparison of monitored and synthetic daily load profiles. Energy Build. **179**(2018), 292–300 (2018)
8. Wang, B., Yuan, Z., Liu, X., Sun, Y., Zhang, B., Wang, Z.: Electricity price and habits: which would affect household electricity consumption? Energy Build. **240**(2021), 110888 (2021)
9. Ofetotse, E.L., Essah, E.A., Yao, R.: Evaluating the determinants of household electricity consumption using cluster analysis. J. Build. Eng. **43**(2021), 102487 (2021)
10. Yu-Wen, S.: Residential electricity demand in taiwan: consumption behavior and rebound effect. Energy Policy **124**(2019), 36–45 (2019)
11. López, J.J., Aguado, J.A., Martin, F., Munoz, F., Rodriguez, A., Ruiz, J.E.: Hopfield–k-means clustering algorithm: a proposal for the segmentation of electricity customers. Electric Power Syst. Res. **81**(2), 716–724 (2011)
12. Räsänen, T., Ruuskanen, J., Kolehmainen, M.: Reducing energy consumption by using self-organizing maps to create more personalized electricity use information. Appl. Energy **85**(9), 830–840 (2008)
13. Zhu, X., Li, L., Zhou, K., Zhang, X., Yang, S.: A meta-analysis on the price elasticity and income elasticity of residential electricity demand. J. Clean. Prod. **201**(2018), 169–177 (2018)
14. Wang, Z., et al.: How to effectively implement an incentive-based residential electricity demand response policy? Experience from large-scale trials and matching questionnaires. Energy Policy **141**(2020), 111450 (2020)
15. Ye, B., Ge, F., Rong, X., Li, L.: The influence of nonlinear pricing policy on residential electricity demand—a case study of anhui residents. Energ. Strat. Rev. **13**(2016), 115–124 (2016)
16. Liu, Y., Gao, Y., Hao, Y., Liao, H.: The relationship between residential electricity consumption and income: a piecewise linear model with panel data. Energies **9**(10), 831 (2016)

17. Halvorsen, B., Larsen, B.M.: How serious is the aggregation problem? An empirical illustration. Appl. Econ. **45**(26), 3786–3794 (2013)
18. Shafiq, M., Tian, Z., Bashir, A.K., Jolfaei, A., Xiangzhan, Y.: Data mining and machine learning methods for sustainable smart cities traffic classification: a survey. Sustain. Cities Soc. **60**(2020), 102177 (2020)
19. Greener, J.G., Kandathil, S.M., Moffat, L., Jones, D.T.: A guide to machine learning for biologists. Nat. Rev. Molecul. Cell Biol. **23**(1), 40–55 (2022)
20. Di, W., Shang, M., Luo, X., Wang, Z.: An $l_1$-and-$l_2$-norm-oriented latent factor model for recommender systems. IEEE Trans. Neural Netw. Learn. Syst. **2021**, 1–14 (2021)
21. Wu, D., Luo, X.: Robust latent factor analysis for precise representation of high-dimensional and sparse data. IEEE/CAA J. Automatica Sinica **8**(4), 796–805 (2021)
22. Wu, X., et al.: Top 10 algorithms in data mining. Knowl. Inform. Syst. **14**(1), 1–37 (2008)
23. Lu, H., Zhang, M., Xu, X., et al.: Deep fuzzy hashing network for efficient image retrieval. IEEE Trans. Fuzzy Syst. **29**(99), 166–176 (2020)
24. Zheng, Q., Zhu, J., Tang, H., et al.: Generalized label enhancement with sample correlations. IEEE Trans. Knowl. Data Eng. **2021**(99), 1 (2021)
25. Lu, H., Zhang, M., Xu, X.: Deep fuzzy hashing network for efficient image retrieval. IEEE Trans. Fuzzy Syst. (2020). https://doi.org/10.1109/TFUZZ.2020.2984991
26. Lu, H., Yujie, L., Min, C., et al.: Brain Intelligence: go beyond artificial intelligence. Mobile Networks Appl. **23**, 368–375 (2018)
27. Lu, H., Li, Y., Mu, S., et al.: Motor anomaly detection for unmanned aerial vehicles using reinforcement learning. IEEE Internet Things J. **5**(4), 2315–2322 (2018)
28. Lu, H., Qin, M., Zhang, F., et al.: RSCNN: a CNN-based method to en-hance low-light remote-sensing images. Remote Sens. **13**, 62 (2020)
29. Huimin, L., Zhang, Y., Li, Y., et al.: User-oriented virtual mobile network resource management for vehicle communications. IEEE Trans. Intell. Transp. Syst. **22**(6), 3521–3532 (2021)

# A SQL Injection Attack Recognition Model Based on 1D Convolutional Neural Network

Jing Jiang[1,2(✉)], Menghan Xu[2], Sen Pan[1,2], and Lipeng Zhu[1,2]

[1] State Grid Smart Grid Research Institute Co., LTD., Beijing 102200, China
395937369@qq.com
[2] Infomation and Telecommunication Branch, State Grid Jiangsu Electric Power Co., LTD., Nanjing 210024, China

**Abstract.** The rapid development of Internet technology and the widespread popularization of web applications have brought a lot of convenience to people's lives. At the same time, due to the interaction of more user information between browsers and servers, attacks on web applications have intensified, and network security issues occur frequently. SQL injection attacks have always been a common tactic of cyber attackers due to their simplicity and high threat level. Nowadays, SQL injection attacks are emerging in an endless stream, and detection models based on traditional machine learning algorithms have been unable to identify effectively and accurately complex SQL injection attacks. In this paper, we propose a SQL injection recognition model based on one-dimensional convolutional neural network (1D CNN) and combining word embedding and ASCII transcoding techniques. The model can recognize all sorts of SQL injection attacks more efficiently and accurately, dramatically lower human intervention, and offer some defense against 0day attacks that never occur.

**Keywords:** SQL injection · ASCII transcoding · 1D convolutional neural network · Attack Recognition

## 1  Introduction

Network attacks targeting web applications have always been widely concerned in the industry [1]. The Open Web Application Security Project, OWASP, is a non-profit organization focused on researching application security and dependable programs. The organization takes the applications of many companies around the world as the research object, summarizes more than hundreds of thousands of vulnerabilities, and publishes security reports to help enterprises and institutions avoid risks in program development and improve the security of web applications. From the top ten security vulnerability reports released by the organization in 2017 and 2021, it can be seen that injection vulnerability has always been the biggest threat to network security [2]. Among injection vulnerabilities, SQL injection attacks are more widespread and have a greater impact on application security. Because SQL injection attackers can use scripts, tools, and even browsers to maliciously implant SQL queries into the query statements of web applications and trick the database engine to execute these malicious SQL queries, attackers

© The Author(s), under exclusive license to Springer Nature Singapore Pte Ltd. 2022
S. Yang and H. Lu (Eds.): ISAIR 2022, CCIS 1700, pp. 281–289, 2022.
https://doi.org/10.1007/978-981-19-7946-0_24

can easily perform some illegal operations, such as stealing, Malicious acts such as tampering and destroying data or changing database permissions [3] (Fig. 1).

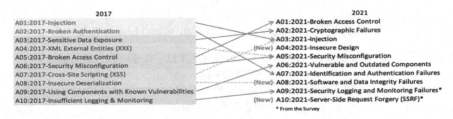

**Fig. 1.** OWASP high-risk vulnerability statistics.

There have been many high-impact SQL injection attacks in recent years [4]. For example, in February 2017, the NextGEN Gallery, a WordPress plugin with millions of installations, was revealed to have a SQL injection vulnerability, which led to the leakage of important data such as the password and key of the website database where the plugin was installed [5]. January 2018, NoraQ downloaded the information of 14 million graduates, including sensitive information such as name and date of birth, through a SQL injection vulnerability on the service website of the Russian Federation of Educational Sciences [6].

At present, there are many and mature researches on the attack methods, detection methods, and defense strategies of SQL injection attacks [7–9], but there is still a lot of research space for the automatic injection detection method based on deep learning. In terms of detection speed and detection rate, the existing methods are still insufficient. A high false positive rate will lead to a very poor user experience of web applications, and a slow detection rate will affect the normal operation of the business, there is still a great gap in the research of SQL injection attack identification model. This paper designs a deep learning model based on a one-dimensional convolutional neural network to classify and learn SQL semantics, which can more accurately identify attack sentences and is not easy to misjudge.

## 2   Relation Works

### 2.1   The Classification of the SQL Injection

Due to the variable attack methods of SQL injection, there are various classifications of SQL injection attacks at present. The classification basis is different, and the classification results are also different. According to current research, SQL injection is divided into the following categories: inline query injection; bool-based blind injection; out-of-band SQL injection [10]. In-band SQL injection means that the attacker can use the same communication channel as the victim to initiate the attack and collect the results and can directly interact with the victim's host. Logical reasoning injection is also known as a blind injection. The attacker cannot directly display data from the target database, nor can he obtain the echo information of the query result. However, logical reasoning can be performed through other information to obtain data. Out-of-band SQL injection is rare and difficult to execute because it depends on the Web application server to enable out-of-band connections to successfully inject.

According to the above description, we found that the classification methods in the current related research cannot comprehensively, quickly, and accurately deal with various SQL types of injection. Therefore, it is necessary to find a better classification method, which can realize comprehensive, fast, and accurate identification in the face of various SQL types of injection.

## 2.2  Related Research on SQL Injection

The traditional SQL injection detection method usually extracts some features based on experience and then detects whether it is an SQL injection attack based on the rule-based matching method, but this method cannot identify the increasingly complex SQL injection statements. With the rapid development of machine learning, more and more researchers try to solve the problems encountered in network security by using machine learning algorithms [11–16]. Deep learning has developed rapidly because it does not have to use complicated feature processing engineering. Its performance usually improves with the increase of training data [17]. It is much more scalable than shallow machine learning algorithms and has a wide range of applications. Fang et al. converting the sample data into word vectors as the input of the model, and using the LSTM model to detect SQL injection, proves that the LSTM-based method has a better detection effect than the traditional RNN and CNN-based methods [18]. The application of deep learning technology in various fields continuously mature applications provide new research directions for SQL injection detection [19], but also face many challenges. Firstly, since there are few public SQL injection datasets, insufficient samples will lead to overfitting during the training process. Secondly, it is necessary to find a way to reasonably convert SQL samples into vectors. In this paper, these two issues have also been deeply studied.

## 3  The Proposed Approach

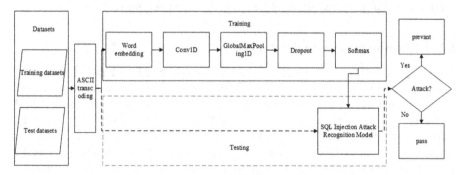

**Fig. 2.** A SQL injection attack recognition model based on 1D convolutional neural network.

Usually, the attacker will package the injected attack code in various ways to bypass the filtering system. Therefore, before model training, it is first necessary to perform ASCII transcoding operation on the data to clean up the training data, then use word embedding to convert it into word vector form, and then input the one-dimensional convolutional neural network model for training (Fig. 2). In this paper, we also added the neural network model and SVM model in reference [20, 21] for comparative experiments. To ensure the fairness of the comparative experiments, we used the same training datasets and test datasets. Once the model is trained, the accuracy of the model can be verified by test data set. Finally, the model determines that the HTTP request is blocked if it is an injection attack, otherwise, it is allowed to pass.

## 3.1  Data Cleaning

To reasonably convert the SQL samples into vectors, we use ASCII transcoding technology to convert the single characters of the input samples into ASCII numbers one by one. Since there are 95 displayable characters, the number of characters in a single SQL sample is almost less than 300 characters, so the number of sample vocabulary is set to 300, and the length of the word vector is set to 95. Samples with less than 300 characters perform Padding operations to make up. The following are examples of ASCII transcoding of SQL injection statements and normal SQL statements:

- Not transcoded SQL injection statement:

  drop table temp –";
  List generated after ASCII transcoding:
  [100, 114, 111, 112, 32, 116, 97, 98, 108, 101, 32, 116, 101, 109, 112, 32, 45, 45, 34, 59, 0, ... , 0]

- Not transcoded normal SQL statement:

  DELETE FROM 'tab' WHERE 'col2' = 'some';
  List generated after ASCII transcoding:
  [68, 69, 76, 69, 84, 69, 32, 70, 82, 79, 77, 32, 96, 116, 97, 98, 96, 32, 87, 72, 69, 82, 69, 32, 96, 99, 111, 108, 50, 96, 32, 61, 32, 39, 34, 41, 41, 59, 0, ... , 0]

## 3.2  1D Convolutional Neural Network

In this paper, the 1D convolutional neural network model consists of a word embedding, a convolutional layer, and a global max-pooling layer, which is finally connected to a fully connected layer. The first convolution layer has 64 convolution kernels, size is 3 * 3, the stride is 1, and the convolution mode is the Same. The ReLu function is used as the activation function in the 1D CNN, and the Softmax function is used as the activation function in the output layer. The model optimizer adopts Adam, its learning speed is 1e-4, and the sparse_categorical_crossentropy is used as the loss function. The epoch of the model is set to 5, and the batch size of its training set is 10, 20, and 30 respectively, in which the number of SQL injection statements and normal SQL statements is half respectively. At the same time, to avoid overfitting, a dropout of 0.5 is used. Figure 3 is the structure of the 1D convolutional neural network.

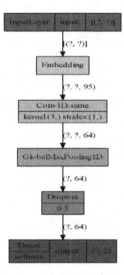

**Fig. 3.** The structure of 1D convolutional neural network.

## 4 Experiments and Comparison

### 4.1 Dataset

Insufficient samples can lead to overfitting during training due to few public SQL injection datasets, this paper uses real datasets to verify the feasibility and effectiveness of our model, and class-balanced data is used to avoid overfitting. The datasets come from the Github repository (https://github.com/blindusername/wafamole-dataset) [22]. First, the data is preprocessed, including cleaning and deduplication. Then, the data is normalized and deduplicated, and finally, 20,000 SQL injection statements and 20,000 normal SQL query statements are screened out for experimentation. The 20,000 SQL injection statements contain the three types of SQL injection mentioned. 10,000 SQL injection statements and 10,000 normal SQL query statements are randomly selected as the test set, and the remaining samples are used as the training set.

### 4.2 Experiments Result

The final confusion matrix results of experiments with three training set sizes are recorded in Tables 1, 2 and 3, respectively. From these tables, we have the following findings:

1) both the TP value and the FN value are completely correct.
2) the TN value is relatively high, and the FP value is relatively low.

**Table 1.** Confusion matrix of 1D convolutional neural network with a training set size of 10.

| Actual class | Predicted class | |
|---|---|---|
| | Positive | Negative |
| Positive | TP = 10000 | FN = 0 |
| Negative | FP = 327 | TN = 9673 |

**Table 2.** Confusion matrix of 1D convolutional neural network with a training set size of 20.

| Actual class | Predicted class | |
|---|---|---|
| | Positive | Negative |
| Positive | TP = 10000 | FN = 0 |
| Negative | FP = 329 | TN = 9671 |

**Table 3.** Confusion matrix of 1D convolutional neural network with a training set size of 30.

| Actual class | Predicted class | |
|---|---|---|
| | Positive | Negative |
| Positive | TP = 10000 | FN = 0 |
| Negative | FP = 329 | TN = 9671 |

From the overall accuracy point of view, the accuracy of the training set and the test set are both above 95.5 (Fig. 4). The accuracy of the test set is higher than that of the training set. The generalization ability of the model is good, and there is no overfitting phenomenon. This is because we include dropout in the model design, which ensures the best test accuracy, better than the training set accuracy. From the point of view of loss, train_loss and test_loss continue to decrease, and there is no over-fitting phenomenon.

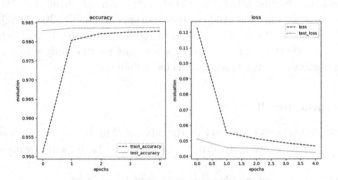

**Fig. 4.** Accuracy and loss of the 1D CNN.

### 4.3 Model Comparison

After comparing the test datasets of the three models, it can be found that the 1D CNN model has better classification performance (Table 4). In terms of precision, the recognition model proposed in this paper has an average precision of 96.83%, which is higher than that of SVM, but when the training set is 20 or 30, the recognition rate is not as high as that of the NN model. In the case of more training sets, the precision is not as high as the NN model, but the precision and stability of the 1D CNN model is relatively high, while the NN model has poor precision when the training set is small; In terms of recall rate, the proposed model has obvious advantages over the other two models. The average recall rate reaches 100%, which is 19 and 15 percentage points higher than the SVM model and the NN model, respectively. It can be seen that the 1D CNN model has very good recognition for the sensitive words and sensitive characters of SQL injection statements; In terms of F1 score, the proposed model is significantly higher than the other two models, with an average F1 score of 98.39, which is 11 and 8 percentage points higher than the SVM model and the NN model, respectively. From the point of view of the stability of the score, the proposed model is very stable in the F1 score, the F1 score of the SVM model is the most unstable, followed by the NN model.

**Table 4.** The results of multiple models on test data.

| Classification | Training set size | f1-score (%) | Precision (%) | Recall (%) |
| --- | --- | --- | --- | --- |
| SVM [20] | 10 | 80.2 | 88.9 | 71.5 |
| | 20 | 89.5 | 94.3 | 84.2 |
| | 30 | 91.7 | 95.2 | 88.1 |
| | Mean | 87.13 | 92.80 | 81.27 |
| NN [20] | 10 | 85.5 | 92.7 | 78.5 |
| | 20 | 92.0 | 97.4 | 86.4 |
| | 30 | 93.9 | 97.4 | 90.2 |
| | Mean | 90.47 | 95.83 | 85.03 |
| 1D CNN | 10 | 98.39 | 96.83 | 100 |
| | 20 | 98.39 | 96.83 | 100 |
| | 30 | 98.38 | 96.82 | 100 |
| | Mean | 98.39 | 96.83 | 100 |

In summary, the comparison experimental results demonstrate that the proposed method can recognize SQL injection attacks more efficiently and accurately.

## 5  Conclusions

The paper implements a SQL injection recognition model based on a 1D convolutional neural network and combines word embedding and ASCII transcoding techniques. The experiments show that the model can recognize all sorts of SQL injection attacks more efficiently and accurately. The next research will consider the real-time response and recognition ability of the model in the case of massive HTTP requests.

**Acknowledgement.** This work is supported by the Science and Technology Project of State Grid Corporation of China (Research on Intelligent Data Management and Feature Engineering Technology for Middle Platform, No. 5700-202058480A-0-0-00).

# References

1. Daoud, R.A., et al.: Risk assessment of SQL injection: an experimental study. In: 2021 7th International Conference on Optimization and Applications (ICOA), pp. 1–4 (2021)
2. Project, O.-O.W.A.S: Top10 Web Application Security Risks (2021). https://www.owasp.org/index.php/Top_10_2021-Top_10
3. Zhang, K.: A machine learning based approach to identify SQL injection vulnerabilities. In: 2019 34th IEEE/ACM International Conference on Automated Software Engineering (ASE), pp. 1286–1288 (2019)
4. Alanda, A., et al.: Web application penetration testing using SQL injection attack. JOIV: Int. J. Inform. Visual. **5**(3), 320–326 (2021)
5. Website, W. More than 1 million WordPress website are at risk due to a critical SQL injection vulnerability in the NextGEN Gallery plugin (2017). http://securityaffairs.co/wordpress/56779/hacking/nextgen-gallery-plugin-flaw.html
6. Wang, F.: Research and Implement of SQL Injection Detection Technology Based on Deep Learning. Beijing University of Posts and Telecommunications, Beijing (2020)
7. Adebiyi, M.O., et al.: An SQL injection detection model using chi-square with classification techniques. In: 2021 International Conference on Electrical, Computer and Energy Technologies (ICECET), pp. 1–8 (2021)
8. Mitra, S., et al.: Prevention of SQL injection and security enhancement in cyber networks. In: 2021 5th International Conference on Electronics, Materials Engineering and Nano-Technology (IEMENTech), pp. 1–6 (2021)
9. Aggarwal, P., et al.: Random decision forest approach for mitigating SQL injection attacks. In: 2021 IEEE International Conference on Electronics, Computing and Communication Technologies (CONECCT), pp. 1–5 (2021)
10. Choudhary, S., et al.: Solving some modeling challenges when testing rich internet applications for security. In: 2012 IEEE Fifth International Conference on Software Testing, Verification and Validation, pp. 850–857 (2012)
11. Wu, D., et al.: A latent factor analysis-based approach to online sparse streaming feature selection. IEEE Trans. Syst. Man Cybern. Syst. 1–15 (2021)
12. Wu, D., et al.: An $L_1$-and-$L_2$-norm-oriented latent factor model for recommender systems. IEEE Trans. Neural Netw. Learn. Syst. 1–14 (2021)
13. Wu, D., Luo, X.: Robust latent factor analysis for precise representation of high-dimensional and sparse data. IEEE/CAA J. Automatica Sinica **8**(4), 796–805 (2021)
14. Wu, D., et al.: A highly accurate framework for self-labeled semisupervised classification in industrial applications. IEEE Trans. Industr. Inf. **14**(3), 909–920 (2018)
15. Wu, D., et al.: Self-training semi-supervised classification based on density peaks of data. Neurocomputing **275**, 180–191 (2018)
16. Yan, H., et al.: Prediction of potentially suitable distributions of Codonopsis pilosula in China based on an optimized MaxEnt model. Front. Ecol. Evol. **9**, 1–17 (2021)

17. Yan, H.-Y., et al.: A fast method to evaluate water eutrophication. J. Central South Univ. **23**(12), 3204–3216 (2016). https://doi.org/10.1007/s11771-016-3386-4

18. Fang, Y., et al.: WOVSQLI: detection of SQL injection behaviors using word vector and LSTM. In: Proceedings of the 2nd International Conference on Cryptography, Security and Privacy, pp. 170–174. Association for Computing Machinery, Guiyang (2018)

19. Ishitaki, T., et al.: Application of deep recurrent neural networks for prediction of user behavior in tor networks. In: 2017 31st International Conference on Advanced Information Networking and Applications Workshops (WAINA), pp. 238–243 (2017)

20. Xie, Y., et al.: Semi-supervised SQL injection detection based on self-training. J. Shaanxi Normal Univ. (Nat. Sci. Ed.) **49**(1), 37–43 (2021)

21. Lu, H., Zhang, M., Xu, X., et al.: Deep fuzzy hashing network for efficient image retrieval. IEEE Trans. Fuzzy Syst. 1 (2020)

22. Demetrio, L., et al.: WAF-A-MoLE: evading web application firewalls through adversarial machine learning. In: Proceedings of the 35th Annual ACM Symposium on Applied Computing, pp. 1745–1752. Association for Computing Machinery (2020)

23. Huimin, L., Zhang, M., Xu, X.: Deep fuzzy hashing network for efficient image retrieval. IEEE Trans. Fuzzy Syst. (2020). https://doi.org/10.1109/TFUZZ.2020.2984991

24. Huimin, L., Li, Y., Chen, M., et al.: Brain intelligence: go beyond artificial intelligence. Mob. Netw. Appl. **23**, 368–375 (2018)

25. Huimin, L., Li, Y., Shenglin, M., et al.: Motor anomaly detection for unmanned aerial vehicles using reinforcement learning. IEEE Internet Things J. **5**(4), 2315–2322 (2018)

26. Lu, H., Qin, M., Zhang, F., et al.: RSCNN: a CNN-based method to enhance low-light remote-sensing images. Remote Sens. 62 (2020)

27. Huimin, L., Zhang, Y., Li, Y., et al.: User-oriented virtual mobile network resource management for vehicle communications. IEEE Trans. Intell. Transp. Syst. **22**(6), 3521–3532 (2021)

# Controlled Makeup Editing with Generative Adversarial Network

Qiurun Cai[1], Hong Pan[2], and Siyu Xia[1]([⊠])

[1] School of Automation, Southeast University, Nanjing, China
xsy@seu.edu.cn
[2] Department of Computer Science and Software Engineering,
Swinburne University of Technology, Melbourne, VIC, Australia

**Abstract.** Although Generative Adversarial Networks has performed well in the field of image generation, previous studies on Generative Adversarial Networks usually explored how to interpolate in the latent space to make the image generation more smoothly, without considering whether the semantic attributes are controllable or not. It fails to completely control the semantic meaning of the generated images as required by many tasks. In this work, we propose a new framework for makeup face editing, called MakeupGAN. This network decouples semantic entanglement in the latent space of Generative Adversarial Networks, learns semantic features of makeup, and achieve a more accurate control of image semantic attributes. A large number of examples show that this method can smoothly generate accurate and controllable facial makeup images.

**Keywords:** Makeup · Generative Adversarial Network · Semantic attributes · Latent space

## 1 Introduction

Makeup plays an important role in today's society. Through makeup, you can beautify your appearance and increase your spirits. In today's essential beauty software, automatic makeup and beautification have been embedded in every photo, live broadcast, and even shopping software [1]. Behind the automatic makeup are the advances in computer vision technology, which allows us to create images of faces with makeup on or off.

GAN (Generative adversarial networks) [2] has achieved great success in the field of image generation in recent years. The basic principle behind GAN is to learn the nonlinear mapping from potential distributions to real data through adversarial training. After learning mapping, GAN is able to generate photo-level real images from the randomly sampled latent code. However, how to obtain the desired semantic meaning from the latent space is still an open question. The key to interpretation of GAN's latent space is to find meaningful subspaces corresponding to human-intelligible properties. In this way, the latent code representing the semantic attributes of the subspace can be expressed as a set of vectors in the subspace plane. By moving this set of vectors, different semantic attributes of GAN are obtained, thereby generating images corresponding to different

S. Yang and H. Lu (Eds.): ISAIR 2022, CCIS 1700, pp. 290–302, 2022.
https://doi.org/10.1007/978-981-19-7946-0_25

semantic states. In the field of face image processing, this technique can be used to generate images with different makeup levels, so that the predicted face images with or without makeup can be obtained. However, due to the high dimensionality of the potential space and the diversity of image semantics, it is extremely challenging to find an effective semantic attribute in the latent space.

In this paper, we propose a novel framework, MakeupGAN, for automatic image generation of makeup faces. It identifies the semantic attributes encoded in the latent space of a trained face generation model, and then employs them for semantic face editing. We further investigate the entanglement between different semantics and prove that some latent spaces of entanglement can represent the desired semantics. These unraveled semantics allow any GAN model to precisely control facial properties without the need for retraining. Our contributions are summarized as follows:

(1) We obtained the attributes corresponding to different makeup levels from the latent spatial semantics of GAN, and used them to edit the facial semantics for generation of heavier or lighter makeup faces.
(2) We unentangled the potential high-dimensional space of GAN and found out a set of automatically generated weights to represent the makeup attribute.
(3) We improved the structure of the generator to include both the latent space domain and the decoupled latent Space domain as inputs to the AdaIN structure to combine both global and local styles.
(4) For some specific makeup attributes, we designed a new loss function, as well as a face analysis method to add local constraints (Fig. 1).

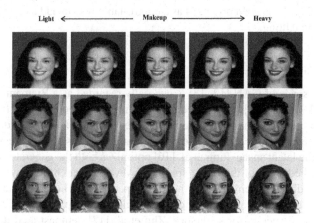

**Fig. 1.** Examples of face images with different levels of makeup, generated from our MakeupGAN model. The level of makeup ranges from light (left) to heavy (right).

The structure of this paper is as follows. Related work will be introduced in Sect. 2, including the study of makeup and the study of Latent space. In Sect. 3, we will focus on the introduction of our network structure. Section 4 is the experimental part to verify the effectiveness of the method. Section 5 summarizes the whole paper.

## 2   Related Work

### 2.1   Makeup Studies

In recent years, more and more attention has been paid to studying how to makeup. Li [3] introduced an adversarial network to generate non-makeup images for makeup face verification. Makeup Transform is another attractive application that aims to transfer style from a reference image while preserving the identity of the source image. BeautyGAN [4] combined global domain-level loss and local instance-level loss to use two GAN networks for makeup migration. PSGAN [5] is the first makeup change algorithm to achieve local makeup change, control of makeup change depth, posture and expression, which can be well applied to the real world environment.

### 2.2   GAN for Image-To-Image Translation

GAN is one of the generation models, which consists of a generator and a discriminator. GAN [6, 7] is widely used in computer vision tasks due to its ability to produce visually realistic images. Most of the existing image translation research aims to learn the mapping from the source domain to the target domain. Recently, a lot of work on using GAN for image generation and transformation has been proposed. For example, Isola et al. [8] developed a classic Pixel2Pixel framework that learns pairs of data and performs domain to domain transitions. To overcome the lack of paired images in training data, CycleGAN [9] was proposed and then added the loss of cyclic consistency to standardize the key attributes between the input and translated images. StarGAN [10] even solves the problem of mapping between multiple fields through a single generator. Recently, InterfaceGAN [11] has been proposed as a controllable way to add a certain attribute of image to image editing.

### 2.3   Latent Space of GAN

To The latent space of GAN [12, 13] is generally regarded as a Riemannian manifold. Previous work [12, 14, 15] has focused on exploring the smooth change from one composition to another through interpolation in the latent space, without considering whether the image is semantically controllable or not. Latent code is a set of vectors that map the image to the latent space. Piotr et al. [16] optimizes both the generator and the latent code to learn better about the latent space. However, research on how a well-trained GAN encodes different semantics in the latent space is still lacking of attention. Shen et al. [11] proposed the classification of high-dimensional space for the first time, and edited the feature vectors for semantics. Zhu et al. [17] demonstrated that decoupled feature Spaces are more capable of single-semantic editing. Yang et al. [18] explored the hierarchical semantics in the deep generative representation of scene composition. Unlike them, we decouple the semantic attributes of the feature space, process each semantic attributes according to the makeup look semantic attribute we need, focus on editing the makeup look semantic attributes that appear in face synthesis, and extend our method to real image processing.

# 3  Methodology

In this part, we introduced the structure of MakeupGAN. MakeupGAN uses StyleGAN as the basic network. Taking an input image sized of $256 \times 256$ pixels as an example, our network uses progressive training, that is starting from training the generator and discriminator of very low resolution images (such as $4 \times 4$). The style-based generator has 14 layers, and each resolution has two convolutional layers (4, 8, 16,..., 256). MakeupGAN first trains the GAN encoder to obtain the hidden space, and decouple the hidden space. Then, uses the semantics of the latent code to edit the makeup face.

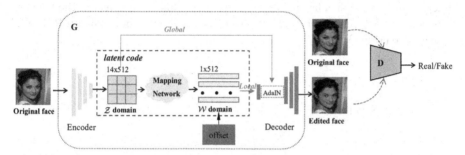

**Fig. 2.** Framework of the proposed MakeupGAN. The upper pipeline shows the overall system. G accepts an image as input: the original photo of the person, and the edited face is generated through the encoder-decode model. The generated face and the original face are sent to the discriminator, and the generator is trained repeatedly according to the adversarial loss. At the same time, we send the feature resulted from the encoder to the AdaIN section of the generator as input instead of constants or latent code.

## 3.1  Framework of the MakeupGAN

As illustrated in Fig. 2, the overall framework consists of one generator G and one discriminator D. The input to the generator is a real face, which is mapped to the latent space by the generator with a randomly initialized latent code and the gradient descent technique. Through decoupling the latent code in the latent space, a group of decoupled latent codes representing the semantic features of different makeup levels are obtained. According to user requirements, one can increase the latent code offset to the desired semantics, and then map the moving latent code back to the image domain. Finally the generated fake face and the real face are fed into the discriminator to train the discriminator and the generator simultaneously.

## 3.2  Disentangled Feature Space in GAN

Given a trained GAN model, the generator can be formulated as a fixed function:

$$\tilde{x} = G(z) \tag{1}$$

where G is the generator and is usually sampled from a Gaussian prior with zero mean and unit variance. Latent code belongs to latent space -domain. Suppose a random value is taken on the distribution of the latent code, and a value is taken for each characteristic dimension. All the eigenvalues are combined to form a picture. We hope each element of the latent codes represent a feature, but actually several latent code represents a feature. In addition, latent code is not necessarily normally distributed, such as eye size. Multiple normal distributions can be fitted into an arbitrary distribution, which gives rise to entanglement of eigenvalues.

In order to solve the problem of feature entanglement, the -domain is proposed and generated through the following module. Specifically, StyleGAN inputs into a mapping structure, yielding another latent space, which is a 512-dimensional vector. The Mapping Network is an 8 layers of MLP (Muti-Layer Perception) is sent to this MLP with L2 regularization (Fig. 3).

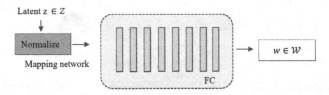

**Fig. 3.** Latent $Z$ is decoupled to the $W$-domain by a mapping network

An image is obtained by sampling multiple distributions and combining these features, and the distribution that each feature follows is weighted and averaged by multiple normal distributions. We decouple the features in the -domain to the -domain, and the latent space of the entanglement should be that each layer or several layers represent a feature. Since the decoupling is not complete, there may be correlations between different layers, which increases the complexity and inconvenience of the task. However, blindly reducing the indicators will lose a lot of information and easily lead to wrong conclusions. Therefore, it is necessary to find a reasonable method to reduce the loss of the information contained in the original index while reducing the indicators to be analyzed, so as to achieve the purpose of comprehensive analysis of the collected data. Assuming that for each vector in, there should be a set of weighting coefficients that makes represents facial makeup characteristics. It is also necessary to satisfy that it should not change other facial attributes. The gradient descent method is used to obtain a set of coefficients, so that changing the coefficient can change the makeup degree and achieve the minimum identity loss.

### 3.3   Edit Semantic Attributes in the Latent Space

First, we assume that this is a binary classification problem (e.g., light makeup and heavy makeup), and there is a hyperplane in the latent space that can separate one class from the other, as shown in Fig. 4. When moving sideways, the binary semantic properties remain the same, but when the underlying code moves to the other side, the semantics change in the opposite direction. Therefore, a metric is needed to define the distance from the current latent code to the hyperplane, and the semantic properties change with the distance. In actual operation, we first mark each makeup image with a semantic score. The thicker the makeup, the higher the score. Then, each image is converted to the latent space, and the two-dimensional semantics are classified by the support vector machine (SVM), so as to obtain the hyperplane.

Given a hyperplane with as the normal vector, the distance is defined as:

$$d(n, w) = n^T w \tag{2}$$

where $W$ is the latent code of the image in the $W$-domain. It is important to note that the distance here is not strictly a distance, because it can be negative, which means the semantic inversion. We want the distance to be proportional to the semantics, i.e.

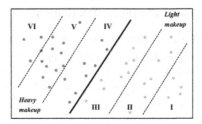

**Fig. 4.** Faces with light makeup and heavy makeup are mapped into the latent space as a vector, separated by a hyperplane between vectors, where I-VI indicate the degree of makeup (I means, the lightest makeup and VI means the heaviest makeup). When shifting the latent code to a specific area, the makeup characteristics were edited to a specific level.

In this case, the normal vector is the direction of one of the features, and moving to this direction will make the feature change in semantic direction:

$$w = w + a * n \tag{3}$$

If a > 0, the semantics move to the same direction, and if a < 0, the semantics move to the opposite direction and the score changes accordingly.

### 3.4 A Hybrid Generator Based on Global and Local Styles

The generator of GAN typically takes latent code $z$ as the input and is trained to synthesize a photo-realistic image $\tilde{x} = G(z)$. StyleGAN first maps $z$ to a decoupled space, where $f$ () denotes the mapping function of the multi-layer perceptron (MLP).

Regarding style-based generators, StyleGAN adds a non-linear mapping network, using the $W$-domain rather than the constant as the input for adaptive instance normalization. In our structure, we also use latent code $Z$ as the input for Adaptive Instance Normalization (AdaIN). In the Fig. 5, $W$ and $Z$ are 512-dimensional vectors. A is an affine transform, and AdaIN is

$$AdaIN(x, y) = \sigma(y)(\frac{x - \mu(x)}{\sigma(x)}) + \mu(y) \tag{4}$$

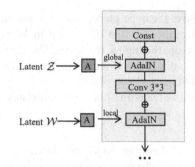

**Fig. 5.** Structure of generator network which takes $w$ and $z$ as inputs to AdaIN

## 3.5 Instance-Level Makeup Face Image Translation

In order to use GAN encoder to generate accurate fake face images, we define the objective function by leveraging both low-level and high-level information. Usually, the traditional encoder uses direct pixel-wise reconstruction error as well as the L1 distance between the perceptual features extracted from the two images as objective function.

$$L_{dis} = ||x - \tilde{x}||_2^2 \tag{5}$$

$$L_{perceptual} = E[\sum_i \frac{1}{N_i} ||\theta_i(x) - \theta_i(\tilde{x})||_1] \tag{6}$$

where $\theta(\cdot)$ denotes the perceptual feature extractor.

In order to further allow the network to learn instance-level makeup transfer, and consider the insights that facial makeup level changes can be seen as changes in color and structure, we proposed a new loss function $S(x, \tilde{x})$ that compares contrast and structure similarity between generated image $\tilde{x}$ and original image $x$.

$$c(x, \tilde{x}) = \frac{2\sigma_x \sigma_{\tilde{x}} + C}{\sigma_x^2 + \sigma_{\tilde{x}}^2 + C} \tag{7}$$

$$s(x, \tilde{x}) = (\frac{1}{\sqrt{N-1}} \frac{x - \mu_x}{\sigma_x}) \cdot (\frac{1}{\sqrt{N-1}} \frac{\tilde{x} - \mu_{\tilde{x}}}{\sigma_{\tilde{x}}})$$

$$= \frac{1}{\sigma_x \sigma_{\tilde{x}}} (\frac{1}{\sqrt{N-1}} \frac{x - \mu_x}{\sigma_x}) \cdot (\frac{1}{\sqrt{N-1}} \frac{\tilde{x} - \mu_{\tilde{x}}}{\sigma_{\tilde{x}}}) \tag{8}$$

$$l(x, \tilde{x}) = \frac{2\mu_x \mu_{\tilde{x}} + C}{\mu_x^2 + \mu_{\tilde{x}}^2 + C} \tag{9}$$

where $c(x, \tilde{x})$ donates the contrast similarity between $x$ and $\tilde{x}$ and $s(x, \tilde{x})$ donates the structure similarity between $x$ and $\tilde{x}$. $\sigma_x$ is the standard deviation of the pixel and $\mu_x$ is the mean of the pixel. $C$ is a small number to avoid the denominator being 0.

Therefore, the similarity loss of the two pictures is:

$$L_{pic} = 1 - c(x, \tilde{x}) \cdot s(x, \tilde{x}) \tag{10}$$

The loss of the generator is:

$$L_G = \lambda_1 L_{dis} + \lambda_2 L_{perceptual} + \lambda_3 L_{pic} \tag{11}$$

Considering the adversarial loss function $L_D$ of the discriminator, the whole loss function is then defined as:

$$L = L_G + L_D. \tag{12}$$

As the makeup level of face images switches from light to heavy, other areas of the images may also varies. At the same time, the appearance variations (e.g., the differences between hair, face shape etc.) of different subjects may also cause subtle changes in facial features. To ensure that the change and makeup area in face images does not affect the identity attributes of a person, we perform face parsing to separate facial features that represent identity information. According to the face parsing, we can obtain a mask covering the above areas, and then a constraint is added to these parts:

$$\Delta_{area} = \angle(p(x), p(\tilde{x})) \tag{13}$$

where, $f(\cdot)$ is an operator that calculates the angle between two colors regarding the RGB color as a 3D vector. Equation 14 sums the angles between the color vectors for every pixel pair in face mask $p(x)$ and $p(\tilde{x})$. If $\Delta_{area} > threshold$, adjust these facial areas to ensure the identity information is consistent.

## 4  Experiment

In this section, we evaluate MakeupGAN and present the experimental results. Specifically, Sect. 4.1 introduces the experimental setup and data set division, Sect. 4.2 explains the latent space of the traditional generator by decoupling the latent code in $\mathcal{Z}$-domain. Section 4.3 studies the effects of various loss and hybrid generator. In Sect. 4.4, we evaluate and analyze the results of makeup face editing.

### 4.1  Implementation Details

We made a dataset by ourselves, and selected 2717 makeup faces in the Makeup transfer dataset and 78,390 pictures with makeup semantics in celebA, [20] a total of 81,107. In order to train GAN model, each image was resized to 256 * 256 pixels. Out of 78,390 images, we randomly selected 1,000 images as the test set. The remaining images are divided into training set and validation set according to the ratio of 4:1. Unlike other GAN that can accept folder input, StyleGAN can only accept TFRecords as input, and it stores each image as an array of different resolutions, resulting in an actual storage size up to 19 times that of the original image. When batchsize is set to 8, the learning rate is 0.002. The training starts from 4 4, then the network layer is added, the resolution is doubled, and the network is trained until the desired output resolution is reached.

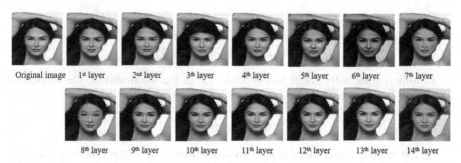

**Fig. 6.** A 14 × 512 vector in $z$-domain is decoupled into 14-layers 1 × 512 vectors in $w$-domain, and each vector is visualized so that the semantic information represented by each layer can be intuitively seen. (Color figure online)

## 4.2 Interpretability of Different Layers of the $W$-domain

We visualized the output images from each layer of the latent code decoupled to the $w$-domain, as shown in Fig. 6. To generate the output images from each layer of the proposed framework shown in Fig. 2, we send the real face into the generator to generate the latent code of the $z$-domain, and then decouple it through the mapping net to decouple it into 14 vectors in the $w$-domain. We mask each layer by setting its value to zero in turn, and decode changed latent code to reconstruct the image. In this way, we can see the impact of this layer on the overall face output. Taking the first layer as an example, the face shape and facial features of a person are different from the original face. It can be judged that the vectors in the first layer are used to generate basic identity information such as contours and facial features. In Fig. 6, the sequence number is the number of layers, and the layer is blocked, leaving the rest of the layers unchanged. The visualization results show that the features learned in shallow layer correspond to the posture, hairstyle and shape of the face, and the deep layer may represent some detailed features and color. We get a set of weights that linearly combine these 14 layers, representing the semantics of makeup.

At the same time, in order to prove that faces generated by decoupling using latent codes in $w$-domain can guarantee less identity information loss, compared with faces generated directly using latent codes in $z$-domain. We also conducted the following ablation experiments at $z$-domain. Since the features of the $z$-domain are not decoupled, while changing the makeup features, it may vary all the facial contours and facial features to change, and even cause the image into a strange face. In this case, the person's identity information will also change accordingly. However, the makeup features of the face generated by MakeupGAN are reduced, and the identity information is basically unchanged.

## 4.3 Ablation Study

To investigate the importance of each component of the overall objective function, we performed ablation studies. We mainly analyze the influence of similarity loss term and adding the $z$-domain as input to the generator (Fig. 7).

Original image    $\mathcal{W}$ domain edit    $\mathcal{Z}$ domain edit    Original image    $\mathcal{W}$ domain edit    $\mathcal{Z}$ domain edit

**Fig. 7.** The latent code of $w$ and $z$ domains were used to edit the makeup face, respectively. The face identity information of $w$-domain was basically unchanged, while the information in $z$-domain changed in addition to the makeup region, and other regions were also changed.

## 4.4 Loss Function Without $L_{pic}$ vs. With $L_{pic}$

To ensure that the other settings are the same, in the loss function, we also remains the same, only change the $L_{pic}$ term. Specifically, we remove the similarity loss term from the Eq. 13. Figure 8 shows the results. It can be seen that due to the characteristics of the color and structure of makeup, the contrast ratio in the generated results with increased similarity loss is higher and makeup is more obvious.

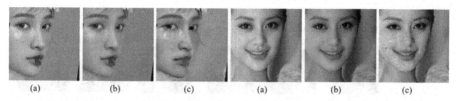

(a)    (b)    (c)    (a)    (b)    (c)

**Fig. 8.** (a) Original image. (b) Image reconstruction with similarity loss *Lpic*. (c) Original image reconstruction without

**Fig. 9.** Original image is on the left. In the middle is the reconstruction with only $w$-domain latent code as input, and on the right is the reconstruction with mixed style with both $w$-domain and $z$-domain latent code as input.

## 4.5 Generators Based on $w$-domain Styles vs. Generators Based on Hybrid Styles

In this experiment, we verify that the addition of $z$-domain as AdaIN input can better keep global information in the reconstructed images. Figure 9 shows the result. It can be seen that the facial features of the reconstructed image generated based only on the $w$-domain style have some changes, such as expression changes, etc. The hybrid style restores the face more closely to the original image.

### 4.6    Comparison with Other GAN-Based Approaches

Currently, there are many other methods, such as CycleGAN, StyleGAN, BeautyGAN etc. In this subsection, we qualitatively and quantitatively compare our method with other popular GAN-based approaches (e.g., CycleGAN, StyleGAN and BeautyGAN) on makeup image generation. Figure 10 shows the effect of editing makeup attributes on three networks. StyleGAN changes other attributes as well as makeup, such as face shape and identity information. CycleGAN can do makeup, but can only be edited in one direction. BeautyGAN also has this problem and it has another drawbacks such as uneven makeup and an unnatural face Our MakeupGAN can control the editing of a makeup face in both directions without changing other properties.

In Table 1, we compare the quantitative metrics, such as PSNR (Peak Signal-to-Noise Ratio) and NIQE (Natural Image Quality Evaluator), among these methods. PSNR is used to measure the pixel level difference between the reconstructed image and the original one, while NIQE compares the reconstructed image to a default model computed from images of natural scenes. As shown in Table 1, our MakeupGAN has the highest PSNR, but by comparison, the images generated by CycleGAN are more natural and match the textures of real images.

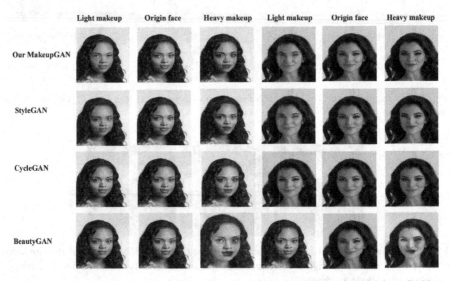

**Fig. 10.** Comparison of the CycleGAN, StyleGAN2, BeautyGAN and our MakeupGAN.

**Table 1.** Quantitative comparison of different face translation methods. Competitors include our MakeupGAN, -domain (StyleGAN), CycleGAN, BeautyGAN. ↑ means the higher the better while ↓ means the lower the better.

| Method | PSNR↑ | NIQE↓ |
|---|---|---|
| MakeupGAN (Ours) | **16.32** | 17.32 |
| Z-domain (StyleGAN) [19] | 11.73 | 23.21 |
| CycleGAN [9] | 12.65 | **15.65** |
| BeautyGAN [4] | 14.01 | 19.45 |

## 5  Conclusion

In this paper, we explain the semantics of GAN's latent space and use the semantic and operational techniques of interpretation to control the edit of makeup face. Experimental results show that the performance of this method is significantly improved compared with existing methods.

## References

1. Intelligence, B.: Go beyond Artificial Intelligence. Mobile Netw. Appl. **23**(2), 368–375 (2018)
2. Goodfellow, I., et al.: Generative adversarial networks. Commun. ACM **63**(11), 139–144 (2020)
3. Li, Y., Song, L., Wu, X., He, R., Tan, T.: Anti-makeup: Learning a bi-level adversarial network for makeup-invariant face verification. In: Proceedings of the AAAI Conference on Artificial Intelligence, vol. 32, no. 1 (2018)
4. Li, T, Qian, R, Dong, C, et al.: BeautyGAN: instance-level facial makeup transfer with deep generative adversarial network. In: Proceedings of the ACM Multimedia Conference on Multimedia Conference, pp. 645–653 (2018)
5. Jiang, W., et al.: Psgan: pose and expression robust spatial-aware gan for customizable makeup transfer. In: Proceedings of the IEEE/CVF Conference on Computer Vision and Pattern Recognition, pp. 5194–5202 (2020)
6. Zhang, H., Goodfellow, I., Metaxas, D., Odena, A.: Self-attention generative adversarial networks. In: International Conference on Machine Learning, pp. 7354–7363. PMLR (2019)
7. Miyato, T., Kataoka, T., Koyama, M., Yoshida, Y.: Spectral normalization for generative adversarial networks. arXiv preprint arXiv:1802.05957 (2018)
8. Isola, P., Zhu, J.Y., Zhou, T., Efros, A.A.: Image-to-image translation with conditional adversarial networks. In: Proceedings of the IEEE Conference on Computer Vision and Pattern Recognition, pp. 1125–1134 (2017)
9. Zhu, J.Y., Park, T., Isola, P., Efros, A.A.: Unpaired image-to-image translation using cycle-consistent adversarial networks. In: Proceedings of the IEEE International Conference on Computer Vision, pp. 2223–2232 (2017)
10. Choi, Y., Choi, M., Kim, M., Ha, J.W., Kim, S., Choo, J.: Stargan: unified generative adversarial networks for multi-domain image-to-image translation. In: Proceedings of the IEEE Conference on Computer Vision and Pattern Recognition, pp. 8789–8797 (2018)
11. Shen, Y., Gu, J., Tang, X., Zhou, B.: Interpreting the latent space of gans for semantic face editing. In: Proceedings of the IEEE/CVF Conference on Computer Vision and Pattern Recognition, pp. 9243–9252 (2020)

12. Arvanitidis, G., Hansen, L.K., Hauberg, S.: Latent space oddity: on the curvature of deep generative models. arXiv preprint arXiv:1710.11379 (2017)
13. Zeng, Y., Fu, J., Chao, H., et al.: Learning pyramid-context encoder networkfor high-quality image inpainting. In: Proceedings of the IEEE/CVF Conference on Computer Vision and Pattern Recognition, pp. 1486–1494 (2019)
14. Chen, N., Klushyn, A., Kurle, R., Jiang, X., Bayer, J., Smagt, P.: Metrics for deep generative models. In: International Conference on Artificial Intelligence and Statistics, pp. 1540–1550. PMLR (2018)
15. Kuhnel, L., Fletcher, T., Joshi, S., Sommer, S.: Latent space non-linear statistics. arXiv preprint arXiv:1805.07632 (2018)
16. Bojanowski, P., Joulin, A., Lopez-Pas, D., Szlam, A.: Optimizing the latent space of generative networks. In: ICML (2018)
17. Zhu, J., Zhao, D., Zhang, B., Zhou, B.: Disentangled inference for gans with latently invertible autoencoder. arXiv preprint arXiv:1906.08090 (2019)
18. Yang, C., Shen, Y., Zhou, B.: Semantic hierarchy emerges in deep generative representations for scene synthesis. Int. J. Comput. Vision **129**(5), 1451–1466 (2021)
19. Karras, T., Laine, S., Aila, T.: A style-based generator architecture for generative adversarial networks. In: Proceedings of the IEEE/CVF Conference on Computer Vision and Pattern Recognition, pp. 4401–4410 (2019)
20. Liu, Z., Luo, P., Wang, X., Tang, X.: Deep learning face attributes in the wild. In: Proceedings of the IEEE International Conference on Computer Vision, pp. 3730–3738 (2015)

# Network Traffic Classification Method of Power System Based on DNN and K-means

Jiange Liu[1] , Pengyu Zhang[1] , Yiming Sun[2,3] , Mao Li[1] , Mengna Jiang[1] ,
Shangdong Liu[2,3(✉)] , and Yimu Ji[2,3] 

[1] State Grid Jiangsu Electric Power Co., Ltd., Huai'an Power Supply Branch, Huai'an, China
[2] School of Computer Science, Nanjing University of Posts and Telecommunications,
Nanjing 210023, China
1220045209@njupt.edu.cn
[3] Jiangsu HPC and Intelligent Processing Engineer Research Center, Nanjing 210003, Jiangsu,
China

**Abstract.** The classification of power system network traffic is the key point of
power system network security protection. Therefore, we propose a power system
network traffic classification method based on deep learning algorithm and K-
means clustering algorithm. Our method uses a deep neural network (DNN) to
classify the pre-processed network traffic data to determine whether it is a server,
and then use the K-means algorithm to perform secondary classification on the data
that has been identified as a server to help users identified the specific server type.
Experiments with real power system network data prove that the classification of
this method has a high accuracy rate and can meet the needs of power system
network traffic classification in real environments.

**Keywords:** Power system network security · Network traffic classification ·
Deep learning · Deep neural network · K-means clustering

## 1 Introduction

With the development and application of power system network technology, the scale
of the power system network is constantly expanding [1], and the network complexity
is also significantly improved, which brings increased power system network security
risks. Power system network security is directly related to urban power supply and is
a major event related to the national economy and people's livelihood. Therefore, the
protection of power system network security is very important. Under the normalization
of power network threats, accurate detection and analysis capabilities and early warning
capabilities have gradually become the key to the new generation of big data security
capabilities [4].

The attack on the power system network is basically carried out in the form of network services, and the attack originator has similar traffic characteristics to the server
of the power system network. Therefore, the identification and classification of power

S. Yang and H. Lu (Eds.): ISAIR 2022, CCIS 1700, pp. 303–317, 2022.
https://doi.org/10.1007/978-981-19-7946-0_26

system network traffic is a key step in network security protection. Traditional network traffic classification methods are mainly divided into four types: port-based methods, statistics-based methods and behavior-based methods, and methods based on Deep Packet Inspection (DPI). Among them, the port-based method has low accuracy [19], and the DPI-based method cannot handle encrypted traffic and has high complexity [20]. Therefore, most current research are based on statistics and behavior-based methods [12], and some researches try to use some big data. Analytical method [13, 14]. Traditional network traffic identification methods often rely on many manual queries and verifications, or require manual determination of rules, and the cost cannot be ignored in the current scenario of millions of big data traffic. At the same time, the traditional method has long query interval, poor real-time performance and low accuracy, so it can only be used for passive defense strategies, and the early warning capability is insufficient, making it difficult to deal with new power system network security threats. Based on this situation, more and more researchers try to use machine learning technology to solve the real-time classification of power system network traffic.

Machine learning is a hot research field now, and deep learning is the most important cutting-edge branch of machine learning. This technology can directly learn abstract features from any data read without manual intervention [5], considering dimensionality reduction and classification without limitation. Considering the impact of hand-set features on learning performance, it greatly simplifies feature learning for traffic. Now, deep learning has been widely used in the field of signal processing and communication, and has achieved many results [6, 7]. The network traffic classification technology based on deep learning is an effective method for network attack detection. Since it can directly process the original data, its efficiency is greatly improved compared with the traditional method [8–10]. [15] analyzed the structure of the input, output and feature network of the target detection model in the power grid, studied the optimization of target detection, model tasks, and feature networks, and applied the target detection algorithm to the power scene to optimize the target detection. [16] proposed an anonymous protocol identification method for fully encrypted traffic based on Convolutional Neural Network (CNN). This method can effectively identify anonymous protocols with full encryption in network traffic. [11] was the first to apply a representation learning method to classify network traffic with good results.

On the network segment of the power grid server, the network traffic classification system using deep learning technology is used to screen and analyze the network traffic flowing through the power grid server, and classify all terminal IPs, which can effectively identify the terminal IPs that provide different services and locate malicious attacks. The abnormal traffic generated, and the end IP is provided to the staff for filing, which improves the security protection of the power grid system and the security of key servers; at the same time, the IP traffic in the network is statistically sorted and data analyzed by using the IP classification of the opposite end. Different types of terminal IP service characteristics and rules can be used to provide information behind IP address traffic behavior for network management and security response [2].

The network traffic classification method based on deep learning can effectively find the suspected server in the network traffic of the power system. However, more scenarios require the service type of the suspected server. This is a multi-classification problem, which can also be solved by deep learning methods, but the deep learning classification method is a supervised method that requires manual labeling of training data, and in multi-classification scenarios, this labeling will increase labor costs. Therefore, another more efficient method is to use an unsupervised machine learning model to perform a secondary classification of the suspected servers found by the deep learning method. K-means, a commonly used machine learning clustering method, has also been proven to be effective in network traffic classification scenarios [17]. [3] clustered the base stations by K-means clustering algorithm based on spatial features and constructed an abnormal detection method based on the network traffic of the power core control system. [18] First used the clustering method to build the optimal network traffic training sample set, and then used the neural network for training, and achieved good results, but the method of first clustering and then deep learning classification may be due to the uncertainty of clustering. In contrast, our method of first classification and then clustering is more accurate.

To sum up, we propose a network traffic classification method in the power system network scenario. This method uses a supervised deep learning method to train the model, determines whether a certain end IP is a server, and then uses the machine learning-based unsupervised clustering algorithm for secondary classification of the end IP data of the suspected server to determine its specific type. Experiments show that our proposed method has a good effect on the classification of power system network traffic. The method we propose can provide a basis for the filing and management of power system network servers, and early detection of abnormal traffic and illegal servers has certain significance for power system network security.

The structure of this paper is as follows: Sect. 1 introduces the background, goal and some previous work of this paper. Sections 2 and 3 introduce some theoretical knowledge of the modules and algorithms used in this paper. Section 4 describes the method proposed in this paper. Section 5 verifies the effectiveness of the method proposed in this paper by some experiments. Section 6 is the conclusion.

## 2   Deep Neural Network Architecture

A deep neural network (DNN) is a very expressive model. A fully trained DNN model can achieve classification and judgment capabilities like those of humans. We study the network traffic classification problem of power system and uses deep learning algorithm to train DNN.

The first is data acquisition. For a set of power system network traffic training data $\{x(n), y(n)|1 \leq n \leq N\}$, where $x$ is a network traffic sample, including the total number of packets, packets per second, total bytes, bytes per second, etc. $y$ is the sample label, which is a manually labeled value, indicating whether the training data is a server; $N$ is the total number of training data. At this time, for a DNN network output function $f$, input the data into the network to obtain a classification result, as shown in Eq. 1:

$$\hat{y} = f(\theta, x) \tag{1}$$

where $\hat{y}$ is the confidence of the classification result, and $\theta$ is the network parameter of the DNN. The schematic diagram of the DNN network structure is shown in Fig. 1. Among them, the input layer packs the data of network traffic into batches and transmits them to the hidden layer neural network. C1 to C$l$ in the hidden layer are neurons, $l$ represents the number of neurons in this layer, only one hidden layer is shown in the figure, and the actual network can have multiple hidden layers. The hidden layer transmits the extracted features to the output layer, and the output layer outputs a result logit, which can finally be converted into probabilities by the Sigmoid function.

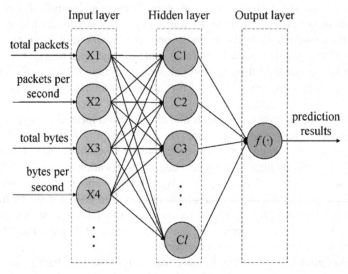

**Fig. 1.** DNN structure diagram.

To make the $\hat{y}$ result as accurate as possible, the DNN needs to be trained iteratively. We use the binary cross-entropy function as the loss function for training, and the binary cross-entropy function is shown in Eq. 2.

$$L(y, \hat{y}) = \sum_{i=1}^{N} y_i \log \hat{y}_i + (1 - y_i) \log(1 - \hat{y}_i) \tag{2}$$

The loss function is used to iteratively train the DNN network model. The training process is an optimization process, and the purpose is to minimize the loss function value, so that the training result value is as close to the label as possible, that is, the objective function $J$ can be expressed as:

$$J = \min L(\theta, x, y) \tag{3}$$

in this process, the network parameter $\theta$ is optimized and updated, and stochastic gradient descent (SGD) is selected as the optimizer. The optimization method can be expressed as:

$$\theta_{t+1} = \theta_t - \lambda_t g_t \tag{4}$$

where $t$ represents a certain iteration, $\lambda_t$ is the optimization weight, generally called the learning rate, and $g$ represents the stochastic gradient, which is expected to be the gradient of $f$, which satisfies $E(g) = \nabla f(\theta, x)$. Iterative training with the above algorithm for a certain number of times can make the DNN fully learn the characteristics of the power network flow data, so that it can make accurate classification in the face of real-time power network flow data.

## 3 K-means Clustering Algorithm

By using the deep learning method to train the DNN, we can obtain the classification result indicating whether a traffic sample belongs to a certain server, but to further explore what kind of server the traffic sample belongs to, we use the K-means clustering algorithm to classify the classified server traffic samples. Perform clustering operations. K-means is an unsupervised machine learning clustering method. The process is as follows: First, a threshold is determined and the classification results are divided. Those above the threshold are considered servers, and those below the threshold are not. Next, find all the original traffic samples of the results classified as servers, add their respective classification confidences to them, and form new sample data $\{\tilde{x}(m)|1 \leq m \leq M\}$, where $M$ is the total number of new samples.

Then, the $K$ value of the cluster is determined to determine $K$ cluster centers $\{c(k)|1 \leq k \leq K\}$, and these cluster centers are randomly initialized. Next, calculate the Euclidean distance from each sample to each cluster center, as shown in Eq. 5.

$$D(\tilde{x}, c) = \sqrt{\sum_{i=1}^{M}\sum_{j=1}^{K}(\tilde{x}_i - c_k)^2} \tag{5}$$

Compare the distances of each sample to each cluster center in turn, and then assign the samples to the clusters with the closest cluster center to obtain $K$ clusters $\{s(k)|1 \leq k \leq K\}$. Then the K-means algorithm will update the position of the cluster center through the cluster. The new cluster center is the mean value of each sample in the cluster in each dimension, which can be expressed as:

$$\tilde{c}_k = \frac{\sum_{\tilde{x}_k \in s_k} \tilde{x}_k}{|s_k|} \tag{6}$$

where $\tilde{c}_k$ is the updated $k$th cluster center. Repeat this algorithm for many times until convergence, then the samples belonging to the server can be divided into $K$ categories.

The optimal $K$ value of the K-means clustering algorithm can be determined through experiments, and the most used determination method is the "elbow method". First, calculate the residual sum of the squared errors (SSE) from the samples in the cluster to the cluster center, which is a commonly used indicator to measure the classification quality of the samples in the cluster, as shown in Eq. 7:

$$SSE = \sum_{p \in s_i} |p - c_i|^2 \tag{7}$$

where $p$ is a sample in cluster $s_i$, and $c_i$ is the corresponding cluster center. The smaller the value of SSE, the better the classification quality of the samples in the cluster.

The core idea of the "elbow method" is as the number of clusters $K$ increases, the sample division will be more refined, and the SSE value of each cluster should be correspondingly smaller. Moreover, when $K$ is less than the optimal number of clusters, since the increase of $K$ will greatly increase the classification quality of each cluster, the decline of SSE is larger, and when $K$ reaches the optimal number of clusters, increase $K$ to obtain the return on classification quality will rapidly become smaller, so the decline in SSE will level off. Therefore, using $K$ as the independent variable and the average SSE as the dependent variable, find the inflection point where the slope of the image decreases rapidly to a gentle decrease, and this point is the optimal $K$ value.

## 4    Network Traffic Classification Method of Power System

We propose a network traffic classification method based on deep learning and K-means clustering algorithm, which aims to solve the problem of server IP classification in the power system, help the power system network to quickly detect abnormal traffic and malicious services, and achieve the purpose of early warning. First, we obtain real-time data from the power system network traffic database and preprocess the data into a form suitable for classification. After preprocessing the data, we use the data to train a two-class DNN network to distinguish whether a certain IP is a server or not. IP. The data to be classified is processed by DNN to output a two-class prediction result, indicating the confidence that the data belongs to a server in the network. The results are filtered according to the confidence level. If the confidence level is greater than a certain threshold, it is a positive sample, that is, server data; otherwise, it is a negative sample, that is, not server data. Subsequently, in order to further know the specific type of the positive server, we add a confidence item to the positive data sample and perform K-means cluster analysis to cluster the multi-classification results representing the specific type of the server. The schematic diagram of the system model is shown in Fig. 2.

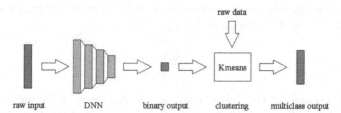

**Fig. 2.** Classification method of power system network traffic based on deep learning and K-means clustering.

### 4.1    Data Preprocessing

There are many data items of data samples in the power network traffic database, some of which are not helpful for network traffic classification, such as TCP synchronization packets and average ACK delay of clients. Therefore, we first screened the original data, selected data items that can provide more information for classification to form data samples, and finally selected the server IP address, port, protocol, client IP address, number of bytes, bit rate, Data items such as the number of packets, the total number of sessions, and time are used as sample data. In all traffic data, we know that some power system network IPs are power system servers, and we also know some IPs that are determined not to be servers. The sample data corresponding to these IPs are extracted as the positive and negative samples of the training set.

Although the number of known server IPs in the power network only accounts for 0.005% of all end IPs, the data samples belonging to known server IPs account for 93.3% of all data samples, which indicates that the vast majority of sessions in the network are generated by extreme It is initiated by a small number of servers, which will cause the number of positive samples to be much larger than negative samples, which will have a great impact on the training effect. Therefore, in response to this problem, we integrated the sample data. Specifically, we use a quadruple such as (server IP, port, protocol, time) as an index to integrate the sample data of the same server IP, same port, same protocol, and the same time period into one piece of data. The number of positive samples is effectively reduced, the number of positive and negative samples after integration is more balanced, and better experimental results are achieved.

Finally, because the order of magnitude difference between data items in the data sample is too large, for example, the total number of bytes of data items can reach the order of $10^6$, but the number of packets per second is only of the order of $10^{-1}$. Using this kind of data for direct training may make Gradient explosion occurs in the neural network, which affects the performance of the model. Therefore, we perform max-min normalization on each sample, and map the sample values to the [0, 1] interval, to achieve fast and stable convergence of the model during training. For a certain sample $x$, the normalization is as shown in Eq. 8:

$$x' = \frac{x - x_{min}}{x_{max} - x_{min}} \tag{8}$$

where $x_{min}$ represents the minimum value of all samples, $x_{max}$ represents the maximum value of all samples, and $x'$ represents the normalized sample.

## 4.2 Construction of DNN

We use the preprocessed training set to train a DNN for preliminary classification of power system network traffic. Since the data to be processed is a one-dimensional vector, the DNN we built is a fully connected network model. The model structure is shown in Fig. 3.

In the figure, except for the input layer, the value marked in each layer is the number of neurons, which is also the data dimension of the output of this layer. The Dense layer is the fully connected layer. The input layer inputs n-dimensional data samples, and the three neurons in the hidden layer are 512, 256, and 128 fully connected layers to output data features to the output layer. The three fully connected layers use a nonlinear activation function Relu:

$$Relu(x) = \max(0, x) \tag{9}$$

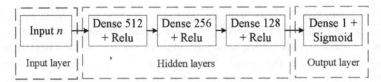

**Fig. 3.** Model architecture.

the output layer outputs a logit value, which becomes the predicted confidence value through the Sigmoid activation function. The sigmoid function is a nonlinear activation function that maps the input to the [0, 1] interval, and its form is as follows:

$$\text{Sigmoid}(x) = \frac{1}{1 + e^{-x}} \tag{10}$$

### 4.3 K-means Multi-classification Scheme

The multi-classification scheme we use is processed by DNN, and the samples determined to be suspected servers are classified by K-means. Therefore, first, the probability value of the result output by the DNN must be determined. We determine a threshold $\delta$ (usually 0.5), and any classification result with a confidence greater than this threshold is judged as a positive example, otherwise it is judged as a negative example. Next, extract all the data samples determined as positive examples, and add the confidence of the DNN output to these data samples as a new "classification confidence" data item. The newly generated data were then subjected to cluster analysis using K-means.

Firstly, the optimal $K$ value of K-means is determined according to the "elbow method" method. We evaluate the case where $K \in [2, 18]$, calculates the value of SSE respectively, and makes a curve diagram, as shown in the Fig. 4. It can be found that the obvious inflection point is at $K = 5$, so the optimal $K$ value should be 5. Therefore, to get the clearest classification discrimination, we choose $K = 5$ as the number of cluster centers. The K-means model is trained according to this $K$ value to classify the new data results.

### 4.4 Model Evaluation Metrics

For DNN classification models, the more commonly used indicators are precision and recall, and their formulas are as follows:

$$\text{precision} = \frac{tp}{tp + fp} \tag{11}$$

$$\text{recall} = \frac{tp}{tp + fn} \tag{12}$$

where $tp$ represents the number of true cases, that is, the number of samples that are actually positive and predicted to be positive; $fp$ represents the number of false positives, that is, the number of samples that are actually negative but predicted to be positive;

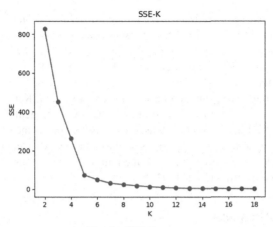

**Fig. 4.** SSE-K curve.

*fn* represents false negative The number of cases, that is, the number of samples that are actually positive but predicted to be negative. The performance of the model can be measured from two dimensions using the precision and recall metrics. Usually, different thresholds are taken as sample points in the experiment, and the precision-recall (P-R) curve is drawn, and the model is judged by the height of the balance point of the curve.

For the evaluation of the K-means clustering algorithm, in addition to the residual sum of squares SSE mentioned above, the evaluation index can also be determined by the silhouette coefficient method. For a certain sample $x$, the silhouette coefficient method is as follows:

$$SC = \frac{b(x) - a(x)}{\max(a(x), b(x))} \tag{13}$$

where $a(x)$ is called the intra-cluster dissimilarity and is the sum of the distances between the sample $x$ and other samples in the cluster. $b(x)$ is the dissimilarity between clusters, which is the sum of the distances between sample $x$ and other samples in other clusters. The value range of SC is $[-1, 1]$, and the closer to one, the better the clustering performance.

## 5   Experiment

### 5.1   Experimental Setup

The data we use comes from the power network flow database, and the training uses the historical data in the database, with a total of 25 days of flow data. The timestamp of the data is divided by hour. We process the data according to the data preprocessing method described in Sect. 4.1. First, we screen out the known intranet server IPs and IPs that are not known to belong to the server, and select a total of 2,257,429 pieces of original data, and mark, integrate, and classify these data. After unification and other operations, 162,952 training data samples are obtained to form a training set. Next, we performed preprocessing operations on the remaining 2,784,335 pieces of unknown data except for labeling, and obtained 698,459 test data samples to form a test set. Finally, we randomly sample the training set and divide it into 10% as the validation set. This part is not used for the training process, but only for the verification and evaluation of the model performance.

Our model is built and evaluated on Ubuntu 18.04 system. Keras and Tensorflow2 deep learning framework are used to build and train the deep neural network, and the scikit-learn machine learning toolkit is used to construct the K-means clustering algorithm. We use data loading as numpy arrays for ease of processing and interaction. When training the deep learning network model, the number of epochs used is 300, the batch size is 128, and the learning rate is 0.02.

## 5.2   Choice of DNN Model

The DNN model proposed in Sect. 4.2 is a four-layer fully connected model with 3 hidden layers and 1 output layer. To evaluate whether the model selection is correct, and to select the low-cost optimal model that meets the performance, we conduct experiments on models with different numbers of hidden layers and analyzes the tested models from the three indicators of training time, inference time and model accuracy. We construct three subject models. In addition to the four-layer model mentioned above, there are also three-layer fully-connected models and five-layer fully-connected models. The difference between them is that the three-layer fully connected model removes the neurons as the hidden layer of 512, and the five-layer fully connected model adds a fully connected layer with 1024 neurons in the front of the hidden layer. The experimental results are shown in Table 1.

**Table 1.** Comparison of three DNN models.

| Model | Training time (s) | Prediction time (s) | Accuracy (%) |
|-------|-------------------|---------------------|--------------|
| 3L    | 270.99            | 1.203               | 94.51        |
| 4L    | 289.29            | 1.339               | 94.61        |
| 5L    | 316.41            | 1.413               | 94.55        |

As shown in the table, we train all three models for 100 epochs. With the increase of the number of model layers, both the training time and the prediction time have been improved to a certain extent, and the prediction time has increased by about 0.1 s, and there will be a significant gap when the amount of data is large. However, in contrast, there is no significant difference in the accuracy of the three models, and the increase in the number of layers may not necessarily lead to an increase in the accuracy. From the data in Table 1, the four-layer DNN fully connected model has both low time Cost and high-accuracy models. Therefore, this paper chooses this model as the classification model.

### 5.3  Model Performance Evaluation

We evaluated the performance of the DNN model based on the validation set data, after the training process, the model training set accuracy and validation set accuracy were 98.82% and 96.34%, respectively. Then, according to the evaluation indicators in Sect. 3.4, we calculated the accuracy and recall rate of the model under the validation set, and by modifying the threshold $\delta$, we drew the P-R curve of the model, as shown in Fig. 5.

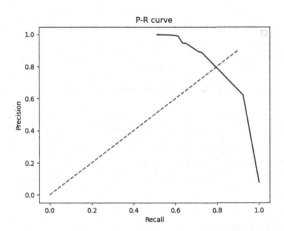

**Fig. 5.**  P-R curve. (Color figure online)

The blue line in the figure is the P-R curve, and the red line is the balance line, where the precision and recall are equal. The intersection of the balance line and the P-R curve can evaluate the performance of the model. In Fig. 5, the intersection is about (0.8, 0.8), indicating that the model has better performance. And when the accuracy rate in the figure is 1, the recall rate can reach 0.4, indicating that the basic recall rate of the model is high, and the server IP can be found as comprehensively as possible while maintaining fewer misjudgments.

For the evaluation of K-means, we also conduct experiments according to the silhouette coefficient index in Sect. 4.4, and the experimental results are shown in Fig. 6.

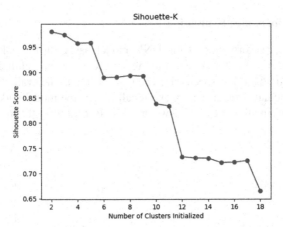

**Fig. 6.** K-means silhouette coefficient.

As shown in the figure, when the $K$ value ranges from 1 to 5, the silhouette coefficient values are all higher than 0.95, which indicates that the classes separated by the clustering algorithm have a high degree of discrimination and have a good clustering effect. Clustering into 5 categories can ensure the effect and efficiency of clustering to the greatest extent.

### 5.4 Validate with the Test Set

We used the constructed model to make predictions on the test set, divided by the threshold $\delta = 0.5$, and got 591 suspected IPs. Since the test set is unknown unlabeled data, we conducted manual verification and found that some of these IPs belong to real business servers, and some are server-like devices, such as monitoring devices, IAD devices, and soft switch devices. The experimental results are shown in Table 2.

**Table 2.** Test set classification results.

| Type | Proportion (%) | Average confidence (%) |
| --- | --- | --- |
| Business server | 25.92 | 97.59 |
| Server-like device | 70.38 | 94.58 |
| Other | 3.70 | 97.00 |

The proportion in the table refers to the proportion of a certain type of equipment in all suspected IPs, and the other types refer to non-grid internal equipment. It can be found that most of the suspected IPs are unregistered devices, accounting for 70.38%, and business servers account for 25.92%, and the average confidence level is high, reaching 97.59%, indicating that the model can accurately detect suspected servers.

In the cluster analysis of the data, we find that there are also different classifications among business servers. Among the suspected IPs found, 66.67% of the business servers were clustered into one category, and the remaining 4 categories of the cluster also included different business servers. Among the server-like devices, cluster analysis successfully distinguishes various devices. The specific cluster analysis results are as follows:

**Table 3.** Test set cluster analysis results.

| Cluster type | Proportion of servers (%) | Server-like device | |
|---|---|---|---|
| | | Device type | Proportion (%) |
| 1 | 66.67 | IAD | 94.73 |
| 2 | 9.52 | Video conference | 25.05 |
| 3 | 4.76 | DVR | 90.91 |
| 4 | 4.76 | None | None |
| 5 | 14.29 | Soft switch | 100.0 |

The proportion in Table 3 represents the proportion of the devices clustered into this class to the total number of such devices. It can be found that in terms of server-like devices, most of the various devices are clustered into the same class, which shows that the clustering analysis has a certain distinguishing effect on device types.

# 6  Conclusion

In this paper, we propose a classification method of power system network traffic based on deep learning and K-means clustering, aiming at the detection and prevention of abnormal traffic and malicious services in the power system network. We first preprocess the power system network traffic data to facilitate model classification, then use the DNN model to classify the data to determine whether it is server traffic, and finally use the K-means clustering algorithm to classify the device traffic that is judged as a server. Experiments show that the proposed model can effectively classify the network traffic of the power system, which has a certain significance for the improvement of the network security of the power system. In future work, we will further refine our method and pursue higher accuracy and faster detection speed.

**Acknowledgements.** This work was supported by the Science Foundation of State Grid Co., Ltd. Headquarters "Research and Application of the Key Cloud-Edge Collaborative Technologies for Smart IoT Secure Access" (5700-202118181A-0), Natural Science Foundation of Jiangsu Province (Higher Education Institutions) (BK20170900, 19KJB520046, and 20KJA520001), Innovative and Entrepreneurial talents projects of Jiangsu Province, Jiangsu Planned Projects for Postdoctoral Research Funds (No. 2019K024), Six talent peak projects in Jiangsu Province (JY02), Postgraduate Research & Practice Innovation Program of Jiangsu Province (KYCX19_0921, KYCX19_0906), Zhejiang Lab (2021KF0AB05), and NUPT DingShan Scholar Project and NUPTSF (NY219132).

# References

1. Tao, L.: Research review of encrypted traffic classification based on deep learning. Comput. Modernization **2021**(08), 112–120 (2021)
2. Shan, Y., Yin, X., Zhang, S.: Research on network security detection based on traffic analysis. Inf. Comput. (Theoret. Edn.) **2018**(6), 205–207 (2018)
3. Li, Z.: Research on anomaly detection method of industrial control system based on network traffic. Beijing Jiaotong University (2020)
4. Zhang, J., Zhang, J., Yang, C., et al.: Detection of abnormal flow in process layer network of intelligent substation based on cyber-physical fusion. Autom. Electr. Power Syst. **2019**(14), 173–184 (2019)
5. Yang, Y., Chen, W., Song, S., et al.: Network traffic classification based on convolutional neural network against attack threats. Comput. Sci. (2021)
6. Zhao, Y., Yin, Y., Gui, G.: Lightweight Deep Learning based intelligent edge surveillance techniques. IEEE Trans. Cogn. Commun. Network. **6**(4), 1146–1154 (2020)
7. Vijayanand, R., Devaraj, D., Kannapiran, B.: A novel Deep Learning based intrusion detection system for smart meter communication network. In: INCOS, 11–13 April 2019, pp. 1–3 (2019)
8. Gui, G., Wang, Y., Huang, H.: Deep learning based physical layer wireless communication techniques: opportunities and challenges. J. Commun. **40**(2), 19–23 (2019)
9. Bendiab, G., Shiaeles, S., Alruban, A., Kolokotronis, N.: IoT malware network traffic classification using visual representation and deep learning. In: NetSoft, 29 June–3 July 2020, pp. 444–449 (2020)
10. Zhao, R., Yin, J., et al.: An efficient intrusion detection method based on dynamic autoencoder. IEEE Wirel. Commun. Lett. (Early access)
11. Wang, W., Zhu, M., Zeng, X., Ye, X., Sheng, Y.: Malware traffic classification using convolutional neural network for representation learning. In: ICOIN, 11–13 January 2017, pp. 712–717 (2017)
12. Xu, J., Zhou, Y., Wang, J., et al.: Anomaly detection of network traffic based on flow time influence domain. J. Northeast. Univ. (Nat. Sci. Edn.) **2019**(1), 26–31 (2019)
13. Li, N.: Research on internet abnormal traffic detection based on big data. J. Chengdu Inst. Technol. **2018**(4), 34–38 (2018)
14. Pu, X.: Research on network traffic anomaly detection in big data environment. Mod. Electron. Technol. **2018**(3), 84–87 (2018)
15. Chen, Z.: Optimization of deep learning target detection model and its application in power grid. North China Electric Power University, Beijing (2021)
16. Bai, H., Ma, X., Liu, W., Liu, G.: Research on anonymous protocol traffic identification technology based on deep learning. Comput. Simul. **38**(07), 360–365 (2021)
17. Wen, W., Hu, Y., Zhao, G., Chen, X.: Design and implementation of abnormal IP identification system based on traffic feature classification. Inf. Netw. Secur. **21**(08), 1–9 (2021)
18. Li, G.: Research on wireless network traffic prediction based on cluster analysis and neural network. Mod. Electron. Technol. **44**(07), 91–94 (2021)
19. Li, W., et al.: Efficient application identification and the temporal and spatial stability of classification schema. Comput. Netw. **53**(6), 790–809 (2009)
20. Wang, H., Cheng, S., Zhang, R., et al.: Research on data bearer network planning method based on deep packet inspection (DPI) and R-squared value. Inf. Commun. **2019**(5), 182–184 (2019)
21. Lu, H., Zhang, M., Xu, X.: Deep fuzzy hashing network for efficient image retrieval. IEEE Trans. Fuzzy Syst. (2020). https://doi.org/10.1109/TFUZZ.2020.2984991
22. Lu, H., Li, Y., Chen, M., et al.: Brain intelligence: go beyond artificial intelligence. Mob. Netw. Appl. **23**, 368–375 (2018)

23. Lu, H., Li, Y., Mu, S., et al.: Motor anomaly detection for unmanned aerial vehicles using reinforcement learning. IEEE Internet Things J. **5**(4), 2315–2322 (2018)
24. Lu, H., Qin, M., Zhang, F., et al.: RSCNN: a CNN-based method to enhance low-light remote-sensing images. Remote Sens. **13**, 62 (2020)
25. Lu, H., Zhang, Y., Li, Y., et al.: User-oriented virtual mobile network resource management for vehicle communications. IEEE Trans. Intell. Transp. Syst. **22**(6), 3521–3532 (2021)

# Research on Server Activity of Power Grid System Based on Deep Learning

Pengyu Zhang[1] , Jiange Liu[1] , Longfei Zhou[2]([✉]) , Mao Li[1] , Jianfei Shao[1] ,
Zhi Xie[1] , Shangdong Liu[2,3] , Liang Zhou[4] , and Yimu Ji[2,3]

[1] Huai'an Power Supply Branch, State Grid Jiangsu Electric Power Co., Ltd., Huai'an, China
[2] School of Computer Science, Nanjing University of Posts and Telecommunications,
Nanjing 210023, Jiangsu, China
1422767499@qq.com
[3] Jiangsu HPC and Intelligent Processing Engineer Research Center,
Nanjing 210003, Jiangsu, China
[4] Nanjing Dingyan Power Technology Co., Ltd., Nanjing, China

**Abstract.** There is a big difference in the change law of the activity between the network services in the power grid server. The traditional single network traffic forecasting method cannot accurately predict the traffic of some network services. In order to predict the grid server activity better, this paper proposes a deep learning-based grid system server activity prediction algorithm which has higher accuracy and adaptability than traditional methods. The algorithm firstly analyzes the grid server traffic data, and proposes a three-dimensional network node activity calculation method based on the total number of bytes, the total data packets and the number of visits. Then based on different deep learning models, the future service activity of the network service is predicted, and an optimal model is obtained through model evaluation and comparison, which is saved in the server for real-time calling. The algorithm proposed in this paper can accurately predict the future activity of the grid system server and has a stronger adaptability to the grid service prediction business with different flow characteristics.

**Keywords:** Network traffic prediction · Deep Learning · LSTM · GRU

## 1 Introduction

With the continuous construction and development of power network systems, business management methods are constantly enriched, and traditional experience-based management methods are gradually transforming into intelligent and scientific management based on data analysis [1], the construction of power monitoring networks in various regions is developing towards digitalization and intelligence. However, the power network is large in scale and high in complexity, and the value of power big data has not been fully utilized. It is urgent to introduce digital means to promote business transformation [2]. At the same time, the problem of network traffic activity is related to the management and maintenance of the network, as well as the discovery and early warning of abnormal services. Timely and accurate analysis and prediction of network activity can intuitively reflect the real situation of grid system service operation status and activity distribution, and can quickly locate faults and assist in optimizing the system, which will help network planning and management, and establish a scientific and efficient power network system management system.

As a typical representative of a new generation of information technology, artificial intelligence technology has unique advantages in flow monitoring, such as abnormal flow identification and power load forecasting. At the same time, due to the development of collection technology, power grid companies have accumulated a large amount of data such as user electricity consumption and power equipment monitoring. Using data mining, artificial intelligence and other technologies to carry out historical data research on power grid systems and forecast future data has become a Possibly [3]. It is necessary, important and feasible to make full use of the historical flow data generated by the power grid to analyze and predict the activity data of the power grid system.

At present, there are mainly the following methods for network traffic prediction: Markov model can clearly describe the whole process of traffic change, but it requires a lot of computation [4] and is not suitable for real-time traffic prediction. The Auto Regressive Moving Average (ARMA) and Auto Regressive Integrated Moving Average (ARIMA) models have simple calculation methods and fast solution speed, but can only predict network traffic with regular traffic changes. However, the prediction accuracy of non-stationary network traffic is low [5]. For non-stationary network traffic prediction, the researchers propose a network traffic prediction method based on Long Short Term Memory (LSTM), which improves the accuracy of prediction, but LSTM has early characteristics in learning network traffic. In the case of insufficient memory [6], the traffic prediction effect for some network services is poor.

Therefore, this paper proposes a power grid system activity algorithm based on deep learning. The algorithm obtains a data set of grid historical activity through data preprocessing, divides and processes the data set to obtain training samples and test samples; The deep learning model predicts the activity; finally, three indicators of MAE (mean absolute error), RMSE (root mean squared error), R2 score are used to evaluate the accuracy of the model and integrate the prediction results into the system for visual display. An optimal prediction model suitable for port service activity prediction, establishes a monitoring system that generates activity evaluation in real time, and predicts the future activity of each service in the power grid system based on historical activity and different deep learning algorithms.

The remainder of this paper is organized as follows. The next section defines important concepts. Section 3 presents the design of the system model and the analysis preparations before the experiments. Section 4 conducts experiments and comparisons and analyzes and evaluates the experimental results. Section 5 summarizes the work.

## 2   Theoretical Basis

### 2.1   Pearson Correlation Coefficient

The Pearson correlation coefficient is an evaluation index used to measure the degree of correlation between data. It is based on the deviation of the two sets of data and their respective averages, and the degree of correlation between two variables is reflected by multiplying the two deviations [7]. The definition of the Pearson correlation coefficient is shown in formula (1):

$$K = \frac{\sum_{i=1}^{m}(X_i - \overline{X})(Y_i - \overline{Y})}{\sqrt{\sum_{i=1}^{m}(X_i - \overline{X})^2}\sqrt{\sum_{i=1}^{m}(Y_i - \overline{Y})^2}} \tag{1}$$

In the formula, $X$ and $Y$ are the two variables for which the degree of correlation is to be calculated, and each variable has m elements; $K$ is the Pearson correlation coefficient, and its value range is $[-1, 1]$, and $K$ is positive means positive correlation, $K$ is negative, indicating negative correlation; the higher the absolute value of $K$, the higher the degree of correlation between variables $X$ and $Y$ [8].

## 2.2 Long Short-Term Memory Networks

The LSTM (Long Short Term Memory) model is called a long short-term memory network, which can transfer the information of the previous state to the next state through increase or decrease. The LSTM model consists of a forget gate, a memory gate and an output gate [9]. The forget gate is used to reduce redundant information and speed up processing; the memory gate is used to retain useful information; the output gate is used to output the current state value [10]. The LSTM network combines short-term memory and long-term memory through gate control, which can process long sequence data and better predict sequence data [11]. The LSTM network structure model is shown in Fig. 1. The mathematical expression of the model is as formula (2)–(6):

$$f_t = \sigma\left(W_f \cdot [h_{t-1}, X_t] + b_f\right) \tag{2}$$

$$\tilde{A} = tanh\left(W_c \cdot [h_{t-1}, X_t] + b_C\right) \tag{3}$$

$$A_t = f_t \cdot A_{t-1} + i_t \cdot \tilde{A} \tag{4}$$

$$O_t = \sigma\left(W_o \cdot [h_{t-1}, X_t] + b_o\right) \tag{5}$$

$$h_t = O_t \cdot tanh(A_t) \tag{6}$$

In the formula: $X_t$ represents the input at time $t$, $h_{t-1}$, $h_t$ respectively represents the memory information at time $t-1$, $t$; $\sigma$ represents the $\sigma$ activation layer in the model; the $f_t$ value range is $(0, 1)$, which represents which information is kept or discarded from the node state; $\tilde{A}$ represents the new candidate state information generated by the $tanh$ activation layer; $i_t$ represents the input of the input gate at the moment $t$; $O_t$ represents the output of the moment $t$; $W$ is the weight matrix of the corresponding gate, and $b$ is the output coefficient of the corresponding gate [12].

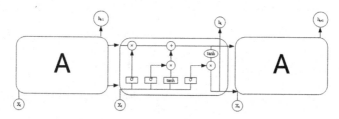

**Fig. 1.** LSTM network structure model

## 2.3 Gated Recurrent Network

The GRU gated recurrent network improves the complex network structure of LSTM. It optimizes the network mainly by merging the input of LSTM and the forget gate to form a new update gate, and at the same time, the unit state and output of LSTM are merged into one state [13]. It only contains two gate control modules (update gate and reset gate), and has the characteristics of simple network structure and fast calculation speed [14]. Figure 2 shows the unit structure of GRU neuron. The mathematical expression of the specific workflow is as follows: (7)–Formula (10):

$$Z_t = \sigma\left(W_Z \cdot \left[h_{t-1}, x_t\right]\right) \tag{7}$$

$$r_t = \sigma\left(W_r \cdot \left[h_{t-1}, x_t\right]\right) \tag{8}$$

$$\tilde{h}_t = tanh\left(W_{\tilde{h}} \cdot \left[r_t \odot h_{t-1}, x_t\right]\right) \tag{9}$$

$$h_t = (1 - Z_t) \odot h_{t-1} + Z_t \odot h_t \tag{10}$$

In the formula, the reset gate $r_t$ determines which information needs to be forgotten at the last moment; the update gate $Z_t$ determines the need to save the hidden state from the previous hidden state to the current hidden state $h_t$ which is the candidate state of the hidden layer at the current moment; $W$ is the weight matrix of the corresponding gate; From the workflow of GRU, it can be seen that GRU only completes the forgetting and retention of memory through the reset gate and update gate, so the efficiency is generally better than the LSTM model [15].

## 3 Prediction Model of Power Grid System Server Activity Based on Deep Learning

### 3.1 System Model

In this paper, a deep learning-based server activity prediction algorithm for power grid systems is designed, and a corresponding activity prediction system is designed and implemented to solve the problem of predicting the activity of server IP ports in the power network system. The main steps are as follows:

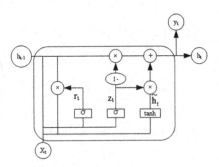

**Fig. 2.** GRU network structure model

(1) The system will obtain the traffic data and the corresponding IP address, port number, time and other information from the interface, and filter out the IP traffic data of the record system.

(2) Retain traffic characteristics that may be related to activity for correlation analysis.

(3) According to the correlation analysis results of the traffic data, the corresponding weights are used to calculate the activity, and the obtained historical activity data is stored in the database.

(4) After data preprocessing, a data set form suitable for the prediction of the system is generated, and several suitable models are selected for activity prediction through the preliminary analysis of the activity data.

(5) Divide the data set into training samples and test samples. The training samples are input into different deep learning models for model training, and the test samples are used to verify the model results.

(6) Use three indicators of MAE, RMSE, R2 score to evaluate the model, debug the model to make the model accuracy the highest, and then compare each model to select the optimal model and save it in the server for real-time calling.

(7) The optimal prediction model corresponding to each IP port will be formed in the final server. The system will automatically obtain and process the activity data of the IP port to be predicted and input it into the model for prediction, and use data visualization technology to make predictions. The results show that. The system model is shown in Fig. 3.

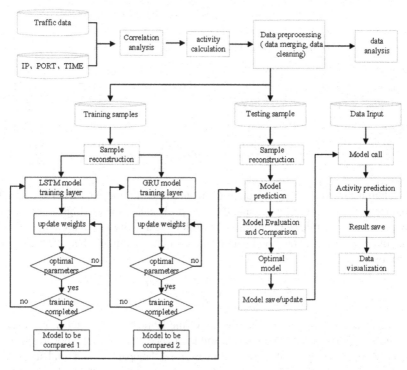

**Fig. 3.** System model

## 3.2 Traffic Feature Correlation Analysis and Activity Calculation

The communication activity is related to the traffic data of both parties in the communication. The original data is the summary of the IP traffic data of a certain terminal every hour after processing by a certain system. It combines the traffic generated by the IP port with all other IP ports that communicate with it within this hour. The data were accumulated, and the original data obtained are shown in Table 1.

**Table 1.** Raw data format.

| IP address | Port | Total bytes | Total packets | Total Bit Rate | ... | Time |
|---|---|---|---|---|---|---|
| | | | | | | |

The data has a variety of information generated by communication, up to 61-dimensional features, and the activity is only related to the size of the traffic and the number of visits, etc. The correlation between them is calculated using the Pearson correlation formula. The coefficients are shown in Table 2.

Through analysis, it can be found that there is a linear relationship between the total number of bytes of the data and the total bit rate, and there is also a linear relationship between the number of visits and the number of sessions. Therefore, for features with a

**Table 2.** Pearson correlation coefficient between traffic data.

|  | Total bytes | Total packets | Total bit rate | Accesses | Sessions |
|---|---|---|---|---|---|
| Total bytes | 1 | 0.993 | 1 | 0.587 | 0.581 |
| Total packets | 0.993 | 1 | 0.993 | 0.667 | 0.660 |
| Total bit rate | 1 | 0.993 | 1 | 0.587 | 0.581 |
| Accesses | 0.587 | 0.667 | 0.587 | 1 | 0.998 |
| Sessions | 0.581 | 0.660 | 0.581 | 0.998 | 1 |

linear relationship, the activity calculation only needs to take the two First, the correlation between the total number of bytes and the total packets is also very high. Based on this, this paper proposes a three-dimensional network node activity calculation method based on the total number of bytes, total data packets and access times. The specific formula is as follows:

$$k = \frac{Bi}{B} \cdot w_1 + \frac{Pi}{P} \cdot w_1 + \frac{Ai}{A} \cdot w_3 \tag{11}$$

In the formula, $k$ represents the activity of the IP port, $Bi$, $Pi$, and $Ai$ represent the total number of bytes, total data packets and total access times of the port respectively; $B$, $P$, and $A$ represent the total number of bytes, total data packets and total access times of all IP ports respectively; $w_i$ represents the weight of each item. Since the total number of bytes has a high degree of correlation with the total number of data packets, but has a low degree of correlation with the total number of visits, the weights in the activity calculation formula are selected as follows:

$$\{w_1, w_1, w_1\} = \{0.3, 0.3, 0.4\} \tag{12}$$

## 3.3 Data Preprocessing

The raw data obtained from the system contains many unwanted traffic characteristics, and only the specified IP port needs to be predicted, and the raw data cannot be directly used for model training. Therefore, a preprocessing operation on the data is required. The specific operation steps as follows:

(1) Read the IP address and port number to be tested from the filing system database, and filter the data of the IP port list from the original data;
(2) Combine traffic data based on IP address, port number, protocol type, and time. Calculate the activity according to the activity calculation formula;
(3) Record the time of each piece of data, merge the IP address and port number, the merged IP port will be used as the column name, and the recorded time will be used as the row index, so that a piece of activity data corresponding to the time of the IP port is obtained;

(4) The above processing is performed by traversing each data file and traversing all rows of data in each data file, and the processed data is merged;

(5) Perform missing value processing on the data set, and replace the null value with 0 to obtain the final activity data set of each IP port corresponding to the time, and divide the data set into training samples and test samples, of which the training samples are used as the inputs of LSTM and GRU model for model training, and the test samples are used to compare with the predicted results.

### 3.4  Activity Characteristic Analysis

**Volatility and Difference of Activity of Different IP Ports**

Different services are running on the power network system server at all times. The types, start times, and running times of these services are different, so their activity data will also have great differences. Figure 4 shows the change of historical activity of different IP ports from June 1st to June 9th. It can be seen from the figure that the change of the activity of each port is highly volatile, and it is impossible to use a linear function to analyze such data. At the same time, there are great differences in the change laws, so it is impossible to evaluate the activity changes of another service based on the activity change laws of one service. Only a nonlinear model for the activity data of a certain port can be considered. Make predictions.

Different services are running on the power network system server all the time. Since the types, start times, and running times of these services are different, their activity data will also be very different. Figure 4 shows the change of historical activity of different IP ports from June 1 to June 9. It can be seen from the figure that the change of the activity of each port is highly volatile, so it is impossible to describe these activities with a linear function. At the same time, the law of activity changes of different IP ports is very different, so it is impossible to evaluate the activity changes of other services based on the activity changes of a certain service. Therefore, only for each port, a nonlinear model can be used to predict the activity.

**Regularity of Activity Changes**

The change of each service activity of the power network system server is dominated by time and date, and its change is regular. Figure 5 shows the historical activity changes of a port from April 14th to June 28th. From this figure, it can be seen that the IP port activity shows a pattern in these two and a half months, that is, every week there will be a spike in activity occurs at a fixed time. Although the size of the peaks varies slightly, the timing of the peaks is periodic, that is, a peak of activity occurs every 7 days. It can be seen that the change of the port activity of the server is closely related to the time and date.

Figure 6 is a graph of the 9-day change in port activity observed at the time granularity of every hour. It can be seen from the figure that the activity changes have a similar pattern in consecutive days, that is, the port activity is basically the same for the first five days. The peak of the day's activity is reached between 12:00 and 1:00 noon. In the last four days, another pattern appeared, that is, there were two valleys of activity at a certain time in the morning and afternoon. Further research found that the change range of port

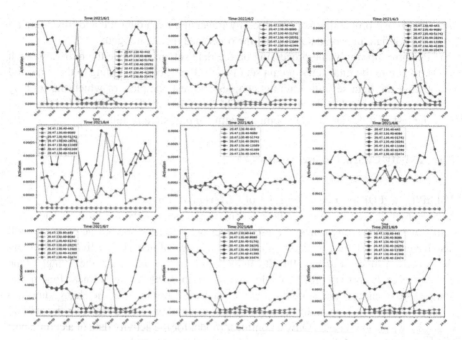

**Fig. 4.** LSTM network structure model

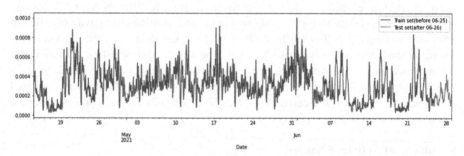

**Fig. 5.** Changes in daily activity of IP port A from April 14 to June 28

activity in the unit of day is too large, while the change range of port activity in the unit of hour is small, and the data is relatively stable; Fig. 7 is a graph of the hourly activity changes of another port within 9 days. The activity changes of this port also show roughly two patterns in one week. For this reason, this paper finds that it is possible to predict the activity changes in the next 72 h with the hour as the time granularity.

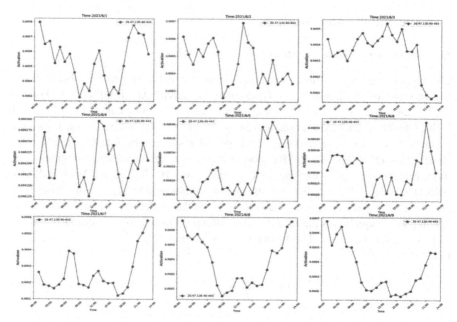

**Fig. 6.** The hourly activity change of IP port A from June 1 to June 9

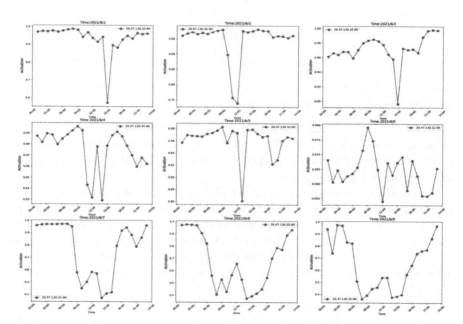

**Fig. 7.** The hourly activity change of IP port B from June 1 to June 9

## 4   Experiments and Analysis

### 4.1   Experimental Data Set and Evaluation Metrics

The experimental data in this paper comes from the real historical flow data collected in a certain area of Jiangsu Power Grid. Take the activity data from 0:00 on April 13, 2021 to 24:00 on July 2 as the training sample, and the activity data from 0:00 on July 3, 2021 to 24:00 on July 4 as the test sample, and the time interval is 1h. In order to evaluate the accuracy of prediction, this paper adopts mean absolute error (MAE), root mean square error (RMSE) and R2 score, which are commonly used in spatiotemporal series prediction tasks, to evaluate model predictions. The RMSE and MAE indicators reflect the actual difference between the predicted value and the actual value. The lower the above results, the better the prediction effect of the model [16]. The R2 score is used to compare the quality of the model under different dimensions. The closer its value is to 1, the better the effect. The formula for calculating MAE, RMSE, R2 score are as follows:

$$MAE = \frac{1}{T} \sum_{t=1}^{T} \left| y_t^i - \hat{y}_t^i \right| \tag{13}$$

$$RMSE = \sqrt{\frac{1}{T} \sum_{t=1}^{T} (y_t^i - \hat{y}_t^i)^2} \tag{14}$$

$$R^2 = 1 - \frac{\sum_i \left( \hat{y}^{(i)} - y^{(i)} \right)^2}{\sum_i \left( \bar{y} - y^{(i)} \right)^2} \tag{15}$$

### 4.2   Comparison of Experimental Results

In order to compare the prediction performance of the prediction model, this paper uses the prediction model based on LSTM and GRU to predict and compare the experimental results of different IP ports. The prediction results of the LSTM and GRU models for different ports are shown in Fig. 8:

The results of evaluating the model with R2 score are shown in Table 3. It can be seen from the results that both the LSTM model and the GRU model can predict the activity changes of different ports in the next 72 h, but there are some delays, and the predicted value lags behind the actual value. At the same time, the prediction effects of the LSTM model and the GRU model for different ports are different. This is due to the difference in the memory modes of the two models. LSTM chooses to expose part of the information and GRU chooses to expose all the information. Therefore, for different data sets, the two models have their own advantages and disadvantages. Therefore, this paper proposes that the combination of LSTM and GRU can be used to predict the service activity of the power network, so that the prediction accuracy of the network activity can be improved.

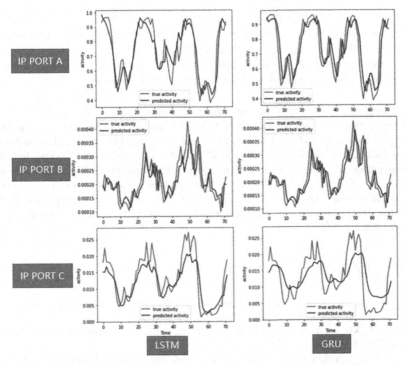

**Fig. 8.** Prediction of different port activity by LSTM and GRU models

**Table 3.** LSTM and GRU models predict and evaluate the activity of different ports.

| Evaluation result | | IP port A | IP port B | IP port C |
|---|---|---|---|---|
| LSTM model | MAE | 0.0605 | 3.4739e−5 | 0.0029 |
| | RMSE | 0.0770 | 4.4569e−5 | 0.0037 |
| | R2 score | 0.8305 | 0.6088 | 0.7406 |
| GRU model | MAE | 0.0696 | 3.3559e−5 | 0.0041 |
| | RMSE | 0.0897 | 4.3127e−5 | 0.0051 |
| | R2 score | 0.7695 | 0.6337 | 0.5152 |

## 5   Conclusion

Aiming at the problem of network service activity in the power network system, this paper proposes a calculation method to evaluate the service activity in the power grid system, then analyzes the characteristics of the network service activity, and uses the LSTM and GRU models to predict the grid service activity. Through the experiment, we obtained the conclusion that the prediction effects of different IP ports LSTM model and GRU model have their own advantages and disadvantages, and then proposed an algorithm based on the combination of LSTM and GRU to predict the activity of power network services. The accuracy and adaptability of the algorithm sex would be better than a traditional single prediction method. On the basis of the algorithm, other different prediction algorithms can be extended or added to further improve the prediction accuracy, and the algorithm can also be applied to other types of data real-time prediction services.

**Acknowledgements.** This work was supported by the Science Foundation of State Grid Co., Ltd. Headquarters "Research and Application of the Key Cloud-Edge Collaborative Technologies for Smart IoT Secure Access" (5700-202118181A-0), Natural Science Foundation of Jiangsu Province (Higher Education Institutions) (BK20170900, 19KJB520046, and 20KJA520001), Innovative and Entrepreneurial talents projects of Jiangsu Province, Jiangsu Planned Projects for Postdoctoral Research Funds (No. 2019K024), Six talent peak projects in Jiangsu Province (JY02), Postgraduate Research \& Practice Innovation Program of Jiangsu Province (KYCX19\_0921, KYCX19\_0906), Zhejiang Lab (2021KF0AB05), and NUPT DingShan Scholar Project and NUPTSF (NY219132).

# References

1. Lin, Z., Cao, X., Ye, S., Zhang, H.: Construction of China southern power grid business flow monitoring system. Electron. World **2020**(22), 28–29 (2020)
2. Wang, Z., Xia, L.: Analysis of the challenges faced by the digital transformation of the power grid [EB/OL], 2021-03-29/2021-04-19
3. Ma, M.: Research and implementation of network traffic prediction system based on deep learning. Beijing University of Posts and Telecommunications (2021)
4. Wang, X., Qi, Y., Li, Q.: Network anomaly detection model based on time-varying weighted Markov chain. Comput. Sci. **44**(09), 136–141+161 (2017)
5. Sheng, H., Zhang, Y.: Research on network traffic modeling and prediction based on ARIMA. Commun. Technol. **52**(04), 903–907 (2019)
6. Du, X., Fan, Z., Lu, Y., Qiu, S.: Network traffic prediction based on bidirectional long short-term memory recurrent neural network. Comput. Appl. Softw. **39**(02), 144–149+156 (2022)
7. Zhang, H., Long, C., Hu, S., Liao, K., Gao, Y.: Distribution network topology verification method based on hierarchical clustering method and Pearson correlation coefficient. Power Netw. Syst. Protect. Control **49**(21), 88–96 (2021)
8. Teng, W., Cheng, L.P., Zhao, K.J.: Application of kernel principal component and Pearson correlation coefficient in prediction of mine pressure failure. In: 2017 Chinese Automation Congress (CAC), pp. 5704–5708. IEEE (2017)
9. Kumar, S.D., Subha, D.P.: Prediction of depression from EEG signal using long short term memory (LSTM). In: 2019 3rd International Conference on Trends in Electronics and Informatics (ICOEI), pp. 1248–1253. IEEE (2019)
10. Park, K., Choi, Y., Choi, W.J., et al.: LSTM-based battery remaining useful life prediction with multi-channel charging profiles. IEEE Access **8**, 20786–20798 (2020)
11. Xu, T.: Research on stock price fluctuation prediction based on LSTM neural network model. Shanghai Normal University (2019)
12. Xue, H., Huynh, D.Q., Reynolds, M.: SS-LSTM: a hierarchical LSTM model for pedestrian trajectory prediction. In: 2018 IEEE Winter Conference on Applications of Computer Vision (WACV), pp. 1186–1194. IEEE (2018)
13. Kumar, S., Hussain, L., Banarjee, S., et al.: Energy load forecasting using deep learning approach-LSTM and GRU in spark cluster. In: 2018 fifth international conference on emerging applications of information technology (EAIT), pp. 1–4. IEEE (2018)

14. Xue, R., Zhang, M., Nan, Y., Zhao, H.: Prediction model of daily average express business volume based on GRU deep learning algorithm. Stat. Decis. **37**(13), 176–179 (2021)
15. Fu, R., Zhang, Z., Li, L.: Using LSTM and GRU neural network methods for traffic flow prediction. In: 2016 31st Youth Academic Annual Conference of Chinese Association of Automation (YAC), pp. 324–328. IEEE (2016)
16. Bao, X., Tan, Z., Bao, B., Xu, C.: A new crown epidemic prediction model based on spatiotemporal attention mechanism. Beijing University of Aeronautics and Astronautics, pp. 1–11 (2021)
17. Lu, H., Zhang, M., Xu, X.: Deep fuzzy hashing network for efficient image retrieval. IEEE Trans. Fuzzy Syst. (2020). https://doi.org/10.1109/TFUZZ.2020.2984991
18. Lu, H., Li, Y., Chen, M., et al.: Brain Intelligence: go beyond artificial intelligence. Mob. Netw. Appl. **23**, 368–375 (2018)
19. Lu, H., Li, Y., Mu, S., et al.: Motor anomaly detection for unmanned aerial vehicles using reinforcement learning. IEEE Internet Things J. **5**(4), 2315–2322 (2018)
20. Lu, H., Qin, M., Zhang, F., et al.: RSCNN: a CNN-based method to enhance low-light remote-sensing images. Remote Sens. **13**, 62 (2020)
21. Lu, H., Zhang, Y., Li, Y., et al.: User-oriented virtual mobile network resource management for vehicle communications. IEEE Trans. Intell. Transp. Syst. **22**(6), 3521–3532 (2021)

# Feature Analysis of Electroencephalogram Signals Evoked by Machine Noise

Hongbin Wang and Mei Wang[✉]

Xi'an University of Science and Technology, Xi'an 710054, China
wangm@xust.edu.cn

**Abstract.** Recently, people who have been working in mines for a long time are affected by the noises of high-power coal mining machines. The noises of machines for a long time may greatly influence people's physical and mental health. To further understand the psychological state of workers working in the mine, and to extract features and analyze the change rule of EEG signals induced by machine noises stimulation. This paper uses the improved singular value decomposition and reconstruction algorithm to process the EEG signal artifact. The improved signal-to-noise ratio is increased from 9.462 to 11.063, the root mean square error is increased from 4.435 to 4.232, and the correlation coefficient is improved to 0.813. Through experiments, the signal generated by the human brain stimulated by machine noises is collected and analyzed after filtering. The results show that the electroencephalography (EEG) of F3, F4 and other electroencephalography (EEG) sensitive electrode potentials tend to be adaptive to a stable state when the frequency of machine noises is different.

**Keywords:** Noises of machine · EEG of human · Electrode potential

## 1 Introduction

According to accident statistics released by the China Coal Mine Safety Administration, 132 people were killed and 37 injured in 54 accidents in coal mines in the first half of 2021. A fresh life, behind the support of large family hope. So, the cause of the unsafe accident, really let us investigate to reflect on, see what the problem is in the end. Timely understanding and adjusting the deployment of sound corresponding measures, which is an effective step to prevent disasters.

From the scientific point of view analyze and judge the cause of the accident, using the existing EEG acquisition equipment [1–3], collect the EEG of the workers working in the mine, and analyze its characteristic change rule [4].We can understand the state of workers in mines by analyzing the characteristics of EEG signals [5]. It is of far-reaching significance to the development of the mining industry in China to observe the activity regularity of the human brain of underground workers and unsafe behaviors before the occurrence of accidents, and further reveal the direct causes of unsafe behaviors of underground workers.

Noise in the coal mine environment is very harmful to human health [6]. Deafness caused by noise is the second largest occupational disease after pneumococcus. Downhole blasting demolition this kind of impulse noise, in a very short period will lead to people tympanic membrane rupture, permanent hearing loss, can also lead to increased blood pressure, nervous system, digestive system has an impact, not ready yet, if the staff suddenly terrified, and even mental disorder, malignant an irregular heartbeat, coma, and death.

In addition, in a large noise environment for a long time, will lead to auditory threshold deviation that can't be alleviated, hearing failure, and irritability increased. Figure 1 shows coal transportation by underground conveyor belt, and Fig. 2 shows coal mining by underground shearer. The influence of noise on coal mine production safety in a noisy environment [7], too much noise will cause workers cannot hear the alarm, cannot escape in time. In the normal production process of coal mines, noise can make workers feel negative and dissatisfied, leading to work mistakes and a series of butterfly effects [8]. To quickly escape from the noise and speed up the production schedule, workers will operate in violation of regulations, which will greatly increase the probability of accidents.

**Fig. 1.** Coal transport down the mine conveyor belt

## 2   The Experimental Paradigm of Machine Noise-Induced EEG was Designed and Implemented

### 2.1   Source and Frequency Induction of Underground Machine Noise

The main sources of machine noise in the underground coal mine: are the noise of conveyor belts, electric drills, point gun explosions, and other complex mechanical equipment noise, strong noise stimulation will make people produce a kind of electrical brain signal (Table 1).

### 2.2   Sensitive Potentials of Humans Brain Electrodes

In this experiment, a 40-lead EEG acquisition cap was used for collection. Among them, the electrical electrodes of the human brain that are sensitive to machine noise are TP7,

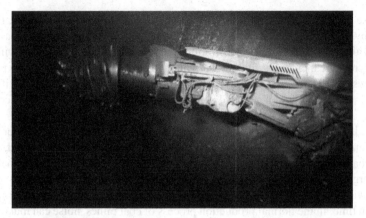

**Fig. 2.** Mining operation of the underground coal shearer

**Table 1.** Frequency distribution of the machine noise

| Source of machine noise | Noises frequency |
| --- | --- |
| The conveyor belt | 2000 Hz–4000 Hz |
| Some drilling rigs | 500 Hz–1000 Hz |
| E point of gun | 500 Hz–1000 Hz |

TP8, CP3, CP4, P7, P8, F3, and F4. The potential difference changes of the above 8 points are obvious and their characteristics are regular, so F3 and F4 can be taken as reference point potentials. Thus, the characteristics of EEG signals were collected and analyzed, and different potential changes were compared.

### 2.3  Improved Singular Value EEG Signal Pretreatment Method Adopts

Artificial deletion, artifact subtraction, principal component analysis [9], independent component analysis, Fourier transform and other filtering algorithms have achieved certain effects, but due to the complexity and particularity of human EEG signal [10], these algorithms still have some limitations. In the independent component analysis of the study, the limitation condition is that the signal source must be non-Gaussian and mutually independent the signal sources of EEG signals are not mutually independent. Fourier transform has some defects in a periodic signal processing.

If the traditional singular value decomposition method is used [11], it can remove the noise, but it is difficult to select the singular value. If the singular value is too high or too low, the experimental data will have a certain influence and deviation. If with the traditional singular value in the dimension of the Hanker matrix [12], the value is selected according to the maximum length, it will not take the frequency into account. Therefore, we adopted the improved singular value decomposition and reconstruction algorithm to deal with the artifact of EEG signal [13]:

(1)  Determination of the dimension of Hankel matrix

Construct a Hankel matrix, which is mainly to transform one-dimensional data into a matrix. Suppose there is auditory EEG induced data X with length N, and the Hankel matrix is constructed as follows:

$$A = \begin{bmatrix} x_1 & x_2 & \cdots & x_n \\ x_2 & x_3 & \cdots & x_{n+1} \\ \vdots & \vdots & \cdots & \vdots \\ x_{N-n+1} & x_{N-n+2} & \cdots & x_n \end{bmatrix} \tag{1}$$

where: $1 < n < N$, when $m = N - n + 1, A \in R^{m \times n}$.

(2)  Reasonable singular value sampling point

Singular Value Decomposition, (SVD) [14], The idea is to project a large matrix into sub spaces that can be decomposed. The principle of SVD: Suppose A is A matrix, and its SVD form is as follows:

$$A = U \sum V^T \tag{2}$$

where: $\sum$ It's a diagonal matrix, U, V; It's an orthogonal matrix, $UU^T = I_{rank(A)}$, $VV^T = I_{rank(A)}$, $u \in R^{rank(A) \times m}$

$$\sum = \begin{bmatrix} a_1 & 0 & \cdots & 0 & 0 \\ 0 & a_2 & \cdots & 0 & 0 \\ \vdots & \vdots & \ddots & \vdots & \vdots \\ 0 & 0 & \cdots & a_{rank(A)-1} & 0 \\ 0 & 0 & \cdots & 0 & a_{rank(A)} \end{bmatrix} \tag{3}$$

where: $a_1 \geq a_2 \geq \cdots a_{rank(A)} > 0$, Is the singular value element of matrix A.
The sub matrix is given by two eigenvectors multiplied by a weight.

$$A = U \sum V^T = \sum_{i=1}^{rank(A)} u_i a_i v^T = \sum_{i=1}^{rank(A)} A_i a_i \tag{4}$$

where: $u_i$ show U the it column vector, $v_i$ show V the ith column vector, $a_i$ represents the singular value of A.

The process of selecting appropriate singular values is as follows: Arrange all singular values from large to small, then,

$$a_i = a_i - a_{i+1} \tag{5}$$

$a_i$ The sequence constituted is a singular value difference spectrum, and the peak value of the difference spectrum is caused by the uncorrelated between noise and useful signal. If the maximum value of the difference spectrum occurs at the point, then singular value reconstruction before I can achieve noise reduction.
The specific calculation steps of the SVD algorithm are as follows:

(1)  Signal column vector or row vector $X = [x_1, x_2, x_3, \cdots, x_n]$;
(2)  Construct Hankel matrix $H = Hankel(x)$;
(3)  Singular value diagonal matrix $V = svd(H)$;
(4)  Singular value row vector $D = (diag(V))'$;

In summary, singular value decomposition and reconstruction of the F7 channel were carried out: for the collected EEG data, EEG software was used for processing and analysis [15, 16], filtering and high-pass filtering, and better EEG data bands were extracted after calibration.

## 3   The Experiment

### 3.1   The Experiment to Prepare

The working environment in the underground coal mine is bad and people are noisy. In the coal mining face, the noise mainly comes from the shearer cutting coal and the machine itself, and with the deepening of the section and the increase of cutting coal speed, the noise increases, about 90–110 dB; In the driving face: the noise mainly comes from drilling rig and drilling rig, which is one of the most serious underground noise impacts. Blasting, although shorter than the machine noise duration, but the huge shock wave, may cause deafness in underground workers because the different intensity can't be measured by a specific sound pressure level range; In the roadway of unified equipment, the noise mainly comes from local ventilators. The noise level of new ventilators is 90–120 dB, and the noise level of ventilators used for about five years is 120–140 dB. If they are not maintained for a long time, the noise may be more serious.

Coal Mine Safety Regulations 2016 stipulate in occupational hazard prevention and noise prevention that the main noise of underground noise includes ventilator, air compressor, local ventilator, coal shearer, pneumatic rock drill, crusher, main water pump, and other equipment. The noise level shall be restricted to 85 dB (A) for more than 8 consecutive hours per day. For less than 8 h, the noise level limit shall be increased by 3 dB (A) to determine the sound level limit. The noise intensity of underground coal mines exceeds the national occupational health standard (Table 2).

**Table 2.**  Main noise source parameters

| The main noise | The construction phase | Noise limited: [dB(A)] | |
| --- | --- | --- | --- |
| | | Day | Night |
| Conditions | Bulldozer, excavator, loader, etc. | 75 | 55 |
| Pile driving | All kinds of pile drivers, etc. | 85 | No working |
| Structure | Concrete mixer | 55 | 70 |
| Decorate | Elevator | 65 | 55 |

In this experiment, the conveyor belt, drilling rig, and blasting are mainly selected for the analysis of the three kinds of sound that are most frequently contacted by the staff and harm people. By Fourier transform, the frequency characteristics of sound are extracted. FFT can be defined as.

$$X(k) = \sum_{n=0}^{N-1} x(n) W_N^{nk} \; 0 \le k \le N - 1 \tag{6}$$

### 3.2 The Experiment to Prepare

In this experiment, a variety of machine noises were used to stimulate human brain EEG signals to generate wavebands for up to 10 min. The sound size was 90d, and the same decibel was mixed with different noises. The principal diagram is shown in Fig. 3.

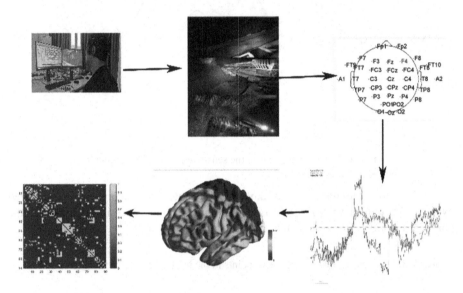

**Fig. 3.** Schematic diagram of EEG induced by machine noise stimulation

In EEG data acquisition, there are many interference factors, the EEG directly collected cannot be used for the analysis of its characteristics. To get a better EEG wave, the Curry7 software system was used in this experiment to process the wavebands, filter, adjust the baseline, remove the interference of EEG signal, and automatically remove the bad wavebands, mean value data, and save data. Finally, through the operation of the data code, using MATLAB software to export EEG image distribution and processing analysis.

## 4 Comparison of Experiments and Results

### 4.1 Changes in the Pattern and Characteristics of Electroencephalogram Induced

As can be seen from Fig. 4, when stimulated by noise for a long time, the EEG generated by the human brain will have different ups and downs, with dynamic peaks and troughs.

It can be seen that when the potential of each electrode is stimulated, the EEG signal of the human brain will fluctuate from −100 ms to 500 ms, and the variation range is slightly different.

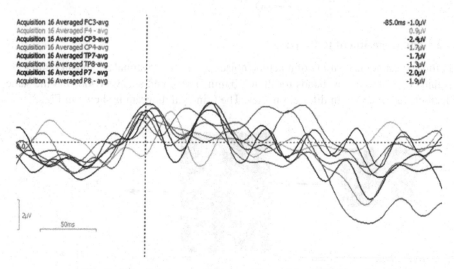

**Fig. 4.** Potential changes at the sensitive points of 40 channels

Table 3 shows the change of EEG amplitude generated by the human brain stimulated by noise. The change value of each point represents the value and minimum value of the point, X direction, Y direction, and Z direction respectively.

**Table 3.** Potential values of a sensitive points in the human brain induced by stimulation

| Point | X | Y | Z | min/UV |
|-------|-------|-------|--------|--------|
| F3 | 51.00 | −81.50 | 86.10 | −0.301 |
| F4 | −53.00 | −82.30 | 84.00 | 0.301 |
| CP3 | 69.00 | 21.00 | 112.30 | −0.365 |
| CP4 | −70.00 | 19.40 | 119.00 | −1.496 |
| TP7 | 84.00 | 22.20 | 42.90 | −3.793 |
| TP8 | −84.00 | 22.20 | 42.90 | −6.425 |
| P7 | 74.00 | 51.60 | 49.30 | −5.750 |
| P8 | −73.00 | 50.60 | 49.20 | −4.424 |

### 4.2  Sensitive Electrode Potential Change Curve

The 8 more sensitive electrode potentials, can be seen in Fig. 4. Based on F3 and F4, the changes of other potentials are compared and referred to. It can be seen that when the human brain is stimulated by noise, the characteristic rule of EEG signal obtained has to be reflected in different changes of stimulation degree, and the rule of change of 8 potentials is relatively stable.

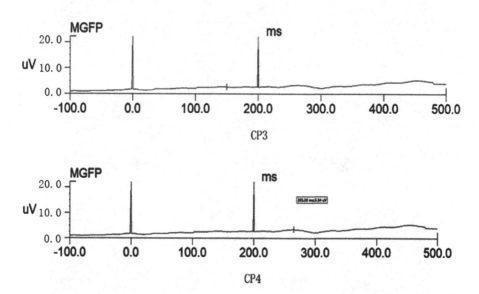

**Fig. 5.** Change curve of CP3 and CP4 potential value

According to the comparison between Fig. 4 and Fig. 5, EEG amplitude changes at about 1.0 UV when it is in a normal state; when it is stimulated by noise, the wave peak can reach 100.0 uvV to 500 ms, and the characteristic change of EEG signal changes at about 2.50 uV.

## 4.3  Three Dimensional Structure EEG

Figure 6 is the three-dimensional structure node diagram obtained by analyzing and processing the collected EEG signals generated by experimentally simulated stimulation and using Brain-Net Viewer data simulation [17–19].The potential difference produced by EEG signal is also different when stimulated by different intensities of noise, and the different color shades represent the potential drop of different nodes.

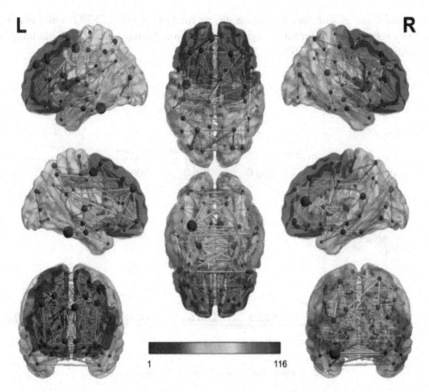

**Fig. 6.** Three-dimensional machine noise long time stimulation-induced EEG model construction (Color figure online)

## 5   Conclusion and Future Directions

The results show that the brain generates EEG signals under long-term noise stimulation, and these signals form an adaptive stationary state. Before hearing the noise, the EEG signals are almost 1.0 uV state, but after hearing the noise, the EEG floating value changes from peak to trough, which is close to 98.0 uV. However, after 10 min of stimulation, the EEG signal gradually subsided into a smooth state and returned to about 2.5 UV. It is a little higher than the previous peak, but still in a smooth and moderate state. The amplitude change of this state also shows an adaptive law of the human auditory system to noise.

**Acknowledgments.** This work is supported by The Chinese Society of Academic Degrees and Graduate Education under grant B-2017Y0002-170, Shaanxi Province Key Research and Development Projects under grant 2016GY-040, and Yulin City Science and Technology Project under grant CXY-2020-026.

# References

1. Zhong, W., Li, D., Zhang, J., et al.: Design of wearable dry electrode brain computer interface system. J. Xi'an Jiaotong Univ. **54**(06), 66–74 (2020)
2. Autthasan, P., et al.: A single-channel consumer-grade EEG device for brain–computer interface: enhancing detection of SSVEP and its amplitude modulation. IEEE Sens. J. **20**(6), 3366–3378 (2020). https://doi.org/10.1109/JSEN.2019.2958210
3. Lin, B.-S., Lin, B.-S., Yen, T.-H., Hsu, C.-C., Wang, Y.-C.: Design of wearable headset with steady state visually evoked potential-based brain computer interface. Micromachines **10**, 681 (2019). https://doi.org/10.3390/mi10100681
4. Zhang, D., Yao, L., Chen, K., Monaghan, J.: A convolutional recurrent attention model for subject-independent EEG signal analysis. IEEE Signal Process. Lett. **26**(5), 715–719 (2019). https://doi.org/10.1109/LSP.2019.2906824
5. Bajaj, V., Taran, S., Khare, S.K., Sengur, A.: Feature extraction method for classification of alertness and drowsiness states EEG signals. Appl. Acoust. **163**, 107224 (2020)
6. Wang, H., Jiang, C., Shi, L.: Saf. Sci. Technol. China **7**(12), 183–187 (2011)
7. Cheng, G., Chen, S., Qi, J., et al.: Analysis of the influence of underground noise on people's unsafe behavior. J. North China Univ. Sci. Technol. **11**(01), 89–93 (2014)
8. Li, J., Wang, Z., Qin, Y., Wang, Z., Luo, J.: The influence of different noise intensity of coal mine workers operation errors research. Chin. J. Saf. Sci. **31**(02), 179–184 (2021)
9. Rahman, M., Hossain, M., Hossain, M., Ahmmed, R.: Employing PCA and t-statistical approach for feature extraction and classification of emotion from multichannel EEG signal. Egypt. Inform. J. **21**(1), 23–35 (2020)
10. Khare, S.K., Bajaj, V.: Constrained-based tunable Q wavelet transforms for efficient decomposition of EEG signals. Appl. Acoust. **163**, 107234 (2020)
11. Yan, Q., Sheng, S., Zhou, J., Lin, Q.: Research on improved singular value decomposition denoising method. Electron. Opt. Control **25**(09), 22–25+41 (2018)
12. Zhao, X., Shao, Q., Ye, B., et al.: Matrix dimension considering frequency factor in singular value decomposition. J. Mech. Eng. **55**(16), 7–16 (2019)
13. Wei, Z.: Early fault diagnosis of rolling bearing based on VMD and singular difference spectrum. Mach. Des. Manuf. **43**(12), 230–234 (2019)
14. Venkatachalam, K., Devipriya, A., Maniraj, J., Sivaram, M., Ambikapathy, A., Amiri Iraj, S.: A novel method of motor imagery classification using EEG signal. Artif. Intell. Med. **103**, 101787 (2020)
15. Wang, M., Ma, C., Li, Z., Zhang, S., Li, Y.: Alertness estimation using connection parameters of the brain network. IEEE Trans. Intell. Transp. Syst. **2021**, 1–10 (2021). https://doi.org/10.1109/TITS.2021.3124372
16. Wang, M., Huang, Z., Li, Y., Dong, L., Pan, H.: Maximum weight multi-modal information fusion algorithm of electroencephalographs and face images for emotion recognition. Comput. Electr. Eng. **94**(107319), 1–13 (2021)
17. Zhang, J., Wang, G.: Emotion recognition based on EEG study. Comput. Appl. Res. **4**(11), 3306–3309 (2019). https://doi.org/10.19734/j.iSSN.1001-3695.2018.05.0295
18. Zhao, L., Bai, X.M., Hu, C.: Research on dimensionality reduction and denoising method of alcohol EEG signal. J. Changchun Univ. Sci. Technol. **42**(06), 78–82 (2019)
19. Runnova, A.E., Zhuravlev, M.O., Kiselev, A.R., et al.: A method of spatiotemporal analysis of brain electrical activity. Tech. Phys. Lett. **46**, 556–559 (2020). https://doi.org/10.1134/S1063785020060127
20. Lu, H., Zhang, M., Xu, X.: Deep fuzzy hashing network for efficient image retrieval. IEEE Trans. Fuzzy Syst. **29**, 166–176 (2020). https://doi.org/10.1109/TFUZZ.2020.2984991

21. Lu, H., Li, Y., Chen, M., et al.: Brain intelligence: go beyond artificial intelligence. Mob. Netw. Appl. **23**, 368–375 (2018)
22. Lu, H., Li, Y., Mu, S., et al.: Motor anomaly detection for unmanned aerial vehicles using reinforcement learning. IEEE Internet Things J. **5**(4), 2315–2322 (2018)
23. Lu, H., Qin, M., Zhang, F., et al.: RSCNN: a CNN-based method to enhance low-light remote-sensing images. Remote Sens. **13**, 62 (2020)
24. Lu, H., Zhang, Y., Li, Y., et al.: User-oriented virtual mobile network resource management for vehicle communications. IEEE Trans. Intell. Transp. Syst. **22**(6), 3521–3532 (2021)

# Cs-YOWO: Human Behavior Detection Model Based on Attention Mechanism

Zhenrong Deng[1], Zhihong Li[1], Da Li[2], Rui Yang[1], Rushi Lan[1(✉)], and Yuxu Xiong[1]

[1] School of Computer Science and Information Security, Guilin University of Electronic Technology, Guilin 541004, China
rslan2016@163.com

[2] Guangxi Construction Industry Mostly Lease Co., Ltd., Nanning 510600, China

**Abstract.** Human behavior detection plays an important role in traffic supervision, medical supervision and social security jurisdiction application requirements. The Cs-YOWO model is the new model put forward in this report, which is improved base on the original video behavior detection model YOWO. By adding Selective Kernel Network and Convolutional block attention module, this model solves the problem of insufficient image feature extraction by convolutional neural network in the original model, and imperfect fusion of spatial information and temporal information in the feature fusion part. On the UCF101-24 and JHMDB datasets test, the average accuracy of the frame level and video level was improved by 1.1% compared with the original model. Meanwhile, on the UCF101-24 dataset, the classification accuracy index was improved 1.9%. The experimental results show that the improved method can fully extract video information and enhance the model detection performance.

**Keywords:** Human behavior detection · Convolutional neural network · YOWO · Selective Kernel Network · Convolutional block attention module

## 1 Introduction

With the widespread use of intelligent monitoring equipment, as well as the development of various new media and short videos, a large number of pictures and video data are generated every day. The current monitoring platform can no longer cope with such a large amount of data and conduct a reasonable and effective analysis of the data. Therefore, it is very important to conduct automatic intelligent analysis of video content.

The existing behavior detection methods are mainly divided into sequential behavior detection and spatiotemporal behavior detection. Among the sequential behavior detection, the current main method is a detection method based on deep learning. For example, Shou et al. [1] were inspired by R-CNN and proposed an efficient neural network segmentation CNN (Segment-CNN, S-CNN) for temporal behavior detection. Xu et al. [2] were influenced by the object detection method Faster R-CNN [3] and developed the Region Convolutional 3D Network (R-C3D) to quickly detect videos of any length. These behavior detection networks can only be limited to processing each individual action, and the relationship between multiple actions cannot be used. However, a

S. Yang and H. Lu (Eds.): ISAIR 2022, CCIS 1700, pp. 343–356, 2022.
https://doi.org/10.1007/978-981-19-7946-0_29

meaningful action contains multiple candidate regions, and the relationship between the candidate regions plays an important role in the positioning of the action. In addition, in spatiotemporal behavior detection, such as Puscas et al. [4] adopt an unsupervised method, use DT algorithm to match and track candidate regions on multiple frames, and then use the optical flow information between two consecutive frames as a weight reference, and finally the frame-level action patterns are connected to form a spatiotemporal action pattern. This method does not make effective use of the timing characteristics of the action, and it is easy to cause the recognition results to be blurred.

In summary, in order to effectively improve the speed and accuracy of behavior detection, this article draws on the idea of the YOWO model [5] to improve the model and implement a new detection algorithm. The YOWO model can be divided into four main parts: 3D-CNN branch, 2D-CNN branch, channel fusion and attention mechanism, and bounding box regression part. The model first uses 3D CNN to extract the spatiotemporal features of the video, and obtains accurate spatial features through 2D CNN at the same time, and then uses the feature features in the channel to reasonably aggregate the features of different branches, and uses the fused features for frame-level recognition. Finally, use regression strategies to adjust the bounding box and classify actions to achieve behavior detection. In order to more accurately extract the 2D CNN branch feature information and better integrate the feature information of the two branches in the feature fusion part, this article proposes to embed SKNet (Selective Kernel Network) [6] into the 2D CNN network and implement the attention mechanism on the convolution kernel, so that the network can obtain different receptive field information. In addition, in the channel fusion part, this article uses the attention mechanism module CBAM (Convolutional Block Attention Module) [7] to replace the original attention mechanism based on the Gram matrix. This module combines the attention mechanism of space and channel, and simultaneously performs global average and global maximum mixed pooling on space and channel, which can extract more effective information.

The following part of this paper is divided into four parts. The first part expounds the development process of behavior recognition and attention mechanism related technologies, and the second part describes each module of the model proposed in this paper in detail. The third part is the experimental part, which uses the new model to conduct experiments and compares it with the existing new models. The Sect. 4 is a summary of the new model.

## 2  Related Work

### 2.1  Behaviour Recognition and Detection

Behavior recognition detection refers to judging the type of behavior action that occurs in the video, and accurately locating the start time of occurrence and the location of the subject. Early research on behavior recognition and detection mainly focused on the field of behavior recognition, and the attention to detection was relatively low. Behavior recognition is the basis of behavior detection, and the development of behavior recognition also promotes the development of recognition and detection [26–30].

Early behavior recognition based on deep learning can be roughly divided into: two-stream convolutional neural network model, spatiotemporal model and time series model. For example, Wang et al. [8] adopted a sparse time sampling strategy and a strategy based on video supervision to realize the recognition of long-term motion and greatly reduce the amount of data. Tran et al. [9] proposed the establishment of C3D (convolutional 3D) on the basis of 3D convolution, which uses 3D convolution and 3D pooling to extract spatiotemporal features in time and space. After training on a large-scale surveillance video data set, it can realize the learning of time sequence information.

The traditional time-series behavior detection method will generate candidate fragments in time-series, and construct local spatio-temporal feature expressions for each paragraph. Then determine the sample label according to the size of the tIoU (temporal IoU) corresponding to Ground Truth of these fragments, and finally realize behavior detection through training and classification. Yuan et al. [10] proposed a Pyramid of Score Distribution Feature (PSDF) based on the iDT feature to capture motion information. Then use PSDF in combination with the latest LSTM, and get the prediction of the behavior segment according to the output frame-level behavior category confidence score. Hou et al. [11] proposed a fully automatic sub-action discovery algorithm, which uses support vector machines to divide sub-actions, uses clustering to merge similar sub-actions, and then iteratively adjusts the action partitions. Finally, the detection results of the detector are calculated to realize real-time timing behavior detection.

## 2.2 Attention Mechanism

In recent years, attention models have been widely used in various types of deep learning tasks such as action recognition, image recognition, and natural language processing. The introduction of attention mechanisms into the network structure can not only improve the feature expression ability of the network model, but also can tell what to pay attention to in the network model, and it can also enhance the representation of a specific area.

The SE-net single-channel attention mechanism proposed by Momenta [12] Hu Jie's team uses the idea of attention mechanism. This mechanism firstly models the relationship between the feature maps and adaptively obtains the weights of the feature maps, and then updates the original data according to the weights. This approach increases the importance of useful features while reducing the importance of useless features. The SK-Net (Selective Kernel Networks) proposed by Xiang Li et al. based on the attention mechanism of the convolution kernel, allows the network to choose the appropriate convolution kernel according to the multiple scales of the input information. Sanghyun Woo et al. proposed the Convolutional Attention Module (CBAM). The mechanism combines the channel attention module and the spatial attention module, and at the same time performs the attention mechanism on the features in the channel and spatial dimensions. Then integrate the information obtained by the two modules to obtain more comprehensive attention information, and finally allocate computing resources more reasonably.

## 3 Action Recognition Model

### 3.1 Overview

The method model in this article is inherited from the YOWO model. The original model is divided into four main parts: 3D-CNN branch, 2D-CNN branch, channel fusion part and bounding box regression part. This article improves the channel fusion part and 2D-CNN branch part. First, the SKNet module is embedded in the 2D-CNN branch, which can generate receptive fields of different sizes according to targets of different scales. In addition, in the channel fusion part, the attention mechanism module (CBAM) of the convolution module is used to replace the original attention mechanism. The attention mechanism is applied to the two dimensions of channel and space at the same time, and the feature extraction ability of the network model is improved without significantly increasing the amount of calculation and the amount of parameters. The detection process is shown in Fig. 1.

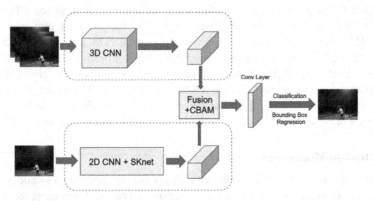

**Fig. 1.** Model architecture

During the detection process, the model will take the current frame of the video and the video sequence as input. The 2D CNN channel network combined with the SKNet attention mechanism will extract the appearance feature information of a single frame of the video from the current frame, and the 3D CNN network will obtain the spatiotemporal feature information of multiple frames from the video sequence. After the 2D CNN and 3D CNN branches, the two feature maps are merged by simply stacking the characteristics along the channel, and then the CBAM hybrid domain attention mechanism is used to perform feature fusion on the two branches of the channel and the space. Finally, a regression method is used to classify the action in the video and regress the bounding box.

### 3.2    Feature Extraction Network

The video feature extraction network in this article uses a dual-branch structure, in which the 3D-CNN branch is used to extract spatiotemporal features and obtain contextual information. The 3D-CNN architecture of the framework uses the ResNeXt-101 network [13]. The basic unit structure diagram of the ResNeXt network is shown in Fig. 2. The network is constructed by repetitive building blocks, using the idea of stacking in the VGG network model [14] and the idea of "split-transform-merge" in the Inception network model [15, 16]. But its scalability is relatively strong, which enhances the performance of the model without increasing the complexity and parameters of the model.

Compared with the traditional method of deepening and widening the network to improve the accuracy of the model, this model improves the effect by increasing the base number. The difficulty and cost of designing the network in this way are relatively low. In addition, the network also replaces the original ResNet's three-layer convolution block with a parallel stack of blocks of the same topology. This method will improve the accuracy of the model without significantly increasing the magnitude of the parameters.

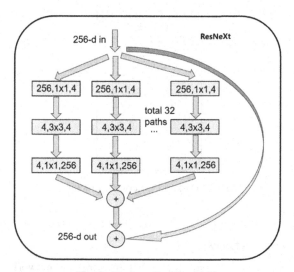

**Fig. 2.** Basic unit of ResNeXt

The 2D-CNN branch of the video feature extraction network is a single-frame feature extraction network used for two-dimensional feature extraction of key frames. The network uses Darknet-53 [17] as the basic structure of a single-frame feature extraction network. This network is a fully convolutional network and uses a large amount of residual network jump layer connections. In order to reduce the negative effects of pooling on gradients, the network does not use pooling operations, but down-sampling is achieved by adjusting the step size in the convolution operation.

The network structure of Darknet-53 is shown in Fig. 3, which contains a common convolution module and multiple residual network modules. The single-frame object recognition framework composed of 2D CNN branch and bounding box regression module has high recognition accuracy and good real-time performance. However, the algorithm has insufficient feature extraction, is not sensitive to small targets, is prone to miss and false recognitions, and also has deviations in the generated recognition result frame. In order to solve these problems and better extract the key frame information, this article adds the SKNet convolutional domain attention module after each module of the Darknet network. It does not directly assign weights to the feature map, but assigns weights to the convolution kernels, and in this way expresses the importance of different kernels. In this way, on the basis of neither changing the original network structure of Darknet-53 nor significantly increasing the amount of calculation, information on different receptive fields can be obtained, and the generalization ability of the network structure can be improved at the same time.

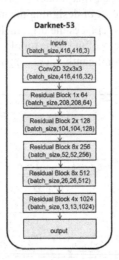

**Fig. 3.** Darknet-53 network structure

### 3.3 Selective Kernel Network

The SKNet embedded in the single-frame feature extraction network is a lightweight model that can be embedded and can be directly embedded in the network structure. When using this model, it will involve the choice of the number and size of the convolution kernel. Simply put, SKNet is equivalent to incorporating a soft attention mechanism into the network, so that the network can obtain information from different receptive fields and has better generalization capabilities. In the network structure using convolution operation, different sizes of perception fields have different effects on targets of different scales. The parameters are fixed while the training is completed, so that the weight of the convolution kernel will be the same. The proposed sknet mechanism uses a non-linear method to aggregate information from multiple convolution kernels, which can make different images have convolution kernels of different importance. Therefore, this article embeds the attention mechanism of the channel domain into the 2D CNN branch, which strengthens the extraction of useful information from the image and compresses the useless information.

The overall structure of SKNet is shown in Fig. 4, which is mainly divided into three operations: Split, Fuse and Select. The Split part is the process of convolving the original feature map using convolution kernels of different sizes. For any given feature map $X \in R^{H' \times W' \times C'}$, the conversion operation of the convolution kernel size of 3 and 5 is performed by default (it can also be divided into more Convolution operation branches with different convolution kernel sizes). The conversion operation at this stage consists of efficient grouping/depth convolution, batch normalization and ReLU functions.

The Fuse part is the part that calculates the weight of each convolution kernel. The basic idea is to use gates to control the information flows from multiple branches, which carry information of different scales to the neurons in the next layer. First, sum the two parts of the feature map by element:

$$U = \tilde{U} + \hat{U} \tag{1}$$

Then, using the global average pooling to obtain the global information. For the global average pooling operation, the calculation of this part of the operation can be expressed as:

$$s_c = F_{gp}(U_c) = \frac{1}{H \times W} \sum_{i=1}^{H} \sum_{j=1}^{W} U_c(i, j) \tag{2}$$

In addition, in order to improve accuracy and adaptability, a fully connected layer is added, which can reduce the dimensionality for better efficiency:

$$z = F_{fc}(s) = \delta(\beta(WS)) \tag{3}$$

where $\delta$ is the ReLU function, $\beta$ represents batch standardization, and the dimension of z is the number of convolution kernels. In addition, we also studied the influence of d on model efficiency:

$$d = \max\left(\frac{C}{r}, L\right) \tag{4}$$

where L represents the minimum value of d, and d represents the feature dimension after full connection.

The Select part is the process of calculating new feature maps based on convolution kernels with different weights. The cross-channel soft attention mechanism is used to adaptively select different spatial scales of information, and the spatial scale is guided by the compact feature descriptor z. Specifically, the softmax operator is applied to channel-wise numbers:

$$a_c = \frac{e^{A_c z}}{e^{A_c z} + e^{B_c z}}, \quad b_c = \frac{e^{B_c z}}{e^{A_c z} + e^{B_c z}} \tag{5}$$

Among $A, B \in R^{C \times d}$, a and b represent the soft attention vector of $\tilde{U}$ and $\hat{U}$, $A_c \in R^{1 \times d}$ is the c-th row of A, and $a_c$ is the c-th element of a. In the case of two branches, matrix B is redundant due to $a_c + b_c = 1$. The final feature map V is obtained through the attention weights of various convolution kernels:

$$V_c = a_c \cdot \tilde{U}_c + b_c \cdot \hat{U}_c, \quad a_c + b_c = 1 \tag{6}$$

Among $V = [V_1, V_2 \ldots, V_c]$, $V_c \in R^{H \times W}$ here is a formula for the double-branch case, and the case with more branches can be easily inferred by extension.

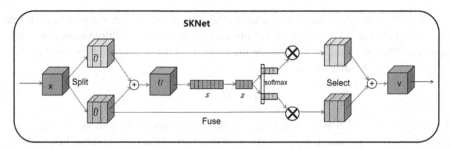

**Fig. 4.** SKNet network structure

### 3.4  Feature Fusion

After passing through the above-mentioned feature extraction network, the two branches will output feature information with the same shape, and only need to connect the two feature maps stacked along the channel. The original YOWO model is based on the channel attention of the Gram matrix to establish the correlation between the features. This article proposes to replace it with the convolutional block attention module of the mixed domain. Convolutional Block Attention Module (CBAM), which is an attention mechanism module used for feedforward convolutional neural networks to combine spatial and channel information. It connects the channel attention module and the spatial attention module serially, compared to the channel attention mechanism only pays attention to the attention information on the channel, and it can also establish associations between the information of the feature map pixels, so as to obtain more comprehensive attention information. For most of the current mainstream networks, it can be directly embedded, which can improve the feature extraction capabilities of the network model without significantly increasing the amount of calculations and parameters.

The overall structure of the convolutional block attention module (CBAM) is shown in Fig. 5. It can be seen that the output result of the convolutional layer will first pass through a channel attention module. After the channel attention is completed, it will pass through again on this basis. A spatial attention module, and finally get the result.

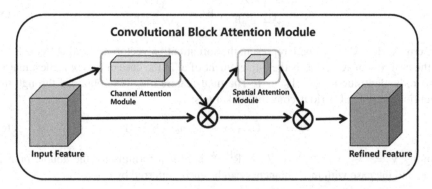

**Fig. 5.** Model of attention mechanism

The structure of the channel attention module is shown in Fig. 6. The channel attention module will first compress the feature map in the spatial dimension to obtain a one-dimensional vector, and then perform subsequent operations. The channel attention mechanism can be expressed as:

$$M_c(F) = \sigma(MLP(AvgPool(F)) + MLP(MaxPool(F)))$$
$$= \sigma\left(W_1\left(W_0\left(F_{avg}^c\right)\right) + W_1\left(W_0\left(F_{max}^c\right)\right)\right) \qquad (7)$$

The execution process of the channel attention module: After the feature map is input, the global maximum pooling and global average pooling are performed based on the width and height, and then the multi-layer perceptron (MLP) is passed through. The feature results output by the MLP layer will be added based on the corresponding elements one by one, and then activated by the sigmoid activation function to generate the output feature map of the channel attention module. The output feature map also performs element-wise multiplication with the input feature map to generate the input features required by the spatial attention module.

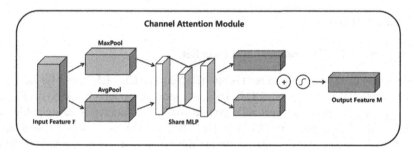

**Fig. 6.** Channel attention Module

Another part of the spatial attention module structure is shown in Fig. 7. Different from the channel attention mechanism, the spatial attention mainly focuses on which part is the information part, which is the supplement after the channel attention. This module applies maximum pooling and average pooling operations to the channel axis, and links them to generate an effective feature map. After this process, important information areas can be effectively displayed. The spatial attention mechanism module can be expressed as:

$$M_s(F) = \sigma\left(f^{7 \times 7}\left(\left[AvgPool(F); MaxPool(F)\right]\right)\right)$$
$$= \sigma\left(f^{7 \times 7}\left(\left[F_{avg}^s; F_{max}^s\right]\right)\right) \qquad (8)$$

The execution process of the spatial attention module: First, take the output feature map of the channel attention module as the input feature map of this module, and perform channel-based global maximum pooling and global average pooling. After the two pools, the output results are connected, and then a convolution operation is performed to reduce the dimensionality to a channel. Then the spatial attention feature will be generated through the sigmoid activation function, and finally the feature and the input feature of the module will be multiplied to obtain the final generated feature.

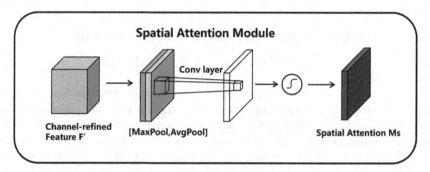

**Fig. 7.** Spatial attention mechanism

## 4  Experiments

### 4.1  Experimental Environment and Data Set

The processor used in this experiment is Intel(R) Xeon(R) CPU E5-2698 v4 @ 2.20 GHz, the GPU is NVIDIA Tesla P100-SXM2 16 G, the network model is based on the Pytorch framework, and the operating system is Ubuntu 16.04. The data sets used are public data sets UCF101-24 [18] and JHMDB [19]. UCF101-24 includes 24 action categories, a total of 3207 videos, and provides corresponding time and space annotations. There may be multiple action instances in the video that belong to the same type of label, but they have different temporal and spatial boundaries. The J-HMDB-21 data set contains 21 categories of daily life actions, a total of 960 short videos, each of which has been well cropped, and there is an action instance in all frames.

### 4.2  Evaluation Criteria

This article uses mAP (mean Average Precision) to evaluate the spatial and temporal positioning performance of the model at the frame level and the video level respectively. mAP is a comprehensive evaluation index of model recognition ability, and the calculation formula of Precision is:

$$\text{Precision} = \frac{\text{TP}}{\text{TP} + \text{FP}} \tag{9}$$

Among them, TP is the number of samples detected as positive in the model, and FP is the number of negative samples detected as positive in the model. The IoU threshold of frame-mAP (frame-mAP) is set to 0.5, and three different thresholds are set for video-mAP (video-mAP) in different data sets.

## 4.3 Experimental Results

**Ablation Experiment**
In order to verify the effects of adding SKNet and CBAM to the YOWO model, this article tests the frame-mAP on the UCF101-24 data set. At the same time, the experiment also studies the positioning and classification effects of the model. For positioning, the recall rate is calculated, that is, the percentage of the number of correct positioning actions to the number of detected areas for all actions is calculated. For classification, calculate its accuracy, that is, the proportion of the number of correct classifications to the total number of recognitions.

Table 1 compares the recognition performance of adding different module combinations in YOWO. The results show that adding the SKNet module and the CBAM module separately can improve the performance of frame-mAP and classification accuracy, which effectively improves the recognition accuracy. When the two modules are embedded in the model at the same time, the improvement of the effect is the most obviously, it shows that the embedding of the two attention mechanisms effectively improves the model's extraction of feature information.

**Table 1.** Performance comparison on UCF101-24 after adding different module combinations (%)

| Model structure | Frame-mAP | Classification accuracy | Location recall rate |
|---|---|---|---|
| YOWO | 87.2 | 94.1 | 94.0 |
| YOWO + SKNet | 88.0 | 95.3 | 92.9 |
| YOWO + CBAM | 87.5 | 94.9 | 93.6 |
| YOWO + SKNet + CBAM | 88.3 | 96.0 | 92.7 |

**Compared with Other Methods**
Table 2 compares this method with other methods on the UCF101-24 data set in frame-mAP and video-mAP. The IoU threshold of video-mAP is set to 0.1, 0.2 and 0.5. The Frame-mAP result of the original model YOWO is 87.2%, while the recognition result of the method in this article is improved by 1.1%, and the effect is improved under all thresholds of video-mAP. Literature [20–25] is an article published in recent years. The experimental results of these recognition models under the same data set are shown in the table. After comparison, it can be found that the model proposed in this article has higher results on multiple indicators. Literature [25] is the latest SOTA method in 2020. The method in this article is significantly better than it in frame-mAP, which is 10.3% higher, which proves that the performance of this article is superior after the improvement of the YOWO model.

**Table 2.** Performance comparison of different methods on UCF101-24

| Method | Frame-mAP | Video-mAP | | |
|---|---|---|---|---|
| | | 0.1 | 0.2 | 0.5 |
| Kalogeiton et al. [20] | 69.5 | – | 76.5 | 49.2 |
| STEP [21] | 75.0 | 83.1 | 76.6 | – |
| Song et al. [22] | 72.1 | – | 77.5 | 52.9 |
| ACT [20] | 69.5 | – | 77.2 | 51.4 |
| PENG et al. [23] | 65.7 | 50.4 | 42.3 | – |
| MPS [24] | – | 82.4 | 72.9 | 41.4 |
| MOC [25] | 78.0 | – | **82.8** | **53.8** |
| YOWO | 87.2 | 82.5 | 75.8 | 48.8 |
| YOWO + SKNet + CBAM | **88.3** | **83.8** | 77.0 | 49.3 |

Table 3 compares this article with other methods on the JHMDB data set. It also compares the two indicators of frame-mAP and video-mAP. The IoU thresholds of video-mAP are set to 0.2, 0.5 and 0.75. The table contains some action recognition methods published in recent years. After comparison, it can be found that the method in this article is higher than other methods in many indicators, which further illustrates the effectiveness of the improved method in this article.

**Table 3.** Performance comparison of different methods on JHMBD

| Method | Frame-mAP | Video-mAP | | |
|---|---|---|---|---|
| | | 0.2 | 0.5 | 0.75 |
| Kalogeiton et al | 65.7 | 74.2 | 73.7 | 52.1 |
| Peng et al. [23] | 58.5 | 74.3 | 73.1 | – |
| Song et al | 65.5 | 74.1 | 73.4 | 52.5 |
| ACT | 65.7 | 74.2 | 73.7 | 52.1 |
| MOC | 70.8 | 77.3 | 77.2 | **71.7** |
| YOWO | 72.7 | 84.1 | 82.3 | 55.9 |
| YOWO + SKNet + CBAM | **73.6** | **84.9** | **83.0** | 56.2 |

# 5  Conclusion

This article improves the single-stage target detection framework YOWO. The 2D-CNN branch single-frame feature information extraction part is embedded in the SKNet module, and the problem of the Darknet network's easy to miss and misdetect small targets by adjusting the size of the convolution kernel is solved. At the same time, in the feature fusion part, the original feature fusion module based on channel attention is replaced with a convolutional attention module. This module summarizes the attention information of space and channel, and obtains more comprehensive and reliable attention information. This article is evaluated on two data sets, UCF101-24 and JHMBD. The experimental results show that the improved method in this article has higher accuracy than the original model, and the detection performance is improved. However, there is still room for improvement in this model. How to make the network continue to improve the detection accuracy without reducing the detection speed is the next problem to be solved.

**Acknowledgment.** This work was supported by the Guangxi key R & D plan (GuiKe AB22035052), the science and technology plan project of Qingxiu District of Nanning City (No. 2020012), and Guangxi Colleges and the Universities Key Laboratory of Intelligent Processing of Computer Images and Graphics (No. GIIP2003).

# References

1. Shou, Z., Wang, D., Chang, S.F.: Temporal action localization in untrimmed videos via multi-stage CNNs. In: Proceedings of the IEEE Conference on Computer Vision and Pattern Recognition, pp. 1049–1058. IEEE, Las Vegas (2016)
2. Xu, H., Das, A., Saenko, K.: R-C3D: region convolutional 3D network for temporal activity detection. In: 2017 IEEE International Conference on Computer Vision (ICCV), p. 17453302. IEEE, Venice (2017)
3. Ren, S., He, K., Girshick, R., et al.: Faster R-CNN: towards real-time object detection with region proposal networks. In: Advances in Neural Information Processing Systems, pp. 91–99. IEEE, Waikoloa (2015)
4. Puscas, M.M., Sangineto, E., Culibrk, D., et al.: Unsupervised tube extraction using transductive learning and dense trajectories. Comput. Graph. **38**(1), 300–309 (2015)
5. Kopuklu, O., Wei, X.Y., Rigoll, G.: You only watch once: a unified CNN architecture for real-time spatiotemporal action localization. arXiv preprint arXiv:1911.06644 (2020)
6. Li, X., Wang, W., Hu, X., et al.: Selective kernel networks. In: IEEE/CVF Conference on Computer Vision and Pattern Recognition (CVPR), Long Beach, CA, USA, pp. 510–519 (2019)
7. Woo, S., Park, J., Lee, J.Y., et al.: CBAM: convolutional block attention module. arXiv:1807. 06521v2 (2018)
8. Tong, M., Wang, H., Tian, W., Yang, S.: Action recognition new framework with robust 3D-TCCHOGAC and 3D-HOOFGAC. Multimed. Tools Appl. **76**(2), 3011–3030 (2017)
9. Tran, D., Bourdev, L., Fergus, R., et al.: Learning spatiotemporal features with 3D convolutional networks. IEEE Access **7**, 19087846 (2015)
10. Yuan, J., Ni, B., Yang, X., et al.: Temporal action localization with pyramid of score distribution features. In: IEEE Conference on Computer Vision and Pattern, pp. 3093–3102. IEEE, Seoul (2016)
11. Hou, R., Sukthankar, R., Shah, M.: Real-time temporal action localization in untrimmed videos by sub-action discovery. In: British Machine Vision Conference. IEEE, Brighton (2017)

12. Hu, J., Shen, L., Sun, G.: Squeeze-and-excitation networks. In: 2018 IEEE/CVF Conference on Computer Vision and Pattern Recognition, pp. 7132–7141 (2018)

13. Hara, K., Kataoka, H., Satoh Y.: Can spatiotemporal 3D CNNs retrace the history of 2D CNNs and image net. In: 2018 IEEE Conference on Computer Vision and Pattern Recognition, pp. 6546–6555. IEEE Computer Society Press, Washington, DC (2018)

14. Simonyan, K., Zisserman, A.: Very deep convolutional networks for large-scale image recognition. In: ICLR (2015)

15. Szegedy, C., et al.: Going deeper with convolutions. In: CVPR (2015)

16. Szegedy, C., Vanhoucke, V., Ioffe, S., Shlens, J., Wojna, Z.: Rethinking the inception architecture for computer vision. In: CVPR (2016)

17. Redmon, J., Farhadi, A.: YOLOv3: an incremental improvement. In: 2018 IEEE Conference on Computer Vision and Pattern Recognition, pp. 89–95. IEEE Computer Society Press, Washington, DC (2018)

18. Soomro, K., Zamir, A.R., Shah, M.: UCF101: a dataset of 101 human actions classes from videos in the wild. arXiv preprint arXiv:1212.0402 (2019)

19. Kuehne, H., Jhuang, H., Garrote, E., Poggio, T., Serre, T.: HMDB: a large video database for human motion recognition. In: 2011 International Conference on Computer Vision, pp. 2556–2563. IEEE (2011)

20. Kalogeiton, V., Weinzaepfel, P., Ferrari, V., Schmid, C.: Action tubelet detector for spatio-temporal action localization. In: Proceedings of the IEEE International Conference on Computer Vision, pp. 4405–4413 (2017)

21. Yang, X., Yang, X., Liu, M.Y., Xiao, F., Davis, L.S., Kautz, J.: STEP: spatio-temporal progressive learning for video action detection. In: Proceedings of the IEEE Conference on Computer Vision and Pattern Recognition, pp. 264–272 (2019)

22. Song, L., Zhang, S., Yu, G., Sun, H.: TACNet: transition-aware context network for spatio-temporal action detection. In: Proceedings of the IEEE Conference on Computer Vision and Pattern Recognition, pp. 11987–11995 (2019)

23. Peng, X., Schmid, C.: Multi-region two-stream R-CNN for action detection. In: Leibe, B., Matas, J., Sebe, N., Welling, M. (eds.) ECCV 2016. LNCS, vol. 9908, pp. 744–759. Springer, Cham (2016). https://doi.org/10.1007/978-3-319-46493-0_45

24. Alwando, E.H.P., Chen, Y.-T., Fang, W.-H.: CNN-based multiple path search for action tube detection in videos. IEEE Trans. Circ. Syst. Video Technol. **30**, 104–116 (2018)

25. Li, Y., Wang, Z., Wang, L., Wu, G.: Actions as moving points. In: Vedaldi, A., Bischof, H., Brox, T., Frahm, J.-M. (eds.) ECCV 2020. LNCS, vol. 12361, pp. 68–84. Springer, Cham (2020). https://doi.org/10.1007/978-3-030-58517-4_5

26. Lu, H., Yang, R., Deng, Z., Zhang, Y., Gao, G., Lan, R.: Chinese image captioning via fuzzy attention-based DenseNet-BiLSTM. ACM Trans. Multimed. Comput. Commun. Appl. **17**(1s), 1–18 (2021)

27. Lu, H., Zhang, Y., Li, Y., Jiang, C., Abbas, H.: User-oriented virtual mobile network resource management for vehicle communications. IEEE Trans. Intell. Transp. Syst. **22**, 3521–3532 (2020). https://doi.org/10.1109/TITS.2020.2991766

28. Lu, H., Qin, M., Zhang, F., et al.: RSCNN: a CNN-based method to enhance low-light remote-sensing images. Remote Sens. **13**, 62 (2020)

29. Lu, H., Zhang, M., Xu, X.: Deep fuzzy hashing network for efficient image retrieval. IEEE Trans. Fuzzy Syst. **29**, 166–176 (2020). https://doi.org/10.1109/TFUZZ.2020.2984991

30. Li, Y., Yang, S., Zheng, Y., Lu, H.: Improved point-voxel region convolutional neural network: 3D object detectors for autonomous driving. IEEE Trans. Intell. Transp. Syst. **23**, 9311–9317 (2021)

# Attention-Based Dynamic Graph CNN for Point Cloud Classification

Junfei Wang[1,2,4], Hui Xiong[1,2,4], Yanli Gong[1,2,4], Xianfeng Wu[1,2,3,4], Shun Wang[1,2,4], Qian Jia[2], and Zhongyuan Lai[1,2,3,4(✉)]

[1] State Key Laboratory of Precision Blasting, Jianghan University, Wuhan 430056, People's Republic of China
laizhy@jhun.edu.cn
[2] School of Artificial Intelligence, Jianghan University, Wuhan 430056, People's Republic of China
[3] Bingling Honorary School, Jianghan University, Wuhan 430056, People's Republic of China
[4] Institute for Interdisciplinary Research, Jianghan University, Wuhan 430056, People's Republic of China

**Abstract.** In this paper, we propose an attention-based dynamic graph CNN method for point cloud classification. We introduce an efficient channel attention module into each edge convolution block of dynamic graph CNN (DGCNN) to obtain more discriminative and stable features. Our experimental results show that, compared with DGCNN, our method improves not only the classification accuracy but also the stability.

**Keywords:** Point cloud classification · Dynamic graph CNN · Edge convolution · Efficient channel attention

## 1 Introduction

Object classification is one of the classic problems in computer vision and pattern recognition. Compared with image, point cloud contains richer spatial information and is hardly affected by illumination changes. Therefore, it is one of the ideal data types for object classification. However, due to its intrinsic properties of disorder, non-structure and non-uniform distribution, it is very challenging to design a deep neural network that directly uses point clouds as inputs.

Generally, the classification methods that directly use point clouds as inputs can be divided into three categories. The first category is the global feature-based methods. The PointNet method [1] is one of the most representative methods in this category. In this method, the feature of each point in the point cloud are generated only by the coordinates or the feature of that point itself, while the interaction relationship between points is not considered. Consequently, the classification accuracy is not high. The second category is the local feature-based methods. The PointNet++ method [2] is one of the most representative methods in this category. In this method, several centroid points are obtained through the farthest point sampling, and then their corresponding local regions

© The Author(s), under exclusive license to Springer Nature Singapore Pte Ltd. 2022
S. Yang and H. Lu (Eds.): ISAIR 2022, CCIS 1700, pp. 357–365, 2022.
https://doi.org/10.1007/978-981-19-7946-0_30

and local features are obtained through the $k$-nearest neighbor algorithm and the vanilla PointNet method. Finally, these local features are concatenated for classification. Compared with the global-based methods, although its classification accuracy is improved, this classification accuracy may be affected by the partial absence or the distribution changes. The third category is the neighborhood-based methods. The dynamic graph CNN (DGCNN) method [3] is one of the most representative methods in this category. This method forms the feature of each point together with the feature of its $k$-nearest neighbors, making full use of the neighbor properties of each point in the point cloud. Therefore, the classification accuracy has been further improved. However, since this method involves the calculation of the neighborhood, the classification accuracy may be affected by the change in the density distribution of the point cloud.

In practical applications such as autonomous driving [20–23], point clouds are obtained by the LiDAR. For the same type of objects, such as vehicles and pedestrians, the closer the object is to the LiDAR, the denser its point cloud is, and vice versa. Therefore, a good point cloud classification method requires not only a high classification accuracy, but also the stability in the case of point cloud density changes.

It has been found that the attention mechanism developed by human vision has the characteristics of natural focus on important regions. With the help of the attention mechanism, the extracted features are more discriminative and stable [4]. Therefore, we introduce the attention mechanism into the DGCNN classification framework and propose an attention-based DGCNN (A-DGCNN) method for point cloud classification. The experimental results show that compared with DGCNN, our method performs better in terms of not only classification accuracy but also stability.

## 2   Our Method

In this section, we first revisit DGCNN [3], then introduce the efficient channel attention (ECA) module [5], and finally show how to embed the ECA module in DGCNN.

### 2.1   Revisiting DGCNN

DGCNN consists of four edge convolution (EdgeConv) blocks, a multi-layer perceptron (MLP), a max-pooling layer and a fully connected (FC) network, as shown in Fig. 1(a). In the process of point cloud classification, the point cloud coordinates matrix of size $n \times 3$ is firstly put into the four cascaded EdgeConv blocks to obtain features of different levels, where $n$ is the number of points in the point cloud. And then these features are cascaded together and put into the MLP to obtain the final feature of each point. After that, these final features are put into the max-pooling layer to obtain the feature of the point cloud. Finally, this feature of the point cloud is pit into the FC network to obtain a $s$-dimensional classification vector.

The core of the above classification network is the EdgeConv block, which maps the input feature matrix of size $n \times D$ into the output feature matrix of size $n \times C$, as shown in Fig. 1(b). It consists of a $k$-nearest neighbor ($k$NN) block, a graph CNN (GCNN) block, and a max-pooling layer. In this mapping process, the input feature matrix of size $n \times D$ is first put into the $k$NN block to construct a $k$NN graph of each point. And then each $k$NN graph is put into the GCNN block to obtain the $C$-dimensional features of $k$ neighbor edges. Finally, theses $k$ features are put into the max-pooling layer to obtain the $C$-dimensional feature of each point.

From the above workflow, we can see that the neighbors of each point in the point cloud dynamically changes in spatial or different feature spaces. This is the origin of the name of dynamic graph CNN. This method considers the point-to-point distance not only in the spatial space but also in in the feature space, so it can capture not only geometrical but also semantical structures in point clouds and thus have a high classification accuracy. However, this method includes the calculation of neighbors, so its classification accuracy is inevitably affected by the density changes of point clouds.

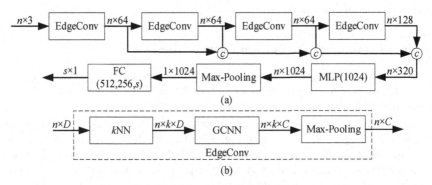

(a)

(b)

**Fig. 1.** (a) Block diagram of DGCNN. (b) EdgeConv block.

## 2.2 Efficient Channel Attention (ECA) Module

As mentioned earlier, attention has the characteristics of natural focus on important regions, which can enhance the discrimination and the stability of the extracted features [4]. There are many attention mechanisms, such as squeeze-and-excitation networks (SENet) [6], convolutional block attention module (CBAM) [7], global correlation network (GCNet) [8], and efficient channel attention (ECA) module [5]. Among them, ECA module can achieve very competitive performance at little additional computational cost. Therefore, we choose ECA module. Next, we briefly introduce the ECA module.

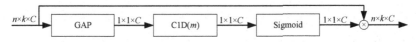

**Fig. 2.** ECA module.

The ECA module consists of a global average pooling (GAP) layer, a one-dimensional convolutional (C1D) layer, and a sigmoid layer, as shown in Fig. 2. In the process of performance boost, the neighborhood feature matrix of size $n \times k \times C$ is firstly put into the GAP layer to obtain a $C$-dimensional aggregated feature vector, where $n$ is the number of points in the point cloud, $k$ is the number of neighbors of each point, and $C$ is the number of channels. And then this aggregated feature is put into the C1D layer of size $m$ and the sigmoid layer to generate a $C$-dimensional channel weight vector, where $m$ is adaptively determined by $C$. Finally, all the features in the input neighborhood feature matrix are weighted by the channel weight vector, resulting in a better performed neighborhood feature matrix of size $n \times k \times C$.

Since the ECA module does not involve the channel dimensionality reduction, it avoids the loss produced by the mapping from channel to weight, and guarantees the performance boost. Since the ECA module make use of cross-channel interaction, it reduces the affection caused by separate channel variation, and improve the feature stability. Meanwhile, the above computation only involves C1D operation, and thus it has extremely high efficiency.

### 2.3  Edge Convolution with Efficient Channel Attention

In order to effectively improve the performance at different feature extraction stages, we effectively combine the EdgeConv block in DGCNN with the ECA module to form an edge convolution with efficient channel attention (ECECA) module.

The ECECA module consists of a $k$NN module, a GCNN module, an ECA module, and a max-pooling layer, as shown in Fig. 3(b). Its workflow is as follows. The input feature matrix of size $n \times D$ is firstly put into the $k$NN module to obtain a neighborhood feature matrix of size $n \times k \times D$. And then this neighborhood feature matrix is put into the GCNN module to obtain a neighborhood feature matrix of size $n \times k \times C$. After that, this neighborhood feature matrix is put into the ECA module to obtain a performance enhanced neighborhood feature matrix. Finally, this neighborhood feature matrix of size $n \times k \times C$ is put into the max-pooling layer to obtain a feature matrix of size $n \times C$.

Since the ECECA module further performs local cross-channel interaction based on the original use of spatial and feature similarity between points, it can improve the classification accuracy as well as the stability.

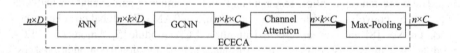

**Fig. 3.**  ECECA module.

## 3  Experiments

In this section, we conduct a series of experiments to verify that our method can improve the classification accuracy while at the same time improving the stability of DGCNN. Firstly, we give the comparison results of our method and the existing methods in terms of classification accuracy. Then we give those in terms of stability. Finally, we give the results of the ablation experiment.

## 3.1  Classification Accuracy Comparison

In order to verify that our method can effectively improve the classification accuracy of DGCNN, we choose ModelNet40 [9] as the dataset. This dataset is split into two parts. One consists 9843 models for training and the other consists 2468 models for testing. For each model, we randomly sample 1024 points. Table 1 shows the overall accuracy and the mean class accuracy of our method and the existing methods. It can be seen that the overall accuracy of our method is 93.8%, which brings 1.6% performance gain compared with DGCNN. Meanwhile, compared with the other methods, our method is second only to the latest PointMLP method [19] in terms of classification accuracy, which further reveals the advantages of our method in classification accuracy.

**Table 1.**  Classification accuracy comparison results on the ModelNet40 dataset. Overall accuracy (OA). Mean class accuracy (MA).

| Models | Year | OA | MA | Frame |
|---|---|---|---|---|
| PointNet [1] | 2017 | 89.2 | 86.2 | PyTorch |
| PointNet++ [2] | 2017 | 90.7 | – | PyTorch |
| KCNet [10] | 2018 | 91.0 | – | PyTorch |
| SRN [11] | 2018 | 91.5 | – | PyTorch |
| DGCNN [3] | 2019 | 92.2 | 90.2 | PyTorch |
| PointWeb [12] | 2019 | 92.3 | 89.4 | PyTorch |
| Point ASNL [13] | 2020 | 92.9 | – | TensorFlow |
| Grid-GCN [14] | 2020 | 93.1 | 91.2 | PyTorch |
| PCT [15] | 2021 | 93.2 | – | Jittor |
| GDANet [16] | 2021 | 93.4 | 90.4 | PyTorch |
| PAConv [17] | 2021 | 93.6 | – | PyTorch |
| PointTransformer [18] | 2021 | 93.7 | 90.9 | PyTorch |
| PointMLP [19] | 2022 | 94.5 | 91.4 | PyTorch |
| Ours | 2022 | 93.8 | 91.3 | PyTorch |

## 3.2  Stability Comparison

In order to verify that our method can ensure the stability against the change of the number of points, we select two representative methods DGCNN [3] and GDANet [17] for our comparison. To this end, we randomly down-sample 1024, 896, 768, 640, 512, 384, 256 points from each testing model. Figure 4 shows some down-sampling results. It can be seen that as the number of points decreases, the resulting point cloud becomes sparser and sparser, and some parts even begin to disappear. Then the above down-sampled points are put into the trained model for testing. The testing results are shown in Fig. 5. It can be seen that when the number of points decreases from 1024 to 768, the overall accuracy of the above three methods is not much different. When the number of points decreases from 768 to 384, the performance of DGCNN decreases rapidly compared with the other two methods. When the number of points decreases from 384 to 256, the performance of GDANet decreases more rapidly than that of our method. In particular, when the number of points is 256, the classification accuracy of our method is 65.3%, which is at least 10% higher than those of DGCNN and GDANet. This validates that compared with the two counterparts, our method is more stable against the changes of the number of points, especially when the number of points is significantly reduced.

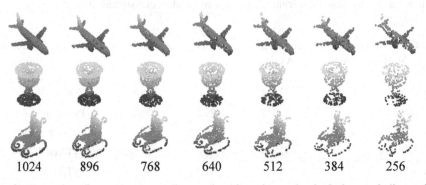

**Fig. 4.** Illustration of some down-sampling results, where the number in the bottom indicates the number of down-sampled points.

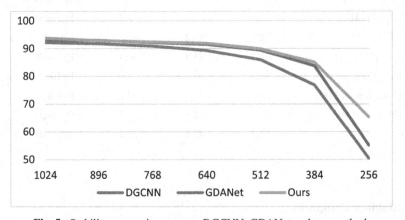

**Fig. 5.** Stability comparison among DGCNN, GDANet and our method.

**Table 2.** Results of ablation experiments for different number of points.

| Model | 1024 | 896 | 768 | 640 | 512 | 384 | 256 |
|---|---|---|---|---|---|---|---|
| DGCNN | 92.2 | 91.8 | 90.9 | 89.3 | 85.9 | 76.8 | 50.4 |
| DGCNN with one ECA | 93.1 | 92.5 | 91.9 | 91.1 | 89.1 | 82.2 | 57.1 |
| DGCNN with two ECA | 93.3 | 92.5 | 92.0 | 91.4 | 89.3 | 82.6 | 60.3 |
| DGCNN with three ECA | 93.5 | 92.9 | 92.1 | 91.5 | 89.5 | 83.7 | 62.1 |
| Our method | 93.8 | 92.9 | 92.4 | 91.9 | 89.9 | 85.0 | 65.3 |

### 3.3  Ablation Study

Table 2 shows the contribution of different number of embedded ECA module to the overall accuracy. It can be seen that when the number of points is 1024, embedding one, two, three and four ECA modules brings 0.9%, 1.1%, 1.3%, and 1.6% performance gain compared with DGCNN. When the number of points drops to 256, embedding one, two, three and four ECA modules brings 6.7%, 9.9%, 11.7%, and 14.9% performance gain compared with DGCNN. This indicates that not only the performance can be steadily improved as the number of embedded ECA modules increases, but also the performance gain can be steadily enhanced as the number of points decreases, which fully demonstrates the clear contributions of ECA modules to the overall performance.

## 4  Conclusion

In this paper, we propose a point cloud classification method based on channel attention. The main idea is to introduce efficient channel attention modules into the EdgeConv blocks of DGCNN. Experimental results show that compared with DGCNN, our method not only improves the classification accuracy, but also improves the stability.

**Acknowledgment.** This work was supported by the State Key Laboratory of Precision Blasting, Jianghan University (No. PBSKL2022201), the Scientific Research Program of Jianghan University (No. 2021yb052), the Graduate Innovation Fund of the Jianghan University, the National College Students' Innovation and Entrepreneurship Training Program of China (Grant No. S202211072042), and the Undergraduate Research Projects of the Jianghan University (Grant Nos. 2021Bczd006, 2021Bczd007, and 2022zd096).

## References

1. Qi, C.R., Su, H., Mo, K., et al.: PointNet: deep learning on point sets for 3D classification and segmentation. In: Proceedings of the IEEE/CVF Conference on Computer Vision and Pattern Recognition (CVPR), Honolulu, USA, pp. 652–660 (2017)
2. Qi, C.R., Yi, L., Su, H., et al.: Pointnet++: deep hierarchical feature learning on point sets in a metric space. In: Advances in Neural Information Processing Systems (NIPS), Long Beach, USA (2017)

3. Wang, Y., Sun, Y., Liu, Z., et al.: Dynamic Graph CNN (DGCNN) for learning on point clouds. ACM Trans. Graph. **38**(5), 1–12 (2019)
4. Vaswani, A., Shazeer, N., Parmar, N., et al.: Attention is all you need. In: Advances in Neural Information Processing Systems, Long Beach, USA, p. 30 (2017)
5. Wang, Q., Wu, B., Zhu, P., et al.: ECA-Net: efficient channel attention for deep convolutional neural networks. In: Proceedings of the IEEE/CVF Conference on Computer Vision and Pattern Recognition (CVPR), Seattle, USA (2020)
6. Hu, J., Shen, L., Sun, G.: Squeeze-and-excitation networks. In: Proceedings of the IEEE Conference on Computer Vision and Pattern Recognition (CVPR), Salt Lake City, USA, pp. 7132–7141 (2018)
7. Woo, S., Park, J., Lee, J.-Y., Kweon, I.S.: CBAM: convolutional block attention module. In: Ferrari, V., Hebert, M., Sminchisescu, C., Weiss, Y. (eds.) ECCV 2018. LNCS, vol. 11211, pp. 3–19. Springer, Cham (2018). https://doi.org/10.1007/978-3-030-01234-2_1
8. Cao, Y., Xu, J., Lin, S., et al.: GCNet: non-local networks meet squeeze-excitation networks and beyond. In: Proceedings of the IEEE/CVF International Conference on Computer Vision Workshops (ICCV), Seoul, Korea (2019)
9. Wu, Z., Song, S., Khosla, A., et al.: 3D ShapeNets: a deep representation for volumetric shapes. In: Proceedings of the IEEE Conference on Computer Vision and Pattern Recognition, Boston, USA, pp. 1912–1920 (2015)
10. Shen, Y., Feng, C., Yang, Y., et al.: Mining point cloud local structures by kernel correlation and graph pooling. In: Proceedings of the IEEE Conference on Computer Vision and Pattern Recognition (CVPR), Salt Lake City, USA, pp. 4548–4557 (2018)
11. Duan, Y., Zheng, Y., Lu, J., et al.: Structural Relational Reasoning (SRN) of point clouds. In: Proceedings of the IEEE/CVF Conference on Computer Vision and Pattern Recognition (CVPR), Long Beach, USA, pp. 949–958 (2019)
12. Zhao, H., Jiang, L., Fu, C.W., et al.: PointWeb: enhancing local neighborhood features for point cloud processing. In: Proceedings of the IEEE/CVF Conference on Computer Vision and Pattern Recognition (CVPR), Long Beach, USA, pp. 5565–5573 (2019)
13. Yan, X., Zheng, C., Li, Z., et al.: PointASNL: robust point clouds processing using nonlocal neural networks with adaptive sampling. In: Proceedings of the IEEE/CVF Conference on Computer Vision and Pattern Recognition (CVPR), pp. 5589–5598 (2020)
14. Xu, Q., Sun, X., Wu, C.Y., et al.: Grid-GCN for fast and scalable point cloud learning. In: Proceedings of the IEEE/CVF Conference on Computer Vision and Pattern Recognition (CVPR), pp. 5661–5670 (2020)
15. Guo, M.H., Cai, J.X., Liu, Z.N., et al.: PCT: point cloud transformer. Comput. Vis. Med. **7**(2), 187–199 (2021)
16. Xu, M., Zhang, J., Zhou, Z., et al.: Learning geometry-disentangled representation for complementary understanding of 3D object point cloud. In: Proceedings of the AAAI Conference on Artificial Intelligence, vol. 35, no. 4, pp. 3056–3064 (2021)
17. Xu, M., Ding, R., Zhao, H., et al.: PAConv: Position Adaptive Convolution with dynamic kernel assembling on point clouds. In: Proceedings of the IEEE/CVF Conference on Computer Vision and Pattern Recognition (CVPR), pp. 3173–3182 (2021)
18. Zhao, H., Jiang, L., Jia, J., et al.: Point transformer. In: Proceedings of the IEEE/CVF International Conference on Computer Vision (ICCV), pp. 16259–16268 (2021)
19. Ma, X., Qin, C., You, H., et al.: Rethinking network design and local geometry in point cloud: a simple residual MLP framework. In: Tenth International Conference on Learning Representations (ICLR) (2022)
20. Zheng, Y., Yang, S., Li, Y., Lu, H.: Global-PBNet: a novel point cloud registration for autonomous driving. IEEE Trans. Intell. Transp. Syst. **23**, 22312–22319 (2022)

21. Li, Y., Yang, S., Zheng, Y., Lu, H.: Improved point-voxel region convolutional neural network: 3D object detectors for autonomous driving. IEEE Trans. Intell. Transp. Syst. **23**, 9311–9317 (2021)
22. Lu, H., Yang, R., Deng, Z., Zhang, Y., Gao, G., Lan, R.: Chinese image captioning via fuzzy attention-based DenseNet-BiLSTM. ACM Trans. Multimed. Comput. Commun. Appl. **17**(1s), 1–18 (2021)
23. Lu, H., Zhang, Y., Li, Y., Jiang, C., Abbas, H.: User-oriented virtual mobile network resource management for vehicle communications. IEEE Trans. Intell. Transp. Syst. **22**, 3521–3532 (2020). https://doi.org/10.1109/TITS.2020.2991766

# Impedance Synovial Control for Lower Limb Rehabilitation Exoskeleton System

Xinyu Zhu, Zhenxing Sun[✉], and Ting Wang

College of Electrical Engineering and Control Science, Nanjing Tech University,
Nanjing 211816, China
sunzx@njtech.edu.cn

**Abstract.** It is very important to improve the working stability and wearing comfort for the lower limb exoskeleton system, so as to increase the rehabilitation effect of patients with lower limb injuries. However, due to the complex structure of the lower limb exoskeleton, there are uncertain disturbances in the system. Traditional control methods cannot meet the requirements of dynamic response and robustness, since there are still many shortcomings in the safety and compliance of the lower limb exoskeleton for rehabilitation wearing. In this paper, an impedance synovial control strategy for the exoskeleton of the lower limbs is proposed. The safety of contact force is considered, and the impedance controller is combined with the improved integral terminal synovial controller (ITSMC) to reduce system's errors, and to ensure system's rapidity. The proposed method reduces the impedance trajectory tracking error by 90% to the conventional linear synovial control (LSMC). The stability is analyzed by a Lyapunov function. The simulation results show that the combination of the synovial controller and impedance controller has superior performances, and the entire system has a good trajectory tracking effect.

**Keywords:** Lower-limb exoskeleton · Impedance control · Synovial control · Trajectory tracking

## 1 Introduction

With the development of society, the number of patients with impaired limb caused by disease, aging, traffic accidents etc. is increasing. Relying on traditional equipment and medical personnel for physical rehabilitation training is inefficient [1]. The exoskeleton robot is a wearable robot, and has been applied in many fields such as military, medical, and industrial. It is mainly divided into two functions: improving personal athletic ability and helping patients with physical disabilities to recover [2, 3].

With the development of robot technology, a variety of advanced control methods have been proposed to improve the control performance of exoskeleton at home and abroad. In [4], Wang et al. proposed a periodic event-trigger sliding mode control method. They performed the wearer's motion prediction under the GA-BP neural network, and the proposed method made the system's error convergence in the finite time. For trajectory

© The Author(s), under exclusive license to Springer Nature Singapore Pte Ltd. 2022
S. Yang and H. Lu (Eds.): ISAIR 2022, CCIS 1700, pp. 366–373, 2022.
https://doi.org/10.1007/978-981-19-7946-0_31

control of multi-joint exoskeleton, in [5], Rafael Pérez-San Lázaro et al. combined high-order synovial control algorithm with adaptive control to design a second-order super-twisting synovial controller. The system's error is reduced under the adaptive control. The chattering problem caused by the synovial control is also decreased.

In order to achieve precise position control and compliance control of the lower limb rehabilitation exoskeleton, we study an impedance synovial control strategy [11–15]. An impedance controller with external feedback is used to obtain the impedance control trajectory and external contact force, so as to improve the dynamic relationship between force and position. Then the inner loop synovial position controller is used to adjust the joint trajectory tracking, which improves the accuracy of the system's position control. Proposed method can improve the safety and stability when patients wear lower limb exoskeleton for rehabilitation exercise, and achieve efficient rehabilitation exercise.

Rest of paper is organized as follows. Section 2 describes the dynamics model of the lower limb exoskeleton. Section 3 proposes a composite control structure composed of impedance controller and synovial controller, and analyzes the stability of the system. Numerical simulations are performed in Sect. 4. Conclusions are given in the last part.

## 2 Dynamical Model of Lower Limb Exoskeleton

According to the Lagrange dynamics equation, the joint space dynamics model of the lower limb exoskeleton robot can be expressed as follows:

$$M(q)\ddot{q} + C(q, \dot{q})\dot{q} + G(q) = \tau, \tag{1}$$

where, $q \in R^n$ is the rotation angle vector of the joint. $M(q) \in R^{n \times n}$ is an inertia matrix. $C(q, \dot{q}) \in R^{n \times n}$ is the matrix of combination of centrifugal force and Coriolis force. $G(q) \in R^{n \times n}$ is the gravitational matrix. $\tau \in R^n$ is torque vector, and n is the degree of freedom.

Since the impedance control is implemented in the Cartesian coordinate system, it is necessary to obtain the dynamics equation in the Cartesian coordinate system through the angular dynamics equation.

Let x be the position vector of the exoskeleton joint of the lower limb. Then the following equation about relationship between robot's angle and position can be obtained as follows:

$$\dot{x} = J(q)\dot{q}, \tag{2}$$

where $J(q)$ is the Jacobian matrix.

In the state of static equilibrium, the relationship between the torque and force of the lower limb exoskeleton joint is as follows:

$$\tau = J^T(q)F_x, \tag{3}$$

where $J^T(q)$ is the Jacobian matrix.

According to formulas (1), (2), (3), and considering the modeling error and disturbance $d$, the model is established as follows:

$$M_x(q)\ddot{x} + C_x(q, \dot{q})\dot{x} + G_x(q) + \Delta(q, \dot{q}, \ddot{q}) = F_x, \tag{4}$$

where,
$$M_x(q) = J^{-T}(q)M(q)J^{-1}(q), C_x(q,\dot{q}) = J^{-T}(q)(C(q,\dot{q}) - M(q)J^{-1}(q)\dot{J}(q))J^{-1}(q)$$
$$G_x(q) = J^{-T}(q)G(q), \|\Delta(q,\dot{q},\ddot{q})\| \leq \eta.$$

## 3  Impedance Model and Design of Synovial Controller

### 3.1  Establishment of Impedance Model

According to the relationship between force and position error, the dynamics model of impedance control is described as follows:

$$M_m(\ddot{x}_r - \ddot{x}) + B_m(\dot{x}_r - \dot{x}) + K_m(x_r - x) = F_e, \tag{5}$$

where, $M_m$, $B_m$, $K_m$ are the inertia, damping and stiffness parameter matrices in the impedance model. $F_e$ is the contact force between the end of the single-leg two-link exoskeleton and the external environment. $x$ is the actual position trajectory. $x_r$ is the ideal position trajectory, and $x(0) = x_r(0)$.

In the impedance model, the target of impedance control is that the actual position trajectory $x$ to track the desired impedance trajectory $x_d$. Let $x = x_d$, the impedance model is expressed as follows:

$$M_m\ddot{x}_d + B_m\dot{x}_d + K_m x_d = -F_e + M_m\ddot{x}_r + B_m\dot{x}_r + K_m x_r, \tag{6}$$

where, $x_d(0) = x_r(0)$, $\dot{x}_d(0) = \dot{x}_r(0)$.

Considering the contact resistance of the external environment, the dynamics model (4) can be transformed as follows:

$$M_x(q)\ddot{x} + C_x(q,\dot{q})\dot{x} + G_x(q) + \Delta(q,\dot{q},\ddot{q}) + F_e = F_x, \tag{7}$$

### 3.2  Design of Synovial Controller

Based on the impedance model of (6), the impedance control trajectory is supposed to be equal to the ideal trajectory in the workspace. Define the position error as follows:

$$e(t) = x_d(t) - x(t), \tag{8}$$

Since disturbances existing in the system, for better finite-time tracking effect, and eliminating steady-state errors, the synovial function is designed as follows:

$$S = \dot{e} + \int_0^t K_1 sig^{\alpha_1}(\dot{e}) + K_2 sig^{\alpha_2}(e)dt, \tag{9}$$

where $sig^r(\xi) = [|\xi_1|^r sign(\xi_1), ..., |\xi_n|^r sign(\xi_n)]^T$, $0 < \alpha_2 < 1$, $\alpha_1 = 2\alpha_2/(\alpha_2 + 1)$, and $K_1$ and $K_2$ are two positive definite diagonal matrices. Derivative the equation (9) with respect to time. We may get the following equation:

$$\dot{S} = \ddot{e} + K_1 sig^{\alpha_1}(\dot{e}) + K_2 sig^{\alpha_2}(e), \tag{10}$$

In order to ensure the system reaching the synovial surface in the finite time, the isokinetic approach rate we use is as follows:

$$\dot{S} = -\eta \text{sgn}(s), \tag{11}$$

where, $\eta > 0$. The general switching function is sign(x). Compared with the sign(x), the hyperbolic tangent function is a relatively smooth switching function. Therefore, we apply this function as the switching function of the approach rate. The improved approach rate function is as follows:

$$\dot{S} = -\eta \tanh(\frac{s}{\varepsilon}), \tag{12}$$

where $\varepsilon$ is the steepness of the switching function. The steepness of the curve can be adjusted by the $\varepsilon$ to achieve better control effect.

Combining (7), (8), (9) and (12), the controller can be designed as follows (Fig. 1):

$$\begin{aligned} F_x &= M_x(q)\ddot{x}_d + C_x(q, \dot{q})\dot{x} + G_x(q) + \Delta(q, \dot{q}, \ddot{q}) + F_e \\ &+ K_1 M_x(q)sig^{\alpha_1}(\dot{e}) + K_2 M_x(q)sig^{\alpha_2}(e) + M_x(q)\eta \tanh(s/\varepsilon). \end{aligned} \tag{13}$$

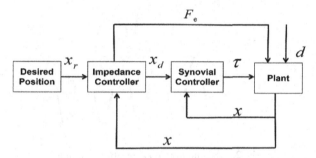

**Fig. 1.** The diagram of the controller.

### 3.3 Proof of Stability

A Lyapunov function V is considered as follows:

$$V = \frac{1}{2}s^2, \tag{14}$$

The derivative of V is as follows:

$$\dot{V} = \dot{s}s = -\eta s \tanh(\frac{s}{\varepsilon}) \leq 0, \tag{15}$$

## 4 Numerical Simulations and Discussions

In the numerical simulation, is calculated by formula (5), while is calculated by (6). The end of the single-leg two-link is in contact with the outer. There are the following two situations:

(1) When $x_1 \leq 0$, there is no external contact force at the end of the single-leg two-link, that is, $F_e = \begin{bmatrix} 0 & 0 \end{bmatrix}^T$.
(2) When $x_1 \geq 0$, there is external contact force at the end of the single-leg two-link, that is, $x_1 = 0, \dot{x}_1 = 0, \ddot{x}_1 = 0$. The damping parameters of the external contact are $M_m = diag[1.0], B_m = diag[10], K_m = diag[50]$.

Considering $\Delta(q, \dot{q}, \ddot{q}) = 1.0 \sin t$, and the controller gain in the synovial controller is selected as $K_1 = \begin{bmatrix} 75 & 0 \\ 0 & 130 \end{bmatrix}, K_2 = \begin{bmatrix} 110 & 0 \\ 0 & 161.1 \end{bmatrix}, \alpha_2 = 0.5, \alpha_1 = 0.67, \eta = 1.2, \varepsilon = 0.5$. Numerical simulations and results are displayed as follows.

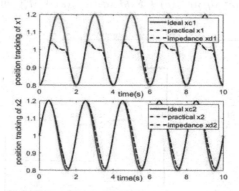

**Fig. 2.** The end joint node position tracking

Figure 2 shows the end joint node position tracking. Figure 3 displays the full trajectory tracking. Figure 4 shows the external contact force of the exoskeleton joint. Since the external contact force of the exoskeleton is at $x_1 = 1.0$, under the influence of impedance control, the position of the joint node rises briefly and then returns to $x_1 = 1.0$. It can be seen from the Fig. 2 and Fig. 3 that the actual trajectory is not tracking the desired trajectory, but is tracking the impedance trajectory. The above three figures show the impedance control can well consider the influence of the external environment. Under the premise of ensuring stability, the joint can safely reach the target position.

Figure 5 shows the actual control torque of the two links. Figure 6 shows the impedance trajectory tracking error under the improved integral terminal synovial control (ITSMC). Figure 7 shows the impedance trajectory tracking error under the general linear synovial control (LSMC). From the Fig. 6, we can see that the error is controlled in a very low range. Compared with the linear synovial control, the error is controlled under the improved integral terminal synovial control in a lower range. From the above

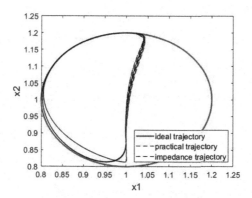

**Fig. 3.** The full trajectory tracking

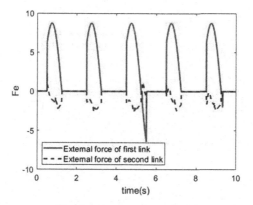

**Fig. 4.** External contact force

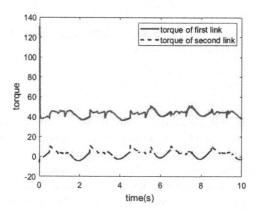

**Fig. 5.** Actual control torque

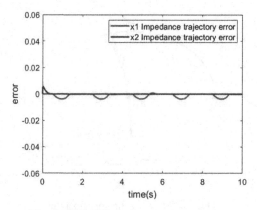

**Fig. 6.** ITSMC Impedance trajectory error

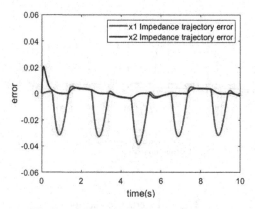

**Fig. 7.** LSMC Impedance trajectory error

three pictures, it is obvious that the designed controller makes the system stable and brings good anti-disturbances performance.

## 5 Conclusion

For the single-leg two-link lower limb exoskeleton system, considering its human-computer interaction force and its disturbances, an impedance synovial controller is proposed. The impedance controller is equivalent to adding feed-forward control to the control system. Under the approach rate based on the hyperbolic tangent function, the integral terminal synovial controller is designed to reduce disturbances and chattering so as to ensure the fast-tracking effect of the system. The simulation results show that the actual control trajectory is continuously adjusted by the synovial controller under the basis of impedance control, and the safe and compliant control is realized. In the future work, we will continue to improve the stability, safety and anti-disturbances ability of lower limb rehabilitation exoskeleton system.

# References

1. Banala, S.K., Kim, S.H., Agrawal, S.K., Scholz, J.P.: Robot assisted gait training with active leg exoskeleton (ALEX). IEEE Trans. Neural Syst. Rehabil. Eng. **17**(1), 2–8 (2009)
2. Yan, T., Cempini, M., Oddo, C.M., Vitiello, N.: Review of assistive strategies in powered lower-limb orthoses and exoskeletons. Robot. Auton. Syst. **64**, 120–136 (2015)
3. Bogue, R.: Exoskeletons and robotic prosthetics: a review of recent developments. Ind. Robot **36**(5), 421–427 (2009)
4. Wang, J., Liu, J., Zhang, G., Guo, S.: Periodic event-triggered sliding mode control for lower limb exoskeleton based on human–robot cooperation. ISA Trans. **123**, 87–97 (2021)
5. Pérez-San-Lázaro, R., Salgado, I., Chairez, I.: Adaptive sliding-mode controller of a lower limb mobile exoskeleton for active rehabilitation. ISA Trans. **109**, 218–228 (2021)
6. Zhang, L., Liu, L., Wang, Z., Xia, Y.: Continuous finite-time control for uncertain robot manipulators with integral sliding mode. IET Control Theory Appl. **12**(11), 1621–1627 (2018)
7. Ma, C., Li, X., Li, Y., Tian, X., et al.: Visual information processing for deep-sea visual monitoring system. Cogn. Robot. **1**, 3–11 (2021)
8. Huimin, L., Li, Y., Chen, M., et al.: Go beyond artificial intelligence. Mob. Netw. Appl. **23**, 368–375 (2018)
9. Sarker, S., Jamal, L., Ahmed, S.F., et al.: Robotics and artificial intelligence in healthcare during COVID-19 pandemic: a systematic review. Robot. Auton. Syst. **146**, 103902 (2021)
10. Pitkäaho, T., Kaarlela, T., Pieskä, S., et al.: Indoor positioning, artificial intelligence and digital twins for enhanced robotics safety. IFAC-PapersOnLine **54**(1), 540–545 (2021)
11. Kang, S., et al.: Discrete-time predictive sliding mode control for a constrained parallel micropositioning piezostage. IEEE Trans. Syst. Man Cybern. Syst. **52**, 3025–3036 (2021)
12. Yang, X., et al.: Dynamics and isotropic control of parallel mechanisms for vibration isolation. IEEE/ASME Trans. Mechatron. **25**(4), 2027–2034 (2020)
13. Lu, H., Zhang, Y., Li, Y., Jiang, C., Abbas, H.: User-oriented virtual mobile network resource management for vehicle communications. IEEE Trans. Intell. Transp. Syst. (2020). https://doi.org/10.1109/TITS.2020.2991766
14. Li, Y., Yang, S., Zheng, Y., Lu, H.: Improved point-voxel region convolutional neural network: 3D object detectors for autonomous driving. IEEE Trans. Intell. Transp. Syst. **23**, 9311–9317 (2021)
15. Lu, H., Yang, R., Deng, Z., Zhang, Y., Gao, G., Lan, R.: Chinese image captioning via fuzzy attention-based DenseNet-BiLSTM. ACM Trans. Multimedia Comput. Commun. Appl. **17**(1s), 1–18 (2021)

# L-FPN R-CNN: An Accurate Detector for Detecting Bird Nests in Aerial Power Tower Pictures

Guolin Dai[1], Rui Yang[1], Zhenrong Deng[1], Rushi Lan[1(✉)], Feng Zhao[2], Guanhong Xie[3], and Kang You[1]

[1] School of Computer Science and Information Security, Guilin University of Electronic Technology, Guilin 541004, China
rslan2016@163.com
[2] Yulin Normal University, Yulin 537000, China
[3] Guangxi Jinghang UAV Co., Ltd., Nanning 530025, China

**Abstract.** Today's power inspection bird's nest detection brings difficulties to object detection due to problems such as few object samples, similar backgrounds, and occlusion by towers. In this paper, an improved Sparse R-CNN model L-FPN R-CNN is proposed. Firstly, an ex-grid initialization method is proposed for learnable proposal boxes in Sparse R-CNN to improve the positioning accuracy of proposal boxes. Then, the SiLU function is introduced into the dynamic detection head of the original Sparse R-CNN network, which makes the network have stronger convergence ability. Finally, a feature pyramid structure L-FPN that fuses low-level features is proposed to improve the richness of feature maps. The experimental results show that the average accuracy of the algorithm is 2.9% higher than the original algorithm, and it has a good detection effect on the bird's nest in the aerial electric power tower image.

**Keywords:** Bird's nest detection · Improved Sparse R-CNN · SiLU · Feature pyramid

## 1 Introduction

Electricity resource is an indispensable resource for the normal operation of our country. The main transmission carrier of power supply in our country is the electric power tower. Due to the good ecological environment protection in my country and the large number of birds, some birds are nesting in power towers. The bird's nest material, bird food and excrement may reduce the outer insulation strength of the tower, posing a serious threat to the safety of power equipment [1]. At present, the bird's nest detection process of the power tower is mainly through the aerial photography of the power tower by the drone, and then the data is brought back for the bird's nest detection operation. This reduces the risks encountered by manual work in the field.

The traditional detection method is manual detection, which has the problems of easy fatigue, low efficiency and high labor cost. With the development of science and

S. Yang and H. Lu (Eds.): ISAIR 2022, CCIS 1700, pp. 374–387, 2022.
https://doi.org/10.1007/978-981-19-7946-0_32

technology, computer technology is gradually used to replace manual detection work [21–25]. Duan et al. proposed a catenary bird's nest detection method based on HOG features of key regions and SVM classifier [2]. Zhang et al. proposed an algorithm based on image contour features, contour area and whether the contour is convex or not for bird nest detection [3]. The above methods are traditional object detection algorithms based on mathematical morphology and digital image processing methods. Compared with manual detection, it solves the problem of high labor cost and improves the detection efficiency to a certain extent. However, the detection accuracy of the above methods is heavily dependent on the feature extraction algorithm, and these feature extraction algorithms have the problems of poor feature extraction ability, limited detection and poor generalization ability.

At present, deep learning technology has been well applied in the direction of object detection. The deep learning object detection algorithms are mainly divided into one-stage and two-stage detection algorithms. The first-stage detection algorithm is an algorithm based on direct regression. The representative algorithm of this type is YOLO [4–6] and SSD [7]. Such algorithms apply a single neural network to the entire image and divide grid regions on the final feature map, while predicting the bounding box and object probability for each region. In recent years, some domestic scholars have also applied subclass algorithms to this field. Zhong et al. proposed the application of an improved algorithm based on YOLOv3 in bird's nest detection [8]. Qi et al. proposed a transmission line bird's nest detection method based on an improved SSD algorithm [9].

Based on the two-stage detection algorithm, the representative algorithm of this type is R-CNN [10]. It is to use the region proposal method rpn algorithm to selectively search the input image and generate the region proposal boxes, and then for each region, the proposed boxes are extracted by the convolutional neural network, and finally classified by classifier. Pang and Wang et al. proposed to use the ZF-NET network or the Faster R-CNN algorithm to improve the ResNet101 object feature extraction network to detect the bird's nest of the transmission towers [11, 12]. Wei et al. proposed a method for infrared image object detection with regional convolutional neural networks (HOG-RCNN) fused with histograms of image orientation gradients [13].

The above-mentioned bird's nest object detection method based on deep learning has higher detection accuracy and detection speed than traditional image processing methods. Among them, the one-stage object detection algorithm has fast detection speed, and the second-stage object detection algorithm has high detection accuracy. However, the bird's nest object in the aerial electric power tower image has the characteristics of small scale, partial occlusion, and complex object features. Moreover, the above-mentioned object detection algorithms all generate a large number of candidate regions, and there are problems of explosion of calculation amount of candidate boxes and redundant calculation of anchor boxes. At the same time, the generation of anchor boxes depends on a large number of hyperparameter settings, and manual parameter adjustment will seriously affect the positioning accuracy and classification effect of the object.

In view of the above problems, this paper proposes an improved object detection algorithm based on Sparse R-CNN. Due to the sparseness of Sparse R-CNN, it solves the computational explosion caused by the generation of a large number of candidate regions and the redundancy of anchor boxes calculation and other issues. The improved network can effectively solve the problems of low detection accuracy caused by insufficient network feature extraction, scale and occlusion. The main improvement points of this paper are as follows: Propose the initialization proposal boxes algorithm "ex-grid", improve the positioning accuracy and reduce the model calculation amount; improve the activation function of the dynamic strength interaction head in the original Sparse R-CNN network, improve the convergence ability of the network model; improve the feature Pyramid network structure, design a feature pyramid structure that fuses low-level features to improve the richness and representation ability of feature maps.

This paper is organized as follows. Section 2 gives a brief introduction to the Sparse R-CNN network structure. Section 3 introduces the improvement points of the model proposed in this paper based on Sparse R-CNN. Section 4 discusses our experimental results and analysis. Section 5 concludes our work.

## 2   Sparse R-CNN

Sparse R-CNN is a purely sparse method for object detection in images. Sparse R-CNN provides a sparse learning object proposal set of length N (N < H × W × K) and a corresponding learnable proposal feature set. The image is extracted through the feature extraction network, and the objects are filtered, positioned and classified by the dynamic instance interaction head. This method omits the design of candidate object anchor boxes, many-to-one label assignment and non-maximum suppression processing. The structure of Sparse R-CNN is shown in Fig. 1.

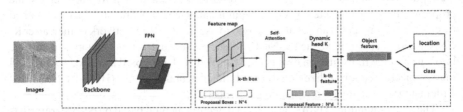

**Fig. 1.** Model structure diagram of Sparse R-CNN. It consists of backbone network, dynamic instance interaction head, and two task-specific prediction layers. The inputs to the network are images, Learnable proposal boxes, and Learnable proposal features.

### 2.1   Backbone

The backbone network is the ResNet-based FPN (Feature Pyramid Networks, FPN) [14] network, through which the multi-scale feature map is extracted from the image, and the 2 to 5 layers of the feature pyramid output the feature map of the corresponding size.

## 2.2 Learnable Proposal Boxes

Sparse R-CNN directly initializes a set of proposal boxes of length N. Each proposal box consists of 4 normalized values, representing the coordinates, length and width of the object. These proposal boxes replace the candidate boxes learned by the anchor boxes of the previous detector. Sparse R-CNN maps these boxes to the feature map generated by the backbone network, and extracts the RoI (region of interest) feature information through the RoIAlign [15] operation. Their parameters are updated in the dynamic instance interaction head. The proposal boxes have 4 initialization methods: "Center", "Random", "Grid", and "Image". "Center" is to place all proposal boxes in the center of the image, and the height and width are set to 0.1 of the image size; "Random" is that the center, height and width of the proposal boxes are randomly initialized with Gaussian distribution; "Grid" means the proposal boxes in the image is initialized to a regular grid; "Image" means that all proposal boxes are set to the full image size.

## 2.3 Learnable Proposal Feature

At the same time, in order to better integrate the detailed features of objects (pose, shape, edge, etc.), a proposal region feature set consisting of N 256-dimensional feature vectors is introduced. These proposal regions feature vectors are in one-to-one correspondence with each learnable proposal box. Finally, it is input into the dynamic instance detection head to interact with the rough ROI feature information extracted from the proposal region, making the features of the RoI feature more conducive to locating and classifying objects.

## 2.4 Dynamic Instance Interactive Head and Prediction Layers

The dynamic instance interaction head is designed, and the classification and positioning of the predicted objects are generated by inputting the ROI feature information and proposal features corresponding to the proposal boxes. The ROI feature $f_i(S \times S, C)$ is matrix multiplied with the corresponding proposal feature $p_i(C)$, and then the output is subjected to Batch Normalization (BN) [16] and ReLU activation, the process is defined as formula (1) shown:

$$Out = ReLU\,(norm(bmm(f_i, P_i))) \tag{1}$$

The above process filters the invalid proposal boxes and the output object feature information C. Then the output feature information C of this time is used as the input of the next detection head. After several iterations of training, the final object feature is generated. The prediction layer includes position regression and classification prediction, a three-layer perceptron constitutes position regression prediction, and a linear mapping layer is used for classification prediction.

## 2.5 Loss

The loss function expression of Sparse R-CNN is shown in formula (2):

$$Loss = \lambda_{cls} \cdot L_{cls} + \lambda_{L1} \cdot L_{L1} + \lambda_{giou} \cdot L_{giou} \tag{2}$$

In the formula, $L_{cls}$ is the focal loss [17] between classification prediction and gt, $L_{L1}$ is the L1 loss of the center point of the object boxes, $L_{giou}$ is the genearlized IoU loss [18] of width and height, $\lambda_{cls}$, $\lambda_{L1}$, $\lambda_{giou}$ are the components of coefficient.

## 3  L-FPN R-CNN

### 3.1  Ex-grid Initialization Method

This paper is a research on the problem of bird's nest detection in aerial images of electric power towers. There is only 1–2 bird nest objects in each original image in the power tower image data set obtained from aerial photography, and they all belong to the small and medium object categories. Sun Peize et al. conducted experiments on the proposed four proposal box initialization methods in the coco dataset. The "Image" proposal box initialization method generates a proposal box covering the entire image. This initialization method has the best effect on medium and small object detection, so it is used as the original proposal box initialization method. The proposal box generated by "Image" is the size of the entire image. If the number of objects to be detected is small, a large number of proposal boxes will be regressed to an object position, resulting in a lot of invalid work of filtering candidate regions. The effect is shown in Fig. 2.

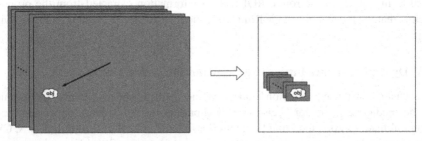

**Fig. 2.** The iterative effect of the proposal box initialized by "Image" in the dynamic instance interaction header.

According to the above problems, we propose the "ex-grid" proposal box initialization method. We set the number N of proposal boxes to 100 and divide the feature map into 10 * 10 grids. The initialization of the proposal boxes is as follows: the center of each grid is used as the center of the proposal box, and the width and height of the proposal box are 0.2. Each proposal box is covered by each other. This initialization method ensures that the object in each grid is covered by at least 4 proposal boxes, and at most 9 proposal boxes. The probability of false detection and missed detection caused by the unreasonable grid division caused by the bird's nest object being cut by several proposal boxes is reduced. At the same time, it also ensures that the proposal boxes which are far away from the object will be filtered out in time, avoiding the occurrence of a large number of proposal boxes returning to an object position, and reduces the amount of calculation. The ex-grid effect diagram is shown in Fig. 3.

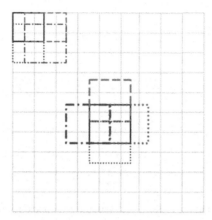

**Fig. 3.** A simplified diagram of the effect of the "ex-grid" initialization proposal box. The upper left graph of the figure represents the generation of proposal boxes in the border corners of the picture. The center of the figure represents the generation of non-boundary corner grid proposal boxes, and rectangles with different colors and lines represent different proposal boxes.

### 3.2 Introduced SiLU Activation Function into Dynamic Instance Interaction Head

The dynamic instance interaction head of the original Sparse R-CNN uses ReLU as the activation function. Its function and its derivative calculation formula are as follows:

$$\text{ReLU}(x) = \max(x, 0) \tag{3}$$

and

$$ReLU\,(X)' = \begin{cases} 1 \; x > 0 \\ 0 \; x <= 0 \end{cases} \tag{4}$$

Compared with the sigmoid and tanh series of activation functions, ReLU has the characteristics of simple form, low computational complexity, no need for exponential operation and faster network backpropagation. However, when the input value is less than 0, the output of ReLU and the first derivative are always 0, resulting in the inability of neurons to update parameters, and the permanent death of some neurons, which affects the convergence ability of the network. The activation function of ReLU and its derivative are shown in Fig. 4.

The improved dynamic instance interaction head in this paper uses SiLU (Sigmoid Weighted Liner Unit) as the activation function, and its function and its derivative formula are as follows:

$$\text{SiLU}\,(x) = x \cdot \frac{1}{1 + e^{-x}} \tag{5}$$

and

$$SiLU'\,(x) = SiLU(x) + \frac{1}{1 + e^{-x}} \cdot (1 - SiLU\,(x)) \tag{6}$$

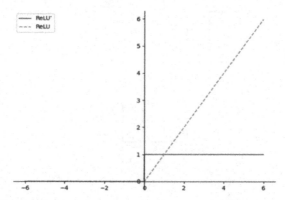

**Fig. 4.** Diagram of ReLU activation function and its derivative.

When the input value is greater than 0, the activation function values of SiLU and ReLU are roughly equal; when the input value is less than 0, the activation function value is close to 0, but not 0, and there will be no permanent neuron death. The SiLU activation function and its derivative are shown in Fig. 5.

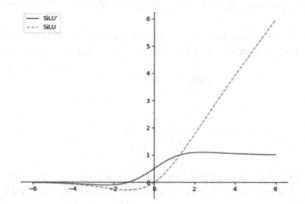

**Fig. 5.** Diagram of SiLU activation function and its derivative.

### 3.3   L-FPN

The original Sparse R-CNN uses image pyramids to solve the multi-scale object detection problem. The image outputs feature maps of different sizes through an image pyramid network, and then predictions are made on these feature maps of different sizes. This method can cope with the impact of size change on the detection performance to a certain extent, but the bird's nest object in the avionics image is small and so many details are in the low-level feature map. Therefore, this paper proposes a feature pyramid structure L-FPN that fuses the low-level features. On the basis of retaining more texture feature information, a maximum pooling operation is performed on the underlying image to increase the receptive field, and it is fused with the semantic information of the high-level feature map, which improves the richness and representation ability of the feature map. L-The FPN structure is shown in Fig. 6.

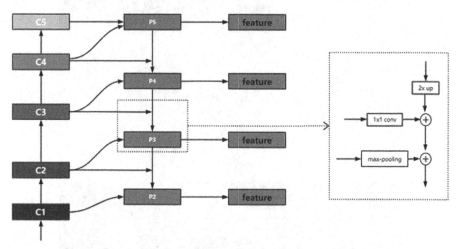

**Fig. 6.** L-FPN structure diagram: $P_n$ is obtained by first convolving $C_n$ with $1 \times 1$ and then fused with the high-level feature map obtained by $P_{n+1}$ upsampling, and then fused with the $C_{n-1}$ image after max-pooling.

## 4  Experiments

### 4.1  Experimental Environment and Parameter Settings

The original image used in this experiment is a sample of drone aerial inspection of a power supply bureau in recent years. There are 180 original images of the power tower with the bird's nest. Select 120 original images as training set, 30 original images as test set, and the remaining 30 as validation set. Each dataset is augmented with data augmentation methods of warping, random rotation, and translation. In the end, the training set has 930 images, the test set has 220 images, and the validation set has 230 images. Part of the dataset is shown in Fig. 7.

The experiment is based on the PyTorch deep learning framework. The experimental environment of our approach was Ubuntu 16.04 system, Tesla P100-SXM2-16 GB, Cuda 10.1, PyTorch 1.7.0 programming framework based on Python 3.7.4; the initial learning rate is $2.5 \times 10^{-5}$, the optimizer is AdamW [19], the weight decay factor is 0.0001, $\lambda_{cls} = 2$, $\lambda_{L1} = 5$, $\lambda_{giou} = 2$, epoch is 100. The default values for the number of proposal boxes, the number of high-dimensional proposal feature vectors, and the number of iterations are 100, 100, and 6, respectively.

**Fig. 7.** Partial data set display.

## 4.2  Evaluation Indicators

IoU (intersection over union) is an important function of object detection algorithm performance mAP calculation. The full name of IoU is the intersection and union ratio. It calculates the ratio of the intersection and union of the predicted box and the real box. The calculation formula is as follows:

$$IoU = \frac{BBox_{pred} \cap BBox_{gt}}{BBox_{pred} \cup BBox_{gt}} \tag{7}$$

The threshold of IoU is set to x. When the IoU value of the predicted box and the real box is greater than the threshold, it is a true case (TP), otherwise it is a false positive case (FP). In this paper, the average precision (Average Precsion, AP) and detection speed (Frames Per Second) commonly used in object detection algorithms are used to evaluate the performance of the model. Calculated as follows:

$$Precision = \frac{TP}{TP + FP} \tag{8}$$

and

$$AP = \frac{\sum_n Precision}{n} \tag{9}$$

## 4.3 Ablation Experiment

This paper takes the original Sparse R-CNN network based on ResNet50 as the Baseline. As shown in Table 1, this paper verifies the effectiveness of each module one by one through 5 groups of progressive experiments. The first set of experiments replaced the original "Image" initialization method with the ex-grid initialization method, and the AP and $AP_{50}$ of the replaced network had 1.056% and 0.541% accuracy improvements respectively. The second set of experiments replaced the ReLU activation function in the dynamic instance interaction head with the SiLU activation function. The result has 0.983 and 1.121% accuracy improvements in AP and $AP_{50}$. As can be seen from Fig. 8, the improved network converges faster and has a better degree of convergence. The third set of experiments replaced the original FPN with L-FPN fused with low-level features, AP and $AP_{50}$ are improved by 2.599% and 1.701%, indicating the importance of low-level feature information for small-scale object detection, but the detection speed is reduced by 1.88 fps. The fourth group of experiments is a combination of the improvement of the first group of experiments and the second group of experiments, it can be seen that the AP and $AP_{50}$ are 1.528% and 1.368% higher than BaseLine respectively, and the detection speed is reduced by 0.28 fps. The fifth group of experiments is a synthesis of the third group of experiments on the basis of the fourth group of experiments, its AP and $AP_{50}$ have 3.505% and 2.01% higher accuracy than BaseLine, and its detection speed is 2.041 fps lower than BaseLine.

**Table 1.** Performance comparison of the modules proposed in this paper.

| Method | AP | AP50 | fps |
|---|---|---|---|
| BaseLine | 46.224 | 95.494 | 13.03 |
| +ex-grid | 47.280 | 96.035 | 12.77 |
| +SiLU | 47.207 | 96.615 | 13.05 |
| +L-FPN | 48.823 | 97.195 | 11.15 |
| +ex-grid+SiLU | 47.752 | 96.862 | 12.75 |
| +ex-grid+SiLU+L-FPN | 49.329 | 97.504 | 10.989 |

## 4.4 Algorithm Comparison

In order to prove the overall effectiveness of the L-FPN R-CNN, we selected a series of representative algorithms for experiments, and the results are shown in Table 2.

As can be seen from Table 2, although the detection speed of the improved network is lower than that of the original Sparse R-CNN to a certain extent. However, the average detection accuracy of L-FPN R-CNN-R50 and L-FPN R-CNN-R101 are better than other models. The AP and AP50 of L-FPN R-CNN-R101 reach 50.1% and 98.2% respectively. Compared with Faster R-CNN-50, Faster R-CNN-101, Cascade R-CNN-R50 [20], Yolov5s, Sparse R-CNN-R50, Sparse R-CNN-R101 and L-FPN R-CNN-R50

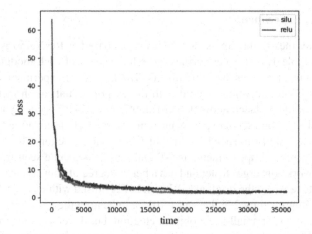

**Fig. 8.** The ordinate is the loss value, and the abscissa is the training time. The blue line is the change of the model loss value with ReLU as the activation function. The red line is the change map of the model loss value with SiLU as the activation function. (Color figure online)

**Table 2.** Comparison of detection results of different feature extraction networks.

| Method | Feature | AP | AP50 | fps |
|---|---|---|---|---|
| Faster R-CNN-R50 | FPN | 43.6 | 95.1 | 14.8 |
| Faster R-CNN-R101 | FPN | 45.7 | 96.2 | 12.4 |
| Cascade R-CNN-R50 | FPN | 46.8 | 96.5 | 12.7 |
| YOLOv5s | PANet | 48.2 | 97.8 | 36.7 |
| Sparse R-CNN-R50 | FPN | 46.2 | 95.5 | 13.3 |
| Sparse R-CNN-R101 | FPN | 48.2 | 96.6 | 10.4 |
| L-FPN R-CNN-R50 | L-FPN | 49.3 | 97.5 | 11.0 |
| L-FPN R-CNN-101 | L-FPN | 50.1 | 98.2 | 9.2 |

algorithms, the AP is 6.5%, 4.4%, 3.3%, 1.9%, 3.9%, 1.9% and 0.8% higher, and the AP50 is 3.1%, 2.0%, 1.7%, 0.4%, 2.7%, 1.6%, 0.7% higher respectively. The results show that the L-FPN R-CNN network can better detect the bird's nest object in the power tower image than other object detection networks.

### 4.5 Algorithm Effect Display

As shown in Fig. 9 of the detection effect, the L-FPN R-CNN-101 method in this paper compared with the Baseline (Sparse R-CNN-R101) method has more accurate prediction box positioning and feature extraction ability Stronger, it has a more significant advantage in detecting small objects and occluded objects.

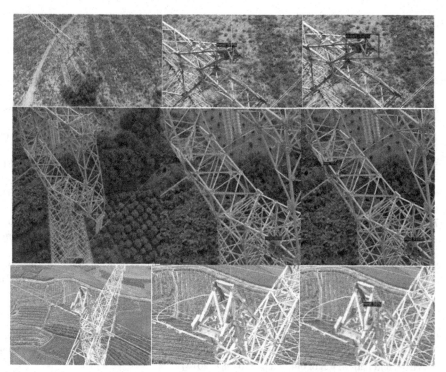

**Fig. 9.** Detection renderings: the left is the original image, the middle is the detection rendering of the L-FPN R-CNN model, and the right is the detection rendering of the Baseline model.

## 5 Conclusion

Experiments show that compared with the original Sparse R-CNN-50, the L-FPN R-CNN-50 model improves AP and AP50 by 2.9% and 2.0%, respectively, but at the cost of 2.3 fps slower detection. L-FPN R-CNN-101 algorithm improves AP and AP50 by 1.9% and 1.6%, respectively, at the cost of 1.2 fps detection speed, and the average accuracy is better than YOLOv5, Faster R-CNN and Cascade R-CNN. Experiments show that the algorithm has a good detection effect on the bird's nest object in the power tower image. However, the model in this paper still has room for improvement. How to make the network improve the detection speed without reducing the accuracy is the next problem to be solved.

**Acknowledgment.** This work was supported by the Guangxi key R & D plan (GuiKe AB22035052), the science and technology plan project of Qingxiu District of Nanning City (No. 2020012), and Guangxi Colleges and the Universities Key Laboratory of Intelligent Processing of Computer Images and Graphics (No. GIIP2003).

# References

1. Wang, J., Li, L., Du, Y., Ma, W., Wang, R.: Analysis and preventive measures on bird damage for overhead transmission lines. Power Secur. Technol. **23**(10), 35–38+42 (2021)
2. Duan, W., Tang, P., Jin, W., Wei, P.: Bird's nest detection of railway catenary based on HOG features of key areas. China Railway, pp. 73–77, August 2015
3. Zhang, Q., Zhao, X., Wang, S., et al.: A kind of transmission line tower bird's nest detection method. CN105095904A[P] (2015)
4. Redmon, J., et al.: You only look once: unified, real-time object detection. In: Proceedings of the IEEE Conference on Computer Vision and Pattern Recognition (2016)
5. Redmon, J., Farhadi, A.: YOLO9000: better, faster, stronger. In: Proceedings of the IEEE Conference on Computer Vision and Pattern Recognition (2017)
6. Redmon, J., Farhadi, A.: YOLOv3: an incremental improvement. arXiv preprint arXiv:1804.02767 (2018)
7. Liu, W., et al.: SSD: single shot MultiBox detector. In: Leibe, B., Matas, J., Sebe, N., Welling, M. (eds.) ECCV 2016. LNCS, vol. 9905, pp. 21–37. Springer, Cham (2016). https://doi.org/10.1007/978-3-319-46448-0_2
8. Zhong, Y., Sun, S., Lv, S., et al.: Recognition of bird's nest on transmission tower in aerial image of high-voltage power line by YOLOv3 algorithm. J. Guangdong Univ. Technol. **37**(03), 42–48 (2020)
9. Qi, J., Jiao, L.: Bird nest detection on transmission tower based on improved SSD algorithm. Comput. Syst. Appl. **29**(05), 202–208 (2020)
10. Girshick, R., Donahue, J., Darrell, T., et al.: Rich feature hierarchies for accurate object detection and semantic segmentation. In: IEEE Computer Society Conference on Computer Vision and Pattern Recognition, pp. 580–587 (2014)
11. Pang, N.: Deep learning based detection and identification of power line tower nest. Autom. Instrum. (4), 5 (2020)
12. Wang, J., Luo, H., Yu, P., et al.: Small objects detection in UAV aerial images based on improved faster R-CNN. J. Meas. Sci. Instrum. **41**(01), 15–20 (2020)
13. Wei, H., et al.: Infrared image object detection of power inspection based on HOG-RCNN. Infrared Laser Eng. **S2**, 242–247 (2020)
14. Lin, T.Y., Dollár, P., Girshick, R., He, K., Hariharan, B., Belongie, S.: Feature pyramid networks for object detection. In: Proceedings of the IEEE Conference on Computer Vision and Pattern Recognition, pp. 2117–2125 (2017)
15. He, K., Gkioxari, G., Dollár, P., Girshick, R.: Mask R-CNN. In: Proceedings of the IEEE International Conference on Computer Vision, pp. 2961–2969 (2017)
16. He, K., Zhang, X., Ren, S., et al.: Deep residual learning for image recognition. In: Computer Vision and Pattern Recognition, pp. 770–778 (2016)
17. Lin, T.Y., Goyal, P., Girshick, R., He, K., Dollár, P.: Focal loss for dense object detection. In: Proceedings of the IEEE International Conference on Computer Vision, pp. 2980–2988 (2017)
18. Rezatofighi, H., et al.: Generalized intersection over union: a metric and a loss for bounding box regression. In: Proceedings of the IEEE/CVF Conference on Computer Vision and Pattern Recognition, pp. 658–666 (2019)
19. Loshchilov, I., Frank, Hr.: Decoupled weight decay regularization. arXiv preprint arXiv:1711.05101 (2017)
20. Cai, Z., Vasconcelos, N.: Cascade R-CNN: high quality object detection and instance segmentation. IEEE Trans. Pattern Anal. Mach. Intell. **43**(5), 1483–1498 (2019)
21. Lu, H., Yang, R., Deng, Z., Zhang, Y., Gao, G., Lan, R.: Chinese image captioning via fuzzy attention-based DenseNet-BiLSTM. ACM Trans. Multimedia Comput. Commun. Appl. **17**(1s), 1–18 (2021)

22. Lu, H., Zhang, Y., Li, Y., Jiang, C., Abbas, H.: User-oriented virtual mobile network resource management for vehicle communications. IEEE Trans. Intell. Transp. Syst. (2020). https://doi.org/10.1109/TITS.2020.2991766

23. Lu, H., Qin, M., Zhang, F., et al.: RSCNN: a CNN-based method to enhance low-light remote-sensing images. Remote Sens. **13**, 62 (2020)

24. Lu, H., Zhang, M., Xu, X.: Deep fuzzy hashing network for efficient image retrieval. IEEE Trans. Fuzzy Syst. (2020). https://doi.org/10.1109/TFUZZ.2020.2984991

25. Li, Y., Yang, S., Zheng, Y., Lu, H.: Improved point-voxel region convolutional neural network: 3D object detectors for autonomous driving. IEEE Trans. Intell. Transp. Syst. **23**, 9311–9317 (2021)

# PBLF: Prompt Based Learning Framework for Cross-Modal Recipe Retrieval

Jialiang Sun[✉] and Jiao Li

University of Electronic Science of Technology of China,
No. 2006, Xiyuan Ave, West Hi-Tech Zone, Chengdu, Sichuan, China
limitlessun@gmail.com

**Abstract.** Nowadays, widespread attention is drawn to cross-modal recipe retrieval due to the various food-relevant applications and the increasing concern on health. This task is addressable through a combination of multi-modal data (e.g., images and texts), which have far-reaching meaning on the merging of vision and language. Early researchers focus on learning joint representation by projecting food images and recipe texts (e.g., ingredients and instructions) to the same embedding space and proposing different cross-modal fusion structure. Recently, most methods adopt a pre-train model and fine-tune strategy to help capture the alignment between modalities. While offering appreciable retrieval performance, two limitations still exist in these methods: 1) with the increasing complexity of the pre-trained model, the data requirements and the cost of calculating in fine-tune stage are also rising. And 2) the down-stream fine-tune tasks they designed for cross-modal recipe retrieval have a gap with the pre-trained model. To this end, we propose a novel fusion framework named Prompt Based Learning Framework (PBLF) to adopt transferable visual model CLIP (Contrastive Language-Image Pre-training) into the recipe retrieval task for the first time, and design an appropriate prompt to train the model efficiently, which bridge the gap between the pre-trained model and the downstream task and transfer the knowledge of the CLIP model to specific recipe retrieval task. The extensive experiments on the large-scale cross-modal recipe dataset Recipe1M demonstrate the superiority of our proposed PBLF model compared to the state-of-the-art approaches.

**Keywords:** Image-recipe retrieval · Fusion strategy · Prompt learning

## 1 Introduction

Food is one of the basic conditions for human existence, it can provide energy, stimulate growth and maintain life. In recent years, due to the rapid development of the electronic devices and social network, digital content of food have quickly become habitual on the Internet, such as food shows or websites that share recipes. Food data are commonly presented in multimedia content, which includes videos, images, user comments, recipes and nutritional information.

Food-related research is not only associated closely with our daily life but also contributes to many central issues of human society. Thus, food computation has received increased attention [1], which including recognition, retrieval, recommendation, etc.

S. Yang and H. Lu (Eds.): ISAIR 2022, CCIS 1700, pp. 388–402, 2022.
https://doi.org/10.1007/978-981-19-7946-0_33

In this work we mainly focus on the task of cross-modal recipe retrieval [2] between food images and textual recipes, which is one of the standard benchmarks of cross-modal retrieval and gives new insights into how multi-modal information should be fused and embedded. This task is challenging for two main reasons. First, approaching this challenge is feasible only through a combination of methods in computer vision and natural language processing. Second, it is difficult to handle unstructured, noisy multi-modal data. Considering the diversity of foods and the complexity of cooking techniques, the images of dishes made from the same recipe may be completely different due to angles, containers and personal tastes, and food images that seemingly identical may be made with completely different ingredients and instructions.

Early works on this task [2–4] mainly aim to learn joint representations of images and recipes, which are projected into a common embedding space. Improvements were made by focusing on the cross-modal fusion strategy, including extracting effective feature representation, proposing complex retrieval frameworks, modifying loss functions, etc. [5–7]. Most of these methods adopt pre-train model and fine-tune strategy to help capture the latent modality alignment. The attention of words and sentences in a recipe is aligned with the image feature in [3]. The modality alignment is imposed using an adversarial loss in [5]. The stochastic latent variables are incorporated to capture the alignments between modalities in [5], and the embeddings of the two modalities are regularized by aligning output semantic probabilities in [7].

These methods achieve considerable results in recipe retrieval. However, most prior works [2, 3, 5–9] simply combine the representations of instructions and ingredients as the recipe embeddings by concatenation operation, then match the image embeddings and the concatenated recipe embeddings in a joint latent space. Two limitations still exist due to the use of pre-train model: the cost of calculating is rising with the increase complexity of the pre-trained model, and the downstream fine-tune tasks have a gap with the pre-trained model. To bridge the gap between the pre-train models and the downstream fine-tune tasks, a method called "prompt-based learning" is proposed in [10]. It is based on language model and used on NLP tasks at first. Prompt based learning model is powerful and attractive for multiple reasons: it allows the model to be pre-trained on massive amounts of raw data, and can be adapted to new scenarios with few or no labeled data. It also bridge the gap between the pre-train process and the downstream training by designing some specific tasks.

CLIP [11] is the first model to adapt prompt-based learning on cross-modal tasks. It jointly trains an image encoder and a text encoder to predict the correct pairings of a batch of image-text training pairs, and use a well-designed prompt template 'A photo of a label' to help bridge the distribution gap in the pre-training dataset.

Based on this idea, we propose a novel fusion framework d **P**rompt **B**ased **L**earning **F**ramework (PBLF) to adopt CLIP model [11] on the recipe retrieval task and design a appropriate prompt template to solve the problems caused by widely used pre-trained models. Our contributions in this paper can be summarized as follows: 1) We introduce transferable visual model CLIP into the recipe retrieval task for the first time, which transfer the knowledge of the CLIP model to the specific task. 2) We design an appropriate prompt to bridge the gap between the pre-trained model and the downstream task. 3) We fine-tune the model which is pre-trained on a dataset of 400 million image-text pairs in an efficient way, we also conduct extensive experiment and ablation study to demonstrate the superiority of our proposed model. The extensive experimental results conducted on the benchmark Recipe1M dataset demonstrate that our proposed PBLF model outperforms the state-of-the-art methods on retrieval performance.

## 2  Related Work

### 2.1  Food Computation

Food has a profound impact on human life. Food computing mainly involves the acquisition and analysis of food data with different modalities, resorting to computer vision, natural language processing, machine learning, data mining and other advanced technologies [1]. In early times, most works focus on food classification and identification [12–15] on the medium-scale datasets such as Food-101 [16]. Other works study different tasks such as nutrition or calorie prediction [17, 18] and recipe recommendation [19–21]. In recent years, the large-scale Recipe1M dataset [2] has become the new benchmark for food computing tasks, which includes over 1m recipes and 800k images. Cross-modal tasks such as recipe generation, image generation from a recipe and question answering of cooking recipes have been explored. In this paper, we concentrate on the task of cross-modal recipe retrieval between food images and recipe texts. In the next section, we introduce the contributions of previous works addressing this task and highlight their differences concerning our PBLF model.

### 2.2  Recipe Retrieval

Cross-modal retrieval has been researched extensively, where the key problem is to measure the similarity between an image and a text [41–45]. This challenging task requires researchers to bridge the gap and capture the latent alignment between different modalities, attracting attention over decades [22]. Canonical Correlation Analysis (CCA) [23] is a typical work in cross-modal data representation learning, it utilizes global alignment to allow the mapping of different modalities. Recently, many efforts have been made to build end-to-end deep learning retrieval systems. The multi-modal embedding is learned via both global and local alignment in [24]. Semantic category labels are exploited to learn discriminative features in [25]. With the development of the generative adversarial networks (GAN) [26], adversarial training methods have also been employed to perform cross-modal retrieval [27, 28].

The baseline of this task is introduced by [2], in which the joint embedding is trained using representations of the cross-modal inputs and regularized via the addition of a high-level classification objective. Early works [4, 5, 8] follow the data processing scheme in [2]. Particularly, the image encoder is based on the pre-trained ResNet-50 [29]. As for the recipes, the instructions are encoded by skip-thoughts [30] and the actual ingredient names are extracted using a separate bi-directional LSTM [31] and further encoded with word2vec [32]. The encoded instructions and ingredients are fed into hierarchical LSTMs and single LSTMs respectively, then concatenated together to generate the encoding of the recipes. Some recent works [3, 6] using raw ingredient text as input, and the Tree-structured LSTM [33] is utilized as the text encoder in CHEF [9].

To capture the latent alignment between modalities, most works place particular emphasis on the fusion strategy. AM [3] models the attention of text in a recipe and aligns them with its image feature. R2GAN [8] learns compatible cross-modal features in an adversarial way. ACME [5] imposes cross-modal translation consistency and aligns modality using an adversarial learning strategy. MCEN [6] incorporates stochastic latent variables to explicitly exploit the interactions between textual and visual features. SCAN [7] regularizes the embeddings of the two modalities by aligning output semantic probabilities. These methods learn the cross-modal fusion from different perspectives. But all of them combine the representation of instructions and ingredients first, then align the composed text modality with images, while ignoring the high-level associations between the three inputs.

Some works [2, 4–6, 8] reconstruct the widely-used triplet loss or ranking loss to adapt to the recipe retrieval task. They utilize cross-entropy or contrastive loss by pseudo-categories extracted from titles to auxiliary the main loss. Some other approaches [5, 6, 8] utilize adversarial losses on top of inputs. While improving the performance of recipe retrieval, these complicated loss functions increase the complexity and difficulty of training.

## 2.3 Prompt-Based Learning

Traditional supervised learning trains a model to take in an input x and predict an output y as $P(y \mid x)$. The main issue with supervised learning is that in order to train a model, it is necessary to have supervised data for the task, which is difficult to be found for many kinds of tasks. Unlike it, prompt-based learning is a new paradigm that model the probability of text directly. To use these models to perform prediction tasks, the original input x is modified using a template into a textual string prompt $x'$ that has some unfilled slots, and then the language model is used to probabilistically fill the unfilled information to obtain a final string $\hat{x}$, from which the final output y can be derived. Prompt based learning have shown remarkable performance by bridging the gap between pre-training tasks and various downstream tasks.

This method is initially proposed to adopt on the language models. A mathematical description of the most fundamental form of prompting is summarized in [10], which encompasses many works on prompting and can be expanded to cover others as well. The basic step for prompting is prompt addition, answer search, answer mapping and design considerations for prompting.

There are many kinds of design considerations for prompting. Pre-trained Model Choice selects pre-trained models that could be used to search over the set of potential answers and calculate the probability of their corresponding filled prompts. Prompt Engineering choosing a proper prompt according to the specific task, which has a large effect not only on the accuracy, but also on which task the model performs in the first place. Answer Engineering designs the answer and possibly along with the mapping function.

Currently, large pre-trained vision-language models like CLIP [11] also show great potential in learning representations that are transferable across different types of downstream task. Therefore, a growing number of researches in the prompt-based learning on cross-modal tasks have been proposed Context Optimization (CoOp) [34] is a simple approach specifically for adapting CLIP-like vision-language models for down-stream image recognition. It models a prompt's context words with learnable vectors while the entire pre-trained parameters are kept fixed. Colorful Prompt Tuning (CPT) [35] reformulates visual grounding into a fill-in-the-blank problem with color-based co-referential markers in image and text, and maximally mitigating the gap.

To our best knowledge, our proposed PBLF model is the first time that prompt-based learning iigs adopted on the cross-modal recipe retrieval task.

## 3   Proposed Method

In this section, we present our proposed cross-modal retrieval PBLF model. The overview architecture of the framework is illustrated in Fig. 1. We use pre-trained CLIP model as our backbone.

### 3.1   Image Embedding

For the image representation, we follow [2] to adopt ResNet-50 [29] as the feature extractor. We incorporate the model by removing the last softmax classification layer, and the rest layers are pre-trained with CLIP. The resulting visual representation is further mapped by a fully connected layer to produce an image embedding with 1024 dimensions, denoted as $I_i$ where $i \in [1, N]$. Here N is the number of samples in a batch.

### 3.2   Prompt-Based Text Embedding

**Prompt Addition.** There are two kinds of data in recipe texts. Instructions consist of multiple sentences and ingredients are sequences with multiple words. [2] uses LSTM

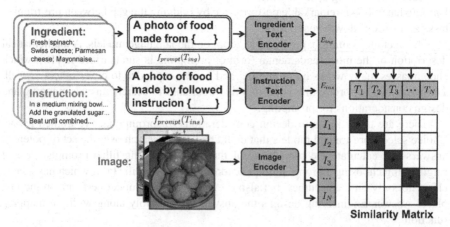

**Fig. 1.** The framework of our proposed PBLF model. The matched image and recipe text pairs are marked by deep color and '*' in the similarity matrix. Our model jointly trains an image encoder and two text encoders to predict the correct pairings of a batch of (image, recipe text) training examples.

to represent the text embedding. Different from it, we introduce prompt-based learning strategy to the recipe retrieval task for the first time. In this step a prompt function fprompt (x) is applied to modify the input recipe text x into a prompt $x' = f_{prompt}(x)$.

In the majority of previous work [11, 34], this prompt function consist of a two step process. The first step is applying a template, which is a string that has a slot: an input slot [X] for input x. For example, the template in CLIP is "A photo of a [X]". Then the second step is fill slot with the input text x. Thus, the input data x will be converted to x' by the prompt function $f_{prompt}(x)$

$$x' = f_{prompt}(x) \tag{1}$$

The structure of instructions and ingredients text is different, here we design two prompt functions for the instructions and ingredients respectively. Here we use the Prompt Engineering strategy mentioned above to decide the prompt template, more details will be described in the experiment section. For the ingredient, $f_{prompt}$ = "A photo of food made from [x]" and for the instructions, $= f_{prompt}$ "A photo of food made by followed instruction [x]".

By this way, the recipe retrieval task is re-adjusted to a form similar to the classification task, thus mitigate the gap between the downstream fine-tune task and the pre-trained task. The converted data x' are fed into the corresponding text encoder to get the representations of instructions and ingredients respectively. Then they are combined by concatenating to get recipe texts embeddings as same as most prior works. Here we follow [11] to use transformer as the text encoder, and the dimension of the text embedding is set to 1024.

**Answer Match.** Most of the standard recipe retrieval models jointly train an image features extractor and a linear classifier to match the image and text embeddings. Different from them, our PBLF model jointly trains an image encoder and a text encoder to predict the correct pairings of a batch of image-text recipe training pairs. This match function could be an argmax match that searches for the highest-scoring matched pairs, or sampling that randomly generates output following the probability distribution of the model. In the recipe retrieval task, we select the argmax match us our function.

In the testing stage, the model will extract the image embeddings and the text embeddings respectively, then go from the highest similarity scoring embeddings to the highest similarity scoring pairs. This is trivial in most of cross-modal retrieval tasks.

### 3.3 Cross-Modal Similarity Learning

Noticed that the image embeddings Ii where i $\in$ [1, N] and the recipe texts embeddings $T_i$ where i $\in$ [1, N] are from the same batch. Thus, the matched image and text pairs are lie in the diagonal of the similarity matrix. Here we use cosine similarity to calculate the similarity scores between a image embedding and a text embedding. The loss in a batch is:

$$L = \left[ S(I_i, T_{i=j}) - S(I_i, T_{i \neq j}) \right] \ where \ i, j \in [1, N] \tag{2}$$

where S is the cosine similarity function, N is the num of samples in a batch.

# 4 Experiment

## 4.1 Experiment Settings

**Dataset.** Following prior works, all experiments are conducted on the Recipe1M dataset [2], which consists of over 1M textual cooking recipes that contain titles, instructions and ingredients. We perform the cross-modal recipe retrieval task based on image-recipe pairs, which means that when the image is used as a query, the ground truth will be the food recipe in the image-recipe pair, and vice versa. We use the official dataset splits which contain 238,999 image-recipe pairs for training, 51,119 pairs for validation and 51,303 pairs for testing.

**Evaluation Metrics.** We measure performance with standard metrics on the cross-modal retrieval task. The median rank (MedR) is the median rank position among where true positives are returned (lower is better). Recall at TopK (R@K) for K = 1, 5, 10 is the percentage of queries for which the true positive is within the top-K retrieved candidates (higher is better). We report average metrics on 10 groups of $N$ randomly chosen samples, where $N = 1000$ (1k setup) or $N = 10000$ (10k setup) as the same in [2].

**Implementation Details.** Our PBLF model is implemented using PyTorch [36]. The experiments are conducted on an NVIDIA GeForce GTX TITAN X with 12 GB RAM. In all experiments, the dimensions of the image embeddings and the recipe texts embeddings are both set to 1024. The batch size is set to 64. As for the optimization, we first freeze the parameters of ResNet and only optimize the rest parameters, thus the PBLF model learns to align to the image representations. After that, we unfreeze all the ResNet weights and fine-tune the entire model until convergence. Adam [37] optimizer is employed and the initial learning rate is $5e-5$ with decay by multiplying 0.3 when the model reaches a plateau. All of the components in our model are trained end-to-end.

## 4.2 Main Results

The cross-modal retrieval performance of our proposed PBLF model is compared with existing works in Table 1, where we take our best performing model on the validation set, and evaluate its performance on the test set. For comparison, we use numbers reported by authors in their respective papers. Our PBLF model outperforms all of the state-of-the-art baselines, which demonstrates the great capability of our trilinear fusion to capture the latent interaction between three inputs. A significant improvement is achieved in all evaluation metrics (MedR and R@K) and retrieval scenarios (image-to-recipe and recipe-to-image) for both 1k-sized and 10k-sized rankings, indicating the robustness of the PBLF model.

Concretely, our model achieves an image-to-recipe R@1 of 61.2 and recipe-to-image R@1 of 61.7 on 1k-sized rankings, which is the best result compared to recent methods. More than that, our method achieves a much better improvement of accuracy for R@5 and R@10. For 1k-sized rankings, the PBLF model achieves an increase by 2.1% and 1.2% for the two retrieval metrics respectively in image-to-recipe retrieval, as well as

2.5% and 1.7% in recipe-to-image retrieval compared with the state-of-the-art methods HT [38]. And the increasing ratios are 6.1% and 8.9% in image-to-recipe retrieval as well as 6.5% and 9.8% in recipe-to-image retrieval for 10k-sized rankings. The incredible improvement for R@5 and R@10 indicates that for most of the queries, our PBLF model ranks the ground-truth results in the top position, which has strong practical significance for the retrieval task. For the 10k-sized test set, the task becomes much harder due to the expansion of diversity, but the PBLF model still achieves state-of-the-art results on it. Results of extensive experiments demonstrate the great capability to capture the latent interaction between three inputs of our trilinear fusion.

### 4.3 Prompt Engineering

The main idea of prompt is to align images and raw text using two separate encoders for different modality. Through large-scale pre-training, vision-language models are allowed to learn visual concepts and can readily be transferred to downstream tasks. CoOp [34] observe that for pre-trained vision-language models the text input, known as prompt, plays a key role in downstream datasets. For example, for Caltech101 dataset, adding "a" to change prompt form "a photo of [CLASS]" to "a photo of a [CLASS]" can increase the accuracy from 78.99% to 84.42%. Moreover, prompt engineering also requires expertise about the task and ideally the language model's underlying mechanism, where adding task-relevant context can lead to significant improvements. For instance, "flower" for Flowers102 dataset, "texture" for DTD dataset and "satellite" for EuroSAT dataset can bring 4.55%, 2.48% and 8.82% increase in accuracy respectively. What's more, tuning the sentence structure could bring further improvements, e.g., putting "a type of flower" after the class token for Flowers102 dataset, keeping only "texture" in the context for DTD dataset, and adding "centered" before "satellite photo" for EuroSat dataset.

**Table 1.** Main results on Image-to-Recipe against baseline methods. The cross-modal retrieval performance is evaluated with MedR (lower is better) and R@K (higher is better). The symbol "–" means the results are not available in the original paper

| Size | Methods | Image-to-recipe | | | | Recipe-to-image | | | |
|------|---------|------|-----|-----|------|------|-----|-----|------|
| | | MedR | R@1 | R@5 | R@10 | MedR | R@1 | R@5 | R@10 |
| 1k | CCA [23] | 15.7 | 14.0 | 32.0 | 43.0 | 24.8 | 9.0 | 24.0 | 35.0 |
| | JE [2] | 5.2 | 24.0 | 51.0 | 65.0 | 5.1 | 25.0 | 52.0 | 65.0 |
| | AM [3] | 4.6 | 25.6 | 53.7 | 66.9 | 4.6 | 25.7 | 53.9 | 67.1 |
| | AdaMine [4] | 1.0 | 39.8 | 69.0 | 77.4 | 1.0 | 40.2 | 68.1 | 78.7 |
| | R2GAN [8] | 2.0 | 39.1 | 71.0 | 81.7 | 2.0 | 40.6 | 72.6 | 83.3 |
| | ACME [5] | 1.0 | 51.8 | 80.2 | 87.5 | 1.0 | 52.8 | 80.2 | 87.6 |
| | DaC [39] | 1.0 | 55.9 | 82.4 | 88.7 | – | – | – | – |

(*continued*)

**Table 1.** (*continued*)

| Size | Methods | Image-to-recipe | | | | Recipe-to-image | | | |
|------|---------|------|-----|-----|------|------|-----|-----|------|
|      |         | MedR | R@1 | R@5 | R@10 | MedR | R@1 | R@5 | R@10 |
|      | MCEN [6] | 2.0 | 48.2 | 75.8 | 83.6 | 1.9 | 48.4 | 76.1 | 83.7 |
|      | SCAN [7] | 1.0 | 54.0 | 81.7 | 88.8 | 1.0 | 54.9 | 81.9 | 89.0 |
|      | CHEF [9] | 1.6 | 49.7 | 79.3 | 86.3 | 1.5 | 49.9 | 78.8 | 86.2 |
|      | HT [40] | 1.0 | 60.0 | 87.6 | 92.9 | 1.0 | 60.3 | 87.6 | 93.2 |
|      | PBLF (Ours) | **1.0** | **61.2** | **89.5** | **94.1** | **1.0** | **61.7** | **89.8** | **94.8** |
| 10k | JE [2] | 41.9 | – | – | – | 39.2 | – | – | – |
|     | AM [3] | 39.8 | 7.2 | 19.2 | 27.6 | 38.1 | 7.0 | 19.4 | 27.8 |
|     | AdaMine [4] | 13.2 | 14.9 | 35.3 | 45.2 | 12.2 | 14.8 | 34.6 | 46.1 |
|     | R2GAN [8] | 13.9 | 13.5 | 33.5 | 44.9 | 12.6 | 14.2 | 35.0 | 46.8 |
|     | ACME [5] | 6.7 | 22.9 | 46.8 | 57.9 | 6.0 | 24.4 | 47.9 | 59.0 |
|     | DaC [39] | 5.0 | 26.5 | 51.8 | 62.6 | – | – | – | – |
|     | MCEN [6] | 7.2 | 20.3 | 43.3 | 54.4 | 6.6 | 21.4 | 44.3 | 55.2 |
|     | SCAN [7] | 5.9 | 23.7 | 49.3 | 60.6 | 5.1 | 25.3 | 50.6 | 61.6 |
|     | CHEF [9] | 7.3 | 20.9 | 44.8 | 56.3 | 7.0 | 21.9 | 45.2 | 56.6 |
|     | HT [40] | 4.0 | 27.9 | 56.4 | 68.1 | 4.0 | 28.3 | 56.5 | 68.1 |
|     | PBLF (Ours) | **3.6** | **29.3** | **59.8** | **74.2** | **3.4** | **30.1** | **60.2** | **74.8** |

Based on this information, we conduct an ablation study to find out the proper prompt engineering for the recipe retrieval task. As shown in 2, the modified template bring improvements in accuracy. We select "A photo of food made from [x]" as our ingredients template and "a photo of food made by followed instruction [x]" as our prompt template.

### 4.4 Scalability

We compare the MedR score of the PBLF model and other baselines against the test set larger than 10k to investigate the scalability of our model. We provide numbers reported in [6]. As shown in Fig. 2, it can be observed that the PBLF model outperforms all baselines on all test sets. As the size of the test set increases, the gap of performance between PBLF and other models becomes larger. A reasonable explanation is that our model transfer the knowledge of the large-scale CLIP model to specific recipe retrieval task, which enhances the robustness of the PBLF model (Table 2).

### 4.5 Visualization

**Recipe-to-Image Retrieval Results.** In Fig. 3, we analyze the typical visualized results on recipe-to-image retrieval obtained by our PBLF model. We select the recipe of three

**Table 2.** Ablation study of the prompt engineering. We try widely-used prompt template then modify it to other task-specific templates.

| Ingredients | Instructions | I-to-R R@1 | R-to-I R@1 |
|---|---|---|---|
| A photo of [X] | A photo of [X] | 52.2 | 52.4 |
| A photo of [X] | A food photo made by [X] | 54.3 | 54.8 |
| A photo of [X] | A photo of food made by followed instruction [x] | 56.6 | 56.9 |
| A food photo of [X] | A photo of [X] | 54.2 | 54.5 |
| A food photo of [X] | A food photo made by [X] | 57.1 | 57.3 |
| A food photo of [X] | A photo of food made by followed instruction [x] | 56.5 | 56.9 |
| A photo of food made from [x] | A photo of [X] | 56.8 | 57.2 |
| A photo of food made from [x] | A food photo made by [X] | 58.9 | 59.1 |
| A photo of food made from [x] | A photo of food made by followed instruction [x] | **61.2** | **61.7** |

different dishes Butternut Squash Bisque, Family Favorite Vegetable Lasagna and Fiesta Mac and Cheese as the query and display the top-5 retrieved images. In all of them, the PBLF model retrieves the correct matched image in the top-3 position.

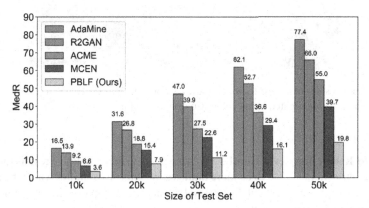

**Fig. 2.** Scalability comparison between different models for image-to-recipe retrieval. MedR is used as the evaluation metric (lower is better).

Generally, we can find that the appearances of the ground-truth image and the retrieved candidates are very similar, which show the difficulty of the recipe retrieval task. We can notice that in the first example, all retrieved images are thick soup in orange and brown color, or the second example, all images contain cheese and the main ingredient in all of them is Lasagna, same as the correct recipe. And for the third example, all images includes pasta. These tasks are indistinguishable even to humans, but our

PBLF model bridge the gap between the pre-trained model and the downstream task, demonstrating the great ability of the recipe retrieval task.

**Fig. 3.** Top-5 results of recipe-to-image retrieval obtained by our TFUN model. The correct retrieved image is highlighted in red color. (Color figure online)

**Image-to-Recipe Retrieval Results.** We also analyze the qualitative results on image-to-recipe retrieval in Fig. 4. To be more intuitive, we choose examples where the ground-truth recipe is ranked second in the retrieval results, and compared the top-1 misleading image-recipe pairs with the query.

As can be observed in Fig. 4, the appearance of the query image and the retrieved image is very similar in each row, and these two recipes both belong to the same category of food. For the first row, both recipes are some kinds of cheese pie with onions, for the second row, both recipes are cupcake and for the third row, both recipes include avocado. The ingredients that appear in both recipes are marked in red, we can notice that for all the queries, more than half of the ingredients are the same in the retrieved results. The failed cases that our model cannot retrieve the ground-truth recipe occurs due to the invisible ingredients, such like milk, pomegranate and parsley, or the fact that in the query recipe and the retrieved result, most of the ingredients are the same and the image looks similar.

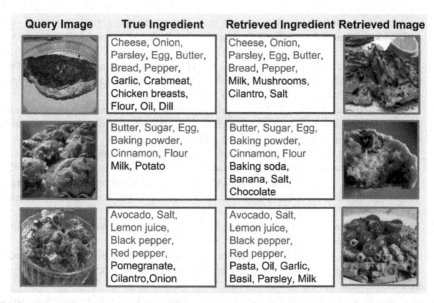

| Query Image | True Ingredient | Retrieved Ingredient | Retrieved Image |
|---|---|---|---|
| | Cheese, Onion, Parsley, Egg, Butter, Bread, Pepper, Garlic, Crabmeat, Chicken breasts, Flour, Oil, Dill | Cheese, Onion, Parsley, Egg, Butter, Bread, Pepper, Milk, Mushrooms, Cilantro, Salt | |
| | Butter, Sugar, Egg, Baking powder, Cinnamon, Flour Milk, Potato | Butter, Sugar, Egg, Baking powder, Cinnamon, Flour Baking soda, Banana, Salt, Chocolate | |
| | Avocado, Salt, Lemon juice, Black pepper, Red pepper, Pomegranate, Cilantro,Onion | Avocado, Salt, Lemon juice, Black pepper, Red pepper, Pasta, Oil, Garlic, Basil, Parsley, Milk | |

**Fig. 4.** Illustration of the image-to-recipe retrieval examples, where the same ingredients in the correct recipe and retrieved recipe are marked in red color

## 5   Conclusion

In this paper, we proposed a novel model named PBLF for cross-modal recipe retrieval. The proposed model focuses on learning image-recipe similarity efficiently by introducing the CLIP model into the recipe retrieval task for the first time. We also design an appropriate prompt to train the model and migrate the gap between the pre-trained model and the downstream task. The extensive experimental results show that the proposed models achieve state-of-the-art results on the large-scale benchmark dataset Recipe1M. In the future, we would like to explore the impact of different prompt-based learning strategies in the recipe retrieval task.

## References

1. Min, W., Jiang, S., Liu, L., Rui, Y., Jain, R.C.: A survey on food computing. ACM Comput. Surv. **52**(5), 92:1–92:36 (2019)
2. Salvador, A., et al.: Learning cross-modal embeddings for cooking recipes and food images. In: 2017 IEEE Conference on Computer Vision and Pattern Recognition, CVPR, pp. 3068–3076 (2017)

3. Chen, J., Ngo, C., Feng, F., Chua, T.: Deep understanding of cooking procedure for cross-modal recipe retrieval. In: 2018 ACM Multimedia Conference on Multimedia Conference, MM, pp. 1020–1028 (2018)

4. Carvalho, M., Cadène, R., Picard, D., Soulier, L., Thome, N., Cord, M.: Cross-modal retrieval in the cooking context: learning semantic text-image embeddings. In: International ACM SIGIR Conference on Research and Development in Information Retrieval, SIGIR, pp. 35–44 (2018)

5. Wang, H., Sahoo, D., Liu, C., Lim, E., Hoi, S.C.H.: Learning cross-modal embeddings with adversarial networks for cooking recipes and food images. In: IEEE Conference on Computer Vision and Pattern Recognition, CVPR, pp. 11572–11581 (2019)

6. Fu, H., Wu, R., Liu, C., Sun, J.: MCEN: bridging cross-modal gap between cooking recipes and dish images with latent variable model. In: 2020 IEEE/CVF Conference on Computer Vision and Pattern Recognition, CVPR, pp. 14558–14568 (2020)

7. Wang, H., et al.: Cross-modal food retrieval: learning a joint embedding of food images and recipes with semantic consistency and attention mechanism. CoRR abs/2003.03955 (2020)

8. Zhu, B., Ngo, C., Chen, J., Hao, Y.: R2GAN: cross-modal recipe retrieval with generative adversarial network. In: IEEE Conference on Computer Vision and Pattern Recognition, CVPR, pp. 11477–11486 (2019)

9. Pham, H.X., Guerrero, R., Li, J., Pavlovic, V.: CHEF: cross-modal hierarchical embeddings for food domain retrieval. arXiv preprint arXiv:2102.02547 (2021)

10. Liu, P., Yuan, W., Fu, J., Jiang, Z., Hayashi, H., Neubig, G.: Pre-train, prompt, and predict: a systematic survey of prompting methods in natural language processing. arXiv preprint arXiv:2107.13586 (2021)

11. Radford, A., et al.: Learning transferable visual models from natural language supervision. In: International Conference on Machine Learning, pp. 8748–8763. PMLR (2021)

12. Chen, J., Ngo, C.: Deep-based ingredient recognition for cooking recipe retrieval. In: Proceedings of the 2016 ACM Conference on Multimedia Conference, MM, pp. 32–41 (2016)

13. Liu, C., Cao, Y., Luo, Y., Chen, G., Vokkarane, V., Ma, Y.: DeepFood: deep learning-based food image recognition for computer-aided dietary assessment. In: Chang, C.K., Chiari, L., Cao, Y., Jin, H., Mokhtari, M., Aloulou, H. (eds.) ICOST 2016. LNCS, vol. 9677, pp. 37–48. Springer, Cham (2016). https://doi.org/10.1007/978-3-319-39601-9_4

14. Lee, K., He, X., Zhang, L., Yang, L.: CleanNet: transfer learning for scalable image classifier training with label noise. In: 2018 IEEE Conference on Computer Vision and Pattern Recognition, CVPR, pp. 5447–5456 (2018)

15. Zhou, F., Lin, Y.: Fine-grained image classification by exploring bipartite-graph labels. In: 2016 IEEE Conference on Computer Vision and Pattern Recognition, CVPR, pp. 1124–1133 (2016)

16. Bossard, L., Guillaumin, M., Van Gool, L.: Food-101 – mining discriminative components with random forests. In: Fleet, D., Pajdla, T., Schiele, B., Tuytelaars, T. (eds.) ECCV 2014. LNCS, vol. 8694, pp. 446–461. Springer, Cham (2014). https://doi.org/10.1007/978-3-319-10599-4_29

17. Kusmierczyk, T., Nørvåg, K.: Online food recipe title semantics: combining nutrient facts and topics. In: Proceedings of the 25th ACM International Conference on Information and Knowledge Management, CIKM, pp. 2013–2016 (2016)

18. Myers, A., et al.: Im2Calories: towards an automated mobile vision food diary. In: 2015 IEEE International Conference on Computer Vision, ICCV, pp. 1233–1241 (2015)

19. Trattner, C., Elsweiler, D.: Investigating the healthiness of internet-sourced recipes: implications for meal planning and recommender systems. In: Proceedings of the 26th International Conference on World Wide Web, WWW, pp. 489–498 (2017)

20. Elsweiler, D., Trattner, C., Harvey, M.: Exploiting food choice biases for healthier recipe recommendation. In: Proceedings of the 40th International ACM SIGIR Conference on Research and Development in Information Retrieval, pp. 575–584 (2017)

21. Yang, L., et al.: Yum-Me: a personalized nutrient-based meal recommender system. ACM Trans. Inf. Syst. **36**(1), 7:1–7:31 (2017)

22. Lew, M.S., Sebe, N., Djeraba, C., Jain, R.: Content-based multimedia information retrieval: state of the art and challenges. ACM Trans. Multimedia Comput. Commun. Appl. (TOMM) **2**(1), 1–19 (2006)

23. Hotelling, H.: Relations between two sets of variates. Biometrika **28**, 321–377 (1935)

24. Jiang, X., et al.: Deep compositional cross-modal learning to rank via local-global alignment. In: Proceedings of the 23rd Annual ACM Conference on Multimedia Conference, MM, pp. 69–78 (2015)

25. Peng, Y., Qi, J., Huang, X., Yuan, Y.: CCL: cross-modal correlation learning with multigrained fusion by hierarchical network. IEEE Trans. Multimedia **20**(2), 405–420 (2017)

26. Goodfellow, I.J., et al.: Generative adversarial nets. In: Annual Conference on Neural Information Processing Systems 2014, pp. 2672–2680 (2014)

27. Peng, Y., Qi, J., Yuan, Y.: CM-GANs: cross-modal generative adversarial networks for common representation learning. CoRR abs/1710.05106 (2017)

28. Wang, B., Yang, Y., Xu, X., Hanjalic, A., Shen, H.T.: Adversarial cross-modal retrieval. In: Proceedings of the 2017 ACM on Multimedia Conference, MM, pp. 154–162 (2017)

29. He, K., Zhang, X., Ren, S., Sun, J.: Deep residual learning for image recognition. In: 2016 IEEE Conference on Computer Vision and Pattern Recognition, CVPR, pp. 770–778 (2016)

30. Kiros, R., et al.: Skip-thought vectors. In: Annual Conference on Neural Information Processing Systems 2015, pp. 3294–3302 (2015)

31. Hochreiter, S., Schmidhuber, J.: Long short-term memory. Neural Comput. **9**(8), 1735–1780 (1997)

32. Mikolov, T., Sutskever, I., Chen, K., Corrado, G.S., Dean, J.: Distributed representations of words and phrases and their compositionality. In: Annual Conference on Neural Information Processing Systems 2013, pp. 3111–3119 (2013)

33. Tai, K.S., Socher, R., Manning, C.D.: Improved semantic representations from tree-structured long short-term memory networks. arXiv preprint arXiv:1503.00075 (2015)

34. Zhou, K., Yang, J., Loy, C.C., Liu, Z.: Learning to prompt for vision-language models. arXiv preprint arXiv:2109.01134 (2021)

35. Yao, Y., Zhang, A., Zhang, Z., Liu, Z., Chua, T.-S., Sun, M.: CPT: colorful prompt tuning for pre-trained vision-language models. arXiv preprint arXiv:2109.11797 (2021)

36. Paszke, A., et al.: PyTorch: an imperative style, high-performance deep learning library. arXiv preprint arXiv:1912.01703 (2019)

37. Kingma, D.P., Ba, J.: Adam: a method for stochastic optimization. In: Bengio, Y., LeCun, Y. (eds.) 3rd International Conference on Learning Representations, ICLR (2015)

38. Salvador, A., Gundogdu, E., Bazzani, L., Donoser, M.: Revamping cross-modal recipe retrieval with hierarchical transformers and self-supervised learning. arXiv preprint arXiv: 2103.13061 (2021)

39. Fain, M., Ponikar, A., Fox, R., Bollegala, D.: Dividing and conquering cross-modal recipe retrieval: from nearest neighbours baselines to SoTA. arXiv preprint arXiv:1911.12763 (2019)

40. Salvador, A., Gundogdu, E., Bazzani, L., Donoser, M.: Revamping cross-modal recipe retrieval with hierarchical transformers and self-supervised learning. In: Proceedings of the IEEE/CVF Conference on Computer Vision and Pattern Recognition, pp. 15475–15484 (2021)

41. Lu, H., Yang, R., Deng, Z., Zhang, Y., Gao, G., Lan, R.: Chinese image captioning via fuzzy attention-based DenseNet-BiLSTM. ACM Trans. Multimedia Comput. Commun. Appl. **17**(1s), 1–18 (2021)

42. Lu, H., Zhang, Y., Li, Y., Jiang, C., Abbas, H.: User-Oriented virtual mobile network resource management for vehicle communications. IEEE Trans. Intell. Transp. Syst. (2020). https://doi.org/10.1109/TITS.2020.2991766

43. Lu, H., Qin, M., Zhang, F., et al.: RSCNN: a CNN-based method to enhance low-light remote-sensing images. Remote Sens. **13**, 62 (2020)

44. Lu, H., Zhang, M., Xu, X.: Deep fuzzy hashing network for efficient image retrieval. IEEE Trans. Fuzzy Syst. (2020). https://doi.org/10.1109/TFUZZ.2020.2984991

45. Li, Y., Yang, S., Zheng, Y., Lu, H.: Improved point-voxel region convolutional neural network: 3D object detectors for autonomous driving. IEEE Trans. Intell. Transp. Syst. **23**, 9311–9317 (2021)

# Predictive Information Preservation via Variational Information Bottleneck for Cross-View Geo-Localization

Wansi Li[✉] and Qian Hu

University of Electronic Science and Technology of China, Chengdu 611731, Sichuan, China
wansil793@gmail.com

**Abstract.** Cross-view geo-localization task, which is to handle the problem of matching two images captured same target building, but from different viewpoints, e.g., satellite-view and drone-view, has received significant attention in recent years. However, this research is impeded by the large visual appearance changes across different views and irrelevant content contained in the background. Previous work mitigates the geo-view gap by some similarity-based constraints or utilizing rich contextual information near the target as auxiliary information. Despite some promising breakthroughs made by such methods, they fail to consider the involvement of irrelevant features retained in the high-dimensional features, which reduces the accuracy of the retrieval result. This paper proposes a simple and efficient model termed Predictive Information Preservation Bottleneck (PIPB), using the variational information bottleneck to discard the irrelevant information and retain the predictive information, enhancing the result performance. In particular, our proposed PIPB consists of two stages. Firstly, we learn the part-based features of each image to make full use of neighbor clues, which is realized by the square-ring partition strategy. Then, at the second stage, these learned representations are fed through the variational information bottleneck module to filter out superfluous information. This step can promote the robustness and generalization of our model and improve experiment performance. Extensive experiments are conducted on the recently-released dataset University-1652 and the fundamental benchmark CVACT, showing remarkable performance results compared to other competitive methods.

**Keywords:** Geo-localization · Variational information bottleneck · Deep neural network

## 1 Introduction

Associating visual appearance from different perspectives and exploring their relations have attracted great interest in recent years. Many relevant image retrieval tasks obtain constantly progress due to their great potential [1–4]. Among them, the cross-view geo-localization task catches the attention [5–9]. It aims to predict whether two images belong to the same geographic target, despite they are captured from different perspectives. As

S. Yang and H. Lu (Eds.): ISAIR 2022, CCIS 1700, pp. 403–419, 2022.
https://doi.org/10.1007/978-981-19-7946-0_34

shown in Fig. 1, if given a satellite-view image of a landmark (query), the system retrieves the drone-view image with the same geo-tagged in the gallery dataset. This ability enables a large number of applications including robot navigation, aerial photography, multi-view coordination, especially facilitating the positioning devices (GPS) [5, 6, 10, 11].

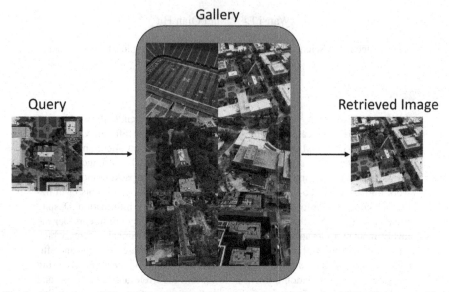

**Fig. 1.** Illustration of Cross-View Geo-Localization task on University-1652. Given a satellite-view image (query), the system retrieves the drone-view images (gallery) with the same landmark.

Since the images are captured by different devices, the large visual appearance variation [6, 8] and irrelevant content [10, 16] in the background are two main problems faced by the cross-view geo-localization task. Most previous approaches put effort to alleviate them by the deep neural network and metric learning [6–9]. They usually deploy a convolutional neural network (CNN) to learn discriminative representations and use some particular constraints (e.g., triple loss) to close the gap between matched images, while pulling apart those with different geo-tags [12–14]. Also, from the position and orientation perspectives, Liu et al. [8] and Shi et al. [15] concentrate on exploring orientation alignment between different viewpoint images to reduce matching ambiguity. They apply a polar transformation strategy to the satellite-view images and use CNN to extract discriminative representations from ground-view images and polar-transformed satellite-view images to align orientation.

It is observed that many methods are employed to obtain invariant representations, but ignore rich contextual information around the target. If this information is not put to good use, they are bootless and superfluous. In this circumstance, Wang et al. [16] utilize the square-ring partition strategy to obtain neighbor information of the target, enabling larger receptive fields. However, in this process, more useless features are extracted inevitably, which can bring a negative influence on the retrieval result. The problem has become how to obtain compressed representations with maximum predictive information of the ground-truth.

In [17], they hold the view that large-scale pretrained natural language models, e.g., BERT, suffer from the overfitting problem on low-resource target tasks. To address this issue, the VIBERT model is proposed, applying the variational information bottleneck [18] to improve the robustness and generalization capability of the model. Inspired by it, we consider using the variational information bottleneck to discard superfluous nuisance and preserve predictive information of the target. The low-dimensional discriminative representations can enhance the retrieval performance on our cross-view geo-localization task. Different from it, we employ the variational information bottleneck to the cross-view image retrieval task. We utilize ResNet-50 as our backbone with a square-ring partition strategy [16] to obtain the part-based features. The contextual information around the geographic landmark is leveraged as auxiliary clues to enrich discriminative information. What's more, to the best of our knowledge, the variational information bottleneck is first introduced to this task with the combination of the CNN.

Based on it, we propose a simple and efficient approach named Predictive Information Preservation Bottleneck (PIPB) for the cross-view geo-localization task, which outperforms other competitive methods. Our work follows the idea of the information bottleneck principle [19] to solve the problem of irrelevant information. This approach is termed the variational information bottleneck which adopts the reparameterization trick, making it possible to compute the gradients during backpropagation.

The overall architecture is shown in Fig. 2, which is made up of two stages. At stage one, images of two views are extracted part-based features with the use of the square-ring partition strategy. It leverages the surrounding information around the target as the auxiliary information to obtain more discriminative representations. Then, at stage two, the variational information bottleneck module is followed to discard the task-independent information while retaining task-dependent information. This concise representation can promote robustness and generalization and improve retrieval performance.

Our contributions are presented as follows:

We propose a simple and efficient cross-view geo-localization method to learn compact and discriminative representations, named Predictive Information Preservation Bottleneck (PIPB) by the use of information bottleneck theory and variational approximation.

We arise a critical problem that has been neglected in previous approaches and tackle it by the variational information bottleneck module. To the best of our knowledge, we first introduce the variational information bottleneck to the cross-view geo-localization task with the combination of the CNN.

Extensive experiments are carried on a newly-proposed dataset University-1652 and a fundamental benchmark dataset CVACT demonstrate the superior retrieval performance of our proposed PIPB method.

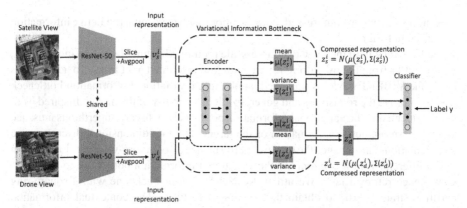

**Fig. 2.** The proposed method PIPB adopts the ResNet-50 as our backbone to extract the representations. The overall framework consists of two stages, i.e., part-based feature extraction and variational information bottleneck module. At the first stage, we exploit the square-ring partition strategy to split the feature maps into part-based feature maps. At the second stage, the variational information bottleneck is employed to abandon the irrelevant information while preserving predictive information, resulting in the improvement of robustness and generalization ability.

## 2 Related Work

### 2.1 Drone-Based Geo-Localization

The drone-based geo-localization task is recently proposed, which refers to drone-view images and drone navigation images retrieved with each other, and has an outstanding prospect. In [5], Zheng et al. pointed out that the drone view met fewer obstacles and proposed a novel dataset namely University-1652, which added drone-view images to the dataset. They claimed that this dataset helped the model to settle the issue of significant visual changes across views and also had good generalization and robustness ability in the practice. Hu et al. [20] proposed to extract aligned partial features [21] and used a style alignment strategy to reduce variant image style and improve the feature unification. In [22], they adopted peer learning to accomplish adaptive alignment during the training process. Moreover, Wang et al. [16] leveraged the contextual information as the auxiliary information, which refers to the features around the target. They applied the partition strategy to learn the part-based representations, resulting in excellent performance improvement.

However, previous work has not taken the superfluous information contained in the learned high-dimensional features into consideration. Such neglect is detrimental to the retrieval result. Different from them, we consider exploring this problem by introducing the variational information bottleneck which provides a variational approximation to the information bottleneck [18, 19].

### 2.2 Ground-to-Satellite Geo-Localization

Ground-to-Satellite geo-localization is a fundamental task in this field, which has been proposed long ago. Given a ground-view image, the network should predict the most similar satellite-view image in the reference dataset. Early work studied on the hand-crafted feature matching [23–25], but was bottlenecked by the large visual variations of different viewpoints. Then, the deep neural network revealed the strong representation learning ability [26]. Workman et al. [27], who first utilized CNN pretrained on ImageNet [28] to the cross-view geo-localization task, attempted to learn discriminative representations from different viewpoints by closing the gap between ground-view and satellite-view features in each pair. Vo et al. [29] designed a soft margin triplet loss to make the model towards the expected triplet embedding learning. To tackle the variant appearance of different perspectives, Zhai et al. [30] proposed a modified Siamese Network [31] by plugging a NetVLAD [32] layer. Later, Liu et al. [8] demonstrated that the orientation was of great importance to enhance the robustness against large viewpoint changes and encoded corresponding coordinate information into the network. Shi et al. [7] explicitly established cross-view domain transfer by the usage of the spatial layout information.

However, there is still little attention paid to the redundancy retained in the learned high-dimensional representations of the cross-view geo-localization task. We utilize the variational information bottleneck theory to abandon the information that is not useful for the given task.

### 2.3 Information Bottleneck

The application of information bottleneck principle traces back to two decades ago, e.g., document clustering [33, 49–53], image segmentation [34] and computer vision [35, 36], due to its ability to learn compact and discriminative representations [37, 38]. This principle was first proposed by Tishby et al. [19]. In this work, they treated it as a theoretic foundation for signal processing, attempting to find a short-code of the input signal while preserving maximum key information. Tishby et al. [39] put forward the idea of using information-theoretic objectives for deep neural networks but left no experimental results. The principle is attractive since it encourages the learned latent representation to be informative of the label and "forget" the original input to the greatest extent. However, the annoying problem of the mutual information computation is intractable [45] and the optimization of the deep neural networks is infeasible [39]. Inspired by the variational auto-encoders (VAE) [40], recent work [18, 35] exploited variational inference to approximate the problem which adopted the reparameterization trick [40], and named the novel method as variational information bottleneck.

Some previous work also employed the information bottleneck theory to the multi-view representation [41–44]. Inspired by it, we consider using this theory to the cross-view geo-localization with the combination of CNN [18, 35].

## 3 Our PIPB Approach

### 3.1 Problem Setting

In the cross-view geo-localization task, the training set is denoted as $\{x_j, y\}$ where $x_j$ is the input image from a particular platform and $y$ is its corresponding label. Particularly, the subscript $j$ in $\{d, s, g\}$, indicating drone-view, satellite-view, and ground-view, respectively. And $y$ in $\{1, 2 \dots N\}$ where $N$ is set to the number of labels. For the University-1652 training dataset, there are 701 buildings with 50,218 images, which implies that $N = 701$. In our experiment, we only use drone-view images and satellite-view images to accomplish two specific, that is, images from these two perspectives are retrieved with each other. Therefore, $x_j$ in $\{x_d, x_s\}$. It is worth noting that the training set and test set share no overlap. Given an image $x_j$, we aim to predict corresponding images from the other viewpoint that contain the same landmark. In our method, we learn cross-view representations via a parameters-shared CNN and divide the feature maps into small parts. Each part contains different information, either from the geographic target or the background in the image. Then, part-based feature maps are bypassed a variational information bottleneck module to filter out excess information while preserving maximum information of the target, which improves the robustness ability of the model and the retrieval performance.

### 3.2 Part-Based Feature Extraction

Due to the strong feature representation capability of deep CNNs, we implement ResNet-50 [45], which is pretrained on ImageNet [28], as our backbone to extract features from drone-view and satellite-view. These two networks are parameter-shared since both views are from the aerial viewpoint. When applying, we remove the last two layers for the subsequent partition strategy. Particularly, we resize input images $x_j$ ($x_j \in \{x_d, x_s\}$) as 256 * 256 and let them pass the backbone to obtain feature maps $f_j$.

After obtaining the extracted representation $f_j$, we use the square-ring partition strategy to slice up the feature map [16], which is to explicitly utilize the contextual information of the geographic target. Based on the assumption that the landmark is usually located in the center of the image, we choose the square-ring partition strategy, denoted as P, to divide the feature maps into i small parts, i.e., $f_j^i = P(f_j)$ ($i = 4$ on University-1652 and $i = 8$ on CVACT). Then, the average pooling operation is performed to transform each part-based feature map to an unified 2048-dim shape $v_j^i = Avg(f_j^i)$.

### 3.3 Variational Information Bottleneck

The information bottleneck principle can help the network learn a low-dimensional representation $z$ of an input $x$ that is maximally informative about the target $y$ [19, 35, 39]. As mentioned in Sect. 3.2, the ResNet-50 and square-ring partition strategy are adopted to extract part-based features $v_j^i \in R^d$. $d$ is the dimension of the part-based features which equals 2048. However, the redundancy retained in the learned features reduces the convergence rate of the model and adversely impacts the retrieval performance. To suppress the task-irrelevant features, we would like to utilize the information bottleneck to obtain lower-dimension representations with maximum predictive information of the target.

$$z_j^i = IB(v_j^i) \tag{1}$$

where represents $z_j^i$ the low-dimensional $i^{th}$ part of the $j$-view feature map. $z_j^i \in R^d$ And $d = 512$.

According to the information bottleneck theory, the mutual information is used to measure the dependence between two variables, i.e., $I(X; Y)$. The objective of employing an information bottleneck is to encourage the model to learn a low-dimensional representation $Z$ of the input $X$ which can predict the label $Y$ correctly. Then, an information constraint $I_c$ is necessary to learn the best representation $Z$ of $Y$, that is, $I(X; Y) \leq I_c$. And we obtain:

$$L_{IB} = I(Z; Y) - \beta I(Z; X) \tag{2}$$

where the first term denotes the predictive ability of $Z$ to $Y$. And the second term measures the dependence between $Z$ and $X$. $\beta \geq 0$ implies the balance between compression and prediction.

The trade-off between the compression and mutual information, however, suffers from computational complexity. We can observe the challenging computation from the following equation.

$$I(X; Y) = \iint_{XY} p(x, y) \log(\frac{p(x, y)}{p(x)p(y)}) dxdy \tag{3}$$

In [18], they applied a variational inference to construct a lower bound of Eq. 2 and leverage the reparameterization trick [40] to obtain a low-dimensional latent representation $Z$. They named this method as the variational information bottleneck and provided the following formulation:

$$L_{VIB} = \beta E_x \big[ KL[p(z|x), r(z)] \big] + E_{z \sim p(z|x)} \big[ -\log q(y|z) \big] \tag{4}$$

where $r(z)$ represents a prior marginal distribution. $q(y|z)$ is a parametric approximation of $p(y|z)$ and $p(z|x)$ is an estimate of the posterior probability of $z$. $KL$ stands for the *Kullback-Leibler divergence*.

The former term is the compression loss $L_{cl}$ and the latter one is the prediction loss according to different given tasks. Based on Eq. 4, we discover that the idea of variational information bottleneck coincides with our goal: if we minimize the $KL - divergence$, the dependence between the input $x$ and the representation $z$ is weak, indicating that $z$ preserves less information from $x$. And the prediction loss ensures that the predictive information of the ground-truth $y$ is retained in $z$.

$$L_{cl(\theta)} = \beta E_x \big[ KL[p(z|x; \theta), r(z)] \big] \tag{5}$$

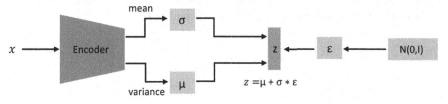

**Fig. 3.** The details of the reparameterization trick.

In training, the compressed $z$ is sampled from the Gaussian distribution $p(z|x; \theta)$ to reduce task-independent nuisance factors and enhance the robustness and generalization of our model. We feed the part-based feature maps through an encoder, followed by two linear layers to extract $\mu$ and $\sigma$. $\mu$ plays a decisive role in our learned compressed representation $z$ and $\sigma$ can be regarded as the noise which helps to improve the robustness. The reparameterization trick [40] is employed to estimate the gradients. The specific implementation detail is shown in Fig. 3. At last, the compressed representation $z$ is sent to the classifier, which is composed of a linear layer.

$$z = \mu + \sigma * \epsilon \tag{6}$$

where $\epsilon \sim N(0, I)$.

### 3.4 Overall Objective

To ensure that our low-dimensional latent representation $z$ is discriminative and predictive to the ground-truth target y, we deploy the standard classification objective loss, i.e., cross-entropy, as our prediction loss:

$$L_{cls} = -\log\left(\frac{\exp(v_j^i(y))}{\sum_{c=1}^{C}(\exp(v_j^i(c)))}\right) \tag{7}$$

where $v_j^i(y)$ denotes the logit score of the ground-truth geo-tag y. C represents the number of the classification objects.

Therefore, the overall objective is the sum of the compression loss and the classification loss:

$$min\, L = \sum_{i,j} (L_{cl} + L_{cls}) \tag{8}$$

which indicates that the loss is a sum of all i parts from both j views.

## 4  Experiments

### 4.1  Datasets and Setup

**Datasets.** We evaluate the effectiveness of our proposed PIPB on a newly-proposed dataset University-1652 [5] and a fundamental benchmark dataset CVACT [8]. A brief introduction of these two datasets is shown in Table 1. And Table 2 provides the number of test images between query and gallery for different tasks.

**Table 1.** Statistical information of the two datasets University-1652 and CVACT used in the experiments.

| Dataset | University-1652 [5] | CVACT [8] |
|---|---|---|
| Training | 701 × 71.64 | 35.5k × 2 |
| Platform | Drone, Satellite, Ground | Satellite, Ground |
| Images/location | 54 + 16.64 + 1 | 1 + 1 |
| Geo-tag | Yes | Yes |
| Evaluation protocol | Recall@K, AP | Recall@K |

The University-1652 dataset is a multi-view dataset that collects 1,652 buildings of 72 universities from satellite, drone, and ground viewpoints. Among them, images from the drone-view are simulated by Google Earth with its 3D models because of the high cost. This dataset is divided into 701 teaching buildings of 33 universities for the training set and 95 teaching buildings of the other 39 universities for the test set. There is no overlap between training and test set. We use University-1652 dataset to implement two tasks, i.e., Drone Satellite and Satellite Drone. And the number of the test image is 37,855 951 for Drone Satellite and 701 51,355 for Satellite Drone.

The CVACT dataset is a standard large-scale cross-view benchmark. Different from the University-1652 dataset, only ground-view and satellite-view images are provided. Besides, the ground views are composed of panoramic images and all images ground-view and aerial-view are all north aligned. This dataset contains 35,532 image pairs for the training set and 8,884 validation image pairs for the test set respectively. The test set is denoted as CVACT_val.

**Table 2.** Statistical information of the test image number on two datasets University-1652 and CVACT used in the experiments. A B denotes query gallery.

| Dataset | University-1652 [5] | CVACT [8] |
|---|---|---|
| Drone → Satellite | 37855 → 951 | – |
| Satellite → Drone | 701 → 51355 | – |
| Ground → Satellite | – | 8884 ⟶ 8884 |

**Implementation Details.** In our experiment, PyTorch is employed to build the whole system with two RTX 3090TI GPUs. The framework is trained end-to-end with the ResNet-50 pretrained weights on ImageNet [28], and the square-ring partition strategy [16] is utilized to extract 2048-dim part-based features from two viewpoints (drone → satellite or ground → satellite). Then, the dimension of the compressed representation is set to 512 based on experience. We use Stochastic Gradient Descent (SGD) as the optimizer with $10^{-3}$ as the initial learning rate of our backbone and $10^{-4}$ of the newly-added layer (e.g., the classifier). After that, we reduce the learning rate by a factor of 10 for each 80 epochs. The batch-size is set to 8.

During training, $\beta$ is initialized as $10^{-6}$ and increases with the epoch. $\beta$ should not be set to a large value at the beginning, otherwise the model is difficult to converge due to unstable $KL - divergence$ loss. Images are resized to $256 \times 256$ pixels and data augmentation is performed such as flipping. The total training epoch is 300 and we save the best model. And it is worth noting that the mean of compressed representation is regarded as the final retrieval feature.

**Evaluation Protocol.** In our experiments, we follow the standard evaluation protocol as previous works [5, 8, 16], Recall@K ($K = 1, 5, 10$) and average precision (AP), to examine the performance for fair comparisons. Recall@K refers to the proportion of correctly matched images in the top $K$ retrieval candidate results given a query view. And AP represents the precision and recall area of the retrieval performance. A higher score of either protocol indicates a better result.

### 4.2 Comparison with the State-of-the-Arts

**Results on University-1652.** We first investigate the geo-localization performance of our proposed method and compare it with the other competitive approaches on the University-1652 dataset, which is a newly-proposed dataset containing drone-view images. As shown in Table 3, PIPB outperforms the baseline [5] by a large margin. Recall@1 increases from 58.49% to 76.76% on Drone Satellite and 71.18% to 87.02% on Satellite Drone. Moreover, it achieves the performance with AP = 79.75% on the drone-view target localization and AP = 76.31% on the drone navigation, which is 0.61 and 1.82 relative improvements compared to a recent approach [16]. In the light of these results, our claim is confirmed that PIPB motivates the model to learn valuable features, rather than redundant task-irrelevant features, resulting in the improvement of robustness and generalization.

**Results on CVACT.** CVACT is a fundamental dataset of this task. We only perform the ground satellite task and evaluate it by Recall@K ($K = 1, 5, 10$) and R@Top1%. We compare our method with the other advanced cross-view localization methods, including CVM-Net [7], Orientation [8]. Zheng [5], CVFT [6] and LPN [16].

The result is illustrated in Table 4. It can be observed that our PIPB acquires competitive results with 81.04% Recall@1 accuracy, 90.63% Recall@5 accuracy, 92.78% Recall@10, and 97.19% R@Top1% accuracy, substantially surpassing the mentioned approaches. As previously indicated, implementing a variational information bottleneck helps the model to retain discriminative information of the target in the latent representations while abandoning those irrelevant factors.

**Table 3.** Comparison results of our PIPB method and the compared approaches on University-1652 dataset. The cross-view geo-localization retrieval performance is evaluated in terms of Recall@1 and AP.

| Method | Drone → Satellite | | Satellite → Drone | |
|---|---|---|---|---|
| | Recall@1 | AP | Recall@1 | AP |
| Instance loss [5] | 58.49 | 63.31 | 71.18 | 58.74 |
| Contrastive loss [46] | 52.39 | 57.44 | 63.91 | 52.24 |
| Triplet loss (M = 0.5) [47] | 53.58 | 58.60 | 64.48 | 53.15 |
| Soft margin triplet loss [7] | 53.21 | 58.03 | 65.62 | 54.47 |
| LPN [16] | 75.93 | 79.14 | 86.45 | 74.49 |
| **PIPB (Ours)** | **76.76** | **79.75** | **87.02** | **76.31** |

**Table 4.**

| Method | Venue | Backbone | CVACT_val | | | |
|---|---|---|---|---|---|---|
| | | | Recall@1 | Recall @5 | Recall@10 | R@Top1% |
| CVM-Net [7] | CVPR'18 | VGG16 | 20.15 | 45.00 | 56.87 | 87.57 |
| Orientation [8] | CVPR'19 | VGG16 | 49.96 | 62.28 | 75.48 | 92.04 |
| Zheng et al. [5] | MM'20 | VGG16 | 31.20 | 53.64 | 63.00 | 85.27 |
| CVFT [6] | AAAI'20 | VGG16 | 61.05 | 81.33 | 86.52 | 95.93 |
| LPN [16] | TCSVT'21 | ResNet-50 | 79.99 | 90.63 | 92.56 | 97.03 |
| **PIPB (Ours)** | – | ResNet-50 | **81.04** | **90.63** | **92.78** | **97.19** |

### 4.3 Further Analysis

**Effect of Different Value of β.** To verify the effectiveness of the variational information bottleneck module, we analyze the effect of β, i.e., whether there is a compression loss or not. As illustrated in Fig. 2, the variational information bottleneck is to obtain a lower-dimensional latent representation z by reparameterization trick, where z is sampled from the Gaussian distribution $p(z|x; \theta)$. And β is a parameter that controls the balance between discarding task-irrelevant information from $z$ and keeping predictive information retained in $z$. During this process, the robustness and generalization capability of the model is enhanced. It is shown in Table 5, we set β = 0 to remove the compression loss, indicating that there is no particular constraint to the part-based feature maps which is compressed to a deterministic dimension and fed to the classifier.

$$L_{(\beta=0)} = \sum_{i,j} E_{z \sim p(z|x;\theta)} \big[ -\log q(y|z; \varphi) \big] \tag{9}$$

The result shown in Table 5 substantiates the variational information bottleneck theory. When β = 0, the performance on two tasks is close to [16], which satisfies our

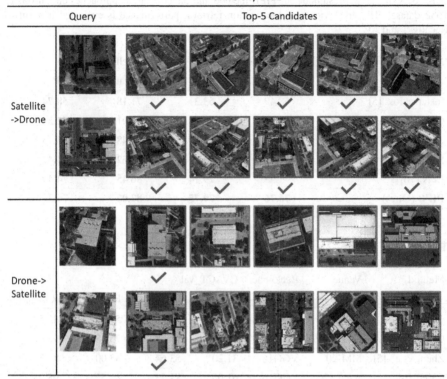

**Fig. 4.** Illustration of cross-view image retrieval results on University-1652, i.e., Top-5 retrieval results of drone-view target localization (Drone → Satellite, i.e., 37,855 → 951) and drone navigation (Satellite → Drone, i.e., 701 → 51,355). The correct matched image is checked in red. (Color figure online)

expectation. Then, we give β a value to make the variational information bottleneck work. As mentioned Sect. 4.1, it is initialized as $10^{-6}$ and increases with the epoch. The number of random seeds is 2021 in our two experiments and all experimental environments are the same except for the value of β, ensuring the absolute fairness of our comparison. As it is presented, the result in the second line is better than that when β = 0. This ablation study confirms that the retrieval performance can be improved by the variational information bottleneck.

**Effect of Different Dimension of the Latent Representation.** As previously mentioned, the goal of the variational information bottleneck is to find a compressed representation with maximum information of the target, achieving better robustness and generalization capability. Therefore, an appropriate bottleneck dimension has huge importance. A small dimension may compromise the discriminative representation learning, while a larger dimension retains more redundancy in the representation. To address this problem, we carry out an experiment on different dimensions of $z$ which are 256, 384, 512 and 600 in this ablation study. The Recall@1 and AP are shown in Fig. 6. Given an

CVACT

| Query | Top-3 Candidates |
|---|---|

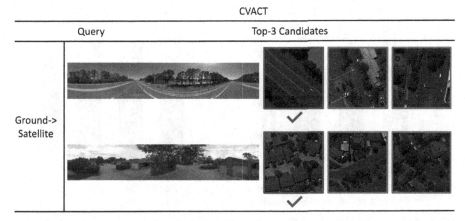

Ground-> Satellite

**Fig. 5.** Illustration of cross-view image retrieval results on CVACT_val, i.e., Top-3 retrieval results of geographic localization (Ground → Satellite, i.e., 8,884 → 8,884). The correct matched image is checked in red. (Color figure online)

**Table 5.** Experimental results of different β on University-1652 dataset. The cross-view geolocalization retrieval performance is evaluated in terms of Recall@1 and AP.

|  | Drone → Satellite | | Satellite → Drone | |
|---|---|---|---|---|
|  | Recall@1 | AP | Recall@1 | AP |
| $\beta = 0$ | 75.81 | 78.93 | 86.73 | 75.51 |
| $\beta \neq 0$ | **76.76** | **79.75** | **87.02** | **76.31** |

overall consideration, we can summarize that when the dimension is 512, it can achieve excellent performance. Therefore, the dimension of the latent representation z is set to 512.

**Visualization of the Learned Feature Distribution.** Finally, we use the t-SNE tool [48] to visualize the distributions of randomly sampled drone-view images of University-1652 in Fig. 5. In our experiment, we choose 10 classes with 54 samples per class from the University-1652 drone-view gallery images. As shown in Fig. 7, (a) visualizes the original feature distributions, and (b) illustrates the learned low-dimensional representations by the variational information bottleneck. It can be observed that the features from the original distributed in the whole visualization map are scattered and there are no compact clusters formed. On the contrary, the representations learned from the variational information bottleneck are grouped by category. Each small cluster represents an identical class. The t-SNE visualization helps to verify the capability of discriminative features learning by our PIPB model in a more intuitive way.

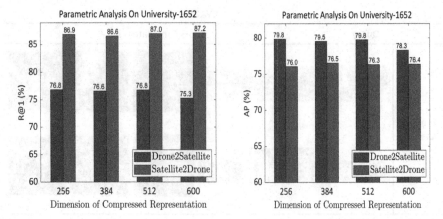

**Fig. 6.** Experimental results of different dimensions of the latent representation on University-1652 dataset. The cross-view geo-localization retrieval performance is evaluated in terms of Recall@1 and AP.

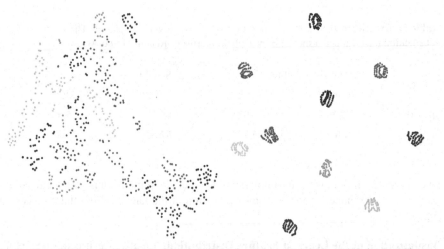

**Fig. 7.** The t-SNE results for the drone-view gallery images on University-1652 dataset. Clusters with different colors are from different classes. (a) The original feature distribution on the dataset. (b) The learned representation distribution on the dataset.

## 5   Conclusions

In this paper, we propose a simply-implemented and efficient model termed PIPB for cross-view geo-localization by leveraging the variational information bottleneck. Different from existing approaches, we view this task from the information bottleneck perspective, devoted to finding the compressed representations which are still predictive and discriminative to the ground-truth, which can enhance the robustness and generalization capability. To verify it, we conduct extensive experiments on two datasets, i.e., newly-released University-1652 (drone satellite) and fundamental benchmark CVACT (ground satellite). The retrieval result confirms the superior retrieval performance of our proposed PIPB. In the future, we will explore more advanced methods to learn cross-view representations and apply the information bottleneck theory to other fields.

# References

1. Wang, W., Shi, Y., Chen, S., Peng, Q., Zheng, F., You, X.: Norm-guided adaptive visual embedding for zero-shot sketch-based image retrieval. In: International Joint Conference on Artificial Intelligence, pp.1106–1112 (2021)
2. Liu, Q., Xie, L., Wang, H., Yuille, A.L.: Semantic-aware knowledge preservation for zero-shot sketch-based image retrieval. In: Proceedings of the IEEE/CVF International Conference on Computer Vision, pp. 3662–3671 (2019)
3. Li, H., Chen, Y., Tao, D., Yu, Z., Qi, G.: Attribute-aligned domain-invariant feature learning for unsupervised domain adaptation person re-identification. IEEE Trans. Inf. Forensics Secur. **16**, 1480–1494 (2020)
4. He, Y., Xiang, S., Kang, C., Wang, J., Pan, C.: Cross-modal retrieval via deep and bidirectional representation learning. IEEE Trans. Multimedia **18**(7), 1363–1377 (2016)
5. Zheng, Z., Wei, Y., Yang, Y.: University-1652: a multi-view multi-source benchmark for drone-based geo-localization. In: Proceedings of the 28th ACM international conference on Multimedia, pp. 1395–1403 (2020)
6. Shi, Y., Yu, X., Liu, L., Zhang, T., Li, H.: Optimal feature transport for cross-view image geo-localization. In: Proceedings of the AAAI Conference on Artificial Intelligence, vol. 34, no. 07, pp. 11990–11997 (2020)
7. Hu, S., Feng, M., Nguyen, R.M., Lee, G.H.: CVM-Net: cross-view matching network for image-based ground-to-aerial geo-localization. In: Proceedings of the IEEE Conference on Computer Vision and Pattern Recognition, pp. 7258–7267 (2018)
8. Liu, L., Li, H.: Lending orientation to neural networks for cross-view geo-localization. In: Proceedings of the IEEE/CVF Conference on Computer Vision and Pattern Recognition, pp. 5624–5633 (2019)
9. Shi, Y., Liu, L., Yu, X., Li, H.: Spatial-aware feature aggregation for image based cross-view geo-localization. Adv. Neural. Inf. Process. Syst. **32**, 10090–10100 (2019)
10. Tomešek, J., Čadík, M., Brejcha, J.: CrossLocate: cross-modal large-scale visual geo-localization innatural environments using rendered modalities. In: Proceedings of the IEEE/CVF Winter Conference on Applications of Computer Vision, pp. 3174–3183 (2022)
11. Olszewska, J.I.: Interest-point-based landmark computation for agents' spatial description coordination. In: ICAART (2), pp. 566–569 (2016)
12. Hadsell, R., Chopra, S., LeCun, Y.: Dimensionality reduction by learning an invariant mapping. In: 2006 IEEE Computer Society Conference on Computer Vision and Pattern Recognition (CVPR 2006), vol. 2, pp. 1735–1742. IEEE (2006)
13. Schroff, F., Kalenichenko, D., Philbin, J.: FaceNet: a unified embedding for face recognition and clustering. In: Proceedings of the IEEE Conference on Computer Vision and Pattern Recognition, pp. 815–823 (2015)
14. Deng, W., Zheng, L., Ye, Q., Kang, G., Yang, Y., Jiao, J.: Image-image domain adaptation with preserved self-similarity and domain-dissimilarity for person re-identification. In: Proceedings of the IEEE Conference on Computer Vision and Pattern Recognition, pp. 994–1003 (2018)
15. Shi, Y., Yu, X., Campbell, D., Li, H.: Where am i looking at? Joint location and orientation estimation by cross-view matching. In: Proceedings of the IEEE/CVF Conference on Computer Vision and Pattern Recognition, pp. 4064–4072 (2020)

16. Wang, T., et al.: Each part matters: local patterns facilitate cross-view geo-localization. IEEE Trans. Circuits Syst. Video Technol. **32**, 867–879 (2021)
17. Mahabadi, R.K., Belinkov, Y., Henderson, J.: Variational information bottleneck for effective low-resource fine-tuning. arXiv preprint arXiv:2106.05469 (2021)
18. Alemi, A.A., Fischer, I., Dillon, J.V., Murphy, K.: Deep variational information bottleneck. arXiv preprint arXiv:1612.00410 (2016)
19. Tishby, N., Pereira, F.C., Bialek, W.: The information bottleneck method. arXiv preprint physics/0004057 (2000)
20. Hu, S., Chang, X.: Multi-view drone-based geo-localization via style and spatial alignment. arXiv preprint arXiv:2006.13681 (2020)
21. Sun, Y., Zheng, L., Yang, Y., Tian, Q., Wang, S.: Beyond part models: person retrieval with refined part pooling (and a strong convolutional baseline). In: Ferrari, V., Hebert, M., Sminchisescu, C., Weiss, Y. (eds.) ECCV 2018. LNCS, vol. 11208, pp. 501–518. Springer, Cham (2018). https://doi.org/10.1007/978-3-030-01225-0_30
22. Zeng, Z., Wang, Z., Yang, F., Satoh, S.: Geo-localization via ground-to-satellite cross-view image retrieval. IEEE Trans. Multimedia (2022)
23. Castaldo, F., Zamir, A., Angst, R., Palmieri, F., Savarese, S.: Semantic cross-view matching. In: Proceedings of the IEEE International Conference on Computer Vision Workshops, pp. 9–17 (2015)
24. Lin, T.-Y., Belongie, S., Hays, J.: Cross-view image geolocalization. In: Proceedings of the IEEE Conference on Computer Vision and Pattern Recognition, pp. 891–898 (2013)
25. Mousavian, A., Kosecka, J.: Semantic image based geolocation given a map. arXiv preprint arXiv:1609.00278 (2016)
26. Russakovsky, O., et al.: ImageNet large scale visual recognition challenge. Int. J. Comput. Vision **115**(3), 211–252 (2015)
27. Workman, S., Jacobs, N.: On the location dependence of convolutional neural network features. In: Proceedings of the IEEE Conference on Computer Vision and Pattern Recognition Workshops, pp. 70–78 (2015)
28. Deng, J., Dong, W., Socher, R., Li, L.-J., Li, K., Fei-Fei, L.: ImageNet: a large-scale hierarchical image database. In: 2009 IEEE Conference on Computer Vision and Pattern Recognition, pp. 248–255. IEEE (2009)
29. Vo, N.N., Hays, J.: Localizing and orienting street views using overhead imagery. In: Leibe, B., Matas, J., Sebe, N., Welling, M. (eds.) ECCV 2016. LNCS, vol. 9905, pp. 494–509. Springer, Cham (2016). https://doi.org/10.1007/978-3-319-46448-0_30
30. Zhai, M., Bessinger, Z., Workman, S., Jacobs, N.: Predicting ground-level scene layout from aerial imagery. In: Proceedings of the IEEE Conference on Computer Vision and Pattern Recognition, pp. 867–875 (2017)
31. Chopra, S., Hadsell, R., LeCun, Y.: Learning a similarity metric discriminatively, with application to face verification. In: 2005 IEEE Computer Society Conference on Computer Vision and Pattern Recognition (CVPR 2005), vol. 1, pp. 539–546. IEEE (2005)
32. Arandjelovic, R., Gronat, P., Torii, A., Pajdla, T., Sivic, J.: NetVLAD: CNN architecture for weakly supervised place recognition. In: Proceedings of the IEEE Conference on Computer Vision and Pattern Recognition, pp. 5297–5307 (2016)
33. Slonim, N., Tishby, N.: Agglomerative information bottleneck. In: NIPS, vol. 4 (1999)
34. Bardera, A., Rigau, J., Boada, I., Feixas, M., Sbert, M.: Image segmentation using information bottleneck method. IEEE Trans. Image Process. **18**(7), 1601–1612 (2009)
35. Peng, X.B., Kanazawa, A., Toyer, S., Abbeel, P., Levine, S.: Variational discriminator bottleneck: Improving imitation learning, inverse RL, and GANs by constraining information flow. arXiv preprint arXiv:1810.00821 (2018)

36. Luo, Y., Liu, P., Guan, T., Yu, J., Yang, Y.: Significance-aware information bottleneck for domain adaptive semantic segmentation. In: Proceedings of the IEEE/CVF International Conference on Computer Vision, pp. 6778–6787 (2019)

37. Yu, J., Xu, T., Rong, Y., Bian, Y., Huang, J., He, R.: Recognizing predictive substructures with subgraph information bottleneck. arXiv preprint arXiv:2103.11155 (2021)

38. Yu, X., Yu, S., Príncipe, J.C.: Deep deterministic information bottleneck with matrix-based entropy functional. In: ICASSP 2021-2021 IEEE International Conference on Acoustics, Speech and Signal Processing (ICASSP), pp. 3160–3164. IEEE (2021)

39. Tishby, N., Zaslavsky, N.: Deep learning and the information bottleneck principle. In: 2015 IEEE Information Theory Workshop (ITW), pp. 1–5. IEEE (2015)

40. Kingma, D.P., Welling, M.: Auto-encoding variational Bayes. arXiv preprint arXiv:1312.6114 (2013)

41. Wan, Z., Zhang, C., Zhu, P., Hu, Q.: Multi-view information-bottleneck representation learning. In: Proceedings of the AAAI Conference on Artificial Intelligence, vol. 35, no. 11, pp. 10085–10092 (2021)

42. Federici, M., Dutta, A., Forré, P., Kushman, N., Akata, Z.: Learning robust representations via multi-view information bottleneck. arXiv preprint arXiv:2002.07017 (2020)

43. Wang, Q., Boudreau, C., Luo, Q., Tan, P.-N., Zhou, J.: Deep multi-view information bottleneck. In: Proceedings of the 2019 SIAM International Conference on Data Mining, pp. 37–45. SIAM (2019)

44. Xu, C., Tao, D., Xu, C.: Large-margin multi-viewinformation bottleneck. IEEE Trans. Pattern Anal. Mach. Intell. $36(8)$, 1559–1572 (2014)

45. He, K., Zhang, X., Ren, S., Sun, J.: Deep residual learning for image recognition. In: Proceedings of the IEEE Conference on Computer Vision and Pattern Recognition, pp. 770–778 (2016)

46. Lin, T.-Y., Cui, Y., Belongie, S., Hays, J.: Learning deep representations for ground-to-aerial geolocalization. In: Proceedings of the IEEE Conference on Computer Vision and Pattern Recognition, pp. 5007–5015 (2015)

47. Chechik, G., Sharma, V., Shalit, U., Bengio, S.: Large scale online learning of image similarity through ranking. J. Mach. Learn. Res. $11(3)$, 1109–1135 (2010)

48. Van der Maaten, L., Hinton, G.: Visualizing data using t-SNE. J. Mach. Learn. Res. $9(11)$, 2579–2605 (2008)

49. Xu, X., Lu, H., Song, J., Yang, Y., Shen, H.T., Li, X.: Ternary adversarial networks with self-supervision for zero-shot cross-modal retrieval. IEEE Trans. Cybern. $50(6)$, 2400–2413 (2020)

50. Liang, P., Yang, Y., Ji, Y., Lu, H., Shen, H.T.: Answer again: improving VQA with cascaded-answering model. IEEE Trans. Knowl. Data Eng. (2020). https://doi.org/10.1109/TKDE.2020.2998805

51. Lu, H., Zhang, M., Xu, X., Li, Y., Shen, H.T.: Deep fuzzy hashing network for efficient image retrieval. IEEE Trans. Fuzzy Syst. $29(1)$, 166–176 (2021)

52. Xu, X., Tian, J., Lin, K., Lu, H., Shao, J., Shen, H.: Zero-shot cross-modal retrieval by assembling AutoEncoder and generative adversarial network. ACM Trans. Multimedia Comput. Commun. Appl. $17$, 1–17 (2021)

53. Wang, G., Xu, X., Shen, F., Lu, H., Ji, Y., Shen, H.: Cross-modal dynamic networks for video moment retrieval with text query. IEEE Trans. Multimedia $24$, 1221–1232 (2022)

# Invariant EKF Based Mobile Robot Simultaneous Localization and Mapping Navigation

Chaoyue Gu, Zhenxing Sun[✉], and Wang Ting

College of Electrical Engineering and Control Science, Nanjing Tech University, Nanjing 211816, China
{sunzx,wangting0310}@njtech.edu.cn

**Abstract.** As robots suffered from magnetic field disturbances, they cannot use satellite navigation such as Global Positioning System to explore the wide unknown area. In this situation, the Simultaneous Localization and Mapping is an efficient choice to obtain the global map by sensors or visions. However, it is inevitable including noises and other disturbances. In this paper, we proposed an Invariant Extended Kalman Filter (IEKF) based navigation method for single mobile robot. The proposed method is simulated on MATLAB platform. Results show good performances of proposed method.

**Keywords:** Mobile robot · Simultaneous Localization and Mapping · Invariant Extended Kalman Filter

## 1 Introduction

In most situations, we can use Beidou, Global Positioning System (GPS) and other satellite navigation systems to construct the map for unknown area [8–12]. Although GPS is vulnerable to the interference of natural factors such as terrain and weather, it cannot normally work. The signal is weak and cannot work under shelter in the indoor environment so that it cannot be used to accurate positioning. In these cases, Simultaneous Localization and Mapping (SLAM) is used for online composition. The so-called SLAM can be described as the robot moving from one position to another position in unknown environment, positioning itself according to the position estimation and sensor data, and constructing an incremental map at the same time [1].

Choi et al. presented a new feature initialization method for monocular EKF SLAM (Extended Kalman Filter Simultaneous Localization and Mapping) which utilizes a 3D measurement model in the camera frame rather than 2D pixel coordinates in the image [2]. As a popular SLAM solution, Fast SLAM suffers from limitation on error accumulation introduced by incorrect odometry model and inaccurate linearization of the SLAM nonlinear functions. To overcome the problem, Li et al. derived a new Jacobian free neural network based FastSLAM [3]. The SLAM algorithm based on laser has stable ranging performance in small static scenes, which is less affected by the light intensity.

© The Author(s), under exclusive license to Springer Nature Singapore Pte Ltd. 2022
S. Yang and H. Lu (Eds.): ISAIR 2022, CCIS 1700, pp. 420–426, 2022.
https://doi.org/10.1007/978-981-19-7946-0_35

Therefore, in order to achieve precise positioning and navigation, Pan et al. applied the laser SLAM algorithm to the sweeping robot indoor [4].

In the process of robot SLAM navigation, many interference and noise points may be generated due to the impact of the environment. Therefore, we introduce Invariant Extended Kalman Filter (IEKF) method to decrease these noises and propose IEKF based SLAM navigation method.

The rest of the paper is organized as follows: Sect. 2 explains the structure of SLAM, Sect. 3 introduces our proposed method and explains details. In Sect. 4, we demonstrate our simulation experiments and discuss results. Finally, conclusions are given in conclusion part.

## 2  Problem Statement

In this section, the description of the SLAM problem and its structure is presented. A process is described in which a mobile robot estimates its own position as it is constructed a map of its surroundings. In the simultaneous localization and map building process, the mobile robot uses a laser or sensor located on the robot to estimate the positions of all waypoint [5].

The process of SLAM includes five steps as follows:

(1) Read information from sensors. The robot reads information from lasers, depth cameras, etc. and pre-processes this information.
(2) Visual odometry. A visual odometer is used to estimate the motion between adjacent images, that is the front end process.
(3) Back end optimisation. It can optimize the information from visual odometry and loop closure, which is known as back end.
(4) Loopback detection. It can verify whether the robot has ever reached the previous position. If the robot passes the previous position, a loopback is proven and the message is sent to the back end for processing.
(5) Construct maps. It may construct relevant maps based on estimated trajectories.

## 3  EKF SLAM and IEKF SLAM

The SLAM algorithm based on EKF is the most popular algorithm to solve the SLAM problem. Its basic idea is to form an extensible joint state vector from the pose state vector of the mobile robot and the position vector of the road signed in the environment for joint estimation. Through the continuous movement of the robot and the continuous observation of the sensor, the new observed road sign vector is added to the joint state vector. Though updating the estimated position of the robot. Since the road signs in the environment are usually static, the position vector of the observed road signs is defined as $M_i = \left(m_1^T, m_2^T, \cdots, m_i^T\right)^T$, $i = 1, 2, \cdots, N$, where $N$ is the total number of road signs in the environment. Therefore, the joint state vector of the system at time $k$ is defined as

$X_k = \left(X_{v,k}^T, M_i^T\right)^T$, where $X_{v,k} = (x_k, y_k, \theta_k)^T$ is the pose vector of the mobile robot. The robot motion equation and observation equation are expressed as follows,

$$
\begin{aligned}
X_{v,k} &= f\left(X_{v,k-1}, u_k\right) + \varepsilon_{k-1} \\
z_k &= h\left(X_{v,k}\right) + \eta_k]
\end{aligned}
\tag{1}
$$

where $\varepsilon_k$ denotes the control noise of the mobile robot and $\eta_k$ indicates observation noise, their average value is zero. EKF SLAM algorithm mainly includes prediction process, observation process, update process and state vector expansion process.

(1) Prediction process. Assume that the estimated value of the system state vector at time $k - 1$ is $\hat{X}_{k-1|k-1}$, the covariance matrix is $P_{k-1|k-1}$ and

$$
P_{k-1|k-1} = \begin{bmatrix} P_{vv} & P_{vm} \\ P_{mv} & P_{mm} \end{bmatrix},
\tag{2}
$$

where $P_{vv}$ is the covariance matrix of robot pose. $P_{mm}$ is the covariance matrix of road signs. $P_{vm}$ is the cross-covariance matrix for the robot and the road sign. $P_{mv}$ is the cross-covariance matrix of road signs and robots. The predicted value and covariance matrix of the system state vector at time $k$ can be obtained from the motion model of the mobile robot, which can be described as follows,

$$
\hat{X}_{k|k-1} = \begin{bmatrix} f\left(\hat{X}_{k-1|k-1}, u_k\right) \\ M_i \end{bmatrix},
\tag{3}
$$

$$
P_{k|k-1} = F_k P_{k-1|k-1} F_k^T + Q_{k-1},
\tag{4}
$$

$$
F_k = \frac{\partial f(X, u_k)}{\partial X}\Big|_{X=\hat{X}_{k-1|k-1}},
\tag{5}
$$

(2) Observation process. The robot obtains the observation value $z_k$ of the road sign at time $k$ through the sensor, by using the predicted observation value $h\left(\hat{X}_{k|k-1}\right)$ obtained from the observation equation, the innovation of the observation value and its covariance matrix can be obtained as follows,

$$
v_k = z_k - h\left(\hat{X}_{k|k-1}\right),
\tag{6}
$$

$$
S_k = H_k P_{k|k-1} H_k^T + R_k,
\tag{7}
$$

$$
H_k = \frac{\partial h(X)}{\partial X}\Big|_{X=\hat{X}_{k|k-1}},
\tag{8}
$$

(3) Update process. Via updating the system state vector and the covariance matrix with predicted and observed values. $K_k$ is described by the Kalman gain as follows.

$$
K_k = P_{k|k-1} H_k^T S_k^{-1},
\tag{9}
$$

$$\hat{X}_{k|k} = \hat{X}_{k|k-1} + K_k v_k, \tag{10}$$

$$P_{k|k} = (I - K_k H_k) P_{k|k-1}. \tag{11}$$

(4) State vector expansion process. The environmental road signs observed by the sensor at time $k$ may have both the existing road signs and the new road signs in the figure. The existing road signs are used to update the state prediction value, and the new road signs are added to the system state vector after initialization. Assuming that the i-th landmark observed at time $k$ is a new landmark, and the observed value is $z_{i,k} = (r_{i,k}, \varphi_{i,k})^T$. Then the position of the new landmark in the global coordinate system is expressed as

$$m_i = g\left(\hat{X}_{v,k} z_{i,k}\right) = \begin{bmatrix} x_k + r_{i,k} \cos(\theta_k + \varphi_{i,k}) \\ y_k + r_{i,k} \sin(\theta_k + \varphi_{i,k}) \end{bmatrix}, \tag{12}$$

By adding the new road sign to the system state vector, the expanded new state vector is obtained as

$$X_{new,k} = \begin{bmatrix} X_k \\ m_i \end{bmatrix}. \tag{13}$$

The covariance matrix of the new state vector is described as follows,

$$P_{new,k} = \begin{bmatrix} P_{vv} & P_{vm} & \nabla g_x P_{vv} \\ P_{mv} & P_{mm} & \nabla g_x P_{vm} \\ (\nabla g_x P_{vv})^T & (\nabla g_x P_{vm})^T & \nabla g_x P_{vv} \nabla g_x^T + \nabla g_z R \nabla g_z^T \end{bmatrix}, \tag{14}$$

$$\begin{aligned} \nabla g_x &= \frac{\partial g(X, z_{i,k})}{\partial X} \Big|_{X = \hat{X}_{v,k}} \\ \nabla g_z &= \frac{\partial g(\hat{X}_{v,k}, z)}{\partial z} \Big|_{z = z_{i,k}} \end{aligned}. \tag{15}$$

The system matrix of the conventional EKF relies on the current state estimate, and the system is inaccurate in predicting the state estimate when there is noise introduced, which makes it difficult to do convergence analysis of the system equations. As the difference between the state estimate and the true value is large, it directly leads to a large deviation. If such a continued calculation is used, it may further amplify the error, causing the system to form positive feedback and eventually leading to filter divergence. In addition, the EKF suffers from inconsistency problems. Namely, the update step of the EKF calculates the covariance matrix of the current state by the old state, but it is not consistent with the actual value of the covariance matrix of the current state [6].

To solve the above problem, the IEKF is based on the Lie algebra and applies the group transformation to the system state variables, so that the state quantities of the IEKF are a matrix and form a group. In order to achieve independence of the system matrix from the state estimates and to solve the problems of the traditional EKF, the errors are also defined on the group, i.e. in the form of both left-invariant and right-invariant errors. The choice between left-invariant and right-invariant errors is based on whether the independence of the system matrix from the state estimates can be achieved [7].

The IEKF algorithm follows the same procedure as the traditional EKF, except that the state update formula is different.

(1) Initialize the robot's state vector $X_0$ and state prediction covariance matrix $P_0$.
(2) Estimate the state of the robot. According to the state transition matrix of the robot system model, the state at time $k + 1$ is inferred by the state quantity at time $k$, The state prediction covariance equation is expressed as

$$P_{k|k-1} = F_k P_{k-1|k-1} F_k^T + Q_{k-1}. \tag{16}$$

(3) Filter gain. Update the system state vector and its covariance matrix.

$$v_k = z_k - h\left(\hat{X}_{k|k-1}\right), \tag{17}$$

$$P_{k|k} = (I - K_k H_k) P_{k|k-1}. \tag{18}$$

Kalman gain is expressed as

$$K_k = P_{k|k-1} H_k^T (H_k P_{k|k-1} H_k^T + R_k)^{-1}. \tag{19}$$

The state error is set as $e_k = K_k v_k$.

Status update formula is described as

$$\hat{X}_{k|k} = \exp(K_k v_k) \hat{X}_{k|k-1}. \tag{20}$$

The parts of the IEKF that can be represented as group elements are updated exponentially and the parts that cannot be represented as group elements are updated in a normal linear way.

## 4   Numerical Simulation

To illustrate the effectiveness of the improved algorithm, we perform numerical simulation experiments on MATLAB platform. We set up the robot in a simulation platform to move in a circular motion on a plane many times and found several unknown features in its motion path. The velocity and angular velocity of the robot's motion maintain constant. The relative position of the features in the robot's reference system is observed once per second. We set the standard deviation of the robot at each speed measurement to be 0.05 times the original speed of the robot.

In Fig. 1, the evaluation of the consistency of two filters uses the NEES indicator in the numerical setting described above. The solid blue line represents EKF SLAM and the magenta dotted line represents IEKF SLAM. We can see that Normalized Estimation Error Squared over the entire time interval is significantly smaller for by using IEKF SLAM than for that uses EKF SLAM. From results, it is indicated that IEKF SLAM has better consistency.

From Fig. 2 and Fig. 3, the evaluation of the performance of the proposed IEKF SLAM algorithm is displayed in terms of RMSE of the vehicle heading and position error. The solid blue line represents EKF SLAM and the magenta dotted line represents IEKF SLAM. It is obvious that the RMSE of IEKF SLAM is significantly smaller than that of EKF SLAM over the entire time interval.

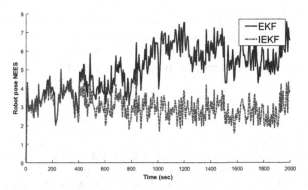

**Fig. 1.** The robot pose NEES of EKF SLAM and IEKF SLAM

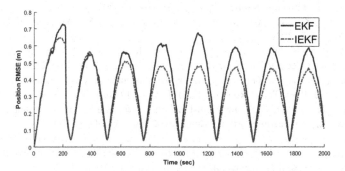

**Fig. 2.** The position RMSE of EKF SLAM and IEKF SLAM

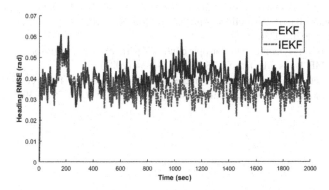

**Fig. 3.** The heading RMSE of EKF SLAM and IEKF SLAM

## 5  Conclusion

For the purpose of solving the problem of error transfer systems forming positive feedback in EKF SLAM, which ultimately leads to filter divergence and inconsistency, IEKF achieves the relative independence of the error transfer matrix. Through the state estimated by changing the way of state errors in the Lie group space, we compared two algorithms on MATLAB platform through numerical simulation. Compared with the EKF method, the proposed IEKF algorithm is superior to the EKF in terms of consistency and convergence.

# References

1. Demim, F., Nemra, A., Louadj, K.: Robust SVSF-SLAM for unmanned vehicle in unknown environment. IFAC PapersOnLine 49(21), 386–394 (2016)
2. Choi, K., Park, J., Kim, Y.-H., Lee, H.-K.: Monocular SLAM with undelayed initialization for an indoor robot. Robot. Auton. Syst. 60(6), 841–851 (2012)
3. Qingling Li, Y., Song, Z.H.: Neural network based FastSLAM for autonomous robots in unknown environments. Neurocomputing 165, 99–110 (2015)
4. Pan, S., Xie, Z., Jiang, Y.: Sweeping robot based on Laser SLAM. Procedia Comput. Sci. 199, 1205–1212 (2020)
5. Zhao, Y., Wang, T., Qin, W., Zhang, X.: Improved Rao-Blackwellised particle filter based on randomly weighted particle swarm optimization. Comput. Electr. Eng. 71, 477–484 (2018)
6. Huang, S., Dissanayake, G.: Convergence and consistency analysis for extended Kalman filter based SLAM. IEEE Trans. Robotics 23(5), 1036–1049 (2007)
7. Coleman, K., Taylor, C.N.: Invariant-EKF design for a unicycle robot under linear disturbances. In: Proceedings of the American Control Conference, vol. 6, pp. 3479–3484 (2020)
8. Yang, S., Lu, H., Li, J.: Multifeature Fusion-based Object Detection for Intelligent Transportation Systems. IEEE Trans. Intell. Transp. Syst. (2022)
9. Teng, Y., et al.: Multidimensional deformable object manipulation based on DN-transporter networks. IEEE Trans. Intell. Transp. Syst. (2022)
10. Wang, P., et al.: Numerical and experimental study on the maneuverability of an active propeller control based wave glider. Appl. Ocean Res. 104, 102369 (2020). https://doi.org/10.1016/j.apor.2020.102369
11. Yang, X., et al.: Dynamics and isotropic control of parallel mechanisms for vibration isolation. IEEE/ASME Trans. Mechatron. 25(4), 2027–2034 (2020)
12. Kang, S., et al.: Discrete-time predictive sliding mode control for a constrained parallel micropositioning piezostage. IEEE Trans. Syst. Cybern. Syst. 52, 3025–3036 (2021)

# Author Index

Printed in the United States
by Baker & Taylor Publisher Services